W9-CMJ-126

Family Systems in Medicine

THE GUILFORD FAMILY THERAPY SERIES
Alan S. Gurman, *Editor*

Family Systems in Medicine

Edited by
CHRISTIAN N. RAMSEY, JR.
University of Oklahoma

Foreword by Kerr L. White

THE GUILFORD PRESS
New York   London

© 1989 The Guilford Press
A Division of Guilford Publications, Inc.
72 Spring Street, New York, NY 10012

All rights reserved

No part of this book may be reproduced, stored in a retrieval system,
or transmitted, in any form or by any means, electronic, mechanical,
photocopying, microfilming, recording, or otherwise, without written
permission from the Publisher.

Printed in the United States of America

Last digit is print number: 9 8 7 6 5 4 3 2 1

Library of Congress Cataloging-in-Publication Data

Family systems in medicine / Christian N. Ramsey, Jr., editor.
        p.   cm.—(The Guilford family therapy series)
    Includes bibliographies and index.
    ISBN 0-89862-103-8
    1. Sick—Psychology.   2. Sick—Family relationships.   3. Family.
  4. System theory.   I. Ramsey, Christian N.
    [DNLM: 1. Family   2. Family Practice.   3. Family Therapy.
  4. Systems Theory.   WB 110 F1985]
  R726.5.F35   1989
  616—dc19
  DNLM/DLC
  for Library of Congress   88-24477
                                                               CIP

Contributors

Troy D. Abell, PhD, MPH, Department of Family Medicine, University of Oklahoma Health Sciences Center, Oklahoma City, Oklahoma

Joel J. Alpert, MD, Department of Pediatrics, Boston City Hospital and Boston University School of Medicine, Boston, Massachusetts

Carol M. Anderson, PhD, MSW, Department of Psychiatry, University of Pittsburgh, Pittsburgh, Pennsylvania

Lisa C. Baker, PhD, Department of Family Medicine, University of Oklahoma Health Sciences Center, Oklahoma City, Oklahoma

Johnye Ballenger, MD, Department of Pediatrics, Boston City Hospital and Boston University School of Medicine, Boston, Massachusetts

W. Robert Beavers, MD, Department of Psychiatry, University of Texas, Dallas, Texas; Southwest Family Institute, Dallas, Texas

Lorne A. Becker, MD, Department of Family and Community Medicine, University of Toronto, Toronto, Ontario, Canada

Donald A. Bloch, MD, The Ackerman Institute for Family Therapy, New York, New York

Joan Borysenko, PhD, Department of Medicine, Harvard Medical School, Boston, Massachusetts

Douglas C. Breunlin, MSW, Institute for Juvenile Research, Chicago, Illinois

Patrick H. Casey, MD, Department of Pediatrics, University of Arkansas for Medical Sciences, Little Rock, Arkansas; Arkansas Children's Hospital, Little Rock, Arkansas

Richard D. Clover, MD, Department of Family Medicine, University of Oklahoma Health Sciences Center, Oklahoma City, Oklahoma

Michelle DeKlyen, MA, Department of Psychology, University of Washington, Seattle, Washington

William J. Doherty, PhD, Departments of Family Social Science and Family Practice and Community Health, University of Minnesota, St. Paul, Minnesota

Robert S. Eliot, MD, The Institute of Stress Medicine, Denver, Colorado

Bernard H. Fox, PhD, Department of Biobehavioral Sciences and Hubert Humphrey Cancer Center, Boston University School of Medicine, Boston, Massachusetts

Stuart T. Hauser, MD, PhD, Joslin Diabetes Center and Department of Psychiatry, Harvard Medical School, Boston, Massachusetts

Raymonde D. Herskowitz, MD, Joslin Diabetes Center, Harvard Medical School, Boston, Massachusetts

Diane P. Holder, MSW, Department of Psychiatry, University of Pittsburgh, Pittsburgh, Pennsylvania

Shih-Tseng T. Huang, MS, Department of Educational Psychology, University of Wisconsin–Madison, Madison, Wisconsin

Alan M. Jacobson, MD, Joslin Diabetes Center and Department of Psychiatry, Harvard Medical School, Boston, Massachusetts

Neil S. Jacobson, PhD, Department of Psychology, University of Washington, Seattle, Washington

Atara Kaplan De-Nour, Department of Psychiatry, Hadassah University Hospital, Jerusalem, Israel

Steven E. Keller, PhD, Department of Psychiatry, UMDNJ–New Jersey Medical School, Newark, New Jersey

Ralph LaRossa, PhD, Department of Sociology, Georgia State University, Atlanta, Georgia

Theodor J. Litman, PhD, School of Public Health, University of Minnesota, Minneapolis, Minnesota

Jay A. Mancini, PhD, College of Human Resources, Virginia Polytechnic Institute and State University, Blacksburg, Virginia

Hamilton I. McCubbin, PhD, School of Family Resources and Consumer Sciences, University of Wisconsin–Madison, Madison, Wisconsin

Marilyn A. McCubbin, PhD, School of Nursing, University of Wisconsin–Madison, Madison, Wisconsin

Mark B. Mengel, MD, MPH, Department of Family Medicine, University of Oklahoma Health Sciences Center, Oklahoma City, Oklahoma

David H. Olson, PhD, Department of Family Social Science, University of Minnesota, St. Paul, Minnesota

Jennifer Orleans, MA, Psychology Department, University of Kansas, Lawrence, Kansas

Joan M. Patterson, PhD, School of Public Health, University of Minnesota, Minneapolis, Minnesota

Lois Pratt, PhD, Department of Sociology, Jersey City State College, Jersey City, New Jersey

Christian N. Ramsey, Jr., MD, Department of Family Medicine, University of Oklahoma Health Sciences Center, Oklahoma City, Oklahoma

John L. Randall, MD, Family Practice Residency Program, Maine Medical Center, Portland, Maine

Donald C. Ransom, PhD, Department of Family and Community Medicine, School of Medicine, University of California, San Francisco, California; Family Practice Residency Program, Community Hospital, Santa Rosa, California

David Reiss, MD, Center for Family Research, George Washington University Medical Center, Washington, D.C.

Steven J. Schleifer, MD, Department of Psychiatry, UMDNJ–New Jersey Medical School, Newark, New Jersey

Karen B. Schmaling, PhD, Department of Medicine, National Jewish Center for Immunology and Respiratory Medicine, Denver, Colorado

David D. Schmidt, MD, Department of Family Medicine, University of Connecticut Health Center, Farmington, Connecticut; Saint Francis Hospital and Medical Center, Hartford, Connecticut

Priscilla M. Schmidt, MA, Department of Family Medicine, University of Connecticut Health Center, Farmington, Connecticut

Stephen J. Spann, MD, Department of Family Medicine, University of Oklahoma Health Sciences Center, Oklahoma City, Oklahoma

John H. Steidl, MSW, The Institute of Pennsylvania Hospital, Philadelphia, Pennsylvania; Department of Psychiatry, Yale University School of Medicine, New Haven, Connecticut

Howard F. Stein, PhD, Department of Family Medicine, University of Oklahoma Health Sciences Center, Oklahoma City, Oklahoma

Marvin Stein, MD, Department of Psychiatry, Mount Sinai School of Medicine, City University of New York, New York, New York

Jeffrey R. Steinbauer, MD, Department of Family Medicine, University of Oklahoma Health Sciences Center, Oklahoma City, Oklahoma

Peter Steinglass, MD, Center for Family Research, George Washington University School of Medicine, Washington, D.C.

Anne I. Thompson, MS, School of Family Resources and Consumer Sciences, University of Wisconsin–Madison, Madison, Wisconsin

Maurine Venters, MPH, PhD, Division of Epidemiology, School of Public Health, University of Minnesota, Minneapolis, Minnesota

Marie Anne Vieyra, MA, Psychology Department, University of Connecticut, Storrs, Connecticut

Donald Wertlieb, PhD, Institute for Health Research, Harvard Community Health Plan, Boston, Massachusetts; Eliot Pearson Department of Child Study, Tufts University, Boston, Massachusetts

Reuben B. Widmer, MD, Department of Family Practice, University of Iowa, Iowa City, Iowa

Joseph I. Wolfsdorf, MD, Joslin Diabetes Center, Harvard Medical School, Boston, Massachusetts

Lyman C. Wynne, MD, PhD, Department of Psychiatry, University of Rochester School of Medicine and Dentistry, Rochester, New York

Foreword

This book may well be a landmark in the evolution of our struggles to understand the origins of health and disease. The wide range of contributors and certainly the editor would be the first to acknowledge that more questions are raised than answered. But that is precisely what is needed. In recent decades, medicine has produced an avalanche of "answers," too many of them half-baked bits and pieces of Lewis Thomas's halfway technology, when what we need most is a broader and deeper set of questions. We need questions that help us understand the complex means by which we perceive, process, integrate, and respond to information generated within the human networks that constitute our "families" and other fellow travelers with whom we interact through time and space.

What we have in this compendium of essays is a vast array of concepts, theories, studies, and methods, representing most of the biologic and behavioral sciences, as well as a variety of practitioners. What seems to be unique is the willingness of each discipline and profession represented to acknowledge the need to integrate its own observations and perspectives into a larger framework, which should make it possible eventually to understand the linkages between family and social systems and the neural, endocrine, and immune systems that mediate our responses and affect our health.

Many of the authors make bold attempts to relate their own findings with those of others and to suggest ways of fostering further collaboration. There even seems to be a collective recognition that it is people—patients and their families—who have the problems and that it is scientists and academicians who have created the departments, disciplines, terms, and definitions that have impeded progress heretofore. The vocabularies of scientists have too often hindered communication among disciplines. When, however, scientists of diverse persuasions focus their collective enquiries, as they do here, on the people who do the striving, struggling, and suffering in living out their allotted life spans, then it is the people's symptoms, complaints, and life experiences that create the common language binding disparate investigators together and compelling clarity of expression as they collaborate.

In contemplating the title of this ambitious work, we may feel trapped by our own traditional terms. The overall contribution of the book is much greater than the sum of its individual chapters. For example, much more than "family"—no matter which of the diverse definitions we choose—is discussed and implied. Networks of interpersonal relationships may extend to neighborhood, occupational, political, and social affiliations and interactions that are accompanied, for example, by joy, euphoria, envy, despair, or anger, with their associated biologic and reverberating psychologic and social ramifications. So "family" in this book becomes a code word, not just for those more intense and sustained sets of human networks with which we usually associate the term, but also for the larger arenas of concentric human systems and patterns that impinge on each of us each day and affect our own and others' well-being and health. Family medicine and its allies in the behavioral sciences and epidemiology have led the way in expanding the horizons of both those who investigate the genesis of health and disease and those who seek to prevent or ameliorate its ravages. In this sense we may speak of the family medicine "movement," since the implications of considering the broader social, cultural, and psychologic contexts in which disease is studied and "medicine" practiced extend far beyond the bounds of one specialty.

Even the term "medicine" gives us problems to the extent that it becomes a code word for the healing professions and even for those social and political interventions that have implications for the health of individuals and their "families." Plant closings, unemployment, natural disasters, information flow, wars, and famines all have impacts through societal and interpersonal shifts, alliances, and tensions that impinge on health. Nurses, social workers, psychologists, and a myriad of other therapists, to say nothing of family and communal support systems, play their therapeutic (and occasionally their destructive) roles, as many of the chapters in this book make clear. Medicine, in the generic sense of a profession, is only one of the actors in an extraordinarily complex drama.

Nevertheless, like it or not, medicine rules the roost! And medicine and physicians have the opportunity and the obligation to change our perspectives. From the organ and the cell, the molecule has been penetrated, and the great bulk of medical research is directed at unraveling its mysteries. Now the available evidence demands that we expand the universe of concern and intensify our studies of individuals and their interactions within family systems and other networks of human associations. What the natural sciences have done for the former dimensions of understanding, the behavioral sciences can do for the latter. But it will take both camps to tackle the most difficult and the most important questions that alone can advance our knowledge of the linkages between the major psychosocial systems that characterize families and other human networks and the body's major regulatory mechanisms, referred to as the psychoneuroendocrine/immune system.

Without in any way detracting from their extraordinary contributions to understanding many of the processes and a few of the precursors of disease, surely many more biologic scientists could foster and support their colleagues in the behavioral sciences as they seek to make their legitimate contributions to understanding the web of causality that finds expression as states of health or disease. True, many elements of the behavioral sciences may be at the same stage Folin was when he diagnosed diabetes mellitus by tasting the patient's urine—but that is no reason to regard them as "soft" and others as "hard." The behavioral and social sciences are as fundamental—as "basic," if you like—as those whose origins are largely biologic. It is the quality, generalizability, and predictability of the findings that determine their credibility, not the site of the research or the stage of the discipline's development.

As many of the contributors from both the behavioral and the biologic sciences make clear in this book, we are at the threshold of potential advances of enormous import. As the authors emphasize, many studies, both biologic and behavioral, are flawed in some way, some fatally flawed, but we need to see where we stand, what we know, and where we go from here. Science is a point of view, an approach to understanding and explaining phenomena. It seeks to minimize bias, error, and wishful thinking of all sorts, but it knows no boundaries—least of all those constructed by academic departments. Indeed, the greatest error of all in science may lie in not asking the important questions—the hard ones.

One reason we produce tomes of this size in medicine is that we lack fundamental understanding of the forces and principles that determine and govern health status. We must resort to partial truths, extrapolations, even anecdotes—as all sciences do, especially in their formative stages. If we had a few general principles at hand, we could organize our observations and practices more parsimoniously. Until that far-off day arrives, we need to consolidate our efforts, integrate our perspectives, clarify our language, and ask the important questions. We must explain to one another, sometimes at great length and in diverse languages, what we think we know, what we think it means, and where we should move next to advance the frontiers of understanding. This book constitutes a substantial contribution to our common task. I hope it will be read by a broad spectrum of scientists and practitioners and will stimulate collaborative research to advance a more encompassing theory of health and disease than that which constrains us now.

Kerr L. White, MD
Stanardsville, Virginia

Acknowledgments

One of the great privileges in my life has been the chance to work with a large number of talented scientists to develop the concept of a Science of Family Medicine. Many people have contributed to my own ideas and have provided professional and personal support throughout the process of bringing seemingly unrelated concepts and data from several disciplines into a unified paradigm. Many others—as evidenced by this volume—have contributed manuscripts in which their work has been reformatted or reoriented to the new paradigm. Space permits acknowledging only a few by name.

Moon Mullins at the University of South Alabama stimulated and confirmed my emerging sense of legitimacy about the study of family systems and biologic outcomes during a postgraduate seminar over 10 years ago. He provided a glimpse of a living, breathing family physician who was systematically exploring family influences on the health care of patients and attempting to teach this to residents. Colleagues in my home environment at that time—Lisa Baker, Troy Abell, Jay Campbell, and Travis Lunceford—provided the initial "family forum" in which to design our first experiments to elaborate the framework for the Science of Family Medicine.

The opportunity of developing a medical school department with medical and family scientists who would work together to further develop the initial ideas of the paradigm came in 1982. During these past 7 years, significant progress has been made in expanding the team beyond Abell, Baker, and Ramsey to include other scholars with expertise in family systems, medicine, and the basic sciences of immunology and biochemistry. One has only to review the academic affiliations of contributors to this book to appreciate the volume and depth of faculty talent within the Department of Family Medicine at the University of Oklahoma College of Medicine. Part of the fun has been observing the refinement of knowledge through experimentation and data analysis and the insinuation of new approaches with the arrival of bright, young recruits. The quality of faculty is a testament to the power and utility of the ideas incorporated in the Science of Family Medicine. The faculty of the Department have provided support, constructive criticism, and review of parts of the manuscript. It is a special privilege for me to be allowed to synthesize many of their ideas into a new paradigm.

Of course, no work such as this can be produced without professional, committed technical assistance. Mary Terrell has typed and retyped my own chapters and those of other faculty in the Department. Laine McCarthy was involved as project director and technical editor from the first and I believe has exceeded even her own expectations of her abilities. We started collection of material for the book by conducting a national conference to bring investigators from many fields together to discuss the state of the Science of Family Medicine. This was to be a 3-day affair that was scheduled for January 1984. Lisa Baker spent untold hours working to help define the program and find the right speakers. Forty invited presentations with discussion were scheduled that covered all aspects of this emerging field. The preparations for the meeting were as detailed as those for a space shuttle launch since we were dealing with people who were well known in their own fields but who didn't know each other or of each other's work. Bringing these world-class scientists together on the condition that they relate their work to a new paradigm was both thrilling and intimidating at the same time.

No one would have been able to predict the 10 inches of snow that arrived in San Antonio, Texas, the night before the meeting was to open. Somehow, Laine got to San Antonio, set up a command post, and spent the next 4 days rearranging the schedule, maintaining contact with stranded speakers from coast to coast, assuring the several hundred attendees that we would not begin until they were all present, cajoling the hotel staff into staying over, and accommodating all of the changes necessitated by the weather. Her greatest accomplishment, however, was constantly reassuring me that it would all work. Those who know my temperament will immediately appreciate the need for this. During the past 5 years, Laine has provided continuity for the entire project by maintaining contact with the authors and has also done a first-class job as technical editor of the volume. Clearly, without her help and leadership, this book would not have been possible.

Of course, my debt to family cannot be adequately expressed in writing. The basis for a Science of Family Medicine started with my own patient families who must be acknowledged but also remain anonymous. Many families allowed me to intrude into their intimate processes, to probe, to question, to support, to intervene. Clinicians will understand the depth of my gratitude to these groups who allowed me to participate in their trials and tribulations. My own biologic family-of-origin contributed substantially to my need to understand certain aspects of family functioning and illness. In addition, being a parent has continuously brought forth new love, gratitude, and respect for my parents.

Finally, my own little family has supported and endured my preoccupation with trying to both (a) formulate the Science of Family Medicine by bringing all of the material together for this book and (b) give it substance by building an academic organization to explore and fill the gaps in knowledge. Anne and Christian have helped me load the computer to take to Aspen during the summer and have allowed me countless weekend days in our little guest house during the past 5 years. Patty has provided exactly the right amount of support to insure that I would get the job done without ever making me feel guilty about the time it required away from her or the children. Somehow, she has provided love in abundant amounts when I wasn't returning nearly enough. To them—Patty, Anne, and Christian—this volume is lovingly dedicated.

C.N.R.

Preface

Teresa, a 13-year-old juvenile-onset diabetic who was encountered early in residency, taught me the importance of the family in the care of patients. This patient was the product of an alcoholic, divorced family. Her mother and two younger siblings were destitute when she presented at the emergency room with her initial episode of ketoacidosis—the mother intoxicated to the point of not being able to give an accurate past history. Constructing ways to help a 13-year-old adapt to a hospital stay, manage her outpatient insulin administration, gain access to a diet alien in the alcoholic culture in which she lived, and deal with the other aspects of medical regimentation without a supporting family system was a real challenge. In this case, lack of family support in the traditional sense forced us to find other, extrafamilial ways to meet the demands of an adolescent with a serious chronic illness. We were successful.

The case of Teresa illustrates the proposition that the practice of primary medicine requires awareness of the impact of the family system on the health, illness, and treatment processes of patients. It provided a vivid lesson of the importance of some things that we often take for granted during the medical care process. During the treatment of many types of problems as a clinician and, subsequently, in experiments that evolved in parallel with my fascination with family systems in medicine, the need for a framework that provided a way to rationalize the interactions of family systems with biologic responses became increasingly apparent. It was intriguing to postulate the mechanisms through which family functioning might be influencing the responses of biologic organs of family members.

The idea of the Science of Family Medicine arose from the need for a new paradigm to explain how family functioning was being transduced and communicated to specific organs of family members. The specific concept of a Science of Family Medicine as proposed herein is the result of more than 10 years of data collection, reflection, and discussion with many colleagues. I believe that clinicians, students, and investigators will find it useful as a framework for codifying, organizing, and integrating the vast amount of information that exists in the field. One has only to examine the number of different journals cited in the reference lists of each of the chapters to begin to comprehend the breadth of thinking that has been pulled together to create this work. Thus, this book is an attempt to reduce the key concepts and studies supporting them to a single, comprehensive treatise that reflects the current state of knowledge in the developing field.

The book is organized into 10 major sections. I have attempted to design each section to be relatively free-standing by including an introductory overview for each section. In this way, the reader can go directly to an area of interest without having to read everything that precedes it. However, as will be apparent from several of the studies cited by various authors, some research suffers from inadequate grounding in either family theory or biologic systems, which then makes it difficult to explain or understand results or to compare the findings to the work of others. Therefore, the introductory chapters dealing with family theory and biologic response systems are recommended to all readers.

Part One consists of three chapters that provide an overview of the Science of Family Medicine and general knowledge about family and biologic systems. The first chapter's purpose is to provide a definition of the Science of Family Medicine and discussions of its impacts on health and illness. The second chapter provides the historic and intellectual background of the fields of family theory and family therapy and reviews the forces that promoted the development of family social science. The third chapter contains the basic anatomy, physiology, and interconnections of the immune and endocrine systems—two of the three major biologic regulatory systems of the Science of Family Medicine.

Part Two is concerned with family theory and its development. Chapter 4 presents an introduction to understanding family theory and the following five chapters cover the major schools of family theory, including perspectives of family development, stress adaptation, typology, and family construction of environmentally sensitive paradigms. The last chapter in this section discusses major family theory issues, including how the status of theory development influences the way in which family health research questions are formulated.

Part Three concerns the methodology of family medicine research. It begins with a comprehensive review of generic and specific methodologic issues that must be countenanced in family medicine experiments. Chapters 12, 13, and 14 contain in-depth discussions of actual methods of measuring family functioning.

Part Four contains material on the family and immune systems. It begins with a review of the interactions between the mind and immune systems, which shows how learning and stress affect immune competence. This is followed by chapters that review the three basic experimental situations that investigators have used in studying family, social, and immune systems: bereavement models, infectious disease models, and neoplasia.

Part Five begins with a review of family systems, stress, and the endocrine system in which the basic interactions between the endocrine and family systems are reviewed. Chapters 20 and 21 contain discussions of two of the major entities that are models for studying family–endocrine system interactions: insulin-dependent diabetes mellitus and cardiovascular risk factors. Substantial work has also been done involving the interaction of family and endocrine systems in eating disorders (obesity, anorexia nervosa, and bulimia) but practical difficulties precluded including this subject.

Part Six is concerned with the family's influence on the fundamental biologic processes of reproduction, growth and development, and aging. It begins with a presentation of a coevolutionary model of the process of symptom development and family development that proposes that symptoms are built into the system through a constructive, iterative, long-term process. This is followed by chapters reviewing the influence of the family system on the outcome of pregnancy, on failure to thrive (childhood growth), and on the aging process. The work presented in this section addresses family system and biologic system growth and development from a longitudinal, interactive perspective.

Thus, the first six sections of the book cover the definition of the Science of Family Medicine and outline the mediators, elements, and results of horizontal and vertical interactions between the family system and biologic systems. The next three sections are concerned with the consequences of these family system–biologic system interactions, including influences on the process of obtaining medical care as well as influences on the course and outcome of both chronic physical illnesses and behavioral and mental disorders.

Part Seven begins with Howard Stein's description of family influences on health behavior. Subsequent chapters cover family influences on the process of medical care from the vantage points of health promotion in the elderly, how decisions to seek medical care are made, and how compliance with a medical regimen is affected. As will be seen, the family system is a major determinant in each of these important areas of the health care delivery process. Today, many health care providers are unaware of the importance of undertanding the family context and dealing with it effectively to help patients obtain maximal outcomes. However, the advent of "managed care" medical delivery systems will probably cause an increased interest in this area by providers and payors, since proper involvement of the family may lead to superior outcomes, a more efficient system, and increased profits.

Chronic illnesses constitute the substantial majority of all physical illness in the United States and present a set of unique challenges to health professionals because of their method of presentation, long course, costs, and influence on family life. Part Eight begins with the presentation of a transactional and developmental model that considers factors in chronic illness of the patient, the family, the illness, and the medical team. Chapters 31, 32, and 33 contain detailed reviews of work done with selected, frequently studied chronic illnesses: end-stage renal disease, hemiplegia resulting from spinal cord injury, and diabetes mellitus.

Beginning Part Nine, Carol Anderson and Diane Holder provide an overview of the commonalities between schizophrenia, depression, and alcoholism which form the basis for our knowledge of the family system's major role in the onset, course, and outcome of these disorders. This is followed by detailed reviews of family system involvement and impacts in each of the three illnesses. I am certain that each chapter will have a major, positive impact on the perspective and ability of every clinician who reads this book. My own knowledge, perceptions, and efficiency in dealing with these illnesses was substantially improved as a result of the editing process.

Part Ten discusses the future of the Science of Family Medicine from four different perspectives. First, Troy Abell discusses the future of research from the viewpoint of the major elements of the research process that come into view once the data are collected: description, inference, and prescription. John Randall's chapter concerns work involving elucidation of the molecular basis of behavior that is genetically (vertically) transmitted in fruit flies and horizontally transmitted through specific molecules in the sea slug. He suggests that these molecular systems represent markers that may be useful in the design and analysis of family medicine experiments. Chapter 40 is a discussion of the implications of differing research traditions, disciplinary backgrounds, and medical orientation of investigators on the design and conduct of future family medicine experiments. The final chapter addresses the notion that the ultimate goal of the Science of Family Medicine is to form a Theory of Family Medicine. The basic requirements for such a theory are presented along with an assessment of progress in meeting them. The conclusion is that while there is much evidence to support theory development, there are still many fundamental questions to be answered.

It is my hope that this book accomplishes three goals: first, to help students at all levels and from many different medical and social science fields learn about family systems in health and illness by providing a comprehensive, organized reference work; second, to provide clinicians and therapists with a paradigm that forms a scientific basis for (a) changing the context of evaluation and treatment, (b) involving other types of professionals in certain cases, and (c) extending treatment efforts to the family itself; and third, to stimulate both new and established investigators to conceptualize new questions, design new experiments, and generally increase the volume of research.

Christian N. Ramsey, Jr.
Oklahoma City, Oklahoma

Contents

Family Systems in Medicine

PART ONE

Introduction

1

The Science of Family Medicine

CHRISTIAN N. RAMSEY, JR.
University of Oklahoma

Clinicians know from experience that family functioning has a significant impact on the risk for or course of illness. The literature of the specialty of family practice contains several exhortations to "put the family into family practice" (Authier, 1978; Authier & Land, 1978; Carmichael, 1978; Schmidt, 1978; Worby, 1971). In a similar vein, the need to enlarge the context of illness to include the family system in treating both physical and mental disease stimulated the development of family therapy and of the family social sciences (Ackerman, 1966a, 1966b; Ackerman, Beatman, & Sherman, 1961; Lewis, 1980; Lewis, Beavers Gossett, & Phillips, 1976; Ransom, Chapter 2, this volume).

Although connections between the family system and the biologic organism have been observed for many years (Crosthwait & Fischer, 1956; Huygens, 1982; Pickle, 1939), investigators have only recently begun to validate their intuition that the functioning of the family system can influence the state of health and health/illness behavior. The fact that biomedical factors account for only half of the cases of a given disease or phenomenon— such as coronary artery disease (Buell & Eliot, 1980) or low birth weight (Ramsey, Abell, & Baker, 1986)—has added impetus to researchers to enlarge the context of investigations to include family system factors.

A new science of family medicine is needed as a paradigm to rationalize the observations of many talented investigators studying the response of the biologic organism to family behavior or functioning. The concept of a science of family medicine includes recognition that the ultimate determinants of biologic status in a given individual are a composite of genetic, biologic, environmental, and behavioral components that can all be provoked, enhanced, or sustained by influences that are beyond simple metabolic or pathophysiologic explanation. It is anticipated that exploration of the science of family medicine will probably prove to be a strong argument toward a biopsychosocial model of medicine (Engel, 1982).

This chapter will define the science of family medicine, review fundamental considerations in understanding and measuring family functioning, and give a broad overview of the physiology and consequences of family–biologic systems interactions.

THE SCIENCE OF FAMILY MEDICINE

The science of family medicine seeks to describe the interactions between the family system and the three major regulatory networks of the body—the nervous, immune, and endocrine systems. There is much evidence that interactions between the family system and the regulatory networks are comprehensive and are major determinants of the physiologic status and functioning of end organs and of individuals. Thus, these interactions play a major role in determining the overall state of health, the onset and/or course of illness, and overall health/illness behavior of an individual and, indeed, of a family.

The goal of the science of family medicine is to develop a theory that explains how the family system influences health or produces illness in a person through its interactions with the nervous, immune, or endocrine system. Health and illness may feed back to the family system to affect family functioning, which may ultimately influence the outcome of illness through recursive interactions with the body's regulatory systems.

Like most emerging disciplines, family medicine is a multidisciplinary field, drawing on both behavioral and biomedical sciences. The social sciences of anthropology, sociology, psychology, and family social science form the crucial family sciences foundation for family medicine. From the biomedical sciences aspect, immunology, biochemistry, genetics, and physiology are the basic physical sciences of family medicine.

A basic proposition of the science of family medicine is that information quanta or stimuli to either the family system or the biologic regulatory networks result in reactions within both systems, which are intimately linked together through both neural and circulatory connections. The reciprocal relationships between the family system and regulatory networks in many conditions suggests that one of the challenges of the field will be to distinguish between the functions and signals that these systems use for communication within and between each other.

Figure 1-1 is a graphic depiction of the interactions between the major systems involved in the science of family medicine.

UNDERSTANDING FAMILY SYSTEMS

A fundamental premise of the science of family medicine is that family functioning can be described using general systems theory or its variants. A number of different approaches have been used by workers in proposing theories to describe family functioning. Family theories have been developed to describe the natural stages of family growth and development (Bowen, 1959, 1960, 1978; Breunlin, Chapter 9, this volume; Hall, 1981; Terkelsen, 1980); the reactions and adaptation mechanisms of the family system to stressors of a variety of different types (Duval, 1977; Hill, 1949; McCubbin & Patterson, 1983a, 1983b); the behavioral typology of families at a given moment in time (Beavers, Chapter 5, this volume; Olson, Chapter 6, this volume; Olson, Sprenkle, & Russell, 1979); and the ways in which families collect, process, and use information from the environment (Moos, 1974; Reiss, 1981, Chapter 8, this volume). Still, enough is not known and a comprehensive theory that is useful in explaining many family system–biobehavioral phenomena is not yet available. As Baker (Chapter 10, this volume) has suggested, perhaps the juxtaposition of descriptions of major theories will promote analysis that will help to uncover connections and similarities, and will lead to the discovery of better theoretical models of family development and functioning.

There is no substitute for proving theory from well-designed experiments. Ultimately, family theory will have to stand such scrutiny in the laboratory. Such testing will require methodology, some of which does not exist at the present time. Methods currently used to analyze family functioning include interviewing, self-report inventories, direct observation, and the completion of tasks and problem solving in naturalistic and laboratory settings. Development of a science of family medicine implies that future methodology may involve the use of biologic markers—alone or in combination with behavioral ones—as accurate, quantiative ways of measuring the functioning of the family system. Biologic markers

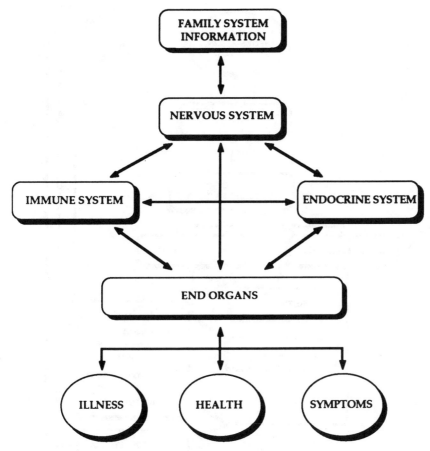

Figure 1-1. Schematic depiction of interactions between the major systems involved in the science of family medicine.

serve as indicators of functional states in many illnesses and disabilities, and it seems logical to assume that they could be harnessed in the service of family systems analysis.

FAMILY/BIOLOGIC SYSTEM PHYSIOLOGY

Family Systems Immunology

Family systems immunology is the study of the interactions between the family and the immune system. The basic area of inquiry involves understanding the immune system's response to family behavior and functioning.

From a theoretical standpoint, a quantum of family system information is processed in the brain of a particular family member. Information processing, depending on its character and message, stimulates the secretion of messenger neuropeptides, which regulate the bone marrow production of T-cells, macrophages, and other elements of the lymphoid system, as shown in Figure 1-2. The general effect is one of activation of the immune

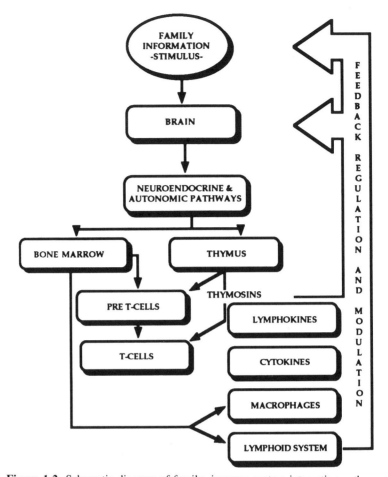

Figure 1-2. Schematic diagram of family–immune system interaction pathways.

system. The cellular components of the immune system secrete a number of cytokines, lymphokines, endorphins, and other inhibitory and stimulatory factors, which provide feedback to both the family and the nervous systems to modulate and regulate the immune response.

Thus, the theoretical framework exists for family systems information to regulate the immune system through the production of neuropeptides or activation of the immune system. Ultimately, the result of activation of the immune system and its consequence (illness, symptom production, defense from illness) would be feedback that would affect family system behavior. The contribution of the science of family medicine to understanding this process will be the explication of whether and how family system information interacts with specific neural circuits to produce a given immune response.

Three general experimental models have been used to study the influence of the family system on immune status. First, workers have looked at the cellular immune response directly to major stressful life events, mainly the death of a spouse. Work with both single individuals and populations shows that immunoincompetence develops in the survivor in response to the death of the female spouse. Schleifer, Keller, Camerino, Thorton, and Stein (1983) and Bartrop, Luckhurst, Lazarus, Kiloh, and Penny (1977) showed that there was decreased lymphocyte functioning in a 6-month period following the death of a spouse. Work with large populations (Kraus & Lillienfield, 1959) has also shown increased morbidity and mortality to infectious disease in the young, widowed, male population of the United States.

The second general model for investigation is more indirect and involves study of the incidence of infectious disease as a response to family behavior. Experimental models utilized include the recurrence of herpes simplex infections (Kemeny, 1985, cited in Turbo, 1987, p. 36; Schmidt & Schmidt, Chapter 17, this volume), the incidence of bacterial and viral infections in natural epidemics (Meyer & Haggerty, 1962) and the incidence of genitourinary and intrauterine infections in pregnancy (work in progress, Department of Family Medicine, University of Oklahoma College of Medicine). The general findings of such experiments are that certain family behaviors predispose to increased rates of infection. This does not necessarily mean that the increased infection rate observed is a direct result of immune incompetence. In fact, at this time, the exact linkage between family behavior, immune response, and incidence of infection has not been conclusively demonstrated, although there is strong suspicion that it does exist.

The third experimental paradigm involves work with neoplasia, both the incidence and the growth rate of tumors, as well as survival time. As with infectious disease, the general hypothesis of such work is that certain behaviors promote tumor growth and dissemination, or decrease survival, or both. Work in the laboratory with animals has shown that social stressors enhance tumor growth (Riley, Fitzmaurice, & Spackman, 1981), but this has not been conclusively demonstrated in human subjects. Also, as Fox points out (Chapter 18, this volume), there is no definitive evidence of the role that family behavior plays in survival.

In each of these conditions, major dislocation or aberration in the functioning of the family system is believed to be related to immune system dysfunction. Attempts to identify the precise physiologic mechanism involved in family system modulation of immunity have not turned up conclusive answers. Most investigators agree that multiple, complex mechanisms and systems are involved. Such factors as the nature of family information, its perception by an individual member, nervous system status, existence of specific neural circuits for family information processing, and nutrition, among others, play an important part in determining the immune response to family behavior.

Family Systems Endocrinology

Family systems endocrinology is the study of interactions between the family and endocrine systems. The basic area of inquiry revolves around how family functioning and behavior affect the physiologic stress reaction, metabolism, water and electrolyte balance, growth and development, reproductive functioning, and other processes under endocrine control. Figure 1-3 is a graphic depiction of family systems endocrinology.

Family systems information is processed in the nervous system and results in the stimulation of one of two basic subdivisions of the endocrine system: hormonal or autonomic. In the hormonal division, stimulation of specific neural circuits (hypothalamic nuclei) causes the secretion of trophic hormones by the anterior pituitary gland, which ultimately control the secretion of hormones by specific end organs. In the autonomic division, stimuli cause a response of the sympathetic nerves with activation of the catecholamine system.

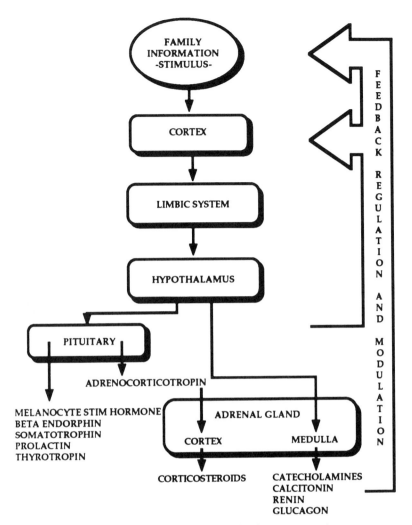

Figure 1-3. Schematic diagram of neuroendocrine stress reaction system.

The family–hormone system components—brain to end organs—display specific messenger molecules for signals, which originate in both systems (Wiedermann & Wiedermann, 1988). These molecules provide the biochemical rationale and matrix for multiple, complex interactions between the family system and specific organs. These pathways and their associated signal molecules allow the tissue, cellular, and molecular levels of the organism to understand and respond to family system inputs.

Major work on the interactions between the family and endocrine systems has centered around diseases of the cardiovascular system, diabetes mellitus, and eating disorders.

Work by Kaplan *et al.* (1983) has shown that, in monkeys, the isolated stress of changing tribes alone is associated with increased atheromatous plaque formation. Medalie and colleagues (Medalie, Snyder, Groen, Neufeld, & Goldbourt, 1973) showed that the incidence of angina increased in a linear relationship to an increase in family problems in Israeli men. Eliot and co-workers (Eliot, Clayton, Pieper, & Todd, 1977; Eliot, Todd, Clayton, & Pieper, 1978) studied the high incidence of sudden death from cardiovascular disease in workers at Kennedy Space Center in the mid-1960s. This population was under great stress, had an unusually high divorce rate, and had the highest alcohol consumption rate in the nation. Postmortem examination revealed a high incidence of hyperfunctional, anomalous contraction bands similar to those seen in animals in whom hyperfunctional necrosis was induced by injecting boluses of catecholamines.

Many of the coronary artery disease risk factors appear to work through or to be activated by catecholamines in concert with hyperlipemia. Catecholamines are secreted as the direct result of stress. In addition, they promote lipid mobilization, platelet adhesiveness, and aggregation; increase the secretion of other hormones (glucagon, thyroxin, calcitonin, parathormone, and renin); and are stimulated by nicotine through smoking. What is not known precisely at this time is what the specific linkages are between family behavior and the end organ response observed in these study populations.

A substantial amount of work with insulin-dependent diabetics shows an association between the family system and the control of this condition. Work with families with an adolescent diabetic have shown that abnormal family dynamics are associated with increased stress and lack of compliance in dietary and insulin procedures (Anderson & Kornblum, 1984; Galazka & Eckert, 1984; Hanson & Henggeler, 1984). Also, Minuchin and colleagues (Minuchin *et al.*, 1975; Minuchin, Rosman, & Baker, 1978) identified a cohort of diabetic families that possessed high cohesion, rigidity in problem solving, overprotectiveness, and lack of acceptable problem-solving mechanisms. Blood fatty acid levels (precursors of diabetic ketoacidosis) in these families were reciprocal between parents and patient. These workers identified specific biochemical reactions that occurred between the parents and patients within this cohort.

Since the family provides the basic context for eating throughout life, it is logical to suspect that family functioning should play a role in the etiology of eating disorders. Work has been done to examine the family role in obesity, anorexia nervosa, and bulimia. Minuchin *et al.* (1978) identified a specific pattern of behavior in families of children with anorexia nervosa and conducted interventions addressed at the family lesions. His results were impressive: Over 85% of the patients treated brought their weight within normal range and maintained normal eating habits for sustained periods (years) after treatment.

Most investigators realize that the interactions between the family and endocrine system involve complex pathways with many feedback loops and controls at several different levels. A further complicating condition is the interconnectedness of the endocrine and immune systems, which increases the levels of complexity tremendously. Although this may be frustrating in attempts to understand the mechanisms involved, the same complexity permits exquisite levels of regulation while also permitting a great degree of individual behavior.

MEDICAL AND HEALTH CONSEQUENCES OF FAMILY–BIOLOGIC SYSTEM INTERACTIONS

Family–biologic system interactions have consequences both in the area of medical care processes and for the course and outcome of illness. As in dissecting the end organ–family system processes, the reciprocal nature of these relationships makes their analysis and understanding very complicated and difficult to approach from an investigational standpoint.

In medical care processes, the family appears to play a major role in at least four areas: (1) in defining what constitutes health versus what constitutes sickness (e.g., the amount of attention that is paid to a symptom); (2) in promoting health and health behavior, through both conscious (nutrition, family physical activity) and unconscious (attitudes, values) efforts; (3) in governing the decision of when to seek or not to seek medical care, as in referral of a family member to a physician; (4) in playing a significant part in determining compliance with a medical or rehabilitation regimen. In other words, the family appears to play a major role in all phases of the health–illness process.

FAMILY INFLUENCE ON THE MEDICAL CARE PROCESS

Definition of Health and Sickness

The family is a major determinant of the individual's view of health and sickness. As Stein points out (Chapter 26, this volume), it is from our families that we bring conscious and unconscious premises, values, attitudes, beliefs, explanations, and expectations (as well as behaviors)—all of which have been patterned in our formative relationships within the family milieu. Many investigators (Eisenberg & Kleinman, 1981; Mechanic, 1978) have proposed that the family context also contributes to the ways in which an individual or family defines a symptom or illness episode, including its meaning, timing, timeliness, organization, and focus.

Health Behavior and Promotion

A number of investigators have studied the role of the family in promoting health. As already mentioned, nutrition is largely determined in the family setting. Also, the family's beliefs about exercise and fitness play a role in determining an individual's participation in these activities. Vaillant (1979) studied a cohort of Harvard undergraduates and found that certain class members shared good health and work success, and experienced fewer divorces than others. Lewis and co-workers (Lewis, 1980; Lewis *et al.*, 1976) studied the characteristics of health within families by comparing those with a sick adolescent to those without. He found that healthy families possessed a multitude of characteristics, including power shared between parents, high levels of psychologic intimacy, highly evolved individuality, and high levels of sexual satisfaction. Pratt (1976), in a study of the health behavior of families in New Jersey, defined the "energized family" as having characteristics similar to those of Lewis's healthy family: a flexible, egalitarian role structure; encouragement of autonomy in individual members; a good community social support network; and active parental efforts to promote a healthful life-style. Pratt (Chapter 27, this volume) has also extended the basic question to examine the family's influence on the health practices of the elderly. Thus, it appears that family functioning plays a major part in health promotion and health behavior across all ages of the family life span.

Decision to Seek Care

A number of workers have investigated the role of the family with reference to the decision to seek medical care. Richardson (1945) first advanced the idea that families play a major role in the decision to seek care in 1945. Medical sociologists, including Mechanic (1978) and Suchman (1965), have developed theories of help-seeking and the stages of illness that provide a basis for the construction of models to study the decision to seek care. Many definitions of health and illness and the responses to them have their basis within the family. Several workers, including Doherty and Baird (1983), have advocated the concept of the "family health expert" who serves as the ultimate family authority on health and refers patients to a medical facility for consultation purposes. Many investigators have pointed out that there is often a relationship between the organization of medical care services and the decision to seek care (Alpert & Ballenger, Chapter 28, this volume; Pratt, 1976).

Compliance

From the standpoint of the medical care process, there is probably no greater problem in caring for patients than in obtaining compliance with a prescribed regimen. Medical regimens often include drug and nondrug therapies, diet, patient education, and physical therapies. Many of these regimens require major changes in life-style, such as stopping smoking or changing diet. The family's role in compliance has been studied from the standpoint of both cause and intervention. For instance, Stuart and Davis (1972) found that lack of support by husbands interfered with compliance in a group of women attempting to lose weight. Family behaviors also inhibit compliance in smoking cessation (Mermelstein, Lichtenstein, & McIntyre, 1983), coronary risk modification (Doherty, Schrott, Metcalf, & Iasiello-Vailas, 1983), and treatment of depression (Strickland, Alston, & Davidson, 1981). A few intervention studies show improved compliance and better outcomes when family members are included in the treatment program (Falloon, Liberman, Lillie, & Vaughn, 1981). Morisky, Bowler, and Finlay (1982) found that teaching a close family member to assist with adherence to the patient's antihypertensive regimen was more effective than individual instruction to the patient or the use of a support group in improving compliance and blood pressure control. Several carefully performed, randomized, controlled trials have shown benefits from family involvement in improving compliance and success in weight loss programs (Brownell, Heckerman, Westlake, Hayes, & Monti, 1978; Brownell, Kelman, & Stunkard, 1983; Saccone & Israel, 1978).

In summary, there is considerable evidence from many investigators, in many different settings, using many different illnesses and methods, that demonstrates that the family plays a major role in every step of the process of medical care. Whether the question is paying attention to a symptom, participating in a health promotion activity, or complying with a prescribed regimen, the family is a major player. Although investigation and analysis of the ways in which the family is involved in these decisions have not been as intensive as many would have liked, the advent of managed care systems for medical care will likely stimulate research into how families participate in the process of care—if for no other reason than for insurers and medical providers to gain competitive advantage, to improve efficiency, and to obtain greater economic rewards for their efforts.

COURSE AND OUTCOME OF ILLNESS

Chronic Physical Illness

Chronic illnesses are unique along the spectrum of sickness. They are generally characterized by insidious onset; ongoing discomfort and constraint; downhill course with or without periods of remission; the potential for extreme expense and unlimited amounts of treatment; and extraordinary demands on family, patient, and medical care system. In analyzing chronic physical illness, Reiss and Kaptan De-Nour (Chapter 30, this volume) have pointed out that it is useful to study the characteristics of the players—patient, family, and medical personnel; the illness itself; and the interaction of the players and the illness across the course of illness. Clearly, isolating family role in this situation becomes a complex enterprise. Workers have studied the family systems' influence on a number of different chronic illnesses and conditions, including end-stage renal disease, diabetes, cystic fibrosis, arthritis, spinal cord injury, and a variety of forms of cardiovascular disease (stroke, hypertensive disease, coronary atherosclerosis).

Investigators have studied the ways in which families influence the course of illness. The data are not clear on the family role; it would seem that there are potential benefits and costs from different types of family involvement with chronic illness patients. Oakes (1970) found that there were benefits for the patient in terms of better health outcomes when families involved all members in meeting multiple system needs and when they attributed positive meaning to the situation. On the cost side, some investigators (Coyne, Wortman, Lehman, & Turnbull, 1985; Monteiro, 1987) have found that overinvolvement of a spouse can undermine patient adaptation to chronic conditions. Reiss, Gonzalez, and Kramer (1986) found that certain families appeared to hasten the demise of patients with chronic renal disease. In summary, the one conclusion on which all investigators can agree is that family functioning influences the course and outcome of chronic illness. The exact mechanisms through which families exert influence on the course and outcome of chronic illness are elusive. Ultimately, it is hoped that better understanding of the ways in which the family system influences the course and outcome of chronic illness will allow for the generation of ways of teaching families how to provide positive assistance to the patient's experience of illness.

Behavioral and Psychologic Disorders

Family dysfunction has been implicated in the cause and course of mental illness. Although there is no conclusive evidence on the single etiology of most mental disorders, the family system, along with biologic and/or genetic factors, has been identified as a factor in several major entities.

Mental illnesses generally have chronic courses in which the patient has a strong impact on the other family members. Anderson and Holder (Chapter 34, this volume) have reviewed the impact of mental illness on family functioning. Depending on the circumstances, family members may be required to take on caretaking roles or extra duties for extended periods of time. In some cases, family relationships are reorganized around the illness, and the family may become isolated from extended family or community. Thus, these disorders have the potential to distort, delay, or subvert phases of family development to a significant degree. The family role in course and outcome of mental illness has been studied extensively in schizophrenia, depression, and alcoholism.

Wynne (Chapter 35, this volume; 1968) has conceptualized schizophrenia as the result of a complex developmental, epigenetic process, which involves multiple system levels—genetic and nongenetic biologic factors, intra- and extrafamilial rearing variables, variations in the fit of intrapsychic processes, and responsiveness of the therapeutic systems—that interface with the family system and the patient. Within this construct, investigators and clinicians have recognized that treatment of schizophrenia requires systems intervention on multiple levels: biomedical, environmental, and family. Several groups have conducted treatment programs with special emphasis on assisting the families of schizophrenic patients with behavioral and educational interventions. Many of these workers have shown impressive results in terms of relapse, symptomatology, and cost of treatment (Anderson, Reiss, & Hogarty, 1986; Falloon, Boyd, & McGill, 1984; Falloon *et al.*, 1981, 1985; Wynne, 1968) when it is carried out in the family context.

Depression is also a complex illness with both physical and mental determinants. Widmer and colleagues (Cadoret, Widmer, & North, 1980; Widmer & Cadoret, 1978; Widmer, Cadoret, & North, 1980) have documented the patterns of medical visits of depressed patients and their family members, showing both an increased number of visits and an increased number of complaints in the period before the diagnosis is made. Thus, family member behavior reflects the pervasive influence of depression on the entire family in those cases in which outside help is sought. Also, several investigators (Biglan *et al.*, 1985; Coyne, 1976a, 1976b; Hops *et al.*, 1987) have reported the importance of interaction style with family members in maintaining patients' symptoms of depression. Clearly, the work of Widmer and his co-workers (Cadoret *et al.*, 1980; Widmer & Cadoret, 1978; Widmer *et al.*, 1980) looking at usage of the health care system for multiple complaints suggests that treating depression in the family context should be effective. A difficulty in designing a comparative study of family versus nonfamily treatment is that making the diagnosis is difficult. As the Widmer work points out, early diagnosis involves family behavior; therefore, simply identifying the need for family intervention is a different proposition than in those situations in which the onset of illness is sudden and discrete and involves only the affected member.

Alcoholism is also a complex illness, which, like schizophrenia and depression, is affected by and has a significant impact on the family system. Steinglass (Chapter 37, this volume) has reviewed work in three areas relating to alcoholism and has drawn three major conclusions. First, studies show that family behaviors vary depending on the specific drinking characteristics of the alcoholic family member (e.g., Jacob, Dunn, & Leonard, 1983; Jacob, Ritchey, Cvitkovic, & Blaine, 1981; Steinglass, 1980, 1981). Second, studies by Wolin and Bennett (1984; Wolin, Bennet, Noonan, & Teitelbaum, 1980) provide evidence that surface behaviors can be used to track the intergenerational course of alcoholism. Third, evidence that the developmental perspective is helpful in understanding the course of designing treatment protocols for alcoholism (Steinglass, Bennett, Wolin, & Reiss, 1987). While most clinicians and treatment protocols recommend involving the family in the treatment process, there has not been a definitive study to show that treating the family as the unit or treating the alcoholic patient in the family context yields superior outcomes (Hazelden Research Services, 1986; Kellerman, 1984; Kirn, 1986).

Interestingly, although a great deal is known about the biology of each of these three entities, few workers have measured family systems, biologic, behavioral, and outcome variables simultaneously. It is hoped that investigators will conduct experiments in which such variables are measured simultaneously in the future. Perhaps such experiments will aid in understanding the relationship between family system functioning and biologic/behavioral course and severity.

CONCLUSION

The promise of a science of family medicine lies in its potential to help us understand the complex ways in which family functioning may determine health and illness. From the available evidence, it is clear that family functioning has the potential to determine one's ability to resist infections, allergies, autoimmune diseases, and cancer, as well as how well one copes with these illnesses or with mental disorders. Family functioning may also determine the course of illness and even whether or how quickly one dies from an illness. Most investigators and clinicians know deep inside that family system influences exist, but feel inadequate in trying to explain how they work or how to harness, predict, or control them. Thus, they cannot usually be addressed in scientific perspective. In the face of these feelings of inadequacy, it is easy to understand the natural tendency not to be bothered with such things. Perhaps development of a science of family medicine will change all this.

This book is evidence that a number of gifted scholars and investigators recognize that a science that focuses on the family system's interactions with the three major regulatory networks of the body is serious. The major questions revolve around how these systems—family, nervous, endocrine, and immune—interact to produce illness or alter its course. The coming years will be a period of intense concentration on the elucidation of the precise mechanisms that produce such suffering. Such investigations and the theory development that will accompany them will surely help solidify the true identity of family medicine as a discipline in its own right.

For the future, it will be of the greatest importance to exercise great care in the development, conduct, and critical interpretation of those experiments that will contribute to the ultimate definition of the science of family medicine.

References

Ackerman NW. Family psychotherapy—theory and practice. American Journal of Psychotherapy 1966a; 20:405–414.

Ackerman NW. Treating the troubled family. New York: Basic Books, 1966b.

Ackerman N, Beatman F, Sherman S, eds. Exploring the base for family therapy. New York: Family Service Association, 1961.

Anderson BJ, Kornblum H. The family environment of children with a diabetic parent: issues for research. Family Systems Medicine 1984; 2:17–27.

Anderson CM, Reiss DJ, Hogarty GE. Schizophrenia in the family: a practitioner's guide to psychoeducation and management. New York: Guilford Press, 1986.

Authier JL. How to put the "family" in family medicine. Presented at the annual meeting of the Society of Teachers of Family Medicine, San Diego, May 6–9, 1978.

Authier J, Land T. Family: the unique component of family medicine. Journal of Family Practice 1978; 7:1066–1068.

Bartrop RW, Luckhurst E, Lazarus L, Kiloh LG, Penny R. Depressed lymphocyte function after bereavement. Lancet 1977; April 16:834–836.

Biglan A, Hops H, Sherman L, Friedman LS, Arthur J, Osteen V. Problem-solving interactions of depressed women and their husbands. Behavior Therapy 1985; 16:431–451.

Bowen M. A family concept of schizophrenia. In: Jackson D, ed. The etiology of schizophrenia. New York: Basic Books, 1960:346–372.

Bowen M. Family relationships in schizophrenia. In: Auerback A, ed. Schizophrenia—an integrated approach. New York: Ronald Press, 1959:147–178.

Bowen M. On the differentiation of self. In: Bowen M, ed. Family therapy in clinical practice. New York: Jason Aronson, 1978:467–528.

Brownell KD, Heckerman CL, Westlake RJ, Hayes SC, Monti PM. The effect of couples training and partner cooperativeness in the behavioral treatment of obesity. Behaviour Research and Therapy 1978; 16:323–333.

Brownell KD, Kelman JH, Stunkard AD. Treatment of obese children with and without their mothers: changes in weight and blood pressure. Pediatrics 1983; 71:515–523.

Buell JC, Eliot RS. Psychosocial and behavioral influences in the pathogenesis of acquired cardiovascular disease. American Heart Journal 1980; 100:723–740.

Cadoret RJ, Widmer RB, North C. Depression in family practice: long term prognosis and somatic complaints. Journal of Family Practice 1980; 10:625–629.

Carmichael LP. Relational model, family, ethics. Presented at the annual meeting of the Society of Teachers of Family Medicine, San Diego, May 6–9, 1978.

Coyne JC. Depression and the response of others. Journal of Abnormal Psychology 1976a; 85:186–193.

Coyne JC. Toward an interactional description of depression. Psychiatry 1976b; 39:28–40.

Coyne JC, Wortman C, Lehman D. Turnbull J. When support fails: miscarried helping processes. In: Caplan RD, chair. Nonsupportive aspects of social relationships. Symposium conducted at the annual meeting of the American Psychological Association, Los Angeles, 1985.

Crosthwait WL, Fischer GE. The last stitch. New York: Lippincott, 1956.

Doherty WJ, Baird MA. Family therapy and family medicine. New York: Guilford Press, 1983.

Doherty WL, Schrott HG, Metcalf L, Iasiello-Vailas L. Effect of spouse support and health beliefs on medication adherence. Journal of Family Practice 1983; 17(5):837–841.

Duvall E. Marriage and family development, 5th ed. Philadelphia: Lippincott, 1977.

Eisenberg L, Kleinman A, eds. The relevance of social science for medicine: culture, illness, and healing: I. Boston: Reidel, 1981.

Eliot RS, Clayton FC, Pieper GM, Todd GL. Influence of environmental stress on the pathogenesis of sudden cardiac death. Federation Proceedings 1977; 36:1719.

Eliot RS, Todd GL, Clayton FC, Pieper GM. Experimental catecholamine-induced acute myocardial necrosis. In: Manninen V, Halonen PI, eds. Advances in cardiology, Vol 25. Basel: S. Karger AG, 1978: 107–118.

Engel GL. The biopsychosocial model and medical education: who are to be the teachers? New England Journal of Medicine 1982; 306:802–805.

Falloon IRH, Boyd JL, McGill CW. Family care of schizophrenia: a problem-solving approach to the treatment of mental illness. New York: Guilford Press, 1984.

Falloon IRH, Boyd JL, McGill CW, Razani J, Moss HB, Gilderman AM. Family management in the prevention of exacerbations of schizophrenia. New England Journal of Medicine 1981; 306:1437–1440.

Falloon IRH, Boyd JL, McGill CW, Razani J, Moss HB, Gilderman AM. Family management in the prevention of morbidity of schizophrenia: clinical outcome of a two-year longitudinal study. Archives of General Psychiatry 1985; 42:887–896.

Falloon IRH, Liberman RP, Lillie FJ, Vaughn CE. Family therapy of schizophrenics with high risk of relapse. Family Process 1981; 20:211–221.

Galazka SS, Eckert JK. Diabetes mellitus from the inside out: ecological perspectives on a chronic disease. Family Systems Medicine 1984; 2:28–36.

Hall MC, ed. The Bowen family theory and its uses. New York: Jason Aronson, 1981.

Hanson CL, Henggeler SW. Metabolic control in adolescents with diabetes: an examination of systemic variables. Family Systems Medicine 1984; 2:5–16.

Hazelden Research Services. Consultation services. Minneapolis, Minn.: Hazelden Foundation, 1986.

Hill R. Families under stress. New York: Harper, 1949.

Hops H, Biglan A, Sherman L, Arthur J, Friedman L, Osteen V. Home observations of family interactions of depressed women. Journal of Consulting and Clinical Psychology 1987; 55(3):341–346.

Huygens FJA. Family medicine. New York: Brunner/Mazel, 1982.

Jacob T, Dunn NJ, Leonard K. Patterns of alcoholic abuse and family stability. Alcoholism: Clinical and Experimental Research 1983; 7:382–385.

Jacob T, Ritchey D, Cvitkovic J, Blaine J. Communication styles of alcoholic and nonalcoholic families while drinking and not drinking. Journal of Studies on Alcohol 1981; 42:466–482.

Kaplan JR, Manuck SB, Clarkson TB, Lusso FM, Taub DM, Miller EW. Social stress and atherosclerosis in normocholesterolemic monkeys. Science 1983; 220:733–735.

Kellerman JL. The family and alcoholism: a move from pathology to process. Minneapolis, Minn.: Hazelden Foundation, 1984.

Kirn TK. Advances in understanding of alcoholism initiate evolution in treatment programs. Journal of the American Medical Association 1986; 256(11):1405, 1411–1412.

Kraus AS, Lillienfeld AM. Some epidemiological aspects of the high mortality rate in the young widowed group. Journal of Chronic Diseases 1959; 10:207–217.

Lewis JM. The family matrix in health and disease. In: Hofling CK, Lewis JM, eds. The family: evaluation and treatment. New York: Brunner/Mazel, 1980: 5–44.

Lewis JM, Beavers WR, Gossett JT, Phillips VA. No single thread. New York: Brunner/Mazel, 1976.

McCubbin HI, Patterson JM. Family stress and adaptation to crises: a double ABCX model of family behavior. In: Olson D, Miller B, eds. Family studies review yearbook. Beverly Hills, Calif.: Sage, 1983a:87–106.

McCubbin HI, Patterson JM. The family stress process: the double ABCX model of family adjustment and adaptation. In: McCubbin HI, Sussman M, Patterson JM, eds. Advances and developments in family stress theory and research. New York: Haworth, 1983b:7–37.

Mechanic D. Medical sociology: a comprehensive test, 2nd ed. New York: Free Press, 1978.

Medalie JH, Snyder M, Groen JJ, Neufeld HN, Goldbourt U. Angina pectoris among 10,000 men. American Journal of Medicine 1973; 55:583.

Mermelstein R, Lichtenstein E, McIntyre K. Partner support and relapses in smoking-cessation programs. Journal of Consulting and Clinical Psychology 1983; 51(3):465–466.

Meyer RJ, Haggerty RJ. Streptococcal infections in families: factors altering individual susceptibility. Pediatrics 1962; 29:539–549.

Minuchin S, Baker L, Rosman BL, Liebman R, Milman L, Todd TC. A conceptual model of psychosomatic illness in children: family organization and family therapy. Archives of General Psychiatry 1975; 32:1031–1038.

Minuchin S, Rosman BL, Baker L. Psychosomatic families: anorexia nervosa in context. Cambridge, Mass.: Harvard University Press, 1978.

Monteiro L. A nursing intervention to improve the functioning of females after myocardial infarction. Report to the Robert Wood Johnson Fellows' Meeting, New Orleans, March 1987.

Moos R. FES—Family Environment Scale (research instrument). Palo Alto, Calif.: Consulting Psychologists Press, 1974.

Morisky DE, Bowler MH, Finlay JS. An educational approach toward increasing patient activation in hypertension management. Journal of Community Health 1982; 7(3):171–182.

Oakes TW. Family expectations and arthritis patient compliance to a hand-resting splint regimen. Journal of Chronic Disease 1970; 22:757.

Olson DH, Sprenkle DH, Russell CS. Circumplex model of marital and family systems: I. Cohesion and adaptability dimensions, family types, and clinical applications. Family Process 1979; 18(1):3–28.

Pickle W. Epidemiology in country practice. Bristol: John Wright & Sons, 1939.

Pratt L. Family structure and effective health behavior: the energized family. Boston: Houghton Mifflin, 1976.

Ramsey CN, Abell TD, Baker LC. The relationship between family functioning, life events, family structure, and the outcome of pregnancy. Journal of Family Practice 1986; 22:521–527.

Reiss D. The family's construction of reality. Cambridge, Mass.: Harvard University Press, 1981.

Reiss D, Gonzalez S, Kramer N. Family process, chronic illness and death. Archives of General Psychiatry 1986; 43:795–804.

Richardson HB. Patients have families. New York: Commonwealth Fund, 1945.

Riley V, Fitzmaurice MA, Spackman DH. Psychoneuroimmunologic factors in neoplasia: studies in animals. In: Ader R, ed. Psychoneuroimmunology. New York: Academic Press, 1981:31–102.

Saccone AJ, Israel AC. Effects of experimenter versus significant other controlled reinforcement and choice of target behavior on weight loss. Behavior Therapy 1978; 9:271–278.

Schleifer SJ, Keller SE, Camerino M, Thornton JC, Stein M. Suppression of lymphocyte stimulation following bereavement. Journal of the American Medical Association 1983; 250:374–377.

Schmidt DD. The family as the unit of medical care. Journal of Family Practice 1978; 7:303–313.

Steinglass P. A life history model of the alcoholic family. Family Process 1980; 19:211–227.

Steinglass P. The alcoholic family at home: patterns of interaction in dry, wet, and transitional stages of alcoholism. Archives of General Psychiatry 1981; 38:578–584.

Steinglass P, Bennett LA, Wolin SJ, Reiss D. The alcoholic family. New York: Basic Books, 1987.

Strickland R, Alston F, Davidson J. The negative influence of families on compliance. Hospital Community Psychiatry 1981; 32(5):349–350.

Stuart RB, Davis B. Slim chance in a fat world: behavioral control of obesity. Champaign, Ill.: Research, 1972.

Suchman E. Stages of illness and medical care. Journal of Health and Human Behavior 1965; 6:114–128.

Terkelsen KG. Toward a theory of family life cycle. In: Carter EA, McGoldrick M, eds. The family life cycle: a framework for family therapy. New York: Gardner Press, 1980:21–52.

Turbo R. Stress and disease: cellular evidence hints at therapy. Medical World News, January 26, 1987: 26–28, 35–36, 39–41.

Vaillant GE. Natural history of male psychologic health: effects of mental health on physical health. New England Journal of Medicine 1979; 301:1249–1254.

Widmer RB, Cadoret RJ. Depression in primary care: changes in pattern of patient visits and complaints during a developing depression. Journal of Family Practice 1978; 7:293–302.

Widmer RB, Cadoret RJ, North CS. Depression in family practice: some effects on spouses and children. Journal of Family Practice 1980; 10:45–51.

Wiedermann CJ, Wiedermann M. Psychoimmunology: systems medicine at the molecular level. Family Systems Medicine 1988; 6(1):94–106.

Wolin SJ, Bennett LA. Family rituals. Family Process 1984; 23:401–420.

Wolin SJ, Bennett LA, Noonan DL, Teitelbaum MA. Disruptive family rituals: a factor in the intergenerational transmission of alcoholism. Journal of Studies on Alcohol 1980; 41:199–214.

Worby CM. The family life cycle: an orienting concept for the family practice specialist. Journal of Medical Education 1971; 46:1971.

Wynne LC. Methodologic and conceptual issues in the study of schizophrenics and their families. Journal of Psychiatric Research 1968; 6(Suppl):185–199.

2

Development of Family Therapy and Family Theory

DONALD C. RANSOM
University of California, San Francisco;
Community Hospital, Santa Rosa, California

This chapter introduces strands from the development of family therapy and family theory that provide an intellectual-historical backdrop for the emerging science of family medicine. To simplify what would be a formidable task if done comprehensively, I will only draw upon selected contributions from the social sciences and medicine from the turn of the century to the period just before the groundswell of interest in family practice that led to its eventual approval as a specialty in 1969. For reasons I will return to later in the chapter, the establishment of family practice training requirements led to a dramatic increase in interdisciplinary cooperation and opened the way to many new developments of the kind reflected by this book. No effort will be made to include here contributions from philosophy, which have been highly influential to the evolving perspective of family systems theory. Theoretical developments after 1970 are also left aside. These are summarized in Chapter 4 by Baker and Patterson and further elaborated by some of their original proponents in the remainder of Part One of this book.

My aim is to sketch the contributions that foreshadowed in various ways what has evolved into the family systems approach. This work constitutes one important conceptual dimension of what is now being constructed as the science of family medicine.

FAMILY MEDICINE AND FAMILY THERAPY

In three earlier papers (Ransom, 1981; Ransom & Vandervoort, 1973; Vandervoort & Ransom, 1973), I outlined a general conception of family medicine and emphasized the importance of introducing the study of family relatedness and health in medical education and research. The great opportunity and promise of the new specialty of family practice lay in focusing on health-relevant processes within primary groups.

Family medicine is a field of inquiry that draws heavily on a broad range of scientific and professional contributors. What can become obscured, however, when the term "family" is used repeatedly as the noun and adjective of choice, is that it is not the family as entity or institution that is of central concern, but "family" as a metaphoric designation for primary, largely self-regulated human systems. Thus, family systems medicine is concerned with processes in any group that make a significant health difference in its members' lives. More important than fixing on any particular corporate group is "family mindedness" (Sluzki, 1974) among both researchers and providers, as problems of health, illness, and care are conceptualized, defined, and addressed in relation to their specific social contexts.

Within the wide-ranging field generally called psychotherapy, the past 30 years have seen the collateral interest in the families of those called patients extend to a focus on families themselves as relevant units of assessment, intervention, and research. This shift to a specific concern with the primacy of ongoing relationships has led to far-reaching conceptual and practical changes in the helping professions. Conceptually, the simplest way to describe this turn is to note the reversal from viewing the family and other primary relationships in terms of the patient to viewing the patient in terms of these relationships. Figure and ground have become reversed and made reversible, and the relevant field of analysis has thereby grown larger, circular, and remarkably more flexible. Practically, the most obvious difference has meant developing new sets of therapeutic techniques aimed at changing patterns of interpersonal relationships directly through working face to face with family members. In time, this shift has included a move away from an exclusive concern with families of psychiatric patients to involvement with families and persons with all types of health and personal problems.

One of the most successful developments that has emerged from and in turn shaped these changes is "family therapy." Quotation marks are used here to note that the term cannot be taken narrowly to hold any one meaning; yet in the larger picture family therapy has assumed the status of a movement in the mental health field. In common usage, family therapy refers to both *a form of therapeutic intervention* and *a conceptual approach to human problems*. It is not a therapeutic method in the usual sense. There is no agreed-on set of procedures followed by practitioners who consider themselves family therapists and no set of techniques to which they jointly adhere. Different therapists approach different families and different problems in a variety of ways. What is consistent is that, at the conceptual level, family therapy embodies the same "family approach" referred to as "family mindedness" above. In its simplest statement, this means that problems are understood and addressed as expressions of the universal constraints and difficulties that arise from the neotonous nature of *Homo sapiens* and from the costs and benefits of maintaining intimate relationships in essential family groups. What unifies family therapists is their search for the source of both problems and solutions within recurring patterns of ordinary life. As outlined by Ramsey in Chapter 1 of this book, what the science of family medicine is now adding to this story is an exploration of how family patterns inform the major regulatory systems of their members' bodies.

Family therapy and family systems medicine share many of the same intellectual roots, even though the practical clinical fields of family therapy and family practice evolved separately until 1969. Next, I will trace a number of early developments that made possible the emergence of our present-day sense of family systems medicine.

THE EMERGENCE OF FAMILY-CENTERED CONCEPTIONS OF HEALTH AND PATHOLOGY

From the beginning, all psychological and social theories of development and nearly all theories of psychopathology have been interested in the family. It is misleading to suggest, as is often done, that only in the past 30 years has the family come to be viewed as an important source of healthy or disturbed individual behavior. What has occurred since the early work on family therapy in the 1950s is not the realization that the family plays an important part in human development, but the elaboration of this insight along new avenues of thought: avenues that define the relationship between person and family in a new set of terms, and focus on the family as a system. This change opened up a central place for families as legitimate subjects for theory, research, and intervention.

This shift in focus constituted a reframing that achieved a new understanding of what had long been observed and suppressed or ignored. Why the family was continually acknowledged as significant but always eluding the grasp of theoreticians and practitioners alike is a complicated story, perhaps best summarized by Spiegel and Bell in their classic review: "The problems of the forced and inhibiting compromise between attending to the individual and attending to the family at the procedural level, and the lack of adequate conceptualization of the interrelations between the family and the individual at the theoretical level, are undoubtedly part of the picture" (1959, p. 116).

The new perspective is impossible to describe precisely. More than a theory in the sense usually meant by the term, the family systems approach employs a new metaphor and a new language in which to converse. As Richard Rorty suggests in the first of his Northcliffe Lectures, interesting philosophy is never an examination of the pros and cons of a thesis, but "a contest between an entrenched vocabulary which has become a nuisance and a half-formed new vocabulary which vaguely promises great things" (1987, p. 4). In the same spirit as Kuhn (1970), Rorty views progress as the process of redescribing things in novel ways until a rising generation is tempted to adopt a new pattern of behavior. So it is with family systems approaches and "normal" medical science vying for usefulness for a large share of the family physician's needs.

The perspective being traced here introduces a language of context and contingency to the medical arena. Patients and family are seen within a seamless web, a reticular system that is clumsily called a biopsychosocial unit.

The patient is no longer viewed as someone on whom a particular history of fragmented two-person relationships and intrapsychic conflicts has simply come to leave its mark. Nor is the patient viewed as a neutral organism to whom biomedical events just happen. Patients are viewed as active, constructive agents whose health and illness are meaningful both within the context in which they have adapted and developed (diachronic axis) and within the context in which they currently live (synchronic axis).

EARLY SOURCES OF INDEPENDENT ACTIVITY

The history of contemporary conceptions of family processes and individual development is difficult to trace because there are so many streams running independently in parallel until the 1950s. Since then, workers interested in health and illness have drawn on all of these sources to construct a transdisciplinary, ecosystemic perspective.

In retrospect, five sources stand out as having contributed to the intellectual climate and provided the practical tools that set the stage for the rapid developments of the past 30 years. These are:

1. Classical psychoanalysis and the subsequent emergence of psychoanalytic ego psychology and object relations theory.
2. The expansion of state mental hospital systems and the accompanying increase in the importance of contact between mental health workers and patients' families.
3. The child guidance movement, born in the 1920s, progressing toward dividing up the work of emotional problems between working directly with the child and working with the parents, and culminating with the example of the Philadelphia Child Guidance Clinic.
4. The influence of American sociological theory.
5. The awakening of an interest in the family's role in physical health.

Early Psychoanalysis

Freud's psychoanalytic writings explored the effect of the family on the potential for healthy or pathological development in the child. The early theory of psychic trauma, difficulties of psychosexual stage transitions, especially the resolution of the oedipal complex, problems of sibling rivalry, and the process of identification all implicate intrafamilial events and family members as central to understanding the developing child. But Freud viewed the family primarily as a by-product of the playing out of intrapsychic forces between people. He described all group and cultural life by extrapolating the terms of an intrapsychic determinism onto social processes.

It is common to hear arguments that psychoanalysis could make only a limited contribution to an evolving family approach because it is essentially atomistic and reductionist in its outlook. The language of psychoanalysis has always preferred terms that describe processes within individuals, such as needs, fantasies, conflicts, anxiety, and wishes, or terms that describe two persons in stylized forms of a complementary relationship, such as symbiosis, dominant–submissive, sadomasochistic, and the like. Another observation is that psychoanalysts resisted dealing with the patient's family directly because it was thought that to involve others would disturb ("dilute") the patient–analyst "transference," the principal modality of treatment, and would thereby prove to be antitherapeutic in the long run. Hence, there were both conceptual and technical preferences that led to the whole family and the real family being ignored in favor of dealing with internalized fragments of that family.

These observations, though accurate enough, merely point out why psychoanalysis was prevented from exploring the other side of the symptoms and pathologic behavioral patterns discovered through analytic treatment. It seems clear today that family connections were made, but they could not be elaborated for lack of a concept of a social system and because of the limitations of the treatment technique. This can be safely said if we observe the discrepancy between Freud the theorist and Freud the astutely observant clinician. In all of Freud's case histories, the family is intricately implicated. The contemporary reader can easily be led to proclaim Freud as the first family theorist, only to find that he follows his observations up a different alley, couching his discoveries and his explanations always exclusively in intrapsychic terms.

In the case of Dora, for example, one could piece together all the evidence presented and describe both the situation and the ultimate change in Dora's "neurotic" behavior completely in contemporary family theoretic terms. In "Fragment of an Analysis of a Case of Hysteria" (1959/1905), Freud presents the elaborate details of 18-year-old Dora's family situation. That situation includes a mother with "housewife's psychosis" (whom Freud actually never met, but whom he describes on the basis of the patient's and the patient's father's account of her); a brother one and a half years older who, when obliged to take sides, would support his mother; a deceitful and philandering father (prone to periods of depression); a psychoneurotic aunt "weighed down by an unhappy marriage"; a "hypochondriacal bachelor" uncle; and a governess who was in love with Dora's father and who befriended Dora only as a means to advance her intentions toward him. Close alliances with a second family, which contained Dora's father's mistress (a woman who had been an invalid and had even been obliged to spend months in a sanatorium for nervous disorders because she was unable to walk, but who became a healthy and lively woman following her affair with Dora's father), and her husband, who had made sexual advances toward Dora and with whom Dora was apparently in love.

There is no question that Freud was aware of the importance of these circumstances. Early in the presentation he says:

> It follows from the nature of the facts which form the material of psychoanalysis that we are obliged to pay as much attention in our case histories to the purely human and social circumstances of our patients as to the somatic data and the symptoms of the disorder. Above all, our interest will be directed towards their family circumstances—and not only, as will be seen, for purposes of inquiring into their heredity. (1959/1905, p. 25)

Freud's account does not stop with a description of the main characters. He portrays a delicately balanced and tightly woven web of relationships between Dora's family and the family of Dora's father's mistress, and he gives the impression that, for several years at least, these families constituted their own miniature world, with its own rules, myths, and intricate structure of reciprocal roles, whose characters were so immured that disclosure or escape did not occur to them.

Freud presents evidence of a quid pro quo that operated at several levels between the principal characters. Most painful to Dora was the implicit bargain that handed her over to "Herr K" as the price of his tolerating the relations between her father and his wife, a cost Dora might have been better able to tolerate had she not also been put into the position of having "imagined" Herr K's advances when she revealed them to her father, an injustice apparently demanded by the delicate situation. This type of deliberate, if not conscious, distortion of one person's experience in favor of another's was called "mystification" by Marx and later adopted as a central concept for the analysis of family process by R. D. Laing (e.g., 1965). Freud seems to appreciate the purpose of such communications as well as the function of what are today called "family myths." Several are described in the case history, including an invented suicide threat story that concealed the true circumstances of Dora's father being discovered for the first time in the woods with his mistress, an event that turned into a tale of a depressed and needy man who thereafter could not do without the regular "companionship" of the woman who had saved his life.

Pushing further into the case, Freud explains the "motive" of one of Dora's symptoms in terms that clearly describe its effects in a sequence of interaction with her father and Herr K, and then reasons backwards to interpret its intention. He goes on to say that every symptom has at least two "functions": the primary one the maintenance of the psychic economy, and the secondary one the maintenance of significant interpersonal relationships. Freud even was able to tell us that Dora's symptoms would come and go as the configuration of persons around her was altered. But he always looked to the unconscious for explanations, turning inward to work; analyzing Dora's dreams, slips of the tongue, and associations; and formulating her neurosis in terms of its internal rather than its external reality. This preference was determined by the importance Freud gave to the role played by fantasies, both conscious and unconscious, in psychologic life. At early stages of development, the mind cannot accurately reflect the reality of the family environment. It reflects ("internalizes") instead an inaccurate version distorted by wishes generated by unconscious instinctual forces that are not yet under the child's control. Thus, while the influence of actual family relations was not denied, it assumed only a secondary and contingent importance in Freud's formulations. The final effect of situational factors was always regarded as contingent upon their influence on the fantasy life of the child. This influence was thought to remain until brought to light to a more mature observing ego during psychoanalysis. Thus, the meaning, the "motive," of the illness was left to be interpreted by Freud and ultimately accepted by Dora rather than to be dissolved as unnecessary by altering her family environment. Musing on the therapist's task, Freud offers the following revealing lament:

> Destiny has an easier time of it in this respect: it need not concern itself either with the patient's constitution or with his pathogenic material; it has only to take away a motive for being ill, and the patient is temporarily or perhaps even permanently freed from his illness. How many fewer miraculous cures and spontaneous disappearances of symptoms should we physicians have to register in cases of hysteria, if we were more often given a sight of the human interests which the patient keeps hidden from us. (1959/1905, p. 56)

That the disposition toward psychological disturbance could be laid at the door of the environment, whether pictured in terms of the family, the community, or the culture, is an idea that can be found in Freud's later speculative and philosophic writings as well as in his early case histories. Spiegel and Bell (1959) observe that Freud's ambiguity and ambivalence over assessing the parts played by our instinctual endowment on the one hand and the environment on the other shows through, but in his later days "the finger of blame lingers longer on the external environment, and mysterious hints are dropped about the possibility of improving the hostile social millieu" (p. 117).

Considering Freud's extreme position toward keeping the relatives of the patient out the analytic setting, his emphasis on intrapsychic dynamics to the exclusion of interpersonal relations in his theoretical writings and yet his vivid descriptions of conflicted and demanding family relations in his clinical studies, it is not surprising that psychoanalysis should have had an inconsistent and confusing effect on the course of thinking about and working with families. It is clear, however, that elaborations of psychoanalysis since the 1920s; the contributions of the neo-Freudians, especially Harry Stack Sullivan (e.g., 1953); and developments within ego psychology have increasingly emphasized the theoretic significance of interpersonal relations and altered the view of the subject's inner world. "Reality" is now seen both as what we remember, or remember and forget, *and* what actually happened that we had to cope with. A natural extension of these ideas is found in the work of Ackerman (1958), Bowen (e.g., 1978), and Lidz (e.g., Lidz, Fleck, & Cornelison, 1965), who among the early family therapists were most closely aligned with the logic of psychoanalytic thinking and the concern for such traditionally important processes as identification, projection, psychologic differentiation, and ego development. Two contemporary examples continuing in this line are Sander (1979) and Scharff and Scharff (1987).

The Expansion of the State Hospital System and the Influence of Social Work

One of the prevailing circumstances that kept the family as a potent system of influence out of the purview of psychiatry was the simple fact that family members were not seen together by the professionals who were responsible for conducting therapy or research on the mentally disturbed. The emphasis on individual treatment combined with the invisibility of the family, except as known through the patient's recollections, prevented psychiatrists from taking note of the often bizarre and generally upsetting quality of the patient's family relations.

Families became implicated in their patient's condition as contact between families and representatives of the mental health field increased. A central channel for new contact opened up with the expansion of the state hospital system, which resulted in two broad areas of exposure. First, families communicated with staff members as they came to visit their hospitalized members. Second, as the social work field increased its specialization in mental health, field workers increasingly contacted the families of hospitalized patients and worked with them to arrange treatment and transition from the hospital to the community. There are scattered reports and anecdotal accounts of early contact with some of these families, and by mid-century the inevitable began to occur. The patient's family became a patient of sorts and was subjected to assessment and treatment by the psychiatric team.

As Spiegel and Bell (1959, p. 116) point out, there was widespread resistance to keeping the focus on the patient's family, even as there is today. At the first round table discussion of the American Orthopsychiatric Association, a psychiatrist, a psychologist, and a social worker spoke about the treatment of behavior and personality problems in children. Alone among the three discussants, Charlotte Towle, the social worker, dealt with the family in systematic terms. She made the case that "Treatment cannot be given to any member of the family without affecting the entire group. In some cases the entire family must be drawn into treatment. Approach to this or that member, or centering treatment on a certain individual, cannot be a random thing" (1948, p. 582). The prolonged discussion that followed dwelt on whether notes should be made in front of the patient. No reference to Towle's earlier remarks was made. The issue of a dynamic formulation and handling of family relations directly was left on the sidelines for the next 20 years.

Interest in the emerging possibility of family treatment was paralleled by an increase in systematic research. By the late 1940s a few studies had looked at the general adequacy of families in which one of the members had been diagnosed as mentally ill. Lidz and Lidz (1949) found only 5 patients in a hospitalized sample of 50 who were considered to have had an adequate home life. In the case of 40% of these patients, one or both of the parents had died before the patient was 19 years old. Ellison and Hamilton (1949) found, in more than 30% of a sample of 100 cases, that the stability of the family was disturbed by the early death of a member or by a divorce or separation.

Research interest in the family reached a zenith at the National Institute of Mental Health with the work of Bowen, begun in 1954. Bowen arranged to have several families, consisting of at least mother, father, and the diagnosed offspring, live on the hospital ward for periods up to two and one half years. The parents assumed the principal responsibility for the care of their patient, and a major effort on the staff was directed toward the creation of a ward milieu that would permit the family to engage in fairly typical interactions. The fascinating results of this project are reported extensively by Bowen (1960) and by Brodey (1959).

The Child Guidance Movement

Child guidance clinics and the child guidance movement provided another institutionalized means for increased contact between families and the psychiatric social service worlds. The movement, initially developed in the 1920s through the efforts of the juvenile court to treat delinquent children, gradually expanded to find convenient and economical means to treat emotionally disturbed children (Jackson & Satir, 1961, p. 32).

In the earliest stages, social workers provided leadership for the therapy "teams" and played an important part both in giving a dynamic focus to emotional problems and in having empirical techniques for investigating the environment. The general approach at that time was for the guidance clinic staff to make an assessment and then work out a plan with the family and community agencies, through which the problem was to be relieved

(Spiegel & Bell, 1959, p. 115). When this approach proved to be incomplete and inadequate, direct psychotherapy with the child was undertaken, and the psychiatrist emerged as the figure with the most authority and responsibility. As the movement progressed, an eventual compromise between the organismic (psychiatrists') and the environmentalistic (social workers') poles was struck (Spiegel & Bell, 1959, p. 116). In practice, this usually meant that someone worked with the mother while someone else worked with the child. Fathers were rarely seen officially, even though a home visitor might gain a good sense of what was going on in the family that shed light on the child's problem (Pollack, 1957). Again, experience proved that a fragmented approach was inadequate. A subsequent effort to involve the father was fraught with resistances, difficulties, and additional staff demands on the overburdened clinics. These pressures combined to result in "a push in the direction of family therapy" (Jackson & Satir, 1961, p. 32).

With regard to research, we can credit the child guidance field with presenting the first studies demonstrating that ramifications were observable in other members of the family following "successful" treatment of the child. Documenting how intervention can shift the balance of family relations so that conflict increases, or another member of the family shows greater disturbance, or the child's therapy is jeopardized, were Burgum, in her classic paper, "The Father Gets Worse" (1942), Beron (1944), and Walton (1940).

The turn toward family therapy in its contemporary sense reached its fullest expression at the Philadelphia Child Guidance Clinic under the leadership of Salvador Minuchin during the decade of the 1970s. Extending the clinical work and research begun at the Wiltwyck School for Boys in New York (Minuchin, Montalvo, Guerney, Rosman, & Schumer, 1967), during this period Minuchin published two influential texts (Minuchin, 1974; Minuchin & Fishman, 1981) and a book outlining the theoretical and research contributions on "psychosomatic families" (Minuchin, Rosman, & Baker, 1978). Looking back, it is clear that in theory, treatment, and research, the child guidance tradition has left a substantial contribution to the current status of the family field.

American Sociological Theory

A significant early conceptual root of present-day family theory and family therapy that extends into family systems medicine can be traced to early developments in sociologic theory in the United States. Freud was not to make an appearance in the United States until 1909, when he gave a series of five lectures under the sponsorship of the Department of Psychology at Clark University in Worcester, Massachusetts. At the time Freud was writing up the case of Dora, the psychiatrist Adolph Meyer was at work trying to persuade his medical colleagues in the United States to view mental illness more in the light of its social context than as the result of an organic defect. Meyer (1906), taking issue with the organic orientation and nosologic rigidity of the 19th century, presented the radical idea that mental illness was a failure in the adjustment of a person to an environment. Meyer recognized the hierarchies of organization in the person and proceeded from a consideration of organismic integrating factors to bridge the gap between biology and psychiatry with the concept of "mentation." He also taught a number of psychiatrists who eventually made their way into the family field, the best known probably being Theodore Lidz, whose first study of the family milieu of schizophrenic patients was carried out on Meyer's private male service beginning in 1940 (Lidz *et al.*, 1965, p. 16). But the necessary conceptual understanding of the social environment or personal situation identified by Meyer was to come from Charles Horton Cooley, professor of sociology at the University of Michigan.

Cooley pushed the limits of social analysis against all traditional views of human nature as he undermined the belief that human nature has some content and meaning superior to the social order of which it is the representative construction. In 1902, Cooley published *Human Nature and the Social Order,* followed in 1909 by *Social Organization* (Cooley, 1964/1902, 1962/1909). In these two works, Cooley developed his conception of the "primary group" and the nature of human communication, firmly establishing what was to become the "symbolic interactionist" tradition in sociology, built on the claim that "the imaginations people have of one another are the solid facts of society, and . . . to observe and interpret these must be a chief aim of sociology" (1964/1902, p. 121).

Many of Cooley's early conjectures are now taken for granted by contemporary family theorists. He argued that human nature and personal behavior should not be viewed as something existing separately in the individual but, rather, as a manifestation of the "primary phase of society." Human nature is developed and expressed

> in those simple, face to face groups that are somewhat alike in all societies; groups of the family, the playground, and the neighborhood. In the essential similarity of these is to be found the basis, in experience, for similar ideas and sentiments in the human mind. In these everywhere, human nature comes into existence. (1962/1909, p. 30)

Thus, Cooley was to leave us with the well-developed suggestion fully elaborated later by Sullivan (e.g., 1953) that personality is shaped and transformed through ordinary interaction within primary, socializing groups, especially the family, and expresses itself in the pattern of relationships that occur in every day life.

Cooley's treatment of communication is also central to our contemporary understanding of family process. In *Social Organization* (1962/1909), he stresses that communication is the means through which human relationships exist and develop. He recognized both its relation to inner life and its societal integrative functions. His suggestion that "The unity of the social mind consists not in agreement but in organization, in the fact of reciprocal influence or causation among its parts, by virtue of which everything that takes place in it is connected with everything else, and so is an outcome of the whole" (1962/1909, p. 4), anticipates Gregory Bateson's work on family communication and Bateson's wider concern with the "ecology of mind" (1972), which, perhaps more than any other source, has influenced the direction that family therapy thinking has taken. In this connection, it is interesting to note that, except for the elaboration of some important technical matters, all of the guiding ideas for the contemporary family systems approach were introduced between 1877 and 1929 by C. S. Pearce, William James, and John Dewey, early American pragmatists who, along with Cooley, not only paved the way for what is now called "contextual thinking," but wait at the end of the road now being traveled by followers of Bateson and devotees of what in family therapy is called the "new epistemology" in the human sciences.

Cooley's ideas did not extensively affect clinical work and research in mainstream social science interest in human development until after Ernest Burgess published "The Family as a Unity of Interacting Personalities" in 1926. For instead of focusing on the actual socializing agents and the primary groups that directly influence the developing person, social scientists skipped over the family to the abstract and "macro" level of "culture and personality" for investigation. Emphasis was placed on the meanings held and the restraints imposed by culture and society on the individual. Through cross-cultural research, attempts were made to learn whether there are any personality processes that are universal, and how particular cultures mold human nature.

It was not until the late 1940s that investigators interested in the linkages between society and the individual began to realize that only a small portion of any culture is "inculcated" into an individual, and that the crucial aspects of personality stem from the particular subset of values, norms, and interaction patterns embodied by the family and other primary groups. When the focus shifted from the broader culture to the immediate interpersonal environment within which a person adapts and develops, a different dimension became central. The actual pattern and process of interaction between mutually significant people itself became the focus of study. The systematic study of family interaction was begun. Here was the place to explore the view that distinctive behavior patterns and roles within the family group foster patterns of perception, language, values and opinions, and self-integration that are *not* necessarily societally or culturally programmed, but arise specifically within the family as the family group and family members reciprocally develop over time.

Burgess's landmark paper on the family referred to earlier was delivered at a meeting of the Section on the Family of the American Sociological Society and later published in a social casework journal in 1926. The paper, which was eagerly taken up by clinical social workers, was widely read and established the central themes in family sociology for the next 25 years. Burgess had called attention to the work of Ernest Mowrer, a former student, whose 1927 book, *Family Disorganization,* initiated a series of influential studies on the family. Mowrer dealt with the problem of "family disorganization" in the light of the process in which the *family complex* breaks up and the ambitions and ideals of the individual members become differentiated, a theme of central importance to family therapists and family physicians today.

Burgess argued convincingly against what he called the prevailing notion of the family as a collection of individuals. By "unity of interacting personalities" he meant a "living, changing, growing" social system connected by sentiments and roles. His paper represents perhaps the earliest conceptualization of the family as a system of roles, including the explicit use of the term.

Following Burgess, other major precursors of contemporary work are Angell's (1936) study of families coping with the Great Depression and Hill's (1949) influential study of war-induced separation and reunion. Hill's classical ABC-X model of crisis formation and resolution (in which A stands for the stressful event, B for the family's resources, C for the family members' appraisal of the potential stressor, and X for the crisis) engendered elaborations by Burr (1973) and a reformulation by McCubbin and Patterson (1983a, 1983b), the double ABC-X model, described by Patterson in Chapter 7 of this book.

In closing this section, it is important to note that the symbolic interactionist approach being traced here gave rise to two research traditions in the study of the family. These reflect the two sides of its theoretical enterprise, individual experience and the social order. Symbolic interactionism conceptually joins the two by demonstrating how each mirrors the other without being reducible to it. On the one side is the fascination with "the imaginations people have of one another" (Cooley, 1964/1902, p. 121) and the persuasiveness of W. I. Thomas's emphasis on the "definition of the situation" and on the dictum that, "If men define situations as real, they are real in their consequences" (Thomas, 1951, p. 81). On the other side, however, is the tenet that "reality is a social construction" built only through face-to-face interaction in socially and historically bounded circumstances. Ways of defining reality emerge to solve problems and coordinate social interaction and thus become the social structure that is partially immanent in each person. The first side, the fascination with the subject's view of the situation, gave rise to the tradition of interview and questionnaire research. The other side, how constructions of reality and "coming to terms'' with novelty and adversity are built up through recurring patterns of communication, gave rise to the tradition of observational studies of family interaction. The science of family medicine needs both of these traditions to pursue its aims.

Family Health Care Theory

In earlier publications (Ransom, 1981, 1983) I commented that the interest in the centrality of family relations to health and well-being has been cyclic, with each renewal adding to our understanding, but failing to generate sufficient thrust to launch family-centered medicine into the mainstream of conventional practice. It is also worth keeping in mind that the history of interest in the family as a "unit of care" and the history of family practice represent separate developments until the early 1970s. It was not until the accreditation requirement by the American Board of Family Practice to create "model family practice units" with their own exclusive identities that the two groups found a place within which to work together on common problems. This organizationally mandated propinquity has been fruitful indeed, creating the necessary conditions and climate for collaborative work of the kind leading to the publication of this collection.

The modern history of self-conscious family-centered care is easily identified with the beginning of the Peckham Experiment in Southeast London in 1926. The explicitness about the "unit of care" issue is significant because it suggests a perceived need by the early project leaders to distinguish what they were up to from how health and illness were conventionally conceived in the 1920s. The issues at stake were the family versus the individual preference for what the fundamental biologic unit of analysis for purposes of health care should be, and, perhaps even more important, a holistic versus a reductionist view of health and illness. The early successes of laboratory biology and bench research had been purchased at the price of increasingly reductive strategies and had set George Scott Williamson into motion with a countervailing theme that was to gain full expression in the Peckham Experiment. Wholes needed to be identified and understood in contrast with mechanically interacting parts. Action in a free environment needed to be observed in contrast with reaction to pertubations in a controlled one. Health was qualitatively different from the absence of disease and needed its own means to be studied.

The Peckham Experiment and its philosophy was the source of several books (Pearse, 1980; Pearse & Williamson, 1931; Williamson & Pearse, 1938, 1980), including a full account of the rationale, methods, experiences, and findings of the project by Pearse and Crocker (1943). A brief summary is provided elsewhere (Ransom, 1983, 1985). For the purpose of this chapter, it is enough to say that the conceptual legacy of the Peckham Experiment is the highly elaborated model of social organicism that infused everything associated with the project. The family-as-organism metaphor is appealing in spite of its excessive biologic analogizing. It is a precursor of the "organismic systems theory" of von Bertalanffy (1968) that was to evolve into a general systems theory.

> As students of *function* in man *(Homo sapiens)*, we must then at the outset be careful not to take anything for granted; not to mistake the individual for the whole organism, for as we have seen, the individual may be but an organ of a more complex organism. By a mistake of this order we should be doomed to miss the manifestations of function that we are seeking . . . man and woman do not work reciprocally as in mechanism, but *mutually* as diverse parts or organs of a unified organism—a "functional organisation." (Pearse & Crocker, 1943, p. 18; emphasis in original)

Three principles central to family systems theory can be found in early forms in the Peckham writings. The first is the idea of *emergent quality*. Pearse and Crocker (1943) offer a series of examples of how members of a family acting together exhibit a new and different quality that cannot be reduced to that of the individuals acting separately.

> When two diverse individuals function as an organism, *all that they encounter* acquires a new significance. It is not merely the addition of the experience of one to that of the other, making the combined view a larger whole seen, but that with new polarity a new *quality* is given to their apprehension. And this quality of perception is given not only to what is experienced at the moment, but that experience itself influences what they in their new functional orientation will in the future experience—hence altering their every action. (p. 19; emphasis in original)

The sophistication of this model already extends beyond the principle that the whole is greater than the sum of its parts. The whole, under continuous construction, shapes the capacities and actions of the parts, which provide the conditions for reconstructing the whole, and so on. The description employs sequential imagery, but both processes occur simultaneously. Identifying two phases is a matter of "punctuation" that helps to convey the dialectical relationship of parts and wholes.

The second principle proposes both a personal and a family "life course" or "life cycle" with a set of stages marked by predictable periods of rapid reorganization. During these times of transition, environmental conditions play an important role in successful and healthy development. In fact, a basic aim of the Peckham Experiment was to provide the kind of environmental conditions that would foster each transition, as the staff understood them, at the opportune moment. Today, no approach to the study of health would be complete without a full discussion of the interplay of individual and family life cycles. Breunlin's model, presented in Chapter 9, is the most recent and advanced elaboration of this family systems process.

The third principle proposes an integrated hierarchy of levels of organization composed of parts that maintain themselves through relations with each other and the environment. The Peckham pioneers made two astute complementary observations about this process. The first is that the development of health requires a "fitness" of the environment. The second, however, adds the qualification that the general state of the environment does not determine in a direct way the health of the individuals within it. That state is mediated by the organized activity of microenvironments—the person's immediate surroundings as represented by the family and the local community. The lesson of many years of observation at the Pioneer Health Centre is that "It is, in particular, this inner environmental circle in its influence on the facilitation or inhibition of health that the health professional requires to understand" (Barlow, 1983, p. 2).

The practical implication is that if influencing an individual's state of health is the goal, intervention must be directed not only toward processes within the person and toward the person as a whole, but also toward the appropriate environment. Seen in this light, family environments are more than background; they are levels within a hierarchy of developmental activity in which all individuals participate. This is the systemic (pragmatic) rationale for the adage that the family is a "unit of care."

A different sort of milestone is "The Study of the Family in Sickness and Health Care," funded by the Josiah Macy, Jr., Foundation, beginning in 1937. The Peckham Experiment, with its Pioneer Health Centre, was an adventure in human cooperative living and community building, a set of resources available for each member family to assimilate in its own way. The Macy-funded study was a research project conducted along more conventional lines. What the Peckham Experiment provided in its commitment to total health and its dedication to establishing the family as the unit of living, the Macy Study matched with formal elegance when it described the family as a system that functions to influence the state of health of its members and to regulate their access to health care and community resources (Ransom, 1984, p. 109).

"The Study of the Family in Sickness and Health Care" was shepherded by Frank Fremont-Smith and Lawrence K. Frank of the Macy Foundation. In a paper first published in 1936 and entitled "Society as the Patient," Frank (1949) advanced an alternative to the prevailing conception that behavioral disorder was best understood as an attribute of individuals. Seeking a basis for reconsidering social theory and revising the notion of deviance and psychopathology, Frank argued that

> The conception of culture and personality, emphasizing the patterned behavior of man toward his group and toward other individuals, offers some promise of help, for it indicates at once that our society is only one of numerous ways of patterning and organizing human life and that what individuals do, for good or evil, is in response to the cultural demands and opportunities offered them. (1949, p. 138)

Although this idea was already available, Frank took the orientation seriously and followed its implications to give a new specification to disorder: It became an *index of group or societal dysfunction*. There was sufficient cause to push further the view that individual disorder is a symptom of the state of a larger system. Today, this pure position is still a fundamental operating principle for a substantial group of family theorists and therapists.

The Macy project was a cooperative venture among members of the faculties of public health, medicine, and psychiatry at Cornell University Medical College, and included representatives from social work and nursing at New York Hospital. A group of 15 families was studied for 2 years with the goals of understanding "the interrelationship between illness and the family situation," learning something about the "implications for treatment" following such an approach, and then "exploring the best methods for cooperative treatment" with the family health care team assembled for the study (Richardson, 1945, p. 312). The report of that study, *Patients Have Families*, was prepared by Henry B. Richardson, the project's director.

The following passage from Richardson's book has become one of the most widely quoted passages in the family medicine literature.

> The idea of disease as an entity which is limited to one person and can be transmitted to another, fades into the background and disease becomes an integral part of the continuous process of living. The family is the unit of illness because it is the unit of living. (p. 76)

Supported by detailed case analyses, *Patients Have Families* presents for the first time the unmistakable notion of the family as a system. Most noteworthy in historical perspective is the suggestion of the dynamic principle that family members sustain their patterns of interacting with one another within the parameters of some kind of equilibrium or homeostasis, the two terms being used interchangeably in the text.

> The application to the family of the concept of homeostasis, by which living organisms maintain a balance between their internal and external environment, is new to doctors in general, but is inherent in the approach to the social sciences. The members of the family may be compared to the organs of the body, in spite of obvious differences. Although the intrafamily relationships are not often essential to life, each individual is profoundly affected by the others

and by the family as a whole. It is necessary here to use a set of concepts taking advantage of developments in the social field and to devise working tools by which the family equilibrium can be understood. How is this equilibrium established, what is its nature, what is its relation to society in general, and how can it be modified for the better? I propose to describe some of the processes by which the dynamic equilibrium is set up and its functional integrity maintained. (p. 79)

This formulation was offered more than a decade before Don Jackson (1957) gave his now classic lecture on ''family homeostasis.'' Richardson is explicit that a ''reciprocating system,'' for example, one of the processes described, ''refers to an interpersonal relationship and is otherwise meaningless'' (1945, p. 324). Richardson even presents some thoughts on formulating family diagnoses instead of talking in terms of the individual patient alone.

What comes through in *Patients Have Families* is further illustrated in Huygen's book, *Family Medicine: The Medical Life History of Families* (1982). Conflicts, tensions, worries, coping with material circumstances, and life transitions—all become inscribed in family patterns, which, in time, are readable in the minds and bodies of those who visit their family physician. F. J. A. Huygen is a Dutch family physician who, for over 30 years, was the only family physician serving three urban villages in a stable, flower-farming district in the Netherlands. Huygen is a meticulous historian whose unique record system allows him to trace both the medical and social histories of the families in his practice and to articulate the relationship between the two accounts of the same lives. Although the publication of his work extends beyond the period covered in this chapter, his contribution to an evolving sense of the family in family medicine is so valuable, yet still so insufficiently known, that a brief introduction is warranted here.

Huygen's work is the best illustration available to us in print of what it means to think of the family as the unit of care. His practice and research reflect a revision of the meaning of health and illness and illustrate what a physician's intervention can be within this new frame. What is remarkable about the assertion that ''family medicine promote a way of thinking about health and illness with revolutionary consequences'' (1982, p. 145) is that it comes at last from a family physician, not from a behavioral scientist or a family therapist. Huygen says little in formal terms beyond suggesting that the ability to identify the family as a unit of coordinated action—a *system*—is sine qua non in the development of family medicine. Yet in case history after case history, he illustrates how the common problems of health and illness are inseparable from the synchronic and diachronic patterns that are the family system and within which each member and his or her physician participate.

What fascinates Huygen is the pattern, the historically situated and mutually constructed relations between family members and their surrounding world that leads inescapably to conflict and pain, to chronic worries, and above all to playing out complementary roles in the family drama. Huygen is able to capture in his case histories how change, which is functional at one level or within one system of essential relations, is simultaneously dysfunctional at another level or in some other system in which the patient participates. Such patterns are an index of *untenability* or *vulnerability,* which he views as the most important factor in understanding changes in health that have taken a negative trajectory.

To give one example, Huygen traces the social and medical effects in a family over a 16-year period of a husband/father who died suddenly and unexpectedly at the age of 58. In describing the health problems in the family that followed, he shows how these are most usefully thought of not as individual disorders, but as aspects of ''a disorder of the family system.'' All members of the family were involved, including a resident servant. Huygen explains that these symptoms were probably not due to grief, since they appeared only after a silent period of 2 years. He focuses on the developing internal tensions between the mother and children resulting from the mother's efforts to take over her husband's roles, especially to maintain rule and order in two contexts at once. As it was, this family had an important socioeconomic function, being not only the unit of living but the unit of working. The father had been the head of the household and head of the firm. This fact gave rise to a peculiar kind of structure identified and described by Huygen, whose vast experience allows him to say, ''It is only in families like this that I can remember having seen similar repercussions after the death of the father'' (1982, p. 39). Thus, Huygen is able to use the system metaphor but also to keep the relevant material and community conditions of the family in full view and to employ them in his analysis. This degree of specificity is not only persuasive and useful for theoretical precision, it is the only hope for the clinician looking for the kinds of details needed to construct an approach to a particular case from the family systems perspective.

Huygen is modest in his suggestions for future work. He says: ''It is imperative to ask oneself when consulted by a patient: why does this particular individual ask my help at this particular moment for this particular symptom or illness?'' (p. 150). Beyond that, he suggests five questions, which orient the whole subsequent process:

1. What do I know of the families of origin?
2. What do I know of the family he or she is living in, including: In what phase of development is this family in its life cycle, and what about its internal and external relationships and communications?
3. What do I know of the medical and social history of this family?
4. What does this particular individual symptom of illness with which I am confronted mean in this particular family?
5. What will be the impact of my modes of action regarding this problem on this particular family?

These are not earth-shattering questions. To answer them, however, would indeed be revolutionary for practice, as well as for research. The point is to focus attention on the level of family relatedness and on the social, economic, and historical realities of patients' lives. In my view, this is what needs to be done most in family medicine today: simply to create opportunities to observe families and to ask questions that focus attention on relations between people rather than only within each person.

THE FUTURE

In this chapter I have tried to provide a conceptual historical background for contemporary family systems medicine by tracing developments from the turn of the century into the 1960s, when these fields began to expand dramatically. Contributions to the current perspective since then can be found summarized in Hoffman (1981) and Nichols (1984) for family therapy; in Burr, Hill, Nye, and Reiss (1979a, 1979b) for family theory; in Doherty and Baird (1983) for family medicine; and in other chapters throughout this book.

The primary focus in the work reviewed here is to understand what is taken to be an irreducible relationship between persons and families. The task has been to develop a language to describe processes at two levels within the same conceptual framework: the personal and the primary social. The science of family medicine, as defined by Ramsey in Chapter 1, is now adding to this project a third level, the major regulatory systems of the body, and is proposing to describe relationships between family systems and psychoneuroendocrine/immune systems. This immediately introduces the question of relating processes between levels, a challenge for the future on which I will close.

In the world of action, an ontologic unity exists between the state (or process) of a person and the state (or process) of a family. That is to say, what the individual is doing, along with any processes (psychologic or physical) that can be identified with or used to describe what that individual and what the relevant family is doing, along with any processes that can be ascribed to the family, are occurring simultaneously as an unbroken unity of action or *process* in the world.

The world is not made up of variables, it is broken down into them. Variables and categories are not properties of the world, they are properties of specialized languages used by scientists of many kinds. At any given moment, a sociologist can describe what is going on between family members, a psychologist can describe what a member is thinking and feeling, a biochemist can describe what hormones are being secreted and inhibited, and a biophysicist can describe what electrical impulses are being fired at the appropriate synaptic junctions. The question is not simply how these specialists learn to talk with each other, but also how we can learn either to translate or to map the "same" molar event into or onto its respective identifiable processes at different levels. This seems to me the greatest challenge to the progress of the ambitious project outlined by Ramsey (Chapters 1 and 41, this volume).

How do we account for the linkages involved in the co-occurrence of a pattern of family relations and the state of an individual's health? Perhaps group-level processes originating within the family are best thought of not as *causing* the state of the individual, but as *being the lived state* in terms appropriate to that level of description. In other words, what we may have here might best be described not as relations of *causality* but as relations of *correspondence*. The reason for introducing this distinction is that, when causal statements cross levels of analysis, the logic involved is problematic. Some contributors who have worked on this general problem, including Piaget (1970) and Rose (1982) suggest that ordinary translations between instantaneous states at different levels of complexity and analysis are possible and call for a kind of "mapping" of the relations of the corresponding processes in question. Others, such as Sinha (1982), argue that Rose's suggestion of partial isomorphism reintroduces reductionism by the back door. He proposes instead that the levels are actually represented in each other through "a relationship of mutual *contextualisation* and material *instantiation*" (p. 37). Bateson (1956, reprinted in Bateson, 1972) is known to have said that relations between logical types cannot be stated. In any case, we can be certain that neither stringing (flattening) out a set of variables on the same logical biopsychosocial plane, nor arranging a set of variables in a simple transitive hierarchy, will do. What a good model and language will be remains to be worked out.

References

Ackerman NW. The psychodynamics of family life: diagnosis and treatment of family life. New York: Basic Books, 1958.

Angell RC. The family encounters the depression. New York: Scribner, 1936.

Barlow K. The Peckham Experiment. Unpublished manuscript, 1983. (Available from Pioneer Health Centre, Maddox Farm, Little Bookham Street, Little Bookham, England.)

Bateson G. Steps to an ecology of mind. New York: Ballantine, 1972.

Beron L. Fathers as clients in a child guidance clinic. Smith College Studies in Social Work 1944; 14:351–366.

Bowen M. A family concept of schizophrenia. In: Jackson D, ed. The etiology of schizophrenia. New York: Basic Books, 1960.

Bowen M. Family therapy in clinical practice. New York: Jason Aronson, 1978.

Brodey WM. Some family operations and schizophrenia. Archives of General Psychiatry 1959; 1:379–402.

Burgess EW. The family as a unity of interacting personalities. Family 1926; 7:3–9.

Burgum M. The father gets worse. American Journal of Orthopsychiatry 1942; 12:474–485.

Burr WR. Theory construction and the sociology of the family. New York: Wiley, 1973.

Burr WR, Hill R, Nye IF, Reiss IL. Contemporary theories about the family: research-based theories, Vol. I. New York: Free Press, 1979a.

Burr WR, Hill R, Nye IF, Reiss IL. Contemporary theories about the family: general theories/theoretical orientations, Vol. II. New York: Free Press, 1979b.

Cooley CH. Social organization: a study of the larger mind (1909). New York: Schocken Books, 1962.

Cooley CH. Human nature and the social order (1902). New York: Schocken Books, 1964.

Doherty WJ, Baird MA. Family therapy and family medicine: toward the primary care of families. New York: Guilford Press, 1983.

Ellison EA, Hamilton DM. The hospital treatment of dementia praecox, Part II. American Journal of Psychiatry 1949; 106:454–461.

Frank LK. Society as the patient: essays on culture and personality. New Brunswick, N.J.: Rutgers University Press, 1949.

Freud S. Fragment of an analysis of a case of hysteria (1905). In: Freud S. Collected papers, Vol. III. New York: Basic Books, 1959.

Hill R. Families under stress. New York: Harper, 1949.

Hoffman L. Foundations of family therapy: a conceptual framework for systems change. New York: Basic Books, 1981.

Huygen FJA. Family medicine: the medical life history of families (1978). New York: Brunner/Mazel, 1982.

Jackson DD. The question of family homeostasis. Psychiatric Quarterly Supplement 1957; 31 (Part I): 79–90.

Jackson DD, Satir V. A review of psychiatric developments in family diagnosis and family therapy. In: Ackerman NW, Beatman FL, Sherman SN, eds. Exploring the base for family therapy. New York: Family Service Association, 1961.

Kuhn T. The structure of scientific revolutions, 2nd ed. Chicago: University of Chicago Press, 1970.

Laing RD. Mystification, confusion and conflict. In: Borzormenyi-Nagy I, Framo JL, eds. Intensive family therapy: theoretical and practical aspects. New York: Harper & Row, 1965.

Lidz T, Fleck S, Cornelison AR. Schizophrenia and the family. New York: International Universities Press, 1965.

Lidz T, Lidz RW. The family environment of schizophrenic patients. American Journal of Psychiatry 1949; 106:332–345.

McCubbin HI, Patterson JM. Family stress and adaptation to crises: a double ABC-X model of family behavior. In: Olson D, Miller B, eds. Family Studies Review yearbook. Beverly Hills, Calif.: Sage, 1983a: 87–106.

McCubbin HI, Patterson JM. The family stress process: the double ABCX model of family adjustment and adaptation. In: McCubbin HI, Sussman M, Patterson JM, eds. Social stress and the family: advances and developments in family stress theory and research. New York: Haworth, 1983b:7–37.

Meyer A. Fundamental concepts of dementia praecox. British Medical Journal 1906; 2:385–402.

Minuchin S. Families and family therapy. Cambridge, Mass. Harvard University Press, 1974.

Minuchin S, Fishman C. Family therapy techniques. Cambridge, Mass.: Harvard University Press, 1981.

Minuchin S, Montalvo B, Guerney BG, Rosman BL, Schumer F. Families of the slums: an exploration of their structure and treatment. New York: Basic Books, 1967.

Minuchin S, Rosman BL, Baker L. Psychosomatic families: anorexia nervosa in context. Cambridge, Mass.: Harvard University Press, 1978.

Mowrer E. Family disorganization. Chicago: University of Chicago Press, 1927.

Nichols MP. Family therapy: concepts and methods. New York: Gardner Press, 1984.

Pearse IH. The quality of life: The Peckham approach to human ethology. Edinburgh: Scottish Academic Press, 1980.

Pearse IH, Crocker L. The Peckham Experiment: a study in the living structure of society. London: Allen & Unwin, 1943.

Pearse IH, Williamson GS. The case for action. London: Faber & Faber, 1931.

Piaget J. Structuralism. New York: Basic Books, 1970.

Pollack O. Family situations and child development. Children 1957; 4:169.

Ransom DC. The rise of family medicine: new roles for behavioral science. Marriage and Family Review 1981; 4:31–72.

Ransom DC. Random notes: the legacy of the Peckham Experiment, Family Systems Medicine 1983; 1:104–108.

Ransom DC. Random notes: Patients have families. Family Systems Medicine 1984; 2:109–113.

Ransom DC. The evolution from an individual to a family approach. In Henao S, Grose N, eds. Principles of family systems in family medicine. New York: Brunner/Mazel, 1985.

Ransom DC, Vandervoort HE. The development of family medicine: Problematic trends. Journal of the American Medical Association 1973; 225:1098–1102.

Richardson HB. Patients have families. New York: Commonwealth Fund, 1945.

Rorty R. The contingency of language. London Review of Books 1987; April 17:3–6.

Rose S. From causations to translations: a dialectical solution to a reductionist enigma. In Rose S, ed. Towards a liberatory biology. London: Allison & Busby, 1982.

Sander F. Individual and family therapy: toward an integration. New York: Jason Aronson, 1979.

Scharff DE, Scharff JS. Object relations family therapy. Northvale, N.J.: Jason Aronson, 1987.

Sinha C. Negotiating boundaries: psychology, biology, and society. In Rose S, ed. Towards a liberatory biology. London: Allison & Busby, 1982.

Sluzki CE. On training to "think interactionally." Social Science and Medicine 1974; 8:483–485.

Spiegel JP, Bell NW. The family of the psychiatric patient. In Arieti S, ed. American handbook of psychiatry, Vol. I. New York: Basic Books, 1959.

Staver N. The use of a child guidance clinic by mother-dominated families. Smith College Studies in Social Work 1944; 14:367–388.

Sullivan HS. The interpersonal theory of psychiatry. New York: Norton, 1953.

Thomas WI. The methodology of behavior study (1932). In Volkart EH, ed. Social behavior and personality: contributions of W. I. Thomas to theory and social research. New York: Social Science Research Council, 1951.

Towle C. Treatment of behavior and personality problems in children. In: The 1930 symposium: the social worker in orthopsychiatry, 1923–1948. New York: American Orthopsychiatric Association, 1948.

Vandervoort HE, Ransom DC. Undergraduate education in family medicine. Journal of Medical Education 1973; 48:158–165.

von Bertalanffy L. General systems theory. New York: Braziller, 1968.

Walton E. The role of the father in treatment in a child guidance clinic. Smith College Studies in Social Work 1940; 11:155.

Williamson GS, Pearse IH. Biologists in search of material. London: Faber & Faber, 1938.

Williamson GS, Pearse IH. Science, synthesis and sanity, 2nd ed. Edinburgh: Scottish Academic Press, 1980.

3

Function of the Endocrine and Immune Systems: A Review

RICHARD D. CLOVER
STEPHEN J. SPANN
University of Oklahoma

An intriguing and delicate process exists in the human body that allows the body to adapt to changes in its environment in order to maintain a level of constancy or homeostasis. The physiologic mechanisms involved in this process are mediated through the neuroendocrine and immune systems. This chapter will provide historic review and the basic foundations of knowledge of the biologic components of these systems.

Our understanding of human physiology and neuroanatomy, from the initial observations of simple physiologic responses (e.g., vasodilation of skin vessels to release heat when an individual is febrile) to the identification of the biologic mediators that produce these responses, has evolved largely in the last century. However, our knowledge of how the human mind may consciously or unconsciously affect these physiologic events has developed only during the last 20 to 25 years.

When studying biologic mediators and their physiologic responses, definition of terms is important. Various authors have used the term "stress" differently. Stress can be used to mean the environmental stimuli that bombard the organism, or the word can be used to describe the organism's response to a stimulus. Stress has also been used to describe the interaction between the individual's perception of the environment and the response, as in "being under stress." In this chapter, we will use the term "stressor" to describe environmental stimuli and "stress response" to describe the organism's homeostatic response to the stressor.

In order to maintain constancy, the organism must sense the stressor and make an appropriate homeostatic response. The nervous system senses and interprets the stressor and then communicates with the endocrine and/or immune system to initiate the appropriate biologic response. Let's consider the homeostatic response to a common physical stressor: exposure to cold. Temperature receptors in the skin and central temperature-sensitive neurons in the hypothalamus, lower brain stem, and spinal column send afferent impulses to the hypothalamus, where they are integrated and stimulate sympathetic outflow, which results in an increase in secretion of norepinephrine. Norepinephrine secretion, in turn, results in increased cardiac output and vasoconstriction of subcutaneous vessels, pilo erections, shivering, and an increase in the energy substrates for heat production, exemplified by increased fat metabolism. The body's internal environment is thus able to maintain its temperature within the narrow range acceptable for survival of the organism (Landsberg & Young, 1985).

NEUROENDOCRINE SYSTEM

History

Claude Bernard (1974), the great 19th-century French physiologist, recognized that the organism consistently faces changes in the external environment (*milieu extérieur*), to which it must respond, because "the constancy of the internal environment (*milieu intérieur*) is the condition for free and independent existence" (p. 84). Walter Cannon (1939) referred to the complex biologic responses necessary to maintain a constant internal environment or steady state as homeostasis. Cannon showed that psychologic stimuli cause stress responses involving both alimentary canal function (Cannon, 1909) and adrenal secretion (Cannon & De La Paz, 1911). These and other findings led him to propose his "fight-or-flight" theory of adrenal–medullary function based on the conclusion that many physiologic consequences of "adrenalin" release are directly related to making the organism more efficient in the struggle that fear, rage, or pain may evoke. He felt that the organism most likely to survive is the one that, aided by increased adrenal secretion, can best master its energies, can best supply sugar to laboring muscles, can best lessen fatigue, and can best send blood to those parts of the body that are essential in the run or the fight for life (Cannon, 1914).

Hans Selye began writing about stress in 1936, when he formulated the concept of the "general adaptation syndrome." He observed that injecting rats with crude extracts of ovary, placenta, pituitary, kidney, spleen, and so forth produced a triad of morphological changes: (1) adrenal cortical enlargement; (2) atrophy of the thymus and other lymphatic structures; and (3) deep, bleeding ulcers of the stomach and duodenal mucosa. He obtained similar results with a variety of other stimuli, such as insulin, cold, heat, X-rays, mechanical trauma, hemorrhage, tubercle bacilli, pain, forced muscular exercise, and nervous stimuli. Selye, concluding that the common triad represented a nonspecific response to essentially all noxious stimuli, called it the "general adaptation syndrome." He hypothesized that noxious stimuli activate some common afferent system of "first mediators," which then carry the message through neural or humoral pathways to integrative centers, which in turn bring about the nonspecific response triad, including stimulation of the pituitary–adrenocortical system (Mason, 1975). Selye's use of the term "stress" evolved over time. Initially he used the word in the sense of stimuli or outside forces acting on the organism. Later he defined stress as a condition within the organism in response to evocative agents. Finally, he entertained the possibility of defining stress in the sense of interaction between stimulus and response. His final definition stated that stress is basically a physiologic response, a total of all the nonspecific changes caused by function or damage (Mason, 1975). His original morphologic observations were later confirmed with hormonal assay techniques that became available in the 1950s, showing that urine and blood levels of corticosteroids were indeed often elevated in response to adverse stimuli (Mason, 1968).

Mason performed a series of experiments to study the endocrine responses to noxious physical stimuli in which he attempted to minimize the animal's psychologic reaction to the stimuli. He found that the psychologic reaction was a major predictor of endocrine response. Fasting monkeys fed non-nutritive, fruit-flavored cellulose fiber "placebo" food showed little or no corticosteroid changes compared with fasting monkeys that were not fed. Mason concluded that the discomfort from an empty gastrointestinal tract and the psychosocial stimuli associated with sudden deprivation of routine food dispensation by the animal caretaker caused the corticosteroid response in the totally fasting monkeys (Mason,

1971). Mason concluded that the endocrine response to "nonspecific" physical stimuli described by Selye was elicited largely by emotional arousal caused by those stimuli. This finding broadened the prevailing concept of a relatively simple "physiologic" arc, involving afferent inputs directly into the final neuroendocrine pathways in the diencephalon, to include the higher, more complex, "psychologic" processes determining emotional arousal (Mason, 1975).

If one thinks of emotional arousal to noxious stimuli as preparation for corrective behavioral actions, or "fight or flight," then adding the psychologic dimension to Selye's general adaptation syndrome concept can be viewed as reconciling the concept of nonspecificity with Cannon's fight-or-flight concept and general theory of homeostasis (Mason, 1975).

Basic Neuroendocrinology

The endocrine and nervous systems regulate most of the metabolic and homeostatic activities of the organism. The two regulatory systems interact with each other: most endocrine secretions are influenced by the brain, and virtually all hormones can influence brain activity. Neuroendocrinology is the study of the relationship between these two systems. The following is a discussion of the components of these systems and their pathways of interaction.

THE HYPOTHALAMIC–PITUITARY UNIT

Figures 3-1 and 3-2 show the location of the pituitary gland and its divisions: the anterior lobe or adenohypophysis; the intermediate lobe, which is rudimentary in humans; and the

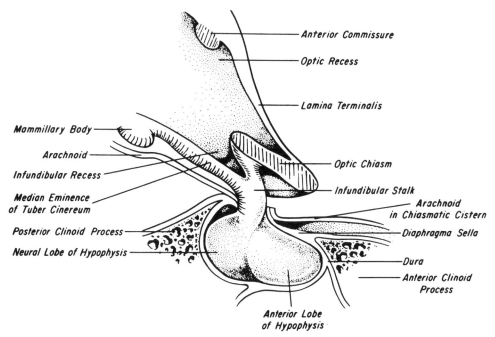

Figure 3-1. Human hypothalamic–pituitary unit. Reproduced with permission from "Neuroendocrinology" by S. Reichlin, 1985, in *William's Textbook of Endocrinology*, edited by J. D. Wilson and D. W. Foster, Philadelphia: W. B. Saunders, pp. 429–567.

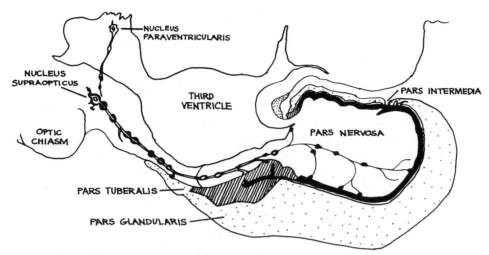

Figure 3-2. Course of neurosecretory substance from hypothalamic cell body. Redrawn from "The Site of Origin of the Hormones of the Posterior Pituitary" by W. Bargmann and E. Scharrer, 1951, *American Scientist*, Vol. 39, pp. 255–259.

posterior lobe, or neural lobe. The neurohypophysis consists of specialized tissue located at the base of the hypothalamus, the neural stalk, and the neural lobe of the pituitary. The neurohypophyseal portion of the hypothalamus is funnel-shaped and is called the infundibulum. Its central portion is enveloped from below by the pars tuberalis of the anterior pituitary gland and is penetrated by numerous capillary loops from the primary portal plexus of the hypophyseal portal circulation. This neurovascular complex forms the median eminence of the tuber cinereum at the base of the hypothalamus (Figure 3-1). The supraopticohypophyseal and paraventriculohypophyseal nerve tracts descend through the infundibulum and neural stalk to terminate in dilated endings in the neural lobe. The cells from which these tracts originate are relatively large and consolidate into paired nuclei above the optic tract (supraoptic) on each side of the ventricle (paraventricular) (Figure 3-2).

Vasopressin and oxytocin are hormones that are synthesized as prohormones in a supraoptic and paraventricular neurons, then transported in membrane-bound vesicles through the axons to the neural lobe, where they are stored and later released. Vasopressin, or antidiuretic hormone, raises blood pressure through vasoconstriction and inhibits renal diuresis; it is regulated by plasma osmolality and "effective" circulating blood volume, as well as by blood pressure, nausea, and emotional stress. Oxytocin causes contraction of the myoepithelial cells in the breast and the milk let-down reflex; this can be inhibited by stress and triggered by sexual excitement and orgasm. Adrenergic influences inhibit secretion of both oxytocin and vasopressin, perhaps explaining the stress-induced inhibition of the milk let-down reflex and stress-induced diuresis.

Tuberoinfundibular neurons secrete the hypothalamic hypophyseotropic factors and terminate in the median eminence, where they are surrounded by capillaries that drain into the portal veins of the anterior pituitary. Hypothalamic hypophyseotropic factors serve as chemotransmitters, traveling the hypophyseoportal system to the anterior pituitary to regulate its function. Thyrotropin-releasing factor (TRH) stimulates release of thyroid-stimulating hormone (TSH) from the anterior pituitary. Gonadotropin-releasing hormone (GnRH or LHRH) stimulates luteinizing hormone (LH) and probably follicle-stimulating hormone

(FSH) release. Growth-hormone-releasing hormone (GHRH) stimulates growth hormone (GH) release, whereas somatostatin inhibits GH and TSH secretion. Corticotropin-releasing hormone (CRH) stimulates adrenocorticotropic hormone (ACTH) secretion. Prolactin-inhibiting factor (PIF) inhibits and prolactin-releasing factor (PRF) stimulates prolactin release.

Virtually all known neurotransmitters can influence the secretion of the tuberoinfundibular neuronal system and can thereby modify anterior pituitary function. The best understood are the biogenic amines: dopamine, norepinephrine, serotonin, and epinephrine. These are involved in many homeostatic functions and in the manifestations of emotion, and can be modified by psychotherapeutic drugs. The dopamine-containing fibers concerned with pituitary regulation arise chiefly in the arcuate nucleus of the hypothalamus. From there, the fibers project to the median eminence. Most of the neurons that synthesize dopamine arise in the midbrain and project to the forebrain. Those projecting from the basal ganglia are involved in extrapyramidal control. Dopaminergic fibers are also directed to various parts of the cerebral cortex and limbic system. Alterations in pituitary function due to changes in dopamine secretion by tuberoinfundibular neurons do not necessarily reflect alterations in the other central dopaminergic systems. Dopamine agonist and antagonist drugs do not act directly on the tuberoinfundibular system. Noradrenergic pathways originate from the locus ceruleus nucleus in the midbrain and project to the forebrain, including the cerebral cortex, the hypothalamus, the limbic system, the brain stem, and the spinal cord. The principal components that regulate the anterior pituitary project either to the median eminence, where they come into contact with the nerve endings of the tuberoinfundibular system, or to the tuberoinfundibular cells. The central noradrenergic system is the site of action of amphetamines and antidepressant drugs (Reichlin, 1985).

NEUROENDOCRINE CONTROL
OF CORTICOTROPIN REGULATION
The release of ACTH can be stimulated by various hormones such as CRH, catecholamines, vasopressin, and vasointestinal peptide hormone. Release of ACTH can be inhibited by glucocorticoids via feedback aimed at both ACTH release (anterior pituitary) and CRH secretion (hypothalamus). Two classes of receptors mediate feedback control: One responds promptly, the other is subject to a delay of several hours. The short-term inhibition likely involves direct changes in membrane function of CRH-secreting neurons and/or pituitary corticotropic cells or glucocorticoid receptor cells in the hippocampus, septum, and amygdala. Delayed inhibition effects probably result from reduction of ACTH messenger RNA activity and synthesis of ACTH (Reichlin, 1985).

Anterior Pituitary Hormones

GROWTH HORMONE
Growth hormone is a one-chain peptide synthesized and stored in somatotropic cells in the anterior pituitary. Growth hormone stimulates skeletal and soft tissue growth, promoting positive balances of nitrogen, phosphorus, potassium, and magnesium. It has an insulin-like action and may stimulate beta cell secretory capacity in the pancreas. Growth hormone promotes protein synthesis, hepatic and muscular glycogenesis, lipolysis, and fatty acid oxidation. Some of the effects of growth hormone are mediated indirectly by inducing the formation of somatomedins, which are insulin-like growth factors. Growth hormone secre-

tion is under the control of GHRH and somatostatin, two hypothalamic peptides. Growth hormone secretion can be augmented or inhibited by a number of neurogenic, metabolic, and hormonal influences. Exercise, stress, and some neurogenic stimuli, for example, stimulate growth hormone secretion.

PROLACTIN

Prolactin is also a one-chain peptide that is synthesized, stored, and secreted by the lactotropic cells of the anterior pituitary. The human placental decidua also synthesizes prolactin, which acts directly on the mammary gland and is responsible for the initiation and maintenance of lactation. Prolactin also acts through dopaminergic and opioid mechanisms on the hypothalamus to inhibit LHRH release. Causes of increased prolactin secretion include nipple stimulation, stress, pregnancy, hypothyroidism, and several medications (Daughaday, 1985).

Endogenous Opioids

Many different peptides in the brain are localized to nerve endings and are released in response to nerve stimulation, with significant effects on the functions of other nerve cells. Endogenous opioids are peptides with morphine-like activity; beta-lipoprotein is the prohormone of several endogeneous opioids, the most potent of which is beta-endorphin. In the anterior pituitary, but not the brain, the secretion of both ACTH and beta-lipoprotein is regulated by the feedback action of glucocorticoids; both are released simultaneously by CRH. The first endogenous opioids to be isolated from brain were pentapeptides and designated as met-enkephalin and leu-enkephalin. Enkephalin-containing neurons, which account for the bulk of endogenous opioids, are distributed in regions correspondingly rich in opiate receptors. Regional concentrations of endorphines correspond to regionally specialized functions. In the spinal cord, for example, opiate receptors and enkephalins are in highest concentration in the dorsal gray matter, corresponding to the centrally directed nerve endings of primary sensory neurons. The principal localization of beta-endorphin is in the pituitary, especially in the intermediate lobe. The endogenous opioids raise the threshold of pain, produce sedation, and influence extrapyramidal motor activity. Endogenous opioids have endocrine effects. Administration of morphine or its analogues brings about a number of endocrine responses, such as release of growth hormone and prolactin, and inhibition of gonadatropin and TSH release. Activity of the endogenous opioids is initiated by binding to specific cell membrane receptors (Reichlin, 1985).

The Adrenocortical System

ANATOMY

The adrenal glands are paired, pyramidal structures adhering to the upper poles of the kidneys. The human adrenal gland is divided into cortex and medulla. The cortex is involved in steroid synthesis and secretion, while the medulla synthesizes and secretes catecholamines. The adrenal cortex can be divided into three zones: the outer zona glomerulosa, the zona fasciculata, and the zona reticularis. The zona glomerulosa is chiefly concerned with the biosynthesis of the mineralocorticoid aldosterone. The two innermost zones synthesize and secrete corticosteroids, progestagens, estrogens, and androgens (Bondy, 1985).

CONTROL OF CORTICOSTEROID SECRETION

Secretion of adrenocorticohormones is controlled by adrenocorticotropin (ACTH). Basal plasma corticosteroid levels fluctuate at regular intervals throughout the day, in a regular pattern. Secretion is minimal during the 4 hours before sleep and the first 2 hours of sleep. Over the next 3 hours there are a few short bursts of secretion in the "preliminary nocturnal secretory episode." In the remaining hours of sleep and in the first waking hour, prolonged bursts of activity contribute the "main secretory phase." There is intermittent secretory activity during waking hours. The concentration of plasma cortisol usually is highest on waking in the morning and falls during the day, reaching a minimum during the first hour or two of sleep. This circadian rhythm results from the diurnal pattern of ACTH secretion by the anterior pituitary, which is intrinsically controlled by the hypothalamic system (Bondy, 1985).

BIOLOGIC EFFECTS OF CORTICOSTEROIDS

Steroid effects can be classified as glucocorticoid and mineralocorticoid. Glucocorticoid effects are those concerned with intermediary metabolism, inflammation, immunity, wound healing, and muscle and myocardial integrity. Mineralocorticoid effects are those concerned with salt, water, and other mineral metabolism. Steroids may be examined for their relative activity in each category and can be classified according to decreasing ratios of glucocorticoid to mineralocorticoid activity. For example, cortisol has a great deal of glucocorticoid but relatively little mineralocorticoid activity. Cortisone and corticosterone have intermediate positions; aldosterone has very little glucocorticoid activity but significant mineralocorticoid activity (Bondy, 1985).

GLUCOCORTICOID EFFECTS

Corticosteroids promote gluconeogenesis (conversion of protein to carbohydrate) and store carbohydrates as glycogen. Corticosteroid administration causes an increase in protein breakdown, a rise in glucose and insulin levels, and a decrease in urinary ketone excretion. The anabolic effect of insulin partially blocks the catabolic effect of the corticosteroids; appetite increases, which may explain the obesity caused by steroids. Cortisol increases blood flow to gastric mucosa and promotes gastric acid secretion, although glucocorticoids in conventional therapeutic doses probably do not increase peptic ulceration. Cortisol increases secretion of growth hormone. Steroids suppress the secretion of TSH in primary myxedema. Corticosteroids potentiate the beta-adrenergic effects of catecholamines, and enhance epinephrine and norepinephrine secretion in the adrenal medulla. Corticosteroids play a role in maintaining normal blood pressure and cardiac output by enhancing myocardial contractility and peripheral arteriolar tone. Glucocorticoids are important in maintaining striated muscle strength and contractility. Corticosteroids in excess impair the normal inflammatory response to infectious or physical agents. Capillaries do not fully dilate, cellular exudate is reduced, transudation and edema occur, deposition of fibrin around the inflamed area is diminished, and healing is delayed. The chief anti-inflammatory effect is achieved by reducing the number of white blood cells mobilized to the inflamed area (Bondy, 1985).

The Sympathoadrenal System

The sympathoadrenal system is made up of the adrenal medulla and the sympathetic nervous system; these form both an anatomic and physiologic unit. The central neural connec-

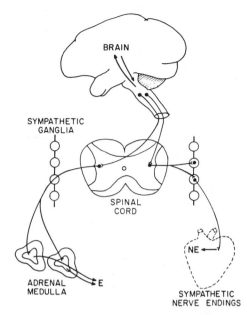

Figure 3-3. Organization of sympathoadrenal system. Reproduced with permission from *Metabolic Control and Disease* by P. K. Bondy and L. E. Rosenberg, 8th edition, 1980, Philadelphia: W. B. Saunders.

tions that regulate sympathoadrenal output are complex and have been only partially characterized. Preganglionic neurons in the interomediolateral cell column of the spinal cord receive inputs directly from several regions of the central nervous system (CNS), including centers within the medulla (reticular formation, raphe nuclei), pons, hypothalamus (particularly the paraventricular nucleus), and ultimately the postganglionic sympathetic neurons in the paravertebral and preaortic and sympathetic ganglia. Preganglionic neurons either synapse with postganglionic sympathetic neurons in the paravertebral ganglia or pass through the ganglia to form the splanchnic nerves that innervate the adrenal medulla or synapse with postganglionic sympathetic neurons in the great preaortic plexuses, such as the celiac and superior mesenteric. Postganglionic sympathetic fibers are distributed widely to blood vessels and viscera (Figure 3-3). The central nuclei that initiate descending impulses are subject to influences by pathways from centers in the hypothalamus, limbic system, and cortex as well as from an array of afferent impulses that initiate reflex changes in sympathetic outflow at the level of the brain stem. The adrenal medulla is enveloped within the adrenal cortex. In the human, the combined weight of both medullae is about 1 gram, or 10% of the total adrenal mass. The adrenal medulla is composed almost entirely of chromaffin cells, which contain numerous chromaffin granules that are important in the storage and secretion of catecholamines. Epinephrine, which accounts for 85% of the adrenomedullary catecholamine stored, functions predominantly as a hormone but is also a neurotransmitter in certain select regions of the CNS. Norepinephrine is the peripheral adrenergic neurotransmitter; it is synthesized and stored in sympathetic nerve endings and released in the innervated tissues. It is also a neurotransmitter in the central nervous system. Dopamine, another biologically important catecholamine, is a CNS transmitter. Catecholamines affect most tissues and influence most body processes. Catecholamine release at the sympathetic nerve endings and from the adrenal medulla is under the direct control of the CNS.

Catecholamines synthesized in the adrenal medulla are stored in chromaffin granules and released by exocytosis (extrusion of the cellular contents of the granules into the extracellular space). Norepinephrine is stored in vesicles in the postganglionic sympathetic nerve terminals. The release of norepinephrine at the nerve ending is triggered by depolarization of the axonal membrane following a propagated action potential. Release is probably by exocytosis.

ADRENERGIC RECEPTORS

The physiologic changes induced by catecholamines are mediated via adrenergic receptors on the surface of effector cells. Catecholamine uptake is not required for expression of the physiologic effect. The interaction between catecholamines and receptors initiates events that begin in the cell membrane, regress into the cell interior, and culminate in a given response.

Two major types of adrenergic receptors are recognized: alpha receptors and beta receptors. Physiologic responses have been characterized as alpha or beta based on differential agonists, potency, and antagonism by specific alpha or beta receptor blocking pharmacologic agents. Distinct subtypes of alpha and beta receptors exist. The alpha adrenergic receptor mediates a variety of responses, including vasoconstriction. Epinephrine and norepinephrine are potent, nonselective, alpha receptor agonists. The beta receptor mediates cardiac stimulation, bronchodilation, and vasodilation. Epinephrine is a nonselective beta agonist. Norepinephrine is a potent beta-1 agonist, but a weak beta-2 agonist. Beta-1 receptors mediate cardiac stimulation and lypolysis; beta-2 receptors mediate bronchodilation, vasodilation, and prejunctional stimulation of norepinephrine release from sympathetic neurons. Beta receptor agonists stimulate adenylate cyclase and increase intracellular cyclic adenosine monophosphate (cAMP), which serves as the second messenger for the beta-receptor-mediated process (Bondy, 1985).

PHYSIOLOGY OF THE SYMPATHOADRENAL SYSTEM

Traditionally, the sympathetic nervous system and the adrenal medulla have been viewed as working in tandem, with circulating catecholamines from the adrenal medulla supporting the effects of the sympathetic nerves. This view is consistent with the pattern of sympathoadrenal involvement in various conditions. During cold exposure and physical exercise, for example, the initial response is mostly sympathetic stimulation, but as the strength of the stimulus increases, the secretion of adrenomedullary catecholamines progressively increases. Enhancement of adrenomedullary secretion occurs when sympathetic function is diminished by drugs, surgery, or fasting. In other circumstances, the relationship between the sympathetic nervous system and the adrenal medulla is more complex. Suppression of sympathetic activity in association with adrenomedullary stimulation has been found to occur in hypoglycemia, acute hypoxia, and acute ischemia. One possible explanation for this is that reduction of sympathetic activity lowers the rate of energy utilization, while an increase in adrenomedullary secretion sustains essential catecholamine-dependent processes at a lower net energy cost.

Catecholamines influence virtually all tissues and vital functions. Generally they are not sole or exclusive regulators, but participate with other hormonal and neuronal systems in regulating a multitude of direct physiologic processes. The sympathetic nervous system regulates the peripheral circulation and the cardiac output according to the requirement of the organism as a whole. Sympathetically mediated adjustments in peripheral resistance maintain the integrity of the circulation in order to provide adequate perfusion of organ systems in the face of changing circulatory metabolic demands. The effects of catecholamines on the heart, mediated by beta receptors, include increased heart rate, enhanced cardiac contractility, and increased conduction velocity, all of which contribute to an increase in cardiac output. Catecholamines have effects on multiple viscera, mostly through actions on the smooth muscle. Beta-2 agonists cause smooth muscle relaxation, and alpha-1 agonists cause smooth muscle contraction. Metabolic effects of catecholamines include facultative thermogenesis (heat production in excess of that required for maintenance of basal functions); fuel metabolism in the form of breakdown of stored fuels into utilizable substrates; and lipoprotein metabolism, including increase in plasma levels of cholesterol and free fatty acids. Catecholamines play a role in water and electrolyte metabolism, and are also involved in regulating the secretion of many hormones (Bondy, 1985).

IMMUNE SYSTEM

The immune system is extremely complicated and plays a variety of roles, including maintaining homeostasis and serving as the body's defense mechanism. The system is similar to the endocrine system in that it exerts its control by virtue of circulating substances capable of acting at sites distant from their point of origin. The immune system's regulatory mechanisms are genetically controlled and have major influences via the neuroendocrine system. Dysfunction of the immune system results in disease (Katz, 1982).

History

Our knowledge of the immune system has advanced greatly in recent years. Even though most of the data on the immune system have been accumulated since the turn of the century, certain observations were made earlier. In an attempt to protect against smallpox, people in ancient China and western Asia used fluid from lesions of individuals with mild forms of smallpox to "vaccinate" healthy ones. An ancient Greek king of Pontus, Mithridates VI, repeatedly administered to himself small amounts of poisonous substances to protect himself from the poisons. Serpa Pinto, who traveled through central Africa in the middle of the 19th century, reported that people protected themselves against snake bites by treatment with a mixture of snake heads and ant eggs (Grabar, 1982). These were all attempts by people to "vaccinate" or "immunize" themselves against more serious forms of disease.

The first true, though crude, immunization was performed by Edward Jenner, an 18th-century English physician who observed that people who recovered from cowpox were subsequently protected against smallpox (Grabar, 1982). Therefore, he proposed to vaccinate people with cowpox as a means of protection against smallpox. Almost a century later, the scientific approach to vaccination was applied by Louis Pasteur and his collaborators on a variety of organisms.

Toward the end of the 19th century, numerous observations were reported by microbiologists that subsequently were formalized into theories on immunity. The cellular immunity theory was originated by a Russian zoologist, Elie Metchnikoff (Grabar, 1982). He demonstrated how microorganisms could be engulfed by leukocytes, a process he called phagocytosis, and later showed the existence of the two types of circulating cells capable of phagocytosis, the polymorphonuclear leukocytes and the macrophages. Metchnikoff's theories were challenged by the proponents of "humoral" theory. Several investigators, including Pfeiffer and Isaeff (1894), Robert Koch (1843–1910), Jules Bordet (1873–1961), and Paul Ehrlich (1854–1915), demonstrated through a variety of experiments that various substances in the blood were able to destroy bacteria without the apparent assistance of white cells. During this period, the terms "antigen" and "antibody" were introduced. Over subsequent years, the interrelationships between "cellular immunity" and "humoral immunity" were discovered.

Since the 1940s, numerous investigators have defined the various components of the immune system, including its various cells and their functions, its molecular components, and its genetic components. The interrelationships of these components are extensive, and the following is a brief overview of each of these subjects.

Polymorphonuclear Leukocytes

The polymorphonuclear leukocytes include neutrophils, basophils, and eosinophils. The neutrophils make up approximately 60% of the circulating leukocytes in humans, although the total number of neutrophils is greater in the bone marrow than in the circulating blood. About half of the cells in the blood vessels are found adhered to or migrating close to the wall of the blood vessel. They have a half-life of about 6 to 20 hours in the peripheral blood, and a survival time in tissues under steady-state conditions of about 4 days (Douglas, 1982).

The primary function of neutrophils is phagocytosis, a process that neutrophils undergo to engulf and destroy foreign materials. The neutrophil migrates toward a stimulus (a process called chemotaxis) which may be produced by bacterial products, tissue proteases, and complement components. This migration involves the neutrophil adhering to the endothelium of the vessel, followed by extravascular immigration and migration toward the particles to be ingested. The membranes of the neutrophil then adhere to the particles, invaginate, and finally enclose them. The pockets or vacuoles produced by the engulfment then fuse with the granules (or lysosomes) within the neutrophil, and the constituents of the lysosome are expelled into the phagocytic vacuole (Figure 3-4).

Phagocytosis is greatly enhanced by opsonization, a mechanism the body uses to allow the phagocytic cells to recognize readily the particles to be ingested as foreign. Opsonins, which include immunoglobulins, complement system components, and other plasma factors, coat or change the particles to be phagocytized and thereby aid in the recognition of particles as foreign and their subsequent ingestion. Defects in opsonization result in reduced phagocytosis.

Basophils and tissue mast cells have oval granules containing biologically active compounds, including heparin, serotonin, SRS-A (slow reacting substance of anaphylaxis), and histamine. These cells are found in connective tissue surrounding small blood vessels throughout the body. Basophils comprise 1% of the circulating leukocytes. Basophils and mast cells have receptors that bind IgE. Their primary function is to release potent inflammatory and repair substances upon injury to the body. Release of the bioactive enzymes by the basophils and mast cells results in a variety of reactions, such as smooth muscle contraction of bronchioles and small blood vessels, increased permeability of capillaries, increased nasal and bronchial mucous secretions, stimulation of pain fibers, and vasodilation (Dvorak & Dvorak, 1975; Frick, 1982).

Eosinophils make up 2% to 5% of the normal peripheral blood leukocytes; some authors, however, argue that this percentage is too high. The half-life of the eosinophil in the blood is approximately 2 hours (Weller & Goetzl, 1980). As with other types of white

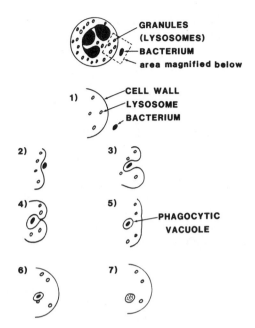

Figure 3-4. Phagocytosis.

cells, the majority of eosinophils are of the respiratory and gastrointestinal systems, along with mast cells and basophils. Eosinophilia is produced by a specific lymphokine released by sensitized T-lymphocytes (Basten & Beeson, 1970) and by an eosinophiloprotein (Mahmond, Stone, & Kellermeyer, 1977). Although they have been demonstrated to phagocytize bacteria, their major roles are in allergic and type I immediate hypersensitivity reactions and host defense against parasites (Weller & Goetzl, 1980).

Mononuclear Phagocytes

Mononuclear phagocytes include circulating peripheral blood monocytes and tissue macrophages. Monocytes are released into the circulation within 60 hours after formation and circulate for 12 to 24 hours, during which they make up 3% to 8% of the circulatory leukocytes. They then emigrate into various tissues, where they mature into tissue macrophages. Macrophages arise not only directly from monocytes, but also by multiplication in the general macrophage population of immature macrophages that retain the ability to respond to mitogens (Werb, 1982).

Macrophages are characterized by their large size, their spreading borders, and their abundant cytoplasmic granules. They exist in many tissues, including lung, spleen, liver, lymph nodes, bone marrow, and peritoneal cavities. Their prominent function is their ability to recognize and ingest foreign or damaged materials—the process called phagocytosis, described previously. They also play a prominent role in initiating and regulating the immune response, which is discussed in more detail later in this chapter.

Lymphocytes

The lymphocytes are the second most numerous white cells in the peripheral blood, although the circulating lymphocytes represent less than 5% of the total body pool of lymphocytes. The majority of lymphocytes are located in the spleen, lymph nodes, and other organized lymphatic tissue. The lymphocytes are divided into two main classes: the T-lymphocytes or thymus-derived lymphocytes, which participate in cell-mediated immunity, and the B-lymphocytes, whose origin in humans is probably from the bone marrow and which are characterized by their ability to differentiate into cells capable of producing immunoglobulins. The T-lymphocytes can be subdivided into two groups based on their functions: regulatory T-lymphocytes and effector T-lymphocytes. The regulatory T-lymphocytes consist of the helper (or inducer) cells that amplify or initiate an effector (lymphocyte or macrophage) function and the suppressor cells that suppress the function of other T-lymphocytes. The effector T-lymphocytes are responsible for delayed cutaneous hypersensitivity response, rejection of foreign tissue grafts and tumors, and elimination of virus-infected cells. The effector lymphocytes are divided into various subgroups based on their functions. Cytotoxic T-lymphocytes directly lyse histocompatible cells that have antigens recognized as foreign on their surface, such as those produced by a virus-infected cell (Blanden, 1970). Killer cells are unsensitized lymphocytes whose surfaces have Fc receptors for IgG and require antibody to lyse cells (Klein, 1982). Natural killer (NK) cells are large granular lymphocytes with distinct surface antigens that are cytotoxic to tumor cells, certain virus-infected cells, and protozoa. There are low levels of endogenous NK cells. Although their complete function is not well established, some data suggest they may be a part of natural resistance to certain infections including herpes simplex virus, vaccinia virus, and Bobesic microti (Herberman, 1981).

The T-lymphocytes may also be subdivided by their surface antigens. Different nomenclatures have been used by various authors (Lanier, Engleman, & Gatenby, 1983; Reinherz & Schlossman, 1980). T-lymphocytes lose and acquire various antigens as they mature in the thymus and when they enter the circulation. Approximately 75% of peripheral blood lymphocytes are T-cells, with 25% of these cells expressing CD8 (also called Leu2) and 65% expressing T4 (also called Leu3) (McLeod, Wing, & Remington, 1985). In general, cells expressing CD1, CD3, CD4 (Leu3) surface antigens usually function as helper/inducer cells (T4 cells), and cells bearing CD1, CD3, CD5, CD8 (Leu2) antigens usually function as cytotoxic lymphocytes or as suppressor (T8 cells), although exceptions to this rule have been reported (McLeod *et al.*, 1985).

The B-lymphocytes can be subdivided on the basis of the immunoglobulins they produce. There is also a subset of B-lymphocytes known as memory B cells that are important for the development of rapid secondary (anamnestic) antibody response upon subsequent antigen exposure.

Cell-Mediated Immunity

All the cellular components of the immune system discussed above function in an integrated manner to produce cell-mediated immunity. A macrophage phagocytizes a foreign antigen, and, after processing the antigen, presents the antigen on its surface to the T-lymphocyte and thereby "sensitizes" the lymphocyte. Furthermore, macrophages produce substances like interleukin 1 (IL1), an antigen-nonspecific lymphocyte activating factor, which induces helper T-lymphocyte activation and proliferation. Different sets of sensitized lymphocytes undergo various reactions. Certain sensitized lymphocytes produce a variety of soluble substances known as lymphokines, which have an overall function to amplify the initial cellular response. For example, interleukin 2 (IL2) enhances lymphocyte transformation and promotes T-cell growth. Other substances attract macrophages to the site of infection (chemotactic factors), inhibit migration of macrophages from that site (MIF), and activate macrophages (MAF). Another population of sensitized T-lymphocytes, the cytotoxic T-lymphocytes, directly lyse histocompatible cells that have antigens on their surface to which the lymphocyte had been sensitized. Other sensitized T-lymphocytes may become long-lived "memory" cells that are responsible for the rapid and heightened response of cell-mediated immunity upon reexposure to the original antigen.

In addition to enhancing cellular response, intercellular communication may suppress the response. High ratios of macrophages to lymphocytes suppress lymphocyte responses. Suppressor T-lymphocytes express their control in a variety of mechanisms, including directly antagonizing the activity of helper T-cells and inhibiting the differentiation of B-cells. Their activity may be interrupted by contrasuppressor cells that render helper T-cells resistant to subsequent suppressor cell signals (Green, Flood, & Gershon, 1983).

The Complement System

The complement system is a segment of the immune system that has the ability to respond immediately to a variety of substances through a series of enzymatic reactions. This system is composed of a series of proteins that are found in the circulation and interstitial fluid in an inactive precursor state that has no physiologic activity. There are two independent pathways that will activate this series of reactions that results in a variety of biologic activities: the classical pathway, which requires the interaction of specific antibodies with an antigen for its initiation, and the alternate pathway, which is initiated by various substances including certain complex polysaccharides and lipopolysaccharides but does not require the binding of antibodies to antigens. For a more detailed explanation of these pathways, the reader is referred to various reviews (Cooper, 1982; Frank, 1979, Ruddy, Gigli, & Austen, 1972).

After activation of the complement systems, the subsequent series of reactions leads to a variety of biologic reactions, including lysis of bacteria, viruses, or cells, and various inflammatory responses, such as smooth muscle contraction, enhanced vascular permeability, and release of vasoactive amines such as histamine from mast cells and lysosomal enzymes from granulocytes. The importance of the complement system is demonstrated in individuals who have a defect or absence of a component of this system. Depending on the exact defect, such individuals may have increased susceptibility to infections, systemic lupus erythematosus or similar syndromes, nephritis, or hereditary angioedema.

Immunoglobulins

The major components of the humoral immunity system are immunoglobulins, which are complex glycoproteins. The five major classes of immunoglobulins are IgG, IgM, IgA, IgD, and IgE, which make up 75%, 10%, 15%, 0.2% and 0.004%, respectively, of the total in the serum (Root & Ryan, 1985). They all have the same basic structure, consisting of two longer peptide chains known as "heavy" or H chains bound by disulfide bridges to two shorter chains known as "light" or L chains (Figure 3-5). Each L chain has a constant region and a variable region. Each region is so named based on the variance of its amino acid sequence. The variability is important in the development of antibody specificity. The H chain also has one variable region but three constant regions that are unique for each

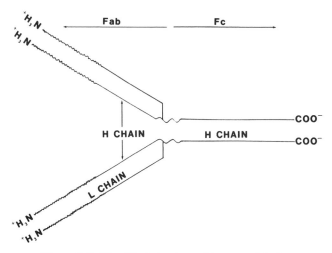

Figure 3-5. Simplified structure of immunoglobulin.

class of immunoglobulin. The variable region of the H chain, like the L chain variable region, is involved in antigen binding.

The immunoglobulins not only function as antibodies to bind antigens but also interact extensively with the cellular immune and the complement systems. Many leukocytes have Fc receptors that, upon binding IgG, initiate a series of events. For phagocytes, the binding of IgG to its surface receptors stimulates endocytosis, lysosome release, and activation of oxidative metabolism (Horowitz, 1982; Weissman, Smolen, & Korchak, 1980). As noted previously, opsonization enhances phagocytosis by allowing IgG or IgM to engage with the Fc receptors of phagocytic cells. For mast cells and basophils, the binding of antigen to IgE attached to their surface receptors triggers the release of the vasoactive amines (Ishizaka, Soto, & Ishizaka, 1973). Furthermore, killer cells require antibody attached to the target cells to be cytotoxic (antibody-dependent cellular cytotoxicity, or ADCC) (Shore, Melewicz, & Gordon, 1977; Waksman, 1976). Finally, immunoglobulins have differing capabilities for binding complement and thus activating the classical complement pathway and subsequent lysis of susceptible organisms. Other functions of immunoglobulins include neutralization of toxins, inhibition of attachment of organisms to host cells, and inhibition of the infectivity of extracellular viruses (Root & Ryan, 1985).

The production and regulation of antibody requires the interaction of many aspects of the immune system. Two categories of antigens are described that require different pathways in the stimulation of B-cells: T-independent antigen, which can stimulate B-cells directly (i.e., bacterial lipopolysaccharides), and a T-dependent antigen (i.e., erythrocytes, serum proteins, hapten carrier complexes), which requires more extensive interaction with the T-cell system. In the latter system, the antigen is presented to helper T-cells by macrophages. As noted previously, helper cells are a source of IL2, which stimulates T-cell proliferation. They also are a source of B-cell growth factors (BCGF), which cause B-cell proliferation, and a B-cell differentiation factor, which enhances immunoglobulin secretion (Muraguchi, Butler, Kehrl, & Fanci, 1983; Okada, Sakaguchi, & Yoshimura, 1983). Once an antigen-reactive B-cell has been stimulated, it may give rise to as many as 1,000 progeny cells. The initial antibody response is of the IgM class, followed by IgG. Plasma cells apparently are capable of production of only one type of immunoglobulin at a time, but they are capable of changing classes; therefore, IgG-producing cells are derived from IgM precursors (Lawton, Asofsky, & Hylton, 1972; Manning & Jutilc, 1972).

As helper T-cells aid in the production of antibody-producing cells, supressor T-cells can readily inhibit this response. Suppressor T-cells can act directly on B-cells or on helper T-cells in inhibiting humoral response. Furthermore, immunoglobulins themselves can inhibit further antibody production, suggesting the operation of a negative feedback control system (Eardley, 1980).

Laboratory Evaluation of the Immune System

Numerous assays are available for measuring various aspects of the immune system. Readily available studies for measuring B-cell function include measuring IgG or IgM responses to various vaccines or common viruses. T-cell functions may be evaluated by skin tests (PPD, candidus, etc.) or contact sensitization with dinitrochlorobenzene; complement systems may be evaluated by measuring only C3 or CH50 (total hemolytic complement).

More in-depth investigation is being performed in several laboratories; many of these studies will be mentioned elsewhere in this book. Measurement of IgG subclasses or the kinetics and immunoglobulin class of antibody that are produced in response to specific immunization may be performed. Assays for evaluating various B-cell membrane antigens and receptors are available. T-cells may be quantified into their subpopulations by assays utilizing monoclonal antibodies against various surface antigens (CD3, CD4, CD8). Lymphocyte transformation to various mitogens (phytohemagglutinin, conA, etc.), which correlates with *in vivo* lymphocyte activations, may be performed. Quantification of lymphokines is also available. Finally, assays for assessing phagocytosis, chemotaxis, and opsonization have been developed.

CONCLUSION

The function of the endocrine and immune systems is to maintain homeostasis. The endocrine, through the hypothalamic–pituitary unit, regulates the body's metabolism, growth and development, and reproductive ability. The sympathoadrenal system, responsible for the fight-or-flight response, affects circulation, thermogenesis, and fuel metabolism.

The two traditional divisions of the immune system are the humoral and cellular systems. Although they are commonly discussed separately, they function in a highly integrated manner as the body's defense mechanism. If the immune system is depressed, by whatever mechanism, infections result. If the system loses its regulation, the immune system may attack "itself," resulting in a spectrum of immunologic diseases.

Both systems are regulated by intraregulatory feedback mechanisms, by genetic influences, and by each other. Only in recent years has the complexity of these systems been partially understood. From this knowledge, we can begin to look at how the family unit may affect these systems. The interactions of the family system with the neuroendocrine and immune systems are subjects for subsequent chapters.

References

Bargmann W, Scharrer E. The site of origin of the hormones of the posterior pituitary. American Scientist 1951; 39:255–259.

Basten A, Beeson PA. Mechanisms of eosinophilia: II. Role of the lymphocyte. Journal of Experimental Medicine 1970; 131:1288.

Bernard C. Lectures on the phenomena of life common to animals and plants, Vol. I. Hoff HE, Guillence R, Guillence L, trans. Springfield, Ill.: Thomas, 1974.

Blanden RV. Mechanisms of recovery from a generalized viral infection: mousepox-I. The efforts of anti-thymocyte serum. Journal of Experimental Medicine 1970; 132:1035.

Bondy PK. Disorders of the adrenal cortex. In: Wilson JD, Foster DW, eds. William's textbook of endocrinology. Philadelphia: Saunders, 1985: 816–890.

Bondy PK, Rosenberg LE. Metabolic control and disease, 8th ed. Philadelphia: Saunders, 1980.

Cannon WB. The influence of emotional states on the functions of the alimentary canal. American Journal of Medical Science 1909; 137:480–487.

Cannon WB. The energizing functions of the adrenal medulla in pain and the major emotions. American Journal of Physiology 1914; 33:356–372.

Cannon WB. The wisdom of the body. New York: Norton, 1939.

Cannon WB, De La Paz D. Emotional stimulation of adrenal secretion. American Journal of Physiology 1911; 27:64–70.

Cooper NR. The complement system. In: Stites DP, Stubo JD, Fudenberg HH, Wells JV, eds. Basic and clinical immunology. Los Altos, Calif.: Lange Medical Publications, 1982: 124–135.

Daughaday WH. The anterior pituitary. In: Wilson JD, Foster DW, eds. William's textbook of endocrinology. Philadelphia: Saunders, 1985: 568–613.

Douglas SD. Development and structure of cells in the immune system. In: Stites DP, Stubo JD, Fudenberg HH, Wells JV, eds. Basic and clinical immunology. Los Altos, Calif.: Lange Medical Publications, 1982: 65–88.

Dvorak HF, Dvorak AM. Basophilic leukocytes: structures, function, and role in disease. Clinical Hematology 1975; 4:651.

Eardley D. Feedback suppression: an immunoregulatory circuit. Federation Proceedings 1980; 39:3114.

Frank MM. The complement system in host defense and inflammation. Review of Infectious Disease 1979; 1:483.

Frick OL. Immediate hypersensitivity. In: Stites DP, Stubo JD, Fudenberg HH, Wells JV, eds. Basic and clinical immunology. Los Altos, Calif.: Lange Medical Publications, 1982: 250–275.

Grabar P. The historical background of immunology. In: Stites DP, Stubo JD, Fudenberg HH, Wells JV, eds. Basic and clinical immunology. Los Altos, Calif.: Lange Medical Publications, 1982: 1–12.

Green DR, Flood PM, Gershon RK. Immunoregulatory T-cell pathways. Annual Review of Immunology 1983; 1:439.

Herberman RB. Natural Killer (NK) cells and their possible roles in resistance against disease. Clinical Immunology Review 1981; 1:1.

Horowitz MA. Phagocytosis of microorganisms. Review of Infectious Disease 1982; 4:104.

Ishizaka T, Soko CS, Ishizaka K. Mechanisms of passive sensitization: 3. Number of IgE molecules and their receptor sites on human basophil granulocytes. Journal of Immunology 1973; 3:500.

Katz DL. The immune system: an overview. In: Sites DP, Stubo JD, Fudenberg HH, Wells JV, eds. Basic and clinical immunology. Los Altos, Calif.: Lange Medical Publications, 1982: 13–20.

Klein J. Immunology: the science of self–non-self discrimination. New York: Wiley, 1982.

Landsberg L, Young JB. Catecholamines and the adrenal medulla. In: Wilson JD, Foster DW, eds. William's textbook of endocrinology. Philadelphia: Saunders, 1985: 891–965.

Lanier LL, Engleman ED, Gatenby P. Correlation of functional properties of human lymphoid cell subsets and surface market phenotypes using multiparameter analysis and flow cytometry. Immunology Review 1983; 74:143.

Lawton AR, Asofsky W, Hylton MB. Suppression of immunoglobulin class synthesis in mice. Journal of Experimental Medicine 1972; 135:277.

Mahmond FAF, Stone MK, Kellermeyer RW. Eosinophilopoietin: a circulating low molecular weight peptide-like substance which stimulates the production of eosinophils in mice. Journal of Clinical Investigation 1977; 60:675.

Manning DD, Jutilc JW. Immunosuppression of mice injected with heterologous anti-immunoglobulin heavy chain antisera. Journal of Experimental Medicine 1972; 135:1316.

Mason JW. A review of psychoendocrine research in the sympathetic–adrenal medullary system. Psychosomatic Medicine 1968; 30(5):631–653.

Mason JW. A reevaluation of the concept of "non-specificity" in stress theory. Journal of Psychiatric Research 1971; 8:323–333.

Mason JW. A historical view of the stress field. Journal of Human Stress 1975; 1:6–12, 22–36.

McLeod R, Wing EJ, Remington JS. Lymphocytes and macrophages in cell-mediated immunity. In: Mandell GL, Douglas RG, Bennett JE, eds. Principles and practice of infectious disease, 2nd ed. New York: Wiley, 1985: 72–90.

Muraguchi A, Butler JL, Kehrl JH, Fanci AS. Differential sensitivity of human B-cell subsets to activation signals delivered by antigen antibody and proliferative signals delivered by a monoclonal B-cell growth factor. Journal of Experimental Medicine 1983; 157:530.

Okada M, Sakaguchi N, Yoshimura N. B-cell growth factors and B-cell differentiation factor from human T hybridomas. Journal of Experimental Medicine 1983; 157:583.

Reichlin S. Neuroendocrinology. In: Wilson JD, Foster DW, eds. William's textbook of endocrinology. Philadelphia: Saunders, 1985: 429–567.

Reinherz EL, Schlossman SF. The differentiation and function of human T lymphocytes. Cell 1980; 19:821.

Riley V. Psychoneuroendocrine influences on immunocompetence and neoplasia. Science 1981; 212:1100–1109.

Root PK, Ryan JL. Humoral immunity and complement. In: Mandell GL, Douglas RG, Bennett JE, eds. Principles and practice of infectious disease, 2nd ed. New York: Wiley, 1985: 31–56.

Ruddy S, Gigli I, Austen F. The complement system of man. New England Journal of Medicine 1972; 287:489.

Selye H. A syndrome produced by diverse noxious agents. Nature 1936; 138:32.

Shore SL, Melewicz FM, Gordon DS. The mononuclear cell in human blood which mediates antibody-dependent cellular cytoxicity to virus-infected target cells: I. Identification of the population of effector cells. Journal of Immunology 1977; 118:729.

Solomon GF, Amkraut AA. Psychoneuroendocrinological effects on the immune response. Annual Review of Microbiology 1981; 35:155–184.

Waksman BH. Immunoglobulins and lymphokines as mediators of inflammatory cell mobilization and target cell killing. Cellular Immunology 1976; 27:309.

Weissmann G, Smolen JE, Korchak HM. Release of inflammatory mediators from stimulated neutrophils. New England Journal of Medicine 1980; 303:27.

Weller PF, Goetzl EJ. The human eosinophil: roles in host defense and tissue injury. American Journal of Pathology 1980; 100:790.

Werb Z. Phagocytic cells: chemotaxis and effector functions of macrophages and granulocytes. In: Stites DP, Stubo JD, Fudenberg HH, Wells JV, eds. Basic and clinical immunology. Los Altos, Calif.: Lange Medical Publications, 1982: 109–123.

PART TWO

Family Systems Theory

4

Introduction to Family Theory

LISA C. BAKER
University of Oklahoma

JOAN M. PATTERSON
University of Minnesota

Family medicine research is just beginning to be influenced by the range of family theories available from other disciplines and to develop its own ideas about the importance of family functioning in relation to physical illness and health. Research on the "family" part of family medicine has centered around a series of questions that have become more and more refined. The thrust of much of our work has been simply to show that family structure and/or function is associated with health outcomes. One series of questions has addressed the family as the victim of unusual difficulties brought on by illness; another line of inquiry has examined the family as an agent of influences on the illness process itself.

Engel's (1977) concept of the biopsychosocial model has expanded our field of vision to include social (family) as well as psychological variables in our study of biologic processes. It has taken quite a while, however, for researchers to move past the stage of including family variables and begin to puzzle about how and why variables are related.

As family and health research flourishes, researchers in family medicine are wisely looking to traditions of family theory and research that could save them from reinventing the proverbial wheel. Not only are we considering ideas from research done outside of family medicine (e.g., Minuchin, Rosman, & Baker's [1978] classic study of psychosomatic families), but we are also turning to the "bench researchers" of family phenomena— family social scientists.

Among the broad conceptual frameworks that have emerged in family studies, this book contains chapters addressing five theories. It is the purpose of this chapter to introduce the reader briefly to these differing frameworks of family functioning: the Beavers systems model of family functioning (Beavers, Chapter 5, this volume), the circumplex model of marital and family systems (Olson, Chapter 6, this volume), the family adjustment and adaptation model (Patterson, Chapter 7, this volume), family problem-solving paradigms (Reiss, Chapter 8, this volume), and the oscillation theory of family development (Breunlin, Chapter 9, this volume.) Family medicine has already shown interest in these frameworks and has begun to produce its own variations of the ideas and research styles that often accompany them.

SUMMARY OF THEORETICAL FRAMEWORKS

Beavers Systems Model

The Beavers Systems Model of Family Functioning (Chapter 5) integrates two levels of systems: an individual psychiatric orientation with family systems theory. There are two dimensions or axes in the model: family competence (in functioning) and family style. Family competence is a continuous linear variable that reflects, first, the degree of family adaptability in effecting change and tolerating differentiation of members and, second, the degree of individual autonomy. Family competence varies from severely dysfunctional to optimal, with three categories (borderline, midrange, adequate) between these extremes. Family style is a curvilinear variable with two poles: (1) centripetal style, where the belief is that major relationship satisfaction comes from within the family and hence the tendency is to pull family members in, versus (2) centrifugal style, where the belief is that the world outside the family holds the most satisfaction and hence the tendency is to push family members out. Families between these two extremes, labeled "mixed," switch styles as needed.

Using the two dimensions of competence and style, nine family categories are constructed. The two dimensions are not weighted equally. In the two extremes of family competence—optimal and adequate—there is only mixed style; similarly, in the two extremes of family incompetence—severely dysfunctional and borderline—there is no mixed style but only rigidly centripetal style or rigidly centrifugal style.

There appear to be two central themes for assessment with this model—conflict and ambivalence—which Beavers considers ubiquitous properties of families and individuals, respectively. The central task for optimal functioning is to resolve these satisfactorily. One method developed for assessing family competence and style is observer ratings of family interaction during task performance. There are 13 subscales for assessing family competence (power, coalitions, boundaries, autonomy, affect, negotiating, etc.) and 8 subscales for assessing family style (aggression, closeness, dependency, appearances, etc.) In addition to its research potential for understanding families, the model has also been elaborated into a family systems approach to psychotherapy.

Circumplex Model of Family Functioning

The original circumplex model developed by Olson, Sprenkle, and Russell (1979) contained two major dimensions, adaptability and cohesion, both considered as continua ranging from very low to very high. The model emerged as a synthesis of clinical and empirical literature about family functioning. The authors added the new idea of putting the two variables into a circumplex that defines various combinations of cohesion and adaptability. Communication was added later as a facilitating dimension, but it is not part of the graphic model of the circumplex itself.

The two dimensions of cohesion and adaptability are conceptualized as curvilinear variables, with better functioning families generally falling in the midrange ("balanced families") and dysfunctional families at the extremes.

A recent expansion of the model has been to combine its concepts with those of the family adjustment and adaptation response (FAAR) stress model (Patterson, Chapter 7) to produce the integrative family system model (Olson, Chapter 6). This model attempts to integrate four areas of family functioning: family stress, family types, family resources, and family adaptation.

The authors of the circumplex model have developed a questionnaire, the Family Adaptability and Cohesion Evaluation Scales (FACES), which has been revised twice since its inception (see Chapter 6). These instruments are designed to assess how an individual perceives his or her family system, and can also be used to assess the person's ideal description. This latter concept has been added more recently to tap family satisfaction as measured by the perceived–ideal discrepancy.

A clinical rating scale has also been developed to measure cohesion, change, and communication (Olson & Killorin, 1985). This scale is used to rate the behavior of a family system based on a semistructured interview with an individual or with several family members.

Family Adjustment and Adaptation Response Model

The family adjustment and adaptation response (FAAR) model discussed by Patterson (Chapter 7) has evolved from three decades of family stress theory building, which began with Hill's ABC-X family crisis model (1949). The original focus on how the stressor (factor A) interacting with the family's resources (factor B) and perceptions (factor C) produced a crisis (factor X) for the family has been expanded to include postcrisis variables.

In the FAAR model, a distinction is made between the pre- and postcrisis stress process, called "adjustment" and "adaptation," respectively, to emphasize the need and ability of families to adapt following a crisis by making discontinuous change in their system. During the adjustment phase, families resist major changes and attempt to maintain homeostasis using their existing capabilities (resources and coping behaviors) and perceptions for meeting demands (stressors and strains). However, when the number of demands increases or the nature of the demands changes (e.g., developmental change occurs) beyond the family's existing capabilities, a crisis emerges in the family system that pushes them into the adaptation phase, where second-order change is called for.

Theoretically, the FAAR model is rooted in systems theory while also incorporating concepts from family development theory (e.g., developmental tasks as stressors), from symbolic interaction theory (e.g., perceptions of demands and capabilities that may be discrepant or congruent within the family), and from structure–function theory (e.g., adjustment/adaptation is evaluated in terms of how well the family meets its functions). In addition, the conceptual definitions for the domains of the stress process (i.e., sources, mediators, and outcomes) reflect some parallels with other stress theories that have been developed by physiologists, psychologists, and epidemiologists. By integrating these related theories focused on different levels of systems (e.g., an organ system, the individual), it is suggested, a paradigm could emerge for examining the relationship between the social processes of the family, the psychologic processes of the mind, and the physiologic processes of the body.

Several self-report instruments have been developed by McCubbin and his colleagues (see Chapter 12, this volume) for assessing different components of this model. In addition, a summary table is presented of other research instruments that could be considered for research studies using the FAAR model.

Family Problem-Solving Paradigms

The family paradigm model (Reiss, Chapter 8, this volume) is based on an ecologic approach to theory building. Its emphasis is on describing differences in family style that may or may not be dysfunctional depending on the particular challenges facing the family and the different settings in which they find themselves.

The three major dimensions of family paradigms identified thus far are configuration, coordination, and closure. Configuration refers to the sense of mastery felt by the family relative to its belief in a patterned, lawful environment. Coordination refers to the family's conception of being regarded by the world as a highly connected group, as opposed to more isolated individuals. Closure has to do with the family's being dominated by tradition versus being open to new experience.

Current theoretical work on family paradigms centers around questions of differences in the ways families respond to challenges. It appears that families with certain paradigms respond characteristically to various kinds of challenges; they may also have different coping styles and may suffer predictable consequences following a failure to cope.

This model has been operationalized by its author using a laboratory problem-solving method called a card-sort procedure. Family members each sit in an isolated booth in contact with each other through a telephone-like device. Each person sorts a deck of cards containing a sequence of symbols. The task is performed individually and again by each family group. From these data, the researcher can measure the subtlety of the patterns seen in the cards, the degree to which family members work together, and the degree to which people change their sorting schemes as the task proceeds.

Oscillation Theory: Family Development and the Process of Change

Family life cycle theory has been one of the most important family theories in the science of family medicine. Two hallmarks of family medicine, continuity of care and treating whole families, have necessitated an understanding of normative needs at each stage of the life cycle and of how individuals and families change over time. Concurrent with family physicians' efforts to integrate knowledge of family development into clinical practice, family therapists have integrated the concept of the family life cycle into their theory-building efforts as an important component for understanding family context. In Chapter 9 (this volume), Breunlin integrates a family therapy perspective with family life cycle theory.

Systemic family therapists have viewed the family as a cybernetic system that attempts to balance stability (through homeostasis) and change (through morphogenesis). Normal developmental transitions have been viewed as occasions calling for second-order (discontinuous) change by the family. Failure to make such changes resulted in symptoms that served as a homeostatic mechanism to keep the family in a pretransition stage. Therapy was directed at altering the context in some way that would activate a positive feedback loop leading to morphogenic change needed to move the family to the next developmental stage.

Bruenlin points out, however, that this assumption of the change–stability dualism in families has been challenged in the 1980s by the view that change–stability is a unitary process, that is, "complementary sides of a systemic coin" (p. 7). Oscillation theory is an attempt to integrate family development theory with this newer cybernetic view of the family as always simultaneously engaged in change while remaining stable.

In Breunlin's view, families do not make an all-or-nothing step change to the next developmental stage, but change more gradually by oscillating between greater than and less than competent behavior relative to each transition. This oscillation reflects the family's effort to change while remaining stable. In normal families, the oscillation gradually dampens, and the family progresses to increased developmental competence. Failure to make the transition leaves the family stuck in the oscillation (in contrast to the older system's view of the family as homeostatically stuck in the prior stage). Symptoms emerge as a function of the oscillation. The clinician's task is to dampen the oscillation so that family members and the family unit can progress in developmental competence. In his chapter,

Breunlin describes the clinical assessment of developmental process and outlines strategies for therapeutically dampening these oscillations. Research methodology using this theory is not presented.

CONCLUSION

The theoretical frameworks introduced above clearly have much to offer family medicine research. It also seems apparent that family medicine can do much to advance and elaborate these ideas in the specific context of family and health research. The theories raise such issues as process versus outcome assessment, change versus stability of family patterns, and the family as victim versus the family as a causal agent. Each chapter also contains the intertwining of theory and method. Not only the preferences and training of the researchers, but sometimes the ideas themselves, seem to influence which methodology is chosen to answer different kinds of questions.

Baker's chapter (Chapter 10, this volume) on "Critical Issues in Family Theory in Family Medicine Research" is organized around three themes. The chapter challenges the often simplistic and romanticized view of the family on which much of family medicine research relies. Second, it attempts to clarify some of the issues in our current thinking about the terms "health" and "illness" as they relate to families. Third, the chapter highlights traditions of family theory that are relevant for family medicine research, focusing on family sociology and on systems theory and cybernetics. Baker's chapter discusses some key concepts and distinctions in systems theory and cybernetics, and she puts into perspective some of the recent discussion about systems theory versus more traditional sociologic theories.

The diversity of these theories should stimulate our thinking to develop even more refined ideas about family issues that are specific, not only to the topic of illness, but also to different kinds of physical conditions.

Painted in the broadest strokes, the similarity of these theories should give us a sense of the state of the art from which we can draw. These broad-based conceptual frameworks demonstrate that thinking about families can be an expansive, sophisticated endeavor.

References

Engel GL. The need for a new medical model: a challenge for biomedicine. Science 1977; 196:129–136.
Hill R. Families under stress. New York: Harper, 1949.
Minuchin S, Rosman BL, Baker L. Psychosomatic families. Cambridge, Mass.: Harvard University Press, 1978.
Olson DH, Killorin E. Clinical rating scale for circumplex model. Department of Family Social Science, University of Minnesota, St. Paul, 1985.
Olson DH, Sprenkle DH, Russell CS. Family inventories. Department of Family Social Science, University of Minnesota, St. Paul, 1979.

5

Beavers Systems Model

W. ROBERT BEAVERS
University of Texas;
Southwest Family Institute, Dallas

A *model* is a representation of reality. As Korzybski (1933) noted, a map is not the territory, but the most useful map—or model—is the one that most nearly reflects the qualities of the territory. The systems model of family functioning to be described reflects 25 years of research and clinical work, merging a clinical psychiatric orientation with general systems theory. It was the framework for a study of families, especially focused on healthy families, that was reported by Lewis, Beavers, Gossett, and Phillips (1976) and subsequently elaborated in a family systems approach to psychotherapy (Beavers, 1977). Since then, several descriptions of the model have been published (Beavers, 1981, 1982; Beavers & Voeller, 1983; Beavers, Hampson, & Hulgus, 1985; Hampson, Beavers, & Hulgus, 1988). Using this family model as the basis, we are in the seventh year of a study of nonlabeled families who have a developmentally disabled child. It is my strong belief that physicians markedly increase their therapeutic skills as they embrace a systems approach to illness and health, and this family assessment schema can be a valuable heuristic device in learning to ''think systems,'' that is, to think of patients and illness as contextual phenomena.

Some years ago, I began a talk addressed to a general medical audience as follows: ''A physician treating pneumonitis in a 75-year-old woman, bedridden with a recently fractured hip, long addicted to cigarettes, habituated to alcohol, and whose husband had died 6 weeks before, knows intuitively that he must deal with a complex array of variables, and if he is successful it will be due to the orchestration of many skills to alter these variables favorably.'' This physician will approach his patient with attention to biology, individual patterns and characteristics, family factors, and social realities.

It is regrettable that such an important systemic integrative orientation must be developed incidentally rather than as an intrinsic part of medical education. There are, however, some basic processes encompassed in a family systems orientation that are already being taught in medical schools. Medical physiology, for example, provides such a foundation. If the physician extrapolates physiologic principles (e.g., homeostasis, circularity, wholes being more than the sum of parts) to the environment beyond the skin, then family systems medicine concepts can take root.

Engel (1977) contrasts the multilevel systems view of illness with what he terms the ''biomedical'' model. The latter has molecular biology as its basic scientific discipline, and assumes that disease can be attributed to deviations from the norm of measurable biologic (somatic) variables. It demands that disease be dealt with independently of social behavior and, further, requires that behavioral aberrations be explained as disordered somatic processes. The biomedical model could be characterized as reductionistic, perpetuating a false mind–body dualism.

The obsessive focus on one system level to explain illness is, unfortunately, not limited to biology. Recently, a colleague visited a family therapy institute and observed the institute director and a trainee jeering at the mother of a 20-year-old manic patient for allowing the medical establishment to "give her son poison." These therapists coerced the mother into reading the warning material from the lithium container, with the apparent goal of enlightening her and abolishing the young man's "irrelevant and dangerous" lithium treatment. Such a procedure is as antithetical to a systems paradigm, which emphasizes the interaction of many levels, as is the biomedical model.

BASIC CONCEPTS OF THE BEAVERS SYSTEMS MODEL OF FAMILY FUNCTIONING

Several underlying principles contributed to the characteristics of this model of family functioning.

1. Family functioning is best described on a continuum rather than by assigning families to discrete "types." Most of the dangers inherent in psychiatric labeling result from trying to put pieces of our varied universe into small boxes and then trying to force some sort of fit. Indeed, such a concept as "family types" encourages noncontextual, nonsystems thinking. To visualize qualities, patterns, and functioning abilities as existing on various continua promotes the conception of health and disease *in relation to* other people and other processes.

2. The model provides for measurement of competence in whole families engaged in current task performance. When family members are asked an open-ended question—for example, "What would you like to see changed in your family?"—the resulting behavior is valuable in determining that family's current negotiating capacity. Some of our previous research has shown that competence in small tasks is closely correlated with competence in the larger family responsibilities, such as raising children (Lewis *et al.*, 1976).

3. In addition to a current level of competence, families also have various styles of functioning that may be unrelated to adaptation or competence. Family assessment must take these stylistic differences into account.

4. The model was designed initially to represent data from direct observations of family interaction rather than from reports of such interaction. This decision was aimed at increasing the clinical relevance of findings. Trained outside raters observing interaction are operating at a level similar to that characteristic of the clinical arena. (The activity requested of families being assessed should make sense to the family members even during times of extreme stress.) Although family self-report scales provide useful information, the relevance of such information to clinical problems is unclear, and family members' personal statements often differ sharply. We have added a self-report scale to this basic observational methodology in order to broaden the dialogue with other family assessment researchers who use self-reports as a basic source of data and to explore the relationships between these two methods of assessment (Beavers *et al.*, 1985; Hampson *et al.*, 1988).

5. The model should be compatible with major clinical concepts of family functioning, which are derived from family therapy. For example, Minuchin's (1974) structural concepts and Bowen's (1978) emphasis on differentiation of self fit easily with this model and are consistent with an assessment approach generated out of clinical material and guided by systems concepts.

The data for evaluating clinical families are usually developed as follows. The interviewer or therapist asks the family to perform a task (usually, to discuss what they would like to see changed in their family) and then leaves the room. The family is observed with a video camera or through a one-way mirror, or both, for approximately 10 minutes. In the home or in clinical settings without such technical advantages, the interviewer can remain silent and inactive during this interval. It is most important for the interviewer not to interact with family members while they are fulfilling this task. The interviewer's participation creates another system with significantly different characteristics, and the resulting interactions reveal a great deal about the interviewer–family system but relatively little about the family itself.

USING THE MODEL

Figure 5-1 is a diagram of this model. The horizontal axis relates to the structure, available information, and adaptive flexibility of the system. In systems terms, this may be called a "negentropic measure": The more flexible and adaptive the system, the more the family can negotiate, function, and deal effectively with stressful situations.

   High adaptability requires both structure and the ability to change structures. There is a complex interaction of morphogenic and morphostatic features. Capable families intuitively have a systems approach to relationships, with an appreciation of the interchangeability of causes and effects, as well as the circularity of systems phenomena. When a family is not bound to rigid behavior patterns and responses, it has more freedom to evolve

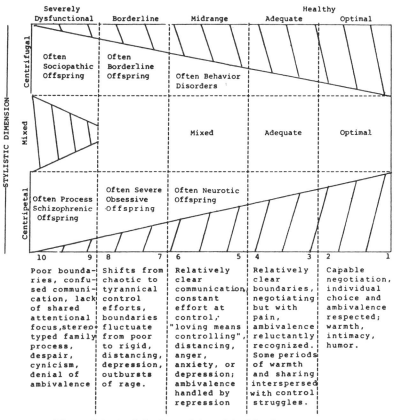

Figure 5-1. A clinically useful model of family assessment.

and differentiate. von Bertalanffy (1969) wisely said that "system sickness is system rigidity" (p. 92).

The vertical axis relates to a stylistic quality of family interaction. Centripetal (CP) family members view most relationship satisfactions as coming from within the family rather than from the outside world. Conversely, centrifugal (CF) family members see the outside world as holding the most promise of satisfaction and the family as holding less. Competent families change and adapt in various ways in order to meet members' needs. For example, a family with small children is appropriately more centripetal; as the family matures and children reach late adolescence, a more centrifugal pattern is optimally adaptive (Combrinck-Graham, 1983). This centripetal/centrifugal (CP/CF) dimension is an old one, dating back to sociologic concepts of the 1930s. Later, Erikson (1963) used the concept in describing Indian tribes in *Childhood and Society,* as did Stierlin (1972) in his studies of adolescent runaways and their families. The diagram combining the two dimensions is in the shape of an arrow to illustrate that although family style is a different dimension than family competence, they are related. That is, the healthier and more adaptive the family, the less significant is its style of the moment, because the family is able to change as needed for adaptation. The extreme forms of CP/CF family styles are seen only in rigid and poorly functioning families whose stereotyped patterning demands a simple style. For the same reason, there is no mixed CP/CF category in the severely dysfunctional and borderline families.

From this two-dimensional grid, nine family groups are constructed that are clinically useful, empirically supported, and able to offer a valid graduation of functioning ability.

Optimal and Adequate Families

GROUP 1: OPTIMAL FAMILIES
These serve as our model for effective functioning. The family members have what can be described as a systems orientation; they realize that many causes interact to produce a given result and that causes and effects are interchangeable (e.g., excessively harsh discipline leads to bad behavior, bad behavior invites harsh discipline).

Intimacy is sought and generally found, a function of frequent, equal-powered transactions combined with respect for each others' viewpoints. Individual choice and perceptions are respected allowing for capable negotiation and excellent group problem solving. Individuation of each person is highly evolved, and boundaries are clear. There is conflict, but it is usually resolved quickly. (Conflict in family systems is comparable to ambivalence in the individual. Both are ubiquitous and inescapable, and health consists in resolving the conflict at the individual or family level, not in avoiding or denying it.)

Accepting limits allows for the resolution of conflict. The family and the individual are not perceived as necessarily at odds but rather in an ongoing tension. This family can be considered as simultaneously both morphostatic and morphogenic. The hierarchic structure of the family is well defined and continues to be accepted. There is concomitant flexibility that permits frequent changes in function and approaches to problems. The family can tolerate its evolution through time, actually encouraging its own demise as a tightly knit unit. In its later stages of development, it becomes a loosely connected, lovingly respectful group of equal adults, with another generation emerging. Each individual knows that he or she needs the family, and this knowledge promotes capable, comfortable negotiation.

GROUP 2: ADEQUATE FAMILIES

These families show many similarities in function and style to the midrange families discussed in the following sections. Adequate families are contrasted with optimal families in that the former are more control-oriented and often attempt to resolve conflict by intimidation and direct force. Therefore, family members seek greater overt power, and the parental coalition is less emotionally rewarding, though usually effective. The interaction in these families, though still adequate, produces less intimacy and trust, less joy, and less spontaneity. Role stereotyping, particularly sex-role stereotyping, with conventional, powerful, unemotive males counterpointed by relatively less powerful, emotive, and frequently depressed women, is usual.

These families, however, seem to have children as competent as those found in the optimal families. Apparently this is due to family members' strong belief in the importance of parenting and of family life. Tenacity and genuine caring are effective in spite of only modest negotiating skills. These families function with pain and some individual loneliness, but they do function, and one sees relatively few psychiatric patients from this group.

Midrange Families

The first group of dysfunctional families are termed "midrange." These families usually rear sane but limited offspring, and both parents and children are susceptible to psychiatric illness. Midrange families are concerned with control and overt power differences; power struggles and discipline without negotiation are typical. These control efforts are believed essential because people are assumed to be basically antisocial and depraved. Family members do not have flagrant boundary problems. Although there are frequent projections, family roles allow for rebuttal, and invasions of one member's inner space by another are resisted. Further, one often sees unresolved oedipal difficulties with "favorite" children. These favorites may be different for each parent—mother selects a son, father a daughter—or they may team up and select an agreed-on favorite and possibly a scapegoat.

Ambivalence is frequently handled by denying half of a pair of strong feelings and using repression or projection for the other, such as "I like to go out and you like to stay at home" or "You are too strict with the kids" versus "No, you are too lenient." There is a pervasive belief that people really have one unambiguous feeling: "He really loves me, though he is contemptuous" or "She really hates me though she tries to be nice." Three types, or styles, of midrange families will be discussed: centripetal (CP), centrifugal (CF), and mixed.

GROUP 3: MIDRANGE CENTRIPETAL FAMILIES

The midrange CP family expects overt, authoritarian control to be successful; parental manipulation or indirect control is minimal. The expression of hostility is not approved and is therefore covert; expressions of caring are approved. There is only modest spontaneity and a great concern for rules and authority. Sex stereotyping is at a maximum in this group; childlike women and strong, silent males abound.

Here are found most of the diminishing breed of the "good psychiatric patients"—those who work hard, pay their bill, develop transference nicely, and keep their pain out of sight of the neighbors if at all possible.

GROUP 4: MIDRANGE CENTRIFUGAL FAMILIES

These midrange families also attempt to use control by intimidation, but they do not expect their efforts to be successful. Unlike members of the midrange CP family, who believe in their own basic malevolence but expect to be successful by fraud, members of this CF group expect to be found out in their sleaziness and lack of genuine values. Open hostility, blame, and attack are frequent; expressions of warmth and caring are anxiety-provoking. Easily unleashed negative feelings provide the energy for CF movement. For example, because of their open hostility, mother and father spend little time in the home, and children move out into the neighborhoods and streets much earlier than the norm. The parental coalition is tenuous, with unresolved power issues openly displayed. All family members make use of manipulation. The children characteristically have difficulty with and contempt for authority, both in the home and beyond it. Control over self and other is sought but never achieved. These families distrust words and are infrequently seen in psychotherapy. They are apt to seek treatment with great ambivalence.

GROUP 5: MIDRANGE MIXED FAMILIES

This midrange group has enough alternating and competing CP and CF behavior to disqualify them for an extreme stylistic position. Thus they are in a mixed position within the midrange.

Borderline Families

These families present with chaotic overt power struggles alternating with ineffective but persistent efforts to establish dominance–submission patterns. Individual family members have little skill in attending to emotional needs, either their own or those of others. The families are neither as flagrantly amorphous as the severely disturbed group nor as effective in establishing control-oriented, stable patterning as the midrange families.

GROUP 6: BORDERLINE CENTRIPETAL FAMILIES

In these families, the chaos is more verbal than behavioral, and control battles are intense but usually covert. Open rebellion or overtly expressed rage is not expected because it is not within the family rules. Severely obsessional and anorectic patients are frequently found in these families.

GROUP 7: BORDERLINE CENTRIFUGAL FAMILIES

This group is much more open in the expression of anger. The parental coalition is notably poor, and stormy battles occur regularly. Children learn to manipulate the unstable but oscillating system and often receive a psychiatric label of "borderline personality."

Severely Disturbed Families

The severely disturbed family's greatest lack and need is communicational coherence. Consequently, this group is quite limited in its negotiating and adapting capacity. Family members have little ability to resolve ambivalence and to choose and pursue goals. There is a lack of a shared focus of attention in discussion, a peculiar distancing that precludes satisfying encounters. No one in the family clearly holds overt power. As one result, family functioning appears chaotic, since control is carried on by a variety of covert and indirect means.

GROUP 8: SEVERELY DISTURBED CENTRIPETAL FAMILIES

Those severely disturbed families with a CP style have a tough, nearly impermeable, outer boundary. These families are usually seen by neighbors as strange or queer. Children are handicapped in their progress through normal sequences of emotional development. For them (with an appropriate genetic contribution), a schizophrenic break is one solution to the conflict between the developmental need for separation/individuation and the family's insistence that everyone remain static and blurred.

GROUP 9: SEVERELY DISTURBED CENTRIFUGAL FAMILIES

This severely disturbed group with an extreme CF style has a tenuous perimeter, with frequent member leave-taking and some lack of clarity about who actually belongs in the family. Members express a lot of direct hostility and great contempt for dependency, vulnerability, tenderness, and warmth. Although these characteristics contrast with those of severely disturbed CP family members, the confused, incomplete transactions of the severely disturbed level of adaptability are similar. Children from severely disturbed CF families are as limited in developmental evolution as those from severely disturbed CP families. Since the necessary tenderness, nurturing, and caretaking behavior is minimal (and not highly regarded) in the severely disturbed CF family, character development is frequently antisocial in nature. Child abuse, sexual deviance, and severe drug problems are common in these families.

Two scales are observer assessment tools; these are the Beavers Interactional Scales I (Competence) and II (Style). Tables 5-1 and 5-2 summarize the Competence and Style subscale content.

The 13 subscales in the Competence instrument used for assessing family competence cover various aspects of family system functioning, including overt power, coalitions, boundaries, autonomy, feeling tone, irresolvable conflict, and negotiating. The scale is useful both as an assessment instrument and as a device for teaching systems concepts to health professionals.

The 8 Style subscales elicit raters' impressions of family members' concern with appearances and their attitudes about aggressiveness, dependency, and distance/closeness.

Table 5-1. Subscale Items for the Beavers Interactional Scales: I. Competence

Item number	Content area	Item description
1	Overt power	From chaotic through authoritarian to shared
2	Parental coalitions	From parent–child through weak to strong
3	Closeness	From vague, amorphous boundaries through isolation to close with distinct boundaries
4	Mythology	Degree of congruence between the family's views of itself and observer's impression
5	Goal-directed negotiation	Degree of efficiency in shared problem solving
6	Clarity of expression	Family members clear in disclosing thoughts and feelings
7	Responsibility	Degree to which members claim their actions
8	Invasiveness	Frequency of members' speaking for each other
9	Permeability	Degree of openness to each other's statements
10	Range of feelings	"Bandwidth" of members' expression of varied feelings
11	Mood and tone	Ranges from warm, optimistic, to cynical, hopeless
12	Unresolvable conflict	Degree of impairment of group functioning from currently unresolvable conflict
13	Empathy	Ability to understand another's feelings
14	Global	Overall impression of family's health/pathology

Table 5-2. Subscale Items for the Beavers Interactional Scales: II. Style

Item number	Content area	Item description
1	Dependency needs	Family encouragement or discouragement of dependency
2	Adult conflict	From overt to indirect
3	Family proximics	How members physically space themselves
4	Social presentation	Degree of apparent concern with appearances
5	Verbal expression of closeness	From consistent emphasis to denial
6	Aggression	Family encouragement or discouragement of aggression
7	Selective feeling expression	Whether members more easily express positive or negative feelings
8	Scapegoating	Degree to which family problems are blamed on only one member
9	Global	Observer's overall impression of this family's style

This stylistic dimension is clinically important, and observers usually agree on family style when historical data are used. The development of this instrument is an attempt to bring the concept into the arena of observed interaction.

We used these instruments in a study of 157 nonlabeled families with developmentally disabled children 3 to 5 years old. Table 5-3 shows the inter-rater reliability figures of two raters using both the Competence and Style subscales to assess these families. Inter-rater

Table 5-3. Inter-rater Reliability for the Beavers Interactional Scales: I. Competence; II. Style

Subscales	Correlation coefficient
I. Competence	
Overt power	.82
Parental coalition	.83
Closeness	.75
Mythology	.90
Goal-directed negotiations	.75
Clarity of expression	.82
Responsibility	.85
Permeability	.87
Range of feelings	.86
Mood and tone	.79
Unresolvable conflict	.75
Empathy	.89
Global	.85
BT average of subscales	.94
II. Style	
Dependency	.73
Adult conflict	.64
Proximity	.83
Social presentation	.62
Expressed closeness	.61
Assertive/aggressive behavior	.67
Expression of positive/negative feelings	.83
Scapegoating	.61
Global	.75
CP/CF average of subscales	.79

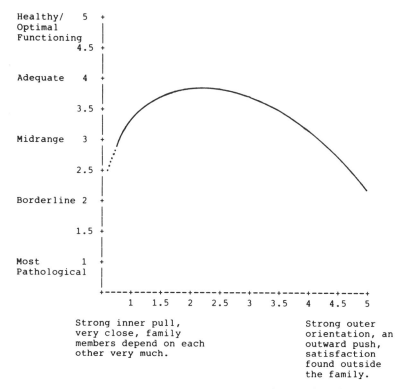

Figure 5-2. The relationship between the empirically derived factors of family health/competence and family style.

reliability of the sum Competence subscales was shown to be highly satisfactory, and the reliability of the Style subscales was acceptable.

We postulate on theoretical grounds that the stylistic dimensions, though distinct and separable from the competence dimension, is not totally unrelated, since the extreme styles should be associated with less functional families. Figure 5-2 provides statistical support for this notion, with data derived from the families with developmentally disabled children. It is apparent that extreme family styles are indeed characteristic of less competent families. Further, we note that the extreme CF style is associated with the most poorly functioning families, as would be expected in this group of families with small children.

Factor Analysis

As a confirmation of the theoretical model for which the scales were constructed, a factor analysis (using Varimax rotation procedure) of the Competence and Style scales was conducted on the data from these families. As Table 5-4 indicates, three principal factors emerged that account for nearly 60% of the variance in individual scores.

Factor 1, Family Health and Positive Feeling, incorporated most of the Competence scales with one—Expression of Positive Feeling—from the Style instrument. In other words, the scales, which were developed theoretically and thought to represent aspects of family competence, held together and were separable from the stylistic dimension. Interviews with

Table 5-4. Varimax Rotated Factor Structure of the Competence Scales and the Style Scales
(*N* = 156)

Subscale	Factor 1: Family Health— Positive Feelings	Factor 2: Family Style	Factor 3: Family Conflict
I. Competence			
Overt power	.55*	.07	.25
Parental coalitions	.53*	.12	.35
Closeness	.81*	−.04	.19
Mythology	.48*	−.01	.08
Goal-directed negotiation	.73*	.19	.30
Clarity of expression	.75*	.01	−.09
Responsibility	.76*	.12	.14
Invasiveness	.21	.07	.11
Permeability	.82*	.09	.15
Range of feelings	.82*	.04	−.12
Mood and tone	.77*	.18	.07
Unresolvable conflict	.43*	.21	.60*
Empathy	.82*	.11	.06
Global	.88*	.01	.17
II. Style			
Social presentation	.11	.62*	−.08
Internal scapegoating	.07	.38	.14
Verbal expression of closeness	.34	.74*	.02
Expression of positive feelings	.59*	.55*	.01
Adult conflict	.08	.15	.54*
Control, clinging	.15	.59*	−.02
Control, aggression	−.26	.43*	.13
Global	.01	.80*	.31

* = All subscales loading above .40.

raters revealed that their own assessment of a family as having a more positive feeling tone was reflected on the subscale of Positive Feelings Easily Expressed, so that this measurement was associated with both Health and Style.

Factor 2, Family Style, consists of items from the Style scale. The clustering of these two subscale groups into two discrete factors is valuable statistical confirmation of the clinical and systems concepts that inspired this theoretical model.

Factor 3, Conflict, emerged as a discrete element in family functioning. Although this construct was originally viewed as being "nested within" measures of Health and Style, it appears to be conceptually and statistically separate. Figure 5-3 illustrates the relationship between Factor 1, Family Health and Positive Feeling, and Factor 3, Conflict. Further research with different family populations will be necessary to determine whether this is a universal finding or simply peculiar to this group.

We have begun to augment the use of raters with self-reports of family member's perceptions of family life. It appears that in nonclinic families with a handicapped child, the breadwinner's self-report rating of family competence is very similar to that of an outside observer. That is, in an intact family with a handicapped child, the father's assessment is the one most congruent with an outsider's view. In single-parent families, however, the mother's view is most closely correlated with an outside observer's. This result also hold for other nonclinical, intact families; mothers tend to view the family's compe-

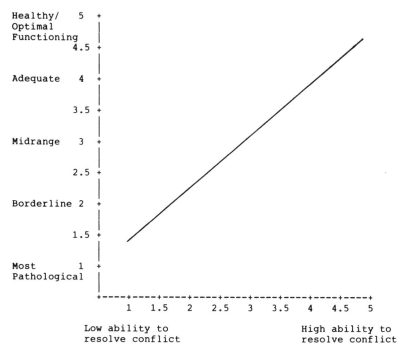

Figure 5-3. The relationship between the empirically derived factors of family health/competence and conflict resolution.

tence in a way similar to that of trained family observers. Interestingly enough, when we look at intact families who come for treatment in our outpatient clinic, *both* parents tend to show moderate agreement with outside observers concerning their family's competence.

We are continuing our research into the relationships of several self-report measures (including our own, designed to reflect our major dimensions of Competence and Style) to outside rater assessments. To date, it appears that, while self-report measures show good test–retest reliability, there is significant intrafamily member variability. We are currently exploring the significance of this variability in relation to overall family competence from both self-report and observational perspectives. We are completing the construction and validation of a standardized family assessment scheme that capitalizes on multilevel assessment.

HEALTH-RELATED STUDIES USING THE MODEL

This model was developed during a study of family health, with the goal of identifying those family qualities associated with success in important family functions, such as the raising of competent children. There was necessarily a contrasting study of families under stress, with an identified psychiatric patient, in which the extremes of the dimensions of competence and style were glimpsed and reported (Lewis *et al.*, 1976). A research team at Southwest Family Institute has recently concluded a study of nonlabeled families with developmentally disabled children in an effort to further explore the qualities found in healthy, coping families (Beavers, Hampson, Hulgus, & Beavers, 1986). The general findings of this study support and follow the theoretical notions of the Beavers systems model.

In our treatment facility, we use the Beavers systems model of family assessment daily while working with families who present all types of difficulties, including behavior problems, psychosomatic illnesses, psychoses, physical abuse, and substance abuse. Through these assessment/research efforts, we have obtained preliminary results that relate initial assessment and a therapist's style of working with a family to treatment outcomes. These initial findings indicate that better outcomes, as rated by both therapists and families, are obtained when therapists tend to match a family's style and competence in the early stages of therapy. Though still tentative, these results highlight the utility of our assessment scheme, while not binding therapists into potentially restrictive intervention strategies and techniques. Additionally, our clinical assessment efforts and strategies are being utilized and tested at sites that literally span the globe. Thus, the practical utility of our model is being widely recognized.

As one example of the utility of family assessment in treatment, severely dysfunctional families have a marked need for assistance in making ambivalent feelings acceptable, and therapists must frequently use strategies that bring out the hidden side of strong opposite emotions. This is in marked contrast to work with midrange families, where family rules tolerate more ambivalence and the therapist can approach family members much more directly regarding their awkward contradictory feelings.

For another example, CF families have difficulty in accepting tender and needful feelings, and hence need frequent reframing of apparently hostile expressions as evidence of caring. Such a strategy is quite effective since these family members often express love as hostility. This is in sharp contrast to CP families, who have difficulty expressing anger and the desire and need to separate; therapeutic effort is well spent in affirming the value of separateness and in assisting family members to experience it during the session and outside, as well as helping these people to express hostility in an effective and nonthreatening fashion. These are but a few of many relationships suggested thus far between family assessment and treatment strategies.

As we have continued to refine our assessment approach, this model has been applied in a wide variety of settings. A slightly modified version of the competence scales has been used by Steidl and co-workers (1980) to study the family qualities associated with several aspects of a family member's behavior and experience as a renal dialysis patient. Steidl has also used the instrument to evaluate family dynamics where one member has bronchogenic cancer (J. H. Steidl, personal communication, 1984). In other studies, families with a retarded child were evaluated (Beavers et al., 1986), as were families with a member with a chronic physical illness (Foote, 1984). There is at least one research group using the instrument with young adult criminal offenders (Green & Kolevson, 1983).

WEAKNESSES AND STRENGTHS OF THE MODEL

The weaknesses of this model were primarily related to the assessment methodology. It is expensive to use experienced raters and video machinery for research purposes; paper-and-pencil methods are far cheaper. Further, observational measures are only as good as their inter-rater reliability, which is far more difficult to establish adequately than is the test–retest reliability necessary for self-report instruments. Within our model, adequate reliabilities have been obtained for observationally rated family competence and style. The stylistic dimension, however, is somewhat less reliable unless clinical and archival information is used to augment the observational data. Fortunately, we have developed a reliable and valid self-report instrument that measures the same general constructs assessed by our observational measures (Hampson & Hulgus, 1986). As we progress in the further development of our multilevel assessment strategy, we hope to simplify the total assessment process so that all relevant information can be integrated and used in ways that are useful in research and clinical practice.

The strengths of this model are related primarily to its clinical usefulness. Grounded as it is in a clinical family systems approach to illness and health, it offers a good map of the territcry. The concepts are immediately applicable to treatment, and the instruments are good teaching tools to help trainees begin to think systemically.

Families assessed directly offer an immediate point of takeoff for intervention. Further, when done as a 10-minute portion of a traditional initial family interview, the process is neither time-consuming nor expensive (assuming a video camera is available). I know of no better model for planning family treatment strategies and methods of intervention. Assessment and intervention are then considered simply as different aspects of a systemic comprehension of the family.

The self-report instrument is valuable in research, in screening for high-risk families, and in determining change following intervention. It is a quick and easy way of applying the model. Finally, the assessment language is simple enough to be learned easily, yet comprehensive enough to allow researchers and clinicians to communicate valuable information about families to each other. Thus, the model facilitates the design and completion of vitally needed outcome studies of family intervention methods.

References

Beavers WR. Psychotherapy and growth: a family systems perspective. New York: Brunner/Mazel, 1977.

Beavers WR. A systems model of family for family therapists. Journal of Marital and Family Therapy 1981; 203:299–307.

Beavers WR. Healthy, midrange, and severely dysfunctional families. In: Walsh F, ed. Normal family processes. New York: Guilford Press, 1982: 45–66.

Beavers, WR, Hampson, RB and Hulgus, YF. Commentary: the Beavers systems approach to family assessment. Family Process 1985; 24:398–405.

Beavers J, Hampson RB, Hulgus YF, Beavers WR. Coping in families with a retarded child. Family Process 1986; 25:365–378.

Beavers WR, Voeller MN. Family models: comparing the Olson circumplex model with the Beavers systems model. Family Process 1983; 22(1):85–98.

Bowen M. Family therapy in clinical practice. New York: Jason Aronson, 1978.

Combrinck-Graham L. The family life cycle and families with young children. In: Liddle HA, ed. Clinical implications of the family life cycle. Rockville, Md.: Aspen Press, 1983:35–53.

Engle GL. The need for a new medical model: a challenge for biomedicine. Science 1977; 196:129–136.

Erikson EH. Childhood and society, 2d ed. New York: Norton, 1963.

Foote MS. Psychological health and chronic illness in the family system. Unpublished doctoral dissertation, Texas Women's University, December 1984.

Green RG, Kolevson MS. Family therapy outcome study. Division of Justice and Crime Prevention (Commonwealth of Virginia), grant no. 78-A4496, 1983.

Hampson, RB, Beavers, WR, Hulgus YF. Comparing the Beavers and circumplex models of family functioning. Family Process 1988; 27:85–92.

Korzybski A. Science and sanity. Lancaster, Pa.: International Non-Aristotelian Library, 1933.

Lewis JM, Beavers WR, Gossett JT, Phillips VA. No single thread: psychological health in family systems. New York: Brunner/Mazel, 1976.

Minuchin S. Families and family therapy. Cambridge, Mass.: Harvard University Press, 1974.

Steidl JH, Finkelstein FO, Wexler JP, Feigenbaum H, Kitsen D, Kliger AS, Quinlan DM. Medical condition, adherence to treatment regimens, and family functioning. Archives of General Psychiatry 1980; 37:1025–1027.

Stierlin H. Separating parents and adolescents. New York: Quadrangle Press, 1972.

von Bertalanffy L. General systems theory—an overview. In: Gray W, Duhl FJ, Rizzo ND, eds. General systems theory and psychiatry. Boston: Little, Brown, 1969:92.

6

Circumplex Model and Family Health

DAVID H. OLSON
University of Minnesota

The health of the family can be a major resource in helping family members cope with physical and mental health problems. On the other hand, dysfunctional families not only can create increasing physical and mental health problems, but can exaggerate already existing symptoms. The Circumplex Model is designed to assess family health and the level of family functioning on three dimensions, cohesion, adaptability, and communication, which have been identified as aspects of a family system by a variety of family theorists and family therapists.

The Circumplex Model enables a physician to assess readily the type of family system using either a self-report assessment, FACES III, or an interview which is evaluated using the Clinical Rating Scale. This assessment of the underlying dynamics and the family system will help a physician better understand how the family operates and how they might be used to facilitate the prescribed treatment program.

There is increasing evidence that the type of family system can have an important impact on how people cope with a variety of health problems (Campbell, 1986). The Circumplex Model is increasingly being used to study the relationship between the type of family system and a variety of physical health problems.

Based on our abstracts of ongoing studies, there are over 100 ongoing studies to date using FACES (versions I, II, and III) to assess family functioning where one member has a physical symptom or symptoms. There are about 15 studies exploring family coping in cancer patients, 10 studies with diabetics, and 5 studies focusing on heart disease. There are over 20 ongoing studies focusing on children with a variety of symptoms including asthma, birth defects, chronic illness, and psychosomatic illnesses. In adults, there are over 20 studies focusing on such topics such as Alzheimer's disease, chronic pain, stroke, premenstrual syndrome (PMS), and dialysis. Future articles will review these studies as they are completed. The goal will be to describe more systematically the relationship between family systems and physical illnesses and how various types of family systems cope with these physical illnesses.

The purpose of this chapter is to provide an update of the recent theoretical developments in the Circumplex Model, to review briefly some of the recent empirical studies validating the model, and to discuss the use of information derived on this model from self-report and clinical assessment. Case illustrations using FACES III, the self-report scale, and the Clinical Rating Scale will be presented. These topics can be used not only for initial diagnosis of family functioning but also for assessing changes over the course of treatment. This chapter reflects the continuing attempt to develop the Circumplex Model and to bridge research, theory, and practice. Some of the theoretical and empirical material that has been discussed elsewhere will be only briefly reviewed (Olson, Russell, & Sprenkle, 1983).

Table 6-1. Theoretical Models and Circumplex Model

	Cohesion	Change	Communication
Beavers	Centripetal	Adaptability	
	Centrifugal	(systemic growth)	
Kantor	Affect	Power	
Epstein	Affective involvement	Behavior control	Communication
		Problem solving roles	Affective responsiveness
Reiss	Coordination	Closure	

CIRCUMPLEX DIMENSIONS: COHESION, CHANGE, AND COMMUNICATION

The salience of these three dimensions is evidenced by the fact that other theoretical models in the family field have relied on concepts related to the three dimensions of cohesion, change (adaptability), and communication. Table 6-1 illustrates the concepts from major theorists that relate to these three dimensions. More specifically, Beavers and Voeller's (1983) description of centripetal and centrifugal forces in families is conceptually related to cohesion. They use the term "adaptability," although their operational definition is somewhat different (Beavers & Voeller, 1983; Olson, Russell, & Sprenkle, 1983). Kantor and Lehr's (1975) concept of "affect" is related to cohesion, and their "power" concept is similar to adaptability. The McMaster model of family functioning (Epstein, Bishop, & Levin, 1978) uses concepts that fit very well into the three major dimensions. Finally, David Reiss's (1981) intensive experimental studies rely heavily on a paradigm focusing on family problem solving. His dimension of "coordination" is conceptually similar to cohesion, and "closure" is similar to the concept of change.

STUDIES VALIDATING THE CIRCUMPLEX MODEL

Although the Circumplex Model has three central dimensions *cohesion* and *change* (adaptability) are the two dimensions graphically used in the model. *Communication* is a facilitating dimension in that it facilitates movement of families on cohesion and change.

The Circumplex Model identifies 16 types of marital and family systems by breaking each of the dimensions of cohesion and adaptability into four levels. The two dimensions are *curvilinear* in that families that appear very high or very low on both dimensions appear dysfunctional, whereas families that are more balanced (the two central areas) seem to function more adequately.

The 16 types can be broken down into three more general types: Balanced, Midrange, and Extreme (see Figure 6-1). *Balanced* types are the four central ones that are balanced on both dimensions. *Midrange* types are those that are extreme on one dimension but balanced on the other. *Extreme* types are those that are extreme on both dimensions.

In order to classify families into the Circumplex Model, a self-report inventory was developed called FACES, an acronym for Family Adaptability and Cohesion Evaluation Scales. FACES III is the most recent version of this inventory, which individual family members can complete to describe how they perceive this family system. This 20-item scale has 10 cohesion and 10 adaptability items, which have proven reliability and validity. A more detailed summary of FACES III and how it can be used in research and clinical work is described later in this chapter.

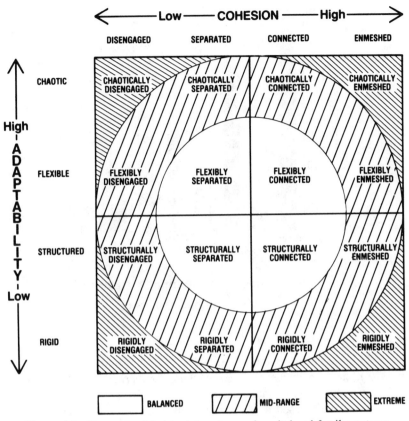

Figure 6-1. Circumplex Model: sixteen types of marital and family systems.

Balanced versus Extreme Families

A central hypothesis derived from the model is that *Balanced families will function more adequately than Extreme families.* This hypothesis is built on the assumption that families that are extreme on both dimensions will tend to have more difficulties functioning across the life cycle. This assumes a *curvilinear relationship* on the dimensions of cohesion and adaptability; that is, too little or too much cohesion or adaptability is seen as dysfunctional to the family system. Families that are able to balance between these two extremes, however, seem to function more adequately.

To test the major hypothesis that Balanced family types are more functional than Extreme types, a variety of studies have been done focusing on range of emotional problems and symptoms in couples and families. A recent study by John Clarke (1984) focused on families including schizophrenics, families with neurotics, families who had therapy sometime in their past, and a no-therapy control group (see Figure 6-2). In general, he found a very high level of Extreme families in the neurotic and schizophrenic groups compared to the no-therapy group. Conversely, he found a significantly higher level of Balanced families in the no-therapy group compared to the other groups.

Figure 6-2 illustrates the differences in the levels of cohesion and adaptability between these groups. While the percentage of Extreme family types *decreased* dramatically from

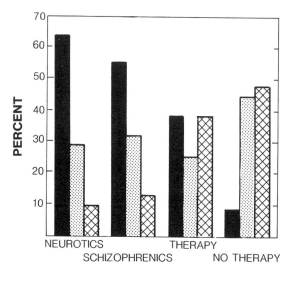

■Extreme ▒ **Mid-Range** ▨ **Balanced**

Figure 6-2. Problem families.

the symptomatic to no-therapy groups (neurotic, 64%; schizophrenic, 56%; therapy, 38%; no-therapy; 7%), the percentage of Balanced families *increased* (neurotic, 8%; schizophrenic, 12%; therapy, 38%; no-therapy, 48%).

Other studies have focused on alcoholic families in which the identified patient was the mother or father. Using the original FACES, significant differences were found between the chemically dependent families and the nondependent families (Killorin & Olson, 1984; Olson & Killorin, 1985a). As hypothesized, the alcoholic families included a significantly higher level of Extreme families compared to the nondependent families. As illustrated in Figure 6-3, 21% of the chemically dependent families were Extreme types, whereas only 4% of nondependent families were Extreme types. Conversely, about two-thirds (65%) of the nondependent families were Balanced, whereas about one-third (38% and 32%) of the dependent families were Balanced.

A study of alcoholics in treatment by James Bonk (1984) assessed 20 families before treatment (pre), after treatment (post), and one month after treatment (follow-up). Although no changes occurred over time on cohesion and adaptability, significant changes did occur between pre–post and pre–follow-up on the *family satisfaction scale* (Olson & Wilson, 1982), which measures satisfaction on cohesion and adaptability.

A recent study by Patrick Carnes (1985) used FACES II to investigate the family systems in sex offenders, and found high levels of *Extreme family types* for both family of origin and current families (see Figure 6-4). Whereas about half (49%) had Extreme family types in their family of origin, and about two-thirds (66%) of their current families were Extreme types, only 19% of the nonoffender families were Extreme types. Conversely, whereas only 11% of their families of origin and 19% of their current families were Balanced types, about half (57%) of the nonoffender families were Balanced types.

Comparing 27 high-risk families with 35 low-risk families, Garbarino, Sebes, and Schellenbach (1985) focused on the type of family system. Using intact families, both parents and one adolescent completed FACES, and a variety of other scales to assess

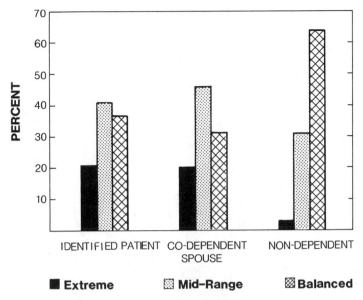

Figure 6-3. Alcoholic families (adults).

family stress, parenting, and family conflict. As hypothesized by the Circumplex Model, they found the majority of the low-risk families were *Balanced* types (mainly flexibly connected type), while the majority of the high-risk families were *Extreme* types (mainly chaotically enmeshed).

A recent study by Rodick, Henggeler, and Hanson (1986) compared 58 mother–son dyads from father-absent families in which half (29) had an adolescent juvenile offender and the other half (29) had adolescents with no history of arrest or psychiatric referral. As graphically illustrated in Figure 6-5, only 7% of the delinquents were Balanced types,

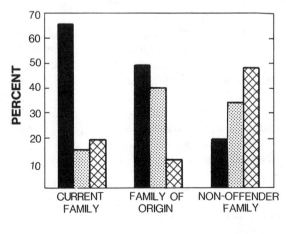

Figure 6-4. Sex offenders.

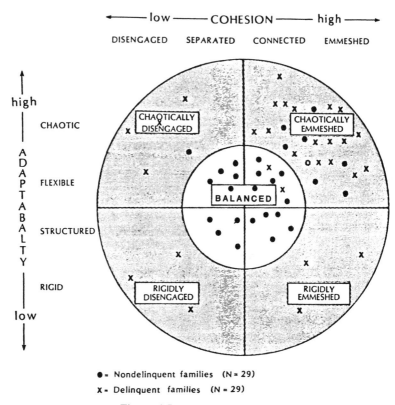

Figure 6-5. Delinquent families.

while 93% of the delinquent families were Midrange or Extreme types. In contrast, 69% of the nondelinquent families were Balanced, while 31% were Midrange or Extreme.

In summary, these studies of clinical samples clearly demonstrate the discriminant power of FACES and the circumplex model in distinguishing between problem families and nonsymptomatic families. There is strong empirical support for the hypothesis that *Balanced families are more functional than Extreme.*

In contrast to the curvilinear relationship found on these dimensions of problem families, there appears to be a *linear relationship between cohesion and change (adaptability) in family functioning with "normal" families.* More specifically, higher levels of cohesion and change seem to be associated with better family functioning. These results were found in a national survey with 1,000 families across the life cycle, which was reported in the recent book by Olson and co-workers: *Families: What Makes Them Work* (Olson, McCubbin, Barnes, Larsen, Muxen, & Wilson, 1983). A primary reason for this finding is that normal families represent only a narrow spectrum of the range of behavior on these two dimensions. As a result, there are very few of the "normal" families that legitimately fall into the Extreme types.

Accounting for Cultural and Ethnic Diversity
Using Family Satisfaction

In order to make the Circumplex Model culturally relevant to a variety of families with different ethnic and cultural backgrounds, a hypothesis was developed to reflect this diversity. The hypothesis states that *if normative expectations of families support behavior extreme on one or both of the dimensions, families will function well as long as all family members are satisfied with these expectations.* In this way, the family serves as its own norm base.

This approach necessitates measuring *family satisfaction* of each family member. There have been two methods developed to measure family satisfaction related to the Circumplex Model. The first method is to have family members complete FACES III twice—once in terms of how they perceive their family system (perceived version), and a second time for how they ideally would like it to be (ideal version). *The greater the ideal–perceived discrepancy, the greater the dissatisfaction with the current family system.*

The second method is a separate 14-item Family Satisfaction scale (Olson & Wilson, 1982), which taps the concepts related to cohesion and change. A study by Caron and Olson (1984) identified, as hypothesized, a high negative correlation between family satisfaction scale and the ideal–perceived discrepancy on cohesion ($r = -.58$) and on adaptability ($r = -.64$).

While it might be more difficult to observe change in cohesion and adaptability (and related family types) related to treatment programs, *family satisfaction* might be due more to treatment change. This was demonstrated in a recent treatment outcome study of alcoholics by Bonk (1984). Although he found no change in mean scores on cohesion or adaptability, significant increases in family satisfaction occurred between pre–post and pre–follow-up.

Balanced Families and Communication Skills

Another useful hypothesis is that *Balanced families will have more positive communication skills than Extreme families.* Communication can be measured at both the marital and the family level. Using data from the national survey of 1,000 families (Olson, McCubbin, Barnes, Larsen, Muxen, & Wilson, 1983; Barnes & Olson, 1985), these researchers investigated parent–adolescent communication and family functioning. Using "nonproblem" families, the hypothesis that Balanced families would have better communication skills was supported when relying on data from the parents. This hypothesis was not supported for adolescents. Future research is needed to test hypotheses at both the marital and family level with both normal and problem families.

In addition to testing the hypothesis regarding Balanced versus Extreme families, Rodick, Henggeler, and Hanson (1986) found strong support for the hypothesis that Balanced families have more positive communication skills. Using observational measures of mother–adolescent interaction, they found that mothers in the Balanced types had significantly higher rates of supportive communication, explicit information, and positive affect than did those in the Extreme type, with the majority of problem dyads (chaotically enmeshed).

INTEGRATIVE FAMILY SYSTEM MODEL

The *Integrative Family System Model* builds on the work of the circumplex model and the FAAR Stress Model (McCubbin & Patterson, 1982). It integrates four areas of family functioning: *family stress, family types, family resources,* and *family adaptation.* It is hypothesized that the impact of stress on the family system is different for Balanced versus

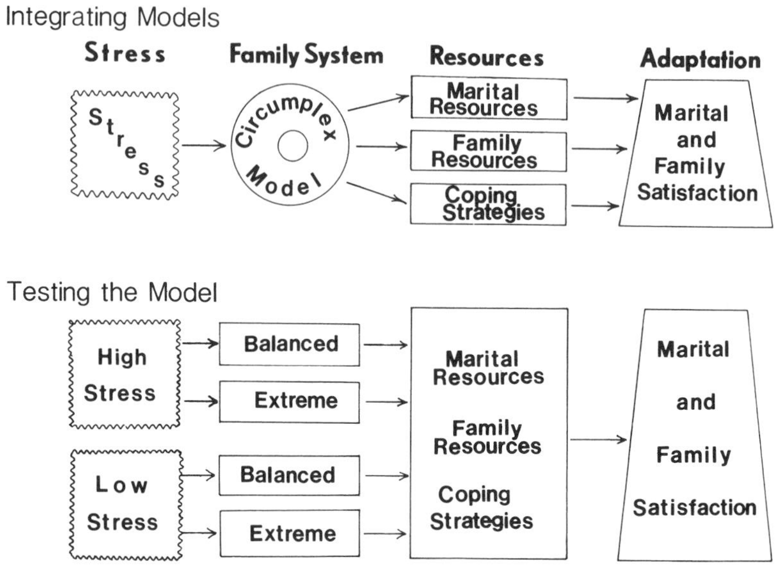

Integrating Models

Figure 6-6. Integrating Circumplex Model and FAAR Model.

Extreme family types. It is further hypothesized that Balanced families will have more marital and family resources and, therefore, will be able to maintain a higher level of adaptation (see Figure 6-6).

The integrative model was tested with the normal families used in the national survey. Examining the four quadrants of the Circumplex Model, it was found that stress was highest in the upper left quadrant (flexibly connected types), and lowest in the upper right quadrant (flexibly separated types).

In order to identify the specific resources in these two quadrants, the stepwise multiple regression analysis was done, with adaptation as the dependent variable. The results clearly indicated that *flexibly connected* families did well because they had many more marital and family resources to rely on than did flexibly separated families. For more details, see Olson, Lavee, and McCubbin (1988).

INVENTORIES FOR RESEARCH
AND CLINICAL ASSESSMENT

In order to assess adequately the three major dimensions of the Circumplex Model and other related concepts, a variety of self-report assessment tools have been developed (Olson, McCubbin, Barnes, Larsen, Muxen, & Wilson, 1982). These assessment tools were designed to provide not only an "insider's perspective" on their own family system, but also an "outsider's perspective." The self-report instrument FACES III provides the insider's perspective, whereas the Clinical Rating Scale provides the outsider's perspective. Both perspectives are useful and often provide conflicting data. Used together, however, the help capture the complexity of marital and family systems (Olson, 1977, 1985).

FACES III: Self-Report Scale

FACES III, acronym for Family Adaptability and Cohesion Evaluation Scales, was developed to tap cohesion and adaptability (Olson, Portner, & Lavee, 1985). FACES III provides an assessment of how individuals *perceive* their family system, as well as their *ideal* descriptions. The scores on cohesion and adaptability can be plotted onto the Circumplex Model to indicate the type of system they perceive and the one they would consider ideal. In addition, the perceived–ideal discrepancy also provides a measure of *family satisfaction,* which indicates how satisfied individuals are with their current family system, regardless of their family type.

FACES III is a 20-item scale from items used in the national survey of 1,000 normal families (Olson, McCubbin, Barnes, Larsen, Muxen, & Wilson, 1983). FACES III overcomes most of the limitations of FACES II, which was developed from the same sample. In FACES II, cohesion and adaptability were rather highly correlated with each other, with social desirability, and with marital and family satisfaction.

Ideally, for two dimensions to be used appropriately in the Circumplex Model, they should be uncorrelated or orthogonal. Cohesion and adaptability in FACES III meets this criterion ($r = .03$). Because social desirability has an impact on most self-report scales, an attempt was made to minimize its impact on these two dimensions. In FACES III the correlation between adaptability and social desirability was reduced to zero ($r = .00$) with some correlation between social desirability and cohesion ($r = .39$).

FACES III is designed to measure both *perceived* and *ideal* descriptions of a marital or family system. The 20-item FACES III is taken *twice,* once for perceived and once for ideal descriptions of the family. The perceived–ideal discrepancy is an indirect measure of *family satisfaction.* The greater the ideal–perceived discrepancy, the less the family satisfaction.

Family satisfaction is a very important variable, which can be useful both empirically and clinically. Empirically, it provided an additional variable from FACES III for any analysis. Clinically, this information regarding both perceived and ideal family is particularly useful. Whereas the perceived description can provide a perspective on the perception of the current system, the ideal can provide directions for change on both dimensions.

A summary evaluation of FACES III in terms of reliability, validity, and clinical utility is provided in Table 6-2. In general, FACES III is a reliable and valid scale that is theoretically based, and is designed for systematic research or clinical work with couples and families. It was designed so that it could be used with a variety of family structures, including nuclear families, blended families, and single-parent families.

An illustration of a graphic representation of perceived and ideal FACES III scores from a father, a mother, and an adolescent is shown in Figure 6-7. Whereas the mother and father both perceived their family as a *structurally separated* type, the adolescent perceived the family as *rigidly enmeshed.* Ideally, the parents both wanted more cohesion, but the mother wanted more adaptability and the father wanted less. The adolescent, however, ideally wanted much less cohesion and more adaptability, as characterized by the *flexibly disengaged* type. As demonstrated by the considerable perceived–ideal discrepancy, the adolescent is the least satisfied. This graphic scheme clearly demonstrates the complexity of the family system in terms of how family members perceive the family and how they would like the family to function.

Self-report instruments were also developed to measure both marital communication and parent–adolescent communication. Marital communication can be assessed by a 10-item scale from the ENRICH inventory (Olson, Fournier, & Druckman, 1982). Family

Table 6-2. Evaluation of FACES III

	Family Adaptability and Cohesion Evaluation Scale (FACES III)
Theoretical domain and model	Family system Circumplex Model
Assessment level	Family as whole
Focus of assessment	Perceived, ideal; satisfaction
Number of scales and items	2 scales; 20 perceived, 20 ideal items
Norms:	
Normative sample	$n = 2,453$ adults across life cycle $n = 412$ adolescents
Clinical	Several type of problem families
Reliability:	
Internal consistency	Cohesion ($r = .77$) Adaptability ($r = .62$) Total ($r = .68$)
Test–retest	FACES II (4–5 weeks) .83 for cohesion .80 for adaptability
Validity:	
Face validity	Very good
Content validity	Very good
Correlation between scales	Cohesion and adaptability ($r = .03$)
Correlation with social desirability	SD and adaptability ($r = .00$) SD and cohesion ($r = .39$)
Concurrent validity	Lack of evidence
Correlation between family members	X = H/W/A ($n = 370$) Cohesion ($r = .41$) Adaptability ($r = .25$)
Discrimination between groups	Very good
Clinical utility:	
Usefulness of self-report scale	Very good
Ease of scoring	Very easy
Clinical Rating Scale	Yes

communication was measured by the Parent–Adolescent Communication Scale (PAC) (Barnes & Olson, 1982). This scale assesses two aspects of communication: open communication and problem-free communication. Parents describe how they perceive their communication with their adolescent, and the adolescent describes the communication (1) with the father and (2) with the mother.

Clinical Rating Scale for the Circumplex Model

The Clinical Rating Scale (CRS) was developed in order to do clinical assessment on *cohesion, change,* and *communication* (Olson & Killorin, 1985b). Copies of the CRS for

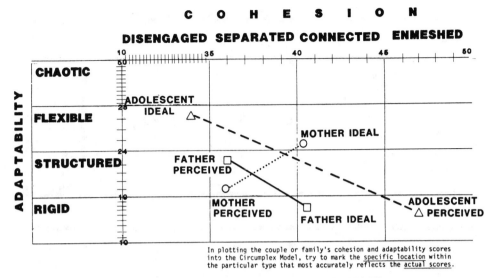

In plotting the couple or family's cohesion and adaptability scores into the Circumplex Model, try to mark the <u>specific location</u> within the particular type that most accurately reflects the <u>actual scores</u>.

Figure 6-7. Circumplex profile: FACES III.

rating cohesion, change, and communication are in Appendix 6A. The CRS can be used for rating the behavior of a family system on the basis of a semistructured interview with an individual family member or several family members. Ideally, it is best to observe the family as they interact while completing some interaction tasks, or during a semistructured interview dealing with the concepts related to the three dimensions.

One useful format for generating information and dynamics about these dimensions is to ask the family member(s) to describe and discuss how they handle daily routines, what a typical weekend is like, what they do separately and together, and how they make decisions.

We have found the CRS easy for practitioners to learn and use in their clinical practice. Inter-rater reliability with this scale has been assessed at rather high levels ($r = .70$–.80) in a recent study by Olson and Logacz (1985).

The Family Profile is used to summarize graphically the ratings on the three dimensions and the concepts related to each dimension (see Figure 6-8). The actual CRS used to do the ratings on cohesion, change, and communication is in Appendix 6A.

Clinical Assessment of a Rigidly Enmeshed Family

The Preston family was seen by a family practice physician initially because the mother, Mary, had symptoms of chronic headaches and insomnia. The Prestons were both in their mid-40s and had been married for 19 years. The father, John, was a recovering alcoholic, and the couple had had several sessions of marriage counseling in the past 2 years but were not currently in therapy. Their 16-year-old son had recently run away and had been known to use drugs.

It became clear from a brief discussion with the mother that a family assessment should be done. The parents and the adolescent were brought together for a clinical family interview, which lasted approximately 45 minutes and focused on a variety of physical and emotional symptoms (see Figure 6-8).

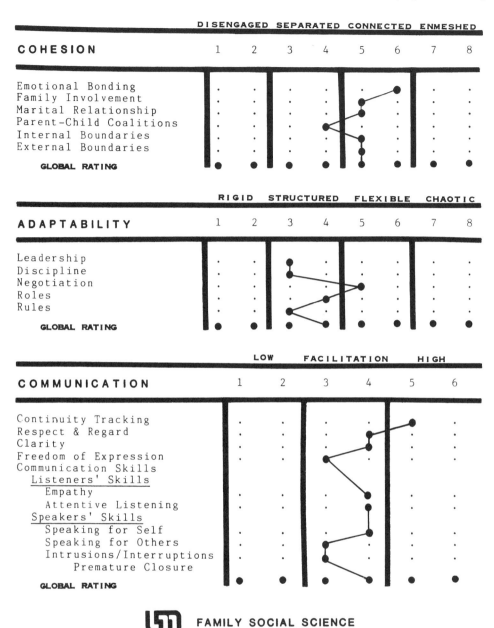

| | DISENGAGED | SEPARATED | CONNECTED | ENMESHED |

COHESION 1 2 3 4 5 6 7 8

Emotional Bonding
Family Involvement
Marital Relationship
Parent–Child Coalitions
Internal Boundaries
External Boundaries
GLOBAL RATING

| | RIGID | STRUCTURED | FLEXIBLE | CHAOTIC |

ADAPTABILITY 1 2 3 4 5 6 7 8

Leadership
Discipline
Negotiation
Roles
Rules
GLOBAL RATING

| | LOW | FACILITATION | HIGH |

COMMUNICATION 1 2 3 4 5 6

Continuity Tracking
Respect & Regard
Clarity
Freedom of Expression
Communication Skills
  Listeners' Skills
    Empathy
    Attentive Listening
  Speakers' Skills
    Speaking for Self
    Speaking for Others
    Intrusions/Interruptions
      Premature Closure
GLOBAL RATING

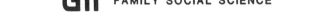

FAMILY SOCIAL SCIENCE

290 McNeal Hall, University of Minnesota, St. Paul, MN 55108 © D. OLSON 1985

Figure 6-8. Family Profile of the CRS.

An assessment was also done on the three dimensions in the CRS. The following is a summary of the family physician's evaluation on the three dimensions. The clinical evaluation is summarized on the Family Profile (Figure 6-8). The final evaluation of this family concluded that they were a rigidly enmeshed family with very poor communication skills.

On *family cohesion,* the global assessment for the family was a 7, indicating that they were an enmeshed family. This global evaluation was based on their overall functioning after looking at the six major areas related to cohesion (see Figure 6-8). More specifically, with regard to *emotional bonding,* the family had extreme emotional closeness, and the parents demanded loyalty. In terms of *family involvement,* members were very dependent on each other and, affectively, were very connected and reactive. Likewise, the *marital relationship* showed high emotional reactivity, and the couple continually battled over issues. There was a strong *parent–child coalition* between mother and son; the mother continually supported her son and often defended him from the father. The *internal boundaries* in the family indicated that they permitted little separate time or space from each other. Their *external boundaries* were mainly focused inside the family. In conclusion, this was clearly an enmeshed family system (see Figure 6-8).

With regard to *family change* (adaptability), the family generally functioned as a rigid family system. In terms of *leadership,* John, the father, was very authoritarian, but the mother tended not to support his leadership. Regarding the *discipline* of Kent, the father had very rigid and often unrealistic rules. The *negotiation* was structured, and the parents continued to make decisions for Kent, which created increasing conflict in the family. The *roles* in the household were traditional, with little attempt to share the roles between the couple. The family *rules* seldom changed and were often enforced in an arbitrary manner. As a result, the Preston family tended to function as a rather rigid family system (see Figure 6-8).

The *family communication* was rather poor in that it did not facilitate mutual understanding or movement on either family cohesion or adaptability. Based on the observation of the family, their *continuity of tracking* of each other was rather poor because they continually interrupted or made frequent and inappropriate topic changes. The *respect and regard* each had for the other was quite low. The *clarity* of their communication was problematic because there was often incongruence between the verbal and nonverbal messages. The *freedom of expression* was limited in that they rarely discussed how they felt personally but tended more to attack and blame each other. Some positive *communication skills* were evident in that they were willing to speak for themselves (assertive). On the other hand, they also often interrupted each other and spoke for the other persons. As a result, their listening and empathy skills were generally low. The Preston family received a global score of 2 on the communication scale, indicating that they had generally poor communication skills (see Figure 6-8).

CHANGES IN A FAMILY SYSTEM RELATED TO PHYSICAL ILLNESS

Although some hypotheses have been developed relating family systems described by the Circumplex Model and family stress (Olson & McCubbin, 1982), little research has been done to date that would help us understand the changes that take place in *family processes* related to physical and emotional illnesses. Short-term longitudinal studies are needed if we are to better understand the changes that occur in the family system, with comparisons between those individuals who recover more quickly and those who have difficulty recovering.

One hypothesis from the Circumplex Model is that Balanced families, compared to Extreme families, will do better because they are able to *change their family system* in order to cope more effectively with the illness in a family member. It is hoped that future studies will begin to provide more systematic information regarding the changes that do occur related to various types of family systems when confronted with a variety of physical illnesses.

An illustration of how the Circumplex Model can be used in graphing the changes in family system over time are demonstrated with a case in which a husband had a heart attack. This illustration is a composite of several case studies completed over the last few years. In this family crisis case, the husband, Peter Mason, age 53, had a massive heart attack. His wife, Martha, had been primarily a homemaker, and they had three teenagers living at home, one of whom was attending college.

The changes in this family system before and after the husband's heart attack are illustrated in Figure 6-9. Before the heart attack (point A) the family was *structurally separated,* which was generally appropriate for that stage of the family life cycle. Once

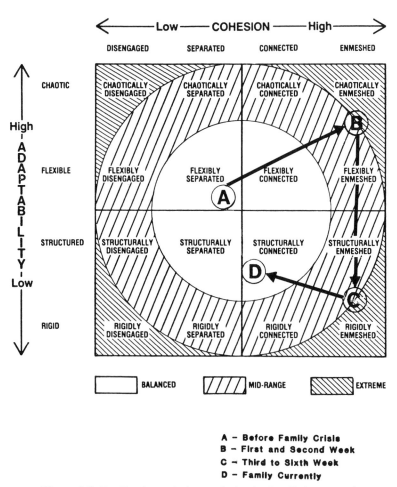

Figure 6-9. Family change before and after husband's heart attack.

the heart attack occurred, however, the family quickly shifted to becoming a more *chaotically enmeshed* family (point B). Very high levels of closeness characterized by enmeshment occurred because the illness brought the family together emotionally but also created chaos in that the family now needed to change many of their traditional ways of handling things and dramatically shift many of their daily routines.

From about the third to the sixth week, the family continued to be enmeshed but became more *rigid* in their structure. This rigidity was an attempt to stabilize the chaos by reorganizing some of the routines in their family system (point C). Six months later the family seemed to be functioning more like a *structurally connected* family. Some of the previous rigidity and extreme levels of cohesion had decreased, but they remained a rather close family with a more structured system because of the father's disability.

In summary, because of the husband's heart attack, this family's system changed several times over the course of the next 6 months as they adapted to this family crisis. They started as a Balanced system (flexibly separated), and moved to two Extreme types (chaotically enmeshed and structurally enmeshed) before ending up once again as a Balanced system (structurally connected).

It is expected that family systems will change in response to a crisis. As hypothesized with the Circumplex Model, it is the *Balanced* families that will have the resources and skills to shift their system in an appropriate way to cope more effectively with a crisis. In contrast, it is hypothesized that *Extreme* families will not have the resources that are needed to change their family and, therefore, will have more difficulty adapting to a crisis. It is hoped that future research will explore more fully the kinds of changes that take place in different family systems over the course of the treatment of physical symptoms.

CONCLUSION

The Circumplex Model can be used for describing family systems with various types of physical illnesses. Patients and their families can be assessed at the beginning of treatment, and changes in family systems that occur during the adjustments to any crisis can be described and plotted onto the model. Ongoing studies are exploring the relationship between various physical symptoms and family systems, both at the onset of physical illness and during the process of recovery.

These ongoing studies are using FACES III to assess the type of family system. Patients with a range of physical symptoms, including bulimia, cancer, coronary disease, diabetes, and pregnancy, are being studied. As these studies are completed, future papers will review the linkage between recovery and coping with a variety of physical illnesses and in various types of family systems.

This chapter updates studies validating hypotheses derived from the Circumplex Model. There is considerable empirical evidence for hypotheses derived from the Circumplex Model, particularly the hypothesis that Balanced family types are more functional than Extreme family types. There is also support for the hypothesis that Balanced families evidence fewer psychologic symptoms in their family members.

Inventories are available that can be used to classify couple and family systems into the model. FACES III is the self report inventory for family members to describe how they perceive their family. A Clinical Rating Scale was developed for physicians, therapists, and researchers to summarize their observation of a family's behavior on the three Circumplex dimensions.

APPENDIX 6A

COHESION	Disengaged		Separated		Connected		Enmeshed	
	1	2	3	4	5	6	7	8
Emotional Bonding	·	·	·	·	·	·	·	·
Family Involvement	·	·	·	·	·	·	·	·
Marital Relationship	·	·	·	·	·	·	·	·
Parent-Child Coalitions	·	·	·	·	·	·	·	·
Internal Boundaries	·	·	·	·	·	·	·	·
External Boundaries	·	·	·	·	·	·	·	·
GLOBAL RATING								

ADAPTABILITY	Rigid		Structured		Flexible		Chaotic	
	1	2	3	4	5	6	7	8
Leadership	·	·	·	·	·	·	·	·
Discipline	·	·	·	·	·	·	·	·
Negotiation	·	·	·	·	·	·	·	·
Roles	·	·	·	·	·	·	·	·
Rules	·	·	·	·	·	·	·	·
GLOBAL RATING								

COMMUNICATION	Low ←	Facilitation	→ High			
	1	2	3	4	5	6
Communication Skills	·	·	·	·	·	·
Listener's Skills						
Empathy	·	·	·	·	·	·
Attentive Listening	·	·	·	·	·	·
Speaker's Skills						
Speaking for Self	·	·	·	·	·	·
Speaking for Others	·	·	·	·	·	·
Intrusions/Interruptions	·	·	·	·	·	·
Freedom of Expression	·	·	·	·	·	·
Clarity	·	·	·	·	·	·
Tracking	·	·	·	·	·	·
Respect & Regard	·	·	·	·	·	·
GLOBAL RATING						

Family Social Science   290 McNeal Hall, University of Minnesota, St. Paul, MN 55108
© D. Olson (Revised, 1988)

Table 6A-1. Family Profile based on the Circumplex Model.

Table with rotated orientation (read as landscape):

COUPLE/FAMILY SCORE	DISENGAGED 1 2	SEPARATED 3 4	CONNECTED 5 6	ENMESHED 7 8
EMOTIONAL BONDING	Extreme emotional separateness. Lack of family loyalty.	Emotional separateness, limited closeness. Occasional family loyalty.	Emotional closeness, some separateness. Loyalty to family expected.	Extreme emotional closeness, little separateness. Loyalty to family demanded.
FAMILY INVOLVEMENT	Very low involvement or interaction. Infrequent affective responsiveness.	Involvement acceptable, personal distance preferred. Some affective responsiveness.	Involvement emphasized personal distance allowed. Affective interactions encouraged and preferred.	Very high involvement. Fusion; over-dependency; High affective responsiveness and control.
MARITAL RELATIONSHIP	Extreme emotional separateness.	Emotional separateness, limited closeness.	Emotional closeness, some separateness.	Extreme closeness, fusion; limited separateness.
PARENT-CHILD COALITIONS	Lack of parent-child closeness.	Clear sub-system boundaries some p/c closeness.	Clear sub-system boundaries with p/c closeness.	Parent-child coalition. Lack of generational boundaries.
INTERNAL BOUNDARIES — PERSONAL	Personal separateness predominant.	Some personal separateness encouraged.	Need for separateness respected but less valued.	Lack of personal separateness.
TIME (physical & emotional)	Time apart maximized Rarely time together.	Time alone important Some time together.	Time together important. Time alone permitted.	Time together maximized. Little time alone permitted.
SPACE (physical & emotional)	Separate space needed and preferred.	Separate space preferred; sharing of family space.	Sharing family space. Private space respected.	Little private space permitted.
DECISION MAKING	Individual decision making. (Oppositional)	Individual decision making but joint possible.	Joint decisions preferred but not necessary.	Decisions subject to wishes of entire group.
EXTERNAL BOUNDARIES — INSIDE vs OUTSIDE	Mainly focused outside the family.	More focused outside than inside family.	More focused inside than outside family.	Mainly focused inside the family.
FRIENDS	Individual friends seen alone.	Individual friendships seldom shared with family.	Individual friendships shared with family.	Family friends preferred limited individual friends.
INTERESTS & ACTIVITIES	Disparate interests. Mainly separate activities.	Separate interests. More separate than shared activities.	Some joint interests. More shared than individual activities.	Joint interests mandated. Separate activities seen as disloyal.
GLOBAL COHESION RATING (1-8)	Very Low	Low to Moderate	Moderate to High	Very High

Table 6A-2. Family cohesion.

Table 6A-3. Family change (adaptability).

COUPLE/FAMILY SCORE	RIGID		STRUCTURED		FLEXIBLE		CHAOTIC	
	1	2	3	4	5	6	7	8
LEADERSHIP (control)	Authoritarian leadership. Parent(s) highly controlling.		Primarily authoritarian but some equalitarian leadership.		Equalitarian leadership with fluid changes.		Limited and/or erratic leadership. Parental control unsuccessful, rebuffed.	
DISCIPLINE (for families only)	Autocratic "law & order". Strict, rigid consequences. Not lenient.		Somewhat democratic. Predictable consequences. Seldom lenient.		Usually democratic. Negotiated consequences. Somewhat lenient.		Laissez-faire and ineffective. Inconsistent consequences. Very lenient.	
NEGOTIATION	Limited negotiations. Decisions imposed by parents.		Structured negotiations. Decisions made by parents.		Flexible negotiations. Agreed upon decisions.		Endless negotiations. Impulsive decisions.	
ROLES	Limited repertoire, strictly defined roles.		Roles stable, but may be shared.		Role sharing and making. Fluid changes of roles.		Lack of role clarity, role shifts and role reversals.	
RULES	Unchanging rules. Rules strictly enforced.		Few rule changes. Rules firmly enforced.		Some rule changes. Rules flexibly enforced.		Frequent rule changes. Rules inconsistently enforced.	
GLOBAL COHESION RATING (1-8)	Very Low		Low to Moderate		Moderate to High		Very High	

LOW ← FACILITATING → HIGH

COUPLE/FAMILY SCORE	1	2	3	4	5	6

COMMUNICATION SKILL
Listener's Skills
  Empathy
  Attentive Listening
Speaker's Skills
  Speaking for Self
  Speaking for Others*
  Intrusions/Interruptions*
(* Note reverse scoring)
	Seldom evident
	Seldom evident
	
	Seldom evident
	Often evident
	Often evident
			Sometimes evident
			Sometimes evident
			
			Sometimes evident
			Sometimes evident
			Sometimes evident
					Often evident
					Often evident
					
					Often evident
					Seldom evident
					Seldom evident	

FREEDOM OF EXPRESSION	Infrequent discussion of self, feelings and relationships.		Some discussion of self, feelings and relationships.		Open discussion of self, feelings and relationships.	
CLARITY	Inconsistent and/or unclear verbal messages. Frequent incongruencies between verbal and non-verbal messages.		Some degree of clarity; but not consistent across time or across all members. Some incongruent messages.		Verbal messages very clear. Generally congruent messages.	
CONTINUITY TRACKING	Little continuity of content. Irrelevant/distracting non-verbals and asides frequently occur. Frequent/inappropriate topic changes.		Some continuity but not consistent across time or across all members Some irrelevant/distracting non-verbals and asides. Topic changes not consistently appropriate.		Members consistently tracking. Few irrelevant/distracting non-verbals and asides; facilitative non-verbals. Appropriate topic changes.	
RESPECT & REGARD	Lack of respect for feelings or message of other(s); possibly overtly disrespectful or belittling attitude.		Somewhat respectful of others but not consistent across time or across all members. Some incongruent messages.		Consistently appears respectful of other's feelings and message.	
GLOBAL FAMILY COMMUNICATION RATING (1 - 6)						

Table 6A-4. Family communication.

References

Barnes H, Olson DH. Parent adolescent communication scale. In: Olson *et al.*, eds. Family inventories. Department of Family Social Science, University of Minnesota, St. Paul, 1982.

Barnes H, Olson DH. Parent–adolescent communication and the circumplex model. Child Development 1985; 56:438–447.

Beavers W, Voeller MN. Family models: comparing and contrasting the Olson circumplex model with the Beavers system model. Family Process 1983; 21:250–260.

Bonk J. Perceptions of psychodynamics during a transitional period as reported by families affected by alcoholism. Unpublished doctoral dissertation, University of Arizona, Tucson, 1984.

Campbell TL. Family's impact on health: a critical review and annotated bibliography. National Institute of Mental Health. Series DN No. 6, DHHS Pub. No. (ADM) 86-1461. Washington, DC: Superintendent of Documents, U.S. Government Printing Office, 1986.

Carnes P. Counseling sexual abusers. Minneapolis, Minn.: CompCare Publications, 1985.

Caron W, Olson DH. Family satisfaction and perceived–ideal discrepancy on FACES II. Department of Family Social Science, University of Minnesota, St. Paul, 1984.

Clarke J. The family types of schizophrenics, neurotics and "normals." Unpublished doctoral dissertation, Department of Family Social Science, University of Minnesota, St. Paul, 1984.

Epstein NB, Bishop DS, Levin S. The McMaster model of family functioning. Journal of Marriage and Family Counseling 1978; 40:19–31.

Garbarino J, Sebes J, Schellenback C. Families at risk for destructive parent–child relations in adolescents. Child Development 1985; 55:174–183.

Kantor D, Lehr W. Inside the family. San Francisco: Jossey-Bass, 1975.

Killorin E, Olson DH. The chaotic flippers in treatment. In: Kaufman E, ed. Power to change: alcoholism. New York: Gardner Press, 1984.

McCubbin HI, Patterson JM. Family adaptation to crises. In: McCubbin H, Cauble A, Patterson J, eds. Family stress, coping and social support. Springfield, Ill.: Thomas, 1982.

Olson DH. Insiders' and outsiders' view of relationships: research strategies. In: Levinger G, Raush H, eds. Close relationships. Amherst: University of Massachusetts Press, 1977.

Olson DH. Struggling with congruence across theoretical models and methods. Family Process 1985; 24:26.

Olson DH, Fournier DG, Druckman JM. ENRICH. Minneapolis, Minn.: PREPARE-ENRICH, 1982.

Olson DH, Killorin E. Chemically dependent families and the circumplex model. Unpublished manuscript, Department of Family Social Science, University of Minnesota, St. Paul, 1985a.

Olson DH, Killorin E. Clinical rating scale for circumplex model. Department of Family Social Science, University of Minnesota, St. Paul, 1985b.

Olson DH, Lavee Y, McCubbin HI. Types of families and family response to stress across the family life cycle. In: Klein DM, Aldous J, eds. Social stress and family development. New York: Guilford Press, 1988.

Olson DH, Logacz E. Reliability of clinical rating scale (CRS) for circumplex model. Unpublished manuscript, Department of Family Social Science, University of Minnesota, St. Paul, 1985.

Olson DH, McCubbin HI. Circumplex model of marital and family systems V: Application to family stress and crisis intervention. In: McCubbin HI, ed. Family stress, coping, and social support. Springfield, Ill.: Thomas, 1982.

Olson DH, McCubbin HI, Barnes H, Larsen A, Muxen M, Wilson M. Family inventories. Department of Family Social Science, University of Minnesota, St. Paul, 1982.

Olson, DH, McCubbin HI, Barnes H, Larsen A, Muxen M, Wilson M. Families: what makes them work. Los Angeles, Calif.: Sage, 1983.

Olson DH, Portner J, Lavee Y. FACES III. Department of Family Social Science, University of Minnesota, St. Paul, 1985.

Olson, DH, Russell CS, Sprenkle DH. Circumplex model VI: Theoretical update. Family Process 1983; 22:69–83.

Olson DH, Wilson M. Family satisfaction. In: Olson *et al.*, eds. Family inventories. Department of Family Social Science, University of Minnesota, St. Paul, 1982.

Reiss D. The family's construction of reality. Cambridge, Mass.: Harvard University Press, 1981.

Rodick, JD, Henggeler SW, Hanson CL. An evaluation of family adaptability and cohesion evaluation scales (FACES) and the circumplex model. Journal of Abnormal Child Psychology 1986; 14:77–87.

7

A Family Stress Model: The Family Adjustment and Adaptation Response

JOAN M. PATTERSON
University of Minnesota

The challenge that faces us as scientists today is to describe, explain, and ultimately predict the linkage between the family system and health and illness in individual family members. The basic question is: How does what occurs in the family environment get inside the human body and make someone sick or well? What are the pathways and mechanisms by which social conditions affect physiologic processes?

One major focus of research and theory building that is germane to these questions, and that has occurred at the biologic, psychologic, and social levels, is in the area of stress. The relationship between the family system and individual health and illness could be examined by linking physiologic, psychologic, and social/family models of stress. The individual and the family function within a hierarchy of systems, as suggested in Figure 7-1. Different models of stress focus on one or more of these levels and, to a greater or lesser extent, allude to or take account of the transactions between one level of system and another. For example, psychologic models of stress may focus on the whole person but often emphasize transactions with the organ system of the brain by way of cognitive processes.

One commonality across the various stress models appears to be the inclusion of three conceptual domains: sources of stress, mediators of stress, and outcomes of stress (see Table 7-1). In addition, the conceptual definitions within these domains have some similarities. For the most part, the *sources* of stress are conceptualized as demands on a system (e.g., the body), physical or psychologic, that upset its normal steady state of functioning. The *mediators* are primarily resources (physical, psychologic, or social) and coping behaviors that influence whether stress is experienced, how it is managed, how long it lasts, and whether it prevents or reduces the outcome. The *outcomes* all focus on changes in functioning of some level of system, for example a body organ (Selye, 1956) or perhaps the family (Hill, 1958). The system of interest in terms of outcome usually reflects the discipline of the theorist—physiology, psychology, or sociology.

Physiologic theorists have been most interested in the biologic impact of stress. They have used primarily a stimulus–response paradigm, elaborating the biochemical response in the pituitary adrenocortical system (Selye, 1956, 1974), with much less attention to what gives rise to that response.

Most other stress theorists have moved away from a stimulus–response paradigm toward an interactional view of stress (i.e, stress emerges from an interaction among factors). The psychologic theorists, most notably Lazarus and Folkman (1984), have emphasized cognitive appraisal for its role in creating, magnifying, or diminishing stressors.

Sociologic theorists have also used an interactional approach to stress, emphasizing aspects of the social environment that either mediate or give rise to stress. For example, Cassel (1976) emphasized psychosocial mediators, particularly social support. Mechanic

Figure 7-1. The "family" as one system in a hierarchy of systems.

(1974) has emphasized cultural solutions for dealing with demands as a mediator and, conversely, how the absence of solutions creates or exacerbates demands. Pearlin, Menaghan, Lieberman, and Mullan (1981) have added the consideration of ongoing strains from roles as a source of demands.

All of the theorists represented in Table 7-1, with the exception of Hill, have focused on the individual level of system or organ systems within the person. The focus of the theory building and research presented in this chapter is the family system and its transactions with other levels of systems. A family stress model, the family adjustment and adaptation response (FAAR) model, is described, which systematically incorporates three levels of systems: the person, the family, and the community. An attempt is made to define the concepts included in the model in a way that establishes linkages to physiologic, psychologic, and sociologic models of stress.

THE FAMILY ADJUSTMENT AND ADAPTATION RESPONSE MODEL

History of the FAAR Model

The theoretical tradition out of which the FAAR model was developed began with the early work of family scholars such as Angell (1936), and Cavan and Ranck (1938), who studied the effect of economic depression on families. Other early investigators studied families experiencing a variety of stressful circumstances, such as bereavement, alcoholism, and war. These scientists asked, "Which families, under what conditions, are adversely affected by stressful experiences?" The first major family stress framework emerged from Hill's (1949, 1958) classic work on the family's response to war separation and reunion, in which he advanced the ABC-X family crisis model: "A (the stressor event) interacting with B (the family's crisis-meeting resources) interacting with C (the definition the family makes of the event) produce X (the crisis)" (p. 141).

Table 7-1. Theoretical Concepts from Physiologic, Psychologic, and Sociologic Models of Stress

Stress theorist	Sources of stress	Mediators of stress	Outcomes of stress
Physiological theories			
Cannon (1929)	Physical or emotional conditions (e.g., fear, rage) which disturb the body's homeostasis		Disturbed homeostasis in the body (e.g., body temperature, blood pH; plasma levels of sugar, protein, fat, calcium, etc.) as a result of neuroendocrine secretions
Wolff (1953)	*Stressor*—physical or psychosocial noxious stimulus	Body's protective reaction pattern that attempts to rid body of noxious threat	Disease or organic abnormality
Selye (1956, 1974)	Any demand, physical or psychologic (affective or cognitive), that places a demand on the body for readjustment or adaptation	Internal or external conditioning factors; *resources*—sleep to restore body physically; *coping*—altruistic egoism; *perception*—turning stressors into something positive (eustress)	General adaptation syndrome—3 stages: alarm (characterized by pituitary–adrenocortical response); resistance (tissue defense); and exhaustion (destruction of tissue, organ, or body)
Psychological theories			
Alexander (1950)	Tensions and *strains* produced by serious life conflicts	Ability to solve these conflicts	Alterations in organic processes viewed as unresolved conflicts being transferred from the psychologic system to the physiologic system
Lazarus & Folkman (1984)	Stimulus that is appraised by the individual as causing him or her harm (including loss), threat (potential for harm), or challenge (potential for gain under difficult odds)	*Coping*—process of managing demands that are appraised as taxing or exceeding the resources of the person Perception—evaluative process that gives *meaning* to what is at stake as well as resources for managing it	Adaptational outcomes: 1. Morale—how person feels about self and life conditions 2. Social functioning—way a person fulfills roles, satisfaction with interpersonal relationships, and social skills 3. Somatic illness
Scott & Howard (1970) Howard & Scott (1965)	Stimulus arising from internal or external, physical or symbolic environment that produces demands on human organism that require it to diverge above or below its ordinary level of functioning	1. Adequate physical and psychological energy 2. General and specific resources for resolving problems 3. Definition of problem as solvable 4. Appraisal of problem 5. *Coping* responses that are assertive, divergent, or inert	Successful mastery of problems as evidenced by dissipated tension and return to usual functioning (homeostasis) vs. stress as excess tension produced by failure of organism to master threats from environment
Eisdorfer (1985)	Activators—endogenous or exogenous events that change an individual's present state	Mediators—process (e.g., appraisal), environmental (e.g., support networks), and person (e.g., personality) elements that filter and modify activators, reactions, and consequences	Two levels: (1) reactions—biological or psychologic responses of an individual to an activator; (2) consequences—prolonged biologic, psychologic, and psychosocial effects of reactions
Sociological theories			
Cassel (1976)	Psychosocial processes as conditioned noxious (symbolic) stimuli	Psychosocial processes as beneficial and protective (especially social supports of primary groups)	Increased susceptibility to disease agents (i.e., direct noxious stimuli) because of altered endocrine balance

(continued)

Table 7-1. (Continued)

Stress theorist	Sources of stress	Mediators of stress	Outcomes of stress
Sociological theories			
Antonovsky (1979)	*Stressor*—a demand made by the internal or external environment of an organism that upsets its homeostasis, restoration of which depends on a nonautomatic and not readily available energy-expending action	1. Generalized resistance *resources*—characteristics of person, group, subculture, or society that are effective in avoiding or combatting stressors 2. Coherence—belief or *meaning* that environment is predictable and things will work out as well as possible	Health ease/dis-ease continuum—multifaceted (e.g., pain, functional limitation, prognostic implication, action implication) state or condition
Mechanic (1974)	Complex set of changing social and environmental conditions, often symbolically created	*Coping*—ability to react to, influence, and control demands *Resources*—intrapsychic (pretenses, motivation) and social (support networks) and institutionalized cultural solutions for dealing with demands	Mastery—sufficient personal and social resources to meet demands vs. discomforting response when there are inadequate resources to meet demands
Pearlin, Menaghan, Liberman, & Mullan (1981)	The occurrence of discrete life events converging with the presence of relatively continuous problems (*strains*) that place demands on individuals and contribute to diminishment of self-concept	*Coping*—behavior that (1) modifies sources of stress; (2) modifies *meaning* or problems; or (3) manages symptoms of stress Social support—access to and use of individuals, groups, or organizations for exchange of intimate communications and presence of solidarity and trust	Response of organism to experienced noxious stimuli as reflected in (1) cell, organ, or organism; (2) biochemical, physiologic, or emotional functioning; (3) endocrine, immunologic, metabolic, or cardiovascular system; or (4) physical or psychologic disease
Hill (1958)	*Stressor*—a crisis-provoking event in a family for which they have no prior preparation and which is thus problematic	*Resources*—characteristics of the family for dealing with stressors that help prevent crisis or help the family recover from crisis Family definition—*meaning* or perception of the seriousness of the stressor	Crisis—the amount of disruptiveness, disorganization, or incapacitatedness in the family social system as a result of the stressor event

This theoretical formulation guided family stress studies for three decades. Numerous variables were introduced to explain differences in family response to stressful circumstances. Burr (1973) synthesized these studies around two central concepts—vulnerability and regenerative power—by identifying factors that help prevent a stressor from creating a crisis (invulnerability) and/or help the family recover from a crisis (regenerative power). The variables identified by Burr were primarily associated with Hill's B factor of crisis-meeting resources, and included concepts such as family integration, family adaptability, marital adjustment, and extended familism.

The FAAR model evolved out of theory-building efforts begun in the 1970s, when the ABC-X framework, was used to guide a longitudinal study of families who had a husband/father missing in action or a prisoner of war in Vietnam (McCubbin, Dahl, & Hunter, 1976). Observations of these families in crisis suggested that additional factors beyond A, B, C, and X were needed to describe and explain the course of family adaptation over time. For example, families appeared to (1) experience a pile-up of demands in addition to the stressor of separation, (2) employ various coping strategies in an effort to manage the demands, and (3) modify their perceptions as a way to adapt (McCubbin & Patterson, 1982a).

As a result of these studies, the double ABC-X model of family behavior (McCubbin & Patterson, 1982a, 1983a) was advanced, which included the original ABC-X model as its foundation, with the addition of postcrisis variables to explain how families recover from crisis and achieve adaptation. In addition, the double ABC-X model was incorporated into a process model, called the family adjustment and adaptation response (FAAR) (McCubbin & Patterson, 1983b), in an effort to describe the *processes* by which families achieve precrisis adjustment and postcrisis adaptation.

In this chapter, a revision of the FAAR model is introduced with two objectives in mind. First, there is an effort to revise and clarify concepts based on more recent empirical findings. Second, there is an attempt to clarify further the linkages to physiologic, psychologic, and sociologic models of stress so as to render the model more salient for family medicine research.

Overview of the FAAR Model

The family adjustment and adaptation response model is presented in Figure 7-2. In the FAAR model, the focus is on family efforts to manage the demands it faces (from stressors

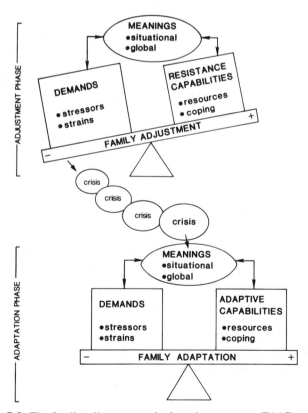

Figure 7-2. The family adjustment and adaptation response (FAAR) model.

and strains) with its capabilities for meeting demands (resources and coping behaviors), mediated by meanings (situational and global) so as to achieve a balance in family functioning (called adjustment or adaptation). There are two distinct phases in the model—adjustment and adaptation—separated by a period of family crisis when the family homeostasis is upset. Three levels of systems are considered—individual family members, the family unit, and the community—each characterized by both demands and capabilities. Over time, families attempt to maintain or arrive at a balance by using capabilities from one level of system to meet demands at another level.

In the paragraphs that follow, these concepts will be described in terms of the three major constructs that interact during both phases, followed by a discussion of the distinction between the two phases and how crisis emerges.

Pile-up of Demands

A family *demand* is defined as a stimulus or condition that produces or calls for change in the family system. Because change is implied, a demand can be viewed as a threat or challenge to the family's existing homeostatic functioning. These demands for change produce tension in the system, which persists until some capability is directed toward meeting the demand. When there is no available capability, a state of stress arises. Thus, stress is *not* defined as the occurrence or presence of the demand; rather, it is an actual or perceived demand–capability imbalance. There are two major conditions that give rise to demands: the occurrence of discrete events or stressors and the relatively continuous presence of strains.

STRESSORS
A *stressor* is defined as a life event that occurs at a discrete point in time and produces, or has the potential to produce, change in the family social system. Although stressor events have a discrete onset (e.g., death), adjustment or adaptation to them may take some time. Stressors may be normative, expectable changes associated with individual or family development over time, such as the onset of puberty or the formation of a family through marriage. Or they may be non-normative events that occur unexpectedly or suddenly, such as a child's death or a natural disaster like a flood or tornado.

STRAINS
Most studies to date have focused only on stressors or the accumulation of discrete events of change. However, family stress studies suggest that there is another important component of demands on the family, which is called strains. A *strain* is defined as a condition of felt tension associated with the need or desire to change something. Stressors happen and produce change. Strains, in contrast, are already there, and the change that is demanded is to get rid of them. Unlike stressors, strains usually do not have a discrete onset, but emerge more insidiously in the family.

There would appear to be at least two sources of strain. First, strain may emerge from the unresolved tension associated with prior stressors. In other words, when the family is unable, or when it is impossible, to resolve a stressor completely (e.g., when a member gets a chronic illness), there is a residue of tension that is carried along by the family over time as a part of their pile-up of demands. Second, strains may emerge from ongoing roles where tension is felt because role performance does not meet one's own or someone else's expectations. For example, if a parent wishes he or she had more time to spend with a child, there may be strain in the parenting role associated with a perceived desire for change. In addition, the nonoccurrence of an event (e.g., trying unsuccessfully to get pregnant) can be more stressful than if the event occurred. Conceptually, the nonoccurrence of an event can be viewed as a role strain—that is, a desire for change in the performance of a role, in this case the reproductive role.

Other investigators have also emphasized the importance of strains in the stress process. Role strains, such as those of a spouse, parent, employee, or economic provider, especially when coupled with discrete life events, are factors that give rise to stress (Pearlin *et al.*, 1981). Kanner, Coyne, Schaefer, and Lazarus (1981) have reported findings suggesting that daily hassles are independent and better predictors of negative psychologic outcomes than is the accumulation of major life events. Their "hassles" appear to be strains associated with the performance of social roles inherent in daily living. In the case of chronic illness, Patterson and McCubbin (1985) found that strains were the aspect of demands more predictive of negative outcomes, when measured as a decline in the health status of a child with cystic fibrosis.

It would appear that stressors interact with strains and contribute to demands in more than an additive way. When a new stressor occurs, it often exacerbates existing strains, making the family more aware of them as demands in and of themselves. For example, when a child member is diagnosed with a chronic illness, marital conflict (an ongoing family strain) may increase as parents struggle in disparate ways to manage this new demand.

SOURCES OF STRESSORS AND STRAINS

The demands that affect the family system emerge from three sources: individual members, the family itself, and the larger community in which the family resides. Though not intended to be exhaustive, four broad categories of demands are noted here because of their relevance for family medicine research.

1. *Individual survival needs and developmental tasks:* Biologic needs (e.g., food and shelter) and developmental tasks (e.g., developing trust, autonomy, etc.) (Erikson, 1950) from birth to death are viewed as demands of individual members for which the family and community provide capabilities. It is important to remember that adult members too have developmental needs (see Levinson, 1978; Sangiuliano, 1978), and that sometimes it is the interaction of adult and child developmental tasks (perhaps in terms of competition for available resources) that pushes the demand level up in families.

2. *Family tasks of maintenance and development:* Over the life cycle, the family unit is faced with tasks such as allocation of resources, division of labor, socialization of family members, reproduction and release of children, and maintenance of motivation and morale (Duvall, 1977). Situational transitions such as divorce and remarriage create additional tasks or demands for families, such as economic settlement, child custody, and the like.

3. *Changing social conditions:* Just as individual members and family units change over time, so do the communities and societies in which the family lives. Changes in the workplace, in the children's schools, in the family's church, in government policy, or in the world economy can have profound effects on family life. Cultural norms such as gender role expectations may change, creating ambiguity and role strain for many men and women.

4. *Acute and chronic illness and handicapping conditions:* An individual member's illness or injury is a stressor that produces change for which the family often turns to the medical community for the needed capability to manage this demand. The seriousness and chronicity of the illness or injury would, of course, influence the intensity of the demand and how much it upsets the family's homeostatic balance. Chronic illnesses and handicap-

ping conditions would also generate chronic strains that would remain an ongoing part of the family's level of demands.

THE MEANING OF PILE-UP

Although most stress research has focused on a single stressor, families usually are dealing with multiple demands and their response can best be understood in this context. These multiple demands change over time as some are resolved and new ones emerge. The family often gives priority to some demands over others. When they seem to be ignoring or not dealing effectively with a particular demand—for example, not following the doctor's orders—it may be because this demand has a lower priority than competing demands. In addition, because demands accumulate and interact with each other, it does not necessarily require a major event to push the demand load beyond the family's threshold to manage it. It is often the proverbial straw that breaks the camel's back. In working with families, it appears they often fail to take account of the "little things" that produce stress. When a family is helped to see this, the realization sheds light on why they feel so tense, and often increases their sense of control about being able to manage things.

Given this perspective on the multiple sources of demands confronting families, it is hard to conceive of a family that can meet all of them perfectly. There will always be some unresolved residue of strain creating a certain level of stress in the family. The family may be able to maintain some kind of balanced functioning by using all or most of their existing capabilities to manage ongoing strains. But, they have little reserve capability to absorb any additional demands, and hence would be more prone to crisis or exhaustion. Howard and Scott (1965) offer a similar perspective; it is failure to master stressors that leads to a residue of tension, called stress, which in turn renders the individual more vulnerable to subsequent stressors.

Capabilities

In the FAAR model, a *capability* if defined as a potentiality the family has available to it for meeting demands. There are two types: resources, which are what the family has, and coping behaviors, which are what the family does.

RESOURCES

A *resource* is a characteristic, trait, competency, or means of an individual, the family, or the community. Resources may be tangible, such as money, or intangible, such as self-esteem. It readily becomes apparent that a listing of potential resources is nearly infinite. However, those that have emerged in the stress literature as most salient for meeting demands, and that may be of particular relevance for family medicine research, are emphasized here.

Personal resources include: (1) innate intelligence; (2) knowledge and skills; (3) personality traits (a sense of humor, extraversion, etc.), that may facilitate efficacious coping behaviors; (4) physical and emotional health, so that intact faculties and personal energy may be available for meeting family demands; (5) time, which all individuals have equally but may allocate differently to manage demands; (6) a sense of mastery—the belief that one has some control over the circumstances of one's life; and (7) self-esteem, that is, a positive judgment about one's self-worth. These latter two are crucial for active, effective efforts at managing demands, and yet are most threatened when the pile-up of demands gets too large, particularly chronic strains that imply a failure at mastery. In fact, one of the important pathways that may link stressors and strains to negative outcomes, such as psychological depression, is through the diminution of self-esteem (Pearlin *et al.*, 1981).

Family resources represent one of the most intensely studied domains of family research. Many of the prominent family theoretical models are focused around variables that could be included as part of "family resources." Two such resources identified by several investigators (see review by Olson, Sprenkle, & Russell, 1979) are cohesion (the bonds of unity running through family life) and adaptability (the family's capacity to meet obstacles and shift courses). Another resource that has received attention is family organization (Hill, 1958; Moos & Moos, 1983), which includes agreement, clarity, and consistency in the family role and rule structure, as well as shared parental leadership and clear family and generational boundaries (Lewis & Looney, 1984).

Communication skill, a frequently identified family resource, includes giving clear, direct messages (Satir, 1972), both instrumental and affective communication capability (Epstein, Baldwin, & Bishop, 1983), and verbal–nonverbal consistency (Fleck, 1980). Quality communication is of particular importance to stress management in families because it enables the group to coordinate their efforts to manage demands and because it helps to reduce ambiguity, which is part of what makes change so stressful.

Based on a survey of family therapists and counselors, Curran (1983) identified 21 traits of a healthy family, such as a sense of humor and play, family rituals and traditions, religious beliefs, and clear values. One other promising conceptualization of family resources that has particular relevance for family medicine research is Pratt's (1976) analysis of characteristics that contribute to the conduct of health behaviors in the family. Families who (1) engaged in regular and varied interaction with each other, (2) had a marital relationship characterized by egalitarian roles, and (3) had members with social ties to the community followed better preventive health practices (balanced diet, exercise, regular doctor visits, brushing teeth, etc.).

COMMUNITY RESOURCES

Community-based resources are all of those characteristics, competencies, and means of persons, groups, and institutions outside the family that the family may call on and use to meet their demands. This includes a whole range of services, such as medical and health care services, as well as schools, churches, employers, and the like. At the macro level, government policies that strengthen and support families can be viewed as community resources.

Of all the community resources, the one that has received the most attention in the stress literature is social support. It is most often viewed as one of the primary buffers or mediators between stress and health breakdown (see reviews by Caplan, 1974; Cassel, 1976; Cassel & Tyroler, 1961; Cobb, 1976; Gottlieb, 1983; House, 1981; Pilisuk & Parks, 1983). Conceptualizations of social support include what is given (e.g., emotional support, information, tangible aid), how supported the recipient feels, and who gives support (i.e., the social network). Network members may not be supportive in all circumstances, and during times of transition they may become more a source of strain than support. For example, divorce may lead to withdrawal of support from extended family members.

The process of acquiring and allocating resources for meeting demands is a crucial aspect of the adjustment and adaptation response. The family is a resource exchange network. In the FAAR model, coping is viewed as the action for this exchange.

Coping

In the context of the FAAR model, a *coping behavior* is defined as a specific effort by which an individual or the family attempt to reduce or manage a demand. Specific coping behaviors can be grouped together into patterns, such as coping directed at ''maintaining family integration and cooperation,'' which is one of the coping patterns that has emerged as important for families with a chronically ill child (McCubbin, McCubbin, Patterson, Cauble, Wilson, & Warwick, 1983). Coping patterns are more generalized ways of responding that transcend different kinds of situations. When coping is placed in the context of multiple family demands (the pile-up), it seems more useful and relevant to view coping as a generalized rather than a situation-specific response.

Although coping most often has been conceptualized at the individual level, family- and even community-level coping can also be considered if we think of collective group action to eliminate or manage demands. Family coping could be viewed as coordinated problem-solving behavior of the whole system (Klein & Hill, 1979), but it could also involve conplementary efforts of individual family members that fit together as a synthetic whole.

The function of coping is to maintain or restore the balance between demands and resources. There are five ways this can be accomplished by the family system:

1. Direct action to reduce the number and/or intensity of demands (e.g., refusing a job promotion requiring a family move, placing a terminally ill grandmother in a nursing home rather than keeping her at home).
2. Direct action to acquire additional resources (e.g., finding medical services for an ill family member, developing self-reliance skills when a spouse dies suddenly).
3. Maintaining existing resources so they can be reallocated to new demands (e.g., maintaining social ties, doing things together as a family to maintain cohesion).
4. Managing the tension associated with ongoing strains (e.g., exercising, using humor appropriately, expressing emotion and affection).
5. Cognitive appraisal to change the meaning of demands (e.g., reducing role expectations) or the meaning of resources (e.g., seeing oneself as competent). Maintaining an optimistic outlook and accepting that this is the best the family can do under the circumstances is an example of a cognitive coping strategy. Cognitive appraisal interacts directly with what is labeled ''meaning'' in the FAAR model.

Resistance versus Adaptive Capabilities

In the FAAR model, a distinction is noted between resistance capabilities in the adjustment phase and adaptive capabilities in the adaptation phase. This distinction is made for two reasons. First, it implies the dynamic process of family change over time as new resources are acquired and new coping behaviors are developed in response to new demands. This natural process reflects the resiliency of families and, in many instances, their voluntary efforts to take on new demands as a way to grow and develop both as individuals and as a family unit. Second, this distinction is intended to imply that some resources and coping behaviors are more generic and could be used to meet most any type of demand. Such behaviors as self-esteem or family flexibility would fall into this category. Other capabilities may be more stressor- or strain-specific. For example, a support group for parents of a child with a congenital heart defect would be a resource specific to that demand.

Meanings

In the original ABC-X model (Hill, 1949), the C factor was the family's definition of the stressor. This factor has been expanded to include meanings at two levels. At the first level, there are *situational meanings,* which include the family's subjective definitions of their demands, of their capabilities, and of these two factors relative to each other. At the second level, there are *global meanings,* which make up the family schema for viewing the relationship of family members to each other, as well as the relationship of the family unit to the larger community.

SITUATIONAL MEANINGS

Demands are interpreted consciously or unconsciously, from the context of prior experience. The interpretation includes many components of the demand, such as valence, degree of controllability, amount of change implied, and the like. In some instances, demands exist only by virtue of the meaning given, as when role strain occurs because expectations are too high or when one believes one has a serious illness in the absence of any clinical evidence for it.

Resources and coping behaviors are also evaluated through the meanings given. When these are viewed as inadequate or insufficient relative to perceived demands, an imbalance results, which in turn produces tension and stress. In some instances, it is the lack of a clear definition of how to cope, or the existence of conflicting definitions, that create ambiguity. While there is some degree of uncertainty and ambiguity inherent in all change, and the management of stress involves reducing this, some strains exist primarily because this ambiguity is so difficult to resolve.

There are two types of ambiguity that create or exacerbate demands: social ambiguity and boundary ambiguity. "Social ambiguity" refers to stressful situations where the community or society provides no clear guidelines or blueprints about what to do (Mechanic, 1974). This is most likely to occur in the face of changing social conditions, where old norms or ways of behaving no longer seem to fit. For example, with medical technology that enables the sustenance of life with machines, families are increasingly confronted with the dilemma of whether to withhold or terminate life support systems for a family member who appears to be terminally ill.

"Boundary ambiguity" (Boss, 1977) refers to the strain associated with being unclear about who the members of a family are. This is a common strain for divorced families and stepfamilies, particularly for the children. Another example would be the struggle of an adult daughter over whether an elderly, dependent parent should move in with her nuclear family.

When an individual or a family experiences a stressor or strain they do not understand (i.e., they don't know what caused it and/or don't know what to do about it), they often turn to someone or something in the community for interpretation and meaning. Some families turn to religious beliefs as a way to provide meaning, especially to seemingly unexplainable events like death or serious illness. Another prime example of this kind of behavior is going to a physician when one is ill and is looking for new perceptions or interpretation. For the physician's diagnosis and prescription to be effective, it will somehow have to fit the patient's and family's existing set of beliefs, or schema, which is the other level of meanings emphasized in the FAAR model.

GLOBAL MEANINGS: THE FAMILY SCHEMA

At a more covert level, families hold a set of core beliefs or assumptions, called the *family schema*, about themselves in relationship to each other and about their family in relationship to the community and to systems beyond their boundaries. The family schema is more stable than situational meanings; it transcends and influences the latter. This way of thinking about family beliefs has been influenced by the work of Reiss and his colleagues (Reiss, 1981; Reiss & Oliveri, 1980), who have emphasized the importance of family paradigms in the stress process, and by other theorists, concerned primarily with individual response to stress, who have emphasized the personal orientations of coherence (Antonovsky, 1979) and hardiness (Kobasa, Maddi, & Kahn, 1982).

In the double ABC-X model, which emerged from the longitudinal observations of POW/MIA (prisoners of war/missing in action) families, the C factor was defined as "family definition and meaning." Based on prior theory-building efforts with McCubbin and on those efforts of the others just noted, as well as on more recent empirical studies of military family stress and coping in West Germany (Lavee, McCubbin, & Patterson, 1985), this definition and meaning factor has been expanded to include the family schema. Although the family schema has not been fully tested empirically, it appears to have five dimensions: shared purpose, collectivity, framability, relativism, and shared control (see Table 7-2 for conceptual linkage to other theorists).

Table 7-2. Conceptual Dimensions and Linkages of Family Schema

Family Schema conceptual dimensions	Family level		Individual level	
	Paradigm (Reiss & Oliveri, 1980)	World view (Fisher *et al.*, 1984)	Coherence (Antonovsky, 1979)	Hardiness (Kobasa *et al.*, 1982)
Shared purpose: Having family values, goals, and commitments that are shared; having a family ideology and identity			*Meaningfulness*— having values and commitments of emotional significance	Commitment vs. hopelessness and alienation; involvement in life
Collectivity: Recognizing that the individual or family is part of something larger; a "we" vs. an "I" orientation	*Coordination*— solidarity of unit; sensitivity to each other	Consensus vs. toleration of differences	*Comprehensibility*—belief that life is ordered and just; it has continuity	
Framability: Viewing life situations optimistically and with hope as well as realism		Optimism vs. pessimism		*Challenge*—view that change is normative and a growth opportunity, not disaster
Relativism: Viewing life in the context of present circumstances, not in terms of absolutes	*Closure*—openness to new information; here-and-now focus	Variety vs. sameness		
Shared control: Balance of personal/family control with trust in others	*Configuration*— sense of mastery and belief that family can learn and gain control	Security vs. insecurity	*Manageability*—belief that things will work out by my efforts and help from others	*Control*—belief that one can influence experiences, not be powerless

Shared purpose is the extent to which the family shares commitments, values, and goals that guide their life and activity. It gives the family its identity as a unit and a guide or ideology for living. Shared purpose does not imply any correct or best values; they can be idiosyncratic to the family.

Collectivity is the degree to which the family unit sees itself as part of something larger than itself, such as the community or the nation, and the degree to which members of the family see themselves as part of the family unit. It is a "we" versus an "I" orientation, and involves a sense of orderliness, patterning, and connection among the human elements of the universe, rather than randomness.

Framability is the degree to which the family views life situations optimistically and with hope while still retaining realism, in contrast to a pessimistic, doomsday orientation.

Relativism is the degree to which the family views their life experience in the context of present circumstances, in contrast to viewing experiences and their responses as absolute, prescribed, and invariant. It influences their judgments of what is good and bad, and whether they are oriented to absolutes of the past or to circumstances as they are in the present and may be in the future. It also involves the extent to which they set their own limits and accept less than perfect solutions to all their demands.

Shared control is the degree to which the family balances personal/family control with trust in others. It involves sharing the burden of demands with appropriate others within and outside the family. Shared control is midrange between belief in high personal control and fatalism.

Interaction of Demands, Capabilities, and Meanings

Demands, capabilities, and meanings are major constructs that interact with each other in the stress process. Strains emerge as a result of individual expectations or meanings, or the discrepancy between family member meanings or beliefs. The difficulty of demands involves subjective appraisal and includes some evaluation of the adequacy of capabilities for dealing with them. Coping behaviors can become a source of demand as well as a way to eliminate demands. For example, using alcohol to release tension can lead to dependency, thereby creating strain for the family.

To illustrate these interactions further, we might consider how social support may buffer the negative impact of stress. Social support may function to reduce ambiguity by giving the family and its members feedback on how well they are doing in social roles. This helps create more realistic expectations, and hence less role strain. Support also can help maintain and build self-esteem, a vital personal resource that often facilitates active coping efforts. During periods of major transition—moving to a new city, starting a new job, or getting a divorce—support networks are often upset (loss of a resource), new roles and rules are unclear (ambiguous perceptions), and all this exacerbates the demand–capability imbalance.

Family Change over Time

In the FAAR model, there is an emphasis on the importance of viewing the family's response over time because, whether in spite of or because of their efforts, families do change as a result of their circumstances. This time perspective has given rise to a two-phase model, separated by a state called family crisis.

ADJUSTMENT PHASE

The precrisis, or adjustment, phase represents a period of relative stability or homeostasis in the family system. The patterns of family interaction, family roles, and rules of relationship are established, and guide day-to-day activity in a fairly predictable pattern, so that members generally know what to expect from each other. This stability does not preclude the possibility of some disturbing patterns of family interaction (e.g., marital conflict, substance abuse). These, too, can become predictable.

Families in the adjustment phase are overtly or covertly trying to resist any major changes in their system. They meet demands with their existing capabilities. If a new demand emerges that is beyond their existing repertoire of abilities, they may ignore or resist dealing with the demand. For example, a family with an alcoholic member who is not ready to change will not hear confrontation (a demand) and will deny there is a problem.

How well the family is able to meet demands is reflected in their level of adjustment, which varies on a continuum from good (bonadjustment) to poor (maladjustment). It reflects the adequacy of the family's internal strengths and capabilities relative to the number and type of demands they face. There are many relatively stable periods in the family life cycle when minor, short-term responses are adequate, and bonadjustment can be maintained.

There are, however, occasions when the family's existing capabilities are inadequate to meet the demands they face. This situation is likely to emerge when (1) a stressor event occurs that calls for new capabilities the family does not have in their repertoire; (2) the number of demands exceeds the family's capabilities; or (3) unresolved strains tax and deplete the family's capabilities. In other words, the demand–capability imbalance increases and persists, functioning is no longer stable, and the family system is in disequilibrium. The family has moved into a state of crisis.

FAMILY CRISIS

Crisis is characterized by family disorganization and disruptiveness (Burr, 1973), where old patterns and capabilities are no longer adequate, and change is called for (Hill, 1949, 1958). It is important to note that a family *in crisis* does not carry the stigmatizing value judgment that somehow the family has failed, is dysfunctional, or needs professional counseling. Rather, many family crises are normative ones that call for changes in family structure and rules.

A family in crisis is uncomfortable and vulnerable. Not uncommonly the crisis will precipitate reaching out for help, often in the form of medical help—a legitimate, nonstigmatizing source of help. Thus, in many circumstances, medical professionals will be dealing with a family in crisis that may be open to some form of intervention because of the desire to bring the family back into balance. A family crisis can be viewed as a turning point because the old family system no longer exists in the same way; something new must emerge. This "something new" is the focus of the adaptation phase.

ADAPTATION PHASE

During the adaptation phase, family efforts are directed at restoring a balance to their system by (1) altering or expanding their perceptions and definitions to take account of their changed circumstances; (2) reducing the pile-up of demands; (3) developing and acquiring new resources (called adaptive resources); and/or (4) developing new coping strategies for dealing with demands. *Adaptation* is defined as a minimal discrepancy between demands and capabilities at two levels of interaction; individual-to-family and family-to community.

At the first level, a balance is sought between individual family member needs, tasks, and demands, and the family system's capabilities to bring the necessary resources, coping behaviors, and meanings into play for meeting members' needs. Reciprocally, the tasks and demands of the family system to create and maintain itself as a unit are met by the capabilities of its individual members. The whole course of family development is an ongoing effort to shape and reshape the fit between the individual members and the family unit. When a new family unit is formed, there is usually some overt or covert understanding of reciprocity and sharing that will be mutually advantageous. This is the beginning of the family schema. The web of fit eventually becomes increasingly complex as adult members change, new members are added to the unit, members leave the family, and myriad unexpected life events occur. Members of the family learn the rules, sometimes help change these rules, and evolve a complex set of reciprocal role relationships. Fitting into a family means making the "raw material"—who we are by virtue of genetic inheritance—fit the circumstances we are in. Conversely, the environment can support or undermine the development of this raw material, influencing the extent to which the person becomes an autonomous individual who can leave the family at some point and begin to fit in someplace else. Stated in this way, failure to individuate (Bowen, 1978) may reflect a situation where balance was achieved, but where family demands precluded certain individual tasks from being met.

This latter point calls attention to an important aspect of adaptational fit—the balancing of multiple, competing demands among different levels of systems. One way to think of this is that each level of system is trying to maintain its own dynamic balance. When, for example, the individual experiences excessive demands, one or more of these demands may be shifted (through feedback loops linking system levels) to the family to be met so that the individual retains his or her integrity or balance. Likewise, family or subsystem demands or strains may be shifted to an individual. This is the kind of situation that gives rise to the "symptom carrier" for the family, as when a deviant child is acting out tension in the marital subsystem. Similarly, if individually experienced demands are absorbed by a system lower on the hierarchy, such as an organ system in the body, illness may occur. The complexity of this kind of systems thinking is readily apparent when we consider the number of systems involved, which increases exponentially as we move up the hierarchy— several organs in one individual, two or more individuals in a family, multiple families in multiple community environments, many communities in a subculture . . .

In addition to individual-to-family fit, adaptation includes family-to-community fit, which occurs in many different contexts—the workplace, the school system, the church, the neighborhood, the peer group, the subculture, the nation. Whenever the family changes membership in one of these community environments, voluntarily or involuntarily, imbalance (i.e., a crisis) would most likely occur until a new fit could be achieved. This new fit would involve a shifting of demands and capabilities across system levels. For example, when a family moves to a new city, adaptation may involve (1) each parent taking on new job demands and making his or her capabilities fit the new workplace; (2) children fitting into a new school with different expectations; (3) fitting into the neighborhood in terms of property maintenance, socializing, and the like; (4) finding new resources in the community for meeting family needs such as medical care, food, clothing, and so on; and (5) possibly trying to find a fit for the family's schema with the new environment's social, political, and economic values and behaviors.

The important distinction about family adaptation, in contrast to adjustment, is that the nature and extent of the demand–capability imbalance has created a situation requiring second-order change in the family system (Watzlawick, Weakland, & Fisch, 1974) involving changes in family roles, rules, patterns of interaction, and/or meanings. Adaptation usually evolves over a longer period of time, and has long-term consequences. It also seems probable that it is during adaptation that families make major changes in their family schema, evolving new ways of thinking about themselves and their world to better fit the circumstances they are in. Reiss and Oliveri (1980) have also suggested that family paradigms become more conscious and possibly shift in the aftermath of major stressful experiences.

The concept of family adaptation is used to describe a continuum of outcomes that reflect family efforts to achieve a balance in functioning at the member-to-family and family-to-community levels. The positive end of the continuum, called "bonadaptation," is characterized by (1) physical and mental health of individual family members, (2) optimal role functioning and continued development of individual members, (3) the maintenance of a family unit that can accomplish its life cycle tasks, and (4) the maintenance of family integrity and its sense of control over environmental influence. Family maladaptation, at the negative end of the continuum, is characterized by a continued imbalance at either level of family functioning (member-to-family or family-to-community) *or* the achievement of a balance at both levels *but at a price* in terms of (1) deterioration of individual member health and/or development or (2) deterioration of family unit integrity, autonomy, or the ability to accomplish left cycle tasks.

OPERATIONALIZING THE FAAR MODEL

McCubbin and his colleagues (see Chapter 12, this volume) have made an effort to systematically develop and test instruments to operationalize most of the major variables of the FAAR model. In addition, there is a vast array of instruments developed by other investigators that also could be used as measures of the FAAR constructs. Table 7-3 lists some examples of possible instruments for each of the FAAR constructs.

The adjustment and adaptation constructs have not been included in the summary table. Based on conceptual definitions of these constructs as "fit" at two levels, individual-to-family and family-to-community, measures of individual and/or family well-being could serve as indices of adaptation. These could include measures of both physical and psychologic health, which are particularly relevant for family medicine research. Measures of physiologic systems in the body, such as the immune, neurologic, or endocrine systems, could be used. In a study of families that have a child with cystic fibrosis, change in pulmonary functioning over a specified time period was used as one index of adaptation, since it measured a vulnerable organ system in one of the family members (Patterson, 1985; Patterson & McCubbin, 1985). More global indicators of health/illness could also be used, such as a checklist of symptoms in a given time period, or measures of height and weight as indicators of growth.

Measures of individual psychologic well-being could provide other indices of how well individuals are doing in the family and community. Such measures have commonly been used in individual stress studies (see, for example, Pearlin *et al.*, 1981) In a similar vein, a measure of family well-being would indicate how well the family is doing. Some investigators may choose to examine this as the family's satisfaction with internal and

Table 7-3. Instruments for Measuring Variables of the FAAR Model

FAAR construct	Instrument	Variable
Demands	FILE—Family Inventory of Life Events and Changes (McCubbin, Patterson, & Wilson, 1981)	Family stressors and strains
	A-FILE—Adolescent–Family Inventory of Life Events and Changes (McCubbin, Patterson, Bauman, & Harris, 1981)	Family and adolescent stressors and strains
	SRRS—Social Readjustment Rating Scale (Holmes & Rahe, 1967)	Individual stressors
	The Hassles Scale (Kanner, Coyne, Schaefer, & Lazarus, 1981)	Individual strains
	Role Strains in Marriage, Parenting, Household Economic and Occupation (Pearlin & Schooler, 1978)	Individual role strains
Capabilities		
Personal resources	Self-Esteem Scale (Rosenberg, 1965)	Individual self-esteem
	Mastery Scale (Pearlin & Schooler, 1978)	Individual sense of mastery
	Locus of Control (Rotter, 1966)	Individual's internal vs. external locus of control
	Personal Hardiness Measurement (Kobasa, Maddi, & Kahn, 1982)	Commitment, challenge, control
Family resources	FIRM—Family Inventory of Resources for Management (McCubbin, Comeau, & Harkins, 1981)	Family esteem and communication, family mastery and health, family social support, family financial well-being
	FES—Family Environment Scale (Moos, 1974)	Cohesion, expressiveness, conflict, independence, active recreation, moral–religious, intellectual–cultural, control, organization, achievement
	FACES II—Family Adaptability and Cohesion Evaluation Scales (Olson, Portner, & Bell, 1982)	Family cohesion and family adaptability
	FAD—Family Assessment Device (Epstein, Baldwin, & Bishop, 1983)	Problem solving, communication, roles, behavior control, affective responsiveness, involvement
	FFI—Family Functioning Index (Pless & Satterwhite, 1973)	Marital satisfaction, decision making, communication, cohesiveness, happiness
Community resources	Social Support Inventory (McCubbin, Patterson, Rossman, & Cooke, 1982)	Emotional, esteem, network, appraisal, and altruistic support from 13 network sources
	Social Support Index (McCubbin, Patterson, & Glynn, 1982)	Community and friend support
	Social Network Questionnaire (Fischer & Phillips, 1982)	Size, density, multiplexity of family social network and type of support received
Individual coping	CHIP—Coping Health Inventory for Parents (McCubbin, McCubbin, Nevin, & Cauble, 1981)	3 coping patterns (maintaining family integration, self-esteem, getting medical consultation)
	A-COPE—Adolescent Coping Orientation for Problem Experiences (Patterson & McCubbin, 1987)	12 coping patterns: (e.g., ventilation, self-reliance, inactivity, family problem solving)
	DECS—Dual Employed Coping Scales (Skinner & McCubbin, 1981)	5 coping patterns: (e.g., modifying work–family interface, managing tensions)

(continued)

Table 7-3. (Continued)

FAAR construct	Instrument	Variable
Family coping	Coping Responses for Marital, Parental, Household Economic and Occupation (Pearlin & Schooler, 1978)	17 coping factors (e.g., self-reliance, positive comparisons, selective ignoring)
	F-COPES—Family Coping Strategies (McCubbin, Larsen, & Olson, 1982)	5 coping patterns (acquiring social and spiritual support, getting help, reframing, passive appraisal)
	Note: Family coping could also be assessed by examining the combination of individual coping patterns in a family	
Meanings		
Situational	Use subjective weighting scale for experienced stressors and strains on FILE (McCubbin, Patterson, & Wilson, 1981)	Family's definition of difficulty of demands
	FIC—Family Index of Coherence (McCubbin & Patterson, 1982b)	Factors of predictability, commitment, controllability, family–community fit for military families
Family schema	Family Paradigm Card Soft Procedure (Reiss, 1981)	Paradigm dimensions of closure, configuration, and coordination
	Family World View Scales (Fisher, Ransom, Kokes, Weiss, & Phillips, 1984)	Security vs. insecurity, optimism vs. pessimism, variety vs. sameness, consensus vs. toleration of differences, child- vs. adult-centeredness

external family functioning. One needs to be cautious in selecting family well-being (or individual well-being) measures so that they are not confounded with the family and individual resource measures used in the same study (often as predictors).

In operationalizing the FAAR model, one methodologically strong approach would be to include family-level measures (e.g., demands, resources), psychologic well-being measures, and individual physiologic measures in a multivariate analysis, since one of the most likely pathways linking the social environment to physiologic outcomes is through cognitions and emotions of the neurologic system.

One other strategy for operationalizing adaptation more completely (as opposed to the partial indicators mentioned above) would be to use multiple scales of individual and family well-being and combine them statistically into one composite index that could be used as a single criterion. This approach was followed in a study of military families using canonical correlational analysis (Patterson, McCubbin, & Lavee, 1984) and using family factor weights for five separate indices to create a single family system adaptation score (McCubbin, Patterson, & Lavee, 1984).

APPLYING THE FAAR MODEL TO HEALTH-RELATED ISSUES

Primary Prevention

Primary prevention issues can be viewed as occurring within the adjustment phase of the FAAR model. Generally speaking, health care settings are already involved in supporting and encouraging families to acquire resistance capabilities and perceptions that could increase their ability to manage whatever demands they face. Promoting coping behaviors that contribute to health (e.g., exercising, eating a balanced diet) and discouraging those that undermine it (e.g., smoking, substance abuse) represents one example. Teaching skills and providing information about ways to prevent the occurrence of unwanted demands (e.g., contraception to prevent pregnancy) is another example.

With the advantage of continuity of care, family physicians are in a position to help families acquire resistance capabilities and anticipate some of the strains associated with normative transitions, such as having a baby or parenting adolescents. In other words, adaptation to some developmental crises can be eased through this kind of anticipatory guidance.

Family physicians often have the unique advantage of managing a family's health care over more than one generation. Hence they may be aware of a family history that could contribute to new medical problems (i.e., new stressors). In addition, a frequently used family medicine history-taking technique, the family genogram, may suggest targets for early intervention. When families have known history of specific illnesses, such as hypertension, or diabetes, the onset of these stressors may be avoided or delayed, or its impact reduced, if resistance capabilities are developed early.

Another way clinics could focus on primary prevention is through routine screening of families to identify families at risk, that is, families with a high level of demands relative to their capabilities. Such screening could become part of regular medical checkups in much the same way that Pap smears are routinely done to detect cancer. A "positive" test for the at-risk family could lead to further clinical evaluation of psychosocial issues to determine ways to reduce the demand–capability imbalance and to bring the family system into better homeostasis.

Research strategies could be developed for any of these primary prevention issues. Prospective studies could be undertaken relating resources and coping training, and early detection and intervention programs, to subsequent health status of family members (in terms of number of clinic visits, episodes of illness, etc.). Evaluation of different types of patient education programs might be done to assess optimal timing for delivery of such programs, involvement of individuals versus whole families or subsystems, or comparisons of different strategies for different types of families (e.g., the relationship of family schemas to different educational strategies).

Acute Episodes of Illness

When a family experiences the stressor of a major episode of illness in one of its members, it could be predicted, on the basis of the FAAR model, that the family would move into a crisis. As defined, this would involve family disorganization where normal routines and roles would be upset. From the perspective of the FAAR model, the family's recovery from crisis could be greatly enhanced by the way the medical team relates to the whole family system. There are at least two strategies that might be helpful in such circumstances. First, the medical team can help the patient *and* the family reduce ambiguity about what is happening (and thereby reduce the strains) by providing information about the medical condition—etiology, treatment, prognosis, and so forth. When this is done with all family members present, it facilitates the family's speedy arrival at a shared definition, which in turn may hasten their additional efforts to adapt. Second, the medical team may be able to facilitate the family's assessment of their demands relative to their capabilities through a clinical interview or with questionnaires like those identified in the previous section. Supporting and guiding the family in developing and acquiring additional resources (such as support groups) would be an additional kind of intervention. This kind of secondary prevention can be viewed as "hurdle help," which does not imply that the family is dysfunctional because they are in crisis but, rather, that they need a little extra help and input to get them over the hurdle.

Research strategies focused on some of these intervention issues could be undertaken to determine what is effective for which types of families and under what conditions. Studies related to the physician's role in the development of shared family definitions and meanings about illness seem particularly promising in expanding our understanding of family adaptation to illness. Or more exploratory studies could be undertaken to identify the nature of strains associated with different kinds of acute illness, how families do cope, and which resources are most important.

Chronic Illness and Handicapping Conditions

If illness in general has a significant impact on families, we know that chronic conditions have an even more profound effect because the ongoing care and management of the condition rests primarily with the family. The FAAR model is especially useful both for examining the impact of these illnesses on the family and for determining what resources, coping behaviors, and meanings in the family facilitate successful adaptation. This latter strategy is particularly important because of the disproportionate emphasis given in prior studies on how chronic conditions create dysfunction in families.

Longitudinal studies examining how families change overtime in response to these chronic strains would be particularly useful and might shed light on the processes of adaptation to stress. One major limitation, of course, is that it is virtually impossible to identify families before the onset of the illness or handicap, and hence it is difficult to get baseline measures of family variables so as to assess change due to the condition. However, if family medicine record keeping included periodic routine assessments of select family variables (such as an abbreviated FILE and key resources), then a study of the effect of chronic illness and handicaps on families may be possible.

Compliance Problems

Compliance with prescribed treatment regimens is an important issue for family medicine research. Using the FAAR model, medical prescriptions can be viewed as "demands" from the community, and whether the patient and family can follow through with them (compliance) could be viewed as one indicator of adaptation (i.e., their ability to meet community demands with family and personal resources). It would be useful to examine what family factors may be associated with lack of compliance, such as other competing demands, family meanings that are discrepant with those of the medical system, inadequate resources or coping strategies. Conversely, what family factors, using the same FAAR variables, are associated with the family's and patient's ability to comply? The fit of the medical prescriptions with the family's schema and with their situational definitions of the medical problem are, again, important issues that could prove fruitful for further research.

STRENGTHS AND LIMITATIONS OF THE FAAR MODEL

The FAAR model has several strengths that make it particularly relevant for the emerging research linking the family system to health and illness in family members.

First, the conceptual definitions of the constructs link biologic, psychologic, and social variables. The FAAR is genuinely a biopsychosocial model with its emphasis on three levels of systems: the individual, the family system, and the community.

Second, it incorporates measures of individual health and illness as one index of family adaptation (or adjustment). The advancement of research of the family system in family medicine depends heavily on our ability to link empirically "hard" biomedical data with psychosocial factors in methodologically sound studies. A relevant theoretical framework with constructs that are conceptually and operationally well defined is an important first step.

Third, the concepts in the FAAR model are linked to physiologic stress theory and research. Very similar conceptual definitions are used to describe the stress process at the family system level. This model sets the stage for us to expand our understanding of the psychosocial context that leads to the physiologic response in the individual.

Fourth, the concepts of this model are clinically relevant for physicians and other health care professionals, as well as family therapists. This will increases the model's utility for intervention research.

Fifth, with its roots in family studies, the FAAR model integrates concepts from other family theoretical perspectives, most notably family systems theory, family development theory, the symbolic-interaction framework, and the ecosystems perspective. This should strengthen its utility as a family assessment model.

Sixth, there is an emphasis on family change and interaction over time that negates static, linear, cause–effect thinking. This should be a better approximation of the true nature of family life, and the course of health and illness.

Seventh, the constructs, as they are defined, are not culture-bound or value-laden. This makes the model relevant for diverse types of families from different ethnic, religious, and economic backgrounds.

Eighth, instruments are already developed to test the FAAR Model. These measures are relevant to medical issues. They measure factors internal to the family, as well as the family's transactions with the community.

There are three major limitations of the FAAR Model for family medicine research. First, it may be that the constructs as defined are too generic in that they do not specify *which* resources, *which* meanings, *which* coping behaviors, and so on. This means that the number of concepts that could be plugged into the model are almost limitless, and this poses problems in identifying the critical concepts to measure. Second, the scope of what needs to be included to test the model adequately may be too great for many studies, especially those that are limited by number of subjects. Third, with three units of analysis included—individual, family, and community—there may be confusion in variable selection and in analysis procedures.

CONCLUSION

The complex nature of the illnesses that confront us today require going beyond the simple, linear, cause–effect thinking that worked well in discovering the etiology of disease in the past. We are at a critical point in advancing research to test the biopsychosocial model (Engel, 1977).

Systematic study of the family is relatively new in the field of social science, but five decades of work have led to important theoretical developments that can be integrated into research designed to explore the relationship between the psychosocial environment, and individual health and illness. In particular, developments in the area of family stress theory offer theoretical constructs that are medically relevant because of their linkage to physiologic stress theory.

The family adjustment and adaptation response model is one very useful family stress model for family medicine research because its concepts bridge physiologic, psychologic, and social domains. The FAAR model emphasizes the individual, the family, and the community. When we consider the feedback loops between these three levels of systems, and when we have concepts that transcend these different levels of systems, we have set the stage for research addressing the question, "How does what occurs in the family environment get inside the human body and make someone sick or well?"

References

Alexander R. Psychosomatic medicine. New York: Norton, 1950.

Angell RD. The family encounters the depression. New York: Scribner, 1936.

Antonovsky A. Health, stress and coping. San Francisco: Jossey-Bass, 1979.

Boss PG. A clarification of the concept of psychological father presence in families experience ambiguity of boundary. Journal of Marriage and the Family 1977; 39: 141–151.

Bowen M. Family therapy in clinical practice. New York: Jason Aronson, 1978.

Burr WF. Theory construction and the sociology of the family. New York: Wiley, 1973.

Cannon WB. Bodily danger in pain, hunger, fear and rage. New York: D. Appleton, 1929.

Caplan G. Support systems and community mental health. New York: Behavioral Publications, 1974.

Cassel J. The contribution of the social environment to host resistance. American Journal of Epidemiology 1976; 104:107–123.

Cassel J, Tyroler HA. Epidemiological studies of culture change: I. Health status and recency of industrialization. Archives of Environmental Health 1961; 3:25–33.

Cavan R, Ranck KR. The family and the depression. Chicago: University of Chicago Press, 1938.

Cobb S. Social support as a moderator of life stress. Psychosomatic Medicine 1976; 38:300–314.

Curran D. Traits of a healthy family. Minneapolis: Winston Press, 1983.

Duvall E. Marriage and family development, 15th ed. Philadelphia: Lippincott, 1977.

Eisdorfer C. The conceptualization of stress and a model for further study. In: Zales MR, ed. Stress in health and disease. New York: Brunner/Mazel, 1985:5–23.

Engel GL. The need for a new medical model: a challenge for biomedicine. Science 1977; 8:129–136.

Epstein N, Baldwin L, Bishop D. The McMaster family assessment device. Journal of Marital and Family Therapy 1983; 9(2):171–190.

Erikson E. Childhood and society. New York: Norton, 1950.

Fischer CS, Phillips SL. Who is alone? Social characteristics of people with small networks. In: Peplou LA, Perlman D, eds. Loneliness: a sourcebook of current theory, research and therapy. New York: Wiley-Interscience, 1982: 21–39.

Fisher L, Ransom D, Kokes R, Weiss R, Phillips S. The California family health project. Presented at the Family and Health preconference workshop of the National Council of Family Relations, San Francisco, October 1984.

Fleck S. Family functioning and family pathology. Psychiatric Annals 1980; 10:46–57.

Gottlieb BH. Social support strategies. Beverly Hills, Calif.: Sage, 1983.

Hill R. Families under stress. New York: Harper, 1949.

Hill R. Generic features of families under stress. Social Casework 1958; 49:139–150.

Holmes TH, Rahe RH. The social readjustment rating scale. Journal of Psychosomatic Research 1967; 11:213–218.

House JS. Work stress and social support. Reading, Mass: Addison-Wesley, 1981.

Howard A, Scott RA. A proposed framework for the analysis of stress in the human organism. Behavioral Science 1965; 10:141–160.

Kanner AD, Coyne JC, Schaefer C, Lazarus RS. Comparison of two modes of stress measurement: daily hassles and uplifts versus major life events. Journal of Behavioral Medicine 1981; 4:1–39.

Klein D, Hill R. Determinants of family problem solving effectiveness. In: Burr W, Hill R, Nye FI, Reiss I, eds. Contemporary theories about the family, Vol 1. New York: Free Press, 1979.

Kobasa S, Maddi S, Kahn S. Hardiness and health: a prospective study. Journal of Personality and Social Psychology 1982; 42:168–177.

Lavee Y, McCubbin HI, Patterson JM. The double ABCX model of family stress and adaptation: an empirical test by analysis of structural equations with latent variables. Journal of Marriage and the Family. 1985; 47:811–825.

Lazarus R, Folkman S. Stress, appraisal and coping. New York: Springer, 1984.

Levinson D. The seasons of a man's life. New York: Knopf, 1978.

Lewis JM, Looney JG. The long struggle: Well-functioning working-class black families. New York: Brunner/ Mazel, 1984.

McCubbin, Comeau J. Harkins J. FIRM—Family Inventory of Resources for Management (research instrument). Department of Family Social Science, University of Minnesota, St. Paul, 1981.

McCubbin H, Dahl B, Hunter E, eds. Families in the military system. Beverly Hills, Calif.: Sage, 1976.

McCubbin H, Larsen A, Olson D. F-COPES—Family Crisis-Oriented Personal Evaluation Scales (research instrument). Department of Family Social Science, University of Minnesota, St. Paul, 1982.

McCubbin H, McCubbin M, Nevin R, Cauble A. CHIP—Coping Health Inventory for Parents (research instrument). Department of Family Social Science, University of Minnesota, St. Paul, 1981.

McCubbin H, McCubbin M, Patterson J, Cauble A, Wilson L, Warwick. CHIP—coping health inventory for parents: An assessment of parental coping patterns in the care of the chronically ill child. Journal of Marriage and the Family 1983; 45:359–370.

McCubbin HI, Patterson JM. Family adaptation to crises. In: McCubbin HI, Cauble AE, Patterson JM, eds. Family Stress, coping and social support. Springfield, Ill.: Thomas, 1982a: 26–47.

McCubbin HI, Patterson JM. FIC—Family Index of Coherence (research instrument). Department of Family Social Science, University of Minnesota, St. Paul, 1982b.

McCubbin HI, Patterson JM. Family stress and adaptation to crises: A double ABCX model of family behavior. In: Olson D, Miller B, eds. Family Studies Review Yearbook. Beverly Hills, Calif.: Sage, 1983a: 87–106.

McCubbin HI, Patterson JM. The family stress process: The double ABCX model of family adjustment and adaptation. In: McCubbin HI, Sussman M, Patterson JM, eds. Social stress and the family: Advances and developments in family stress theory and research. New York: Haworth, 1983b: 7–37.

McCubbin HI, Patterson JM. Stress: the family inventory of life events and changes. In: Filsinger E, ed. A sourcebook of marriage and family assessment. Beverly Hills, Calif.: Sage, 1983c: 275–297.

McCubbin HI, Patterson JM, Bauman E, Harris L. A-FILE—Adolescent Family Inventory of Life Events and Changes (research instrument). Department of Family Social Science, University of Minnesota, St. Paul, 1981.

McCubbin HI, Patterson JM, Glynn T. Social Support Index (research instrument). Department of Family Social Science, University of Minnesota, St. Paul, 1982.

McCubbin HI, Patterson JM, Lavee Y. Black military family adaptation in stressful environments: critical strengths and supports. Presented at annual meeting of National Council on Family Relations, San Francisco, October 1984.

McCubbin HI, Patterson JM, Rossman M, Cooke B. Social Support Inventory (research instrument). Department of Family Social Science,University of Minesota, St. Paul, 1982.

McCubbin HI, Patterson JM, Wilson L. FILE—Family Inventory of Life Events & Changes (research instrument). Department of Family Social Science, University of Minnesota, St. Paul, 1981

Mechanic D. Social structure and personal adaptation: some neglected dimensions. In: Coelho GV, Hamburg OA, Adams JE, eds. Coping and adaptation. New York: Basic Books, 1974: 32–44.

Moos R. FES—Family Environment Scale (research instrument). Palo Alto, Calif.: Consulting Psychologists Press,1974.

Moos R, Moos B. Clinical applications of the family environment scale. In: Filsinger E, ed. Marriage and family assessment: a sourcebook for family therapy. Beverly Hills, Calif.: Sage, 1983: 153–273.

Olson D, Portner J, Bell R. FACES II—Family Adaptability and Cohesion Evaluation Scales (research instrument). Department of Family Social Science, University of Minnesota, St. Paul, 1982.

Olson D, Sprenkle D, Russell C. Circumplex model of marital and family systems, I. Family Process 1979; 18:3–28.

Patterson JM. Critical factors affecting family compliance with cystic fibrosis. Family Relations 1985; 34:79–89.

Patterson JM. McCubbin HI. Adolescent coping style and behaviors: conceptualization and measurement. Journal of Adolescence 1987; 10:163–186.

Patterson JM, McCubbin HI. Family adaptation to cystic fibrosis. Presented at the annual meeting of the North American Primary Care Research Group, Seattle, April 1985.

Patterson JM, McCubbin HI, Lavee, Y. Assessment of family adaptation to stressful environments: army families in Europe. Presented at the annual meeting of the National Council on Family Relations, San Francisco, October 1984.

Pearlin LI, Schooler C. The structure of coping. Journal of Health and Social Behavior 1978; 19:2–21.

Pearlin LI, Menaghan EG, Lieberman MA, Mullan JT. The stress process. Journal of Health and Social Behavior 1981; 22:337–356.

Pilisuk M, Parks SH. Social support and family stress. In: McCubbin H, Sussman M, Patterson J, eds. Social stress and the family: advances and developments in family stress theory and research. New York: Haworth, 1983: 137–156.

Pless IB, Satterwhite B. A measure of family functioning and its application. Social Science and Medicine 1973; 7:613–621.

Pratt L. Family structure and effective health behavior: the energized family Boston: Houghton Mifflin, 1976.

Reiss D. The family's construction of reality. Cambridge, Mass: Harvard University Press, 1981.

Reiss D, Oliveri ME. Family paradigm and family coping: a proposal for linking the family's intrinsic adaptive capacities to its responses to stress. Family Relations 1980; 29:431–444.

Rosenberg M. Parental interest and children's self-conceptions. Sociometry 1965; 26:35–49.

Rotter J. Generalized expectancies for internal vs. external control of reinforcements. Psychological Monographs 1966; 80 (609):1–28.

Sangiuliano I. In her time. New York; William Morrow, 1978.

Satir V. Peoplemaking. Palo Alto, Calif.: Science & Behavior Books, 1972.

Selye H. The stress of life. New York: McGraw-Hill, 1956.

Selye H. Stress without distress. Philadephia: Lippincott, 1974.

Scott R, Howard A. Model of stress. In: Levine S, Scotch NA, eds. Social stress. Chicago: Aldine, 1970: 259–277.

Skinner D, McCubbin H. DECS—Dual Employed Coping Scales (research instrument). Department of Family Social Science, University of Minnesota, St. Paul, 1981.

Watzlawick P, Weakland J, Fisch R. Change: principles of problem formation and problem resolution. New York: Norton, 1974.

Wolff HG. Stress and disease. Springfield, Ill.: Thomas, 1953.

8

Families and Their Paradigms: An Ecologic Approach to Understanding the Family in Its Social World

DAVID REISS
George Washington University Medical Center

For some years, investigators have explored several different ways of understanding the events and processes displayed in families dealing with central problems of physical health and illness. In broad strokes, there have been two major approaches.

The first approach begins by making clear distinctions between competent families, on the one hand, and dysfunctional families—those that have more than the usual difficulties in dealing with major tasks. Functional or competent families are viewed as similar to one another—in Tolstoy's words, "Happy families are all alike." Thus, the Beavers model (see Chapter 5) specifies what well-functioning families have in common: adequate autonomy for their members; open, affective expression; warmth; humor; freedom from dominating family myths; and so forth. Likewise, Olson (see Chapter 6) identifies the competent family as one that lives in the midrange on the dimensions of adaptability and cohesion.

Both Olson and Beavers reserve their fine distinctions and discriminations for pathologic or dysfunctional families. For example, the Olson model permits a clear, dramatic discrimination between the "disengaged" and the "enmeshed" family—both of them pathologic. But the model can barely discriminate among different types of functional or competent families; they are all clustered together in the middle of the circumplex. The same general features—an emphasis on distinguishing between pathologic and nonpathologic families, and making the finer discriminations among the former—are generally true of the Beavers model as well. For example, very sharp distinctions are made between two pathologic family types: the "centripetal family," where a schizophrenic patient is common, and the "centrifugal family," where antisocial character disorders are frequent. The Beavers model does not yield a comparably sharp distinction among "normal" families. Both models, because of their emphasis on distinguishing normal from abnormal, and then making fine distinctions among the abnormal, can be regarded as examples of a *diagnostic approach* to understanding families.

In sharp contrast to this diagnostic approach is a second approach, which focuses on differences among *all* families. The primary emphasis here is to delineate sharply different family styles. There is less of a focus on distinguishing competent from incompetent families. Indeed, there is an emphasis on family situation fit. Some kinds of families can manage some situations quite well but do very poorly in others. Thus, this perspective can be termed the *ecologic approach*. As an example, my team has studied families with highly collaborative and consensus-oriented problem-solving styles. As will be detailed more completely below, when faced with the acute admission of a teenager for serious psychiatric problems, these families appear to do very well. They become rapidly and effectively engaged in the milieu of the inpatient treatment service. Apparently, their group solidarity wins them the respect of staff and other families. In contrast, the very same kind of family has difficulty coping with chronic, physical illness in one of its members (Reiss, Gonzalez, & Kramer, 1986). Here, it seems as if their tendency to stick together makes them over-solicitous and overinvolved in the emotionally and physically draining sequelae of chronic illness; other family members' needs are not met, and over time the family may run into severe trouble.

This second approach, then, to the analysis of family process emphasizes differences among families in basic style, organization and values; identifies sources of stress that are most problematic for each type of family; and focuses on the coping responses most typical of that family type, and the forms of family dysfunction that might characterize a particular family type if its coping mechanisms fail.

This chapter describes one model that exemplifies the ecologic approach: the family paradigm model. The work summarized in this chapter uses the research of other investigators who have followed the same approach. For example, Kantor and Lehr (1975) described three different family styles: open, closed, and random. On the basis of extensive home observation of a number of families of each kind, they were able to hypothesize situations that were most problematic for each type, as well as the consequences, for each type, of failures to cope with those specific situations. Earlier work that has influenced our own includes Strodtbeck's (1958) characterizations of different family problem-solving styles, and their fit with broader cultural designs, and Hess and Handel's (1959) work on different "family worlds."

This approach to the analysis and understanding of families can be illustrated by two brief case vignettes.

THE DAKOS FAMILY

The Dakos family consists of a father and mother in their late 40s, two sons in their early 20s, and a 14-year-old daughter. Mr. Dakos has owned a chain of women's high-fashion clothing stores. Both sons are in training to enter the family business; the father's brother is a co-owner. The daughter wants to be either a fashion model or a fashion designer; the mother, a snazzy dresser herself, is heavily involved in church groups and charitable enterprises. The family is very conspicuous in the Greek-American community in which they live. Indeed, the envy they generate is sometimes a burden to the family.

Within the family, there is a good deal of closeness both within and across the generations. The two sons, for example, are planning to move out of the family home and share an apartment with each other. In a similar vein, Mr. Dakos is very closely tied to his aging father, whom he visits ever night although his father lives several miles away. The death of Mr. Dakos's mother 5 years previously is still felt deeply by the family, and produces an anxious sadness during the rare moments when it is mentioned explicitly. Likewise, Mrs. Dakos is very close to her mother, who, although she had been in the United States for 45 years, can barely speak English. Mrs. Dakos continues to do all her mother's shopping and banking.

The family, though it is successful in a material sense, and also emotionally close and supportive, is not without its problems. Tension occasionally erupts between the two boys, usually around issues of competition. Mrs. Dakos complains that her husband works too long and too late. Recently, the daughter had some difficulty in school. As they usually do when faced with a problem, the Dakoses had a family conference (which was held, as usual, in one of the best and most expensive restaurants in town). After a thorough discussion, the family decided the daughter should drop her extracurricular activity, lacrosse, and concentrate on her studies until her grades improved. By the next report card she had shown significant improvement.

THE SWENSON FAMILY

Now let us contrast this family with another. Whereas the Dakos family does not currently face any severe crisis or challenge, the Swensons, by contrast, face a monumental one. Mr. Swenson, in his mid-50s, has end-stage renal disease. He must undergo hemodialysis three times a week, take a number of medications, and adhere to a very strict diet. In addition, he has many physical limitations.

Even before Mr. Swenson's kidney failed, the family had begun organizing around the demands of his medical condition. Severe atherosclerosis had led to the amputation of one of his legs below the knee, and was beginning to affect the other leg. During an arteriogram to investigate the severity of his circulatory impairment, Mr. Swenson went into shock and emerged from the critical episode with no kidney function. Mrs. Swenson, a talkative, efficient woman with seemingly boundless energy, added three round trips to a downtown dialysis center to a weekly routine that already included driving herself and her husband to full-time jobs every day; maintaining a large suburban home; and caring for the couple's 13-year-old son, Eric. During the preceding year she had nursed her husband through two major hospitalizations, the first time arranging to have him released to spend Thanksgiving at home, with a turkey dinner served around the hospital bed that had been set up in the living room. Despite a second hospitalization, the Swensons went forward with plans for their daughter's wedding; once again, Mrs. Swenson arranged to have her very sick husband released from the hospital long enough to give the bride away. Because he works full time, Mr. Swenson dialyzes three evenings a week. His wife drops him off at the center on the way home from work, then drives home 25 miles to have dinner with Eric, and returns at 10:30 P.M. when the dialysis session is finished. The nephrologist has told Mrs. Swenson that work is what is keeping her husband alive, so she is determined that he will continue to work.

Mr. Swenson, an intellectual man with a degree in laboratory science, catalogued the course and state of his medical condition in detail. He told the research interviewer, in a matter-of-fact manner, that he probably would not be alive at the 6-month follow-up interview. Constant pain and restricted mobility kept him from the recreational and home maintenance activities he had always enjoyed. Mr. Swenson said his son was an utter disappointment to him, had not lived up to his talents, and was always in trouble at school. The two could never talk without the father eventually berating the son for his failures.

Eric arrived an hour and a half late for the home interview, and contributed little. He was obviously put off by his father's detailing of his medical problems; he said, at one point, "Dad, you don't have to give us all the gory details."

As an ecologic approach, the family paradigm model begins by asking what these families might have in common, and then what the circumstances are that make for relatively smooth, enjoyable, and nonproblematic family life in the Dakos family but for serious difficulty in the Swenson family.

First, these two families can be understood as being similar in their underlying family paradigm. This concept is a metaphor borrowed, with considerable license, from the philosophy of science (Kuhn, 1962), but it is applied to families to emphasize the shared, unspoken, and unquestioned assumptions family members hold in common about their social environment. These are not assumptions about any particular situation, event, relationship, or circumstance; rather, they are abiding conceptions of the environment in which these discrete events are embedded. Our two brief vignettes reveal some similarities in the assumptions and world views of these two families. First, both believe in the importance of mastery—in ordinary circumstances—of their immediate environment. Not only is it important, but—again, under ordinary circumstances—it is also possible. The Dakoses believe that clever (and, I might say, at times ruthless) business practices can not only establish a highly renumerative business but also can keep that business and its profits in the family for at least two generations. In a more faltering way, we see evidence of the same thirst for mastery in Mrs. Swenson's drive to overcome the imminence of death through keeping her husband employed, even if, in an almost literal sense, it kills her. Likewise, Mr. Swenson is continuing to work at a very competitive pace until the very last days of his life. Both children, too, in their own worlds, displayed the family thirst for mastery.

A second theme also unites these families—a sense of group responsibility and solidarity. More particularly, both families see the world as expecting them to behave as a group. This assumption seems more tattered and paradoxical for the Swensons. Hostility and friction are more conspicuous there, and the family seems to be coming apart at the seams, but the basic conception of solidarity is still evident. For example, Eric can still express his anger by arriving late for a family interview; this maneuver would be ineffective in a more individualistically oriented family, where members lead their own lives and are not constrained by the assumption that the world expects them to do otherwise.

Finally, these two families appear similar in the importance they attach to intergenerational ties; or, to put it another way, they have an important sense of the family continuing across time, and a common belief that the present experience of the world must be tempered by memories of the past and anticipation of the future. For the Dakoses, this sense is vividly conveyed both by the nature of the family business and by the tight bonds between parents and grandparents. For the Swensons, at least two events speak to this issue: the extraordinary efforts that Mrs. Swenson exerted to hold her daughter's wedding, and the preservation of the family ritual of Thanksgiving dinner. Indeed, the past was not to be a victim of the present but, instead, provided familiar ritual experiences through which the pain of the present could be filtered.

In contrast to the Dakoses, however, the Swenson family seems beset by rancor, overdevotion, belittling, pathologic behavior, and rigidity mixed with a sense of isolation and impending defeat. An ecologic approach, though not insensitive to these differences, maintains its primary focus on the family situation fit for both families. Two differences are striking: First, the difference in the severity of the challenges facing the two families, and, second, major differences in the social environments in which they are embedded. The Dakoses face the ordinary and expectable developmental challenges of a midlife family: father reassessing his role in his business, mother contemplating the empty nest, all three children making important transitions. For these transitions, both the family history and the cultural community provide a rich and detailed script to help the family anticipate the problems of these transitions and elaborate coping strategies to deal with them.

The Swensons are another matter altogether. They face a unique challenge in dealing with a debilitating illness, with the added stress of ambiguity—Mr. Swenson's life is maintained entirely by a machine. Moreover, the family's primary community now is the medical one, which is acting in a paradoxically disruptive way. The doctor, speaking on behalf of this community, unwittingly rallies the family around its own flag. The instruction is to get the family organized, appealing to its already well-developed solidarity, to keep Mr. Swenson at work, and hence alive. This last appeals also to the family's already well-developed thirst for mastery. In fact, however, these instructions are a recipe for disaster. Overfocusing on Mr. Swenson's illness means that other family needs (e.g., Eric's needs) are being sacrificed. Moreover, falsely securing the family's sense of potential mastery over the illness means that the seeds are sown for feelings of bitter disappointment and self-doubt when the illness inevitably worsens.

I have suggested that the underlying paradigm of the Dakos and Swenson families is similar, and I have used this example to emphasize that families with similar paradigms may be both troubled and untroubled. As an ecologic approach, however, the paradigm model has sought to discriminate sensitively among different kinds of family paradigms. Indeed, paradigms can be thought of as almost infinite in their variety. For simplicity's sake, however, a finite number of dimensions is necessary to study this variety, and its consequences, systematically. Thus far, paradigm theory has identified three dimensions, although there are probably more.

Configuration expresses the degree of patterning and lawfulness the family perceives in its environment. It reflects the degree to which the family believes there are stable, discoverable, noncapricious laws that underlie the crucial phenomena in their experienced world. Both the Swensons' and the Dakoses' paradigm would be judged high on this dimension. We see a purer picture in the Dakos family: evidence of mastery not only of the business world, but of their ethnic community as well. The same belief system operates for the Swensons, but in a more poignant, if not tragic, sense. They are hanging on, quite literally for dear life to a sense that they can control the inexorable progression of Mr. Swenson's illness.

Coordination refers to the family's conception of how it is regarded by the social environment. Families that are high on this dimension are convinced the world sees them as a group: What one member does reflects equally on all the rest. Firm, dense connectedness among family members is both a consequence and a cause of this conception. Again, the Swenson and Dakos families are both high on this dimension. Both families also illustrate that the dimension of coordination is not to be confused with such similar-sounding dimensions as "cohesion," which are heavily weighted by lack of conflict, of anger, of arguments, of conflicting perspectives, and so forth. There is plenty of anger in both families, and, in the Swenson family, there is complaining, undercutting, protest, and even minor rebellion as well. The dimension of coordination, in contrast to Olson's "cohesion," refers to a set of standards that determine the causes of conflict, how it is expressed, and the ways in which it should be resolved. Thus, because the Swensons are a high-coordinated family, Eric's failure to make his family look good is a major source of conflict with his father. For Eric, coming late to a family interview is an effective expression of rebellion. There is strong family pressure to resolve or suppress conflicts so that everyone can pull together—and can be seen as pulling together by the outside world.

Closure refers to the balance between openness to new experience (delayed closure), and being dominated by tradition (early closure). Again, both families would be high on this dimension, but not as high as others. We have already pointed out ways in which both families filter present experience through intense ties to the past; current experience is not entirely novel, fresh, or unprecedented, but has a familiar ring or seems evocative of significant past or recurrent events.

We have sketched some of the basic concepts of paradigm theory. We will, in the remaining sections, provide data to answer four questions:

1. What is the evidence for the existence of family paradigms, and the three principal dimensions by which they are distinguished?

2. Is there evidence of specific challenges or situations being worse for families with one kind of paradigm than for those with other kinds?
3. In what ways do families with different paradigms elaborate different coping styles?
4. Are there different consequences, following failure-to-cope, for families with differing paradigms?

The first question, of course, is intrinsic to paradigm theory itself; the last three questions are ones to be posed by any model within the ecologic approach.

EVIDENCE FOR THE FAMILY PARADIGM

Entirely by happenstance, an eccentric laboratory problem-solving method called the "card-sort procedure" has emerged as a good estimate of aspects of the family paradigm. While our group is exploring a number of other approaches to assessing a family's paradigm, the card-sort procedure remains the most thoroughly investigated effort to operationalize the concept of paradigm. The card-sort procedure asks each member to sit in an isolated booth in contact with other members by a telephone-like device. Each member is asked to sort one deck of cards as an individual and a second deck in concert with his or her family. Each card contains a patterned sequence of symbols. The procedure permits measurement of the subtlety of pattern a family recognizes in the symbols of the cards, the degree to which they work together in the second phase of the task, and the degree to which—either as individuals or as a family group—they change their sorting schemes as new evidence becomes available.

As detailed elsewhere (Reiss, 1981), this procedure was developed for entirely different purposes: to explore the relationship between family interaction and the thought disorder of schizophrenic patients. In the course of early work, it was discovered that most families regularly developed "mistaken" conceptions about what the researcher expected of them. Usually this was expressed in the family's "misunderstanding" of experimental instructions. These misunderstandings, however, turned out to be a gold mine in disguise. For example, all the members of one family regularly misheard the researcher as instructing them that they must agree on all phases of the task's solution, although no such instruction was ever given. This family turned out to be terrified of the whole research procedure, which they viewed as a covert effort to split and thereby humiliate the family. Their misunderstanding served to enforce family cohesiveness in the face of this perceived threat. Our group hypothesized that all families had their own intensely personal views of what the research staff was really up to. Even those who trusted the staff seemed to do so on the basis of their own convictions; there was hardly enough adequate information available to the family for them to test systematically the trustworthiness of the staff. The critical notion was that these misunderstandings, which expressed the family's subjective view of the research project, were vividly portrayed by their task performance, performance that was easy to measure with precision. An intriguing possibility, still being pursued 15 years later, is that these perceptions of the research staff by the family are not unique to the research situation, but express latent tendencies in the family for construing idiosyncratically all novel or ambiguous circumstances.

This possibility has been pursued in several steps. First, it was important to know if the procedure did yield several dimensions or clusters of behavior that, on their face, seemed to express theoretically sensible dimensions of paradigm. This, in fact, has been a repeated finding in our group (Oliveri & Reiss, 1981) and in a brief version of the task conducted in Israel (Shulman & Klein, 1982). The pattern-recognizing behavior seems to reflect configuration, the shared pacing reflects coordination, and the ability to respond to new information reflects (delayed) closure. These dimensions are unrelated to intelligence, education, social class, family size (Oliveri & Reiss, 1981), a wide variety of individual perceptual styles (Reiss & Oliveri, 1983b), and several personality measures such as Hogan's measure of empathy and Rotter's internal locus of control scale (unpublished data). Taken together these data suggest that the card-sorting procedure measures at least three dimensions that are not simply reflections of individual members' skills or some major social or family structural variables: coordination, closure, and configuration.

Second, it was important to know whether these dimensions did reflect aspects of the family's experience of its personal world. This question is particularly pressing, since the underlying social process being measured refers to a deep, emotional, subjective experience, but the procedure on the surface appears to be measuring cognitive processes and information processing. Three studies addressed this. A projective test—requiring the family to arrange figures of a family, strangers, and geometric figures—suggested that in the card sort, configuration did indeed express a sense of comfort and mastery, and (delayed) closure did reflect openness to experience (Oliveri & Reiss, 1982). A second study assessed how subject families perceived other families in a therapeutic multiple-family group (Reiss, Costell, Jones, & Berkman, 1980). Card-sorting configuration was correlated with a detailed and subtle grasp, by the subject families, of the dynamics of relationships within the other families. Coordination was correlated with a shared view, by all members of these families. A third study measured the family's view of an inpatient psychiatric service into which an adolescent member had recently been admitted (Costell, Reiss, Berkman, & Jones, 1981). Configuration on the card sort predicted the subtlety of the family's perception of emotional details in the ward's social system, and coordination predicted the similarity of the family's conception—subtle or coarse—of the social system.

Third, it was important to know that dimensions of paradigm are distinct from similar-sounding but conceptually distinct dimensions. This is, in other terms, a matter of discriminant validity. For example, we have already stated that coordination reflects an underlying belief that the social environment expects the family to behave as a group. To be logically and empirically precise, this is not the same as saying that the family has no conflict, disagreement, dissent, or fighting. Thus, as a way of probing further the empirical validity of the basic dimensions of paradigm, it is important they they do not correlate with certain other variables. We have already mentioned the importance of distinguishing Olson's concept of "cohesion" (Chapter 6, this volume) from our concept of coordination. For the same reason it is important, for example, to distinguish coordination from "conflict" as measured by Moos and Moos (1976). Likewise, Olson has a formulated concept of "adaptability." At its extremes, this latter dimension is designed to distinguish between families that are pathologically rigid and never change their rules of response patterns, no matter what the situation, and those families that are always in chaos, changing capriciously and on impulse. Our dimension of closure is aimed at a very different distinction: families who are absorbed by their own traditions versus families who are deeply embedded in the richness and novelty of fresh experiences. This is an important difference in style, not a distinction between two forms of pathology. To date, we have reported two studies addressing these questions. The first compared a small sample of families in their performance on the card-sort procedure and on the Moos Family Environment Scale (Oliveri & Reiss, 1984). The second (Sigafoos, Reiss, Rich, & Douglas, 1985) did a similar comparison of the card-sort procedure and the Olson FACES (Family Adaptability and Cohesion Evaluation Scales) procedure, which is the best measure of "cohesion" and "adaptability." Both studies showed no significant correlations between any of the three paradigm dimensions on the one hand, and any of the dimensions on either the Family Environment Scales or on FACES on the other.

Fourth, it was important to inquire about the stability of families' performance on our three dimensions. The paradigm model argues that the three dimensions assess an enduring style of pattern of family experience. Hence, under most circumstances we would expect family performance to be stable. In one study, we measured family performance on the card sort at two intervals separated by 6 to 7 months. As the strictest test of durability of response styles, we used two alternative forms of the card sort in a randomized, counterbalanced fashion. Pearsonian correlations from time 1 to time 2 were .72 ($p < .0001$) for configuration; .86 ($p < .0001$) for coordination; and .43 ($p < .04$) for closure. These statistics probably underestimate the underlying stability. Since all families have some experience with the test situation by time 2, we cannot expect them to behave as if the test is an entirely fresh experience. We did, in fact, observe that some families that showed delayed closure on time 1 showed early closure on time 2 (we did not observe the reverse); it was as if these delayed-closure families were saying, ''Oh, we've seen a puzzle very similar to this one just 6 months ago. This time we needn't keep ourselves in suspense for the whole task.''

Fifth, having established many of the properties of family behavior of this kind in the laboratory, it is important to know what its implications are for families in the ordinary setting in which they live. In other words, can a laboratory analysis of behavior—and particularly the subjective experience that lies behind it—help us understand the dilemmas of ordinary family life? The next sections of this chapter will present a few examples, from a much larger corpus of work to answer this question.

THE FIT BETWEEN FAMILY AND SITUATION

As mentioned previously an ecologic model focuses on the fit between families of a particular type and situations of a particular type. No family is regarded as uniformly or consistently pathologic or healthy. Rather, some families find certain challenges much more difficult than others. This perspective leads naturally to two closely related questions. First, how should we classify or describe settings in ways that are most useful for understanding family functions? Second, once we have at least a sketch for an approach of this sort, what types of families do best in some situations but more poorly in others? Let us consider each of these questions in turn.

Describing Situations

The example of the Dakoses and the Swensons helps us begin our analysis. Note that there are two very different kinds of situations that are crucial to understanding and comparing these two families. In the broadest possible terms, the first kind of situation may be termed a ''challenge.'' Perfectly serviceable synonyms here are ''stressors,'' ''life events,'' and ''predicaments.'' Challenges may either rise up within the family or be externally imposed from without; most are probably both. In the simplest sense, the Dakoses are dealing with a range of developmentally expectable challenges of midlife in the parents, and those of adolescence and young adulthood in the children. In sharp contrast, the Swensons are dealing with a severe, chronic illness that is not ordinarily expected in the course of development (although we have seen a number of families with a history of severe illness in the past who almost seem to expect lightning to strike a second time).

The summaries of these two families also provide us examples of another kind of situation, which we may call a "setting," although "social community," "support network," and "social environment" are all serviceable alternatives. In general, challenges are delineated, delimited, preemptory experiences that require some sort of discrete or specifiable acknowledgment from the family. Settings, as the word implies, may also make demands on the family, but these demands are more subtle background requirements rather than specific and delimited requirements for response.

CHALLENGES

In our first attempts in this area, our team sought to begin with some very broad distinctions among challenges to families. First, we have been concerned with the magnitude of the challenges families face. Intuitively, the Swensons are facing challenges of greater magnitude than the Dakos family. Second, we have sought to assess the externality of challenges—whether they arise within the family and are, in fact, products of the family's own processes or, in contrast, are thrust on the family from the outside. On the surface, at least, the Dakoses and the Swensons differ as well: The Dakoses are dealing with problems that are engendered, in part, through their own developmental progress, whereas the Swensons' life is dominated by an illness over which they have little or no control. The distinctions here, of course, cannot be too tightly drawn, as even our two examples make plain. For example, part of the developmental problems facing the Dakoses arise from how the family is perceived in the Greek community. Likewise, we cannot be sure that family process played no role in the evolution or maintenance of Mr. Swenson's illness.

In beginning work in this area, the paradigm perspective has been particularly helpful. Most attempts to measure stressful challenges to families have foundered on a serious logical problem (see, e.g., reviews by Hansen & Johnson, 1979, and McCubbin, Joy, Cauble, Comeau, Patterson, & Needle, 1980). A stressful challenge, according to all these approaches, must ultimately be defined only by its impact on the family. That is, we have no way of anticipating whether or not an event constitutes a stressful or major challenge for a particular family until that event occurs and we can ask them about it and watch their response to it. This is a obvious predicament: It gives us no way to distinguish the family's response to a challenge from the challenge itself. The paradigm approach offers a way out of this difficulty. Following from the work by Goffman (1974), and utilizing the basic conceptual tools of paradigm theory, Reiss and Oliveri (1983b) proposed that social communities (e.g., hospital communities, professional or workplace communities, or neighborhood communities) provide a frame for understanding the meaning and potential threat in virtually any event or circumstance. For example, the work of Scotch (1963) showed that traditional Zulu communities regarded childbirth as a nonstressful blessing demonstrating a woman's fertility in a traditional culture in which fertility was highly valued. In sharp contrast, urban Zulus were threatened by childbirth, since it increased considerably the strain on their marginal capacities to adjust to a strange new world.

Not only does the community provide a frame for judging the threat in any event, it also provides a frame of expectations for each family of what coping, if any, they are responsible for in responding to the event. For example, the communal healing rights of the traditional Navajo clarify that it is the community's, not the family's, responsibility to support and heal the physically ill. In an effort to explore this hypothesis about stress empirically, Reiss and Oliveri (1983b) studied a group of 48 families from a homogeneous suburban community, and found very high agreement among them in their rating of the threat to families inherent in a large list of events and in the family's accountability for each event. The very high levels of agreement suggested that there was, indeed, a common community frame for evaluating events.

SETTING

Our initial approach to the analysis of settings has taken an analogous turn. So far, we have been concerned with three kinds of settings: (1) communities, including neighborhoods and other residential settings; (2) organizations, including hospitals and places of employment; and (3) the characteristics of the extended kin, considering the family's relatives as an important parallel between families and these larger social groups. The larger social groupings can also be distinguished by their shared conceptions of reality. To illustrate, I will review only a small portion of our work here.

In one study, we asked whether it would be possible to identify paradigm-like structures in psychiatric hospitals. Following from the work of Silverman (1970), we decided to call such a hypothetical structure an "organizational objective." For the life of the organization, we posit that the organizational objective is the analogue to the family paradigm. All organizations have tasks and, in a broad sense, a product. At its core, an organization is structured by the shared definitions among its members of what precisely that task might be. Close inspection of variations among organizations as to how the task is conceived will provide clues to variations in organizational structure, values, and the interaction patterns among their members.

Reiss, Costell, and Almond (1976) carried out such a study of two psychiatric hospitals. They gave virtually all patients and staff a detailed questionnaire that sought to delineate each respondent's conception of what mental illness 'really is,'' and what, as a consequence, the fundamental task of the organization (i.e., the organizational objective) should be.

From this work, two major dimensions, orthogonal to each other, emerged that can distinguish among organizational objectives. The first is called *belief in the technical order.* Psychiatric hospitals can be organized around the belief that mental illness is a breakdown in a complex, discoverable mechanism, which may be neurochemical, psychologic, or both. The fundamental premise, however, is that this mechanism is discoverable by properly trained experts, and that, as research progresses, defects in the mechanism can be treated, also by competently trained professionals. Somatotherapy and psychotherapy, administered by highly trained professionals, then become the treatments of choice, and the hospital is organized to place these therapies at the center. Its practitioners (usually physicians) are given the most authority and prestige; the rest of the staff and patients are subordinated in a relatively hierarchical arrangement.

A contrasting dimension, called *belief in the moral order,* reflects a view that mental illness arises first and foremost from a breakdown in human relationships, not a failure of some arcane mechanism. At its core, the concept is moral: People have an intrinsic, unquestionable importance to one another. This is not an object of research but a universal given of experience. In this view, "sociotherapy" (which would include some forms of family therapy, but not all forms) is the treatment of choice. The primary qualification for the practice of this form of therapy is personal openness, warmth, and a capacity to engage others—skills that do not reside uniquely in certified professionals, but may be possessed by a broad variety of professional staff, as well as by patients themselves. Psychiatric hospitals high on this dimension are not hierarchically organized. There is a dedifferentiation of authority levels, as expressed, in extreme form, in the therapeutic community.

These two dimensions, which describe the differences among organizations, have clear conceptual relationships to dimensions of the pardigm: Belief in the technical order is a parallel to configuration; belief in the moral order is similar to coordination. Paradigm theory has proposed that these dimensions may predict a good or poor fit between an institution and a family. Thus, we hypothesize that a low-coordination family entering a high-coordination psychiatric hospital may feel as estranged as an immigrating family in a strange culture.

Fitting Family to Situation

This is a new area of study for our team, and we are only starting to exploit some of the distinctions among settings described in the previous section. Let me give some examples from completed studies to illustrate rather surprising findings when one takes the fit between family and setting into account. A particularly interesting example is a pair of studies each of which, in part, sought to explore the adaptive advantages of high coordination. In other words, we asked: What is the value to a family of being high in coordination, and does this "value" depend on the family's situation—its challenges and setting? We have already anticipated these findings in the introduction to this chapter.

In the first study we examined prospectively how families adjusted to a psychiatric inpatient service after the hospitalization of an adolescent for severe psychiatric difficulties. The inpatient service we studied focused on treatment of the whole family. We examined adjustment from a variety of perspectives: the family's subjective feelings of comfort in the ward community, the quality of their relationships with staff and other families, and the nature of their internal interaction patterns (Costell, Reiss, Berkman, & Jones, 1981; Reiss, Costell, Jones, & Berkman, 1980). In this study we found that high coordination predicted very successful adaptation by families. For example, high-coordination families attended therapy sessions (consisting for the most part of large and small multiple-family groups) more regularly; were liked more by other families; participated in therapeutic sessions more actively; felt more more involved; and experienced less danger in the full range of their interactions with staff, other families, and patients.

A second study produced very contrasting results for coordination (Reiss *et al.*, 1986). In this study, we prospectively observed families facing a very different sort of challenge in a very different setting. Rather than the relatively time-limited crisis of a psychiatric hospitalization, the families in this study faced year after year of an unremitting chronic illness—end-stage renal disease—of the type and severity that the Swensons faced. Also, in contrast to the psychiatric inpatient service, which fostered growth and development in the whole family, the major setting was a medical one in which only the patient's needs were recognized. Faced with this challenge and in this setting, high-coordination families had a much more malignant course. The most important of our findings in this study was that the duration of patient survival was actually *shorter* in high-coordination families. Our data suggested a mechanism: high-coordination families, just like the Swensons, may overfocus on the illness. By a series of steps, this stress ultimately leads to severe strains in the family relationships, and to an early death for the already vulnerable patient.

This pair of studies does not constitute a perfectly controlled experiment. For example, the families in the psychiatric study were not the same (except for coordination) as those in the dialysis study. Moreover, we cannot delineate sharply what the differences were in the situations they faced. We have pointed to two differences—the nature of the challenge, and the therapeutic setting in which it was faced—but there are probably many others. Nonetheless, these data are an interesting suggestion of what the ecologic approach can provide. As is often the case, more data are urgently needed.

SPECIFIC FAMILIES AND SPECIFIC RESPONSES

Our work in this area is just beginning. Nonetheless, some of our first findings are intriguing, and gave some hint of the prospects for work here.

The analysis of differences among situations faced by families is a useful point of departure for our analysis. Recall that we drew one very broad distinction between delineated, preemptory challenges and more long-term, subtle, and background factors in which the family is embedded: Each of these two different situations may be thought of as leading to different kinds of responses or stances in the family. Challenges require some form of specific response ranging from, at least, passive acknowledgement to active, tactically effective strategies. All of these may be grouped together as *coping responses*. In contrast, settings do not necessarily lead to any specific responses or even to acknowledgment, nor can they be ignored. Rather, over time, the family develops a pattern of experience and behavior that is shaped by the setting and, in turn, actively shapes the setting as well. We may call these sutble, long-term family processes *adaptation patterns*.

We are in the midst of a study on the relationship between family paradigm and family coping. Following from the work of Dewey (1910), Brim (1962), Argyris (1965a, 1965b), and Aldous (1971), and within a frame suggested by paradigm theory, we proposed that a family's response to any event or circumstance may be divided into three phases. First, the family defines the event and searches for additional information: Is the event routine or problematic? Is it the family's fault, or does it come from outside? Does the family have a responsibility to deal with the event? Then the family makes an initial response and/or fashions several trial solutions. Finally, the family comes to a closing position: If the event had been conspicuous, this process includes the integration of the event and the family's responses to the event into the family's conception of its own history. These shared memories of the family's response to stress may serve as a guide for future action. These phases may overlap and can occur in any order.

Paradigm theory has proposed that a family's coping responses to challenges are determined by its cognitive and emotional appraisal of the event or circumstance, of the efficacy of its own responses, and of the relationship of the event to the family's conception of its own development (Reiss & Oliveri, 1980). This process of appraisal is similar to those we have already described as shaped by a family's paradigm. Thus, the three dimensions of paradigm—configuration, coordination, and closure—should each determine how the family copes in each of the three phases of their response.

For example, families high in configuration, we hypothesize, will feel a sense of volition, confidence, and potential mastery in ambiguous situations—including stressful ones. They are likely to own up to their responsibility to deal with most stressful events on the basis of conviction that the family, through its own efforts, can master them. With this basic objective, they will vigilantly search for information; initiate may trial solutions; and, once they have coped with the event, take credit for their own success. This leads to an enrichment of the family's conception of its own vigor, imaginativeness, and competence. Families high in coordination will, in the first phase, see the event as relevant for their members. In these families, members will quickly integrate their own coping efforts with those of others, and consensus will loom large in the family's closing position. Finally, delayed-closure families will, in the initial phase, focus on current experience rather than using the past as an orientation. They will continually develop new repertoires of responses to crisis rather than depend on previous patterns. Integrating their experiences of stress will lead to change in their conceptions of themselves, in contrast to early-closure families, which see in their response to stress a confirmation of their previous conceptions about themselves.

We have begun to explore this model empirically. We have already shown that it is possible to use standardized, structured family interviews to reconstruct, in detail, the three phases of the family's response to a stressful event. Coders can identify reliably the kinds of coping responses we proposed. Finally, on a completely blind basis, it has been possible to determine post hoc some of the details of the family's coping response on the basis of their detailed reports of how they coped with a stressful life event. For example, high-configuration families became more fully engaged in actual coping responses, more thoroughly organized themselves as a group, altered their responses based on new information, and regarded their efforts to cope with a difficult event as an experience from which they learned something valuable.

We have also begun work on delineating longer term adaptational responses of families. Here, in our first efforts, we have found that families are more active than we expected. They not only respond more actively to the social settings in which they find themselves, but they also actively shape those settings to conform to their own particular needs. We found this level of activity in a surprising place: our studies of kinship networks of families.

On first thought, a family's kinship system—its size, diversity, and interconnectedness—should be a given for any nuclear family; that is, a nuclear family cannot choose its kinship system. Rather, at best, it must put up with what it has. We found, however, that, although families cannot refashion their own kin in major ways, they do vary a great deal in how they attach themselves to kin. In effect, the family seems to create its own kinship world by attaching itself to only a portion of available blood relatives. We focused on three dimensions describing this variation: (1) the breadth and diversity of kinfolk with whom members of the same nuclear families had important ties; (2) the extent to which members of the nuclear family formed strong ties to the same (or different) kin; and (3) the extent to which a nuclear family formed close ties with that part of its kinship system where kinfolk were closely bound together or, conversely, were emotionally isolated from one another. Variation along these three dimensions was closely linked to the three dimensions of paradigm. For example, families whose paradigm showed delayed closure, suggesting an openness to a breadth of experience, had a greater breadth and diversity of ties to kinfolk (often, for example, choosing kin from both maternal and paternal wings of the family). Reiss and Oliveri (1983a) presented data that supported a reciprocal mechanism in these ties: Families with a particular paradigm form ties consistent with that paradigm, but these ties serve to reinforce or stabilize the paradigm itself. Thus, delayed-closure families pick a broad and diverse set of kinfolk with whom to have important relationships, and this diversity and breadth, in turn, sustain the delayed-closure characteristics of their paradigm.

THE FAILURE OF COPING AND ADDITIONAL PATTERNS

When the full range of coping and adaptational patterns fail, are there specific consequences for specific families? In many ways, this is the most interesting and important of the four major questions we have posed in our chapter. As an ecologic approach, paradigm theory emphasizes that when families fail to cope adequately with particular challenges, and when their adaptational patterns no longer fit with their settings, they will show signs both of disorganization and of severely painful and dysfunctional efforts to overcome that disorganization. More than that, paradigm theory would suggest that particular families would display particular forms of disorganization and overcompensation and, further, that a knowledge of the family's paradigm could predict, in part, the special characteristics of family distress. We have already presented a fragment of data to suggest that this sequence might be true. We have seen how high-coordination families get into trouble when faced with the challenges of chronic illness; we have suggested (although the data are by no means clear) that they may overfocus on the illness to the exclusion of other family needs.

Unfortunately, despite the importance of this question, I cannot report any solid findings in response to it. It is, however, the most active area of investigation by our group. Currently, we are engaged in several studies of a variety of severe, chronic illnesses in both adults and adolescents and in a longitudinal study of the family's response to residential relocation following a major natural disaster. These studies are guided by two major hypotheses, which I will state here, very briefly, as a way of anticipating future directions in our work.

The first hypothesis concerns the levels of stages of family disorganization. Paradigm theory points to three levels. In each stage the family attempts to deal with the challenges and problem settings that besiege it. In addition, the family must deal with the internal conflicts, alienation, dissension, scapegoating, and deceptions that have been fueled by its prior difficulties in coping with both challenges and settings. If the family's efforts fail, then it falls back to a lower stage where, again, there is a mixture of both distress and efforts at coping. This hypothesis has been outlined in more detail elsewhere (Reiss, 1981; Reiss & Klein, 1987), and therefore I will only summarize it here.

The three hypothesized stages are as follows.

1. *The emergence of rules:* Where stress is chronic, and the family's initial coping strategies are unsuccessful, the coping strategies themselves begin to harden. Behaviors that once were flexible and responsive to the demands of the challenge or the setting now become more entrenched and established; they become constraints that each member places on the other. For example, early in the course of dealing with Mr. Swenson's illness, his wife, with his consent, established a rule that Eric must fix breakfast for himself; initially, this was an effort to cope with the pressures of getting Mr. Swenson to work. Later, however, it became rigid, so that Eric's occasional failure to fix himself breakfast was perceived by both parents as a traitorous act.

2. *The explicit family:* When rules coalesce, they become an explicit, constraining, and oppressive expression of the family's underlying perspective or paradigm.

3. *Rebellion and action:* This stage follows inexorably from the last. If the family cannot right itself, then either someone rebels or someone is excluded. This final stage was reached by the Swensons. At first it was Eric who was excluded. The process here was the familiar one of scapegoating; it was Eric who, as the family perceived it, could not live up to what had become, in the stage of the explicit family, a grotesque caricature of family standards. Both parents expressed their disappointment in him, and he responded with a broad range of behavior and school problems. Later, we think, Mr. Swenson himself was excluded by quite a different process. Date from our study of renal patients (Reiss *et al.*, 1986) suggests that as a final coping effort, severely distressed families undergo a major realignment. The well members become more highly invested in each other while, at the same time, the ill member withdraws emotionally. In emotional terms, the sick member leaves the family as the healthy members draw a new boundary around themselves. We suspect that this is a psychosocial mechanism that contributes to death in these patients.

A second hypothesis is even more speculative. We have wondered if families with different pardigms take different paths through the stages of family disorganization. For example, the Dakos family is marked by a respect for its own family traditions (witness the intense ties between the generations). This sense of binding to tradition is what we think early closure expresses in families (although the data are far from conclusive here).

We wonder whether, if the Dakoses must confront major challenges or a significant interruption in the family unit's relation with its setting, intergenerational conflict will then come to the foreground. We have already suggested, in considering the Swenson family, how high coordination and high configuration might, under severe stress, become specific liabilities. The overfocusing on the illness and the belief in mastery were central to this family's distress.

CONCLUSION

I have presented the outlines of an ecologic approach to families. First, I described the core concept of the family's paradigm and presented evidence for its role in family life. Second, I described some concepts and evidence to show how a theory of family paradigms could account for specific fits between a family, on the one hand, and the challenges and settings it must encounter in its everyday life on the other. Third, I presented evidence that specific families—those with particular paradigms—elaborate different types of coping and adaptational responses when faced with challenges of everyday life. Finally, I speculated on the consequences—for families with different paradigms—when coping fails. The specific theory of paradigms, and the ecologic perspective it represents, is far from proven fact. Both more research and more clinical experience are necessary before the theory can be regarded as established empirically. Nonetheless, as ideas about family process, and ideas about the practice of medicine come together—and this book is the best example of that to date—I am hopeful that this perspective on family life may accomplish three things. First, it will enhance clinicians' appreciation of the pluralism of family life: Families are remarkably different, and need to be regarded as such. Second, I hope it will deemphasize the clinicians' thirst to find pathology, not only in the body's organs but in families themselves; families are more remarkable for their ability to cope with a broad variety of challenges, including serious illness, than they are for their pathology. Finally, I hope this perspective contributes to the planning of interventions for families who clearly need help. Specifically, paradigm theory argues that families differ remarkably in their goals, standards, and qualities of relationships. Paradigm theory gives the clinician specific, measurable dimensions to clarify some of these differences. There is no one "normal" family toward which all interventions should be aimed. Rather, treatment must be tailored to return each family to its own version of normality and comfort. In terms of the theory I have proposed, where necessary, the clinician must help the family to repossess its own paradigm so that it is no longer external and projected as a caricature, but it can once again be held inside the family as an implicit, ineffable, unspeaking guide to the family's experience and behavior.

References

Aldous J. A framework for the analysis of family problem solving. In: Aldous J, Condon T, Hill R, Strauss M, Tallman I, eds. Family problem solving: a symposium on theoretical, methodological and substantive concerns. Hinsdale, Ill.: Dryden, 1971:128–135.

Argyris C. Explorations in interpersonal competence I. Journal of Applied Behavioral Science 1965a; 1:58–83.

Argyris C. Explorations in interpersonal competence II. Journal of Applied Behavioral Science 1965b; 1:147–177.

Brim OG. Personality and decision processes studies in the social psychology of thinking. Palo Alto, Calif.: Standford University Press, 1962.

Costell R, Reiss D, Berkman H, Jones C. The family meets the hospital: predicting the family's perception of the treatment program from its problem solving style. Archives of General Psychiatry 1981; 38:569–577.

Dewey J. How we think. New York: Heath, 1910.

Goffman E. Frame analysis. Cambridge, Mass: Harvard University Press, 1974.

Hansen DH, Johnson VA. Rethinking family stress theory: definitional aspects. In: Burr WR, Hill R, Nye FI, Reiss IL, eds. Contemporary theories about the family. New York: Free Press, 1979:582–603.

Hess R, Handel G. Family worlds. Chicago: University of Chicago Press, 1959.

Kantor D, Lehr W. Inside the family. San Francisco: Jossey-Bass, 1975.

Kuhn TS. The structure of scientific revolutions. Chicago: University of Chicago Press, 1962.

McCubbin HI, Joy CB, Cauble AE, Comeau JK, Patterson JM, Needle RH. Family stress and coping: a decade review. Journal of Marriage and the Family 1980; 42:855–871.

Moos RH, Moos BA. A typology of family social environments. Family Process 1976; 15:357–371.

Oliveri ME, Reiss D. A theory based empirical classification of family problem solving behavior. Family Process 1981; 20:409–418.

Oliveri ME, Reiss D. Families' schemata of social relationships. Family Process 1982; 21:295–311.

Oliveri ME, Reiss D. Family concepts and their measurements: things are seldom what they seem. Family Process 1984; 23:33–48.

Reiss D. The family's construction of reality. Cambridge, Mass: Harvard University Press, 1981.

Reiss D, Costell R, Almond R. Personal needs, values and technical preferences in the psychiatric hospital: a replicated study. Archives of General Psychiatry 1976; 23:795–804.

Reiss D, Costell R, Jones C, Berkman H. The family meets the hospital: a laboratory forecast of the encounter. Archives of General Psychiatry 1980; 37:141–154.

Reiss D, Gonzalez S, Kramer N. Family process, chronic illness and death: on the weakness of strong bonds. Archives of General Psychiatry 1986; 43:795–804.

Reiss D, Klein D. Paradigm and pathogenesis: a family-centered approach to problems of etiology and treatment of psychiatric disorders. In: Jacob T, ed. Family interaction and psychopathology: theories, methods and findings. New York: Plenum Publishing 1987:203–252.

Reiss D, Oliveri ME. Family paradigm and family coping: a proposal for linking the family's intrinsic adaptive capacities to its responses to stress. Family Relations 1980; 29:431–444.

Reiss E, Oliveri ME. The family's construction of social reality and its ties to its kin network: an exploration of causal direction. Journal of Marriage and the Family 1983a; 45:81–91.

Reiss D, Oliveri ME. Sensory experience and family process: perceptual styles tend to run in but not necessarily run families. Family Process 1983b; 22:289–308.

Scotch NA. Sociocultural factors in the epidemiology of Zulu hypertension. American Journal of Public Health 1963; 53:1205–1213.

Shulman S, Klein MM. The family and adolescence: a conceptual and experimental approach. Journal of Adolescence 1982; 5:219–234.

Sigafoos A, Reiss D, Rich J, Douglas E. Pragmatics in the measurement of family functioning: an interpretive framework for methodology. Family Process 1985; 24:189–203.

Silverman D. The theory of organizations. New York: Basic Books, 1970.

Strodtbeck FL. Family interaction, values and achievement. In: McClelland DC, Baldwin AL, Bronfenbrenner U, eds. Talent and society. Princeton, N.J.: D. Van Nostrand, 1958:85–101.

9

Clinical Implications of Oscillation Theory: Family Development and the Process of Change

DOUGLAS C. BREUNLIN
Institute for Juvenile Research, Chicago

Family therapists effect change by altering context. Although this fundamental axiom has remained fairly constant since family therapy's inception some 30 years ago, the assumptions underpinning both the process of change and the definition of context to be altered have constantly evolved. During these three decades, the emphasis given to family development as a necessary component of context has varied considerably. Initially, family therapists completely failed to recognize the role played by family development in the formation and maintenance of symptoms. Then, in the 1970s, nearly all family therapy models adopted a view of context that relied heavily on family development. More recently, new theories of family functioning have emerged that challenge the relevance of family development.

I believe that family development should still be viewed as a vital component of context, but there currently exists no theory of family development that is compatible with current views of family functioning. In this chapter, I will propose that oscillation theory (Breunlin, 1981, 1982, 1988) serves as a clinically relevant theory of family development that is compatible with contemporary theories of family functioning, and, hence, can be used as a framework to enable family therapists to effect change by altering context.

IN SEARCH OF A DEVELOPMENTAL MODEL FOR FAMILY THERAPY

Family therapy began in the 1950s where individual therapy left off—with a view that clinical problems are caused by pathology. Family therapists simply replaced individual pathology with family pathology, giving birth to concepts such as the "double bind" (Bateson, Jackson, Haley, & Weakland, 1956), "schism" and "skew" (Lidz, Cornelison, Fleck, & Terry, 1957), "contagious affect" (Ackerman, 1966), and "perverse triangle" (Haley, 1967). To effect change, it was deemed necessary to redress the pathology in the family context. Family development played little or no role in these formulations.

In the 1970s, through a more sophisticated application of systems theory, a number of family therapy models emerged, each offering a theory of family functioning that specified the relevant component of context to be changed. Hence, Minuchin (1974) specified structure; Haley (1976), organizational sequences; the Mental Research Institute (MRI) (Watzlawick, Weakland, & Fisch, 1974), attempted solutions; and Bowen (1978), triangles. These models relied heavily on the systems theory concept of "homeostasis," which purports that a system maintains its stability by returning to a steady-state condition when it is disturbed. The family was described as an error-activated, self-correcting homeostatic system regulated by negative feedback (Dell, 1982). A symptom, it was argued, serves as a homeostatic mechanism by appearing whenever a disturbed family's delicate balance is threatened with change. Such homeostatic mechanisms resulted in system rigidity, making it impossible for a family to produce alternative behaviors in the service of change.

To produce change, family therapists attempted to override the system's homeostasis by introducing positive feedback to create a deviation-amplifying process that would force the system to exceed its usual threshold (Hoffman, 1971). Therapy was viewed as a crisis induction, and families were viewed as changing only after they had been shifted off their homeostasis with powerful interventions. Minuchin, for instance, described the use of intensity to "exceed the family's threshold of deafness" (Minuchin, 1974); and paradox, particularly symptom prescription, came to be viewed as an accepted way to introduce a system runaway (Hoffman, 1976, 1981).

Speer (1970) and Haley (1981), among others, questioned the wisdom of using a theory purporting to explain how systems do *not* change as a basis for a therapy intended to promote change. To address this concern, the concept of "morphogenesis" was introduced to further explain how families change (Speer, 1970). Families, it was argued, possess two states: a homeostatic (or morphostatic) state that characterizes stability, and a morphogenic state that characterizes change. Therapy was said to access the family's morphogenic state, enabling positive rather than negative feedback to be introduced into the system and thereby producing change. This view, however, had the same clinical implications insofar as the intent of therapy was to trigger a family from a stable state to a state of change.

Two 1973 publications proposed that a model of family development, which came to be known as the family life cycle, also be considered a relevant component of context (Haley, 1973; Solomon, 1973). This stage transition model of the life cycle argued that symptoms emerge when a family experiences difficulty in making a transition from one stage of the life cycle to the next. For each stage, families must master a set of tasks that are specific to that stage. A transition signals the need for change in the family, enabling it to leave a previous stage to begin negotiating the tasks of the next stage. Transitions correspond to points of nodal change, involving primarily changes in family composition, such as birth, marriage, leaving home, and death, but also major shifts in autonomy, such as going to school, entering adolescence, and retirement. Henceforth, I will refer to such transitions as "nodal" transitions. A transition threatens a family if the subsequent stage implies disastrous consequences (e.g., the last child leaving home), or if the family functions rigidly in the existing stage. A symptom enables the family to stabilize in the present stage and thereby avoid the transition.

The stage transition model of the life cycle fit well with prevailing views of family functioning based on homeostasis. Faced with a threatening transition, a family could develop a symptom that then served as a homeostatic mechanism that rigidified the family in the pretransition stage and prevented the transition. Therapy, therefore, was still geared toward disrupting the family homeostasis, but with a view toward forcing the family to negotiate the failed transition in order to allow it to continue developing.

The family life cycle was an enormously important contribution to the field of family therapy because it provided a conceptualization that enabled the field to transcend the pathological views that originally organized thinking about context. Clearly, symptoms generated by the family's inability to negotiate the transitions of the life cycle were more easily and hopefully resolved than were those produced by family pathology. The stage transition model of the life cycle was incorporated as a relevant component of context by nearly all the major models of family therapy (Carter & McGoldrick, 1980; Haley, 1973, 1976, 1981; Minuchin, 1974; Watzlawick *et al.*, 1974).

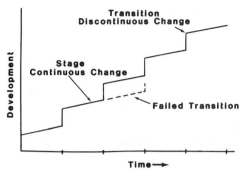

Figure 9-1. The MRI theory of change applied to the stage transition model of the family life cycle.

During the 1970s, the clinical application of the family life cycle was advanced considerably by juxtaposing the stage transition model of the life cycle with the MRI theory of change (Watzlawick *et al.,* 1974). The MRI group argued that there are two types of change: first-order change, which is gradual and continuous and within the current rules of a system; and second-order change, which is abrupt and discontinuous and involves a change in the rules of the system. First order change, it is argued, is quantitative, whereas second-order change is qualitative. The marriage between the MRI concept of change and the family life cycle seemed ideal. Hughes, Berger, and Wright (1978) argued that during a stage when specific tasks are being mastered, first-order change is involved, whereas a transition requires a fundamental change in the family (in terms of rules, structure patterns, etc.) and, therefore, necessitates second-order change.

Expressing family development as a function of time, the curve that results from applying the MRI theory of change to the life cycle would be a step function, as depicted in Figure 9-1 (Breunlin, 1988). This curve, though seldom depicted graphically, became the organizing metaphor for how life cycle transitions are made, and also for how therapeutic change takes place in general. The clinical hypothesis derived from this curve could be stated as follows: Families with symptoms are rigidly stuck at points of transition; therefore, the therapist must intervene to create second-order change that will enable the family to make a discontinuous leap to a new organization and a subsequent stage of development.

During the past decade, the widely accepted model of family functioning based on the view of a family maintaining stability through homeostasis and change through morphogenesis has been questioned. Keeney (1983), for instance, applied second-order cybernetics to family functioning and concluded:

> The potential problem with this view is that it too easily depicts change and stability as a dualism of polar opposites. Families are described as either change-oriented, homeostatic, or a balanced combination of these distinct processes. This division is simply not a cybernetic view. One cannot, in cybernetics, separate stability from change—both are complementary sides of a systemic coin. Cybernetics proposes that change cannot be found without a roof of stability over its head. Similarly, stability will always be rooted to underlying processes of change. (p. 70)

With a second-order cybernetic view, the therapist does not shift the family from a homeostatic to a morphogenic state but, rather, addresses the patterns of change by which a family maintains stability.

The stage transition model of the family life cycle that blended so well with the homeostatic model of family functioning does not fit well with this cybernetic view of family functioning. Hence, what is needed now is a theory of family development that is compatible with the current cybernetic view of family functioning. Such a theory would address the following: (1) how families change while remaining stable as they develop; (2) how symptoms can emerge and be maintained as a result of this developmental process; and (3) how family therapy can produce change by altering context, including the developmental process. I am proposing that oscillation theory serve as a starting point for creating such a clinically applicable theory of family development.

OSCILLATION THEORY AND FAMILY DEVELOPMENT

In a family there exists a recursive relationship between the development of individual members and family development. As each family member develops, he or she increases the potential to possess additional competence that can be used in the service of increasing the flexibility and complexity of the family. But for that potential to be realized, the family must be able to accommodate and nurture constantly the new competence. Hence, a family must constantly change in response to the development of its members while still maintaining an overall stability that enables it to preserve its identity. When development is progressing well, individual and family competence recursively foster each other.

The stage transition model argues that at nodal transitions a family either does or does not accommodate the development. If it does not, then no change takes place. If it does, then a discontinuous leap is made to a higher level of functioning. I believe that a family accommodates to development not in this step function manner but, rather, through an *oscillation* between levels of functioning, as shown in Figure 9-2. A family cannot *not* make a transition. It can only accommodate to it in a more or less successful manner. The oscillation represents the family's inevitable attempt to accommodate to change while remaining stable. In normal families, oscillations appear and then dampen, with each oscillation producing an increment in developmental competence for the individual and additional complexity for the family. In symptomatic families, rather than dampening, the oscillation stabilizes and becomes a part of the family's pattern of interaction. Subsequent accommodations to development are, therefore, made in relation to an existing oscillation, with the likelihood that these accommodations will intensify rather than dampen the oscillation. Although the family is still changing, the accommodation between individual and family development fails to work well. The oscillation limits rather than increases the

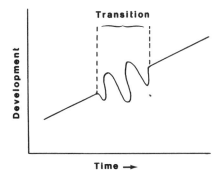

Figure 9-2. An oscillation in the developmental process.

complexity of the family; and the family, in turn, is less able to accommodate subsequent development. In such a context, the identified patient's behavior oscillates between less than and greater than expected competence. Symptoms emerge and are maintained as a function of this oscillation. The task of the family therapist is to alter the context by dampening the oscillation, thereby restoring both individual and family development.

To arrive at an operational model of oscillation theory that is clinically applicable, I will next describe how I arrived at competence as a useful variable to specify what changes as a family develops, and describe in detail how oscillations emerge in the developmental process.

What Changes

Oscillation theory proposes that it is the competence of each family member that changes over the course of the life cycle, thus enabling a family to develop by becoming increasingly differentiated and complex. Competence is broadly defined as the ability to behave in a manner appropriate for one's age, potential, and culture. One may question whether competence is sufficient to provide the relevant information about a developing family system. Just as the presenting problem is often used as a point of entry to obtain information about the leverage in a complex family system, so also does the level of behavioral competence of the identified patient serve the same function with regard to family development.

The relationship between individual behavior and the family is defined by family sequences that regulate these behaviors (Haley, 1976). The total pattern of a family is composed of a myriad of such sequences, many of which regulate levels of behavioral competence (Breunlin & Schwartz, 1986). Such family variables as structure and rules are nothing more than midlevel constructs (Sluzki, 1983) that are inferred from sequences. They cannot, of themselves, be operationalized except through observations of behavior. I believe that it is preferable, therefore, to use behavioral competence as the operational variable for what changes as a family develops, recognizing that all aspects of competence are regulated by sequences, and that these sequences in turn allow us to infer any midlevel construct associated with family functioning. A more complete discussion of competence can be found elsewhere (Breunlin, 1988).

How Oscillations Emerge

At any point in time, the level of complexity of a family is defined by a pattern of interlocking sequences that regulates the competence of all family members. Each developmental increment, dictated by biology or the demands of socialization, necessitates a change in the associated sequences such that competence is regulated from its present level to a higher level (Terkelson, 1980). Development necessitates that competence changes throughout the life cycle, and not only at nodal transitions. Terkelson (1980) noted that "even very small incremental developments can produce surprisingly widespread perturbations in family structure" (p. 35). For example, a small child learns to be apart from a parent when the parent leaves the child for progressively longer periods of time. This allows the parents more time to relate to each other and to do other things. I refer to the process by which a competence behavior is regulated to a different level through change in the sequences regulating it as a "microtransition."

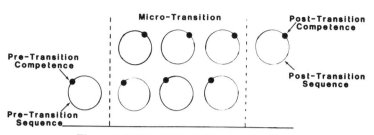

Figure 9-3. The process of a microtransition.

A microtransition, then, consists of a period of time during which both sequences and their associated levels of competence exist simultaneously such that an oscillation exists between the two sequences and the two levels of competence. For instance, when a child first walks, walking does not abruptly replace crawling in a discontinuous fashion. Rather, the child sometimes walks (and frequently falls) and sometimes crawls. Likewise, during the microtransition, family sequences that regulate crawling/walking exist simultaneously. Sometimes the parents offer a hand or encourage and praise the child for walking; at other times it is more convenient for the parents if the child crawls. The oscillation persists until sequences that regulate walking predominate and crawling is abandoned. The process of a microtransition depicted in Figure 9-3 is very similar to the three phases of developmental change described by Terkelson (1980).

In every family there is a myriad of competence behaviors that must change as various family members grow and develop. For children, these behaviors include such diverse activities as relating to adults, playing, coming and going from home, sleeping, doing chores, toileting, and doing their schoolwork. For adults, they include interacting with children, spouses, home, friends, and work.

With oscillation theory, the distinction between a stage and a transition is dropped in favor of the concept of a microtransition. Family development is viewed as relentless, with significant microtransitions always taking place. At points of nodal transition, the process is similar but intensified because the number of microtransitions clustered at a given time is greatly increased. These microtransitions involve sequences that regulate existing competence to higher levels as well as those that generate newly required competence. When a child starts school, for instance, sequences that regulate existing behaviors, such as getting up, going to bed, dressing, and leaving a parent, must all change in the direction of higher levels of competence. New sequences must also emerge that regulate behaviors newly acquired for school, such as going to and coming from a strange place.

Behaviors, however, are not automatically regulated at an appropriate level of competence. The microtransition may involve one of three outcomes:

1. The sequence may continue to regulate behavior at a pretransition level of competence, such that what may once have been an appropriate level of competence becomes, over time, less than competent.
2. The sequence may regulate behavior at a level of competence that exceeds what is appropriate.
3. The sequence may regulate competence at an appropriate level.

A microtransition, therefore, may result in a too low, too high, or appropriate level of competence for a particular behavior.

For example, as a child grows older, his or her competence about safety should become increasingly complex. For a small child with little competence about safety, the parents rightly make almost all decisions to the point of child-proofing the house. A 7-year-old possesses more competence and should be allowed more decisions—for instance, deciding when it is safe to cross a street. Older adolescents should possess the competence to make decisions about safety in complex social situations, such as driving while dating. If a child is 7 and the parents continue to make all decisions about safety, the outcome of microtransitions around safety will produce less than competent behavior, whereas if the parents allow the 7-year-old to enter into situations where an adolescent's competence about safety is required, the outcome is likely to be greater than competent behavior. Finally, parents may correctly assess what safety decisions a 7-year-old can handle, and thus regulate competence at an appropriate level.

When a microtransition results in a sequence regulating behavior at a less than or greater than competent level, the potential for an oscillation emerges. With each successive microtransition, the family then searches for an accommodation in a context that includes a less than or greater than competent behavior. The result is likely to be further less than or greater than competent behaviors, and an emerging oscillation. For example, a child with an illness may be legitimately limited in some areas of competence, but if the illness organizes the parents to be protective, microtransitions around developmental issues that need not be affected by the illness may result in clusters of less than competent behaviors. The child, on the other hand, may react to his accommodation by attempting to act in a greater than competent manner, thus pushing the oscillation in the other direction. The potential for an oscillation is realized when a significant number of microtransitions produce outcomes of less than or greater than competent behavior, and the oscillation becomes detectable. Detectable oscillations are most likely to occur at nodal transitions because of the large number of microtransitions clustered at such times, but they may also arise from other stressful events, such as chronic illness, or gradually, over time, as successive microtransitions fail to regulate behavior at an age-appropriate level of competence.

Once a detectable oscillation is produced, it can become a stable part of the family's total pattern. It will continue to evolve and change any subsequent microtransitions that occur, but it will not easily dampen. The oscillation then becomes a part of the family belief system. We often hear parents say, in effect, "Our son is 2 going on 22, and we don't know what to do about it."

Although the terms "less than competent" and "greater than competent" are not commonly used in the literature and are a bit awkward, I have selected them because they are neutral and do not reflect a deficit-based view of behavior. Moreover, the terms, connected as they are to sequences, are context-specific and, therefore, are not to be viewed as traits. If the sequences change, the level of competence will change.

Such terms as "immature," "developmentally delayed," or "regressed" suggest, but are not synonymous with, less than competent behavior because these terms generally refer to a presentation of self that is pervasive and not easily changed, whereas less than competent behavior refers to a context-specific act wherein an individual at a given age behaves as if he or she is less than competent because such a behavior is the logical outcome of the sequence by which it is regulated.

Although it is easy to see how a microtransition that results in less than competent behavior will adversely affect family development, one may rightly question whether an outcome of greater than competent behavior is problematic. It may be argued that there is no such thing as too much competence—reading three grades above grade level is better than reading at grade level. I believe, however, that in symptomatic families, the identified patient almost always exhibits some behaviors that are too competent for his or her age. For example, a 6-year-old latchkey child who lets himself or herself into the house after school in order to allow a single parent to work longer hours is acting in a greater than competent way.

In the field of family therapy, a number of concepts describe greater than competent behavior. The term "incongruous hierarchy" (Madanes, 1981) suggests that at one level a child is higher in the hierarchy than the parents. The violation of a generational boundary (Minuchin, 1974) suggests that a child is allowed to share inappropriately in the world of adults. The term "parental child" (Minuchin, 1974) suggests that a child, by acting as a parent, is behaving in a greater than competent manner. Finally, the function of a symptom suggests that a behavior somehow serves to protect the family. I would suggest that any time a child behaves in a symptomatic way in order to protect the family, that child is acting in a greater than competent manner.

Of course, in any pattern of oscillation, appropriate levels of competence can also be detected. These behaviors are quite important because they signal the potential for a family to negotiate microtransitions in a manner that does not produce oscillations. These areas of appropriate competence point toward individual and family strengths and often serve as a starting point for dampening the oscillation.

It is theoretically possible that microtransitions only result in sequences regulating competence at one extreme or the other, but my clinical experience suggests this rarely happens. Even when a child presents with an apparently pervasive set of less than competent behaviors, the family has usually organized around these behaviors in a way that produces an incongruous hierarchy or results in symptoms that serve a protective function. Hence, there exists greater than competent behavior. When microtransitions consistently regulate behavior in the direction of greater than competent behavior, the individual usually compensates by also finding ways in which to act less than competently or by exhibiting a symptom that metaphorically expresses less than competent behavior. For instance, an adolescent who acts much older than her age may be enuretic. The following clinical vignette is a typical example of oscillation between extremes of less than and greater than competent behavior.

> A pediatrician requested a family consultation for a case of abdominal pain in a 13-year-old girl. She was seen with her parents, who complained about the girl's immaturity: She wouldn't help at home, performed poorly at school, and had few friends. When she failed to get her way, she had temper tantrums. The parents reported the girl was the youngest of 14 children. The girl was large for her age, appearing to be 16 or 17. She also wore a dress that seemed too old for her. When the consultant inquired about the dress, the mother said it belonged to the girl's 30-year-old sister. When asked why she wore her sister's clothes, the father replied that he encouraged her to wear the dress, hoping that she would learn to act more like her sister. Of course, the clothes put her age at 30 when in fact the girl was only 13. In this case, the clothing and appearance combined with the less than competent behaviors established the oscillation. Further exploration revealed both parents to be ill and unable to provide consistent care for the girl. It was as though they were saying, "We've already raised 13 children. Please hurry and grow up because we're afraid we can't go the distance with you, the 14th."

CLINICAL APPLICATION

Oscillation theory hypothesizes that symptoms arise as a result of a family's attempt to accommodate to developmental demands by regulating behavior at inappropriate levels of competence. Through the microtransitioning process sequences regulate significant numbers of less than and greater than competent behaviors such that a detectable oscillation exists. The symptom may appear as a metaphor for the oscillation, as an attempted solution, or as a manifestation of one of its extremes.

The basic clinical hypothesis is quite simple: *Since a symptom is maintained by an oscillation, interventions must be targeted to dampen and eliminate the oscillation, thereby eliminating the symptom and restoring normal development.*

For any theory to be clinically applicable, it should guide the therapeutic process in four ways. First, it should specify the relevant information to be gathered in the assessment process. Second, it should provide a redefinition of the problem in interactional and solvable terms. Third, it should suggest a plan of action for producing change. Fourth, it should define parameters for recognizing change during the course of therapy, and for establishing a successful outcome.

Assessment

The goal of assessment is to detect an oscillation in the developmental process. In my experience, oscillations in clinical families are easily detected. At the therapist's disposal are an enormous wealth of immediate data obtained from in-session observations and out-of-session reports. The therapist looks for short sequences regulating competence, behavioral indicators of competence, and metaphorical expressions of oscillations. Perhaps the most powerful and succinct evidence of an oscillation is conveyed through metaphor. For instance, a 10-year-old may be dressed like a teenager yet answer the therapist in a whining, insecure voice.

Information about the time of onset and persistence of an oscillation is useful because it can orient the therapist to the severity of the problem and guide the choice of intervention. If the oscillation is of recent origin and caused by the sequence-generating events of a nodal transition, or if it appears to involve a small number of competence-regulating sequences, the interventions may be quite straightforward. If, however, an oscillation has lasted for a number of years and has persisted through several nodal transitions, or if the number of competence-regulating sequences at the greater than and less than competent level are many, then the problem is more severe and interventions must be carefully selected. Moreover, in such cases the oscillation, having persisted for some time, gives rise to real deficiencies in behavioral competencies such as social skills and academic performance. For instance, an adolescent whose presenting problem is school-related may have spent years in a behavior disorders class and thus may possess language skills that are several grades below grade level. Such an adolescent is often terrified at the prospect of having to function in a regular class. The interventions, therefore, must take into account the fact that the adolescent can't read, and fears the success (or failure) of moving to a regular class.

The following vignette provides an example of how a therapist use the assessment process to detect an oscillation.[1]

> A 6-year-old girl was referred for enuresis and encopresis. Her status as a first-grader, and the correspondence of symptom onset with the birth of the 2-year-old sister, served as strong evidence that the symptoms were related to at least two nodal transitions. The following sequences, observed in the first interview, enabled the therapist to hypothesize how less than competent behavior had emerged from microtransitions associated with the birth of the sister.

While the mother held the sister on her lap, the 6-year-old sat alone and somewhat separate. At one point, the girl moved closer to her sister and, in an age-appropriate way, began to play patsy with her. Then she attempted to take the sister off the mother's lap. When she reached for the sister, the mother pushed the girl and then gave a bottle to the sister. Simultaneously, the girl began to suck her thumb. The outcome of this sequence, then, was to regulate the girl's behavior at a less than competent level. One could hypothesize that the mother accommodated to the birth of the second child by continuing to treat her older daughter as a baby. This excluded the girl, who was distanced from her mother and left with little option but to continue to act like a baby. The mother described additional sequences that confirmed less than competent behavior. She never let the girl play outdoors and rarely expected her to help around the house. At one point she said, "At home, it's just me and the two babies."

Later in the interview, the mother also described her efforts to secure employment. Each day she looked for work without success. She returned home frustrated, and engaged her daughter in conversations about her search for employment. This sequence required greater than competent behavior from the girl and resulted in the girl feeling somehow part of the mother's quest for work, but unable to make any contribution. Indeed, she couldn't even help out by acting her age.

There existed, therefore, an oscillation, with the daughter sucking her thumb, whining, and acting less than competently in many ways, but also functioning in an adult way with regard to the mother's employment. The symptoms of enuresis and encopresis could be viewed as a metaphor for less than competent behavior, but also as a stressful outcome of the greater than competent behavior.

Problem Redefinition

Having detected an oscillation, the therapist confirms its existence using the language of the family, and then reframes the symptoms as a manifestation of an oscillation. Developmental reframing has been used often by family therapists (Coopersmith, 1981; Minuchin & Fishman, 1981) and is now afforded additional theoretical backing by oscillation theory. The basic message is: Your child's problem arises because he or she sometimes acts too old and sometimes too young. When he or she learns to act his or her age consistently, the problem will be solved.

In cases where the parents have no previous explanation for symptoms, this type of redefinition is usually far preferable to one that conveys madness or badness. It reduces fear that the child is defective, and does not appear to blame the parents. Families are less likely to accept the reframing, however, if they have an investment in an alternative (and usually medical) explanation. Biochemical explanations accompanying the diagnosis of schizophrenia or neurologic explanations for hyperactivity are but two examples. The difficulty is compounded if the medical explanations have been reinforced by long-standing contact with an institution whose experts adopt that view. A child whose parents have attended staffings at a behavior disorders school for years may have been convinced by the experts that their child's less than competent behavior has a neurologic base. In such instances, the therapist must move more slowly and gain the trust of the family before a reframing is attempted.

When the family staunchly adheres to its medical explanation, the therapist can define the illness as part of the context, and then state that even with an illness, the child should still be expected to live up to his or her potential. Once the parents accept the problem redefinition, they can be included as part of the solution: Therapy will help them find ways for their child to act his or her age.

Dampening the Oscillation

Theoretically, an oscillation can be dampened by arresting either one of the extremes of greater than or less than competent behavior. Arresting one extreme sometimes eliminates the other, but in more severe oscillations interventions must be targeted to both extremes. This is particularly true when interventions target greater than competent behavior that serves a protective function. The identified patient may then give up the primary symptom only to remain handicapped by less than competent behaviors. Any treatment that fails to address the associated less than competent behavior in this context is likely to fail. In fact, many treatment failures occur in cases where chronic oscillations of this sort exist.

Having assessed the severity of the problem in terms of the chronicity and intensity of the oscillation, four options exist:

1. Increase the number of sequences regulating appropriate levels of competence.
2. Make direct requests to change sequences that regulate less than or greater than competent behavior.
2. Paradoxically encourage less than competent behaviors and/or their associated sequences.
4. Paradoxically encourage greater than competent behaviors and/or their associated sequences.

The option chosen depends somewhat on the initial assessment and the preference of the therapist. Interventions selected from the models of family therapy may be used appropriately for a given option.

1. *Increase the number of sequences regulating appropriate levels of competence.* If the family is motivated, the number of sequences involved in the oscillation are limited, and the oscillations appear to be of recent origin almost any intervention is likely to work. Many one-session cures are the result of a judiciously targeted intervention designed to interrupt a budding oscillation. In such cases there is little need to employ elaborate or paradoxical interventions. All the therapist needs to do is help the family accommodate to developmental changes by making microtransitions in a manner that produces appropriate levels of competence. Straightforward education, such as telling a parent to give a child more or less responsibility or even simply to give the child more sleep, can work. Social learning theory can also be used effectively where contingency contracts reinforce appropriate levels of competence. When a sufficient number of sequences regulate competence at an appropriate level, their preponderance will eliminate the oscillation and dictate normal development.

2. *Make direct requests to change sequences that regulate less than or greater than competent behaviors.* If an oscillation is well established but the family appears motivated and well engaged in therapy, this option may be most successful. For this option to work, the parents not only must accept the problem redefinition but must also buy the logic that their child can and should act his or her age. In this approach, the family is challenged directly to change behavior by changing the associated sequences. Structural family therapy interventions such as enactment, unbalancing, and working complementarity can be used during the session to produce altered sequences that eliminate less than or greater than competent behaviors (Minuchin & Fishman, 1981). Likewise, direct strategic interventions, such as giving tasks, can be assigned between sessions to continue to dampen the

oscillation (Haley, 1976; Madanes, 1981). The intervention may involve the whole family, the parents, the identified patient, or the sibling subsystems.

Using this option, it is particularly helpful to initiate change by challenging the identified patient to act competently. This process is initiated when the therapist treats the identified patient in a manner that elicits competence. Once the patient is well joined, the therapist can also challenge the patient to reject parental behaviors that keep the patient young. Minuchin (Minuchin & Fishman, 1981) is a master at eliciting statements from children intended to convince parents that they wish to be treated their age. In the vignette, for instance, the daughter was challenged to convince her mother that she wanted a relationship with her younger sister. As a result, the two were allowed to play together successfully in the session. The therapist may also challenge a child's perception that the parents need protection; or, if the child is a worrier, the parents may be told to convince the child that they, and not the child, will worry for the family. As sequences that regulate less than or greater than competent behavior change, the oscillation will begin to dampen and the symptoms will remit.

3. *Paradoxically encourage less than competent behaviors.* When the family accepts the problem redefinition, but believes that less than competent behavior is outside the child's control, paradoxical interventions are in order. If the family is well engaged and compliant with the therapist's directives, compliance-based symptom prescription can be used (Rohrbach, Tennen, Press, & White, 1981). Using compliance-based interventions, the therapist encourages the parents to continue to treat the child as younger, with the expectation that they will attempt to comply but will find it very difficult to do so. The less than competent behavior can be scheduled for certain times or places. For instance, the parents may instruct a 10-year-old to have temper tantrums in a temper tantrum room (Hare-Mustin, 1975). Using the pretend techniques of Madanes (1981), a child can also be asked to pretend to act in a less than competent manner.

If the family is highly reactant to the therapy, and likely to oppose the therapist's directives, defiance-based strategies can be used (Rohrbach *et al.*, 1981). Parents may be instructed to encourage their child to act young, with an expectation that they will then do the opposite. Defiance-based strategies are particularly successful when directed toward children. Most children, although they may act young, do not like to be designated as such. For example, a therapist may say to a child, "You are not ready to act your age, you should continue to have your problem. . . ." The child's response is likely to be defiance, with the less than competent behavior replaced by more appropriate behavior.

Paradoxical strategies are most useful to demonstrate that at least one less than competent behavior can be changed. Following this initial change, parents often become more invested in therapy and open to an oscillation view of symptoms. The therapist may then choose to restrain the family from becoming too optimistic, or shift to option 2.

4. *Paradoxically encourage greater than competent behaviors.* The criteria for this option are essentially the same as for option 3, with the addition that greater than competent behavior also serves a protective function for the family, and sometimes even appears essential for the family's survival. For example, an adolescent may parent his younger siblings and protect his mother from an alcoholic father. In such cases, the greater than competent behavior represents a sacrifice of normal development. For the adolescent to give up that behavior, the family context must change dramatically.

Systemic prescriptions are very effective in such cases. By defining greater than competent behavior as a necessary sacrifice on behalf of the entire family, the therapist prescribes it, hoping the family will reorganize without it. If this is successful, the behavior will be abandoned and the identified patient will have a chance to grow up properly.

Unfortunately, many users of systemic prescriptions do not go beyond the initial prescription, believing instead that the family should be allowed to reorganize in its own way. This view ignores the fact that the greater than competent behavior is always part of an oscillation that also includes less than competent behavior. This is particularly the case when an oscillation has persisted through several nodal transitions. A young adult may, for instance, abandon a long-standing role of protecting her parents' marriage only to find that she lacks the skills to function independently. Therapy, therefore, must also provide support to enable the patient to function competently in the adult world.

Read the Feedback and Define Success

Regardless of the option selected for intervention, the therapist must determine whether change is occurring. The feedback should include evidence that the oscillation is beginning to dampen. This can be determined from direct observation of and reports about the patient's behavior. When the patient behaves more consistently with an appropriate level of competence, and extremes of less than and/or greater than competent behavior become less frequent, the therapist can conclude that the oscillation is dampening. As the oscillation dampens, the family will also evidence a different accommodation to individual developmental issues, and individual and family development will once again recursively foster each other. During this process, the presenting problems or symptoms will remit, sometimes spontaneously, sometimes gradually. Remission of the problem may signal a sudden end to an oscillation, but in some cases therapy must continue beyond symptom removal if the oscillation is to be truly dampened. Sometimes, a small shift in behavior will enable a family to accommodate to developmental issues in a manner that is dramatically different and does not involve an oscillation. At other times, the oscillation dampens gradually as interventions systematically target long-standing less than and greater than competent behaviors. The therapist needs to hold the family long enough to assess that the family's patterns of accommodating to change are changing, but not so long that therapy becomes a stable part of that pattern.

A family's efforts to remain stable while constantly changing and accommodating to the development of its members will never be easy. There is no cure for development. The therapist can only hope to part company when the family has a sense that it can successfully accommodate to the constant need for change. Not all cases are successful. Sometimes the price a family must pay to relinquish an oscillation may appear to one or more members to be prohibitively high. It may appear that, for one person to be competent, another person must be sacrified. The compromise reached by the family is partial incompetence for all. The result is a persisting oscillation, with no one exercising appropriate competence.

CONCLUSION

Oscillation theory has several strengths that commend it for clinical application. First, it is dervied from direct observation of family development and does not require the juxtaposition of a separate theory to account for change. Second, oscillation theory has the flexibility to analyze development at the level of detail essential to formulate a useful clinical picture. Sometimes a simple metaphor is sufficient to define the oscillation, whereas in other cases considerable detail may be needed. Third, oscillation theory, by postulating swings between less than and greater than competent behaviors, affords a coherent explanation for many of the inconsistencies often apparent in clinical families. Fourth, oscillation theory draws a distinction between acute and chronic problems: Acute problems are associated with a recent onset of a detectable oscillation; chronic problems are maintained by oscillations that have persisted for some time and generally through more than one nodal transition. Finally, oscillation theory can explain failure and relapse. Unless an oscillation is dampened successfully, symptoms may not remit, or may remit only temporarily and then return as a function of a recurrent oscillation.

Note

1. The therapist in this case was Stephen Christian-Michaels. The supervisor was Howard A. Liddle.

References

Ackerman NW. Treating the troubled family. New York: Basic Books, 1966.
Bateson G, Jackson D, Haley J, Weakland J. Toward a theory of schizophrenia. Behavioral Science 1956; 1:251–264.
Bowen M. Family therapy in clinical practice. New York: Jason Aronson, 1978.
Breunlin DC. Panel on the family life cycle. With: Falicov C, Schnitman D, Hoffman L, Sluzki C, Breunlin D, McGoldrick M. Meeting of the American Orthopsychiatry Association, New York, 1981.
Breunlin DC. Clinical dimensions of the family life cycle. Presented at the annual conference of the American Association for Marriage and Family Therapy, Dallas, 1982.
Breunlin DC. Oscillation theory and family development. In: Falicov C, ed. Family transitions: continuity and change over the life cycle. New York: Guilford Press, 1988.
Breunlin DC, Schwartz RC. Sequences: toward a common denominator of family therapy. Family Process 1986; 25:67–87.
Carter EA, McGoldrick M. The family life cycle: a framework for family therapy. New York: Gardner Press, 1980.
Coppersmith EI. Developmental reframing: he's not bad, he's not mad, he's just young. Journal of Strategic and Systemic Therapies 1981; 1:1–7.
Dell P. Beyond homeostasis: toward a concept of coherence. Family Process 1982; 21:21–41.
Haley J. Toward a theory of pathological systems. In: Zuk G, Nagy I, eds. Family therapy and disturbed families. Palo Alto, Calif.: Science and Behavior Books, 1967:11–27.
Haley J. Uncommon therapy: the psychiatric techniques of Milton Erickson. New York: Norton, 1973.
Haley J. Problem solving therapy. San Francisco: Jossey-Bass, 1976.
Haley J. Leaving home: the therapy of disturbed young people. New York: McGraw-Hill, 1981.
Hare-Mustin R. Treatment of temper tantrums by paradoxical intervention. Family Process 1975; 14:481–486.
Hoffman L. Deviation-amplifying processes in natural groups. In: Haley J, ed. Changing families: a family therapy reader. New York: Grune & Stratton, 1971:285–311.
Hoffman L. Breaking the homeostatic cycle. In: Guerin P, ed. Family therapy theory and practice. New York: Gardner Press, 1976:501–519.
Hoffman L. Foundations of family therapy. New York: Basic Books, 1981.
Hughes S, Berger M, Wright L. The family life cycle and clinical intervention. Journal of Marriage and Family Counseling 1978; 4:33–40.
Keeney B. Aesthetics of change. New York: Guilford Press, 1983.
Lidz T, Cornelison AR, Fleck S, Terry D. The intrafamilial environment of schizophrenic patients: II. Marital schism and marital skew. American Journal of Psychiatry 1957; 114:241–248.
Madanes C. Strategic family therapy. San Francisco: Jossey-Bass, 1981.
Minuchin S. Families and family therapy. Cambridge, Mass.: Harvard University Press, 1974.
Minuchin S, Fishman C. Family therapy techniques. Cambridge, Mass. Harvard University Press, 1981.

Rohrbach M, Tennen H, Press S, White L. Compliance, defiance and therapeutic paradox: guidelines for strategic use of paradoxical interventions. American Journal of Orthopsychiatry 1981; 51:454–467.

Sluzki C. Process, structure and world views: toward an integrated view of systemic models in family therapy. Family Process 1983; 22:469–476.

Solomon M. A developmental conceptual premise for family therapy. Family Process 1973; 12:179–188.

Speer DC. Family systems: morphostasis and morphogenesis, or, ''is homeostasis enough?'' Family Process 1970; 9:259–278.

Terkelson K. Toward a theory of the family life cycle. In: Carter EA, McGoldrick M, eds. The family life cycle. New York: Gardner Press, 1980:21–52.

Watzlawick P, Weakland J, Fisch R. Change: principles of problem formation and problem resolution. New York: Norton, 1974.

10

Critical Issues in Family Theory in Family Medicine Research

LISA C. BAKER
University of Oklahoma

This chapter is an assessment of theory, or how we think about families and illness and how we conceptualize our particular research questions. In spite of a sizable body of literature, theory in this area suffers from: (1) a simplistic and romanticized view of the family; (2) muddled thinking about the terms "health" and "illness"; and (3) an unawareness of the theoretical traditions which we build, which results in shallow thinking and impeded progress. The first section of this chapter offers historical and demographic evidence that challenges common notions about the family. The second section raises issues about the concepts of family health and illness along with the relationship between illness in the family system and in the individual's body. The third section discusses traditions of family theory that are relevant for family medicine research, focusing on family sociology and on systems theory and cybernetics. Within family sociology, five conceptual frameworks will be highlighted, with references to the five theories to be discussed in the chapters that follow. Some attention will be given to sorting through the labyrinth of terms and distinctions that characterize scientific writing about theory. Having examined these points, we may be in a position to suggest some steps to take so that the field can move ahead at the best pace possible.

AN ADEQUATE VIEW OF THE FAMILY

American families today are dealing with circumstances that are absolutely new. The continual increase in human life span means that married couples can expect to have many healthy years together after their children are grown and their working years completed. Paradoxically, never has marriage been so fragile because of its foundation on companionship instead of economic survival. Never have there been more single people living alone without the immediate economic and social matrix of a family. For the first time, sexuality and parenthood can be separate issues because of the widespread use of effective contraception. Major changes like these are overshadowed by a still more astonishing fact: All cultures have struggled with scarce resources and threats to their survival, but ours is the first to have the capability and even the probability of destroying the planet.

In the face of bewildering change and intractable problems, the political and social efforts of today are aimed in part at trying to reinstate the "good old days" when life supposedly was better. As participants in the culture, family medicine researchers are subject to the same tendency. The problem is that the families we study have little in common with what Goode (1963) has labeled "the classical family of Western nostalgia." Whether the referent for the good old days is an idyllic preindustrial group of extended kin, or some later version—the "Father Knows Best" family of the 1950s—neither is a true picture of our social reality today. The romanticized image is a kin network with the heritage of an agricultural past in which parents marry once and for always, sex roles are distinct and traditional, the extended family is congenial and available, and the children are wholesome and happy contributors to the family economy. The later version moves the grandparents out of the house (although they remain close by) and decreases family size, but roles and rules remain similar.

The problem with this "ideal" family is that there is doubt as to whether it ever existed. Even if it did, it would be impossible to recreate it today. But in fact, there is little convincing evidence that things were better for families in the past.

Historical data have now soundly refuted the standard theory that the extended family was the dominant preindustrial household structure, and that the nuclear family is the product of industrializaton. Demos (1970), Greven (1970), and the Cambridge group (Laslett & Wall, 1972) have shown that the nuclear family was the dominant form even in the preindustrial period. What *is* new is the turning inward of the family. The shift has not been from extended to nuclear, but from openness to privacy (Hareven, 1982). In the past, even the conjugal family that lived apart from the extended family group had a steady stream of boarders, workers, and visitors who went in and out of the family's permeable boundaries and with whom the family shared responsibilities, resources, and an identity with the wider community.

There are also significant differences between contemporary families and the more recent ideal coming out of the post-World War II era (i.e., the "Father Knows Best" family of the 1950s). Major demographic changes have occurred that demand that researchers at least start with a definition of the family that includes many more divorced or never-married people, single parents, blended families, gay families, childless families, and dual-earner families. A number of these trends have been going on in this country since the Civil War, but using the yardstick of the post-World War II generation of parents makes it seem that the current shifts that are aberrant. The exception, however, was the temporary decrease in divorce and increase in marriage and fertility that occurred among the cohort born between 1920 and 1940—the parents of the "baby boom" generation. As Masnick and Bane (1980) put it, "Had the 1940s and 1950s not happened, today's young adults would appear to be behaving normally" (p. 2).

At present, not only is there a pluralism of family structure within our culture, but there is also more variety in any one individual's life experiences. Consider the hypothetical life history of Sue Parkerson (adapted from Cherlin, 1981). Sue lived with both parents until they divorced when she was 12 years old. When she went to college, she met and married a classmate, and they had a child 2 years later. They separated after 5 years and divorced after the birth of their second child. Sue and her children moved in with Sue's sister until Sue could get a good job. She soon met another man, who was also divorced, and they married after living together for 6 months. Their marriage lasted 21 years, until Sue's husband died of a heart attack. She lived alone for 16 more years and then moved to a nursing home where she lived until her death.

It is not unusual for a person to move from a family of origin to living alone or with someone else (of either sex), to marriage, to divorce, to a blended family, and then to divorce again, or to widowhood. The family systems associated with a life history like this one can be extremely complicated.

One final point about diversity: Cherlin (1981) has done a careful analysis of demographic data showing a sharp divergence in marriage patterns between blacks and whites since 1960, which brings into question the conventional theories about present black family structure being determined by slavery and its consequences. He reports a marked increase among blacks in a family structure characterized by a strong network of kin, but fragile ties between fathers and mothers. Changes appear to be greater among lower-class families. The proportion of black families maintained by women has increased sharply and these households have fallen further behind economically. Thus, Cherlin suggests that the lower-class black family is becoming even less integrated into the mainstream of American life than ever before.

Since family medicine research often concerns the needs of these families, it behooves us to look carefully at the normative assumptions we use when we study them. The fact is that there is no American family that is a gold standard today, except in our minds—and sometimes in our research.

CLEAR THINKING ABOUT "HEALTH" AND "ILLNESS"

Scholars (Litman, 1974; McEwan, 1974) have pointed out the ambiguity of the term "family health." It can be taken to mean the sum of the physical health statuses of the individuals in the family, or it can be used in a broader sense to mean the overall psychosocial functioning of the family, which may or may not include reference to their physical health. Since family medicine research will be done both by health care professionals, who commonly think of the former, and by social scientists, who tend to forget that people have bodies at all and refer only to the latter, it is necessary to examine more closely the use of the terms "health" and "illness." The issue is even more important when we consider the interaction between psychosocial and physical health.

In the psychosocial realm, healthy families are defined in a number of ways. One common definition is based on traditional family structure; that is, a family is healthy if it has two parents (one of each sex) who are in their first and only marriage, and two children (one of each sex). Another popular conception relies on the children's behavior. If the fruit of the tree is good, then the tree itself must be good. Thus, if children are not deviant and misbehaving, the family must be doing something right. Some would link healthy functioning with a particular life-style—one in which father is a middle-class breadwinner; mother is a homemaker; and their life in the suburbs is complete with two cars, a single-family dwelling, and various accoutrements, including processors for both words and food. Some radical feminists would say that "healthy family" is a contradiction in terms because it is impossible to find a healthy example of a structure grounded in patriarchy. The most familiar conception of health is the absence of pathology, which is often easier to specify than health. Families without violence or abuse, for example, may be considered healthy. But even the definition of pathology is hard to agree on. Is divorce unhealthy? Some would say yes, and others, no. The same would be true of homosexual families, single-parent families, and other forms that differ from the traditional norm. This brings up a favorite point of debate in family theory: that "health" may be defined differently by the family, the researcher, and society.

Partly in response to the plurality highlighted earlier, another approach to defining healthy families has focused less on membership and more on process. The chapters in this section present five theories that have emerged in this area. These theories emphasize clear communication; family rules, roles, and boundaries that are clear but not rigid; and the ability of a family to assimilate new information and adapt according to changing needs while maintaining some continuity and predictability.

For both physical and psychosocial health, context is what determines if a condition is dysfunctional. High blood pressure is a healthy sign if a woman is about to be hit by a car or if she sees smoke pouring out of her study. But if her blood pressures remains high under normal circumstances, she may be diagnosed as having hypertension. By the same token, extremely high cohesion among her family members may be adaptive if the woman is seriously injured in a car accident, but that same interaction style may become smothering after she begins rehabilitation and works her way back to independence.

The question is, then, just how we describe the relationship between health or illness in the family and in the individual's body. Our conceptualization involves a number of choices. One is whether the family will be seen primarily as the independent or the dependent variable. When viewed as the dependent variable, the family is seen as the victim that encounters a stressor (the illness) and must cope. When the family is seen as the independent variable and physical illness as the outcome, then family relationships are seen as factors that cause or exacerbate the illness. Variations on this theme are found in studies of family characteristics as they affect intervening variables in health outcomes, such as adherence to medical regimens or success in behavioral interventions (diets, smoking cessation programs, etc.).

Another choice in theory development is the question of where to generalize and where to make differentiations. For example, sometimes we generalize about biologic illness, as when we group diseases together under the term "neuromuscular diseases." Rolland (1984) has pointed out that physical illnesses, normally grouped together according to biomedical criteria such as diagnosis or treatment, may be grouped differently if we emphasize their psychosocial aspects. He suggests these categories: crisis/chronic/terminal phase; progressive/relapsing/constant; incapacitating/nonincapacitating; acute/gradual onset; and fatal/possibly fatal/nonfatal. We have yet to learn which ways of generalizing will yield what information.

We also generalize about psychosocial illness, as when we talk about the psychosomatic family model that originated from the work of Minuchin and colleagues (Minuchin, Rosman, & Baker, 1978). On other occasions, it may be more meaningful to draw contrasts. Family patterns that lead to problems with pregnancy outcome, for example, may be very different from those associated with infectious disease or chronic illness.

A third choice is whether to look for change or stability. One study might look for past family coping strategies, assuming that premorbid functioning is the best predictor of functioning during illness. A second study might assume that illness would be the impetus to alter long-time family patterns, while a third might study illness as a special case that demands situation-specific coping styles in families.

All approaches to studying families are only arbitrary punctuations of the process Weakland (1977) called "family somatics." To say they are arbitrary, however, does not mean that our distinctions are meaningless ones. How we choose to punctuate a phenomenon may be influenced by a combination of factors, including a process or outcome of interest, a method of interest, a sample of interest, or self-interest (e.g., what the funding agencies happen to be funding).

Most if not all of the research on the family in family medicine has been built on the theoretical assumption that dysfunctional family systems are associated with dysfunctional biochemical systems in the individual. The basic idea is that families and bodies are isomorphic, in part because they are overlapping systems and there is a parallelism in their status. This theory is so embedded in our thinking that it is hard even to perceive it as a theory. Yet the study of body systems and some clinical work with family systems show that one member of a system may also compensate for another. The question may become: If someone is sick and gets better, what is the cost, and who pays the price? These two ideas echo Bateson's (1958) concepts of symmetric and complementary relationships. Perhaps illness is a case of symmetric escalation of the biochemical system and the psycho-social system, both individual and family. Or illness may function in a more complementary fashion, as presented in Reiss, Gonzalez, and Kramer (1986), possibly suggesting that at times the sick person dies so the family can survive. In this study, it was the highly collaborative and consensus-oriented healthy families whose members with renal disease were more likely to die.

These thoughts about the family in changing circumstances, and models of family health and illness, require that research begin to address the following "unequivalences," to use Starfield's (1983) term:

1. The household versus the extended family
2. The common stereotypic image of families versus the demographic realities of who families are
3. Blood and marriage relationships versus the people who function daily as the family
4. A family poor in material resources versus a family that functions poorly
5. The perception of the family by family members versus its perception by outsiders
6. Family health defined as the sum of individual health states of the members versus family psychosocial functioning that promotes well-being of the group and its members

TRADITIONS OF FAMILY THEORY RELEVANT FOR FAMILY MEDICINE RESEARCH

The study of the family is, like family medicine, an interdisciplinary field, and as such draws its theories from many sources. There are what might be called "theoretical vantage points," which differ by academic discipline. Anthropology and history take the long look; sociology views the family from closer at hand; psychology is closer still, focusing on the individual in the family.

Among the social sciences, anthropology offers the widest cross-cultural understanding of the family against the backdrop of human evolution. Structure–functionalism and an understanding of kinship groups in their cultural context have been major contributions to family theory.

Particularly in the last decade, historians have added new depth to our ideas of the family as they became interested in the everyday life of common people rather than only the history of the elite. Hareven (1974) notes that most of this work has focused on the questions: (1) What constitutes a family? (2) What is the relationship between family structure and parental authority? (3) What are the family's mechanisms for adapting to social change?

Sociologic theories applied to the family have focused on variations in modern family patterns, and social psychology concentrates on studying individuals in group contexts. These two closely related areas offer theories about the contemporary family most likely to be used in family medicine research. These will be explored in more detail below.

From the field of psychology, social learning theory such as that advanced by Bandura and Walters (1963) has had a profound influence, especially in the area of parent–child relations. A second contribution of psychology has been developmental theory, which has given us the notion of the individual life cycle, later expanded by family specialists to the parallel concept of the family life cycle. Another branch of psychology that finds its way into family theory comes from philosophy and cognitive psychology. In the wake of Piaget's studies of cognitive development (e.g., Piaget, 1971), and with the influence of phenomenology in psychology and sociology, family scholars (e.g., Berger & Kellner, 1964; Kantor & Lehr, 1975; Reiss, 1981) began to talk about the family's created reality.

Family Sociology

Of these social sciences, the one from which family medicine is most likely to adapt its own theories about families and health and illness is family sociology, which draws from both sociology and social psychology. This tradition is characterized by ideas about theory rooted in logical positivism. Merton (1945) was a strong influence, calling for "middle-range theory," which means the systematic linking of propositions concerning interrelated variables applicable to a limited range of data. Zetterburg's contribution in 1965 was to set forth a method for theory development that emphasizes formal logic and propositional networks. *Contemporary Theories about the Family,* edited by Burr, Hill, Nye, and Reiss (1979a, 1979b), is a major two-volume summary work by family scholars following in this tradition. Volume 1 contains 24 chapters, each of which is an inventory of empirically based propositions and an attempt at diagramming a causal model. Topics include families' social networks, marital timing, fertility, family problem solving, child behavior, and family violence. The authors specify that theorizing "is not merely a matter of finding empirical relationships that happen to occur in the real world, but rather of learning the circumstances under which variation in variables brings about variation in other variables in a way that acquires multiple levels of generality" (Burr *et al.,* 1979a, p. 20).

Family sociologists make the distinction between three kinds of scholarship: *theory* (as discussed above), *atheoretical work* (sometimes called descriptive research), and *conceptual frameworks* (also called theoretical perspectives or orientations).

ATHEORETICAL RESEARCH

Atheoretical research, that is, accumulating data about individual variables or trends, may be a useful process as an end in itself or as a step toward generating theory. Atheoretical research may discover covariation between variables, and decisions made concerning interpretation may be generated after the results are in. A study showing that "Reaganomics" results in increased infant mortality and morbidity (Edelman, 1983) is most likely information aimed at changing policy, and the only theory guiding the study is the belief that there is a direct relationship between two things. This belief is translated into a testable hypothesis, and the results may be used, for example, to influence lawmakers. In the medical world, discovery of a drug may result in a changed protocol based on its effectiveness in treating a condition, even if the explanation of why it works is still partially or wholly unknown. Much of family medicine research on the family and illness fits these criteria. We have shown that there is a relationship between the family and illness, but there is little explanation as to how and why these variables covary. This does not mean, however, that authors of these studies are free from theoretical assumptions that guide their choice of questions, variables, and operationalization. It does mean that these assumptions are sometimes not explicit and are not tied to a larger body of connected propositions known as a theory.

Family sociology also differentiates between theories and conceptual frameworks. The more general conceptual frameworks serve as our guide to which landmarks are important and which can be temporarily ignored. A theory about a specific phenomenon directs itself to a particular landmark and tries to explain how it is related to the things and events surrounding it. Conceptual frameworks specify the way a problem is to be considered; midrange theories specify which circumstances and variables are to be studied.

Before the early 1900s, ideas about the family were mainly philosophic statements, or macrotheories, that were not designed to be subjected to empirical verification. Grand theory, as it was sometimes called, did generate other ideas from its assumptions about human beings and society, but the concepts remained on a nonempirical level. At present, theories and conceptual frameworks are differentiated primarily on the basis of their relative scope and on their emphasis on an inductive or deductive process. Theory is aimed at explaining more specific phenomena, and it is constructed inductively from empirical regularities—hence the term "theory building." The use of conceptual frameworks, however, is a deductive process arriving at more specific implications of large-scale concepts that may or may not be testable.

There has been a 40-year debate over the relationship between these two levels of theory and the need of one for the other. More recent texts on theory construction, such as those by Hage (1972) and Burr (1973), portray conceptual frameworks as useful but distinct from theory building itself. An exchange between Rodman (1984) and Klein (1984) typifies the two sides of the debate. Rodman (1984) argues that conceptual frameworks are not only unnecessary, but also a diversion that may detract from building formalized networks of testable propositions. He believes that the principal value of conceptual frameworks is that they draw attention to variables that are usually overlooked. Klein (1984) believes that without conceptual frameworks, theories would be little more than abstract empiricism with total emphasis on prediction or on explaining variance.

Volume 2 of *Contemporary Theories about the Family* (Burr *et al.,* 1979b) covers some of these general theoretical orientations, including exchange theory, symbolic interaction, systems theory, conflict theory, and phenomenology.

The argument can be made that the difference between description, theory, and conceptual frameworks is one of degree only, not of kind. The inductive–deductive distinction is only relative, since both are at work in either generalizing or specifying. Furthermore, the difference between *describing* and *explaining* the relationship between two variables may be no more than a difference in how many other variables can be specified to fill in the details of the relationship on multiple levels. Initial studies may show that a drug accomplishes a desired effect through a hypothesized mechanism. Subsequent studies may elaborate on that hypothesis and may study more carefully the biochemistry of the drug action. The biochemical pathway is both an explanation of why the drug works and a more detailed description of how the drug works on a different level of analysis.

CONCEPTUAL FRAMEWORKS

Of the broad theoretical frameworks in family sociology, several should be highlighted. Five theoretical frameworks will be described briefly below, with comments about their applicability for family medicine research. Special note will be given to the theories presented in later chapters of this book as they fit into these larger frameworks. This compilation is not intended to be exhaustive. Others, such as conflict theory or game theory, could also have been included. These theories may show promise for family medicine research but have not been used as much to date.

Social Exchange Theory. Social exchange theory, originally developed by Thibaut and Kelley (1959), Homans (1961), and Levi-Strauss (1969), deals with the changing balance of costs, benefits, and alternatives that explains some decision making and behavior. The general principle of exchange theory is that people choose the best outcome available on the basis of their perception of rewards and costs. In family social science, this framework has been applied to such areas as dating (Murstein, 1980), marital cohesiveness (Levinger, 1976), and contraceptive decision making (Luker, 1975). Since exchange theory deals with decision points—be they conscious or unconscious, rational or nonrational—it may be particularly useful in the study of family health care decision making.

Symbolic Interactionism. Symbolic interactionism, also called role theory, grows out of philosophical work by James, Cooley, Dewey, and Mead (cited in Burr, Leigh, Day, & Constantine, 1979). This framework gives us the concept of a person acting in a role, following scripts for certain prescribed and chosen behaviors that are integrated into a sense of self. A major contribution of symbolic interactionism is its emphasis on the importance of people's symbols and, consequently, their perceptions. This framework offers to family medicine research the concept of the "sick role" and the "health expert role," and the legitimacy of studying people's perceptions of these and other health-related experiences.

Phenomenologic Sociology. Phenomenologic sociology, which assumes a constructivist world view, emphasizes human perception to an even greater extent. The philosophic foundation of this work is the writing of Schutz (1967) and Husserl (1962), and it has been developed in sociology primarily by Berger, Luckmann, Cicourel, and Garfinkel (cited in McLain & Weigert, 1979). According to this orientation, the family must be approached as it is perceived and experienced by its members. As we study the family, we are inevitably a part of the social reality we study. Sociology, then, is a reflexive form of knowledge (McLain & Weigert, 1979).

In the area of families and illness, Reiss's (1981; see also Chapter 8, this volume) theory of family problem-solving paradigms draws heavily on the phenomenologic perspective as well as on small-group research. This work, developed primarily from studying families dealing with chronic illness, has much to offer future family medicine research. Our understanding will be enhanced as family paradigms are examined in family structures other than the one with which the theory was primarily developed (i.e., two-parent families with an adolescent child). Also, it will be useful to pursue the process of paradigm formation and paradigm shift as it applies to health and illness issues, since serious illness may be able to jolt the family into fundamentally new ways of organizing and viewing the world.

Stress and Adaptation Theories. Stress and adaptation theories are a fourth contribution from family sociology that have promise for family medicine research on the family system. Most of the concepts in current family stress theories trace their heritage back to Hill's (1949) ABC-X model: A (stressor event) interacting with B (the family's resources) interacting with C (the family's definition of the event) produces X (the crisis). Social support, an important component of many theories, is most often conceived of as the buffer or counteraction against stress.

One issue generic to stress frameworks is difficulty with circularity and tautology—is something stressful because it affects the family in a particular way, or does it affect the family in a particular way because it is stressful? A vulnerability of the stress framework (and possibly the reason for its enthusiastic adoption into popular culture) is it makes it possible to see the family or individual as a passive recipient, instead of seeing people as actively involved in creating and diffusing their own stress and social support.

One theoretical direction that may be helpful is to address stress and social support as *relationship patterns* (Coyne & Holroyd, 1982); that is, how does a stressing/supporting relationship develop and how and under what circumstances is it mobilized by the givers and receivers?

When applied to health issues, McCubbin and Patterson's (1983; see also Chapter 7, this volume) elaboration of the stress framework at the family level has been used with such diseases as cystic fibrosis (Patterson, 1985) as a model of chronic disease, but the theory may be more useful in understanding acute illness as it affects the family (M. A. Baird, personal communication, January 15, 1984). As this theory develops, it raises new questions: What do we gain by viewing illness as the stressor, and some other family behavior or feeling as the outcome, as opposed to viewing illness as the outcome in response to some other family stresses? Can it be argued that illness as an outcome may not be "bad" if it is a congruent mirroring of distress in a larger system?

Family Developmental Theory. Family developmental theory is the sociologic framework most often used in family medicine teaching about the family, and its themes guide much of our research. As an adaptation from psychologic theory, the family life cycle (Duvall, 1971) carried with it the assumptions of predictable stages with associated tasks or issues that need to be resolved for successful transition to the next state (Erikson, 1963). As long as family developmental theory is tied to traditional shifts in household composition, which are increasingly non-normative, this theory will become obsolete. However, Breunlin (see Chapter 9, this volume) has followed the trend mentioned earlier, by moving the emphasis from family structure to family functioning, adding the concepts of oscillation theory to better describe how families develop over time.

SUMMARY

These theories and theoretical orientations are implicit in much of the thinking about families that is most applicable to family medicine research. The main advantage of the family sociology approach as an extension of the logical positivist tradition is the rigor that accompanies careful codifying of empirical findings into clusters of research-based ideas. This attempt to bridge studies and to ground our theory in data is important for early research efforts like those in family medicine in which we can be dazzled simply by showing associations between variables not previously studied together. The contribution of family sociology is a call for more careful thinking about how, when, and under what circumstances variables are linked.

Of the five theories discussed, we have referred only to three so far: Reiss's family paradigms, McCubbin and Patterson's family stress theory (called the family adjustment and adaptation response, or FAAR, model), and family developmental theory as interpreted by Breunlin. The Beavers systems model (1981; Chapter 5, this volume) and Olson and colleagues' circumplex model (Olson, Sprenkle, & Russell, 1979; Chapter 6, this volume) fit less easily into one of the general sociologic frameworks mentioned earlier, although they draw concepts from several of them. Instead, these models claim systems theory as their primary theoretical orientation. The circumplex model uses the dimensions of cohesion and adaptability as curvilinear variables, with healthy families operating in the midrange. The Beavers systems model considers cohesion as a stylistic dimension, and adaptability as a continuum ranging from dysfunctional to optimal. These concepts and differences will become more meaningful as we discuss systems theory as a major tradition.

Systems Theory and Cybernetics

Systems theory and cybernetics together form the other major tradition, besides family sociology, influencing the study of families in family medicine research. Many bits and pieces of their vocabulary are already a part of our work, and some of the most exciting ideas we are dealing with come from this tradition. All five of the theories presented in the following chapters use the language and concepts of systems theory, though in slightly different ways.

Many people say that Western science and social science are in the midst of a paradigm shift, in the sense that Kuhn (1970) used the term; that is, assumptions about the world, so basic that they usually go unrecognized, are being challenged by a fundamentally different view of things. The revolution began in nuclear physics with the shift from Newton's theories to Einstein's, showing that observations are relative to an observer's point of view, and with the elaboration of ideas such as Heisenberg's uncertainty principle. More recently, the changes have moved into communications theory and biology with the study of information processing in living systems. The introduction of the language of systems theory was the beginning of the shift in the family field, which has now also moved to include some cybernetic concepts.

The distinction between cybernetics and systems theory is a significant one. Keeney (1983) points out that systems theory is a change of focus from parts to wholes, whereas cybernetics is the shift from material to pattern. Thus, a person can analyze a phenomenon by looking at wholes instead of parts, but still not have made the paradigmatic shift to look at patterns of organization. For example, using systems theory, much of family therapy has made the first-order change of viewing the family instead of the individual as the locus of pathology. Family medicine is in danger of making the same epistemologic mistake. A cybernetic point of view is the punctuating our frame of reference so as to encircle the family is convenient, but arbitrary. Relevant patterns of organization may be at *any* level, including the health care system, the school system, the larger culture, or the individual person.

The basic idea of cybernetics is that of "feedback," that is, a method of controlling a system by reinserting into it the results of its past performance. It is in this sense that an enduring family system is self-corrective (Keeney, 1983). In this perspective, we realize that in observing a system's feedback process, we are also a part of a higher order feedback loop. This idea of feedback at multiple levels, which includes a self-referential component, is called *recursion*. The construction of patterns that connect the individual and the family is a collaborative effort of the observer (clinician, researcher) and the family, and the patterns depend on the categories brought to the data by both the observer and the observed.

Arguments abound and rebound as to the implications of this thinking for social science theory and research. Some spokespersons for cybernetics believe that most of social science is misguided because of its goal of objectivity in findings that are supposedly observer-independent (Umpleby, 1975, cited in Keeney, 1983). They remind us that in the human sciences, the higher order cybernetic process necessarily includes the observer. Others, like Gurman (1983), argue that standard social science methods are not antithetical to systems and cybernetic thinking. Cybernetics itself leads to the position that the answer is not either/or.

Both of the traditions we have discussed, family sociology and systems theory/cybernetics, are apparent in family medicine research, and each has its own characteristic dangers. The danger of family sociology is in relegating cybernetics to the level of a conceptual framework and not seeing it as a critical paradigm shift. Because there are still many implications to be worked out in translating cybernetics into research vocabulary and strategies, the danger is in compartmentalizing it and continuing to do studies that ignore context. On the other hand, the danger of cybernetics is that we will take the observer and the context so seriously that we will believe we can never recreate them, so that every experience is idiosyncratic and science is impossible.

Either position is untenable. Both traditions are searching for patterns by carefully studying the world. Cybernetics says that we need a study of the observer. This does not mean that we should forego a systematic study of what has traditionally been observed but, rather, that we should expand what is observed to include the observer. The cybernetic emphasis on the creative perception that humans have of their world gives fresh vitality to the sociologic study of people's self-report about their families, as well as to our studies observing family interaction. There is encouragement here to look at *patterns* of perceptions, including the researcher's own construction of reality, in setting up the definitions and parameters of the study. For instance, by looking for patterns of similarities and discrepancies among family members' reports of family interaction, we can generate a second level of description approximating what Bateson (1979) called "binocular vision." By reflecting on our own categories for this description and what that creation says about us and the process, we may be combining the best of both traditions.

The answer to the challenge of cybernetic thinking is not to quit doing carefully designed and controlled studies, but to realize that every study is an intervention study. We perturb a system, and we see how it responds. We describe our context (setting, procedure, and sample) as carefully as we know how, and we count on enough people describing their own interaction with the phenomenon that eventually a pattern will emerge. As Abell (Chapter 38, this volume) has said, ". . . nobody goes into research to explain zero percent of the variance." The real test of our theories is whether they can predict clinically important outcomes.

Keeney (1983) uses the analogy of building a tennis court to describe the usefulness of both approaches. We know that the earth is round, but if we were to build a tennis court, we would build it as if we believed the earth were flat, and appropriately so. In the same way, linear thinking is useful in designing our research. The key is recognizing that this way of thinking is encompassed by larger reflexive patterns, which we are a part of creating. If many tennis courts were built next to each other, eventually they would form a circle around the globe. As Bloch (1983) put it,

> Linear, cause and effect, single factor science may be seen as a special case which depends on a number of simplifying assumptions that are useful under specified conditions. . . . [Sometimes] it may be better to act *as if* the symptom had a single cause and cure. (p. 4; emphasis in original)

What we need to develop is a paradigm about shifting paradigms; that is, what are the conditions under which we switch from one to another? Both paradigms are useful, as are the five theories we have discussed. But if we are to be eclectic, we need to be as articulate as possible about the theory that guides our eclecticism.

CONCLUSION

Currently, family medicine research struggles to have its own defined theories, which may be applications of general theories but are worked out in the domain of a specific problem to be solved. For example, the circumplex model suggests that, in general, balanced families are more functional than extreme families. In spinal cord-injured patients and their families, however, a more specific application of the circumplex model leads us to hypothesize that families and patients do better when the families are enmeshed during the acute stage, and then become more disengaged as rehabilitation progresses and the patient tries to regain some functional independence (Baker, 1985). All of these theories will take new twists and turns as they are worked out in new contexts.

Part of the design in this book is to encourage the blending or contrasting of ideas, and to discover what the theories and theorists may say to each other to move the field in new directions. The five theories that will be presented in the chapters that follow have much to offer each other, and ideas may be further developed by juxtaposing them. For example, what is the relationship between "cohesion" from the circumplex model or the Beavers model, "coherence" in the FAAR model, and "coordination" in family paradigms? What is the relationship between cohesion and social support? Is enmeshment a case of runaway escalation of social support? Can there be *over*support? The circumplex model and Beavers systems model share some things in common, and have already been in formal dialogue about their differences (Beavers & Voeller, 1983; Olson, Russell, & Sprenkle, 1983), one of which is the dimension of adaptability and whether it is linear or curvilinear. There have been attempts to blend the circumplex and the FAAR model, which Olson described (Chapter 6, this volume). The developmental framework has been a consistent theme that all the other models have included to some degree in the consideration of family change over time.

The Beavers, Olson, and Reiss models focus on family patterns that persist over time. Up to this point, less attention has been given to ways in which those patterns develop or how they persist. Because of this emphasis on consistencies in family interactions, these theories result in classification schemes, such as typologies. Thus, family paradigms give us categories such as configuration, coordination, and closure. The circumplex model generates 16 combinations of cohesion and adaptability. Beavers's model constructs nine family types ranging from severely disturbed to optimal. To the degree that developmental theories and stress theories focus on family *change*, which is by definition a break in pattern, they will *not* generate typologies. Of course, it is possible to move to a meta-level and look for patterns of change, asking if families have styles of changing, and thus of creating a typology on that dimension. That level, in turn, could be subject to questions about the evolution of pattern, and so on. The point is that change and stability are points of view, both useful for dealing with various questions.

We must keep asking ourselves where our blind spots are. What is it that we are *not* focusing on? Subjects who do not agree to participate in our study or who drop out may be as informative as those who do participate. Have we wondered about the family member who is *not* the "health expert" in the family, or the person who is *not* sick? An understanding of multifinality and multicausality would lead us to ask, "Beyond the ones we studied, what other outcomes could these variables lead to?" and "What other variables could explain this outcome?"

Finally, taking the observer into account means that we bring all of ourselves to the research process. Clinical research at its best is fueled by human emotion, the passion to correct a problem or solve a puzzle that is important to peoples' lives. When we are designing studies on family coping styles as a family member is dying, we should also be reading Dylan Thomas's (1963) "Do Not Go Gentle into That Good Night." Then our research becomes another way to express the "rage against the dying of the light"—and may, indeed, make a small difference in human existence.

References

Baker LC. Predicting medical, functional, and psychosocial outcomes of spinal cord injured patients. Presented at the annual meeting of the North American Primary Care Research Group, Seattle, Washington, April 1985.

Bandura, A, Walters RH. Social learning and personality development. New York: Holt, Rinehart and Winston, 1963.

Bateson G. Naven. Stanford, Calif.: Stanford University Press, 1958.

Bateson G. Mind and nature: a necessary unity. New York: E. P. Dutton, 1979.

Beavers WR, Voeller MN. Family models: comparing and contrasting the Olson circumplex model with the Beavers system model. Family Process 1983; 22:85–98.

Berger PL, Kellner H. Marriage and the construction of reality. Diogenes 1964; 46:1–24.

Bloch DA. The sun also rises. Family Systems Medicine 1983; 1(3):3.

Burr WR. Theory construction and the sociology of the family. New York: Wiley, 1973.

Burr WR, Hill R, Nye FI, Reiss IL, eds. Contemporary theories about the family, Vol. 1: Research-based theories. New York: Free Press, 1979a.

Burr WR, Hill R, Nye FI, Reiss, IL, eds. Contemporary theories about the family, Vol. 2: General theories/theoretical orientations. New York: Free Press, 1979b.

Burr WR, Leigh GK, Day, RD, Constantine J. Symbolic interaction and the family. In: Burr WR, Hill R, Nye FI, Reiss IL, eds. Contemporary theories about the family, Vol. 2: General theories/theoretical orientations. New York: Free Press, 1979.

Cherlin AJ. Marriage, divorce, remarriage. Cambridge, Mass.: Harvard University Press, 1981.

Coyne JC, Holroyd, K. Stress, coping, and illness. In: Millon T, Green C, Meagher R, eds. Handbook of clinical health psychology. New York: Plenum Press, 1982.

Demos J. A little commonwealth: family life in Plymouth colony. New York: Oxford University Press, 1970.

Duvall EM. Family development, 4th ed. New York: Lippincott, 1971.

Edelman MW. Death by poverty, arms, or moral numbness. American Journal of Orthopsychiatry 1983; 53(4):593–601.

Erikson EH. Childhood and society. New York: Norton, 1963.

Goode WJ. World revolution and family patterns. New York: Free Press of Glencoe, 1963.

Greven P. Four generations, population, land, and family in colonial Andover, Massachusetts. Ithaca, N.Y.: Cornell University Press, 1970.

Gurman A. Family therapy research and the "new epistemology." Journal of Marital and Family Therapy 1983; 9(3):227–234.

Hage J. Techniques and problems of theory construction in sociology. New York: Wiley, 1972.

Hareven TK. The history of the family as an interdisciplinary field. Journal of Interdisciplinary History 1974; 2:399–414.

Hareven TK. American families in transition: historical perspectives on change. In: Walsh F, ed. Normal family processes. New York: Guilford Press, 1982.

Hill R. Families under stress. New York: Harper and Row, 1949.

Homans G. Social behavior: Its elementary forms. New York: Harcourt Brace Jovanovich, 1961, 1974.

Husserl E. Ideas: general introduction to pure phenomenology. New York: Collier, 1962.

Kantor D, Lehr W. Inside the family. San Francisco: Jossey-Bass, 1975.

Keeney BP. Aesthetics of change. New York: Guilford Press, 1983.

Klein DM. Commentary on the linkages between conceptual frameworks and theory development in sociology. In: Olson DH, Miller BC, eds. Family studies review yearbook, Vol. 2. Beverly Hills, Calif.: Sage Publications, 1984.

Kuhn T. The structure of scientific revolutions. Chicago: University of Chicago Press, 1970.

Laslett P, Wall R, eds. Household and family in past time. Cambridge: Cambridge University Press, 1972.

Levinger G. A social psychological perspective on marital dissolution. Journal of Social Issues 1976; 32:21–47.

Levi-Strauss C. The elementary structure of kinship. Boston: Beacon Press, 1969.

Litman TJ. The family as a basic unit in health and medical care: a social behavior overview. Social Science and Medicine 1974; 8:495–519.

Luker K. Taking chances. Berkeley: University of California Press, 1975.

Masnick G, Bane MJ. The nation's families: 1960–1990. Cambridge, Mass.: Joint Center for Urban Studies of MIT and Harvard University, 1980.

McCubbin HI, Patterson JM. Family stress and adaptation to crisis: a double ABCX model of family behavior. In: Olson DH, Miller BC, eds. Family studies review yearbook, Vol. 2. Beverly Hills, Calif.: Sage Publications, 1983.

McEwan PJM. The social approach to family health studies. Social Science and Medicine 1974; 8:487–493.

McLain R, Weigert A. Toward a phenomenological sociology of family: a programmatic essay. In: Burr WR, Hill R, Nye FI, Reiss IL, eds. Contemporary theories about the family, Vol. 2. New York: Free Press, 1979.

Merton R. Sociological theory. American Journal of Sociology 1945; 50:462–473.

Minuchin S, Rosman BP, Baker L. Psychosomatic families. Cambridge, Mass.: Harvard University Press, 1978.

Murstein BL. Mate selection in the 1970s. Journal of Marriage and the Family 1980; 42(4):777–792.

Olson DH, Russell CS, Sprenkle DH. Circumplex model of marital and family systems: VI. Theoretical update. Family Process 1983; 22(1):69–83.

Olson DH, Sprenkle D, Russell C. Circumplex model of marital and family systems: I. Cohesion and adaptability dimensions, family types and clinical applications. Family Process 1979; 18:3–15.

Patterson JM. Critical factors affecting family compliance with cystic fibrosis. Family Relations 1985; 34:79–89.

Piaget, J. Biology and knowledge. Chicago: University of Chicago Press, 1971.

Reiss D. The family's construction of reality. Cambridge, Mass.: Harvard University Press, 1981.

Reiss D, Gonzalez S, Kramer N. Family process, chronic illness and death: on the weakness of strong bonds. Archives of General Psychiatry 1986; 43:795–804.

Rodman H. Reply to Klein. Sociological Quarterly 1984; 21:455–457.

Rolland JS. Toward a psychosocial typology of chronic and life-threatening illness. Family Systems Medicine 1984; 2:245–262.

Schutz A. The phenomenology of the social world. Evanston, Ill.: Northwestern University Press, 1967.

Starfield B. Patients and population: advancing knowledge in primary care by linking two levels of research. Keynote address at the 1983 annual meeting of the North American Primary Care Research Group, Banff, Alberta, Canada, April 19, 1983.

Thibaut JW, Kelley HH. The social psychology of groups. New York: Wiley, 1959.

Thomas D. Miscellany one: poems, stories, broadcasts. London: J.M. Dent & Sons, 1963.

Weakland JH. "Family somatics": a neglected edge. Family Process 1977; 16:263–272.

Zetterburg HL. On theory and verification in sociology, 3rd ed. Totawa, N.J.: Bedminster Press, 1965.

PART THREE

Research Design and Methods for Family Medicine Research

11

Some Methodological Problems and Issues in Family Health Research

THEODOR J. LITMAN
University of Minnesota

The role of the family and family members in health and health care continues to hold empirical as well as theoretical fascination for researchers in both the behavioral and the medical sciences. As the basic unit of interaction and transaction in health and medical care, the family has variously been treated as not only an independent, dependent, and intervening variable, but also a precipitating, predisposing, and contributory factor in the etiology, care, and treatment of both physical and mental illness (Alpert, Kosa, & Haggerty, 1967; American Academy of Pediatrics, 1965; Fink, 1969; Kaplan & Cassel, 1975; Litman, 1974; Schwenk & Hughes, 1983; Young, 1983). Despite its potential contribution and value to both theory and practice, however, empirical research in this area has tended to be relatively limited, plagued by methodologic imprecision and a minimal integration with family theory. Moreover, little attempt has been made at either longitudinal or intergenerational analysis of family health patterns and practices (Litman & Venters, 1979).

Over the course of the past 15 years, considerable progress has been made in the field, ostensibly in the areas of family reaction and response to illness of one of its members (Elliott, 1983; McCubbin, 1979; McCubbin, Cauble, & Patterson, 1982; McCubbin, Joy, Cauble, Comeau, Patterson, Needle, 1980; Patterson & McCubbin, 1984b; Shapiro, 1983; Venters, 1980, 1981); the provision of social support (Brody, Johnson, Fulcomer, & Lang, 1983; Pilisuk & Parks, 1983; Poulschock & Deimling, 1984; Robinson, 1983; Shanas, 1979; Thompson & Doll, 1982; Zarit, 1982; Zarit, Reeves, & Bach-Peterson, 1980); and patient compliance (Becker & Green, 1975).

More recently, Doherty and McCubbin (1985) have offered a six-phase model of the family health and illness cycle within which they anticipate most, if not all, current and future research on the family and health will likely fall. Major elements of the model include: (1) the family health promotion and risk reduction phase; (2) the family vulnerability and illness onset phase; (3) the family illness appraisal phase; (4) the family acute response phase; (5) the family and health care system–critical choice phase; and finally (6) the family adaptation to illness phase (Doherty & McCubbin, 1984).

As rich and insightful as the efforts and activities to date have been, however, much still needs to be done. Research and publication in the field, unfortunately, still remain relatively limited, confined to a small, energetic, and productive coterie of medical and behavioral scientists. Moreover, like other areas of family research, research on family health has been subject to a number of methodologic problems and issues, some of them generic to the broader field and others peculiar to the study of family health. In addition to the continuing problems of measurement, far too often research on health care and the family has proved to be inconsistent, impressionistic, descriptive rather than explanatory, limited in both scope and techniques, reliant on rather small and unrepresentative samples of limited generalizability, and plagued by simplistic conceptualizations as well as methodologic weaknesses in study design (Kreisman & Joy, 1975). Since many of these problems will be explored in greater depth by others elsewhere in this book, our discussion here will focus on three areas of concern: (1) access, (2) sample selection, and (3) research design and data collection. In this way, it is hoped that this discussion will not only stimulate additional methodologic inquiry in this area, but also lead to some mutually agreed-on and arrived-at solutions.

ACCESS

The inviolability of the family and family life has long posed problems of access for the conduct of research on the family (Christensen, 1965). Only in the past 40 years or so have social scientists effectively penetrated the methodologic and sociomoral impediments to family research per se (Hill, 1958; Hobbs & Sussman, 1965).

In addition to the constraints it imposes on research in this area, as LaRossa and co-workers have observed (LaRossa, Bennett, & Gelles, 1983), the private and intimate nature of the family also raises several distinct ethical issues, namely those of informed consent and, in the case of more intrusive projects, the risk–benefit equation.

The latter is, of course, a major ethical concern confronting all researchers and involving an assessment of the relative risks and potential benefits accruing from the research itself. According to LaRossa *et al.* (1983), the private or secret character of family life, and the importance of family life to self-esteem (i.e., the potential threat that exposure of a family to itself via participation in the research endeavor may hold for the self-esteem of its members) constitute two aspects of the family that create special contingencies within which a balanced risk–benefit ratio must be achieved and maintained in qualitative family research.

In seeking to achieve an acceptable risk–benefit equation, however, LaRossa *et al.* (1983) note that qualitative researchers on the family must consider not only the standard risks of human subjects research, but also the risk of public exposure as well as the delicate problem of exposure of a family to itself. ''The fact that many people consider their family both a sanctum and their most precious possession,'' they caution, ''is something that qualitative (and, we would add, family health) researchers should never forget and never abuse'' (LaRossa *et al.*, 1983, p. 312).

Comparably, the pervasiveness and inaccessibility of family life, as well as the physical setting in which family research is conducted, create special contingencies within which research investigators must seek and maintain the informed consent of their study participants (LaRossa *et al.*, 1983). The main problem, as LaRossa and colleagues have observed, is that of ''balancing the need to penetrate the private, pervasive and emotional back regions of family life, against the tempting, and often easy, violation of a family's privacy and hospitality'' (LaRossa *et al.*, 1983, p. 312).

Finally, on a somewhat different note, the adoption of increasingly restrictive institutional policies on human subjects review, ostensibly in the name of protecting and preserving patient privacy, as well as both institutional and physician resistance to providing access to patient populations for study, has made sample selection and the pursuit of record linkages more difficult, though not insurmountable. Although such practices do in fact pose potentially serious problems for family health research, our own experience suggests that in most cases, reasonable requests, reasonably made, with assurances of adequate safeguards, usually form grounds for mutual negotiation and accommodation. Nevertheless, greater effort needs to be made to try to reduce such impediments to research in this area.

THE PROBLEMS OF SAMPLE SELECTION AND RESEARCH DESIGN

Closely associated with the problem of access in family health research are the problems of sample selection and research design. As in other areas of family study, a good share of the research in family health to date has involved the use of small, often self-selected, convenient, disease-specific samples assessed at a single point in time in the absence of either cross-sequential, time-sequential, or longitudinal designs, with little, if any, comparability between studies.

Sample Selection

To a large extent, the nature and selection of the sampling method used is dependent on the purpose of the research being done. The accuracy of a probability sample, for instance, is a function of the sample size and the number of population subgroups to be sampled; the larger the number of subgroups to be studied, the larger the size of sample needed. As a result, a particularly difficult problem in the use of cross-sectional or panel-based samples for the study of relatively rare events or family types, such as in family health research, is the need either to select a sufficiently large sample, or to provide for a sufficiently long period of study, so as to assure acquisition of an adequate number of cases (Kitson *et al.*, 1982).

Although probability samples facilitate description, as well as prediction and generalization, to the larger population from which the sample is drawn, their major disadvantage lies in the time and costs involved in their selection, including the development of the sampling frame. Nonprobability samples, on the other hand, whether accidental, convenient, purposive, quota, haphazard, or fortuitous, though subject to the danger of producing possible spurious results, offer a relatively low-cost, convenient, and useful approach for not only gaining an in-depth, insightful look at issues and exploring low-frequency or sensitive behavior, but also developing hypotheses for further study (Kitson *et al.*, 1982).

Unfortunately, the very nature of their selection makes generalization from such samples beyond the special characteristics of the population being studied very difficult, if not impossible. Their lack of generalizability, however, as Kitson and colleagues have argued, need not necessarily preclude their research value and utility, as long as a clear explanation is given of the underlying rationale for why and how the sample selection was made, and any interpretations of the data are carefully limited (Kitson *et al.*, 1982). Toward this end, they have suggested that description of the sampling procedures used in any such endeavor should include the following:

1. Stipulation of how the study population was defined, how the sample was selected, and any limits on generalizability this produces.
2. A clear description of the methods used to select, train, and supervise the data collection staff.

3. A description of the methods used for tracking respondents and obtaining a high rate of response, as well as any problems encountered.

4. Full disclosure and discussion of the response rate, including demographic comparisons, where possible, between respondents and nonrespondents. Response rate is defined in this sense as the total number of persons selected for study who live in the geographic area to be surveyed, minus all interviews not completed, regardless of cause, divided by the total number of eligible subjects (see Kitson *et al.*, 1982, p. 972). Sources of nonresponse may include refusals, persons not at home despite repeated efforts to contact, persons who have moved without leaving a forwarding address, and persons unable to respond because of language barriers or physical or mental problems. Overall, the response rate has tended to decline over the course of the past decade or so, with research on sensitive issues, such as intra- and interfamily relations, particularly susceptible to the problems of nonresponse.

5. Finally, placement of the study findings within the context of other available data on the topic, in order that limitations of the sampling methods may be interpreted (Kitson *et al.*, 1982).

Diversity of Family Form and Type

Equally important, if not more so, however, is the need for greater recognition of differences in family form and type in family health research. Largely as a result of a host of social and technologic changes in society, including the rise of the women's movement, the sexual revolution, a faltering economy, and the increased social acceptance of divorce, we have witnessed a gradual transformation in the nature and form of the American family such that at any given point in time the traditional nuclear family no longer is representative of the nation's households (Macklin, 1980). Over the course of the past few decades, for instance, the nation has experienced a slow but steady increase in the proportion of the population residing in either single-parent or dual-career families, as well as those living alone or in households comprising nonrelated individuals. According to data from the 1980 census, over 18% of all children in the United States are currently being raised in female-headed households, and over 20% of all families with children in this country are headed by single women (McLanahan, 1983). Moreover, it has been estimated that stepfamilies now make up between 10% and 15% of all the nation's households (Espinoza & Newman, 1979).

Despite these changes, including the dramatic rise in marital dissolutions in this country, there has been little research directed at determining the consequences and problems, if any, that variant or alternative family forms hold for health and health care. Such nontraditional family forms include: (1) Binuclear or shared-parent and joint-custody families in which the child is seen as part of a family system composed of two nuclear households, with or without parents sharing legal custody; (2) step versus blended families in which one or both of the married adults have children from a previous union with primary residence in the household (Macklin, 1980).

Unfortunately, not only have there been few studies of family health among diverse family forms and varied class and ethnic types, but our knowledge of the impact of divorce and remarriage on the health and health care of family members remains largely based on anecdotal and clinical data.

Similarly, although ethnic families have been the focus of concern for researchers and practitioners in the family field for nearly a century, the influx of legal and illegal immigrants to our shores in the 1970s, along with the resurgence of racial pride and cultural identity among various minority groups in the population, has resulted in a new infusion into our society of ethnic diversity and ethnic families who need to be taken into account in the study of family health and health care (Allen, 1978; Bernardo, 1980). Toward that end, several workers (Allen, 1978; Staples & Mirande, 1980) have made excellent contributions to the body of literature on minority families. In addition, Aday and colleagues (Aday, Chu, & Anderson, 1980), and Habermacher (1980) have addressed specifically the problems associated with survey research on the health of Hispanic populations.

The absorption of non-kin into the existing familial structure, for instance, has long been an attribute of black family life. Yet, as Malson (1982) has noted, prior to the work of Robert Hill (1972), large-scale social surveys to examine the characteristics of the social support system of black families were practically nonexistent. The latter's *The Strengths of Black Families* (Hill, 1972) and *Informal Adoption among Black Families* (Hill, 1977) represent some of the first efforts to employ secondary analyses of large-scale data to describe the black family kin system (Malson, 1982).

On the whole, the assumption of responsibility for child care and child rearing by immediate kin (mothers, siblings, older children, or extended kin such as aunts and mothers- and sisters-in-law) in black families has been well documented (Malson, 1982). McAdoo (1980), for instance, found that 71% of the subjects in her study of the support networks of single black mothers had relationships with "fictive kin," who took the roles of sisters, brothers, aunts, and uncles. Such familial arrangements, moreover, tend to serve as a mutual aid system that has been particularly beneficial to black single-parent families, permitting the mother to work and providing greater economic security through the "doubling up" and sharing of resources (McAdoo, 1981). Less well known, on the other hand, is how and in what ways such systems of familial support perform in times of health and illness including their interaction with more formalized systems of care.

Unfortunately, because of their relatively small numbers within the general population and their geographic dispersion, broad-based representative samples of minority families and family groups are not easily found. Nevertheless, in the case of black families, two surveys begun in the late 1970s would seem to hold promise of greatly increasing our knowledge of this population group. The first of these, the National Survey of Black Americans, directed by James Jackson at the University of Michigan's Institute for Social Research, is based on data collected from a national probability sample of 2,000 black Americans. The other, the National Black Pulse Survey, was conducted by the National Urban League (Malson, 1982).

Research Design

In addition to the concerns and deficiencies already mentioned, a further problem involved in family health research is that associated with research design. As we have noted elsewhere, although research on health care and the family has embraced a variety of designs, longitudinal or intergenerational analyses of family health patterns and practices, for the most part, with but a few notable exceptions, have been relatively limited (Litman & Venters, 1979).

Although the interrelationship of the family and health is a fairly dynamic, ongoing process, most research on family health and health care has revolved around the use of cross-sectional data in which the family is viewed at only one point in time. Such an approach, however, greatly limits our understanding of process and causation. On the other hand, although retrospective data can recapture some of the processional dimension, the accuracy of such data may be distorted by the difficulty of accurate recall. With this in mind, our attention now turns to a consideration of the applicability of more longitudinal approaches to the study of family health.

Perhaps one of the best methods for assessing the impact of change over time, as Kitson and colleagues (1982) have noted, is the use of some form of panel study in which the same subjects are surveyed or observed two or more times over a given period. Such an approach, they point out, offers a useful method for obtaining reliable information on causally related situations and events, especially when there is little variation in confounding variables over time.

In addition to their high costs, however, panel studies are subject to several sources of bias that can detract from their utility, ranging from respondent attrition and failure to complete follow-up interviews, to possible response contamination due to test–retest effects (Kitson *et al.*, 1982). (A number of suggested solutions to these problems, incidentally, have been offered by Marcus and Telesky, 1983, Schaie, 1977, and Kitson *et al.*, 1982, and need not be gone into here.)

In the area of family health, one of the earliest efforts to employ the use of a longitudinal design was Downes's (1952) study of chronic illness in the Eastern Health District of Baltimore, Maryland. Using data derived from a study of 951 families over a 5-year period, she noted that such a design not only afforded a description of the family patterns of disease, as well as the growth and decline of the family as a biologic, social, and economic unit, but also facilitated an opportunity to gain a better understanding of family attitudes toward health and illness (Downes, 1952; Downes & Mertz, 1953).

Such attributes aside, however, the longitudinal approach is not without its methodologic problems. Foremost among these are the rather high rates of attrition and nonresponse experienced and the difficulty of retaining staff and securing the family's long-term cooperation and commitment. Very long projects, for instance, may be subject to premature termination or lack of completion due to the loss of either the subjects and/or key staff over the course of the project. As a result, financial and organizational costs of such studies may frequently prove burdensome, if not prohibitive. In addition, a further concern with such designs is the possibility that repeated observation or interviewing may serve to condition or "contaminate" the subjects and affect their orientations and behavior in such a way as to alter the outcome of the research (Christensen, 1958, 1965).

Finally, as Glenn and Frisbie (1977) have noted, although behavioral scientists have long yearned for more opportunities for longitudinal and trend studies, there is increasing evidence that such diachronic approaches have neither the utility for causal inference nor even the establishment of direct causation that they formerly were believed to have. Concomitant with the growth of opportunities for such studies has been an increased awareness of their limitations for providing explanation and understanding of causal processes, and their inadequacy to provide definitive evidence of cause and effect.

Intergenerational Analysis

A potentially effective alternative to the pure logitudinal design in family health research, which tends to minimize many of its disadvantages while still providing insight into the process, is that of intergenerational analysis. Such an approach, as we have noted elsewhere, lends itself to an examination of the interaction of family members, as well as the totality of intrafamilial transactions in the context of historical time. Moreover, in the case of health and health care, such a design facilitates assessment of not only the socialization of health attitudes, values, and beliefs, but also the dynamic aspects of health behavior of families and their members, within and throughout the various phases of the family life cycle (Litman & Venters, 1979).

But as promising and insightful as this approach has proved to be (Brody, Johnson, Fulmer, & Lang, 1983; Hill, Foote, Aldous, Carlson, & MacDonald, 1970; Litman, 1970, 1971; Litman & Venters, 1979) it too has been fraught with a number of methodological weaknesses. Acock (1984), for example, has noted that few areas of social research have used less appropriate sampling designs than intergenerational analyses. Not only are sampling frames so narrowly circumscribed that generalization is severely limited, but the interdependence of one generational linkage on another greatly heightens their vulnerability to loss. Thus, the refusal or loss of one generational line within the family potentially threatens the retention of the entire family line and the ultimate loss of all three family lineages. As a result, considerable effort needs to be expended in order to assure cooperation and participation, including careful selection and training of interviewers as well as the maintenance of close, friendly contact between project staff and participating families. In the process, one runs the risk of overly sensitizing or conditioning the respondents to give socially acceptable responses. The latter, however, can be overcome in part by the careful wording and framing of questions, and the cross-validation of data with other sources.

An additional methodologic concern with such an approach, cited by Connell (1972), is that most of the comparisons made in such studies have been of aggregates of grouped members of each generation rather than true lineages (i.e., parents with their own children). Although this is admittedly often blurred in actual practice, he points out the need to distinguish between pair and group correspondence. The former, for instance, is usually represented in terms of a correlation coefficient, and refers to measures of intrafamilial, lineage similarities. Group correspondence, on the other hand, involves comparisons of cohorts as aggregates (i.e., parents as a group with children as a group), and is often represented by a *t*-test or analysis of variances.

Finally, although the financial cost and time-consuming nature of prospective, longitudinal research in an era of fiscal restraint is an obvious constraint on the development and implementation of such designs, these drawbacks should not be allowed to blind us to their value, nor deter our efforts to pursue them. Nor does the availability and use of new, highly sophisticated, and powerful analytic techniques preclude the need for sound design and data collection procedures. One must guard against the temptation, however unintentional it may be, to rely on the use of such statistical techniques to hide bad or poorly collected data.

DATA COLLECTION

This brings us to the final set of issues concerning the process of data collection. On the whole, as in other areas of family study, the methods used in the collection of family-related health data tend to be largely dependent on the particular purpose of the study and the availability and accessibility of the sources of information. Since several of these techniques (health diaries and telephone interviews) have been well addressed elsewhere (Aneshensel, Frerichs, Clark, & Yokopenic, 1982; Groves & Kahn, 1979; Henson, Roth,

& Cannell, 1972; Litman & Venters, 1979; Marcus & Telesky, 1983; Marquis, 1981; Pless & Miller, 1979; Roghmann & Haggerty, 1974; Siemiatycki, 1979; Verbrugge, 1980; Wright, Beisel, Doliver, & Gerzowski, 1976), and others, namely self-reports and direct observation, will be discussed at greater length later (see McCubbin *et al.*, Chapter 12, this volume; Schmaling *et al.*, Chapter 13, this volume), the following discussion will be confined to the problems associated with two areas of concern—the use of official records and record linkages, and the survey interview in family health research.

Official Records and Record Linkages

The potential value official records and record linkages hold in the repertoire of techniques available for the study of families and family life was recognized long ago by Christensen (1958, 1965). Although limited by inaccuracies of recall and the recording of missing data, as well as a lack of standardized recording conventions (Berkanovic, 1974; Litman & Venters, 1979), vital records, such as those on births, marriages, divorces, and deaths, can provide helpful insights into family health experiences, relationships, and trends.

The restriction of the data recorded in such official documents to categories that are clearly defined and unambiguous, however, may serve to mask other important information. For example, as the work of Venters, Schacht, and Ten Bensel (1976), has shown, the mere recording of "yes" or "no" on a birth certificate to depict the presence or absence of congenital abnormalities tends not only to lack sufficient specificity about the type of condition in question, but also to hide the degree of severity involved (Litman & Venters, 1979). Moreover, since the data obtained from records are a reflection of the sociocultural conditions in the larger society, what is included may vary from time to time and place to place. For instance, sudden infant death syndrome (SIDS) was rarely, if ever, listed as a cause of death on state death certificates until a decade or so ago. Similarly, the recording of data concerning socially frowned on conditions or stigmatized behavior (e.g., child abuse or unwed motherhood) may be either ignored, mislabeled, or misrepresented by overly sensitive public officials.

Institutional records, on the other hand, like those maintained by hospitals, pharmacies, and nursing homes, though useful as a source of information concerning an individual patient's illness or illness experience, are normally not collected or stored by families or family units. As a result, their value for family health research is fairly limited except in terms of record linkages. Such linkages, as Glick (1964) has noted, offer a number of advantages over other forms of data collection on the family. For instance, the basic data are generally available in relatively uniform quality, and the information obtained from different record sources may be cross-checked to safeguard against errors of recording. In addition, distortions that may arise in the direct questioning of persons about previous events of a sensitive nature may be avoided or at least minimized through the use of matched vital records. Finally, they also afford an excellent vehicle for tracing certain diseases in families as well as along patrilineal and matrilineal lines.

The utility of such linkages, however, may be limited by the restricted nature of the data available on the record; by the completeness and accuracy of the information provided; by physician, institutional, and bureaucratic resistance to making such data accessible for study; and by biases introduced through the loss of cases in the search process. As a result, it is recommended that record linkages be used in concert with other data-gathering techniques in order to obtain more definitive results than would be possible through any one approach alone (Christensen, 1965).

The Survey Interview

The survey interview affords another useful technique for collecting family-related health data. In view of the intimate nature of family life and the sensitive nature of many health and illness problems, it is not surprising that researchers in family health have relied on the field survey rather than direct observation as the primary method of data collection.

As noted elsewhere (Litman & Venters, 1979), perhaps one of the more confounding problems encountered in the surveys of family health has been the difficulty of obtaining accurate information about the health and related behavior of various family members. A common practice in studies of the family in general, as well as in the area of health and illness, has been the heavy reliance placed on the responses of the wife/mother as the primary, if not sole, source of data (Bokemeier & Monroe, 1983). Few studies, for instance, have included the responses of both husbands and wives, let alone other family members (Ball, Mckenry, & Price-Bonham, 1983). As a matter of fact, in an analysis of some 444 empirical articles drawn from 12 family-related journals by Ruano, Bruce, and McDermott (1969), the wife/mother was found to have served as a source of information on the family six times as often as her male counterpart—the husband/father.

Among the basic assumptions and justifications given for reliance on the wife/mother as the sole or primary source of data on the family have been the following:

1. Wives are more often available because they are home more often (an increasingly questionable assumption, we might add).
2. Wives are more cooperative.
3. Differences between partners in one marriage tend to compensate for differences between partners in another marriage.
4. There are no significant differences in the responses of wives and those of other family members (Ball *et al.*, 1983).

Nevertheless, there is considerable evidence that the responses and views of spouses may well be discrepant (Ball *et al.*, 1983; Bokemeier & Monroe, 1983). Although such discrepancies have been attributed by some to systematic differences in perceptions between husbands and wives, they have been dismissed by others as a reflection of nonsystematic measurement error (Bokemeier & Monroe, 1983). But whatever the case, the continued reliance on a single respondent in studies of the family has tended to be based essentially on grounds of pragmatism and convenience. That is, not only is the collection and analysis of data from more than one family member increasingly expensive and more complex, but more time is required to gather data and to arrange interviews with several family members (Bokemeier & Monroe, 1983).

On the other hand, although intrafamily differences are more difficult and complicated to interpret or explain than are similarities or perceptions of a single family member, Ball and associates (1983) have suggested that family researchers must begin to use methodologic and statistical designs that allow a "whole family perspective." Toward this end they have proposed the use of repeated measures (analysis of variance, or ANOVA, and multivariate analysis of variance, or MANOVA) "within family" designs. Such designs, they note, are generally more statistically efficient in detecting not only differences between family members, but also the extent to which these differences vary across different family types (Ball *et al.*, 1983).

As far as the study of family health and health care is concerned, although it is not surprising that given her role as the central agent of cure and care in the family setting, the wife/mother is frequently called on to serve as the primary source of information on the family and its members, she is not without her faults in this regard. Mechanic (1964), for instance, found that mothers under stress tended to report more symptoms of illness not only for themselves, but for their children as well. Moreover, mothers with less education were also more fatalistic about illness and less concerned about detecting and reporting it in their children. Similarly, Cartwright (1961) found discrepancies in the wives' estimates of their spouses' symptoms as compared to those of the husbands themselves.

In addition, such reports may be plagued by biases engendered by the normative values of medical relevance and social desirability. Kosa and colleagues (Kosa, Alpert, & Haggerty, 1967), for instance, found a tendency on the part of mothers to invoke a selective censorship involving norms of relevance, social desirability, privacy, and decency in separating reportable events from and those to be suppressed. Moreover, in response to questions concerning the temporal aspects of health, their replies tended to be structured in accordance with the implied reference and current health status of the family member involved. As a result, data collected about the same family, but at different points in time or in reference to various aspects of health and related behavior, may not necessarily be correlated.

Perhaps even more important, reliance on the wife/mother as the primary, if not sole, informant in surveys of family health serves to ignore the role played by other family members in times of health and illness, and to underestimate their potential contribution to our understanding of family health and health care. In fact, less tends to be known about the role of the husband/father vis-à-vis health and illness than about any other family member. Yet much can and should be learned from and about this often ignored family resource, and more consideration should be given to incorporating him in the data collection endeavor. The same is true for sibling children, as the work of Leonard (1983) has demonstrated. Using a sample of 77 healthy siblings of children newly diagnosed as being afflicted by one of four chronic illnesses (cancer, epilepsy, diabetes, or cystic fibrosis), she found that such children provided valuable insights about not only their own behavior but also that of their parents and affected brothers and/or sisters, and served as an important source of information on the impact of the sick child's illness on family relations.

Finally, although this chapter has focused on the need for more sophisticated, large-scale, longitudinal studies in family health, there is also a genuine and ongoing need for carefully crafted, small-scale, qualitative, exploratory research in this area. As Davis's (1963) classic study of family adjustment to polio well attests, such efforts not only can provide meaningful theoretical and practical insights, but, indeed, can also suggest a number of promising hypotheses to be tested and avenues of investigation to be pursued. Moreover, as Hill (cited in Menaghan, 1983, p. 130) has argued, such studies may well generate more discoveries per hour expended than can be gleaned from large-scale, quantitative verification or experimentally designed laboratory studies.

CONCLUSION

In conclusion, although much has been accomplished and great progress made over the past 10 years or so since we last assessed the state of the field, a number of methodologic problems and issues still remain to be overcome. With this in mind, the following recommendations are proposed:

1. There is a need for a greater merging of theory and methods in family health research, including the testing of hypotheses derived from research propositions

devised from a sound theoretical base. Just as Rogers (1973) noted in his critique of research in family development, if research on family health is ever to move beyond the current hit-or-miss, eclectic approach to data gathering and analysis, it must begin to seek a better formulated theoretical grounding.

2. As Sussman (1969) noted long ago, there remains a continuing need for cross-cultural validation of our findings. Without such efforts, much of what we know about the family in health and health care will remain culturally bound and constrained, limited both conceptually and theoretically.

3. There is also a need for development of a more extensive data base in family health, incorporating both the husband/father and member children into the data collection process.

4. Consideration should also be given to exploring the research potential of medical records maintained in health maintenance organizations (HMOs) as a source of behavioral and epidemiologic data in the study of family health.

5. Heeding Haggerty's (1965) call of nearly two decades ago, there remains a need not only for more epidemiologic studies of healthy families, but also for a greater incorporation of family-related variables in epidemiologic research.

6. Similarly, greater attention needs to be paid and better use made of family variables in surveys conducted by the National Center for Health Services Research, as well as the inclusion of health- and health care–related items as part of the federal census. (For an excellent compilation of available national health care data bases, see Mullner, Byre, & Killingsworth, 1983)

7. Exploration is also needed of the feasibility of using various observational techniques to record the involvement of family members in the care and treatment of institutionalized patients.

8. Finally, there is a need for the development of more extensive longitudinal and intergenerational studies of the family and health care, including:

    a. Studies of larger, more diverse samples, with multiple assessment points and repeated measures of outcome variables. In reviewing the family coping literature, for instance, Menaghan (1983) has noted that not only has multivariate assessment been rare, but when multiple regression methods have been used, nonlinear or nonadditive forms of relations were seldom examined. As a result, she has suggested that future studies would be more useful if they would consistently report basic distributions of variables, including their summary statistics as well as selected interrelationships, and examine the data for indications of nonadditivity or nonlinearity.

    b. Such studies, moreover, should embrace family units of more diverse structural forms (e.g., single-parent, dual-earner, reconstituted or blended families and of varying cultural and class characteristics.

Such suggestions, however, are not meant to underestimate the difficulty, both empirical and financial of accomplishing them. But if our quest for knowledge and understanding of the family's role in health and ilness is to be fulfilled, one can do no less.

References

Acock AC. Parents and their children: the study of intergenerational influence. Sociology and Social Research 1984; 69(2):151–171.

Aday LA, Chu GY, Anderson R. Methodological issues in health care surveys of the Spanish heritage populations. American Journal of Public Health 1980; 70:367–374.

Allen W. Black family research in the United States: a review, assessment and extension. Journal of Comparative Family Studies 1978; 9:167–189.

Alpert JJ, Kosa J, Haggerty RJ. A month of illness and health care among low-income families. Public Health Reports 1967; 82:705–713.

American Academy of Pediatrics. Family epidemiology: report of a symposium. Pediatrics 1965; 35:856–863.

Aneshensel CS, Frerichs RR, Clark VA, Yokopenic PA. Telephone versus in-person surveys of community health status. American Journal of Public Health 1982; 72:1017–1021.

Ball D, Mckenry PC, Price-Bonham S. Use of repeated-measures designs in family research. Journal of Marriage and the Family 1983; 45:885–896.

Becker MH, Green LW. A family approach to compliance with medical treatment: a selective review of the literature. International Journal of Health Education 1975; 18:2–11.

Berkanovic E. An appraisal of medical records as a data source. Medical Care 1974; 12:590–595.

Bernardo FM. Decade preview: some trends and directions for family research and theory in the 1980s. Journal of Marriage and the Family 1980; 42:723–728.

Bokemeier J, Monroe P. Continued reliance on one respondent in family decision-making studies: a content analysis. Journal of Marriage and the Family 1983; 45:645–652.

Brody EM, Johnson PT, Fulmer MC, Lang AM. Women's changing roles and help to elderly parents: attitudes of three generations of women. Journal of Gerontology 1983; 38(5):597–607.

Cartwright A. Some methodological problems encountered on a family morbidity survey. Unpublished doctoral dissertation, London University, 1961.

Christensen HT. The method of record linkage applied to family data. Marriage and Family Living 1958; 20(1):38–42.

Christensen HT. New approaches in family research: the method of record linkage. In: Sussman MB, ed. Sourcebook in marriage and the family. New York: Houghton Mifflin, 1965:530–535.

Connell RW. Political socialization in the American family. Public Opinion Quarterly 1972; 36:323–333.

Davis F. Passage through crisis. Indianapolis: Bobbs-Merrill, 1963.

Doherty WJ, McCubbin HI. Family and illness cycle. In: Patterson JM, McCubbin HI, eds. Family systems and health network. Family Stress, Coping & Health Project, Department of Family Social Science, University of Minnesota, St. Paul, 1984; 1(2):4–5.

Doherty WJ, McCubbin HI, eds. The family and health care [special issue]. Family Relations 1985; 34.

Downes J. The longitudinal study of families as a method of research. Milbank Memorial Fund Quarterly 1952; 30:101–118.

Downes J, Mertz JC. Effect of frequency of family visiting upon the reporting of minor illnesses. Milbank Memorial Fund Quarterly 1953; 31:371–390.

Elliott B. Families managing chronic stress: role enactment with physically disabled children. Unpublished doctoral dissertation, University of Minnesota, Minneapolis, 1983.

Espinoza R, Newman Y. Step parenting. DHEW publication no. (ADM) 78-579. Washington, D.C.: U.S. Government Printing Office, 1979.

Fink R. The family as a unit of medical care behavior, treatment, and of utilization analysis. In: Greenlick MR, ed. Conceptual issues in the analysis of medical care utilization and behavior [conference series]. Presented at Kaiser-Permanente Medical Care Program, Health Services Research Center, Portland, Oregon, October 29–31, 1969.

Glenn ND, Frisbie WP. Trend studies with survey sample and census data. Annual Review of Sociology 1977; 3:79–104.

Glick PC. Demographic analysis of family data. In: Christensen HT, ed. Handbook of marriage and family. Chicago: Rand McNally, 1964: 300–334.

Groves RM, Kahn RL. Surveys by telephone: a national comparison with personal interviews. New York: Academic Press, 1979.

Habermacher J. Hispanic health services: research conference proceedings. Department of Health and Human Services, Office of Health Records, Statistics and Technology. DHHS publication no. (PHS) 80-3288. Washington, D.C.: U.S. Government Printing Office, 1980.

Haggerty RJ. Epidemiology of health in families. Pediatrics 1965; 35:856–863.

Henson R, Roth A, Cannell C. Personal versus telephone reinterviews on reporting of psychiatric symptomatology in experiments. In: Interviewing techniques: field experiments in health reporting: 1971–77. DHEW publication no. (HRA) 78-3204. Washington, D.C.: U.S. Government Printing Office, 1972: 205–291.

Hill R. Sociology of marriage and family behavior: a trend report, 1945–56. Current Sociology 1958; 7(1):5.

Hill R. The strengths of black families. New York: Emerson Hall, 1972.

Hill R. Informal adoption among black families. Washington, D.C.: National Urban League, 1977.

Hill R, Foote N, Aldous J, Carlson R, MacDonald R. Family development in three generations. Cambridge, Mass.: Schenkman, 1970.

Hobbs DF Jr, Sussman MB. Impediments to family research: a symposium. Journal of Marriage and the Family 1965; 27:410–416.

Kaplan BH, Cassel JC, eds. Family and health: an epidemiological approach. Chapel Hill, N.C.: Institute for Research in Social Science, University of North Carolina, 1975.

Kitson GC, Sussman MB, Williams GK, Zeehandelaar RB, Shickmanter BK, Steinberger JL. Sampling issues in family research. Journal of Marriage and the Family 1982; 44:965–981.

Kosa J, Alpert JJ, Haggerty RJ. On the reliability of family health information. Social Science and Medicine 1967; 1:165–181.

Kreisman D, Joy VD. The family as reactor to the mental illness of a relative. In: Guttentag M, Struening EL, eds. Evaluation of mental health programs. Beverly Hills, Calif.: Sage Publications, 1975:483–518.

LaRossa R, Bennett LA, Gelles RJ. Ethical dimensions in qualitative family research. Journal of Marriage and the Family 1983; 45:303–313.

Leonard BJ. Psychosocial consequences on siblings of children with chronic illness. Unpublished doctoral dissertation, University of Minnesota, Minneapolis, 1983.

Litman TJ. Health care and the family: a three generational study. An exploratory study conducted under grant no. CH00167-02, Division of Community Health Services, U.S. Public Health Service, 1970.

Litman TJ. Health care and the family: an intergenerational analysis. Medical Care 1971; 9:67–81.

Litman TJ. The family as a basic unit in health and medical care: a social–behavioral overview. Social Science and Medicine 1974; 8:495–519.

Litman TJ, Venters M. Research on health care and the family: a methodology review. Social Science and Medicine 1979; 13a:379–385.

Macklin E. Nontraditional family forms: a decade of research. Journal of Marriage and the Family 1980; 42:905–922.

Malson M. The social support systems of black families. Marriage and Family Review 1982; 5:37–57.

Marcus AC, Telesky CW. Nonparticipation in telephone follow-up interviews. American Journal of Public Health 1983; 73:72–77.

Marquis KH. Evaluation of health diary data in the health insurance study. In: Sudman S, ed. Health survey research methods. National Center for Health Services Research. DHHS publication no. (PHS) 81-3268. Washington, D.C.: U.S. Government Printing Office, 1981: 159–164.

McAdoo H. Black mothers and the extended family support network. In: Rodgers-Rose LAF, ed. The black women. Beverly Hills, Calif.: Sage Publications, 1980.

McAdoo H. Stress and support networks of working single black mothers. Boston: Society for Research on Child Development, 1981.

McCubbin HI. Integrating coping behavior in family stress theory. Journal of Marriage and the Family. 1979; 41:237–244.

McCubbin HI, Cauble AE, Patterson JM, eds. Family stress, coping and social support. Springfield, Ill. C. C. Thomas, 1982.

McCubbin HI, Joy CB, Cauble AE, Comeau JK, Patterson JM, Needle RH. Family stress and coping: a decade review. Journal of Marriage and the Family 1980; 42:855–871.

McLanahan SS. Family structure and stress: a longitudinal comparison of two-parent and female-headed families. Journal of Marriage and the Family 1983; 45:347–357.

Mechanic D. The influence of mothers on their children's health attitudes and behavior. Pediatrics 1964; 33:444–453.

Menaghan EG. Individual coping efforts and family studies: conceptual and methodological issues. In: McCubbin HI, Sussman MB, Patterson JM, eds. Social stress and the family: advances and developments in family stress theory and research. Marriage and the Family Review 1983; 6:130–138.

Mullner RM, Byre C, Killingsworth CL. An inventory of U.S. health care data bases. Review of Public Data use 1983; 2:85–188.

Patterson JM, McCubbin HI, eds. Family systems and health network 1984; 1:4–5.

Patterson JM, McCubbin HI. Gender roles and coping. Journal of Marriage and the Family 1984; 46:102.

Pilisuk M, Parks SH. Social support and family stress. In: McCubbin HI, Sussman MB, Patterson JM, eds. Social stress and the family: advances and developments in family stress theory and research. Marriage and Family Review 1983; 6:137–156.

Pless IB, Miller JR. Apparent validity of alternative survey methods. Journal of Community Health 1979; 5:22–27.

Poulschock SW, Deimling GT. Families caring for elders in residence: issues in the measurement of burden. Annals of Gerontology 1984; 39(2):230–239.

Robinson BC. Validation of a caregiver strain index. Journal of Gerontology 1983; 38:344–348.

Rogers RH. Family interaction and transaction: the developmental approach. Englewood Clifs, N.J.: Prentice-Hall, 1973.

Roghmann KJ, Haggerty RJ. Measuring the use of health services in household interviews: a comparison of procedures used in three child health surveys. International Journal of Epidemiology 1974; 3(1):71–81.

Ruano BJ, Bruce JD, McDermott MM. Pilgrim's progress: II. Recent trends in family research. Journal of Marriage and the Family 1969; 31:688–698.

Schaie KW. Quasi-experimental research designs in the psychology of aging. In: Birren JE, Schaie KW, eds. Handbook of the psychology of aging. New York: Van Nostrand Reinhold, 1977: 39–58.

Schwenk TL, Hughes CC. The family as patient in family medicine: rhetoric or reality? Social Science and Medicine 1983; 17(1):1–16.

Shanas E. The family as social support systems in old age. The Gerontologist 1979; 19:169–174.

Shapiro J. Family reactions and coping strategies in response to the physically ill or handicapped child: a review. Social Science and Medicine 1983; 17(14):913–931.

Siemiatycki J. A comparison of mail, telephone and home interview strategies for household surveys. American Journal of Public Health 1979; 69:238–244.

Staples R, Mirande A. Racial and cultural variations among American families: a decennial review of the literature on minority families. Journal of Marriage and the Family 1980; 42:887–903.

Sussman MB. Cross-cultural family research: one view from the catbird seat. Journal of Marriage and the Family 1969; 31:203–208.

Thompson E, Doll W. The burden of families coping with the mentally ill: an invisible crisis. Family Relations 1982; 31(3):379–388.

Venters M. Chronic childhood illness/disability and familial coping: the case of cystic fibrosis. Unpublished doctoral dissertation, University of Minnesota, Minneapolis, 1980.

Venters M. Familial coping with chronic and severe childhood illness: the case of cystic fibrosis. Social Science and Medicine 1981; 15a:289–297.

Venters M, Schacht L, Ten Bensel R. Reporting of Down's syndrome for birth certificate data in the state of Minnesota. American Journal of Public Health 1976; 66:1099–1100.

Verbrugge L. Health diaries. Medical Care 1980; 18:73–95.

Wright RA, Beisel RH, Doliver J, Gerzowski MC. The use of multiple entry diary in a panel study on health care expenditure. Proceedings of the Social Statistics Section of the American Statistical Association 1976:848–852.

Young RF. The family–illness intermesh: theoretical aspects of their application. Social Science and Medicine 1983; 17(7):395–398.

Zarit JM. Predictions of burden and distress for caregivers of senile dementia patients. Unpublished doctoral dissertation, University of Southern California, Los Angeles, 1982.

Zarit S, Reeves KE, Bach-Peterson J. Relatives of the impaired elderly: correlates of feelings of burden. Gerontologist 1980; 20:649–655.

12

Family Assessment and Self-Report Instruments in Family Medicine Research

HAMILTON I. McCUBBIN
MARILYN A. McCUBBIN
ANNE I. THOMPSON
SHIH-TSENG T. HUANG
University of Wisconsin—Madison

The use of self-report family assessment measures in family medicine research is based on the premise that family functioning interacts with individual physiologic and psychologic processes in a discernible and predictable manner, and consequently affects the health status of the family members. Additionally, while family social scientists, epidemiologists, and physicians have pursued their research separately, we believe that in the context of family medicine they can mutually enhance each other's work, and collectively advance our knowledge of the relationship between the family environment and health-related outcomes. This emerging and interdisciplinary interest in family environment influences on health and disease can be linked to three important developments in health research: public health investigations, socioecologic research, and psychosomatic research.

This linkage between the family and health or disease can be traced to the origins of public health and social medicine, which grew out of research leading to the discovery that various diseases and plagues occurred more frequently in densely settled cities, in polluted air, and through rapid population growth. Nutrition, housing, poverty, social class, and other variables were also related to the occurrence of disease, and were shown to have an impact on growth and physique (Moos, 1977). With the major crowd diseases effectively controlled for, we enter into the third revolution of medicine, and struggle with physical "disorders engendered by malign environments and man's corrupt relations to his immediate world and his individual existence" (Moos, 1977).

Furthermore, because the majority of people are relatively healthy most of the time, even in association with biologic agents of disease thought to be ubiquitous in the environment (Dubos, 1965), there is reason to hypothesize that the social and interpersonal environment in which people live does play a critical catalytic role in promoting disease or in strengthening our resistance to disease. Environmental factors, including family relationships, may transform an innocuous relationship between agents of disease and the host person into one in which clinical disease is an outcome. Therefore, we need to examine family and environmental factors that alter or change the relationship between the person and these ubiquitous agents of disease (Cassell, 1976).

Psychosomatic medicine has also played a vital role in linking the environment, including the family unit, to clinical disease. Lipowski (1973a, 1973b), who assumed that individuals are psychobiologic entities in interaction with the environment, hypothesized that the social and physical environment influences the disease process in four distinct, but overlapping ways:

1. By creating symbolic stimuli that result in social communications that inform individuals as to the environment's noxious influence. This contributes to people viewing the physical environment as threatening, if not potentially lethal.
2. By introducing noxious, biologic, chemical, or physical pollutants that can cause tissue damage or mutations.
3. By directly affecting an individual's psychic processes, and changing a person's habitual modes of perceiving, thinking, and feeling.
4. By providing stimulus overload and, in turn, causing stress, and thus linking people's social and physical environment to their physiologic functioning.

Clearly, the family system is but one of a host of interrelated environmental influences that can and do have a profound impact on individual family members, and particularly on their physical and psychologic health status. But the research to substantiate this relationship is in an embryonic state of development. The jury remains in session deliberating the merits of current research that is offered in support of family research in health settings and the value of family interventions as a part of health care. However, until such research has been accumulated to guide family in-the-clinic interventions, the training of family physicians, and family-based prevention-oriented interventions (promoting health practices, etc.), we will continue to operate on the basis of faith, experience, clinical insights, and unconfirmed hypotheses. By discussing the various self-report measures of family functioning for use in family systems medicine research, we expect to reinforce extant investigations, and to encourage new and creative efforts in both instrument construction and hypothesis testing in this emerging arena of family systems medicine research.

CHALLENGES IN THE SELECTION OF SELF-REPORT MEASURES OF FAMILY FUNCTIONING FOR HEALTH RESEARCH

The selection of self-report measures of family functioning for health research linking the family system to health outcomes is a major challenge for social and biosocial scientists for several important reasons. First, we struggled with *the problem of conceptualization and definition.* To the practicing physician and to family therapists, the concept of family functioning has heuristic value and hence meaning. Yet, as we discuss family functioning, this apparent understandable phenomenon becomes increasingly slippery; we have many different definitions of family functioning, and each means different things to different professionals. Some would describe family functioning in terms of structure—the single-parent, two-parent, or binuclear family; the reconstituted family, the gay family, the lesbian family, and so on. Others would point to the interactional nature of families, with an emphasis on family communication, cohesion, adaptability, conflict, expressiveness, control, and affective involvement, to name a few. Still others would describe family functioning in terms of its transactional processes—coping, adaptation, social support, assimilation, and accommodation. Finally, some family specialists would emphasize the psychologic characteristics of family members, such as esteem, depression, and denial, as indices of family functioning. The systematic assessment of family functioning by self-report measures is limited by the lack of agreed-on concepts and definitions. Consequently, we have narrowed our selection of instruments to those that have well-defined family-system-oriented constructs and that appear to fit the broad range of concepts used to describe how families respond to change, stress, and their developmental tasks.

Second, we are challenged by the rather elusive responses given to the basic question, "Why are we interested in family functioning in health research?" Up to this point in the chapter we have presented only one research question to be studied: the role of the family in shaping the conditions leading to the onset of disease in a family member. But is this the only research question of interest to the family physician, or the family physician turned researcher? There is reason to believe that *family medicine research involves a host of related research questions that call for alternative self-report measures of family functioning.* Specifically, family physicians might also be interested in the systematic assessment of (1) family functioning in response to acute illnesses; (2) family functioning in shaping the adjustment of member-patients with specific medical conditions, such as coronary bypass surgery or renal transplantation; and (3) family functioning in the long-term rehabilitation of member-patients with chronic health conditions such as diabetes, cystic fibrosis, and cerebral palsy. It is important to determine what aspects of family functioning are to be evaluated or assessed for the different research questions. Therefore, we selected self-report measures that encompass a range of dimensions associated with family functioning, and that would be applicable to a wide range of relevant questions and hypotheses in family medicine research.

Third, we are challenged by the *methodologic limitations and strengths of self-report measures.* Any review of the various methods of measuring families would surface the laundry list of difficulties associated with self-report measures, including (1) distortion in the recall of family information, (2) lack of objectivity in perceptions that guide the recording of self-report observations, and (3) the difficulty of deriving family-level measures from individual self-report assessments of family functioning. Additionally, we were sensitive to the fact that self-report measures have unique and positive properties of interest to health researchers. Specifically, self-report measures have the potential for capturing family dynamics across a period of time. Family members are called on to sample their life experiences, across time and across events, and to use these recollections to describe, evaluate, and record their assessment of how the family behaves. Therefore, in selecting self-report measures to be reviewed here, we focused on those instruments that operationalized family dynamics, interpersonal properties, and processes that evolved over time, and which we felt the self-report measures were best suited to capture.

Fourth, if family medicine research is to build on previous research and to maximize the accretion of research data and findings, it is vital that *medicine-oriented family systems theories be used* to guide the development of self-report assessment of family functioning. Idiosyncratic measures that are unique to a specific study have immediate value to the family physician but may present major obstacles to a group of professionals *searching for common threads of evidence that point to the importance of the family in health research.* Instruments based on theories about family functioning, particularly in relationship to health outcomes, have a greater potential for being refined and improved on while remaining focused on the family property or dimension being measured. This process of developing and refining self-report instruments is a vital and valued part of family medicine research, and is enhanced by a strong linkage between the instruments and a systems-oriented theoretical foundation. It follows that the basic assumptions of this systems model would emphasize (1) the parts of the family that are interrelated; (2) that one part of the family cannot be understood in isolation from the rest of the system; (3) that family functioning cannot be fully understood by simply understanding each of the parts; (4) that a family's structure and organization are important factors determining the behavior of family members; and (5) that transactional patterns of the family system shape the behavior of family members. Therefore, we limited our selection of self-report instruments to those that were based on a documented theoretic framework.

Finally, we are challenged by the ever-present need to refine and confirm the strengths of self-report measures through standardized procedures establishing the instruments' reliability and validity. Although this seems to be an obvious criterion in the selection of instruments, this matter takes on added complexity and importance in family health research. Certainly, the standard psychometric procedures used to confirm an instrument's reliability (test–retest, internal consistency, split-half, etc.) and validity (concurrent, discriminatory, construct, etc.) apply to family health research. But we are also challenged by the need to validate these measures in relationship to specific health outcomes. We must accumulate evidence that confirms that measures of family functioning are sensitive to physiologic changes, changes in health status, and medical conditions of family members. In this review we selected those self-report measures that already have confirmatory statistics as to their link to health outcomes. Additionally, recognizing that some of the strongest self-report measures are now being used in health research, we selected those we felt had the greatest potential of validation against criterion indices of physiologic changes and health status.

In the final analysis, three self-report instruments and three sets (i.e., grouping of instruments designed to assess different dimensions of family functioning defined by the same theoretic framework or variations of the same instrument) of instruments were selected for this review:

1. The Family APGAR (FAPGAR) (Smilkstein, 1978)
2. The Family Environment Scales (FES) (Moos, 1974)
3. The Family Assessment Device (FAD) (Epstein, Levin, & Bishop, 1976)
4. The Family Assessment Measure (FAM-III) (Steinhauer, Santa-Barbara, & Skinner, 1984)
5. The Family Adaptability and Cohesion Evaluation Scales (FACES I, II, and III) (Olson, Portner, & Bell, 1982; Olson, Portner, & Lavee, 1985)
6. The typology model of family adjustment and adaptation measures—Demands, Resources, Coping, Support, and Appraisal (FILE, FIRM, CHIP, FHI, and FTRI) (McCubbin & Patterson, 1981; McCubbin, McCubbin, & Thompson, 1987)
7. The Beavers System of Family Assessment—Self-Report Family Inventory (SFI) (Beavers, 1987)

At the outset it is important to underscore the unique importance and value of each instrument or set of instruments in family systems medicine research. Although this review may appear critical and will reference apparent discrepancies between the ideal expectations and the limitations of each instrument, we also point to the embryonic nature of instrument development and testing in family medicine. As already noted, the jury is still in session and is not likely to render any firm judgment until a sufficient body of empirical data is presented and reviewed. This chapter introduces six instruments or clusters of instruments with the intention of encouraging new and creative research, with the ultimate goal of advancing our understanding of family relationships and its impact on and response to the health status of its members. Over time we will accumulate the empirical verifications or refutations we seek about these self-report instruments. But until then we indicate our total support for and appreciation of these six instruments, note their relative value to a wide range of research questions, and acknowledge their contribution to this valuable line of scientific inquiry.

In an effort to introduce the six self-report instruments (or sets of instruments) in a brief but meaningful manner, we have introduced the appropriate conceptual frameworks for each, described the instruments and their major dimensions, and discussed their psychometric properties. In summary, we compared and contrasted the self-report measures, and highlighted their apparent value to family medicine research.

THE FAMILY APGAR (FAPGAR)

Smilkstein (1978), of the University of Washington, was challenged by the observation that whereas a host of examinations and tests were available to the physician for evaluating a diseased organ's functional state, there were few tools for evaluating the family unit of which the patient is a part. Furthermore, although questionnaires and procedures existed to establish the state of functional integrity of the family, none had proved of practical value for daily use in the physician's office.

In response to this challenge, Smilkstein (1978, 1984) introduced a brief screening questionnaire called the Family APGAR, which was designed to elicit a data base that would reflect a patient's view of the functional state of his or her family. The APGAR acronym was applied because the author felt that APGAR was familiar to physicians involved in the evaluation of the newborn.

Since family structure and family function play a part in understanding and managing the complaint of the individual patient as well as of the family in trouble, Smilkstein (1978, p. 1232) focused on the family unit as part of "medical" care and treatment. He defined the family as a psychosocial group consisting of the patient and one or more other persons, children or adults, in which there is a commitment for members to nurture each other. This definition allows for a wide range of family life styles, including the traditional nuclear family, communal groups, and nonmarried partners, whether heterosexual or homosexual. The process of nurturing included in the definition is equated with family function that promotes emotional and physical growth and maturation of its members.

Five basic components of family function were selected, defined, and operationalized in the development of the Family APGAR. These components and their definitions appeared to represent common themes dealing with families in the social science literature. These dimensions may also be likened to the body's organ system, in that each component had a unique function, yet each was interrelated with the whole. The family in health may be considered to be a nurturing unit that demonstrates integrity of the components of (1) *A*daptability, (2) *P*artnership, (3) *G*rowth, (4) *A*ffection, and (5) *R*esolve.

The Family APGAR, a questionnaire that features five closed-ended questions, is introduced by the author as a screening test to give a rapid overview of the components of family function. The questionnaire is designed so that it may be given to members of either nuclear or alternative life-style families. The questions are designed to permit qualitative measurement of the family member's satisfaction with each of the five basic components of family function. The functional components of the Family APGAR are as follows:

1. *Adaptation:* How resources are shared, or the degree to which a member is satisfied with the assistance received when family resources are needed

2. *Partnership:* How decisions are shared, or the member's satisfaction with mutuality in family communication and problem solving
3. *Growth:* How nurturing is shared, or the member's satisfaction with the freedom available within the family to change roles and attain physical and emotional growth or maturation
4. *Affection:* How emotional experiences are shared, or the member's satisfaction with the intimacy and emotional interaction that exists in a family
5. *Resolve:* How time (and space and money) is shared, or the member's satisfaction with the time commitment that has been made to the family by its members

Psychometric Properties

Smilkstein, Ashworth, and Montano (1982) describe the reliability and validity of the Family APGAR. Initial validation was done by correlating global scores on this five-item questionnaire with the Pless-Satterwhite Family Function Index (validity correlation of .80), and with estimates of family function made by psychotherapists (validity correlation of .64). Internal reliability (Cronbach alpha) estimates range from .80 to .86. The authors concluded that the Family APGAR was a reliable, validated, and utilitarian instrument. Further studies are now underway to examine the use of the Family APGAR to correlate family function with utilization of medical facilities, somatization, compliance, and outcome of health problems. The authors present a strong and persuasive argument for the use of the Family APGAR in family practice. Through the use of medical case studies, Smilkstein (1978) points out the importance of family assessment in medical care and the viability of the Family APGAR in the conduct of these family-focused evaluations.

Research/Clinical Applications

Three situations have been identified in which the physician may need information on the functional state of the patient's family:

1. When functional information is needed where the family will be involved with the patient's care, as in the case of a patient with coronary artery disease, knowledge of family functioning would assist in ascertaining the family's ability to support the patient's return home.
2. When a new patient is introduced to a physician's practice, the Family APGAR would permit the physician to establish a baseline view of family function.
3. When the physician is involved in managing a family in trouble, the Family APGAR would provide necessary information on family function.

Smilkstein (1978) recommended that the Family APGAR be used as part of a broader data base to be collected regarding (1) identifying and evaluating the family's crises, present and past; (2) the level of family function; and (3) the family's resources through assessment of those resources. In support of this line of reasoning, the author proposes a modification in the problem-oriented record so that the format (data base, numbered problem list, titled plan, and follow-up) can be applied to the family.

THE FAMILY ENVIRONMENT SCALES (FES)

In elaborating on environmental factors that have an impact on health, Moos (1974) introduced a comprehensive socioecologic perspective designed to advance our understanding of and to explain the complex but important linkage between the environment and health status. Specifically, Moos (1979) discussed the central importance of the personal and the environmental systems in determining the individual's health status. The *personal system* includes age, socioeconomic status, sex, intelligence, cognitive and emotional development, ego strength, self-esteem, attitudes, values, traits, and expectations. The *environmental system* includes the physical setting, organizational factors, the human aggregate, and the social climate. The family system, which is an integral part of the social climate, is characterized by the relationship dimension, the personal growth or goal orientation dimension, and the system maintenance and system change dimensions.

The Family Environment Scale (FES) is a 90-item true–false questionnaire that focuses on the interpersonal relationships among family members, on the directions of personal growth emphasized in the family, and on the organizational structure of the family. It consists of 10 subscales that measure three domains of the family milieu: *relationship* dimensions (cohesion, expressiveness, conflict); *personal growth* or *goal orientation* dimensions (independence, achievement orientation, moral–religious emphasis, and intellectual–cultural and active–recreational orientation; and *systems maintenance* and *change* dimensions (organization, control). These three domains, which characterize a variety of settings ranging from classrooms to work environments (Moos, 1974), provide the clinician with a conceptual framework to help organize many disparate observations about a family system (Eichel, 1978; Moos & Fuhr, 1982). The 10 FES subscales are shown in Table 12-1. A description of the logic underlying the FES, the steps involved in its construction, its

Table 12-1. The Family Environment Scale and Subscales

I. Relationship dimensions	
1. Cohesion	Commitment, help, and support family members provide for one another
2. Expressiveness	How much family members are encouraged to act openly and to express their feelings directly
3. Conflict	The amount of openly expressed anger, aggression, and conflict among family members
II. Personal growth dimensions	
4. Independence	Extent to which family members are assertive, self-sufficient, and able to make their own decisions
5. Achievement orientation	Extent to which activities (e.g., school and work) are cast in an achievement-oriented or competitive framework
6. Intellectual–cultural orientation	Degree of interest in political, social, intellectual, and cultural activities
7. Active–recreational orientation	The extent of participation in social and recreational activities
8. Moral	Emphasis on ethical and religious issues
III. System maintenance dimensions	
9. Organization	The importance of clear organization and structure in planning family activities and responsibilities
10. Control	The extent to which set rules and procedures are used to run family life

psychometric characteristics, and a review of relevant research is provided elsewhere (Moos, 1974, 1979).

Psychometric Properties

In brief, an initial pool of 200 items was reduced to the final 90-item self-report questionnaire after analysis of the responses of a diverse sample of 285 families. The subscales have internal consistencies ranging from .64 to .79, 8-week test–retest reliabilities ranging from .68 to .86, and average intercorrelations of about .20. The scale has been used with more than 1,600 families in over 45 studies focused on its construct validity, its relationship to other dimensions of family functioning, and its implications for treatment outcome (Moos, Bromet, Tsu, & Moos, 1979; Moos & Moos, 1984). Normative data are also available to the family physician to facilitate the identification of those "at-risk" families. There is a Real Form and an Ideal Form of the FES. Family members use the Real Form (Form R) to describe the current family environment and the Ideal Form (Form I) to describe their preferred or ideal family.

Research/Clinical Applications

Over the past 9 years, the FES has been used as a complement to ongoing family therapy. Typically, the Real and Ideal Forms of the FES are administered early in therapy, and the Real Form is given again both at the end of therapy and several months later. The authors have made a concerted effort to render clarity to the Family Environment Scale and to demonstrate its utility in clinical settings.

In summarizing the clinical value of the FES, we can expand on Fuhr, Moos, and Dishotsky's (1981) conclusions, and argue that:

1. Since the FES focuses on the present family situation, it can help shift attention from exclusive concern with medical problems of the "identified patient" to a consideration of family issues and concerns.
2. The FES can be used to organize and objectify the discussion of family issues in relationship to medical treatment.
3. Through the use of the Ideal Form of the FES, family members can take an active part in shaping the nature of their goals. It can be used to foster consensus on needed change, or, at minimum, to clarify the nature and extent of discrepancies in family goals.
4. The FES can be used to monitor the progress and outcome of family changes, particularly in relationship to improvements or deterioration in the patient's medical condition.

THE FAMILY ASSESSMENT DEVICE (FAD)

The McMaster model of family functioning (MMFF) has developed over a period of 25 years from studies of normal as well as clinical populations. The initial research that contributed to the model's evolution was conducted in the late 1950s at McGill University (Westley & Epstein, 1969). In the late 1960s and through the 1970s, work on the model took place at McMaster University. Currently, research and theory-building activities are taking place at both McMaster and Brown universities.

The model is based on concepts from the family therapy literature, as well as from the authors' clinical, teaching, and research experience. Consequently, the model has been continually refined and reformulated. The concepts have been tested in clinical work, re-search, and teaching. Inconsistencies in observations and empirical invalidations have become the basis for reformulations in the MMFF. The model has been used extensively in a variety of psychiatric and family practice clinics (Comley, 1973; Sigal, Rakoff, & Epstein, 1967; Westley & Epstein, 1960, 1969). The framework has also been used successfully in a number of family therapy programs (Bishop & Epstein, 1979).

Like all the instruments discussed in this chapter, the MMFF is based on a systems perspective.

> The family is seen as an open system consisting of systems within systems (individual, marital, dyad, etc.) and relating to other systems (extended family, school, industry, etc.). The unique aspect of the dynamic family group cannot be simply reduced to characteristics of the individual or interaction between pairs of members. Rather, there are explicit and implicit rules, plus action by members, which govern and monitor each other's behavior. (Epstein & Bishop, 1973, p. 176)

The McMaster model is based on the assumption that the primary function of today's family unit is to provide a setting for the development and maintenance of family members on the social, psychologic, and biologic levels (Epstein, Levin, & Bishop, 1976, p. 1411). In the course of fulfilling this function, families will have to deal with a variety of issues and problems, or tasks, which the authors group into three areas: basic tasks, developmental tasks, and hazardous tasks. The most fundamental, the *basic tasks,* involve the provision of food, money, transportation, and shelter. The *developmental tasks* encompass those family issues that arise as a result of development over time. These developments are associated with individual and family stages. The *hazardous tasks* involve the management of crises that arise as a result of illness, accident, loss of income, and other major and minor life events and changes. Families that are able to deal effectively with these three task areas are most likely to endure and thrive and less likely to develop clinically significant problems and/or chronic maladaptive problems.

To advance the development of the MMFF around structure, organization, and transaction patterns of the family, the authors focused on six dimensions: problem solving, communication, roles, affective responsiveness, affective involvement, and behavioral control. The same MMFF dimensions served to guide the development of a self-report instrument called the Family Assessment Device.

The McMaster Family Assessment Device (FAD) was designed as a paper-and-pencil, self-report questionnaire that can be filled out by all family members over the age of 12. The 53 items in the questionnaire are statements a person could make about his or her family. The FAD measures structural and organizational properties of the family group and the patterns of transactions among family members that have been found to distinguish between healthy and unhealthy families. Specifically, in addition to a measure of *General Functioning,* FAD assesses six dimensions of family functioning, as follows:

1. *Problem Solving:* This dimension of the MMFF refers to the family's ability to resolve problems. Seven steps of effective problem solving are identified.
2. *Communication:* This dimension is defined as the exchange of information among

family members. The focus is on whether verbal messages are clear in content and direct in the sense that the person spoken to is the one for whom the message is intended.

3. *Roles:* Here the MMFF focuses on whether the family has established patterns of behavior for handling a set of family functions that includes providing resources, providing nurturance and support, supporting personal development, maintaining and managing the family system, and providing adult sexual gratification. In addition, assessment of Roles dimension includes consideration of whether tasks are clearly and equitably assigned to family members, and are carried out responsibly by family members.

4. *Affective Responsiveness:* This dimension assesses the extent to which individual family members are able to experience appropriate affect over a range of stimuli. Both welfare and emergency emotions (Rado, 1961) are considered.

5. *Affective Involvement:* This dimension is concerned with the extent to which family members are interested in and place value on each other's activities and concerns. The healthiest families have intermediate levels of involvement, neither too little nor too much.

6. *Behavior Control:* This final dimension assesses the way in which a family expresses and maintains standards of behavior of its members. Behavior in situations of different sorts (dangerous, psychologic, and social) are assessed, as are different patterns of control (flexible, rigid, laissez-faire, and chaotic).

The scales and related items are presented in Table 12-2.

Table 12-2. Family Assessment Device: Major Subscales and Sample Items

Problem solving:
  We usually act on our decisions regarding problems.
  After our family tries to solve a problem, we usually discuss whether it worked or not.

Communication:
  When someone is upset, the others know why.
  You can't tell how a person is feeling from what they are saying.
  People come right out and say things instead of hinting at them.

Roles:
  When you ask someone to do something, you have to check that they did it.
  We make sure members meet their family responsibilities.
  Family tasks don't get spread around enough.

Affective responsiveness:
  We are reluctant to show our affection for each other.
  Some of us just don't respond emotionally.
  We do not show our love for each other.

Affective involvement:
  If someone is in trouble, the others become too involved.
  You only get the interest of others when something is important to them.
  We are too self-centered.

Behavioral control:
  We don't know what to do when an emergency comes up.
  You can easily get away with breaking the rules.
  We know what to do in an emergency.

General functioning:
  Planning family activities is difficult because we misunderstand each other.
  In times of crisis we can turn to each other for support.
  We cannot talk to each other about the sadness we feel.

Psychometric Properties

The Family Assessment Device (FAD) was based on the responses of a sample of 503 individuals. Of these individuals, 294 came from a group of 112 families. This group includes 4 families of children in a psychiatric day hospital, 6 families of patients in a stroke rehabilitation unit, and 9 families of students in advanced psychology courses. The remaining 93 families in this group contained one member who as an inpatient in an adult psychiatric hospital. The total sample was selected so that it would contain individuals from families varying considerably in their level of functioning.

The reliability coefficients for the seven scales range from .72 to .92. The intercorrelations of the FAD subscales range from .4 to .6, indicating only a moderate degree of independence. However, the authors reported that the partial correlations between the dimensions approach zero when General Functioning is held constant. The variance shared between the dimensions is, for the most part, accounted for by the variance that each shares with the General Functioning Scale.

The authors report two general findings that suggested that the FAD has validity. First, using data from a sample of 503 individuals, they compared the FADs for 218 nonclinical families and 98 clinical families in a discriminant analysis to determine whether family scores on the FAD could predict whether the family came from the clinical or the nonclinical group. Sixty-seven percent of the nonclinical group and 64% of the clinical group were correctly predicted. Second, they examined the retirement adjustment of 178 couples in their 60s. To assess concurrent validity, they used regression analysis. The FAD explained 28% of the variance on couple marital satisfaction for both husbands and wives analyzed separately. The FAD also explained 22% of the variance in the moral scores for husbands and 17% of the variance for wives.

Research/Clinical Applications

The authors have argued persuasively for the usefulness of FAD:

1. It is an economical paper-and-pencil test containing 53 items.
2. It provides assessment of families in terms of a well-described specific model that has itself been proved useful in clinical work.
3. It provides a more detailed picture of families than do other available scales, because it contains seven different scales, each having acceptable reliability.

THE FAMILY ASSESSMENT MEASURE (FAM)

The process model of family functioning, on which the Family Assessment Measure is based, differs from the McMaster model of family functioning and from their common source, the family categories schema, by its increased emphasis on the dynamic interaction between the major dimensions of family functioning, and by its emphasis on the interface between intrapsychic subsystems and the interpersonal dimension of the family system.

While respecting the McMaster model of family functioning's contributions to providing an organizing structure, Steinhauer, Santa-Barbara, and Skinner (1984) felt the need for a more process-oriented and dynamic model that would satisfy the following four criteria:

1. The model would be capable of describing successful and unsuccessful patterns of family structure and functioning.
2. The model would allow a summary and integration of various clinical and research findings.
3. The model would provide a dynamic and process-oriented conceptual framework to guide clinical assessment and ongoing treatment.
4. The model would encourage the generation of new and researchable hypotheses and insights into the structure and functioning of families.

The process model of family functioning (PMFF) is an attempt to meet these four criteria. Consequently, the model emphasizes the dynamic interaction between the major dimensions of family functioning by its greater emphasis on the ongoing and interrelated development of individual and family. It goes beyond merely describing family structure to describing family process. Additionally, it systematically begins the task of integrating systems theory with theories of individual psychopathology. It emphasizes the important linkage between the individual subsystems and the family system. Finally, the model emphasizes a systematic attempt to define the interface between the family and the greater social system of which it is but a part.

The family process model of family functioning (FPMFF) underscores the basic assumption that the family and its members share common goals or objectives without which the family would not exist (Skynner, 1969; Tallman, 1970). The overriding goals of the family are to provide for the biologic, psychologic, and social development and maintenance of family members, thereby ensuring the survival of both the family and the species (Ackerman, 1958; Murdock, 1960; Parsons & Bales, 1955). These overriding goals require the execution of certain tasks. Steinhauer, Santa-Barbara, and Skinner (1984) assume that these tasks may vary over the course of the family life cycle, but they involve the same basic skills and processes. It is through successful task accomplishment that families achieve their biologic, psychologic, and social goals, including ensuring the continuing development of all family members, providing reasonable security and autonomy for all, adapting usual patterns of functioning to meet environmental and developmental demands for change, and supplying the cohesion needed to hold the family together.

The PMFF focuses on three types of tasks to be accomplished. *Basic tasks* are those related to day-to-day survival (food, shelter, health care, etc.). *Developmental tasks* provide for the continuing development of all members evolving constantly over the course of the family's life cycle as members' developmental needs change. *Crisis tasks* include the family's way of dealing with the periodic crises that result when the number and intensity of stressors confronting the family exceed the combined skills and resources (psychologic, familial, and social) available to deal with them. In crisis situations, the family's capacity for successful task accomplishment is undermined or curtailed as the basic skills on which family problem solving and tension management depend may be overwhelmed or at least diverted.

Family values and norms will shape every aspect of a family's functioning. A family's norms are the sum total of what is or is not considered acceptable within the family. The family's values may be either consonant with or dissonant from those of society. While the PMFF identifies which characteristics are conducive to healthful or pathologic family functioning, it is not possible to take such a position with values and norms. Nevertheless, understanding a family's values and norms is crucial for understanding that family's functioning.

To accomplish these tasks, family members are called on to achieve a high level of *role performance*. Roles are prescribed, and repetitive behaviors involving a set of reciprocal activities with other family members are measured. Collectively, these roles and their performance either facilitate or interfere with successful task accomplishment. The authors classify roles into either *traditional* or *idiosyncratic*. Traditional roles contribute to the accomplishment of essential family tasks, but the definition of a traditional role (father, wife, teenager, etc.) may vary depending on the values and norms of the society and of those subcultures in which the individual or family is involved. There is no one "correct" definition of traditional roles; each family arrives at a definition that works for it. Idiosyncratic roles do not contribute directly to task accomplishment, and are often the expression of individual and/or family pathology. Some families, for example, delegate one member to the role of family scapegoat, sacrificing his or her development to allow the family as a unit to exist in relative comfort.

Effective role performance and definition and task accomplishment in the family unit necessarily involves family *communication* and *affective expression*. It is through communication that the information required for effective role performance and task accomplishment is exchanged. The goal of communication—the achievement of mutual understanding—will occur if messages sent are clear, direct, and sufficient, and if receivers are psychologically available and open to receiving them with minimal distortion. In content, a characteristic can be affective (expression of feeling), instrumental (related to the ongoing task of everyday life), or neutral (neither instrumental nor affective). The more disturbed the family system, the greater the disturbance in affective communication.

Concomitantly, the family members' affective (emotional) involvement with each other and family control or way of influencing one another play a critical role in helping or hindering role performance and definition, communication, and ultimately task accomplishment. *Affective involvement* refers to the degree and quality of family members' interest and concern for one another. Optimally, the family will meet all members' emotional needs—thus providing the cohesion, security, and sense of being valued that contribute to the development of self-esteem and independence—while at the same time valuing and protecting each member's right to independent thought and behavior. *Control* is a PMFF concept used to describe a variety of interpersonal strategies or techniques to influence members' behavior. Family members will need to influence each other in two distinct situations, either to sustain ongoing functioning or to allow the family to adapt to changing task demands. Ideally, family control should emphasize consistency of style, educational and nurturing techniques, and achievement and internalization of a sense of personal responsibility.

The process model of family functioning focuses on family function rather than structure, and thus defines six universal criteria of family functioning. A self-report test—the Family Assessment Measure III (FAM-III)—developed from the model is being widely used both as a research tool and as a clinical adjunct.

THE FAMILY ASSESSMENT MEASURE III (FAM-III)

The Family Assessment Measure III was aimed at providing an operational definition of the constructs in the process model. The present version of the FAM-III assesses the family from three different perspectives. The General Scale (50 items, 9 subscales) focuses on the level of health-pathology in the family from a systems perspective. This scale provides an overall rating of family functioning, seven measures relating to the process model, plus two response style subscales (Social Desirability and Denial). The Dyadic Relationship

Scale (42 items, 7 subscales) focuses on relationships among specific pairs (dyads) in the family. For each dyad, an overall rating of functioning is provided, along with an index (subscale) for each construct of the process model. The Self-Rating Scale (42 items, 7 subscales) focuses on the individual's perception of his or her functioning in the family. An overall index is provided, along with seven measures relating to the process model.

Psychometric Properties

Preliminary analyses have been conducted on FAM-III using a heterogeneous sample of 475 families who were tested at various health and social service settings in the Toronto area. The reliability estimates are provided for the overall rating and various subscales. The estimates for the overall ratings are substantial: *adults*—.93 General Scale, .95 Dyadic Relationships, and .89 Self-Rating; *children*—.94 General Scale, .94 Dyadic Relationships, and .86 Self-Rating (Steinhauer, Santa Barbara, & Skinner, 1984).

A multivariate comparison of problem and nonproblem families was conducted to provide evidence on the diagnostic power of the FAM-III General Scale. "Problem" families were defined as currently having one or more family members receiving professional help for psychiatric/emotional problems, alcohol/drug problems, school-related problems, or major legal problems. These groups were contrasted with nonproblem families. A multiple discriminant analysis was conducted to identify linear combinations of the nine General Scale measures that significantly differentiated among the six groups. The two discriminant functions differentiated children from adults and problem from nonproblem families. Problem families in general are likely to report family dysfunction in roles and affective involvement. Nonproblem families have a tendency to be somewhat higher in social desirability and denial, although these differents appear to be minor. The discriminatory power of FAM-III has not been established for the Dyadic and Self-Rating Scales. Test–retest reliabilities are now being examined.

Research/Clinical Applications

Although the FAM-III provides a comprehensive overview of family functioning and an objective and independent verification of the clinical assessment, it is not intended as a substitute for clinical assessment. At present, normative data are being collected on various clinical and nonclinical populations. The instrument has the advantage of being grounded in a comprehensive model of family functioning and offers considerable promise as a brief assessment tool for the clinician and the researcher interested in the assessment of major strengths and weaknesses in a family.

THE FAMILY ADAPTABILITY AND COHESION EVALUATION SCALES (FACES)

The circumplex model of family behavior, which will be presented in greater depth elsewhere in this book (see Olson, Chapter 6, this volume), provided the basic foundation and overriding framework in the development of the three versions (FACES I, II, and III) of the Family Adaptability and Cohesion Evaluation Scales (FACES). Olson and associates (Olson & McCubbin, 1982; Olson, McCubbin, Barnes, Larsen, Muxem, & Wilson, 1983;

Olson, Sprenkle, & Russell, 1979; Russell, 1979; Sprenkle & Olson, 1978) have advanced the development of one of the major conceptual frameworks in family therapy and family research. Family cohesion, adaptability, and communication are three dimensions of family behavior that emerged from a conceptual clustering of over 50 concepts developed to describe marital and family dynamics. After reviewing the conceptual definitions of many of these concepts, Olson and associates argued that the terms were conceptually similar, and dealt with closely related family processes. One family process focused on the degree to which an individual was separated from or connected to his or her family system, and was called *cohesion*. The second dimension focused on family *adaptability*, the degree to which the family system was flexible and able to change. The third dimension was *communication* between various members.

Family cohesion is defined as the emotional bonding that family members have toward one another. There are four levels of cohesion ranging from disengaged to separated to connected to enmeshed. The developers of this framework hypothesized that the central levels of cohesion (separated and connected) are the most viable for family functioning. The extremes (disengaged and enmeshed) are generally seen as problematic.

Family adaptability is defined as the ability of a marital or family system to change its power structure, role relationships, and relationship rules in response to situational and developmental stress. The four levels of adaptability range from rigid to structured to flexible to chaotic. As with cohesion, it is hypothesized that central levels of adaptability (structured and flexible) are more conducive to marital and family functioning throughout the family life cycle than are the extremes (rigid and chaotic).

Communication, the third dimension in the circumplex model, is the facilitating dimension of family functioning. Communication is considered crucial to movement on the other two dimensions. Positive communication skills (empathy, reflective listening, supportive comments) enable couples and families to share with each other their changing needs and preferences as they relate to cohesion and adaptability. Negative communication skills (double messages, double binds, criticism) minimize the ability of a couple or family members to share their feelings and thereby restrict their movement on these dimensions.

The family cohesion and adaptability dimensions were integrated into the circumplex model as formulated by David H. Olson, Candyce Russell, and Douglas Sprenkle (1983). When cohesion and adaptability are placed orthogonally to each other, 16 distinct types of marital and family systems are identified by combining the four levels of the cohesion and four levels of the adaptability dimensions. Four of the 16 family types are moderate *(Balanced types)* on both cohesion and adaptability dimensions. Eight types are extreme on one dimension and moderate on the other *(Midrange types)*, and four types are extreme on both dimensions *(Extreme types)*.

The Family Adaptability and Cohesion Evaluation Scales (FACES) were initially developed and tested as part of doctoral dissertation research. Sprenkle and Olson (1978) focused on the adaptability dimension and examined the interaction processes of 25 couples in marriage counseling and 25 nonclinical married couples. Russell (1979) studied both the cohesion and adaptability dimensions, testing 31 clinical families with adolescent girls. As hypothesized, high-functioning families were moderate on cohesion and adaptability, while low-functioning families scored at extremes of cohesion and adaptability.

The Family Adaptability and Cohesion Evaluation Scales (FACES I, FACES II, FACES III) were designed to enable the researcher or clinician to place individual families or groups of families within the circumplex model. This assists in further understanding the dynamics of particular kinds of families and in setting treatment goals and program objectives. The three versions of FACES were designed so that individual family members can describe how they perceive their family. The reading level for the instruments was about 7th grade so that children as young as 12 can understand and respond to the items.

FACES I

FACES I (Olson, Portner, & Bell, 1978) was developed to provide an assessment of cohesion and adaptability as perceived by each family member. FACES I items were developed to tap each of nine concepts (emotional bonding, independence, boundaries, coalitions, time, space, friends, decision making, and interests and recreation) related to cohesion, and six concepts (assertiveness, control, discipline, negotiation, role, rules) related to adaptability. Additionally, two items were selected for the high, moderate, and low levels of each concept related to cohesion and adaptability. As a result, there were 54 items for cohesion and 42 items for adaptability, making a total of 96 items in FACES I. In addition, 15 items from the Edmonds Social Desirability Scale were included, making a total of 111 items in FACES I.

PSYCHOMETRIC PROPERTIES

A factor analysis of the adaptability and cohesion scales was done using data from 201 families with a father, a mother, and an adolescent, making a total of 603 family members. The factor analysis replicated the initial foundation of the scales where items were written for high, moderate, and low levels of cohesion and adaptability. The internal consistency (alpha) reliability for adaptability was .75, and for cohesion .83.

Portner (1980), who was involved in the development of all the versions of FACES, compared 55 families (parent and one adolescent) in family therapy with a matched control group of 117 nonproblem families. As hypothesized, nonclinic families were more likely to fall in the Balanced areas of the circumplex model on cohesion and adaptability than clinic families (58% and 42%, respectively). Clinic families tended to be more toward the chaotic disengaged extreme (30%), with fewer nonclinic families at that extreme (12%). Bell (1982), also one of the co-developers of FACES, studied 33 families with runaways and compared them with the same 117 nonproblem families used in the Portner (1980) study). As hypothesized, he found significantly more nonproblem families as described by the mother and adolescents (but not by the fathers) in the Balanced area compared to the runaway families. Conversely, he found more runaway families at the Midrange and Extreme levels then nonproblem families. Also, significantly more runaway families (29%) were disengaged than nonproblem families (7%). A higher percentage of runaway families (23%) were also chaotic compared to nonproblem families (7%).

FACES II

FACES II (Olson, Portner, & Bell, 1982) was developed in order to overcome some of the limitations of the original FACES. More specifically, the authors wanted to develop a shorter instrument with simple sentences so that it could be used with children and those with limited reading ability. They wanted to reduce the number of double negatives and provide a 5-point response scale. They wanted to develop a scale with two empirically reliable, valid, and independent dimensions. After initial testing with 464 adults and on the basis of factor analysis and reliability (alpha) analysis, the initial scale (90 items) was reduced to 50 items.

PSYCHOMETRIC PROPERTIES

Factor analysis was done separately for the cohesion and adaptability items. Although there were 13 factors for cohesion and 9 factors for adaptability, the first four factors for each dimension accounted for about 75% of the variance. For the reduced scale of 50 items, the Cronbach alpha reliability figure for cohesion was .91, and .80 for adaptability.

The 50 items of the initial FACES II were administered to 2,412 individuals in a national survey (Olson, McCubbin, Barnes, Larsen, Muxem, & Wilson, 1983). On the basis of the factor analysis and reliability checks, the 50-item scale was reduced to 30 items, with 2 or 3 items for each of the content areas. The final 30-item scale contains 16 cohesion items and 14 adaptability items. There are two items for the following eight concepts related to the cohesion dimension: emotional bonding, family boundaries, coalitions, time, space, friends, decision making, and interest and recreation. There are two or three items for the six concepts related to the adaptability dimension: assertiveness, leadership, discipline, negotiation, roles, and rules.

The total sample of 2,412 respondents was divided into two equal subgroups. Cronbach alpha figures for each of these groups and the total scale were as follows: (1) total sample: cohesion (.87), adaptability (.78); (2) subsample 1: cohesion (.88), adaptability (.78); and (3) subsample 2: cohesion (.86), adaptability (.79). The test–retest reliability study was conducted in the fall of 1981, using the 50-item version. The time lapse between the first and second administration of FACES II was between 4 and 5 weeks. Respondents included 124 university and high school students who were not currently enrolled in a family studies course. They were asked to describe their "family of origin." The Pearson product–moment correlation for the 50-item FACES II scale was .83 for cohesion and .80 for adaptability. The norms on FACES II were based on the parents and adolescents participating in the national survey. Using only cases where there were complete data for all 30 items, a total of 2,082 parents and 416 adolescents were used as the normative sample.

FACES III

The new version, FACES III (Olson, Portner, & Lavee, 1985) has been developed and tested along with the development of national norms in response to the recognition that the two scales, cohesion and adaptability, as measured by FACES I and II are highly intercorrelated. Because measures of family functioning in the circumplex model call for orthogonal dimensions—cohesion and adaptability—the developers of FACES III have been able to isolate these two dimensions, which meet this important criterion. The intercorrelation between cohesion and adaptability was a low of .05.

RESEARCH/CLINICAL APPLICATIONS

For those using FACES I, II, or III, the developers recommend that it be administered twice in order to assess both the perceived and the ideal descriptions from as many family members as possible. By comparing the perceived–ideal discrepancies for each person, it is possible to assess each individual's level of satisfaction with the current family system.

The authors recommended the use of "family satisfaction" in the application and interpretation of FACES information in clinical settings. The alternative hypothesis states that families classified at the extreme on both dimensions will function "well" as long as all individuals indicate satisfaction while with the family situation. Therefore, the perceived–ideal discrepancy on the family satisfaction scale, which is recommended to be used along with FACES, are two methods for assessing how individuals feel about their current family system.

THE TYPOLOGY MODEL OF FAMILY ADJUSTMENT
AND ADAPTATION MEASURES

The typology model of family adjustment and adaptation (McCubbin & McCubbin, in press) emerges as part of a long tradition of theorizing and systematic research linking illness in the body to stress experienced in life, particularly family life (see also Croog, 1970). Dating back to the work of Adolph Meyer (cited in Lief, 1948), who used life charts with his patients to establish the association between the occurrence of particular or multiple life events and the onset of illness, scientists (e.g., Holmes & Rahe, 1967; Jenkins, 1979; Patterson & McCubbin, 1983) have continued to pursue this line of inquiry in an effort to provide an individual and family-based explanation for the variability in individual susceptibility to illness and disease.

The typology model, which builds on the family adjustment and adaptation response framework (Patterson, Chapter 7, this volume), focuses on the family's efforts to manage the demands it faces (from stressors and strains) with its capability for meeting demands (resources and coping), mediated by the family's appraisal (situational and schema) so as to achieve a balance in family functioning (called adjustment and adaptation). The model recognizes two distinct and important phases, adjustment and adaptation, separated by a period of family crisis when the family's homeostasis is upset. Unlike the traditional models of family functioning, which focus on internal family dynamics, the typology model considers three levels of family functioning: the individual, the family unit, and the community. Each is characterized by both demands and capabilities. This is not a static model; rather, there are dynamic interactions (inside the family) and transactions (outside the family) over time as families attempt to maintain or arrive at a balance by using capabilities from one level of the family system to meet demands at another level.

To highlight the important aspects of family functioning, particularly as they apply to self-report measures of functioning, we turn our attention to the critical dimensions of the typology model as they apply to health and illness research: (1) *pile-up of demands*—stressors and strains, and (2) *family capabilities*—resources, coping, and appraisals.

Pile-up of demands is a condition that produces or calls for change in the family system. Because change is implied, a demand can be viewed as collection of threats or challenges to the family's existing homeostatic functioning. These demands may come from individual family members (psychologic problems, developmental needs, etc.), from the community (work pressures, etc.), or from the family (marital conflicts, etc.) and may take the form of discrete *stressors* (events that occur at a discernible point in time) or *strain* (a condition of tension associated with a residual unresolved problem from the past or with a need or desire to change something). These demands for change produce tension in the family system, and, if this tension is not mediated by the family's own capabilities, a state of stress arises. Because demands accumulate and interact with each other, it does not necessarily require a major event to push the family demand load beyond the family's threshold to manage it. What is implied in this concept of pile-up is the dynamic nature of family demands; stressors and strains are constantly changing over the course of time.

Family capabilities are defined as the family's potentiality for meeting demands. *Family resources,* the first of three types of capabilities, are defined as characteristics, traits, competencies, or tangible items that may be brought into play in eliminating or mediating the impact of demands. Resources may be tangible, such as money, or intangible, such as self-esteem, and may come from individual members (innate intelligence, personality strengths, etc.), from the family unit (cohesiveness, flexibility, communication, etc.), or from the community (esteem support, network support, medical care, etc.).

Coping is the second type of capability that serves to eliminate or mediate the impact of demands. Coping is defined as a specific effort (covert or overt) by which an individual member or the family unit eliminates, reduces, or manages a set of demands. Although coping most often has been conceptualized at the individual level, we can also consider family- and even community-level coping if we think of collective group action to eliminate or manage demands. Because the family is a system, coping may be conceptualized as the simultaneous management of competing demands, and therefore may include a combination of the following strategies: (1) direct action to reduce the number and/or intensity of demands (e.g., home treatments for a child with cerebral palsy); (2) direct action to acquire additional resources not already available to the family (medical assistance and diagnosis, respite care, etc.); (3) maintaining or strengthening existing resources so they can be allocated and reallocated to meet demands (e.g., doing things together as a family to maintain cohesiveness); (4) managing tension associated with ongoing strains (exercising, using humor, engaging in enjoyable activities, etc.); and (5) reframing the situation to make it more tolerable or manageable (lowering expectations in the home while caring for an ill member, emphasizing spiritual beliefs to build hope, etc.)

Family appraisals, specifically situational perceptions and family schemas, have also received additional and appropriate emphasis in the typology model as important factors in the management of demands. Situational appraisals are assessments done by individual family members, or collectively by the family unit, of the interactional relationship between the *family pile-up of demands*—their intensity, controllability, resulting expectations, and potential short- and long-term consequences—and *the family's capabilities*—their availability, utility, potential mediating or buffering impact, the family's costs in the use of their resources, and the resulting short- and long-term consequences when these capabilities are utilized to meet the demands. Understandably, situational appraisals play a central role in shaping the family members' and the family unit's response(s) to the total stressful, and possibly distressful, situation.

The typology model of family adjustment and adaptation calls for a constellation of family measures designed to assess the complex relationship between the family's demands and the mediating influences of the family's capabilities—resources, coping, and appraisals. In this chapter we will limit our presentation to three select indices of family functioning that have already been utilized in family medicine research. This brief review is suggestive of the current and future potential of self-report measures in both family systems medicine research and family-oriented medical–clinical interventions. Specifically, we will introduce the Family Inventory of Life Events and Changes (FILE), the Family Inventory of Resources for Management (FIRM), and the Coping Health Inventory for Parents (CHIP), which are designed to assess family demands, resources, coping, and appraisal. Before reviewing each of the three typology measures, it is important to restate the underlying assumption and hypotheses of the typology model as it applies to family medicine intervention and research.

1. The relationship between family functioning and the health status of family members can be examined through the systematic assessment of the *demands* placed on the family system and the *resources, coping behaviors,* and *appraisals* family members have and use to manage these demands.
2. The demands on the family unit, if not mediated or buffered by capabilities (resources, coping, and appraisal) *will increase the probability of emotional and/or health problems.*
3. In the face of a diagnosed acute or chronic medical condition, additional or con-

current family demands that are not mediated by family capabilities, *will compli-cate medical treatment and the long-term rehabilitation or recovery of the ill family member.*

4. These assessments of family capabilities *may guide the family physician's inter-ventions and supportive interactions,* which in turn may shape the family's re-sponse and ultimately the family's environment, to be more supportive of family life and medical intervention.

FILE: Family Inventory of Life Events and Changes

The Family Inventory of Life Events and Changes (McCubbin, Patterson, & Wilson, 1981) was designed to record the pile-up of stressors and strains—demands that may contribute to the onset of a disease and/or, in interaction with a specific medical diagnosis, treatment, or medical condition, may render the family vulnerable or incapable of responding in a constructive manner to the needs of a family member who is acutely or chronically ill. This linkage between demands and family stress is predicated on understanding the family as a "system" in terms of the interconnectedness of its members. What affects one person in the family affects the others to some degree. Change in any one part of the system requires some readjustment by the whole family system and by its individual members. Life events and strains experienced by the family as a whole or by any one member, when added together, will have a negative impact on the stability of the family unit, the health of its members, and the family's response to concurrent or future medical situations.

FILE is a 71-item self-report instrument designed to record normative and non-nor-mative family demands such as stressors, hardships, or prior strains that a family unit may experience within a year. Families usually are dealing with several stressors and strains simultaneously, and FILE provides an index of this pile-up, which in turn is an index of a family's vulnerability to crisis. The questionnaire is to be completed by adult family mem-bers (together or separately), a single parent, or a cohabiting couple (together or sepa-rately). The selection of family stressor and strain items was guided, in part, by those life changes appearing on other individual life change inventories (Coddington, 1972; Dohren-wend, Krasnoff, Askenasy, & Dohrenwend, 1978; Holmes & Rahe, 1967). In addition, situational and developmental changes experienced by families at different stages of the life cycle were included. These items were derived from clinical and research experience of the investigators, and from a careful review of family stress research from the previous decade (McCubbin *et al.,* 1980). This inventory has been used in a wide range of studies including rural farm and nonfarm families, and families faced with childhood chronic ill-ness such as cystic fibrosis, myelomeningocele, or cerebral palsy.

The first version of FILE consisted of 171 items, but in our efforts to adapt this inventory for use in prevention-oriented settings (family practice clinics, pediatric clinics, family life education centers, and the like) and in other medical and family counseling clinics, we reduced FILE (Form C) to 71 items grouped into nine subscales and a total scale. Intrafamily Strains focuses on sources of tension and conflict between family mem-bers and on parenting strains and the increased difficulty in enacting the parenting role. Marital Strains focuses on the strains associated with the marital role arising from sexual or separation issues. Pregnancy and Childbearing Strains relates to pregnancy difficulties or adding a new member to the family unit; Finance and Business Strains focuses on sources of increased strain on a family's money supply and sources of strain arising from a family-owned business or investments. Work–Family Transitions and Strains focuses on strains associated with a member moving in and out of the work force and on intrafamily demands related to work difficulties. Illness and Family Care Strains focuses on family demands associated with injury or illness to a family member or friend or problems with child care, and strains associated with having a chronically ill member or relative/member requiring more help or care. Family Losses focuses on demands due to the loss of a family member or a friend, or to a breakdown in relationships. Family Transitions In and Out focuses on family members moving out of or back into the family, or a member beginning a major involvement outside the family unit. Family Legal Strains focuses on a family member's violation of the law or mores. Total Family Pile-up (71 items) focuses on the total number of family demands associated with the accumulation of stressors and strains in the nine areas of family life.

PSYCHOMETRIC PROPERTIES

The total index of family pile-up of deamands is reliable with a Cronbach alpha of .81. Select subscales of Family have respectable reliabilities—Intrafamily Strains, Finance and Business Strains, and Family Legal Strains. Additionally, test–retest reliabilities (4 to 5 weeks apart) ranged from a low of .64 to a high of .84 for the various subscales. The overall test–retest reliability for FILE was .80.

Factor analyses were completed on data obtained on two independent samples of husbands and wives ($N = 1,330$ and $N = 1,410$, respectively) representing families from all stages of the family life cycle. The results (McCubbin & Thompson, 1987) revealed the same factor structure of nine subscales reported in the initial publication of FILE. Several additional indices of validity have been reported. Specifically, total pile-up of family life stressors and strains was significantly and inversely correlated with measures of changes in the health status of children (e.g., pulmonary functioning) of children with cystic fibrosis (Patterson & McCubbin, 1983). A greater number of family stressors and strains in a 12-month period was associated with a subsequent decline in the children's pulmonary functioning as recorded during two clinic visits that occurred 3 to 6 months later. Additionally, the pile-up of demands was correlated significantly with measures of family functioning. Through the use of data obtained on 1,140 couples, or 2,280 married individuals, who were representative of seven stages of the family life cycle, we were able to obtain normative data so that families completing FILE could be compared with other families at their respective stages of development (McCubbin & Patterson, 1983b). The normative data are separated into three levels—Low Demand, Moderate Demand, and High Demand—on the basis of cutoff scores determined by mean and one standard deviation.

RESEARCH/CLINICAL APPLICATIONS

The Family Inventory of Life Events and Changes (FILE) provide family physicians, educators, and researchers with a brief (approximately 10 minutes completion time) but meaningful index of the pile-up of stressors and strains in a family. It is useful as an initial intake or screening test to determine the family's vulnerability. The family physician is able to: (1) identify some of the major stressors and hassles that chip away at the family's flexibility and resiliency; (2) foster the family's own awareness of what stressors and strains they have been struggling with, which may predispose a family member to illness or impede or compete with family compliance with a medical regimen in the home environment; and (3) encourage the family to examine these demands, their consequences, and what stressors and strains deserve attention in the prevention of illness or in the rehabilitation or long-term care of a family member who is acutely or chronically ill.

FIRM: Family Inventory of Resources for Management

In an attempt to assess the family's basic repertoire of resources, FIRM, the Family Inventory of Resources for Management (McCubbin, Comeau, & Harkins, 1981), was developed. In order to describe or predict how a family adapts to stressful events and strains, the typology model calls for information about which resources a family has, does not have, or has depleted. It is hypothesized that families possessing a larger portfolio of resources will manage more effectively and will be better able to adapt to stressful situations.

The selection of items for FIRM was influenced by literature and theory in three major areas: (1) personal resources, (2) the family system's internal resources, and (3) community support. *Personal resources* refer to the broad range of resources, qualities, and aids characteristic of individual family members that are available to any family member in need. They include financial (economic well-being), education (contributing to cognitive ability, facilitating realistic perceptions and problem-solving ability), health, and psychologic attributes (personality characteristics) (George, 1980; Pearlin & Schooler, 1978).

Family system resources encompass primarily the original concepts identified by Hill (1958), and in Burr's (1973) synthesis of the literature—family communication and family cohesiveness. Managerial ability (resource management) has been emphasized by proponents of family management frameworks (Deacon & Firebaugh, 1975; Paolucci, Hall, & Axinn, 1977), along with the ability to identify resources (Paolucci *et al.*, 1977). Problem-solving ability has been examined as a key family system resource (Aldous, Condon, Hill, Straus, & Tallman, 1971; Hill & Joy, 1979; Reiss, 1981).

Community support, often referred to as "social support" as defined by Cobb (1976), is information exchanged between people that provides emotional support, resulting in the individual feeling loved and cared for; esteem support, resulting in the individual feeling esteemed and valued; and network support, resulting in the individual feeling he or she is part of a network of mutual obligation and understanding.

FIRM consists of 98 self-report items, and the respondent is asked to evaluate on a 0-to-3 scale how well the items "describe our family." The four major resources (subscales) identified in FIRM are:

1. *Family Strengths I: Esteem and Communication.* This family resource reflects the presence of a combination of personal, family system, and community resources in six areas: (a) family esteem (respect from friends, relatives, and co-workers, and among family managements); (b) communication (sharing feelings, discussing decisions); (c) mutual assistance (helping each other and relatives); (d) optimism (maintaining a positive outlook on matters); (e) problem-solving ability; and (f) encouragement of autonomy among family members. (Cronbach alpha = .85.)
2. *Family Strengths II: Mastery and Health.* This family resource includes items that reflect personal, family system, and community support resources along three dimensions: (a) sense of mastery over family events and outcomes (fate control, flexibility, managerial abilities); (b) family mutuality (emotional support, togetherness, cooperation); and (c) physical and emotional health of family members. (Cronbach alpha = .85.)
3. *Extended Family Support.* This family resources index contains items that indicate the mutual help and support given to and received from relatives. (Cronbach alpha = .62.)
4. *Financial Well-Being.* This family resource reflects the family's perceived finan-

cial efficacy along the dimensions of: (a) ability to meet financial commitments; (b) adequacy of financial reserves; (c) ability to help others (relatives, the needy); (d) optimism about the family's financial future (adequacy of insurance, employment benefits, retirement income, earning power, and the family's financial progress). (Cronbach alpha = .85.)

PSYCHOMETRIC PROPERTIES

FIRM has been subjected to factor analyses involving a samples of 322 families responding to having a child with either cerebral palsy or myelomeningocele. Additionally, FIRM has been used in the study of a normative sample of approximately 2,000 families in the Midwest. The findings reported to date indicate the stability of the four resources described above. Additionally, the alpha reliabilities for the four major resources ranged from a low of .62 for Extended Family Social Support to a high of .85 for the three remaining sources. The authors report low to moderate intercorrelations among the four major resources and only a modest association with social desirability.

RESEARCH/CLINICAL APPLICATIONS

FIRM was designed as a self-report hand-scoreable instrument, and, although initially developed and tested with a population of families with a chronically ill handicapped child, was designed for use with any type of family. As a research and counseling tool, FIRM can be used diagnostically to pinpoint the family's resources or strengths for dealing with a medical condition and to identify resources that may need attention immediately or in the future. FIRM may be viewed as a viable index of the family's basic strengths—esteem and communication, mastery and health, financial well-being, and extended family support.

CHIP: Coping Health Inventory for Parents

One of the major mediating factors and buffering influences to the impact of demands on the family system and its potentially adverse consequences is the parental coping strategies they employ to manage tensions and strains. Parental coping takes on added importance as a critical aspect of family functioning in the case of families struggling with a member with chronic illness. Managing the long-term treatment of a member with a chronic illness usually involves a complementary relationship between the health care team and the family unit. The successful care of a chronically ill member depends on the family's willingness to modify family life in response to a complex and usually time-consuming regimen of continuous therapy. Therefore, how the parents cope with the situation could make a difference in the health status of chronically ill children over time.

The Coping Health Inventory for Parents (CHIP) (McCubbin, McCubbin, & Cauble, 1979) is an 80-item questionnaire checklist developed to provide information about how parents individually perceive their overall response to the management of a chronically ill child in the family. The coping behaviors, such as "Believing that my child(ren) will get better" or "Talking with the medical staff (nurses, social worker, etc.) when we visit the medical center," are listed, and the parent(s) are asked to record how "helpful" (on a 0-to-3 scale) the coping behavior items were to them in managing the home illness situation.

Following the methodology outlined in earlier family coping studies (Boss, McCubbin, & Lester, 1979; McCubbin, Dahl, Lester, Benson, & Robertson, 1976), the construction of CHIP was guided by the inclusion of important behavior items used in previous studies of family response to stress. The development of additional items focused on: (1)

network and social support theory (Caplan, 1974; Cobb, 1976), that is, the family's relationship to the community and to family members for emotional, esteem, and network support; (2) individual psychology of coping (Lazarus, 1966; Pearlin & Schooler, 1978), that is, the personal, active, and passive psychological adjustments needed to manage anxieties and emotional tensions; and (c) family medical support, that is, the parents' efforts to communicate with the medical staff and with other parents, as well as their attempts to master medical illness and home care issues in order to understand and manage the chronically ill child in the home.

The development of CHIP (McCubbin, 1984) was influenced by a hierarchic approach to the organization of behavior. In the application of this approach, two general levels of abstraction were defined: (1) coping behaviors (operationally defined through 80 specific items) and (2) coping patterns (combination of coping behaviors into specific patterns). After careful analysis of the items, the initial list was reduced to 45 items, which were grouped by factor analysis into three subscales or three distinct parental coping patterns.

1. *Coping I: Maintaining Family Integration, Cooperation, and an Optimistic Definition of the Situation* is composed of 19 behaviors that center on the family and the parents' outlook on life and illness, keeping the family together, encouraging cooperation, investing in the children, an encouraging independence in the family.
2. *Coping II: Maintaining Social Support, Self-Esteem, and Psychologic Stability* involves 18 coping behaviors which focus on the parents' efforts to maintain a personal sense of well-being through obtaining social support, maintaining self-esteem, and managing psychologic tensions and strains.
3. *Coping III: Understanding the Medical Situation through Communication with Other Parents and Consultation with Medical Staff* involves eight coping behaviors and focuses on the interface between the parent, other parents in a similar situation, and the medical staff and its program, as well as parental efforts to understand and master the medical information needed to cope with the illness.

PSYCHOMETRIC PROPERTIES

The psychometric details of CHIP are presented elsewhere (McCubbin, 1985; McCubbin & Patterson, 1981; McCubbin, *et al.*, 1983). Briefly, three coping patterns derived from factor analysis represented 71% of the variance of the original correlation matrix. Cronbach alphas, computed for the items on each coping pattern, indicated respectable reliabilities of .79 (Coping I), .79 (Coping II), and .71 (Coping III).

Additionally, the CHIP subscales were correlated with independent assessments of family functioning and changes in the health status of children with cystic fibrosis. When used by mothers, all three coping patterns were significantly correlated with the family interpersonal relationships dimensions of family life. Briefly, the mother's three coping patterns were validated by their positive association with family cohesiveness and expressiveness. The father's coping patterns were validated by their association with family cohesiveness, conflict, organization, and control.

Parental coping, as measured by CHIP, was also validated against health status indices. Specifically, mother's efforts to maintain family integration, cooperation, and an optimistic definition of the situation (Coping I) was validated against the criterion index of positive gains in the child's height and weight. Additionally, mother's Coping II—maintaining social support, self-esteem, and psychologic stability—was significantly correlated with positive changes in the child's pulmonary functioning. Father's coping pattern—maintaining social support, self-esteem, and psychologic stability—was significantly correlated with positive gains in the child's height/weight index and pulmonary functioning index.

RESEARCH/CLINICAL APPLICATIONS

The evidence presented regarding CHIP emphasizes the value of systematic assessments of parental coping patterns and the need to examine what parents can do in a positive way to manage the strains of caring for a chronically ill child, as a part of health care to families. Consequently, the results suggest that parental coping is a viable target for family medicine, both practice and research. Strengthening or reinforcing parental coping efforts is a legitimate objective for physicians, nurses, and other health professionals. CHIP may be viewed as part of the battery of family assessment tools designed to provide family physicians with a reasonably reliable and valid picture of parental efforts to manage a stressful situation.

FHI: Family Hardiness Index

In order to measure the characteristic of hardiness as a stress resistance and adaptation resource in families, the Family Hardiness Index was developed. Family hardiness especially refers to the internal strengths and durability of the family unit that would function as a buffer or mediating factor in mitigating the effects of stressors and demands, and a facilitation of family adjustment and adaptation over time. Since family hardiness is characterized by a sense of control over the outcomes of life events and hardships, changes are viewed as beneficial and growth-producing, and parents have an active rather than a passive orientation in adjusting to and managing stressful situations.

The construction of the Family Hardiness Index was guided by the concept of individual hardiness (Kobasa, 1979), which is a personality characteristic that encompasses both cognitive and behavioral components, serves as a stress resistance resource, and has the potential to offset the illness-producing effects of stress on individuals. Individual hardiness consists of three interrelated components: commitment, challenge, and control. When applied to the family's typical patterns of appraising the impact of life events and changes on family functioning, four interrelated components were found to compose family hardiness: co-oriented commitment, confidence, challenges, and control.

The Family Hardiness Index (FHI) (McCubbin, McCubbin, & Thompson, 1987) is a 20-item questionnaire consisting four subscales (co-oriented commitment, confidence, challenges, and control) which calls for respondents to reflect the degrees to which each statement describes their current family situation. The four major components (subscales) identified in FHI are:

1. *Co-oriented commitment subscale* assesses the family's sense of internal strengths, dependability, and ability to work together.
2. *Confidence subscale* measures the family's sense of being able to plan ahead and of being appreciated for efforts, as well as their ability to endure hardships and experience life with interest and meaningfulness.
3. *Challenges subscale* focuses on the family's efforts to be innovative and active, to experience new things, and to learn.
4. *Control subscale* reflects the family's sense of being in control of family life rather than being shaped by outside events and circumstances.

PSYCHOMETRIC PROPERTIES

FHI has been subjected to investigation involving a sample of 304 nonclinical families (McCubbin, Thompson, Pirner, & McCubbin, 1988). The internal reliability for FHI is .82 (Cronbach alpha). The factor loading of the hardiness factors and behaviors ranged from .52 to .85. Examinations of the association between hardiness and other criterion indices such as *family flexibility* (the ability to change to meet challenges), *family time and routines* (the ability to maintain stability and continuity), and *quality of family life* (family satisfaction, marital satisfaction, and community satisfaction) confirmed the hypothesis that family hardiness would be positively correlated with the other criterion indices.

RESEARCH/CLINICAL APPLICATIONS
As mentioned earlier, the FHI was designed to measure the characteristic of hardiness as a stress resistance and adaptation resource in families. Although it was developed in a non-clinical family population, it can be used in any type of family. As a research and counseling tool, FHI can be utilized to assess the internal strengths and durability of the family unit in response to life events and hardships.

FTRI: Family Time and Routines Index

Family time together and the routines families adopt and practice are relatively reliable indices of family integration and stability, which includes effective ways of managing common problems and the ability to handle major crises (McCubbin, McCubbin, & Thompson, 1987). The development of the FTRI was based on the assumption that even in the face of illness and other medically related crises, families need to maintain continuity and stability (Jensen, James, Boyce, & Harnett, 1983). The FTRI includes 16 additional items, with greater emphasis on including teenage members, and eliminates 10 items from the original Family Routines Inventory.

The Family Time and Routines Index contains 30 self-reported items and 8 subscales: Parent–Child Togetherness, Couple Togetherness, Child Routines, Meals Together, Family Time Together, Family Chores Routines, Relatives Connection Routines, and Family Management Routines.

1. *Parent–Child Togetherness* assesses the family's emphasis on establishing predictable communications between parents and children and adolescents.
2. *Couple Togetherness* measures the family's emphasis on establishing predictable routines to promote communication between couples.
3. *Child Routines* relates to the family's emphasis on establishing predictable routines to promote children's and teenagers' sense of autonomy and order.
4. *Meals Together* assesses the family's efforts to establish predictable routines to promote togetherness through family mealtimes.
5. *Family Time Together* measures the family's emphasis on family togetherness, including special events, caring, quiet time, and family time.
6. *Family Chore Routines* reflects the family's emphasis on establishing predictable routines to promote child and adolescent responsibilities in the home.
7. *Relatives Connection Routines* relates to the family's efforts to establish predictable routines that promote a meaningful connection with relatives.
8. *Family Management Routines* indicates the family's efforts to establish predictable routines to promote a sense of family organization and accountability needed to maintain family order in the home.

PSYCHOMETRIC PROPERTIES
The psychometric research on FTRI involved a sample of 304 nonclinical families. The internal reliability for Family Time and Routines is .88 (Cronbach alpha). The factor

loadings of the factors structure for routines range from .30 to .85. Positive correlations between FTRI and criterion indices of family bonding, family coherence, and family celebrations, as well as with indices of family satisfaction, marital satisfaction, and community satisfaction (McCubbin, Thompson, & Pirner, 1986) confirmed the hypotheses of validity tests of FTRI.

RESEARCH/CLINICAL APPLICATIONS

Family life is punctuated by normative and non-normative transitions and changes. At the same time, family units are called on to provide a well-organized system of behaviors which ensures stability and predictability. Family stability has been treated as an essential part of family life, allowing family units to bridge generations, establish continuity in the present and in the midst of disruptions, and build a solid foundation of interpersonal supports needed to negotiate major transitions and transformations. The FTRI suggests a psychologic measure to provide information on family patterns of stability, including tradition (continuity across time), celebrations (continuity in the present, which lays the groundwork for the future), and family routines (stability on a day-to-day basis).

THE BEAVERS SYSTEM MODEL OF FAMILY ASSESSMENT

The Beavers system model (BSM) has three instruments—the Beavers–Timberlawn Family Evaluation Scale (BT) for assessing family competence, the Centripetal/Centrifugal Family Style Scale (CP/CF) for evaluating family stylistic constructs, and the Self-Report Family Inventory (SFI) for obtaining information from family members' perceptions of their family. The Beavers system model has developed over 20 years based on general systems theory, clinical work with families, and research into family systems qualities (Beavers, 1987; Beavers, Blumberg, Timken, & Weiner, 1965). This review will be limited to the Self-Report Family Inventory (SFI).

The Beavers system model of family assessment is designed to provide a quantitative index of family health/competence on continua representing a family system framework. The model incorporates clinical and theoretic background and concepts that can be summarized as follows:

Systems concepts:

1. Families have repetitive interactional patterns, which influence the developmental unfolding of children.
2. Separating and developing autonomy are vital developmental challenges for individuals and families.
3. Communication, behavior, feeling tone, and negotiating are both individual and family phenomena, with each level of human experience influencing the other.
4. Therapeutic intervention can be considered as family therapy regardless of how many people are in the room. Individual treatment, for example, can be one strategy available to assist the family processes of separation and differentiation (Beavers, 1987).

Clinical interpretations of systems concepts:

1. Living systems are most competent when they have maximum organization and available energy to bring to bear on adaptive challenges.

2. Chaotic systems are the most resistant to change, since they possess little capacity to forge an energetic, coherent, and effective response to change within and without the family system.

3. The next most limited systems are rigidly control-oriented structures in which intimidation is the major mode of interpersonal communication.

4. Intimacy, or the ability to share one's innermost feelings, is a human quality that greatly reduces the risk of people becoming emotionally ill. This experience is only obtained in relationships with little or no overt power differences.

5. Negotiation is the key to adaptive, healthy, or competent family functioning. Negotiation requires boundary clarity, resolution of individual ambivalence, and little overt power indifferences. Families of similar competence levels observed in negotiating and problem solving may differ greatly in style (Beavers, 1987; Beavers *et al.*, 1965).

SFI: Self-Report Family Inventory

The Self-Report Family Inventory (SFI) was designed to obtain information concerning family members' perceptions of their family. SFI is a 36-item *self-report* inventory to reflect the family's relational and systemic qualities as seen by each member of the family. The SFI assesses six areas of family functioning: Family Health, Conflict, Family Communication, Family Cohesion, Directive Leadership, and Expressiveness. This instrument represents the self-report level of the Beavers model of family functioning. It is most beneficially used in conjunction with the Beavers-Timberlawn Family Evaluation Scale and the Centripetal/Centrifugal Family Style Scale. Combined, these three scales would provide a multimethod, multilevel family systems evaluation.

PSYCHOMETRIC PROPERTIES
The internal consistency for this scale has been assessed at between .84 and .88 (Cronbach alpha). Test–retest reliability for the SFI was assessed over 30- and 90-day periods, and moderate correlations across time indicate temporal stability for the SFI. Correspondence of Health/Competence and Style with SFI factors by type of family member indicates that mothers tend to correspond most closely with external observers, followed by children ages 9 to 16, fathers, and children over 16 years of age. In addition, "insider" versus "outsider" ratings of family functioning constructs indicate that more competent families show a greater variation of views than do clinical families. This is suggested by lower correlations found for nonclinical families between observational and self-report measures, compared to higher correlations for clinical families. The influences of social desirability motives and responses to the SFI has been investigated. Results indicate that responses on the SFI are not significantly related to giving socially desirable responses.

The SFI shows good convergence with other measures of family functioning, including the Locke-Wallace Marital Satisfaction Scale, the FACES II and FACES III, the Bloom Family Evaluation Scale, the Moos and Moos Family Environment Scale, and the Family Assessment Device.

The relationship between marital satisfaction (measured by the Locke–Wallace Marital Satisfaction Scale) and the SFI factors indicates a range from $-.610$ to $.092$ (with both parents combined). And marital satisfaction is significantly related to the Family Health, Conflict, Communication, and Cohesion dimensions measured by the SFI.

Correlations of SFI factors with the Adaptability scale of FACES II range from $-.30$

to −.79 (significant on all six factors of SFI), and correlations of SFI with the Cohesion scale of FACES-II range from −.12 to −.93 (significant on five SFI factors, except Family Communication). Correlations of SFI with the Adaptability scale of FACES III range from −.39 to .02 (significant on Family Health and Directive Leadership) and correlations of SFI with the Cohesion scale of FACES III range from −.18 to −.78 (significant on five SFI factors, except Family Communication).

Ranges of the correlations of Bloom Family Evaluation Scale factors with SFI factors are summarized as follows: Health (range from −.862 of Family Idealization to .726 of Conflict), Conflict (from −.685 of Family Idealization to .776 Conflict), Communication (from −.562 of Conflict to .256 of Organization), Cohesion (from −.744 of Cohesion to .577 of Conflict), Leadership (from −.409 of Authoritarian to .552 of Laissez-Faire Family Style), and Expressiveness (from −.601 of Family Idealization to .434 of Laissez-Faire Family Style).

Correlations of Self-Report Inventory factors and the Moos and Moos Family Environment Scale indicate wide ranges on SFI factors: Health (from −.733 of Cohesion to .656 of Conflict), Conflict (from −.484 of Cohesion to .676 of Conflict), Communication (from −.403 of Expressiveness to .369 of Control), Cohesion (from −.648 of Cohesion to .494 of Conflict), Leadership (from −.376 of Control to .174 of Conflict), and Expressiveness (from −.708 of Cohesion to .594 of Conflict).

Finally, correlations of SFI factors and Family Assessment Device factors show significant relationship between SFI factors—Health (from .080 of Behavior Control to .766 of General Functioning), Conflict (from .143 of Behavior Control to .531 of General Functioning), Cohesion (from −.107 of Behavior Control to .612 of General Functioning), and Expressiveness (from .118 of Behavior Control to .693 of Affective Responsiveness) and all dimensions of the Family Assessment Device except Behavior Control. The SFI factor of Leadership (from .132 of Affective Responsiveness to .360 of Behavior Control) is significant related to the Problem Solving, Roles, Affective Involvement, Behavior Control, and General Functioning dimensions of the FAD. The SFI factor of Communication (from −.212 of Behavior Control to .352 of Communication) is significant related to the Communication, Affective Involvement, Behavior Control, and General Functioning dimensions of the FAD.

RESEARCH/CLINICAL APPLICATIONS

SFI has shown promise in screening high-risk families, and for an inexpensive and reliable assessment of perceived family change after intervention. Family members' views of family competence or health are statistically correlated with outsiders' (raters' and/or therapists') perceptions, but are qualitatively different. Style is a concept most appliable to an outsider's viewpoint. Family members have important things to say about their family structure, but questions regarding style are best answered from a different perspective. Further research is needed in studying the interrelationships between insider and outsider perspectives on family interaction.

CONCLUSION

Family medicine research has much to gain from investing in systematic assessments of family functioning. Self-report measures of family functioning are but one among many strategies used to make these important assessments. By introducing, discussing, and to some degree appraising extant self-report measures, we hope to shed light on this devel-

Table 12-3. Overview of Family Assessment and Self-Report Measures in Family System Medicine Research

Family measures	Theory base	Major scale	Unit of assessment	Norms	Reliabilities	Validities
Family APGAR	Clinical	Adaptability Parternship Growth Affection Resolve	Family system			Case studies, face validity
Family Environment Scales	Family climate, social ecology	Cohesion Expressiveness Conflict Independence Achievement Moral–Religious Intellectual Active–Recreational Organizational Control	Family system	1,498 adults, 612 children	Internal, test–retest	Face, concurrent, content, discriminant, health status
Family Assessment Device	McMaster model	Problem Solving Communication Roles Responsiveness Involvement Consistency Behavioral Control General Functioning	Family system	503 adults, clinic samples	Internal, test–retest	Face, discriminant, content
Family Assessment Measure III	Process model of family functioning	Affective Involvement Control Role Performance Task Accomplishment Communication	Family system	475 families, 933 adults, 502 children	Internal	Face, concurrent
Family Adaptability and Cohesion (I, II, III)	Circumplex model	Cohesion Adaptability	Family system	2,453 adults, 412 adolescents, life cycle stage	Internal, test–retest	Face, content, discriminant, health status

Family adjustment and adaptation response measures	FILE Stressors and strains	Family system	2,453 adults, life cycle stage	Internal, test–retest	Face, content, discriminant, health status
	FIRM Family Strengths: Esteem, Mastery Support Financial	Family system	454 parents of chronically ill child	Internal, test–retest	Face, content, discriminant, health status
Family adjustment and adaptation response framework	CHIP Illness coping: I: Family integration II: Support and esteem III: Medical consultation		454 parents of chronically ill child	Internal, test–retest	Face, content, discriminant, health status
	FHI Co-oriented commitment Confidence Challenge Control		304 nonclinical families	Internal, test–retest	Face, content, discriminant, health status
	FTRI Child Routines, Couple Togetherness, Meals Together, Parent–Child Togetherness, Family Togetherness, Relatives Connection, Family Chores, Family Management		304 nonclinical families	Internal, test–retest	Face, content, discriminant, health status
Beavers system model of family assessment	BT: Beavers–Timberlawn Family Evaluation Scale CP/CF: Centripetal/Centrifugal Family Style Scale SFI: Self-Report Family Inventory		42 midrange competent families	Internal, test–retest	Concurrent

oping but very complex arena of family measurement and, more important, to encourage further research in this area. A brief review of all the instruments presented in this chapter is outlined in Table 12-3.

We have much to gain from the continued use of self-report measures of family functioning, and, over time, we will be able to advance the development of these measures, improve their reliabilities and validities, and further substantiate the linkage between the family environment and the health of family members. With this in mind, we can anticipate major developments and constructive findings in the immediate future.

Although all the instruments and sets of instruments discussed here are in need of continued refinement and rigorous assessment, there appears to be a growing commitment to advance the development of instruments grounded in theory, supported by empirical tests of reliability and validity, and with a direct link to the health status and physiologic changes in family members. Although it may be premature to express excitement at the prospect of uncovering or discovering the pathways between the family and the human body, it is reassuring to note the emergence of encouraging efforts to examine this linkage.

Family research, and family systems medicine research in particular, has much to gain from this line of scientific inquiry. It is possible that self-report measures can be central in understanding the family's role in producing physiologic changes, in understanding why some families fall apart in the face of chronic illnesses, in understanding the role of the family in supporting or undermining medical interventions, and in understanding the role of the family system in promoting rehabilitation and recovery of patients afflicted with an illness or those who have received medical treatment requiring home care. Surely the emergence of self-report measures, even with all their psychometric limitations, has served and will continue to serve an important function in the advancement of research linking the family environment to the present and future health status of family members.

References

Ackerman N. The psychodynamics of family life. New York: Basic Books, 1958.

Aldous J, Condon T, Hill R, Straus M, Tallman I. Family problem-solving. Chicago: Dryden Press, 1971.

Beavers WR, Blumberg S, Timken KR, Weiner MD. Communication patterns of mothers of schizophrenics. Family Process 1965; 4:95–104.

Beavers WR. The Beavers System Model for family assessment: norms, validity, and reliability. Dallas, Tex.: Southwest Family Research Institute, 1987.

Bell R. Parent–adolescent interaction in runaway families. Unpublished doctoral dissertation, University of Minnesota, St. Paul, 1982.

Bishop DS, Epstein NB. Research on teaching methods. Presented at the International Forum for Trainers and Family Therapists, Tavistock Clinic, London, 1979.

Boss PG, McCubbin HI, Lester G. The corporate executive wife's coping patterns in response to routine husband-father absence. Family Process 1979; 18:79–86.

Burr WF. Theory construction and the sociology of the family. New York: Wiley, 1973.

Caplan G. Support systems and community mental health. New York: Behavioral Publications, 1974.

Cassell J. The contribution of the social environment to host resistance. American Journal of Epidemiology 1976; 104:107–123.

Cobb S. Social support as a moderator of life stress. Psychosomatic Medicine 1976; 38:300–314.

Coddington RD. The significance of life events as an etiologic factor in the diseases of children: II. A study of a normal population. Journal of Psychosomatic Research 1972; 16:205–213.

Comly A. Family therapy and the family physician. Canadian Family Physician 1973; 38:78–81.

Croog S. The family as a source of stress. In: Levine S, Scotch N, eds. Social stress. Chicago: Aldine, 1970.

Deacon R. Firebaugh F. Home management context and concepts. Boston: Houghton Mifflin, 1975.

Dohrenwend BS, Krasnoff L, Askenasy AR, Dohrenwend BP. Exemplification of a method for scaling life events: the PERI life events scale. Journal of Health and Social Behavior 1978; 19:205–229.

Dubos RJ. Man adapting. New Haven, Conn.: Yale University Press, 1965.

Eichel E. Assessment with a family focus. Journal of Psychiatric Nursing and Mental Health Services 1978; 16:11–15.

Epstein NB, Bishop DS. State of the art—1973. Canadian Psychiatric Association Journal 1973; 18:175–183.

Epstein NB, Levine S, Bishop DS. The family as a social unit. Canadian Family Physician 1976; 22:1411–1413.

Fuhr RA, Moos RH, Dishotsky N. The use of family assessment and feedback in ongoing family therapy. American Journal of Family Therapy 1981; 9:24–36.

George L. Role transition in later life. Belmont, Calif.: Brooks/Cole, 1980.

Hill R. Generic feature of families under stress. Social Casework 1958; 49:139–150.

Hill R, Joy C. Conceptualizing and operationalizing category systems for phasing of family development. Unpublished manuscript, University of Minnesota, 1979.

Holmes TH, Rahe RH. The social readjustment rating scale. Journal of Psychosomatic Research 1967; 11:213–218.

Jenkins CD. Psychosocial modifiers of response to stress. Journal of Human Stress 1979; 5:3–15.

Jensen, EW, James SH, Boyce WT, Harnett, SA. The family routines inventory: development and validation. Social Science Medicine 1983; 17(4):201–211.

Kobasa S. Stressful life events, personality, and health: an inquiry into hardness. Journal of Personality and Social Psychology 1979; 37:1–11.

Lazarus RS. Psychological stress and the coping process. New York: McGraw-Hill, 1966.

Lief A, ed. The commonsense psychiatry of Dr. Adolf Meyer. New York: McGraw-Hill, 1948.

Lipowski ZJ. Affluence information inputs and health. Social Science and Medicine 1973a; 57–529.

Lipowski ZJ. Psychosomatic medicine in changing society: some current trends in theory and research. Comprehensive Psychiatry 1973b; 22:203–215.

McCubbin MA. Nursing assessment of parenting coping with cystic fibrosis. Western Journal of Nursing Research 1984; 6:405–422.

McCubbin HI, Comeau J, Harkins J. FIRM—Family Inventory of Resources for Management. University of Wisconsin–Madison, 1981.

McCubbin HI, Dahl B, Lester G, Benson D, Robertson M. Coping repertoires of families adapting to prolonged war-induced separations. Journal of Marriage and Family 1976; 38:461–471.

McCubbin HI, Joy C, Cauble A, Comeau J, Patternson J, Needle R. Family stress, coping, and social support: a decade review. Journal of Marriage and the Family 1980; 42:855–871.

McCubbin M, McCubbin H. Theoretical orientations to family stress and coping. In: Figley C, ed. Treating stress in families. New York: Brunner/Mazel, in press.

McCubbin HI, McCubbin MA, Cauble AE. CHIP—Coping Health Inventory for Parents (Form A). University of Wisconsin–Madison, 1979.

McCubbin HI, McCubbin MA, Patterson J, Cauble AE, Wilson L, Warwick W. CHIP—Coping Health Inventory for Parents: an assessment of parental coping patterns in the care of the chronically ill child. Journal of Marriage and the Family 1983; 45:359–370.

McCubbin HI, McCubbin MA, Thompson AI. FTRI—Family Time and Routines Index. In: McCubbin HI, Thompson AI, eds. Family assessment inventories for research and practice. Madison: University of Wisconsin, 1987.

McCubbin HI, Patterson JM. Systematic assessment of family stress, resourses and coping. Department of Family Social Science, University of Minnesota, St. Paul, 1981.

McCubbin HI, Patterson JM. Family transitions: adaptation to stress. In McCubbin H, Figley C, eds. Stress and the family: I. Coping with normative transitions. New York: Brunner/Mazel, 1983b.

McCubbin HI, Patterson JM, Wilson L. FILE—Family Inventory of Life Events and Changes. University of Wisconsin–Madison, 1981.

McCubbin H, Thompson A, eds. Family assessment inventories for research and practice. Madison: University of Wisconsin, 1987.

McCubbin HI, Thompson AI, Pirner P, McCubbin M. Family types and strengths: A life cycle and ecological perspective. Edina, Minn.: Burgess, 1988.

McCubbin MA, McCubin HI, Thompson AI. FHI—Family Hardiness Index. In: McCubbin HI, Thompson AI, eds. Family assessment inventories for research and practice. Madison: University of Wisconsin, 1987.

Moos R. Family Environment Scale preliminary manual. Palo Alto, Calif.: Consulting Psychologists Press, 1974.

Moos R. Coping with physical illness. New York: Plenum, 1977.

Moos R. Evaluating family and work settings. In: Ahmed P, Coelho G, eds. New directions in health. New York: Plenum, 1979.

Moos R, Bromet E, Tsu V, Moos B. Family characteristics and the outcome of treatment for alcoholism. Journal of Studies in Alcohol 1979; 40:78–88.

Moos R, Fuhr R. The clinical use of social ecological concepts: the case of an adolescent girl. American Journal of Orthopsychiatry 1982; 52:111–122.

Moos R, Moos B. Family Environment Scales manual. Palo Alto, Calif.: Consulting Psychologists Press, 1984.

Murdock GP. The universality of the nuclear family. In: Bell NW, Vogel EF, eds. A modern introduction to the family. Glencoe, Ill.: Free Press, 1960.

Olson DH, McCubbin HI. Circumplex model of marital and family systems: V. Application to family stress and cirsis intervention. In: McCubbin HI, Cauble AE, Patterson JM, eds. Family stress, coping and social support. Springfield, Ill.: Thomas, 1982.

Olson DH, McCubbin HI, Barnes H, Larsen A, Muxem M, Wilson M. Familes: what makes them work. Beverly Hills, Calif.: Sage Publications, 1983.

Olson, DH, Portner J, Bell R. Family Adaptability and Cohesion Evaluation Scales. Department of Family Social Science, University of Minnesota, St. Paul, 1978.

Olson DH, Portner J, Bell R. FACES II—Family Adaptability and Cohesion Evaluation Scales. Department of Family Social Science, University of Minnesota, St. Paul, 1982.

Olson DH, Portner J, Lavee Y. FACES III—Family Adaptability and Cohesion Evaluation Scales. Department of Family Social Science, University of Minnesota, St. Paul, 1985.

Olson DH, Russell C, Sprenkle D. Circumplex model: VI. Theoretical update. Family Process 1983; 22:69–83.

Olson DH, Sprenkle D, Russell C. Circumplex model of marital and family systems: I. Cohesion and adaptability dimensions, family types, and clinicial application. Family Process 1979; 18:3–28.

Paolucci B, Hall OA, Axinn NW. Family decision making: an ecosystem approach. New York: Wiley, 1977.

Parsons T, Bales RB. Family: socialization and interaction process. Glencoe, Ill.: Free Press, 1955.

Patterson, JM, McCubbin HI. The impact of family life events and changes on the health of a chronically ill child. Family Relations 1983; 32:255–264.

Pearlin LI, Schooler C. The structure of coping. Journal of Health and Social Behavior 1978; 19:2–21.

Portner J. Parent–adolescent interaction of families in treatment. Unpublished doctoral dissertation, University of Minnesota, St. Paul, 1980.

Rado, S. Towards the construction of an organized foundation for clinical psychiatry. Comprehensive Psychiatry 1961; 2:67–73.

Reiss D. The family's construction of reality. Cambridge, Mass.: Harvard University Press, 1981.

Russell CS. Circumplex model of marital and family systems: III. Empirical evaluation with families. Family Process 1979, 18:29–45.

Sigal JJ, Rakoff V, Epstein NB. Indicators of therapeutic outcome in conjoint family therapy. Family Process 1967; 6:215–226.

Skynner, AC. A group-analytic approach to conjoint family therapy. Journal of Child Psychology and Psychiatry 1969; 10:81–106.

Smilkstein G. The family APGAR: a proposal for a family function test and its use by physicians. Journal of Family Practice 1978; 6:1231–1239.

Smilkstein G. The physician and family function assessment. Family Systems Medicine 1984; 2:263–278.

Smilkstein G, Ashworth C, Montano D. Validity and reliability of the family APGAR as a test of family function. Journal of Family Practice, 1982; 15(2):303–311.

Sprenkle DH, Olson DH. Circumplex model of marital systems: IV. Empirical study of clinc and non-clinic couples. Journal of Marriage and Family Therapy 1978; 4:59–74.

Steinhauer PD, Santa-Barbara J, Skinner HA. The process model of family functioning. Canadian Journal of Psychiatry 1984; 29:77–88.

Tallman I. The family as a small problem group. Journal of Marriage and the Family 1970; 32:94–104.

Westley WA, Epstein NB. Report on the psychosocial organization of the family and mental health. In: Willner E, ed. Decisions, values and groups, Vol. I. New York: Pergamon Press, 1960.

Westley WA, Epstein NB. The silent majority. San Francisco, Calif.: Jossey-Bass, 1969.

13

Direct Observational Methods for Studying Family Functioning

KAREN B. SCHMALING
National Jewish Center for Immunology
and Respiratory Medicine

MICHELLE DeKLYEN
NEIL S. JACOBSON
University of Washington

Direct observational methods of assessment have been called the hallmark of behavioral psychologists (Ciminero, Calhoun, & Adams, 1977). Direct observation involves data collection in the natural environment, or in settings in which the behavior of interest is believed to be similar to behavior in natural settings. It is a rigorous approach to data collection because of the emphasis on measuring *samples* of overt behavior, rather than relying on inference and the interpretation of *signs* believed to reflect real behavior. Johnson and Bolstad (1973) state that direct observational methods are "the greatest contribution of behavior modification to the treatment of human problems" (p. 7). Direct observation is important in two contexts: for use by researchers to test experimental hypotheses, and for clinicians working in applied settings to monitor problem behaviors for evaluation of progress and outcome of interventions.

Haynes (1983) states that the history of behavioral observation dates back to Pavlovian experimenters (cf. Jones, 1924) and may be traced to the Hellenic and Egyptian eras. The recent increasing interest in behavioral assessment is largely a reaction to more traditional assessment methods. Direct observation methods emphasize assessment of current rather than historic behaviors. This is in contrast to the focus of psychodynamically oriented persons. Traditional assessment procedures include self-report measures and assessment by interview, both of which usually involve global rating scales. The need for more objective, sensitive, and specific assessment methods, with less bias and inferential qualities, grew out of dissatisfaction with these traditional assessment procedures.

There are few examples of applied observational methods in the research literature on interaction in families with physical presenting problems. Reports of the use of observational methods in the psychologic literature, however, have greatly increased over the past 15 years, for example in the treatment outcome literature on families with children with conduct problems (McIntyre *et al.*, 1983). The methodology presented in this chapter could be applied to assess many medical complaints—for example, any physical complaints that develop from the family system or are maintained or exacerbated thereby. Psychosomatic disorders such as Raynaud's disease, ulcerative colitis, asthma, hypertension, hyperthyroidism, neurodermatitis, rheumatoid arthritis, migraine, and paroxysmal tachycardia (Adams, 1983, p. 66) are examples of the ubiquity of psychologic factors in medicine. Psychosomatic diseases are defined as such according to

(1) a large series of observations which have revealed that the malfunctioning organ is susceptible to changes in function by influences mediated via the autonomic nervous system, (2) the

discovery in the biographies of some patients of an inordinately high incidence of resentment, hostility, and suppressed emotionality, (3) a demonstrable relationship between onset and successive exacerbations of disease and the presence of disturbing and frustrating incidents in the patient's life. (Adams, 1983, p. 66)

We interpret these statements to mean that observational methods could be used to assess the psychologic concomitants of *many* physical illnesses—that observational methods have great potential utility and applicability.

   This chapter will present an overview of methodology and application of direct observation methods to the assessment of family interaction and therapy. The goal of providing a discussion of methodologic concepts, issues, and problems with observational methods is to give the reader some perspective with which to evaluate applications.

DESIGNING THE OBSERVATION SYSTEM

Designing a method for systematically observing behavior involves (1) specifying and developing a behavioral coding system; (2) selecting an observation setting, modality, and behavior sampling technique; and (3) choosing data collection and storage technology (see Figure 13-1).

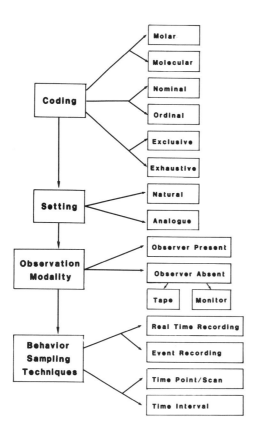

Figure 13-1. Behavioral coding system.

Developing the Coding System

The coding system should be designed to measure the salient behaviors in a way that will permit analysis and unambiguous interpretation, with a balanced concern for the limits of the human observer. The objectivity of the coding system depends in part on the degree to which the observers must infer or interpret events. The number of categories is generally a function of the specificity of the behaviors of interest as conceptualized on a molar to molecular continuum (Sackett, Ruppenthal, & Gluck, 1978).

MOLECULAR VERSUS MOLAR

First, what level of inference is required of the coders? Are the variables being coded relatively simple motor behaviors, or do they require the coder to make a judgment concerning the actor's intention or the function of the behavior? Systems involving comparatively simple behaviors have been called "molecular," as opposed to "molar" scales, which require a higher level of abstraction, often combining actions into classes defined by intent, function, or outcome (Sackett *et al.*, 1978).

Examples of molecular items include "words spoken," "looks," and "paraphrase." Such behaviors should be relatively easy to define so that all observers can consistently discriminate the intended action and agree on whether or not it has occurred.

In contrast, molar scales are more frequently designed in the context of a particular theoretic framework, so that the relationship between data and theoretic hypotheses may be clearer. A molar code might include items such as "conveyed warmth," "reviewed homework," "gave interpretation based on past relationships," or "related client's affective state to thoughts." Each of these items involves a sequence of many specific actions whose intention or function must be assessed.

For purposes of data analysis it is best to err in the direction of coding on a more molecular level of behavior, because codes can always be collapsed and combined into more molar categories, but the level of analysis cannot be made more molecular than the original code categories. It should be noted that observers' ability to code behavior reliably decreases as the complexity of the coding system (i.e., the number of categories) and interaction increases (Reid, Skindrud, Taplin, & Jones, 1973; Taplin & Reid, 1973).

NOMINAL VERSUS ORDINAL CODING SYSTEMS

Nominal coding systems involve strictly qualitative judgments about the presence or absence of given behaviors or events. Nominal scales tell what occurred, and with what frequency or duration. For example, a coder may be asked to determine whether the therapist "challenged," "taught," or "disagreed." Ordinal scales, by contrast, require coders to make quantitative judgments (e.g., to what degree the therapist was "warm" or "formal," or whether the therapist explored the client's thoughts "not at all," "some," or "extensively" during the session). Ordinal scales are well suited to answer questions of degree about variables that do not occur as "all or none." They can also allow rough and relatively inexpensive estimates of frequency and/or intensity. Some variables lend themselves to ordinal measures, while others are better tapped by nominal codes. A therapist's skill in using a particular technique, for instance, is probably best assessed by an ordinal system; but whether or not a technique was used at all in a particular session is a nominal scale question.

EXCLUSIVE AND EXHAUSTIVE CATEGORIES

A rule of thumb for coding system development is the definition of mutually exclusive and exhaustive categories. A coding system is mutually exclusive if none of the categories overlap, that is, if two codes cannot both occur. A system is exhaustive if *every* behavior can be coded into one of the categories. The conditions of exclusivity and exhaustivity are not necessary, but they make analysis and interpretation more straightforward (Sackett, 1979).

A system can be designed to include all possible jointly occurring events; such a system can record two behaviors that occur at the same time. In the large and cumbersome system that results, the categories are mutually exclusive. Another, less desirable approach to this problem is to define an elaborate hierarchy of categories so the observer knows which behavior to code and which to ignore when two behaviors occur at the same time.

It is useful to develop a training manual for new observers that provides operational definitions and positive and negative examples of each code for identification and discrimination learning. Patterson and Moore (1979) provide a detailed account of the development of a widely used coding system, the Family Interaction Coding System (FICS). Reid (1978) has published a training manual for this coding system.

Selecting an Observation Setting

The validity of observation data depends in part on the relationship between the observational setting and the environment where the behaviors of interest naturally occur. If the investigator wishes that the coding system capture the essence of naturally occuring behaviors, then the observations should take place in those settings. If the behaviors of interest occur in many settings, the observations optimally should include samples from the range of natural settings. The assumption that behavior observed in one setting will be the same in all naturally occurring settings may not be valid. Observing in natural settings, however, may not be feasible.

Analogue observation is the observation of behavior in contrived settings that have been modified and structured to increase observational efficiency (Haynes, 1983). An example includes the work of Patterson, Reid, Jones, and Conger (1975), who observed families in their natural setting in the home, but placed restrictions on the families' behavior so as to *increase* the likelihood of interaction. Family members could make no outgoing phone calls, could answer incoming calls only briefly, could not turn on the radio or television, and were all confined to one room.

A study by Jacobson (1977) provides another example of analogue observation. Couples were asked to discuss a problematic topic in their relationship in a structured clinic setting. It is possible to manipulate the stimuli as well as the setting by, for example, assigning a topic for discussion. Hughes and Haynes (1978) provide a comprehensive methodologic critique of structured laboratory observation. Cataldo, Bessman, Parker, Reid-Pearson, and Rogers (1979) discuss specific issues relevant to observation in hospitals, as do Bakeman and Brown (1977).

In addition to the artificial qualities of the setting and the situation, observer and/or equipment obtrusiveness may affect the generalizability of observational data. This phenomenon is called "reactivity" and is discussed below.

CHOOSING THE OBSERVATION MODALITY

As noted above, *in vivo* observation in the natural environment may not be feasible or cost-efficient. There are several alternative ways of collecting observational data. Alternatives to observer-present *in vivo* observation include audiotaped or videotaped interaction for subsequent coding, or observer-absent *in vivo* observation (i.e., observation through a two-way mirror). Studies have demonstrated the equivalence of live, via mirror, and via television observation by comparing the frequencies of coded behavior in each category (Kent, O'Leary, Dietz, & Diament, 1979).

Another data collection innovation was described by Christensen (1979), who designed a system to make randomly sampled audio recordings of family interaction. His system monitored several locations in the home where interaction was likely to occur (e.g., living room, den, kitchen, and dining room). The family designated periods of time when they were most likely to be in the home together. A tape recorder was connected to a multiple interval timer to send random 15-minute bursts of power to the tape recorder. The advantage of this system is that it requires very little intrusion into the family system, which probably results in less reactivity to the observation procedures. Additionally, the system was designed so that it was possible for the family to censor interaction, an important ethical consideration.

The advantages of the collection technique described above is that coders can review the tapes multiple times or use multiple coding systems, and thus facilitate reliability assessment. Some loss of behavioral clarity, however, is a distinct disadvantage of using recordings. Coding from recordings may be necessary when the behavior of interest is of short duration, some short-duration behaviors might be missed if coded *in vivo*.

SUBJECT REACTIVITY

Subject reactivity is a phenomenon in which the assessment procedures themselves produce changes in the subjects' behavior (Haynes & Horn, 1982). Reactivity may threaten the internal and external validity of the observational data. It is important to note, however, that "no study has yet addressed the significance of the reactive effects or the proportion of variance in behavior change that can be accounted for by reactive effects as compared to other independent effects" (Haynes & Horn, 1982, p. 381). Several studies of family interaction in the home or analogue settings have examined changes in frequencies of behavior code categories as a function of observer presence or absence. The results are equivocal. Some studies (e.g., Johnson & Bolstad, 1973) found no significant differences in behavioral frequencies. Others (e.g., White, 1977) found that observer presence tends to reduce general activity level. There is some evidence that families get used to ("habituate") observer presence with time. Zegiob, Forehand, and Resick (1979) found that mothers' prosocial behavior decreased over several sessions with the same observer, but increased when a new observer was introduced. This effect could be due to the mothers' concern with presenting a socially desirable picture to the observers. Harris and Lahey (1982b) have noted that reactivity effects are more likely to be found in home observation than in analogue and laboratory settings because it is easier to observe covertly in these latter settings.

Choosing a Behavior Sampling Technique

It is important to measure the salient properties of the behavior to be observed. These properties should be identified on the basis of a careful consideration of the response properties that are important to the research question (Foster & Cone, 1980); for example, does the investigator need frequencies, rates, durations, or proportions of specific code categories? Will behavior sequences be examined? The most popular methods of sampling behavior are real-time recording, event recording, time point or scan sampling, and time interval sampling (Sackett, 1979; Sanson-Fisher, Poole, Small, & Fleming, 1979). The use of different sampling methods in observational studies of family interaction has been evaluated by Roberts and Forehand (1978).

Data Collection Equipment and Technology

Real-time coding can be accomplished through the use of portable electronic coding devices that record events, their sequence or relationships to one another, and their duration. Two of the most popular and widely used systems that are commercially available are the Datamyte and OS-3.[1] Computer software is also available to facilitate direct data transfer from the coding devices to storage devices or direct computer entry and to generate frequently used summary statistics (e.g., frequencies, rates, and durations). Sackett (personal communication, 1984) suggests using commercially available microcomputers (such as Radio Shack's RS-100) as less expensive alternatives to such systems as the OS-3 and Datamyte.

Hartmann and Wood (1982) suggest several points to consider in the choice of observational equipment: obtrusiveness of behavior sampling, ease of data storage and retrieval, and feasibility of statistical analysis. These guidelines apply to the choice of a behavior sampling technique as well. Hartmann and Wood (1982) also provide selected references for information on ways to record data other than the systems discussed above.

Statistical Analysis

A review of analysis techniques for observational data is beyond the scope of this chapter. For a discussion of this subject, the reader is referred to Sackett's (1979) book, which includes good introductory material on sequential and nonsequential scoring and analysis methods.

OBSERVERS

The issues involved in the use of human observers include observer selection and training, and control of potential sources of bias that observers contribute to error in the data.

Selection and Training

Recent reviews of the literature on the selection of observers (Hartmann & Wood, 1982; Reid, 1982) summarize the characteristics and skills of observers who produce the most reliable data. These include high levels of verbal, scholastic, and intellectual ability; motivation; analytic and scientific detachment; compulsivity and attention to detail; introspection; intensity; and ability to focus attention without habituating to the surroundings.

Some authors (Hartmann & Wood, 1982; Reid, 1982) suggest a multistep model of observer training. The first step is a general orientation to observation. This might include sensitizing the observers to research issues, such as the need for them to be naive about experimental hypotheses by refraining from attempting to generate any hypotheses by or among themselves. Reid (1982) suggested that observers need to understand that every coding system requires that they be particularly vigilant about certain behaviors while ignoring others or coding such events that are extraneous to the behaviors of interest into a "junk" category. Weinrott, Reid, Bauske, and Brummett (1981) developed an Observer Impression Inventory to allow observers room to express their subjective impressions of family behavior. The need for this sort of instrument arose when observers criticized the coding system for not capturing the elements of behavior that seemed most important to the observers (Reid, 1982). In addition to decreasing observers' resistance to using the coding system, Weinrott *et al.* (1981) found the inventory to contain four clusters of items that possessed satisfactory psychometric properties and were related to the observed behavior of interest.

Observer orientation should also include a discussion of ethical issues, particularly confidentiality. Furthermore, if the observers will be working in naturalistic settings and will have contact with the families, expectations regarding their dress, appearance, and etiquette should be made clear. Observers should also be told how to deal with observed or suspected child or spouse abuse.

The next step is learning the observation code. This may be accomplished through didactic training and study of the observation manual. Observers may practice by using flash cards, homework, oral drills, and written tests. Reid (1982) reported that 10% to 20% of potential observers are dismissed at this point in training because they cannot learn the code definitions. Observers must also be trained how to record the data, including how to use whatever technologic aids are necessary.

Practice with analogue and live observations constitutes the next steps in training. Reid (1982) suggests that videotapes, audiotapes, or role plays can move the trainees from coding slow and simple behavioral interactions to fast and complex sequences. Observers should reach a high level of agreement; Reid (1982) suggests that observers should train to 100% agreement with a criterion, that is, with the "correct" codes as coded by an expert observer.

Feedback is an important part of the training process. Observers should be compared to each other and to a criterion so that corrective information can be given to the group and to individuals. One very good method of comparing two sets of data is the *confusion matrix* (House, 1980; Reid, 1982) This tool can be used for any data that can be matched in time, either exactly, as in real-time coding, or roughly, as with interval sampling. The procedure is to create an $n \times n$ where n equals the number of categories in the coding system. The trainee's codes are represented on one axis of the matrix and the criterion observer's codes (or other observer's codes) are on the other axis. When one observer codes a category, the other observer's protocol is examined to see what, if anything, she or he coded. Tallies are made so that the diagonal represents point-by-point agreements and the off-diagonal cells represent confusions. One can examine the nature of the confusions and look for systematic errors. Further practice can focus on discriminating the confused categories. Other issues in the assessment and control of reliability and their implications for monitoring observers are discussed in the next section.

Direct observation can be quite costly. Some of the most popular family interaction coding systems require 60 hours of training per observer (Weinrott & Jones, 1984). The expense of a portable electronic coding device for each observer must be added if the data are to be collected in that fashion. Imagine a study that calls for 50 families to be observed for 10 hours each, 1 hour a week. If 5 observers worked half-time (i.e., did two hour-long observations a day, including preparation, travel time, and data collection and storage), the data collection phase of the study would take 10 weeks. The total cost for data collection would be $24,000, assuming the coding devices cost $2,500 each and the observers are paid $5 per hour during training and $10 per hour during data collection. This figure does not include costs for data storage and analysis. This estimate would rise considerably if the interactions were coded from videotapes because of the added cost of a high-quality camera, videotapes, television monitors, and video players/recorders.

Sophisticated and costly observational codes and technologic aids are not necessary when the behaviors of interest can be measured in simpler ways. Event, time point, and time interval sampling methods generally entail less observer training, and recording only requires pencil and paper and a timing device.

Factors That Influence Reliability

There are several sources of observer bias that result in errors in the data. These include drift, consensual drift, reactivity of evaluation, and expectancies.

Simply, observer drift refers to decay in observers' performance (i.e., reliability) after the end of the training period. In other words, observers use categories in different ways subsequent to training. While Johnson and Bolstad (1973) suggest that this appears to be due to the passage of time, as in a study by Taplin and Reid (1973), Harris and Lahey (1982a) caution that passage of time and agreement checking were confounded in the Taplin and Reid (1973) study. The problem of observer drift can be dealt with by initial overtraining, periodic drills, and retraining (e.g., to standard criterion tapes), and by providing motivation (e.g., promising involvement in the data analysis after the data collection phase) (Reid, 1982).

One cannot assume that a reliable observer is an accurate observer (Wahler & Leske, 1973). The phenomenon of consensual observer drift occurs when interobserver reliability remains high after the end of training but reliability with a criterion decays (Johnson & Boland, 1973). In other words, all observers have changed their interpretations of code categories, but in agreement with one another (Wildman, Erickson, & Kent, 1975). This problem may be particularly salient for investigators who are using standardized coding systems developed by other observers.

Reliability Measures

There are three measures of assessing reliability that, taken together, express the quality of observational data. These three measures are interobserver agreement, reliability, and generalizability.

Interobserver agreement is the most commonly (and generally the only) reported measure of reliability. It is usually expressed as percentage agreement (Mitchell, 1979): the number of time units that two observers coded the same behavior (agreements) divided by the total of agreements plus disagreements, multiplied by 100. The percentage agreement score is generally calculated for each code category and averaged across categories. This measure may be artificially inflated when there is little variability in the coded behavior or the behavior occurs frequently (Hartmann, 1977). It does not correct for agreement that can be expected by chance. Since observer agreement is moderately related to the frequency of category use, an averaged percentage agreement score overestimates the interobserver agreement on low-rate behaviors of primary interest (Johnson & Bolstad, 1973). Some investigators report percentage agreement of correlation coefficients calculated on category frequencies for the observation as a whole, not point-by-point agreement. The reliability statistics should be calculated at the same level as the study's dependent variables. For example, if the dependent variable of interest is the proportion of observed time units the child was crying, then it is appropriate for reliability statistics to be given for that measure, not for a more molar measure. Gottman (1980), however, argues that matched point-by-point sequences are too severe a reliability criterion for sequential analysis, and offers an alternative.

The second measure of reliability, psychometric reliability, refers to traditional methods of assessing an instrument's psychometric soundness (Nunnally, 1978), that is, interobserver reliability, intraobserver or split-half reliability, internal consistency, and stability over time or test–retest reliability. Split-half reliability may be determined by examining scores at the beginning and end of an observation or the scores from odd and even blocks of time during the observation. Test–retest reliability refers to the extent to which a measure is stable over time. Some studies have shown high intrarater test–retest reliability over periods as long as 6 months (Wessberg, Coyne, Curran, Monti, & Corriveau, 1982).

Berk (1979) and Mitchell (1979) point out that most commonly reported reliability statistics (e.g., percentage agreement) are really agreement statistics because they examine differences among observers. This is only one potential source of error. Traditional reliability statistics differentiate variance due to observed scores (error) and variance due to true scores (individual differences). Berk (1979) examines the advantages and disadvantages of 16 agreement statistics and 6 reliability statistics. The generalizability coefficient is the proportion of variance accounted for by individual differences in the subjects' scores (true score variance) partitioned from the variance due to interobserver and intraobserver effects.

Berk (1979), Coates and Thoresen (1978), and Winer (1971) are good sources for examples of how to calculate reliability estimates from analysis of variance.

Finally, it should be noted that interobserver agreement and reliability can be reported either between observers (consistency) or between an observer and a criterion (accuracy).

Hartmann and Wood (1982) note that an "acceptable value" for observer reliability depends on the coding system and the statistics used to evaluate reliability, but recommended acceptable minimums range from 70% to 90% for percentage agreement scores, and .60 for kappa-like coefficients.

Validity

A valid instrument measures what it was designed to measure. Campbell and Fiske (1959) state that "reliability is the agreement between two efforts to measure the same trait through maximally similar methods. Validity is represented in the agreement between two attempts to measure the same trait through maximally different methods" (p. 83). Several different types of validity have been defined: discriminant validity, content validity, construct validity, and criterion-related validity.

Discriminant validity refers to the instrument's ability to differentiate groups that are formed on the basis of their scores on the independent variable. For example, if children are classified as normal or problematic based on their mother's reports, an observation system has discriminant validity if those groups can be differentiated on the basis of their observed proportions or rates of that specific problematic behavior.

Content validity is established when it is demonstrated that the coding system includes the behaviors of interest in the typical situations in which they occur. Content validity is inferred from criterion-referenced validity. A measure with low content validity will not be concurrently valid (Nunnally, 1978).

Construct validity refers to the accuracy with which observations measure a psychologic construct, such as "prosocial" or "deviant" behavior. Johnson and Bolstad (1973) point out that one way to test construct validity is to examine if observed behaviors are related to important variables external to the observation. These authors report an innovative method for measuring construct validity. They asked parents to rate the behaviors in their coding system on a "clearly deviant" to "clearly nondeviant and pleasing" scale. The average parent ratings were highly correlated with the observed proportion of negative consequences for each behavior. This indicated that parents were in agreement with the developers of the coding system about what constituted deviant behavior.

Criterion-related validity refers to the ability of the observational scores both to predict a criterion (predictive validity) and to be equivalent to an established measure (convergent or concurrent validity). It is particularly important to assess concurrent validity when using analogue observation settings or structured procedures to examine the representativeness of data gathered in those settings versus those gathered in natural settings (Hughes & Haynes, 1978). An example of the assessment of predictive validity would be to correlate the observed behavior of interest (e.g., rate of children's inappropriate nonattentive classroom behavior) with a criterion (e.g., scores from a standardized academic achievement test). A good example of establishing criterion-related validity for a coding system can be found in Robin and Weiss (1980).

CONCLUSION: FUTURE DIRECTIONS

A final topic should be addressed because of its relevance to the use of observational methods to medical problems: the importance of comparing treated individuals to normative data to assess treatment outcome.

Kazdin (1977) suggests an additional direction for future work that seems particularly salient for the assessment of treatments (medical, psychologic, or both) for medical problems. Social comparison procedures (Kazdin, 1977) are methods for assessing the clinical significance of treatment intervention. Most intervention studies assess the effects of treatment by comparing the average score on the dependent variable of the treated group to that of the control group. The treatment group may be *improved,* but are they within the normal range? Treatment outcome results based on group statistics may be misleading. Skewed and extreme scores of a few greatly improved individuals in the treatment group will bias the group's average score such that it may appear that the group improved as a whole, even when the majority of individuals show little improvement or are even deteriorated.

Jacobson *et al.* (1984) suggest that investigators look at individuals (or marital dyads) as another unit of analysis (i.e., what proportion of treated *individuals* are functioning within the normal range on the dependent variable). Jacobson, Follette, and Revenstorf (1984) outline methods for calculating the normal range of a score and assessing treatment effects on individuals.

The successful application of social comparison procedures depends on being able to quantify the range of normal functioning as measured by the dependent variable of interest. For direct observation procedures, this entails standardization of the coding system. Specification of normative rates or proportions of each category in a coding system has rarely been done (cf. Reid, 1978).

This chapter presented an overview of direct observation methodology, its advantages and disadvantages, and examples of applications in the assessment of therapy process and outcome studies, and of physical problems. Not enough work has been done to apply observation methods to topics in the field of medicine. It it hoped that this chapter will encourage practitioners and researchers in family medicine to use observational methods to assess behaviors of interest when the application is appropriate.

Note

1. For information on the Datamyte, the reader is referred to *Behavior Research Methods and Instrumentation* (1977), Vol. 9, no. 5, which includes a series of articles on portable coding systems, particularly the Datamyte. Information about the OS-3 is available from Observational Systems Inc., 15014 N.E. 40th, Redmond, WA 98052, (206) 883-3804.

References

Adams RD. Alterations in nervous system function. In: Petersdorf RG, Adams RD, Braunwald E, Isselbacher KJ, Martin JB, Wilson JD, eds. Harrison's principles of internal medicine, 10th ed. New York: McGraw-Hill, 1983:66.

Bakeman R, Brown JV. Behavioral dialogues: an approach to the assessment of mother–infant interaction. Child Development 1977; 48:195–203.

Berk RA. Generalizability of behavioral observations: a clarification of interobserver agreement and interobserver reliability. American Journal Mental Deficiency 1979; 83:460–472.

Campbell DT, Fiske DW. Convergent and discriminant validity by the multitrait–multimethod matrix. Psychological Bulletin 1959; 56:81–105.

Cataldo MG, Bessman CA, Parker LH, Reid-Pearson JE, Rogers MC. Behavioral assessment for pediatric intensive care units. Journal of Applied Behavior Analysis 1979; 12:83–97.

Christensen A. Naturalistic observation of families: a system for random audio recordings in the home. Behavior Therapy 1979; 10:418–422.

Ciminero AR, Calhoun KS, Adams HE., eds. Handbook of behavioral assesment. New York: Wiley, 1977.

Coates TJ, Thoresen CE. Using generalizability theory in behavioral observation. Behavior Therapy 1978; 9:605–613.

Foster SL, Cone JD. Current issues in direct observation. Behavioral Assessment 1980; 2:313–338.

Gottman JM. Analyzing for sequential connection and assessing interobserver reliability for the sequential analysis of observation data. Behavorial Assessment 1980; 2:361–368.

Harris FC, Lahey BB. Recording system bias in direct observational methodology: a review and critical analysis of factors causing inaccurate coding behavior. Clinical Psychology Review 1982a; 2:539–556.

Harris FC, Lahey BB. Subject reactivity in direct observation assessment: a review and critical analysis. Clinical Psychology Review 1982b; 2:523–538.

Hartmann DP. Considerations in the choice of interobserver reliability estimates. Journal of Applied Behavior Analysis 1977; 10:103–116.

Hartman DP, Wood DD. Observational methods. In: Bellack AS, Hersen M, Kazdin AE, eds. International handbook of behavior modification and therapy. New York: Plenum, 1982:109–138.

Haynes SN. Behavorial assessment. In: Hersen M, Kazdin AE, Bellack AS, eds. The clinical psychology handbook. New York: Pergamon, 1983:397–425.

Haynes SN, Horn WF. Reactivity in behavioral observation: a review. Behavorial Assessment 1982; 4:369–385.

House AE. Detecting bias in observational data. Behavioral Assessment 1980; 2:29–31.

Hughes HM, Hynes SN. Structured laboratory observation in the behavioral assessment of parent–child interactions: a methodological critique. Behavior Therapy 1978; 9:428–447.

Jacobson NS. Problem solving and contingency contracting in the treatment of marital discord. Journal of Consulting and Clinical Psychology 1977; 45:92–100.

Jacobson NS, Follette WC, Revenstorf D. Psychotherapy outcome research: methods for reporting variability and evaluating clinical significance. Behavior Therapy 1984; 15:336–352.

Jacobson NS, Follette WC, Revenstorf D, Baucom DH, Hahlweg K, Margolin G. Variability in outcome and clinical significance of behavioral marital therapy: a reanalysis of outcome data. Journal of Consulting and Clinical Psychology 1984; 52:497–504.

Johnson SM, Bolstad OD. Methodological issues in naturalistic observation: some problems and solutions for field research. In: Hamerlynck LA, Handy LC, Mash J, eds. Behavior change: methodology, concepts and practice. Champaign, Ill.: Research Press, 1973:7–67.

Jones MC. The elimination of children's fears. Journal of Experimental Psychology 1924; 7:383–390.

Kazdin AE. Assessing the clinical or applied importance of behavior change through social validation. Behavior Modification 1977; 1:427–452.

Kent RN, O'Leary KD, Dietz A, Diament C. Comparison of observational recordings *in vivo,* via mirror, and via television. Journal of Applied Behavior Analysis 1979; 12:517–522.

McIntyre TJ, Bornstein PH, Isaacs CD, Woody DJ, Bornstein TP, Lucas TJ, Long G. Naturalistic observation of conduct-disordered children: an archival analysis. Behavior Therapy 1983; 14:375–385.

Mitchell SK. Interobserver agreement, reliability, and generalizability of data collected in observational studies. Psychological Bulletin 1979; 86:376–390.

Nunnaly JC. Psychometric theory. New York: McGraw-Hill, 1978.

Patterson GR, Moore D. Interactive patterns as units of behavior. In: Lamb ME, Suomi SJ, Stephenson GR, eds. Social interaction analysis: methodological issues. Madison: University of Wisconsin Press, 1979: 77–96.

Patterson GR, Reid JB, Jones RR, Conger RE. A social learning approach to family intervention. Vol. 1 of Reid JB, ed. Families with aggressive children. Eugene, Ore.: Castalia, 1975.

Reid, JB, ed. A social learning approach to family interaction: Vol. 2. Observation in home settings. Eugene, Ore.: Castalia, 1978.

Reid JB. Observer training in naturalistic research. In: Hartmann DP, ed. Using observers to study behavior: new directions for methodology of social and behavioral science, no. 14. San Francisco: Jossey-Bass, 1982:37–50

Reid JB, Skindrud KD, Taplin PS, Jones RR. The role of complexity in the collection and evaluation of observation data. Presented at the meeting of the American Psychological Association, Montréal, Québec, Canada, August 1973.

Roberts MW, Forehand R. The assessment of maladaptive parent–child interaction by direct observation: an analysis of methods. Journal of Abnormal Child Psychology 1978; 6:257–270.

Robin AL, Weiss JG. Criterion-related validity of behavioral and self-report measures of problem-solving communication skills in distressed and nondistressed parent–adolescent dyads. Behavioral Assessment 1980; 2:339–352.

Sackett GP, ed. Observing behavior: data collection and analysis methods, Vol 2. Baltimore: University Park Press, 1978.

Sackett GP, Ruppenthal GC, Gluck J. Introduction: an overview of methodological and statistical problems in observational research. In: Sackett GP, ed. Observing behavior: data collection and analysis methods, Vol. 2. Baltimore: University Park Press, 1978.

Sanson-Fisher RW, Poole AD, Small GA, Fleming IR. Data acquisition in real time—an improved system for naturalistic observations. Behavior Therapy 1979; 10:543–554.

Taplin PS, Reid JB. Effects of instructnal set and experiemental influence on observer reliability. Child Development 1973; 44:547–554.

Wahler RG, Leske G. Accurate and inaccurate observer summary reports. Journal of Nervous and Mental Disease 1973; 156:386–394.

Weinrott MR, Jones RR. Overt versus covert assessment of observer reliability. Child Developoment 1984; 55:1125–1137.

Weinrott MR, Reid JB, Bauske BW, Brummett B. Supplementing naturalistic observations with observer impressions. Behavioral Assessment 1981; 3:151–159.

Wessberg HW, Coyne NA, Curran JP, Monti PM, Corriveau DP. Two studies of observers' ratings of social anxiety and skill. Behavioral Assessment 1982; 4:299–306.

White, GD. The effects of observer presence on the activity level of families. Journal of Applied Behavior Analysis 1977; 10:734.

Wildman BG, Erickson MT, Kent RN. The effect of two training procedures on observer agreement and variability of behavior ratings. Child Development 1975; 46:520–524.

Winer BJ. Statistical principles in experimental design. New York: McGraw-Hill, 1971.

Zegiob LE, Forehand R, Resick PA. Parent–child interaction: habituation and resensitization effect. Journal of Child Clinical Psychology 1979; 7:69–71.

14

In-Depth Interviewing in Family Medicine Research

RALPH LaROSSA
Georgia State University

The purpose of this chapter is to discuss in-depth interviewing in social science and to show how in-depth interviewing can be used in family medicine research.

In-depth interviewing is a face-to-face conversation that is designed to gather information. By emphasizing the face-to-face nature of in-depth interviewing, I am excluding from my definition all questionnaires (no matter how open-ended the items) and all telecommunications (i.e., phone and computer interviews). By noting the conversational aspect of in-depth interviewing, I am distinguishing it from standardized interviewing in which respondents are asked a predetermined set of multiple-choice questions. In-depth interviewing, like most conversations, is less directive than standardized interviewing and consequently more likely to include a number of unanticipated questions and raise a variety of unforeseen issues. By asserting that in-depth interviewing is a data-gathering strategy, I am highlighting the fact that in-depth interviewing is a unique kind of conversation. To get the information they need, in-depth interviewers routinely do things that they would not do if they simply were talking with someone. They will, for instance, appear to be ignorant about a topic, even when they are not, and will avoid focusing on themselves unless they feel that doing so will increase the informant's willingness to divulge information. Finally, by making in-depth interviewing a form of qualitative research, I am establishing that verbal rather than numerical data are what primarily interest the in-depth interviewer.

First, I will discuss the rationale behind in-depth interviewing, explaining why someone would choose in-depth interviewing in addition to or instead of other methodologic strategies. Second, I will describe the techniques and steps involved in in-depth interviewing. Although my focus here will be on the interview situation, some attention will be given to sampling and data storage. Third, I will cover the kinds of skills that in-depth interviewers should have, the equipment needed to do the job right, and the expenses involved in carrying out an in-depth interview study. Last, I will talk about the major ethical dilemmas that are likely to arise.

RATIONALE BEHIND IN-DEPTH INTERVIEWING

In-depth interviewing is one of the oldest and most venerable data collection strategies in social science. Frederick LePlay—who may very well have been the first social scientist (Périer, 1970)—used the method in his 19th-century study of working-class families (LePlay, 1855). And the well-known Chicago school of sociology, spawned in this century, owes a great deal to the in-depth interview studies (often called life history studies) carried out under its name (Cavan, 1983).[1]

The relationship between the Chicago school and in-depth interviewing as a research strategy is especially important, since it is the symbolic interactionist perspective of the

Chicago school that provides the rationale for in-depth interview research (Spradley, 1979, pp. 6–7). Symbolic interactionism, the brainchild of the philosopher George Herbert Mead (1863–1931), is a favorite of many family researchers (Hays, 1977) and has been extensively reviewed and critiqued (e.g., Burr, Leigh, Day, & Constantine, 1979; Hutter, 1985; Stryker, 1959). The summary statement penned by Herbert Blumer (1969), a former student of Mead and the individual who coined the term ''symbolic interactionism,'' is in my opinion one of the best. Besides clearly and concisely capturing the main tenets of a symbolic interactionist perspective, it also helps us to see how someone who considered her- or himself a symbolic interactionist would favor in-depth interview research.

According to Blumer (1969), symbolic interactionism rests on three premises:

1. Human beings act toward things on the basis of the meanings that the things have for them. . . .
2. The meaning of such things is derived from, or arises out of, the social interaction that one has with one's fellows. . . .
3. These meanings are handled in, and modified through, an interpretative process used by a person in dealing with the things he encounters. (p. 2)

The ''things'' to which Blumer refers can be physical or social; hence not only do trees or chairs qualify as things, but so do people, categories of people, elements of culture, institutions, activities, and situations. By saying that meanings arise out of social interaction, Blumer is contending that meanings are socially constructed realities. And by insisting that when people attribute meaning to things they do so through an interpretative process, Blumer is maintaining that there is an improvisational element to social life. Thus, people are role-making as well as role-taking when they act as parents, children, spouses, and so forth (Turner, 1962).

In keeping with the first premise, in-depth interviewing is a methodologic strategy that gives considerable weight to people's thoughts and feelings (i.e., meanings). Of course, you could rightly argue that all self-report measures, and especially all attitude scales, give considerable weight to people's thoughts and feelings, and that one does not necessarily have to conduct in-depth interview studies to be able to call oneself a symbolic interactionist. The difference is a matter of degree. In-depth interviewing, by only minimally structuring how informants report their thoughts and feelings, is a strategy that is more likely than survey interviewing to uncover meanings that, for whatever reason, the researcher failed to anticipate, and thus it is more likely to uncover the different ways that people cognitively organize the things around them.

As for the second premise, a good in-depth interviewer will constantly strive to tie meanings to interaction—directly, by asking the people who are being interviewed how they see their attitudes tied to their behavior, and indirectly, by inferring attitude–behavior connections from the interview transcripts (e.g., two sentences that at the time of the interviews seemed unrelated may later on be analyzed in conjunction with one another). A symbolic interactionist study is not complete until the investigator has linked meanings and interactions (Denzin, 1978, p. 9). The same can be said of the in-depth interview study—indeed, of any study that claims to be operating within the symbolic interactionist tradition, which brings us again to a comparison between survey research and in-depth interview research. Although you could argue that an attitude scale is designed to measure meanings, if you failed to include any measures of interaction in your interview schedule, you would be violating the second of Blumer's premises.

The third premise—that meanings are handled in, and modified through, an interpretative process—is the most controversial of the three. Symbolic interactionists do not even agree among themselves on this point. Those symbolic interactionists who place a lot of stock in this axiom (e.g., phenomenologists) tend to emphasize the emergent qualities of social life (and perhaps are guilty of presenting an undersocialized view of human behavior), whereas those symbolic interactionists who place less stock in this axiom (e.g., functionally oriented role theorists) tend to emphasize social life's deterministic qualities (and perhaps are guilty of presenting an oversocialized view of human behavior) (Wrong, 1961; Yoels & Karp, 1976). This last premise is probably also the axiom that separates symbolic interactionists who prefer in-depth interviewing (and other qualitative methodologies) from those who prefer survey interviewing (and other quantitative methodologies).[2]

Up to now I may have given the impression that in-depth interviewing is in competition with other research strategies, and that qualitative and quantitative research are incompatible. This is not the case, however. Although there have been numerous philosophic discussions about the conflicts between qualitative and quantitative research, when the studies carried out by the two camps are examined, it is difficult to discern significant epistemologic differences. In other words, it is not unusual to find qualitative elements in a largely quantitative study (e.g., "juicy quotes" to make the numerical analysis more interesting) or quantitative elements in a largely qualitative study (e.g., statements like " 'Most' of the people with whom I talked . . .") (Bryman, 1984). Yet, despite the fact that both qualitative and quantitative analysis seem to be appreciated (if only subconsciously) by all social researchers, whatever their avowed methodologic persuasion, investigators, at least in the family field, generally seem unwilling to carry out studies that give equal weight to qualitative and quantitative research. A content analysis of articles published in the *Journal of Marriage and the Family* from 1965 to 1983 revealed that in this journal combined studies are extremely rare: Of the 633 research articles surveyed, only 7 were based on studies that gave equal weight to qualitative and quantitative research (LaRossa & Wolf, 1985). What is especially disappointing about this trend is that it violates both the spirit and the letter of family social science as it was conceived and practiced by such luminaries as Robert Angell, Ernest W. Burgess, Ruth Cavan, Leonard Cottrell, E. Franklin Frazier, Ernest Mowrer, and Katherine Howland Ranck. In other words, the men and women who during the 1920s and 1930s were principally responsible for making family studies a *scientific* enterprise almost always relied on both qualitative and quantitative methods in their own work (Howard, 1981), and would probably be disheartened to learn that family scholars today do not appear to be making much of an effort to combine the two.

I believe that family studies has suffered because of the infatuation family scholars seem to have with quantitative methods (in the study just cited, 84% of the research articles were based on studies that were *exclusively* quantitative in design [LaRossa & Wolf, 1985]), and unless we begin soon to strike a better balance between qualitative and quantitative research, the field of family studies will become stagnant. Given my views about family studies in general, it should come as no surprise that I also believe that family medicine research, in order to remain viable, must include both qualitative and quantitative elements. Thus, as far as the rationale behind in-depth interviewing in family medicine research is concerned, let me simply say that whenever it appears that the three premises of symbolic interactionism can be brought to bear on an issue in family medicine, then in-depth interviewing is a methodologic strategy worth considering.

Putting it this way makes it understandable why, in my opinion, in-depth interviewing should be included in any family medicine researcher's "tool kit," for there are a host of issues in family medicine research that are amenable to a symbolic interactionist analysis. The meanings that families associate with pregnancy, birth, aging, and death are central to family medicine, as are the family interactional and interpretative processes that are constituent parts of a variety of illnesses, physiologic and otherwise. Although standardized instruments can shed some light on these cognitions and processes, they are not sufficient to capture the complex connections between the family system and the body's major networks. In short, in-depth interviewing cannot help but be viewed as an indispensable tool in family medicine research.

TECHNIQUES AND STEPS INVOLVED IN IN-DEPTH INTERVIEWING

Selecting Informants

SAMPLING

In-depth interview studies typically are based on somewhere between 20 and 50 interviews (Lofland & Lofland, 1984, p. 62). Perhaps the major reason that so few interviews are used is that verbal data are more cumbersome to analyze than numerical data. Each hour of interview time will yield approximately 20 pages of single-spaced transcript material. Thus, if you were to do 50 90-minute interviews, you would have 2,500 pages of transcripts to analyze. Working with other researchers would allow you to distribute the interviewing load, but when it came to making sense of the data, all members of the research team would still have to immerse themselves in the material. No matter how sophisticated and flexible your filing system is, there is no substitute for reading the interview transcripts over and over again.

In-depth interview studies also typically are based on nonprobability samples. Nonprobability samples include accidental samples (wherein one takes the cases that are available), quota samples, and purposive samples (Selltiz, Wrightsman, & Cook, 1976, pp. 517–521). There are two reasons that, more often than not, nonprobability samples are used. One is that the topic under investigation may be so sensitive that the only kind of sample possible is a nonprobability sample (Gelles, 1978). Bear in mind that the more in-depth a study is, the more likely prospective informants are to assume that they will be asked sensitive questions. Thus, it is generally more difficult to persuade people to participate in an in-depth interview study than in a survey study. The second reason that nonprobability samples are common in in-depth interview research has to do with hypothesis generation versus hypothesis testing. Nonprobability samples, especially purposive (theoretical) samples, which emerge during data collection, are especially suited for hypothesis-generating research (Glaser & Strauss, 1967). Since the quasi-inductive elements of qualitative research also make it well suited for hypothesis generation (Filstead, 1970), one can understand why qualitative researchers would tend to rely on nonprobability samples. Nonprobability samples are typically less expensive and easier to assemble. Unfortunately, they may not be representative, making it impossible to generalize beyond the specific individuals being studied. If, however, your goal is to generate rather than test hypotheses, generalizability is less of an issue. The bottom line, as always, is that *"The choice of sampling methods depends on the purpose of the research being conducted"* (Kitson *et al.*, 1982, p. 968; emphasis in original).

CHOOSING GOOD INFORMANTS

It is important in an in-depth interview study to find people from whom you will learn something, that is, people whose transcripts will have a lot of useful information (''useful'' being determined by your conceptual framework). How can you tell good informants from bad informants? Essentially, there are three criteria (Spradley, 1979, pp. 45–54). First, good informants are people who are thoroughly familiar with a group or situation because of their involvement with that group or situation. Bluebond-Langner (1978), for example, realized that if she wanted to understand how terminally ill children learn that they are dying, she would have to interview the children themselves. Second, good informants are people who are willing to be interviewed at length. It takes time for informants to feel comfortable with the idea of being scrutinized, and it takes time to gather information when you are deliberately trying not to structure your informants' responses. Thus, informants must sometimes commit themselves to not one but a series of interviews, each of which may last 2 to 3 hours. If someone can only "give" you half an hour, or if throughout the interviews he feels he is "wasting" his time, then that individual is not a good informant. In my own studies of pregnancy and the transition to parenthood (LaRossa, 1977; LaRossa & LaRossa, 1981), I dealt with this problem by telling the couples that in order for me to understand how parenthood changed their lives, I would have to gather longitudinal data. Hence, the "logic" of the studies (the taken-for-granted assumption that the second half of pregnancy is different from the first, and that being a parent of a 9-month-old child is different from being a parent of a newborn) made it easier for the couples to accept a multiple-interview design. Finally, good informants generally are people who do not look at themselves as they believe the interviewer does; in other words, they do not constantly analyze their responses, as an outsider would. Here again is why Bluebond-Langner's (1978) decision to interview children proved to be so fruitful. As sensitive as the children were to death, they were not sophisticated enough to try to outguess why an anthropologist would want to study them.

INDIVIDUAL VERSUS CONJOINT INTERVIEWS

In the process of selecting your informants you must decide whether you are going to conduct individual or conjoint interviews or some combination of the two. Family therapists long ago recognized the value of conjoint interviewing; they realized that a systemic conceptual approach to family groups demanded a systemic empirical approach, one that acknowledged the importance of studying not only all the elements in a system but also the interaction among those elements (e.g., Satir, 1964). Family researchers have been more reluctant to rely on conjoint interviewing, but they are beginning to recognize the value of this approach (see Allan, 1980; Bennett & McAvity, 1985).

I am a staunch advocate of conjoint interviewing in qualitative family research, if for no reason other than my feeling that conjoint interviewing is one of the best ways to collect data on mutually understood *meanings* in a family (i.e., a family's culture) and on family *interaction* (admittedly influenced by the presence of the interviewer) (LaRossa, 1977, p. 25; LaRossa, 1978).

The Interview Itself

HOW MUCH STRUCTURE?

The difference between survey interviewing and in-depth interviewing, as I mentioned earlier, is a matter of degree: What distinguishes the two is the amount of structure imposed by the interviewer. There are as many interviewing strategies as there are points on a continuum. At one pole of the continuum is the totally directive interview, in which all questions have been decided in advance and in which the responses of informants are forced into one choice or another. An example of a totally directed interview is a multiple-choice survey that includes no probes and no open-ended questions. At the other end of the continuum is the totally nondirective interview in which no questions have been decided beforehand and in which the informants, and *only* the informants, choose what to discuss. Perhaps the closest thing to a totally nondirective interview is Carl Rogers's client-centered therapeutic approach (Rogers, 1951).

In-depth interviewing is sometimes considered the same as nondirective interviewing—in fact. Rogers himself argues that his nondirective method can be used for research as well as therapeutic purposes (Rogers, 1945)—but the truth is that no interview conducted for research purposes can be totally without structure (Whyte, 1960). This does not mean that there will not be times during a particular interview when the informant will appear to be in charge, but generally in-depth, research-oriented interviews are controlled by the interviewer.

Whyte (1960), following Dohrenwend and Richardson (1956), has devised a six-point scale to conceptualize the different degrees of interviewer direction that may be present at any time in an in-depth interview. Basically, the scale lists the various ways that an in-depth interviewer can respond to what an informant is saying.

(1) "Uh-huh," a nod of the head, or "That's interesting." Such responses simply encourage the informant to continue and do not exert any overt influence on the direction of his conversation.

(2) Reflection. Let us say the informant concludes his statement with these words: "So I didn't feel too good about the job." The interviewer then says: "You didn't feel too good about the job?"—repeating the last phrase or sentence with a rising inflection. This adds a bit more direction than response 1, since it implies that the informant should continue discussing the thought that has just been reflected.

(3) Probe on the last remark by the informant. Here, as in response 2, attention is directed to the last idea expressed, but the informant's statement is not simply reflected back to him. The interviewer raises some question about this last remark or makes a statement about it.

(4) Probe of an idea preceding the last remark by the informant but still within the scope of a single informant statement. In one uninterrupted statement an informant may go over half a dozen ideas. If the interviewer probes on the last idea expressed, he follows the informant's lead. In turning to an earlier remark, the interviewer is assuming a higher degree of control over the interview.

(5) Probe on an idea expressed by informant or interviewer in an earlier part of the interview (that is, not in the block of talking that immediately preceded the interviewer's probe). By going further back in the interview to pick up a topic, the interviewer has a much broader choice, and consequently exercises more control than is the case if he simply limits his choice to immediately preceding remarks. It seems logical to distinguish between probes on ideas earlier expressed by the informant and those by the interviewer. However, . . . in practice . . . this is a difficult discrimination to make because most probes of this type can be related back to remarks made both by the informant, and by the interviewer.

(6) Introduction of a new topic. Here, the interviewer raises a question on a topic that has not been referred to before. (Reprinted by permission from "Interviewing in Field Research" by W. F. Whyte, in *Human Organization Research: Field Relations and Techniques*, edited by R. N. Adams and J. J. Preiss, 1960, Homewood, Ill.: Dorsey Press, pp. 354–355. Copyright 1960 by Dorsey Press.)

Skilled in-depth interviewers use all six responses. In other words, it is not a good idea to "sit" on a response and "ride it" throughout an interview.

Should you decide to take a strong nondirective tack, relying exclusively on the first and second responses, you are basically leaving to chance whether your informants will discuss the topics that you consider important, and making it difficult for yourself later on when you will want to compare one informant with another. Moreover, free-flowing interviews can make people uneasy. Bott (1971), for example, found that she had to introduce more structure into her interviews because, with the nondirective approach she was using in the beginning of her study, her interviewers were "confusing at least three largely incompatible and partly inappropriate roles, those of friend, research worker, and therapist." Her informants also were anxious about the fact that "they did not know what [Bott and her colleagues] found significant or what they [the informants] were revealing about themselves" (Bott, 1971, pp. 20–21).

Too much structure is not a good idea, either. In-depth interviews that rely exclusively on the sixth response may yield information that can more easily be subjected to numerical analysis, but the information obtained probably lacks the necessary intensity to be subjected to case analysis. More important, interviews that are too structured—especially those where sixth-level questions are asked in quick succession—may "become like a formal interrogation" and destroy whatever rapport may have been established with an informant (Spradley, 1979, p. 58).

In my opinion, qualitative family researchers tend to make the mistake of sacrificing depth for breadth rather than vice versa, with the result that much of what passes for in-depth family research does not have much "depth" to it at all. I suspect that family researchers gravitate toward the upper end of Whyte's scale in part because of the survey mentality that permeates family social science. It is not uncommon to find researchers who decide to do an in-depth interview study and who then, paradoxically, put together an elaborate interview guide of some 75 questions—all of which they expect to ask in the span of an hour and a half. These researchers are not conducting in-depth interviews; they are conducting surveys. What they apparently do not realize is that their refusal to abandon the security of a structured guide increases the probability that their study will ultimately be invalid. Too structured to qualify as a good in-depth project and too unstructured to qualify as a good survey, their study will end up satisfying no one.

PHENOMENAL IDENTITY VERSUS CONCEPTUAL EQUIVALENCE

Although there are certainly similarities between survey interviewing and in-depth interviewing—both are self-report measures, for example—the differences between the two should not be minimized. Survey interview research is almost always based on the assumption that informants must be presented with phenomenally identical questions; in other words, it is assumed that informants must be asked the same questions in the same order, with the same tone of voice, and so on. In-depth interview research, on the other hand, operates on the assumption that phenomenal identity is subordinate to conceptual equivalence; in other words, it is assumed that asking each informant phenomenally identical questions is not as important as collecting conceptually equivalent data. Sometimes, of course, phenomenally identical questions yield conceptually equivalent data. But sometimes they do not. We know, for example, that when it comes to doing cross-national research, an insistence on phenomenal identity can mean a loss of conceptual equivalence. Straus, for example, argues that the "use of the identical procedures in different societies for eliciting and quantifying data ('phenomenal identity') does not necessarily result in the measurement of the same variable ('conceptual equivalence') since the stimuli (questions, tasks, items) used to elicit data may have different meanings in different societies" (1969, p. 233). If we substitute the words "informants" or "families" for "societies," Straus's statement can be used to justify the kind of flexible interviewing that characterizes in-depth interviewing (LaRossa & LaRossa, 1981, p. 240). (See Straus, 1969, for other methods of handling the problem of conceptual equivalence.) In-depth interviewers approach each interview with a *concept* of the kind of information that they want to gather. They then proceed to ask questions that allow them to capture that concept. If that means asking in the beginning of an interview a question that in another interview was asked at the end, so be it. If that means probing with one informant more than was done with another, that is all right, too.

Data Storage

TO TAPE OR NOT TO TAPE?

Before tape recorders were invented, qualitatively oriented symbolic interactionists would preserve their informants' stories by asking them to write their autobiographies (Plummer, 1983, p. 94). For example, W. I. Thomas and Florian Znaniecki's *The Polish Peasant in Europe and America* (1918–1920)—the study that was instrumental to the development of symbolic interactionism and qualitative methods (LaRossa & Wolf, 1985)—included a 312-page life history. Today, however, tape recorders are commonplace, and their availability has transformed life history research. Whereas written autobiographies can go through several drafts, with each draft perhaps presenting an increasingly artificial picture, whatever is said during a tape-recorded interview can only be clarified or expanded; deletions are not possible (unless, of course, the interviewer gives the informant final-cut rights on the interview transcript) (Matthews, 1983). Hence, everything that is said is stored, from the off-the-cuff remark to the convoluted rationalization.

Some interviewers prefer not to use a tape recorder because they feel that doing so "constrains interactions already made somewhat unnatural by [their] presence" (Cottle, 1977, p. 190). Others believe that a tape recorder is "imperative" because it allows interviewers to focus their full attention on the informant and at the same time chronicle what is being said (Lofland & Lofland, 1984, pp. 60–61).

No doubt there are interview situations where informants might find a tape recorder threatening, and many of these situations are likely to arise in family medicine research. Featherstone (1980), for example, reported that, in her studies of families with a disabled child, the fact that she did not use a tape recorder during the parent group meetings not only increased the validity of her data but also preserved the privacy of the group. As one woman told her, the parent group "was the one place where [she] could be completely honest," which was something she "really needed" at the time (Featherstone, 1980, p. 246). And Hannam (1975), who used a tape recorder in his study of parents with a retarded child, discovered that the fathers and mothers spoke more eagerly once he turned off the recorder at the end of the interview session.

I personally think that whenever possible a tape recorder should be used in in-depth interview research. As indicated, there are situations where a tape recorder would make informants uneasy, but typically people grow accustomed to its presence. The problem is that you simply cannot rely on your memory or shorthand skills to reproduce faithfully the transcript of an interview, and there really is no substitute for a transcript when you are trying to analyze meanings, interactions, and interpretative processes.

TRANSCRIPTS

Some researchers require a verbatim transcript—one that includes every stutter and every interruption—because they are interested in analyzing grammar, syntax, and form as well as interview content. Ethnomethodologists, for example, typically demand meticulously produced transcripts (see Mehan & Wood, 1975). Other researchers are happy to work with transcripts that basically capture the essence of what was said and are not concerned if a word or sentence is left out or if repetitions are deleted.

The kind of analysis that I typically do requires a transcript that, though not perfect, is reasonably detailed. Syntax and grammar are not important to me, but other cues, such as hesitancy, timing, verbosity, and logic, are. I also tend to favor conjoint over individual interviews and case analysis over a "juicy quote" approach, so it is important that I preserve the subtleties of a family's give-and-take and biographic reconstruction.

Analysis

One of the most difficult and least understood aspects of an in-depth interview study is the data analysis. First of all, as a form of qualitative research, an in-depth interview study is subject to the same rules that apply to qualitative studies in general. For example, whereas in a quantitative study data collection and data analysis are temporally segregated, in a qualitative study the two overlap (Lofland & Lofland, 1984, p. 132). Also, as I mentioned earlier, a qualitative study is more likely than a quantitative study to have hypothesis generation as its principal goal (Filstead, 1970; Glaser & Strauss, 1967).

The fact that qualitative analysis is nowhere near as standardized as quantitative analysis means that subsuming in-depth interviewing under qualitative research goes only so far in reducing the uncertainty involved in analyzing in-depth interview materials. Some people believe that qualitative analysis is as much an art as a science and that, consequently, qualitative research will never achieve the level of standardization characteristic of quantitative research. Others argue that, unless qualitative researchers move to make their procedures more systematic, qualitative research will never be taken seriously in scientific circles.

I believe that both qualitative and quantitative research entail some measure of artistry, and that trying to remove intuition and personal style from qualitative research is not only impossible but also detrimental to the scientific process. On the other hand, I do feel that too often qualitative researchers use the "more-art-than-science" rationale as an excuse not to publicize their procedures. Since science is a communal enterprise, not describing how one got from point A (in this case, the interview transcripts) to point B (the finished book or journal article) is unacceptable.

So, how do you get from point A to point B when you are doing in-depth interview research? As indicated, there is no single, generally accepted path. However, here is how one researcher, Bob Blauner, goes about analyzing his data. I present his approach because I suspect that others follow a similar, though probably not identical, route. I know I do.

> I begin—and this first, preparatory phase is extremely critical—by consulting my "field notes," listening to the tapes, and reading one or more times the transcripts. . . . My impulse is to begin writing immediately, and I have to check such impatience in order to first listen to the tapes in a loose way, to be open and receptive almost as one listens to music. My purpose in this stage is to get an intuitive feel for the "whole person" and his or her story. . . . The second step is to read the transcript in a more focused way, alert for details as well as general impressions. I'm looking now for those sociologically relevant issues that I will want to bring out. I underline passages that strike me as interesting, those that I sense I will want to include. I take note also of material that seems tedious or extraneous or highly repetitive, penciling the word "out" in the margins where I find this, since I'm going to have to boil down an average of 50 transcript pages [per informant] into no more than 10 to 15. . . . Now I'm

ready to get to my typewriter, to write an introduction and to begin actually lifting material from the original transcript to my first rough draft. . . . I may do five or six pages and see that it's not flowing, not hanging together. I start again, usually at a different point in the interview, with a different topic, and sometimes go through two or three false starts before I like what I've got. . . . In each interview I look for the person's unique story, the special focus or issues which set that person off, add something new to the unfolding "cast of characters" who make up the book as a whole. . . . It's the story line above all that organizes "raw data." Through unearthing or imposing a central theme or story line, the editor becomes an active creator or interpreter of the materials. (Reprinted by permission from "Problems of Editing 'First Person' Sociology" by B. Blauner, 1987, *Qualitative Sociology,* Vol. 10, pp. 53–54. Copyright 1987 by Human Sciences Press.)

Blauner (1987) says that analyzing his transcripts involves unearthing or imposing a "story line." Davis (1974, p. 311) thinks it is "essential" to try to find "some kind of story which will give you an opening, a beginning working stratagem with respect to the data." Lofland and Lofland (1984, p. 135) talk about finding "general designs," analytic structures that give coherence to your materials. All of them seem to be saying basically the same thing, namely that the research process involves a cycle between ideas and data. Or to put it another, perhaps more familiar way: The data do not speak for themselves.

In the course of writing for publication, the in-depth interviewer will also have to deal with the following dilemmas: How much of a balance should there be between the informant's voice and the researcher's voice? When transcripts are reproduced, should the interviewer's questions and comments be included or deleted? How much of the informant's grammar and sentence structure should be preserved? Should repetitions be deleted? Should one present full-length case studies and/or brief, typically out-of-context excerpts? If case studies are to be presented, who will be selected for case analysis? How does one deal with contradictions within a single interview and between periodic interviews? How does one decipher evasions, deceptions, and lies? (For help in answering these questions, see Plummer, 1983; Spradley, 1979.)

PERSONNEL AND EQUIPMENT

Personnel

Whereas survey interviewers need only an overview of the theoretic issues that have spawned their interview schedule, in-depth interviewers must be thoroughly familiar with the conceptual issues that motivated their project, and must have enough acumen to know how to use their questions and probes to explore uncharted theoretic terrain. Also, whereas survey interviewers must be able to establish and maintain rapport with their respondents, the interpersonal skills required of in-depth interviewers are more stringent. What Young (1952) said over 30 years ago is still true today:

The competent [in-depth/life history] interviewer must possess keen perceptive faculties and an accurate memory. Not only should he hear correctly what is said to him, but he will be alert to the overtones of the informant's verbal and overt reactions, noting changes in voice, indications of feeling-emotional states from facial or other gestures, and any other possible clues to inner states which may subsequently be exposed. And, while he must know how to direct the session with skillful and revealing inquires, he must also possess the capacity for sympathetic listening. (Young, 1952, p. 308)

All of which means that, if you are going to assemble a team of in-depth interviewers, you should (1) anticipate having to draw from a fairly educated pool of candidates; (2) set up a fairly extensive training program, one that continues throughout the data collection phase at least (you probably will want your interviewers to join in the analysis, too); and (3) be prepared to pay wages that are competitive enough to attract qualified people.

You will also need a good transcriber, someone who not only can type well but also has the ear, foot, and hand coordination to work a transcribing machine and a keyboard simultaneously, and who is compulsive about wanting to get an accurate and neat transcription. Skilled, conscientious transcribers are in demand, so expect to pay top dollar. Furthermore, if you "farm out" the job to a free-lance transcriber, I recommend that you pay by the page rather than by the hour. This not only will make your expectations clearer, but also will serve as an incentive for the transcriber not to leave anything out.

Equipment

Portable cassette recorders can cost anywhere from $30 to $300. Invest in a high-quality model. Also, even if your recorder has a built-in microphone, use an extension microphone or possibly several lapel microphones to ensure that everyone is heard clearly. (Miniature microphones are an especially good idea if you intend to conduct conjoint or group interviews.)

Cassette tapes also vary in price. Buy cartridges that can be taken apart and put back together again so you can splice tapes that break. Also, tapes that you plan to transcribe will be subjected to a lot of stop–start abuse, so avoid brittle or excessively thin tapes.

Transcribing machines cost between $250 and $400. The more expensive models have indexing and cueing features. If your budget allows, buy the best.

Up to now, a qualitative researcher's analytic equipment basically consisted of a lot of paper and a bunch of file folders (Lofland & Lofland, 1984). With the advent of personal computers (PCs), however, electronically assisted text analysis has become more popular. If your budget allows for a PC, I strongly recommend that you consider using one of the text-search software programs currently available when the time comes to analyze your data (see Bermant, 1987; Conrad & Reinharz, 1984).

ETHICAL DILEMMAS

The social-scientific study of family medicine can take a toll on both researcher and subjects. It is not easy to observe families trying to deal with cancer, diabetes, prematurity, or senility; and it certainly is not easy to be scrutinized when these tragedies strike.

Typically, researchers can do little to change the physical reality with which their subjects are trying to cope. They cannot wish away the cancer, nor can they reverse the aging process. But they can and should be sensitive to the ethical dilemmas associated with studying these issues.

One ethical dilemma that in-depth interviewers should be prepared to face is that in-depth interviewing tends to magnify the uneasiness that researchers and subjects may encounter in family medicine research. It is not unusual, for example, for informants to cry or show emotion in other ways during in-depth interview sessions. After all, you are asking them to review *in depth* their thoughts and feelings about things like being the parent of a child with spina bifida or being the child of a parent with cancer (see Darling, 1979, p.

90). It is also not unusual for informants to find the in-depth interview sessions therapeutic and, in fact, to look upon the interviewer as a therapist. Who can blame them? Caught in "a medical system that often is too busy caring for the illness to notice the emotional needs of the victim and his grief-stricken loved ones" (Speedling, 1982, p. 8), families sometimes feel that you are the only person *willing to listen to them*. Finally, it is not unusual for informants to view the in-depth interviewer as a close friend simply because you are there, *no matter what they say* (Bluebond-Langner, 1978, p. 247).

Being a shoulder to cry on, a therapist, or a friend is not, in and of itself, a bad thing, but adopting these roles can pose serious ethical dilemmas if you (1) are unprepared to deal with these responsibilities (e.g., you are taken by surprise or are not qualified to handle them) or (2) deliberately exploit the role ambiguity for personal ends (LaRossa, Bennett, & Gelles, 1981).

I have less of a problem with the first of these two possibilities because I think that interviewers can be trained to anticipate being thrust into one role or another, and to know when people should be referred to a therapist or agency.

The second possibility—that of exploiting the informant—is, to my mind, the more serious. Family medicine research, like all medical research, places subjects in an unfavorable power–dependency relationship (Kelman, 1972). Relying on an in-depth interviewer for emotional nourishment can mean that informants may divulge more about themselves than they had planned to when they signed the informed-consent forms, or, worse, may feel compelled to continue on a project, against their better judgment, because they feel they owe the interviewer something.

Although guidelines for dealing with ethical dilemmas in research do exist (the American Medical Association, American Psychological Association, and American Sociological Association all have codes of ethics), these guidelines rarely address the distinctive ethical dilemmas associated with in-depth interview family medicine research, or with qualitative family research in general. More often than not, researchers must deal with each situation on an ad hoc basis and hope for the best (LaRossa, Bennett, & Gelles, 1981).

CONCLUSION

The object of this chapter has been to discuss the whys and hows of in-depth interviewing in family medicine research. The major strengths of an in-depth interview design are its compatibility with a symbolic-interactionist approach—an approach that cannot be ignored by family medicine researchers—and its capacity to generate hypotheses for further study. The major weaknesses are that typically one must rely on small, nonprobability samples and be satisfied with analytic procedures that, for the present, are less reliable than those used in quantitative research.

I do not think that these pros and cons can be weighed against each other to compute some kind of net value of in-depth interview research. In other words, I do not think it makes much sense to decide, for example, that the costs outweigh the rewards and, therefore, in-depth interview research is not worth doing. *Family medicine researchers have no choice but to encourage in-depth interview research—the nature of family medicine requires it*. Thus, the question is not whether we should do in-depth interview family medicine research, but how we can do *good* in-depth interview family medicine research.

Right now, there is no simple answer to this question. My hope is that the increased interest in qualitative family research (see Hill, 1981; Sprey, 1982) will result in more public and private funding for qualitative work, and that a stronger financial base will not only support more representative samples but also serve as an incentive to develop more standardized procedures for analyzing qualitative data. If this happens, in-depth interview research will become more common and be of higher quality. And the better able we are to do in-depth interview research, the healthier the field of family medicine will be.

Notes

1. The "Chicago school" does not refer to *any* sociology carried out at the University of Chicago. Rather, it denotes "a particular worldview and fieldwork research method preferred by many, but by no means all Chicago analysts in the 1920s and 1930s" (Thomas, 1983, p. 387).

2. Some theorists would disagree with the implication that phenomenology and role theory are opposite poles of a symbolic interactionist continuum because they would say that phenomenology, role theory, and symbolic interactionism are qualitatively different (see, e.g., Gubrium & Buckholdt, 1977, pp. 1–31). In my opinion, however, the difference is a matter of degree, not kind—specifically, the degree to which these *cognitive* sociologies emphasize either the emergent or the deterministic aspects of social life (cf. Burr *et al.*, 1979, p. 311).

References

Allan G. A note on interviewing spouses together. Journal of Marriage and the Family 1980; 42:205–210.

Bennett, LA, McAvity K. Family research: a case for interviewing couples. In: Handel G, ed. The psychosocial interior of the family, 3rd ed. New York: Aldine, 1985:75–94.

Bermant C. Finding it fast: new software features that search your system. Personal Computing 1987; 11:125–131.

Blauner B. Problems of editing "first person" sociology. Qualitative Sociology 1987; 10:46–64.

Bluebond-Langner M. The private worlds of dying children. Princeton, N.J.: Princeton University Press, 1978.

Blumer, H. Symbolic interactionism: perspective and method. Englewood Cliffs, N.J.: Prentice-Hall, 1969.

Bott, E. Family and social network: roles, norms, and external relationships in ordinary urban families. New York: Free Press, 1971.

Bryman A. The debate about quantitative and qualitative research: a question of method or epistemology. British Journal of Sociology 1984; 35:75–92.

Burr, W, Leigh GK, Day RD, Constantine J. Symbolic interaction and the family. In: Burr WR, Hill R, Nye FD, Reiss IL, eds. Contemporary theories about the family: II. General theories/theoretical orientations. New York: Free Press, 1979: 42–111.

Cavan, RS. The Chicago school of sociology, 1918–1933. Urban Life 1983; 11:407–420.

Conrad, P, Reinharz S, eds. Computers and qualitative data. Qualitative Sociology, special issue, Spring–Summer 1984; 7.

Cottle TJ. A middle-American marriage. In: Stein PJ, Richman J, Hannon N, eds. The family: functions, conflicts, and symbols. Reading, Mass.: Addison-Wesley, 1977:190–191.

Darling RB. Families against society: a study of reactions to children with birth defects. Beverly Hills, Calif.: Sage, 1979.

Davis F. Stories and sociology. Urban Life and Culture 1974; 3:310–316.

Denzin NK. The research act: a theoretical introduction to sociological methods. New York: McGraw-Hill, 1978.

Dohrenwend BS, Richardson SA. Analysis of the interviewer's behavior. Human Organization 1956; 15:29–32.

Featherstone H. A difference in the family: life with a disabled child. New York: Basic Books, 1980.

Filstead WJ. Qualitative methodology: firsthand involvement with the social world. Chicago: Markham, 1970.

Gelles RJ. Methods for studying sensitive family topics. American Journal of Orthopsychiatry 1978; 48:408–424.

Glaser B, Strauss AL. The discovery of grounded theory. Chicago: Aldine, 1967.

Gubrium JF, Buckholdt DR. Toward maturity: the social processing of human development. San Francisco: Jossey-Bass, 1977.

Hannam C. Parents and mentally handicapped children. Baltimore: Penguin Books, 1975.

Hays WC. Theorist and theoretical frameworks identified by family sociologists. Journal of Marriage and the Family 1977; 39:59–65.

Hill R. Whither family research in the 1980s: continuities, emergents, constraints, and new horizons. Journal of Marriage and the Family 1981; 43:255–257.

Howard RL. A social history of American family sociology, 1865–1940. Westport, Conn.: Greenwood Press, 1981.

Hutter, M. Symbolic interaction and the study of the family. In: Farberman HA, Perinbanayagam RS, eds. Studies in symbolic interaction: Supplement 1. Foundations of interpretive sociology. Greenwich, Conn.: JAI Press, 1985.

Kelman, HC. The rights of the subject in social research: an analysis in terms of relative power and legitimacy. American Psychologist 1972; 27:989–1016.

Kitson GC, Sussman MB, Williams GK, Zeehandelaar RB, Schickmanter BK, Steinberger JL. Sampling issues in family research. Journal of Marriage and the Family 1982; 44:965–981.

LaRossa R. Conflict and power in marriage: expecting the first child. Beverly Hills, Calif.: Sage, 1977.

LaRossa R. Conjoint marital interviewing as a research strategy. Case Analysis 1978; 1:141–150.

LaRossa R, Bennett LA, Gelles RJ. Ethical dilemmas in qualitative family research. Journal of Marriage and the Family 1981; 43:303–313.

LaRossa R, LaRossa MM. Transition to parenthood: how infants change families. Beverly Hills, Calif.: Sage, 1981.

LaRossa R, Wolf JH. On qualitative family research. Journal of Marriage and the Family 1985; 47:531–541.

LePlay F. Les ouvriers europeens. Tours, France: Alfred Mame et Fils, 1855.

Lofland J, Lofland LH. Analyzing social settings: a guide to qualitative observation and analysis, 2nd ed. Belmont, Calif.: Wadsworth, 1984.

Matthews SH. Analyzing topical oral biographies of old people. Research on Aging 1983; 5:569–589.

Mehan H, Wood H. The reality of ethnomethodology. New York: Wiley, 1975.

Perier P. Foreword. In: Brooke MZ: LePlay: engineer and social scientist. New York: Longman, 1970.

Plummer K. Documents of life: an introduction to the problems and literature of a humanistic method. London: George Allen and Unwin, 1983.

Rogers, C. The nondirective method as a technique for social research. American Journal of Sociology 1945; 50:279–283.

Rogers C. Client centered therapy. Boston: Houghton Mifflin, 1951.

Satir V. Conjoint family therapy. Palo Alto, Calif.: Science and Behavior Books, 1964.

Selltiz C, Wrightsman LS, Cook SW. Research methods in social relations, 3rd ed. New York: Holt, Rinehart and Winston, 1976.

Speedling EJ. Heart attack: the family response at home and in the hospital. New York: Tavistock, 1982.

Spradley JP. The ethnographic interview. New York: Holt, Rinehart and Winston, 1979.

Sprey J. Editorial comments, Journal of Marriage and the Family 1982; 44:5.

Straus MA. Phenomenal identity and conceptual equivalence of measurement in cross-national comparative research. Journal of Marriage and the Family 1969; 31:233–239.

Stryker S. Symbolic interaction as an approach to family research. Marriage and Family Living 1959; 21:111–119.

Thomas J. Chicago sociology: an introduction. Urban Life 1983; 11:387–395.

Thomas WI, Znaniecki F. The Polish peasant in Europe and America. Boston: Gorham Press, 1918–1920.

Turner RH. Role-taking: process versus conformity. In: Rose AM, ed. Human behavior and social processes. Boston: Houghton Mifflin, 1962:20–40.

Whyte WF. Interviewing in field research. In: Adams RN, Preiss JJ, eds. Human organization research: field relations and techniques. Homewood, Ill.: Dorsey Press, 1960:352–374.

Wrong, D. The oversocialized conception of man in modern sociology. American Sociological Review 1961; 26:183–193.

Yoels, WC, Karp DA. A social psychological critique of "oversocialization": Dennis Wrong revisited. Presented at the meeting of the American Sociological Association, New York, August 1976.

Young, K. Personality and problems of adjustment. New York: Appleton-Century-Crofts, 1952.

PART FOUR

Family Systems Immunology

15

Psychoneuroimmunology

JOAN BORYSENKO
Harvard Medical School

The rapidly emerging field of psychoneuroimmunology studies the impact of psychological factors on disease. . . . While there is an abundance of material documenting that the mind/body connection exists, there is a paucity of material on the mechanisms involved. . . . [T]he following chapter . . . surveys the mechanisms of the immune response and the data that support the mind's role in enhancing that response.

MODULATION OF DISEASE EXPRESSION BY BEHAVIORAL FACTORS

According to tradition, keeping well is usually concerned with care of the body through appropriate nutrition and exercise, avoidance of tobacco, moderation of alcohol, immunization against disease, and adequate medical advice or treatment. This approach, while entirely valid, may not be complete. A growing body of evidence, comprising epidemiological studies of humans as well as laboratory experiments with animals, indicates that psychological factors can often cause disease or modulate the expression of disease caused by other factors.

The premise that the immune system can be compromised behaviorally, leading to a transient acquired immunodeficiency, underlies the rapidly expanding field of psychoneuroimmunology. The nomenclature reflects interest in exploring the causal connection between psychological events, endocrine secretion, and modulation of immunity. Early animal studies in this area fit into the more general rubric of psychosomatics, paralleling human research. Once the effect of behavioral factors on disease susceptibility was substantiated, the search for intermediary mechanisms began. These mechanisms currently comprise two categories: an indirect pathway whereby behavioral parameters affect immunity through hormonal changes, and a putative direct pathway involving bidirectional communication between the central nervous system and the lymphoid organs.

Interaction of Behavioral and Environmental Risk Factors: An Example

There is no doubt that cigarette smoking is a direct cause of lung cancer. In the 1960s, Kissen studied over 1,000 men with undiagnosed pulmonary disease and concluded that

Reprinted by permission from *Behavioral Health: A Handbook of Health Enhancement and Disease Prevention,* edited by J. D. Matarazzo, S. M. Weiss, J. A. Herd, and N. E. Miller, 1984, New York: John Wiley and Sons, Inc., pp. 248–260. Copyright 1984 by John Wiley and Sons, Inc.

those found to have cancer displayed an inability to express emotions that differentiated them statistically from men with other types of lung disease (Kissen, 1963, 1967). Such studies are not conclusive, however, since bodily effects of cancer can cause personality changes as can emotional reactions to a suspected cancer diagnosis. In other words, it is hard to distinguish whether personality changes are a cause of or an effect of the disease. More recently, psychosocial risk factors in lung cancer were evaluated on the basis of a composite scale assessing stability of childhood, marriage, and job, plans for the future, and recent significant loss (Horne & Picard, 1979). The psychosocial scale accurately predicted diagnosis of benign or malignant disease 73% of the time ($p < .0001$). A multiple regression analysis, with actual diagnosis as the dependent variable and psychosocial scale and smoking history as the independent variables, indicated that psychosocial factors were 1 to 2 times as important as smoking history in predicting cancer. This does not imply that cigarette smoking is harmless. Rather, it emphasizes the interaction between physical and psychological determinants of disease.

A Model of Hereditary, Environmental, and Behavioral Factors in Disease Susceptibility

The role of personality and psychosocial factors in determining health was a foremost consideration before the development of the current mind/body dualism that developed during the time of Descartes. As medical knowledge increased, however, the direct causes of many diseases were traced to external agents such as bacteria, viruses, chemicals, and vitamin deficiencies. These discoveries helped to extricate science from superstition, but they also led to the premature conclusion that mind and body were entirely separate. It is only within the past decade that new research in health psychology and behavioral medicine has begun to bridge the gap between mental and physical events.

As Figure 15-1 indicates, there are two main biological causes of disease—hereditary predispositions and environmental factors. The hereditary predispositions include inherited weaknesses in certain body tissues or organs that increase susceptibility to disease. The environmental factors include bacteria and viruses, chemical pollutants in the air or water, and even some natural ingredients of the food we eat, such as saturated fats. Some diseases are caused by hereditary or environmental factors alone, while others occur only when there is both a hereditary predisposition and subsequent exposure to an environmental agent. But behavioral factors can also contribute to the disease process. Psychological reactions are sometimes the primary determinants of disease, as in certain types of headache and gastrointestinal disturbances. In other cases, psychological factors interact with biological factors in producing disease; that is, states of mind can sometimes determine whether processes that are initiated by hereditary or enivronmental factors will cause disease. The interaction of psychological factors and smoking-related cellular changes in the development of lung cancer is a case in point.

In recent years, several comprehensive reviews have evaluated the extensive literature concerning the effects of both physical and psychological stress on the immune system and on host resistance to disease (Ader, 1981; Borysenko & Borysenko, 1982; Rogers, Dubey, & Reich, 1979). Most studies have demonstrated that a variety of stresses predispose one to diseases associated with immunologic responses. Where mechanisms have been explored, there is frequently an association between endocrine changes and inhibition of certain immune parameters. Some studies, however, have found no change; others have found an enhancement of outcome measures as a function of stress. Inconsistent experi-

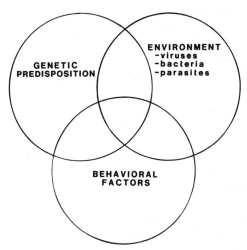

Figure 15-1. A model of hereditary, environmental, and behavioral factors in disease susceptibility. Disease can be caused by any of the three variables acting alone, or by two or more of the variables in conjunction. As an example, some diseases involve genetic factors and are associated with particular histocompatibility types. Such diseases may further involve exposure to an environmental agent like a pathogen or chemical before they appear clinically. Behavioral variables may interact by compromising immune function, predisposing to infection by the disease-specific pathogen, and increasing the likelihood of disease expression.

mental use of stress and timing of the stress relative to the measurement are obviously important variables. Furthermore, stress cannot be used generically for any environmental demand that challenges adaptation. Biological effects vary not only with type and chronicity of the stress, but also with the degree of control available to the organism.

Behavioral Epidemiology

The publication of the Social Readjustment Rating Scale by Holmes and Rahe in 1967 inaugurated a period of intense interest in the effects of stressful life change on disease susceptibility. Such research is methodologically complex. Stress is difficult to define, and situations that are stressful to one person do not necessarily provoke similar responses in others (Lazarus, 1970; Mason, 1975). Both inborn psychobiological differences and past experience ensure a divergence of psychological and physiological reactions to similar challenges, a point we will return to later. Nonetheless, large studies show that in general the more life stresses a person experiences, the higher the probability of developing physical disorders including cardiovascular symptoms, infections, allergy, and even cancer (Dohrenwend & Dohrenwend, 1974; Jenkins, 1976). Psychiatric symptoms also increase as life stress mounts. As the ability to cope diminishes, both mental and physical health suffer, often in unison. In a large prospective study, Vaillant (1979) found that poor mental health predicted subsequent poor physical health even when the obvious variables of alcohol, tobacco, and obesity were statistically controlled.

One of the most powerful stresses is the death of a spouse. We often read or hear accounts of people who die within weeks or even minutes after the death of a loved one. In the 18 months following such a loss, people have a greater risk of death from a variety of illnesses, including infections, heart attacks, and cancer, than do others of the same age and sex (Kraus & Lillenfield, 1959). Some of the more immediate deaths may involve changes in the autonomic nervous system that can lead to heart attack and stroke (Engel, 1971). Others, such as infectious disease and cancer, are more directly associated with impairment of immune function. Recent studies have shown definitively that lymphocytes from bereaved people have a diminished ability to divide in response to mitogens, agents that cause lymphocytes to multiply in number (Bartrop, Luckhurst, Lazarus, Kiloh, & Penny, 1977; Schleifer, Keller, Camerino, Thornton, & Stein, 1983).

MODULATION OF IMMUNITY AND DISEASE SUSCEPTIBILITY

The immune system is subject to complex regulation. The immune response genes affect collaborative cell-to-cell interactions and control the magnitude and specificity of immune reactions. These genes are located within the major histocompatibility complex; their products are thought to be expressed as specific glycoprotein markers on the lymphocyte surface. Susceptibility to some diseases, particularly viral neoplasms in mice, has been shown to depend on genes of the major histocompatibility complex. Likewise, certain human histocompatibility types are associated with increased incidence of specific diseases, particularly those with an autoimmune component.

Given a particular genetic composition, a number of environmental factors can modify the basic immunocompetence of the host to produce a temporary acquired immunodeficiency. Some cases of immunodeficiency may lead to overt disease, while other cases pass with no apparent sequelae. Physical factors leading to acquired immunodeficiency have been well studied, and include trauma, malnutrition, infection, neoplasia, irradiation, and a variety of drugs which are used to depress the immune system following organ transplantation. Aging itself is associated with involution of the thymus and a concomitant decline in both cellular and humoral immunity. Perhaps the most prevalent and least well appreciated of the environmental modulators of immune competence, however, are behavioral factors.

Overview of Immunity

In order to understand how behavioral events might influence susceptibility to or course of disease, it is necessary to understand how the immune system functions normally (Eisen, 1980). Immune mechanisms underlie resistance to all diseases in which the body must recognize and spare components of "self" while identifying and destroying foreign or "nonself" elements or antigens. The immune system develops in late fetal and neonatal life and diversifies into several distinct populations of immune effector cells, the lymphocytes.

Stem cells arise from the yolk sac islets and later from the bone marrow (Figure 15-2). Some of these cells travel through the bloodstream to establish temporary residence in the thymus. Secretory cells within the thymus produce a hormone that induces maturation of the lymphocytes. These cells acquire unique surface markers that distinguish T-cells (thymus-derived cells) from other lymphocyte types. Other lymphocytes mature in the microenvironment of the fetal liver and the bone marrow itself and are termed B-cells, since they were originally discovered in birds where maturation occurs in an out-pouching of the

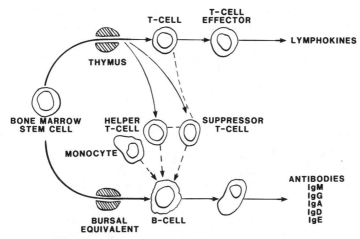

Figure 15-2. The development and basic functions of the immune system.

gut called the bursa of Fabricius. B-cells are distinguished by the presence of immunoglobulins on their surface that function as receptors. These two lymphatic types are for the most part responsible for two basic types of immune reactions: cell-mediated (T-cell) and humoral (B-cell) immunity. In addition to T-cells and B-cells, there is another immune effector cell, the null lymphocyte cell. This cell lacks the distinctive surface features of T- or B-cells, but participates in a special form of cell-mediated, natural killer cell activity. Macrophages, large scavenger cells, also play an important role in immunity by ingesting and degrading antigenic material, by aiding lymphocytes in their specific functions, and by performing direct effector cell functions.

In classical cell-mediated immunity, T-cells "sensitized" to an antigen undergo proliferation and form a clone of cells that carry receptors specific to the sensitizing antigen on their cell surface. Sensitized T-cells then migrate to the antigenic source, for instance an incompatible skin graft, where they release a number of soluble chemicals known as lymphokines. Among the lymphokines are factors that are toxic to the foreign tissue. Other lymphokines attract and activate macrophages and other white blood cells. These, in turn, release more chemicals that perpetuate the immune response.

In humoral immunity, neutralization of the antigen is accomplished by the production and release of specific antibodies. Sensitized B-cells proliferate into special antibody-producing cells, plasma cells. Plasma cells then produce and secrete the specific antibody required. The blood-borne antibodies act in several ways: They combine with and neutralize soluble antigens; they coat particulate antigens (e.g., bacteria) to enhance their ingestion by macrophages. Other types of leukocytes perform ancillary roles: the control of blood vessel permeability; the manufacture of agents that bring effector cells to the site of the tissue reaction; the ingestion of bacteria and cellular debris; and the removal of antigen–antibody complexes.

T-cells collaborate with B-cells in some immune responses. Humoral antibody production is also regulated by subpopulations of T-cells (Figure 15-2). "Helper" T-cells are sometimes required to induce B-cells to proliferate into antibody-producing plasma cells. "Suppressor" T-cells, on the other hand, inhibit antibody formation. Immune regulation is further determined by a number of genetic factors. Immune response (IR) genes affect collaborative cell-to-cell interactions and help control the magnitude and specificity of immune reactions. In addition to genetic control, recent evidence suggests that the immune system is further modulated by both direct central nervous system activity and by hypothalamic regulation of the pituitary and the autonomic nervous system. These neuroendocrine events can either enhance or depress immune function, and are altered significantly by stress.

Stress, Endocrine Response, and Immunity

The psychological and concomitant physiological changes accompanying readjustment to a life event comprise stress (Gutmann & Benson, 1971). Mason (1975) has emphasized the specificity of hormonal responses to different types of stress. Furthermore, Frankenhaueser and Rissler (1970) have shown that a person's ability or perceived ability to master (cope with) a stress is a potent modulator of physiological response. Stress comprises a variety of different bodily responses arising to various stimuli, modulated by the individual's ability to adapt. The specific nature of the stress and its controllability are critical issues in psychoneuroimmunology. For instance, fear is easily conditioned. If rats are signaled before a shock, they show fear only when the danger signal is on. In rats receiving the same total amount of shock, those who are signaled prior to its occurrence and can thus discriminate safe from unsafe conditions have lower levels of the stress hormone, corticosterone, and a reduced incidence of stomach ulcers compared to those in a state of chronic fear (Weiss, 1971).

Given the variability of stressful stimuli, the learned component of control or coping, and the chronicity of the stress, bodily response is not stereotyped. There is, however, a basic core of integrated hormonal changes induced by stress that support the "fight-or-flight" response originally described by Cannon (1914).

A potentially stressful stimulus is processed by the cortex of the brain, and the emotional impact is determined by past experience. The limbic system is responsible for relaying emotional information to the hypothalamus, which is concerned with the regulation of homeostasis. Neurosecretory cells in the hypothalamus are stimulated by the perception of stress, releasing small neuropeptides which then travel to the pituitary gland and other parts of the brain as well. These messages modulate the release of several hormones, including adrenocorticotropic hormone (ACTH) (Figure 15-3). ACTH in turn amplifies the distress signal by causing release of potent systemically active corticosteroids from the cortex of the adrenal gland. Hypothalamic neurons in lower brain centers simultaneously increase activity of the sympathetic, or activating branch, of the autonomic nervous system. Increased sympathetic tone causes secretion of catecholamines (epinephrine and norepinephrine) from the adrenal medulla. The outpouring of catecholamines is then responsible for a secondary cascade of release, liberating an additional eight hormones. It has been hypothesized that the catecholamines have a major role in the integration of endocrine secretion and that their release during stress allows an *anticipatory* change in hormonal milieu initiated by the central nervous system (Landesberg, 1977). The primary effect of this coordinated hormonal symphony is to heighten alertness and provide energy for a fast response. However, the anticipation of an imagined stress provokes the same widespread hormonal changes.

Recent advances have led to a rudimentary understanding of how emotional factors, leading to hormonal changes, can sometimes decrease the efficiency of the immune system and consequently enhance susceptibility to disease. The corticosteroids and catecholamines are key elements in this regard (Borysenko & Borysenko, 1982). Corticosteroids inhibit

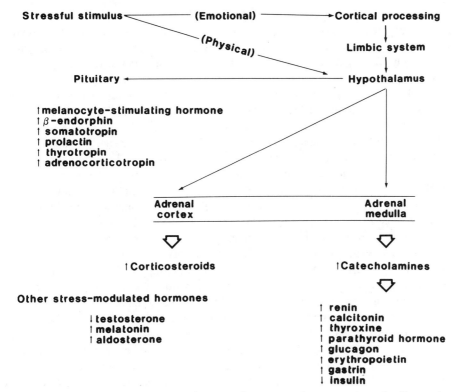

Figure 15-3. Neuroendocrine sequelae of stress—the stereotypic response to stimuli arousing the need for "fight or flight."

the function of both macrophages and lymphocytes as well as inhibiting lymphocyte proliferation. Sufficient exposure to corticosteroids can thus cause atrophy, or withering away, of critical lymphoid tissues. This basic response to chronic stress was originally described by Selye (1936). Whereas lymphoid tissues atrophy, the adrenal glands hypertrophy, or enlarge, in response to constant stimulation. Selye called these stress-induced changes the "general adaptation syndrome." The affect of adrenal corticosteroids on the lymphoid tissue of common laboratory animals and man has been well reviewed (Claman, 1977). Corticosteroids actually destroy lymphocytes in the thymic cortex of sensitive species, such as the mouse, rat, rabbit, and hamster, as well as inhibit the metabolism of other lymphocytes. In "corticosteroid-resistant" species, including humans and monkeys, corticosteroids inhibit lymphocyte metabolism, interfering with their ability to multiply. Thus, with chronic stress, lymphoid organs progressively wither because cell multiplication is retarded. In the test tube, steroid hormones inhibit the multiplication of human peripheral blood lymphocytes after stimulation with agents known as mitogens. In addition to decreasing the total number of lymphocytes, several specific immunological functions are also impaired by physiological doses of corticosteroids.

The release of catecholamines by the adrenal medulla also effects immune function. Epinephrine binds to specific receptor sites on mature lymphocytes and other leukocytes, usually inhibiting their function. In recent years, lymphocytes have been demonstrated to have membrane surface receptors for a number of different hormones. These include the catecholamines, E-type prostaglandins, somatotropin, histamine, insulin, endorphins, antidiuretic hormone, and parathyroid hormone, among others. All these hormones stimulate cell membrane adenylate cyclase and generate cyclic adenosine monophosphate (cAMP) as a second messenger. Elevation in cAMP increases metabolism in immature cells, stimulating maturation. While such hormones stimulate proliferation and differentiation of immature cells, they have a distinct inhibitory effect on mature, immunocompetent cells (Bourne, *et al.*, 1974). Both human and mouse lymphocyte reactivity to mitogens is depressed by agents that raise intracellular cAMP. Similarly, elevated cAMP inhibits killing of bacteria and cancer cells, interferon production by human lymphocytes, histamine release by human basophils, and antibody formation (Bourne *et al.*, 1974). Cyclic guanosine monophosphate (cGMP), which is liberated as a second messenger by parasympathetic stimulation of cholinergic agonists, generally enhances the immune response, opposing the specific actions of cAMP (for review, see Borysenko, 1982b). Recent work from our laboratory has investigated the effect of a small, physiological dose of epinephrine injected into normal human volunteers (Crary *et al.*, 1983). Fifteen minutes after injection, different subsets of lymphocytes are released into the bloodstream at 2 to 4 times their normal numbers. Suppressor lymphocytes, which function to inhibit the activity of other white blood cells, are released in the greatest number and are actively immunosuppressive. Helper cells, which in contrast help amplify some aspects of immune function, are reduced in number. These changes may be an important part of stress-induced immunosuppression. It is important to realize, however, that the immune system is an extremely complex system of cells with a variety of checks and balances. Chronic stress, where epinephrine is released at a high level over time, may produce different changes than those seen after a single injection.

These data suggest that the autonomic nervous system has immunomodulatory effects, and that sympathetic stimulation with its attendant release of catecholamines and corticosteroids has an overall inhibitory effect on the function of immunocompetent effector cells. Following prolonged stress there are fewer circulating lymphocytes, suggesting that the inhibitory effect of corticosteroids on lymphocyte proliferation outweighs the promoting effect of the catecholamines. Furthermore, the function of the existing pool of mature cells is subject to inhibition both by circulating epinephrine and corticosteroids. In addition to effects on lymphocytes, both agents also inhibit functions of macrophages, basophils, mast cells, neutrophils, and eosinophils, which all interact in immune mechanisms.

ANIMAL MODELS

We can get a fuller appreciation of the mechanisms linking stress with disease susceptibility by focusing on experiments with animals in which key factors can be systematically manipulated in ways that would be impossible with human subjects. Locke (1982) has recently reviewed the entire literature on stress and immunity in humans, most of which relies on opportunistic stress because of the ethical constraints in such studies. Even in animal studies, however, a diversity of effects have been observed. While stress generally increases disease susceptibility, sometimes it serves as a protection against infection of neoplasia. The nature and chronicity of the stress, the time at which the infective agent is introduced relative to the stress, the housing, and social conditions of the animals and the nature of the cellular interactions involved in the immune response to the pathogen under investigation are critical to outcome. Overall, cause-and-effect relations between stress and susceptibility to infection are reproducibly demonstrable in adequately controlled animal experiments.

"Behavioral Epidemiology" in Animal Models

Exposure to experimental stress generally decreases host resistance to infection. A variety of stressors have been evaluated in early behavioral epidemiological studies. No direct measures of immune function were performed (for review, see Ader, 1981; Borysenko & Borysenko, 1982; Rogers *et al*, 1979). Mice subjected to experimental stress by avoidance conditioning in a shuttle box or by physical restraint are more susceptible to infections with herpes simplex virus, poliomyelitis virus, Coxsackie B virus, and polyoma virus. Similarly, the stress of crowding markedly increases susceptibility to *Salmonella typhimurium* and trichinosis infection. Predator-induced stress (cat versus mouse) increases infectivity with parasite *Hymenolepis nana* in animals that have been previously immunized. More recently, we reported that the stress of crowding and exposure to inescapable shock increases both the incidence and severity of dental caries in rats infected intraorally with *Streptococcus mutans* and maintained on a high-sugar diet (Borysenko, Turesky, Borysenko, Quimby, & Benson, 1980). In a few cases, however, stress has been demonstrated to protect against infection.

Stress and Immunity in Animal Models

In animal studies designed to evaluate specific immune functions following stress, deficiencies in both cell-mediated and humoral responses have been demonstrated (for review, see Ader, 1981; Borysenko & Borysenko, 1982; Rogers *et al.*, 1979). Decreased responsivity to mitogen stimulation, antigen stimulation, and reduced lymphocyte cytotoxicity have been observed following stress. Prolongation in time to rejection of skin allografts, reduced graft-versus-host responsiveness, and diminished delayed hypersensitivity reactions indicate suppression of cell-mediated immunity following stress in animals. When animals are stressed prior to or directly after immunization, there is also reduced antibody titer to flagellan, a bacterial antigen, reflecting suppression of humoral immunity.

Experimental Design in Animal Models

While stress is most frequently associated with immunosuppression, it can sometimes have an augmenting effect on the immune system (Folch & Waksman, 1974; Mettrop & Visser, 1969). Some of these contradictory findings can be explained by differences in experimental design. The nature of the stress, its duration, and the interval between the stress and the immune measurements are extremely important. For example, mice subjected to chronic auditory stress show a biphasic response. During the first 2 weeks, there is a 50% decrease in lymphocyte cytotoxicity and mitogen responsivity, followed by a significant increase (above baseline) in the same immune functions for 2 weeks thereafter (Monjan & Collector, 1977). This is an example of the rebound overshoot, indicating the importance of timing the stress relative to the measurement.

The comprehensive investigations of Riley (1981) have clarified some of the seemingly contradictory effects of stress on immunity and disease in animals. Rodents living in standard animal quarters are subjected to noise, pheromones, and ultrasound distress signals from other animals undergoing capture and manipulation. The corticosterone levels of such animals are *10 to 20 times* higher than those of rodents housed in a protected, low-stress environment (Riley, 1981). Variables such as population density and proximity of males and females that are usually uncontrolled are capable of modulating impressive changes in corticosterone levels. When apparently ''baseline'' endocrine parameters are in actuality already highly elevated, the effects of additional experimental stress cannot be adequately assessed. It is thus of utmost importance to keep animals in a low-stress, well-controlled environment.

In extensive, meticulously controlled experiments using either virally induced or transplanted tumors, Riley (1981) has shown that stress (either living in a standard animal facility or exposure to a mild, anxiety-provoking rotation) consistently increases tumor growth. These effects can be mimicked by injection of natural or synthetic corticosteroids into the animals (Riley, 1981). The apparently contradictory results of some early animal experiments showing inhibition of tumor growth by stress become understandable in view of the timing of the stress relative to the tumor implant. Both tumor suppression and tumor enhancement can be demonstrated in the same system as a function of such timing. Steroid injection into mice 7 days after implantation of a tumor promotes growth; injection 7 days before implantation retards tumor growth. These differences probably reflect an initial hormonally sustained immune inhibition followed by a rebound recovery and overshoot of cell-mediated immunity (Monjan & Collector, 1977).

Riley also explored the interaction between heredity, environmental factors, and psychological factors in cancer etiology (Riley, 1975). He studied a strain of mice infected with a virus that causes mammary gland cancer in about 80% of females by 400 days of age. One group of these mice was housed in standard animal quarters where they were exposed to the moderate stress characteristic of such facilities. Another group was housed in a special, low-stress facility where animals were protected from pheromones and ultrasound distress signals. At 400 days of age, over 90% of the moderate stress group, compared to less than 10% of the low-stress group, had developed cancer. By 600 days, when the mice reached old age, the incidence of cancer rose to expected levels in the low-stress group, presumably due to the decreased immunity that normally accompanies aging. Although genetic and environmental (virus) factors were the same in both groups, stress had a highly significant effect on latency period—the time in the animals' lives that the cancers appeared.

Additional experiments with animals have shown that control is an important modulator of outcome in stress experiments. In one study, Sklar and Anisman (1979) first injected three groups of mice with the same number of cancer cells. One group was then exposed to an electric shock that they could learn to escape by jumping over a barrier to safety. A second group, the yoked controls, were exposed to the same duration of shock as the first group, but they had no means of actively coping with the stress. Instead, their shock terminated noncontingently when a mouse from the *first* group jumped over the barrier. A third group was never shocked. Cancers grew fastest and led to earliest death among the yoked controls who had no means of coping with their stress. In contrast, the animals in the first group who received the same amount of shock, but who could mount an adaptive escape response, did not differ significantly in tumor growth from those who had never been shocked at all.

In a series of differential housing experiments, social isolation enhanced tumor growth in mice (Sklar & Anisman, 1980). It was the abrupt change in social conditions, rather than isolation per se, however, that was responsible for increased tumor growth. In mice who were reared in isolation and then switched to group housing following tumor implant, behavior modulated tumorigenesis. Specifically, some mice remained passive after the transfer while others fought. The fighters had significantly smaller tumors than the nonfighters.

Sklar and Anisman (1980) hypothesized that fighting may comprise an adaptive coping response. Indeed, fighting is known to prevent some of the neurochemical changes induced by stress, as well as to ameliorate the ulcerogenic effects of shock stress. These data parallel human studies. Stress alone does not apparently lead to increased tumor growth. Rather, inability to cope with stress seems most important (for review, see Borysenko, 1982a).

INTERACTION BETWEEN THE CENTRAL NERVOUS SYSTEM AND THE IMMUNE SYSTEM

Studies involving specific hypothalamic lesions or electrical stimulation of hypothalamic regions suggest that the central nervous system influences immune responses directly (for review, see Stein, Keller, & Schleifer, 1981). Both humoral and cell-mediated immunity are depressed following lesioning of the dorsal hypothalamus in rabbits. Furthermore, such effects are specific to particular hypothalamic regions. Anterior hypothalamic lesions protect against lethal anaphylaxis in guinea pigs, while posterior hypothalamic lesions do not. Anterior hypothalamic lesions also inhibit both humoral and cell-mediated immunity in guinea pigs. While reproducible, lesioning studies may be confounded by unintentional damage to nearby feeding and thermoregulatory centers. Alterations of dietary intake and thermoregulation per se are associated with immunological deficits. Experiments involving electrical stimulation of the central nervous system, however, further safeguard against this problem. Stimulation of the mesencephalon enhances the humoral immune response (Korneva & Khai, 1967). When the lateral hypothalamus is stimulated in rats, serum gamma globulins are doubled without further antigenic challenge (Fessel & Forsyth, 1963). Thus, there is a body of evidence suggesting that the central nervous system can modulate immunity. Recent studies further suggest that information from the immune system feeds back directly to the central nervous system. For example, an increase in the firing rate of neurons in the ventromedial nuclei can be recorded in rats following specific immunization (Besodovsky & Sorkin, 1977).

Mediating mechanisms underlying a potential reciprocal communication of the central nervous system and immune system are currently under intense investigation. Sympathetic and parasympathetic neurons arising from the hypothalamus that directly innervate both the thymus and spleen have been traced using the retrograde transport of horseradish peroxidase (Bullock & Moore, 1980; Williams *et al*, 1981). The mast cell, located at the periphery of small blood vessels, may be an intermediary that transduces the nerve impulse into a chemical signal read locally by thymic or splenic lymphocytes (Locke, 1982). As in the case of hormonal modulation of immunity, sympathetic stimulation has immunoinhibitory effects. Chemical sympathectomy, for example, enhances the immune response to sheep erythrocytes in mice (Williams *et al.,* 1981). Such studies provide evidence for a direct functional link between the nervous and immune systems.

Further evidence for a direct communication between the central nervous system and the immune system derives from Ader's well-replicated finding that immunosuppression can be conditioned behaviorally in the rat (Ader, 1981; Ader & Cohen, 1975; Rogers, Reich, Strom, & Carpenter, 1976). Using a Pavlovian paradigm, taste aversion is conditioned by pairing a novel taste (saccharin water) with injection of cyclophosphamide, an immunosuppressive cytotoxic drug that produces gastrointestinal upset. Subsequently, conditioned animals exposed to saccharin alone, following antigen injection, are significantly immunosuppressed compared to well-conceived control groups. When lithium chloride, a nonimmunosuppressive, illness-inducing agent, is substituted for cyclophosphamide, no immunosuppression ensues. Thus, the immunosuppression appears to be truly conditioned and cannot be accounted for indirectly by the stress of conditioned gastrointestinal upset.

THE CHALLENGE FOR HEALTH PSYCHOLOGY

The notion that behavioral factors can alter immunity and disease susceptibility through direct central nervous system mechanisms or through endocrinological intermediaries has been adequately demonstrated. While immunologists and physiologists are defining the parameters of these interactions, they are limited by the dearth of knowledge concerning the relation between individual differences, psychological response, and endocrine change. McClelland, Floor, Davidson, and Saron (1980) have recently studied the relation between a specific personality trait, the inhibited power motive syndrome, urinary epinephrine excretion, salivary secretory Immunoglobulin A (sIgA) levels, and severity of upper respiratory tract infection. The inhibited power motive syndrome consists of a high need for power (higher than the need for affiliation) in combination with high activity inhibition as reliably and reproducibly measured by the Thematic Apperception Test. Individuals high in activity inhibition stringently control the expression of the power motive. Such individuals have a lower concentration of salivary secretory IgA than do controls, report more severe episodes of upper respiratory tract infection, and excrete more epinephrine in urine (McClelland *et al.*, 1980). Recent longitudinal research in our laboratory and McClelland's conducted on a sample of 64 first-year dental students confirmed and extended these findings (Jemmott *et al.*, 1983).

The prognosis of cancer has also been related to individual differences, but endocrinological and immunological correlates' have not yet been reported. For example, women who can express hostility survive metastatic breast cancer longer than nonassertive, compliant women (Abeloff & Derogatis, 1977). In a similar vein, 5-year outcome after mastectomy for early-stage breast cancer correlates with psychological reaction at diagnosis. Women who have either a "fighting spirit" or who are absolute deniers have a statistically significant advantage in both disease-free interval and mortality compared to those who are helpless/hopeless or stoic acceptors (Greer, Morris, & Pettingale, 1979). These recent prospective studies corroborate older retrospective studies showing that the inhibition of anger is associated with poor prognosis in both men and women with a variety of different cancers (Blumberg, West, & Ellis, 1954; Stavraky, Buck, Lott, & Wanklin, 1968). Knowledge of the mechanisms by which personality influences physiology may lead to the design of interventions that both preserve health and lead to a better prognosis in the diseased individual.

References

Abeloff MD, Derogatis LR. Psychologic aspects of the management of primary and metastatic breast cancer. Progress in Clinical and Biological Research 1977; 12:505–516.

Ader R, ed. Psychoneuroimmunology. New York: Academic Press, 1981.

Ader R, Cohen N. Behaviorally conditioned immunosuppression. Psychosomatic Medicine 1975; 37:333–340.

Bartrop RW, Luckhurst E, Lazarus L, Kiloh LG, Penny R. Depressed lymphocyte function after bereavement. Lancet 1977; 1:834–836.

Besodovsky H, Sorkin E. Network of immunoneuroendocrine interactions. Clinical and Experimental Immunology 1977; 27:1–12.

Blumberg EM, West PM, Ellis FW. A possible relationship between psychological factors and human cancer. Psychosomatic Medicine 1954; 16:276–286.

Borysenko JZ. Behavioral–physiological factors in the development and management of cancer. General Hospital Psychiatry 1982a; 4:69–74.

Borysenko JZ. Higher cortical function and neoplasia: psychoneuroimmunology. In: Levy S, ed. Biological mediators of behavioral disease: neoplasia. New York: Elsevier Science, 1982b: pp. 29–53.

Borysenko M, Borysenko JZ. Stress, behavior and immunity: animal models and mediating mechanisms. General Hosptal Psychiatry 1982; 40:59–67.

Borysenko M, Turesky S, Borysenko JZ, Quimby F, Benson H. Stress and dental caries in the rat. Journal of Behavioral Medicine 1980; 3:233–243.

Bourne HR, Lichtenstein LM, Melmon RL, Henney CS, Weinstein Y, Shearer GM. Modulation of inflammation and immunity by cyclic AMP. Science 1974; 184:19–28.

Bullock K, Moore RY. Nucleus ambiguous projections to the thymus gland: possible pathways for regulation of the immune response and the neuroendocrine network. Anatomical Record 1980; 196:25.

Cannon WB. The emergency function of the adrenal medulla in pain and the major emotions. American Journal of Physiology 1914; 33:356.

Claman HN. Corticosteroids and lymphoid cells. New England Journal of Medicine 1977; 287:388–397.

Crary B, Borysenko M, Sutherland DC, Kutz I, Borysenko JZ, Benson H. Decrease in mitogen responsiveness of mononuclear cells from peripheral blood following epinephrine administration. Journal of Immunology 1983; 130:694–697.

Dohrenwend BS, Dohrenwend BP, eds. Stressful life events: their nature and effects. New York: Wiley, 1974.

Eisen H. Immunology, 3rd ed. Baltimore: Harper & Row, 1980.

Engel G. Sudden rapid death during psychological stress. Annals of Internal Medicine 1971; 74:771–782.

Fessel NJ, Forsyth RP. Hypothalamic role in control of gamma globulin levels. Arthritis and Rheumatism 1963; 6:771–772.

Folch H, Waksman BH. The splenic suppressor cell: activity of thymus dependent adherent cells: changes with age and stress. Journal of Immunology 1974; 113:127–139.

Frankenhaueser M, Rissler A. Effects of punishment on catecholamine release and efficiency of performance. Psychopharmacologia 1970; 17:378–390.

Greer S, Morris T, Pettingale KW. Psychological response to breast cancer: effect on outcome. Lancet 1979; 13:785–787.

Gutmann MC, Benson H. Interaction of environmental factors and systemic arterial blood pressure: a review. Medicine 1971; 50:543–553.

Holmes TH, Rahe RM. The social adjustment rating scale. Journal of Psychosomatic Research 1967; 11:213–218.

Horne RL, Picard RS. Psychosocial risk factors for lung cancer. Psychosomatic Medicine 1979; 41:503–514.

Jemmott JB III, Borysenko JZ, Borysenko M, McClelland DC, Chapman R, Meyer D, Benson H. Academic stress, power motivation, and decrease in salivary secretory immunoglobulin: a secretion rate. Lancet 1983; June 25:1400–1402.

Jenkins CD. Recent evidence supporting psychologic and social risk factors for coronary disease. New England Journal of Medicine 1976; 294:987–994.

Kissen D. Personality characteristics in males conducive to lung cancer. British Journal of Medical Psychology 1963; 34:27–36.

Kissen D. Psychosocial factors, personality and lung cancer in men aged 55–64. British Journal of Medical Psychology 1967; 40:29–43.

Korneva EA, Khai LM. Effect of stimulating different mesencephalic structures on protective immune response patterns. Fizioloicheskii Zhurnal SSR Imeni I M Sechenova 1967; 53:42–47.

Kraus AS, Lillienfeld AM. Some epidemiological aspects of the high mortality rate in the young widowed group. Journal of Chronic Diseases 1959; 10:207–217.

Landsberg L. The sympathoadrenal system. In: Ingbar SH, ed. The year in endocrinology. New York: Plenum Press, 1977:291–344.

Lazarus RS. Cognitive and personality factors underlying stress and coping. In: Levine S, Scotch N, eds. Social stress. Chicago: Aldine, 1970:143–164.

Locke SE. Stress, adaptation, and immunity: studies in humans. General Hospital Psychiatry 1982; 4:49–58.

Mason JW. Emotion as reflected in patterns of endocrine integration. In: Levy L, ed. Emotions: their parameters and measurement. New York: McGraw-Hill, 1975:143–181.

McClelland DC, Floor E, Davidson RJ, Saron C. Stressed power motivation, sympathetic activation, immune function, and illness. Journal of Human Stress 1980; 6:11–19.

Mettrop PJ, Visser P. Exteroceptive stimulation as a contingent factor in the induction and elicitation of delayed-type hypersensitivity reactions to 1-chloro-2 and 4-dinitrobenzene reactions in guinea pigs. Psychophysiology 1969; 5:385–388.

Monjan AA, Collector MI. Stress-induced modulation of the immune response. Science 1977; 196:307–308.

Riley V. Mouse mammary tumors: alteration of incidence as an apparent function of stress. Science 1975; 189:465–467.

Riley V. Neuroendocrine influences on immunocompetence and neoplasia. Science 1981; 211:1100–1109.

Rogers MP, Dubey D, Reich P. The influence of the psyche and the brain on immunity and disease susceptibility: a critical review. Psychosomatic Medicine 1979; 41:147–164.

Rogers MP, Reich P, Strom TB, Carpenter CB. Behaviorally conditioned immunosuppression: replication of a recent study. Psychosomatic Medicine 1976; 38:447–451.

Schleifer SJ, Keller SE, Camerino M, Thornton JC, Stein M. Suppression of lymphocyte stimulation following bereavement. Journal of the American Medical Association 1983; 250:374–377.

Selye H. A syndrome produced by diverse nocuous agents. Nature 1936; 138:32.

Sklar LS, Anisman H. Stress and coping factors influence tumor growth. Science 1979; 205:513–515.

Sklar LS, Anisman H. Social stress influences tumor growth. Psychosomatic Medicine 1980; 42:347–365.

Stein M, Keller SE, Schleifer SJ. The hypothalamus and the immune response. In: Weiner H, Hofer M, Stunkard S, eds. Brain, behavior and bodily disease. New York: Raven Press, 1981:45–65.

Stavraky KM, Buck CW, Lott JS, Wanklin JM. Psychological factors in the outcome of human cancer. Journal of Psychosomatic Research 1968; 12:251–259.

Vaillant GE. Natural history of male psychologic health: effects of mental health on physical health. New England Journal of Medicine 1979; 301:1249–1254.

Weiss JM. Effects of coping behavior in different warning signal conditions on stress pathology in rats. Journal of Comparative and Physiological Psychology 1971; 77:1–13.

Williams JM, Peterson RG, Shea PA, Schmedtje JF, Bauer DC, Felten DL. Sympathetic innervation of murine thymus and spleen: evidence for a functional link between the nervous and immune systems. Brain Research Bulletin 1981; 6:83–94.

16

Bereavement and Immune Function

STEVEN J. SCHLEIFER
STEVEN E. KELLER
UMDNJ–New Jersey Medical School

MARVIN STEIN
Mount Sinai School of Medicine

The immune system is a major integrative network involved in biologic adaptation and is of central importance in health and illness. An extensive literature has described associations between psychosocial processes and the development, onset, and course of medical disorders, and it has been suggested that stress and other behavioral effects on the immune system contribute to susceptibility to illness. A number of studies concerned with the relation of biobehavioral states to immune processes have been undertaken in recent years, facilitated by advances in immunology and immune methodology. This research, though focused primarily on demonstrating the existence of associations between behavior and the immune system, has also begun to consider some of the mechanisms that may be involved.

Many of the major life events that appear to affect biologic systems and health occur within the context of the family and can have a profound psychosocial and biologic impact on family members. Conjugal bereavement, one of the most potentially stressful of commonly occurring life events, provides a model to test for stress effects within families on immune function. Conjugal bereavement is of additional interest in that it has been associated with increased medical morbidity and mortality. For example, Helsing, Szklo, and Comstock (1981), in a prospective epidemiologic study, found that the relative risk of mortality in widowers was significantly greater than in a group of married matched controls. In contrast, no differences in mortality were found when widowed and married women were compared.

We have investigated immune function in relation to bereavement, assessing lymphocyte functional activity as well as the number of peripheral blood lymphocytes and lymphocyte subsets. Lymphocyte activity was measured by means of functional challenges using lymphocyte stimulation, an *in vitro* correlate of cellular immune function. This technique measures the proliferation of either T- or B-cells in response to a variety of stimulants. Sensitized lymphocytes can be cultured and activated with specific antigens, or nonsensitized cells can be activated with nonspecific stimulants, known as "mitogens." Phytohemagglutinin (PHA) and conconavalin A (ConA) are predominantly T-cell mitogens, and pokeweed mitogen (PWM) is primarily a B-cell mitogen. The proliferative response of stimulated lymphocytes can be assessed by labeling stimulated cultures with a radioactive nucleoside precursor, which is incorporated into newly synthesized DNA. The determination of the amount of precursor incorporated provides a measure of DNA synthesis and is employed as a standard measure of lymphocyte responsiveness.

BEREAVEMENT AND LYMPHOCYTE FUNCTION

The first report of an association between bereavement and the immune system was that of Bartrop, Lazarus, Luckhurst, Kiloh, and Penny (1977), who assessed PHA- and ConA-induced lymphocyte stimulation in a group of bereaved spouses and in matched controls. The investigators found that, under some of the experimental conditions, the bereaved group had lower lymphocyte stimulation responses than did controls.

We have investigated the effect of bereavement on immunity in a prospective longitudinal study of spouses of women with advanced breast carcinoma (Schleifer, Keller, Camerino, Thornton, & Stein, 1983). The study was undertaken to determine whether lymphocyte stimulation after the death of spouse differed from responses found prior to bereavement. The prospective design permitted the determination of whether lymphocyte responses are suppressed following bereavement as a direct consequence of that event, or whether they represent preexisting alterations of lymphocyte function. Changes in lymphocyte responses during the year following the death of the spouse were also assessed.

Twenty spouses of women undergoing treatment for advanced metastatic disease in the Department of Neoplastic Diseases, Mount Sinai Hospital, New York, were studied. Spouses were entered into the study during a 3-year period, and each subject was studied at approximately 6- to 8-week intervals over the course of the patient's illness. All subjects were drug-free and were free of acute and chronic medical disorders associated with immune alterations. Lymphocyte measures were obtained for 15 of the spouses during the first 2 months after bereavement, and 12 of the 15 were also studied during the 4- to 14-month postbereavement period. On entry into the study, the subjects had a mean age of 57 years and had been married a mean of 30 years; the spouse's diagnosis had been made, on average, 2.5 years prior to entry into the study. Subjects were followed for a mean of 6 months from entry into the study to death of spouse.

The number of peripheral blood lymphocytes and the percentage and absolute number of T- and B-cells were not significantly different after the death of spouse compared with levels found prior to bereavement. Mitogen-induced lymphocyte stimulation responses, measured prior to bereavement, during the first 2 postbereavement months, and during the latter half of the postbereavement year are shown in Figure 16-1. The responses to the mitogens PHA, ConA, and PWM were significantly lower during the first 2 months after bereavement compared with prebereavement responses.

Follow-up during the remainder of the postbereavement year revealed that lymphocyte stimulation responses had returned to prebereavement levels for the majority, but not for all the subjects. For the group overall, follow-up measures were not significantly different from either the prebereavement or the 1- to 2-month postbereavement mitogen responses.

These findings demonstrate that suppression of mitogen-induced lymphocyte stimulation is a direct consequence of the bereavement event, and that a preexisting suppressed immune state does not account for the depressed lymphocyte responses in the bereaved. Furthermore, in an additional retrospective comparison, we found no differences between the 20 spouses and age- and sex-matched controls when their first visit (prebereavement) mitogen responses were compared. This preliminary observation suggests that the chronic stress of a spouse's illness is not in itself associated with altered immunity. Moreover, since the superimposition of the bereavement event did result in suppressed lymphocyte function, it appears that the stress of a spouse's illness did not result in a habituation of lymphocyte stress responses so as to mitigate the effects of bereavement. The long-term stress may, in fact, have sensitized the subjects to the bereavement experience (Burchfield, 1979).

Further research is required to determine the processes linking the experience of bereavement with effects on lymphocyte activity. We found that bereavement effects on lymphocyte function in our sample were not homogeneous, with some subjects having a greater than 50% suppression of mitogen response, while several showed little or no change.

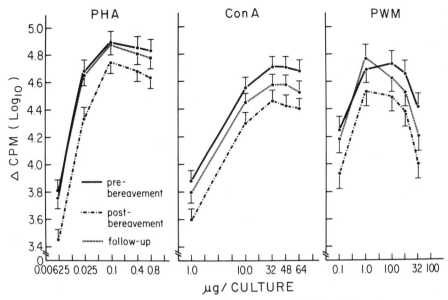

Figure 16-1. PHA-, ConA-, and PWM-induced lymphocyte stimulation before bereavement, after bereavement (1 to 2 months), and during follow-up (4 to 14 months). Each point represents group mean ± SEM ($n = 12$) of each subject's mean log change in counts per minute (Δ CPM) for each period. (Reprinted by permission from "Suppression of Lymphocyte Stimulation following Bereavement" by S. J. Schleifer, S. E. Keller, M. Camerino, J. C. Thornton, and M. Stein, 1983, *Journal of the American Medical Association,* Vol. 250, p. 376.)

However, subjects not showing lowered mitogen responses 1 to 2 months postbereavement tended to have *decreased* levels when restudied during the latter half of the postbereavement year. This contrasted with the majority of subjects, who showed higher levels at follow-up than at 1 to 2 months after death of spouse. Although the sample size precludes more than anecdotal comment, it is of interest that two of the three subjects showing the atypical, delayed pattern of immune changes were the youngest members of the sample, and the only subjects who had young children in their household at the time of bereavement. These observations suggest a need to study systematically the role of factors such as age and coping behavior in relation to bereavement and immunity.

A number of behavioral manifestations of the bereavement experience may have been related to the effects of bereavement on immunity. Changes in nutrition (Bistrian, Blackburn, & Scrimshaw, 1975), activity and exercise levels (Eskola *et al.*, 1978), sleep (Palmblad, Petrini, Wasserman, & Akerstedt, 1979), and drug use (Baker, Santalo, & Blumenstein, 1977; Tennenbaum, Ruppert, St. Pierre, & Greenberger, 1969) which are often found in the widowed (Clayton, 1979), could influence lymphocyte function. Our subjects, however, did not report major or persistent changes in diet or activity levels, or in the use of medication, alcohol, tobacco, or other drugs, and no significant changes in weight were noted. Nevertheless, subtle changes on these variables may have been related to the effects of bereavement on lymphocyte function.

The effects of death of spouse on lymphocyte function could result from centrally mediated stress effects. Stressful life experiences may be related to changes in central nervous system (CNS) activity manifested by psychologic states, such as depression, and associated with neuroendocrine changes such as increased adrenal activity. Bereaved subjects have been described as characteristically manifesting depressed mood (Clayton, Halikes, & Maurice, 1972; Parkes, 1972), and a subgroup of bereaved individuals have been reported to have symptom patterns consistent with the presence of a major depressive disorder (Clayton *et al.*, 1972).

Studies in lymphocyte function in clinically depressed individuals suggest that depression may be related to the effects of bereavement on immunity. There have been several reports of altered lymphocyte function in patients with depression (Cappel, Gregoire, Thiry, & Sprecher, 1978; Kronfol *et al.*, 1983). We have investigated mitogen-induced lymphocyte stimulation and the number of peripheral blood lymphocytes in hospitalized patients with major depressive disorder compared with age- and sex-matched controls. All subjects were in apparently good health and were drug-free. Lymphocyte stimulation by PHA, ConA and PWM, respectively, was significantly lower in the depressed patients than in controls, as were the total number of T- and B-cells (Schleifer *et al.*, 1984). Further studies suggested that the decreased lymphocyte function in depressed patients may be related to the severity of the depression (Schleifer, Keller, Siris, Davis, & Stein, 1985) as well as to age (Schleifer, Keller, Cohen, & Stein, 1985). The findings of altered immunity in depression are consistent with a hypothesis that depressive states following bereavement are related to the changes in immunity found in the bereaved.

BIOLOGIC MEDIATORS OF BEREAVEMENT EFFECTS ON IMMUNITY

A variety of factors may be involved in mediating associations among bereavement, depression, and immunity. The endocrine system is highly responsive both to life experiences and to psychologic state, and has a significant, though complicated, effect on immune processes. Most widely studied are the hormones of the hypothalamic–pituitary–adrenal (HPA) axis. A wide range of stressful experiences are capable of inducing the release of corticosteroids (Coe, Mendoza, Smotherman, & Levine, 1978; Hofer, Wolff, Friedman, & Mason, 1972), and increased HPA activity is characteristic of major depressive disorder (Sachar, 1975).

Secretion of corticosteroids has long been considered to be the mechanism of stress-induced modulation of immunity and of stress-induced changes in illness susceptibility (Riley, 1981; Selye, 1976). Altered immune function in response to stress, however, may not be limited to effects of corticosteroids. We have found, in rats, that while some stress effects on immunity, such as lymphopenia, are adrenal-dependent, stress-induced suppression of mitogen response can be demonstrated in the absence of adrenal activity (Keller, Weiss, Schleifer, Miller, & Stein, 1983). Other possible mechanisms that may contribute to stress effects on immunity include changes in the secretion of thyroid hormones, growth hormone, and sex steroids, and of peptides such as B-endorphin (Gilman, Schwartz, Milner, Bloom, & Feldman, 1982; Stein, Keller, & Schleifer, 1981). Moreover, we and others have shown that the hypothalamus, which plays a central role in neuroendocrine function, can modulate both humoral and cell-mediated immune processes (Cross, Brooks, Roszman, & Markesbery, 1982; Keller, Stein, Camerino, Schleifer, & Sherman, 1980; Stein *et al.*, 1981).

There is good evidence that processes not mediated by classical endocrine pathways are also involved in CNS regulation of immunity. It has been demonstrated that anterior hypothalamic lesions in hypophysectomized rats result in an increase in the number of thymic lymphocytes and a decrease in mitogen response (Cross *et al.*, 1982), and we have found stress-induced suppression of immunity in hypophysectomized rats (Keller, Schleifer, & Stein, 1987). A direct link between the CNS and immunocompetent tissues is suggested by the demonstration of nerve endings in the thymus, spleen, and lymph nodes (Giron, Crutcher, & Davis, 1980; Williams *et al.,* 1980) and by the presence of adrenergic and cholinergic receptors on the lymphocyte surface (Bourne, Lichtenstein, & Melmon, 1974; Pochet, Delesperse, Gauseet, & Collet, 1979).

Recently, it has been shown that there is decreased norepinephrine turnover in the hypothalamus of the rat at the peak of an immune response, and it has been suggested that the immune response exerts an inhibitory action on central noradrenergic neurons as a result of mediators released by immunologic cells (Besedovsky *et al.,* 1983). Furthermore, the lymphocyte may secrete an ACTH-like substance following viral infection (Smith, Meyer, & Blalock, 1982). These findings suggest the presence of a neuroendocrine–immunoregulatory feedback process associated with aminergic circuits within the CNS. It may be, therefore, that alterations in the immune system following stressful life experiences induce secondary changes in the CNS, thereby influencing psychologic state.

CONCLUSION

Stressful life experiences within the family, such as the death of a spouse, appear to have an impact on biologic as well as psychologic processes. Men experiencing bereavement following a spouse's chronic illness (breast cancer) show evidence of altered lymphocyte function, although for most subjects the effect appears not to persist beyond several months. Indirect evidence suggests that the depressed state often found in the bereaved may be involved in the effects of bereavement on immunity. Research is needed to determine whether the effects on immune function are specific to particular types of bereavement experiences, such as those following an extended debilitating illness, and whether stressful life events other than bereavement have similar immune effects. The effects of bereavement on immunity in women and in individuals at different stages of life require investigation. Furthermore, the clinical significance of the observed effects of bereavement on lymphocyte function is unknown and in need of careful study.

Acknowledgment

This research was supported in part by project grants MH37774 and MH39651 from the National Institute of Mental Health, and by the Chernow Foundation.

References

Baker GA, Santalo R, Blumenstein J. Effect of psychotropic agents upon the blastogenic response of human T-lymphocytes. Biological Psychiatry 1977; 12:159–169.

Bartrop RW, Lazarus L, Luckhurst E, Kiloh LG, Penny R. Depressed lymphocyte function after bereavement. Lancet 1977; 1:834–836.

Besedovsky J, del Ray A, Sorkin E, DaPrada M, Burry R, Honegger C. The immune response evokes changes in brain noradrenergic neurons. Science 1983; 221:564–566.

Bistrian BR, Blackburn GL, Scrimshaw NS. Cellular immunity in semistarved states in hospitalized adults. American Journal of Psychiatry 1975; 28:1148–1155.

Bourne HR, Lichtenstein LM, Melmon KL. Modulation of inflammation and immunity by cyclic AMP. Science 1974; 184:9–28.

Burchfield SR. The stress response: a new perspective. Psychosomatic Medicine 1979; 41:661–672.

Cappel R, Gregoire F, Thiry L, Sprecher S. Antibody and cell-mediated immunity to herpes simplex virus in psychotic depression. Journal of Clinical Psychiatry 1978; 39:266–268.

Clayton PJ. The sequelae and nonsequelae of conjugal bereavement. American Journal of Psychiatry 1979; 136:1530–1534.

Clayton PJ, Halikes JA, Maurice WL. The depression of widowhood. British Journal of Psychiatry 1972; 120:71–78.

Coe CL, Mendoza SP, Smotherman WP, Levine S. Mother–infant attachment in the squirrel monkey: adrenal response to separation. Behavioral Biology 1978; 22:256–263.

Cross RJ, Brooks WH, Roszman TL, Markesbery R. Hypothalamic–immune interactions: effect of hypophysectomy on neuroimmunomodulation. Journal of Neurological Sciences 1982; 53:557–566.

Eskola J, Ruuskanen O, Soppi E, Viljamen MK, Jarvinen M, Toivonen H, Kouvalainen K. Effect of sport stress on lymphocyte transformation and antibody formation. Clinical and Experimental Immunology 1978; 32:339–345.

Gilman SC, Schwartz JM, Milner RJ, Bloom FE, Feldman JD. β-endorphin enhances lymphocyte proliferative responses. Proceedings of the National Academy of Science USA 1982; 79:4226–4230.

Giron LT, Crutcher KA, Davis JN. Lymph nodes—a possible site for sympathetic neuronal regulation of immune responses. Annals of Neurology 1980; 8:520–555.

Helsing KJ, Szklo M, Comstock GW. Factors associated with mortality after widowhood. American Journal of Public Health 1981; 71:802–809.

Hofer, MA, Wolff CT, Friedman SB, Mason JW. A psychoendocrine study of bereavement: II. Observations on the process of mourning in relation to adrenocortical function. Psychosomatic Medicine 1972; 34:492–504.

Keller SE, Stein M, Camerino MS, Schleifer SJ, Sherman J. Suppression of lymphocyte stimulation by anterior hypothalamic lesions in the guinea pig. Cellular Immunology 1980; 52:334–340.

Keller SE, Schleifer SJ, Stein M. Stress-induced alterations of immunity in hypophysectomized rats. Presented at the annual meeting of the Society of Biological Psychiatry, Chicago, May 1987.

Keller SE, Weiss JM, Schleifer SJ, Miller NE, Stein M. Stress-induced suppression of immunity in adrenalectomized rats. Science 1983; 221:1301–1304.

Kronfol Z, Silva J Jr, Greden J, Dembinski S, Gardner R, Carroll B. Impaired lymphocyte function in depressive illness. Life Sciences 1983; 33:241–247.

Palmblad J, Petrini B, Wasserman J, Akerstedt T. Lymphocyte and granulocyte reactions during sleep deprivation. Psychosomatic Medicine 1979; 41:273–278.

Parkes CM. Bereavement: studies of grief in adult life. New York: International University Press, 1972.

Pochet R, Delesperse G, Gauseet PW, Collet H. Distribution of beta-adrenergic receptors on human lymphocyte subpopulations. Clinical and Experimental Immunology 1979; 38:578–584.

Riley V. Psychoneuroendocrine influences on immunocompetence and neoplasia. Science 1981; 212:1100–1109.

Sachar EJ. Neuroendocrine abnormalities in depressive illness. In: Sachar EJ, ed. Topics in psychoendocrinology. New York: Grune and Stratton, 1975: 135–154.

Schleifer SJ, Keller SE, Camerino M, Thornton JC, Stein M. Suppression of lymphocyte stimulation following bereavement. Journal of the American Medical Association 1983; 250:374–377.

Schleifer SJ, Keller SE, Cohen J, Stein M. Depression and immunity: role of age, sex, and severity. Presented at the annual meeting of the Society for Neuroscience, Dallas, October 1985.

Schleifer, SJ, Keller SE, Meyerson AT, Raskin MJ, Davis KL, Stein M. Lymphocyte function in major depressive disorder. Archives of General Psychiatry 1984; 41:484–486.

Schleifer SJ, Keller SE, Siris SG, Davis KL, Stein M. Depression and immunity: lymphocyte function in ambulatory depressed, hospitalized schizophrenic, and herniorrhaphy patients. Archives of General Psychiatry 1985; 42:129–133.

Selye H. Stress in health and disease. Boston: Butterworths, 1976.

Smith EM, Meyer WJ, Blalock JE. Virus-induced corticosterone in hypophysecomized mice: a possible lymphoid adrenal axis. Science 1982; 218:1311–1312.

Stein M, Keller S, Schleifer S. The hypothalamus and the immune response. In: Weiner H, Hofer MA, Stunkard AJ, eds. Brain, behavior and bodily disease. New York: Raven Press, 1981:45–65.

Tennenbaum JI, Ruppert RD, St. Pierre RL, Greenberger N. The effect of chronic alcohol administration on the immune reponsiveness of rats. Journal of Allergy 1969; 44:272–281.

Williams JW, Peterson RG, Shea PA, Schmedtje JF, Bauer DC, Felton DL. Sympathetic innervation of murine thymus and spleen: evidence of a functional link between the nervous and immune systems. Brain Research Bulletin 1980; 6:83–94.

17

Family Systems, Stress, and Infectious Diseases

DAVID D. SCHMIDT
University of Connecticut Health Center, Farmington;
Saint Francis Hospital and Medical Center, Hartford, Connecticut

PRISCILLA M. SCHMIDT
University of Connecticut Health Center, Farmington

This chapter begins with a dramatic case history that raises many generic questions. There follows a discussion of the distinction between exogenous and endogenous infections, followed by a presentation of a select group of endogenous infections about which there is evidence to suggest that psychosocial factors influence and onset and/or course of the clinical disease state. Building on this background material, a possible mechanism by which events in the psychosocial environment can influence biologic susceptibility to infection will be offered. The chapter will conclude with some data from a research project that utilizes the disease model recurrent herpes simplex type 1. This work explores the field of psychoneuroimmunology, which is a newly appreciated mind–body connection.

CASE HISTORY

Figure 17-1 is a genogram of a family cared for by one of the authors (D.D.S.) in his private practice during the 1970s. Michael was reared in a series of foster homes and knew nothing about his biologic parents. He left high school after the 11th grade and moved to our community to pursue a job opportunity in a factory. He soon met Ruthann, who had

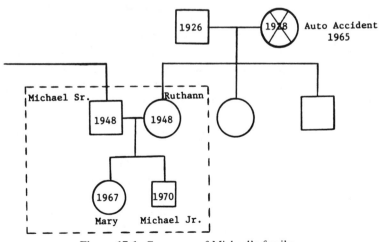

Figure 17-1. Genogram of Michael's family.

recently lost her mother, had a distant relationship with her father, and had two siblings who were living out of state (see Figure 17-1). Michael and Ruthann married when Ruthann was several months pregnant with their first child. In 1973, Ruthann presented to her family physician with the complaint of increasing weight gain and increasing abdominal girth. It was determined that she had abdominal ascites. A medical evaluation led to abdominal exploration, at which time carcinoma of the ovary was found, with multiple metastases throughout the abdominal cavity. Despite extensive surgery and chemotherapy, the patient died within the year.

Nine months after his wife's death, Michael came to the office with a 2-month history of cough. He was most frightened by recent episodes of bright red hemoptysis. A chest X-ray showed a cavitary lesion in the left upper lobe of the lung, which proved to be active tuberculosis. He responded well to therapy, and both children had negative skin tests and normal chest X-rays.

The basic question raised by this illustrative case is the following: Is this temporal relationship between the death of Ruthann and Michael's development of active tuberculosis mere chance, or is the relationship one of cause and effect? Throughout the rest of this chapter, data will be presented to support the premise that a major stressful life event, such as the death of a spouse, does increase biologic susceptibility to infections in general and to tuberculosis in particular.

THE DISTINCTION BETWEEN EXOGENOUS AND ENDOGENOUS INFECTIONS

In a series of lectures given at Yale and later compiled in a book called *Man Adapting,* Rene Dubos emphasized the distinction between exogenous and endogenous infections (1980). Most severe infectious diseases are the direct result of exposure to virulent pathogens. In addition, there is a predictable length of time between the exposure and the onset of signs and symptoms. Classic examples include smallpox, diphtheria, and typhoid fever. These are the truly infectious microbial diseases of exogenous origin. Although these infectious diseases continue to cause havoc throughout the world, they have become less of a menace for the advanced Western nations, which have adopted public health measures, immunization practices, and improved nutrition. Western societies also have readily available methods for prompt diagnosis and effective treatment of the major infectious diseases.

With these major infections under control, we have the luxury of turning our attention to the more subtle infections caused by microbes that are endogenous to humans. Dubos identifies a number of organisms that can exist and persist in human tissue, apparently without causing disease (1955). These include viruses, rickettsia, fungi, bacteria, protozoa, and even helminths. The human host and the parasite have developed a biologic equilibrium. What is the significance of this distinction between exogenous and endogenous infections?

For infections of exogenous origin, the cause of the disease is simple exposure to the pathogen. For infections of endogenous origin, the onset of the disease is caused by environmental factors that upset this biologic equilibrium. The old methods designed for controlling classic epidemics, such as sanitation and vaccination, are not helpful in managing diseases of endogenous origin. New research designs that incorporate both biologic and psychosocial factors are needed for identifying appropriate management. Accomplished biomedical scientists often criticize efforts to quantify stress and other psychosocial factors. On the other hand, psychologically oriented researchers have difficulty comprehending complex biologic systems. Advancement in the area of psychoneuroimmunology will require fruitful collaboration between behavioral scientists and biologists.

RELATIONSHIP BETWEEN ENDOGENOUS INFECTIONS
AND PSYCHOSOCIAL FACTORS

Five examples of endogenous agents for which there is evidence to suggest that psychosocial factors influence the onset and/or course of the infectious disease will be discussed. These include tubercle bacillus, beta-hemolytic streptococcus, common cold viruses, Epstein-Barr virus, and herpes simplex type 1 virus. With the exception of the beta-hemolytic streptococcus, these infectious agents are all handled in the human host by the same arm of the immune system.

The tubercle bacillus can act as both an exogenous and an endogenous microbe. When the human host inhales an infected droplet, a focus of bronchopneumonia develops; this is usually asymptomatic and lasts for approximately 2 weeks. On rare occasions, the infection progresses to widespread necrosis and dissemination. This rapid progression would be an example of classic exogenous infection. In most instances, however, the focus of bronchopneumonia resolves and becomes a granuloma. Within this granuloma, the tubercle bacilli are viable but dormant. This infection can be dormant (endogenous) for years or even a lifetime. Only 5% to 15% of individuals with the granuloma actually develop clinical tuberculosis. Even at the turn of the century, when virtually everyone living in urbanized industrial areas of the United States had such a granuloma, relatively few developed clinical tuberculosis (Glassroth, Robins, & Snider, 1980). Are there psychosocial factors that have been shown to influence this equilibrium between humans and the tubercle bacillus?

Kraus and Lilienfeld (1959) demonstrated a high mortality rate from tuberculosis in young widowed males—12.7 times higher than in young married males. This was confirmed by Holmes, Hawkins, Bowerman, Clarke, and Joffe (1957), who also demonstrated that stressful life events preceded the development of clinically detectable tuberculosis in a group of employees at a tuberculosis sanitarium.

The beta-hemolytic streptococcus is frequently found in the pharynx of schoolchildren who do not have clinical evidence of disease (Cornfeld & Hubbard, 1961). This carrier state represents another form of endogenous infection. More than 20 years ago, Meyer and Haggerty (1962) published a landmark study demonstrating that psychosocial factors were associated with the onset of streptococcal infections. They studied 16 families over a 1-year period. Each family had at least two children, with at least one child of school age. There were 100 individuals in the study. Throat cultures were taken twice monthly, and antistreptolysin-O (ASO) titers were drawn every 3 months. The mothers kept detailed diaries of life events and illnesses within the family. Each illness was seen by project physicians. Thirty-six percent of the beta-hemolytic streptococcal illnesses were associated with acute stress. These were major life events, including deaths and serious illnesses, minor illness with serious implications, and other major family crises. When this group of investigators assessed the level of chronic stress in each family, they demonstrated that as the level of stress increased from low to medium to high, there was a gradual increase in the number of positive cultures, clinical illnesses, and ASO titer responses. Once an individual acquired the beta-hemolytic strep, the ASO response was directly related to the level of chronic family stress.

Upper respiratory tract infections (the common cold) have been studied extensively. Boyce and his colleagues (1977) demonstrated that children from families with rigid routines were most susceptible to the influence of stressful life events on the development and severity of upper respiratory tract infections. Military recruits frequently have been subjects of study. Voors, Stewart, Gutekunst, Moldow and Jenkins (1968) found that the recruit at greatest risk for developing a cold is the individual with a high level of civilian education, high test scores on aptitude intelligence tests, and tardy promotion from private to private first class. These investigators believed that status incongruity was the major factor that increased the risk for developing the common cold. In a prospective study, Mason, Buescher, Belfer, Artenstein, and Mongey (1979) showed that 3 days before the development of clinical signs and symptoms of a retrovirus upper respiratory tract infection, subjects secreted elevated levels of corticosteroids, epinephrine, and norepinephrine in their urine. McClelland, Floor, Davidson and Saron (1980) studied male college sophomores. Students with a great need for power they couldn't obtain had a high incidence of respiratory tract infections. These investigators also found that this subgroup of students excreted a high level of epinephrine and a low level of salivary IgA secretion. Finally, a group of Swiss investigators (Landmann, *et al.*, 1984) stressed 15 healthy subjects, and looked at plasma adrenalin levels and subsets of T cells. As the level of adrenalin increased, there was a fall in the T4:T8 ratio that approached 1.0. This decreasing ratio indicates increasing suppression of the T-cell immune system, which could increase susceptibility to infections.

During the past few decades we have learned so much about the Epstein-Barr virus (EBV). A number of points are relevant to the current discussion. Most individuals have a silent EBV seroconversion during childhood (Henle & Henle, 1979). Of those who enter adolescence and adulthood before contracting the virus, the majority will develop a clinical case of infectious mononucleosis when infected with this virus. There is a transient and dramatic inversion of the T4:T8 ratio during an acute bout of infectious mononucleosis (Reinherz, O'Brien, Rosenthal, & Schlossman, 1980). Lifelong viral latency develops once infected by this virus (Henle & Henle, 1982) and a syndrome of chronic mononucleosis is emerging with defined abnormalities of T-cell subsets (Ballow *et al.*, 1982). This new knowledge suggests that EBV is yet another example of an endogenous infection.

Kasl, Evans, and Niederman (1979) had the rare opportunity to merge two extensive data sets. One data set was a prospective epidemiologic surveillance of the cadets of the class of 1973 at the United States Military Academy at West Point. The second was an extensive collection of psychosocial data obtained on these same students at the time of admission. Two thirds of the 1,327 cadets arrived at West Point immune with antibodies to EBV. Of the susceptible one-third remaining, approximately 20% per year developed positive antibodies. One-quarter of those who experienced a seroconversion during their career at West Point had a clinical case of infectious mononucleosis. The psychosocial factors that increased the risk for expression of the EBV infection as clinical infectious mononucleosis included: (1) having fathers who were "overachievers," (2) having a strong commitment to a military career, and (3) having strong motivation and doing poorly academically. Forty-four percent of those individuals who had a high level of motivation but were doing poorly academically developed infectious mononucleosis.

A WORKING HYPOTHESIS

How can events that occur in the psychosocial environment influence the biologic susceptibility to infections? A blue-ribbon committee of stress researchers (Elliot & Eisdorfer, 1982) convened by the Institute of Medicine utilized as a stress model the conceptualization of Hamburg (1981) diagrammed in Figure 17-2. Referring back to the case history (see the

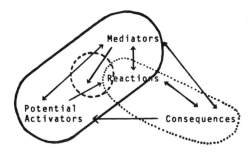

Figure 17-2. Stress model with superimposed Venn diagram.

genogram in Figure 17-1), the following illustration is offered. Potential activators (such as the death of Ruthann) are capable of producing reactions (such as blunting of the immune system) that can progress to consequences (such as the development of clinical tuberculosis). The entire chain of events can be modulated by mediators (such as support from the larger social community or family). On this model, we have superimposed a Venn diagram. The dotted line represents reactions that occur within the individual human host, the solid line represents the larger psychosocial environment in which the individual exists, and the broken line represents the individual's family.

This text is primarily concerned with the family systems, but at this time there is no published study that simultaneously examines family function and infectious disease susceptibility. The most familiar instruments of family function, such as the Family APGAR, the Beavers system model (see Beavers, Chapter 5, this volume), or the circumplex model (see Olson, Chapter 6, this volume) have not been applied to research in the area of infectious disease processes. This virtually untapped area of research offers exciting opportunities for the future. At this point, we will venture a speculation, which will then be illustrated by two contrasting scenarios. In this speculation, we will exclude genetic properties transmitted within the family and specific infectious agents that are passed from one family member to another. The biologic susceptibility to infections (changes in host defense that occur within the dotted line) may be influenced by one's family (that is, the broken line) to the extent that the family influences the individual's perception of himself or herself and/or of the situation (see Figure 17-2). Two contrasting examples may clarify the meaning of this statement:

Scenario 1. A young man loses his job. His wife is extremely understanding. She points out that they have a few dollars in savings, that she is more than willing to work part time, and that the husband has been waiting to spend more time with their child. She reassures the young man that they will do well. The two spend the night in one another's arms.

Scenario 2. A young man loses his job. His wife reacts by creating a scene, shouting that she should have listened to her father, who told her that the young man would never amount to anything. If they use their savings, they will not be able to have the luxuries she wants. She takes the child and goes home to her parents, leaving the young man alone and awake all night fretting about his situation.

We suggest that there are accompanying biologic changes that would increase susceptibility to infection for the young man in the second scenario. What are the biologic effects that might be occurring within the individual human host encountering psychosocial stress that is not neutralized by effective support?

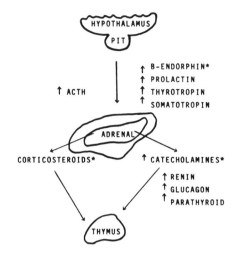

INVOLUTION OF THYMUS GLAND
*SUBSTANCES KNOWN TO HAVE AN INHIBITORY EFFECT ON CELLULAR
IMMUNITY (PREDOMINANTLY IMMUNOCOMPETENT T-CELLS)

Figure 17-3. The principal neuroendocrine reactions to stress.

There are some early hints in the work done by Selye over 40 years ago (1946). When Selye stressed and subsequently sacrificed animals, he repeatedly found hypertrophy of the adrenal gland and involution or atrophy of the thymus gland. Figure 17-3 summarizes the neuroendocrine responses that occur following stress. After the stressful event is processed in the cortex (in other words, once the individual develops his or her own unique perception of the event), lower brain levels (hypothalamus and pituitary) initiate a cascade of neuroendocrine responses. These responses include an outpouring of adrenocorticotrophic hormone (ACTH), which stimulates the adrenal gland. From the adrenal cortex there is an outpouring of corticosteroids, and from the adrenal medulla there is an outpouring of epinephrine. Both of these hormones are capable of producing an involution of the thymus gland. Other agents, such as the endorphins, somatotropin, and parathyroid hormone, are capable of affecting the immune system (Stein, Keller, & Schleifer, 1985). To summarize, stress in the psychosocial environment leads to a cascade of neuroendocrine responses that, in turn, could blunt the immune system and increase the risk of developing infectious disease.

HERPES SIMPLEX TYPE 1: A DISEASE MODEL FOR STUDYING PSYCHONEUROIMMUNOLOGY

Figure 17-4 is a more specific working hypothesis for the disease model recurrent herpes simplex type 1 (HSV). We hypothesize that individuals who experience increased stressful life events that are not neutralized by effective support in their psychosocial environment, have an outpouring of catecholamines and/or corticosteroids. This increased secretion of catecholamines (predominately epinephrine) may lead to an increase in the percentage of circulating T8 suppressor cells and/or a decrease in T4 helper cells, resulting in a rapid decrease in the T4:T8 ratio and decreased production of lymphokines. Dr. Crary and colleagues (1983) have shown a decrease in the T4:T8 ratio within 30 minutes after administration of a single dose of 0.2-mg epinephrine hydrochloride. The combination of these immunologic changes leads to a reactivation of the dormant herpes simplex type 1 virus.

From 1981 to 1984, we conducted a collaborative study of patients with recurrent herpes simplex type 1. The collaborative group had included Jerrold Ellner (immunologist), Steven Zyzanski (psychometrician), Mary Lou Kumar (virologist), Janet Arno (research fellow), Priscilla Schmidt (medical anthropologist), and David Schmidt (family physician).

We obtained psychologic data on 68 subjects, all young, healthy, highly educated graduated students or professionals who worked in or near the university. The majority of these patients experienced three to six herpes infections per year. The psychologic data were obtained through a self-administered questionnaire developed by our group. This methodology is detailed in a previous publication (Schmidt, Zyzanski, Ellner, Kumar, & Arno, 1985).

We now have 23 individuals who completed this questionnaire during the dormant and active stages of infection. At the time of active infection, these individuals had not experienced confounding variables that are known to precipitate HSV infections, such as sunburn, a concomitant viral infection, lip trauma, or menses. Psychologic traits that were measured (behavior type, coping skills, global support, spouse support) did not vary between the dormant and active state of infection. These psychologic traits tend to be stable and would not be expected to change over a short period of time. However, psychologic states did vary between the dormant and active states of infection. The psychologic states were measured by events or states of mind that can vary from week-to-week or day-to-day. Table 17-1 shows these differences. In summary, individuals with recurrent herpes simplex type 1 experienced increased stressful life events and hassles and were in a state of high anxiety just before the appearance of the recurrent infection.

The investigation of biologic factors in this study has occurred at several stages. We first looked at lymphocyte blastogenesis during the inactive and active states of infection. This previously published work (Arno *et al.*, 1983) suggests that during the active state of infection, there is a predominance of suppressor cell activity that is blunting the immune response. In the second phase of the study, we measured T-cell subsets directly using monoclonal antibodies for labeling the T cells. We determined the percentage of T4 helper/inducer cells and T8 suppressor/cytotoxic cells and the total peripheral mononuclear cell

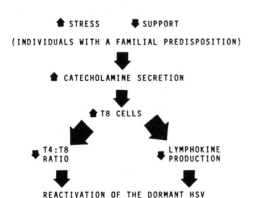

Figure 17-4. A working hypothesis for the disease model recurrent herpes simplex type 1.

Table 17-1. Psychologic "States" during Dormant and Immediately Preceding the Active Stages of Recurrent Herpes Simplex Type 1

Psychologic measures	Herpes status		t-test*	p
	Dormant	Active		
Life events	10.0	14.1	−2.02	.03
Hassles	7.8	10.1	−4.63	.04
P.O.M.S. anxiety	7.4	13.0	−4.16	.00
Anxiety	5.3	7.0	−2.14	.02

*Paired t-test, one-tailed.

$n = 23$.

population. Table 17-2 shows zero-order correlations between psychologic states, the level of T8 cells, and the T4:T8 ratios during an active herpes infection. There is a strong positive correlation with life events and the Profile of Mood States anxiety, and a strong negative correlation between life events, anxiety, and the T4:T8 ratio. Finally, Table 17-3 shows interleukin 2 activity during the dormant and active states of herpes simplex virus type 1 infections. Interleukin 2, one of many lymphokines that are important in the cellular immune system, is necessary for the generation of cytotoxic and helper T cells. This assay involves first stimulating total peripheral mononuclear cells to produce interleukin 2 by incubating them with herpes simplex 1 antigen. This supernatant, which contains interleukin 2, is then incubated with a radioactive indicator and a special murine T-cell line that can grow only in the presence of interleukin 2. As the cells multiply, they incorporate the indicator so that the radioactive counts per minute are related to the number of cells that proliferate. The radioactive counts are much lower for the active state, representing less interleukin 2 produced than during the dormant state of infection.

We are slowly exploring each step in the proposed chain of events. We are confident that there is a correlation between psychologic factors and the appearance of recurrent infections. We have data that support two of the intermediate steps: an increase in the number of circulating T8 cells (with a drop in the T4:T8 ratio), and a decrease in the production of interleukin 2. There is considerable work left to be done before we can claim a definite cause–effect relationship. The most difficult problem that we are currently addressing is whether or not these immunologic changes precede and cause the recurrent infection, or are merely a reaction to the active viral infection. We are now conducting a study involving an intensive examination of a small number of patients prospectively on a weekly basis for an 8-month period.

We would like to conclude by quoting from an earlier review of this subject. When-

Table 17-2. Correlations between Psychologic State and Level of T8 Suppressor Cells and T4:T8 Ratio at Time of Active Herpes Simplex Type 1 Infection

	T8 r value	T4:T8 r value
Life events	.77	−.69
Hassles	.61	−.54
P.O.M.S. anxiety	.55	−.47

$n = 8$.

Table 17-3. Interleukin 2 Activity in the Dormant and Active Stages of Recurrent HSV 1 Infections*

Dormant	Active
24,797 + 7,587**	3,491 + 1,100**
$n = 15$	$n = 7$

*Counts per minute from murine T cells incubated with the supernatant from peripheral mononuclear cells stimulated with HSV 1 antigen.

**$p = .02$.

ever we think we are clever and have discovered something new, it is sobering to realize that others before us had similar ideas.

> "Men renouned in our art . . . are moved by the weight of observation to hold that the origin of pestilences and the like spread by contagion ought especially to be attributed to terror and fear . . ." The increased susceptibility to contagious disease as a result of emotional disturbance . . . is described also by Corp, who states that those "whose minds are depressed by fear" are most frequently attacked when epidemic or contagious disorders prevail. . . . Valangin, too, agrees that fear may increase susceptibility to contagious diseases. "Those who were most afraid of the plague were soonest taken with it." . . . Plechlin suggests that . . . nothing is more dangerous when disease is abroad than to occupy oneself with fearful or sad ideas . . . in epidemic diseases, the fearful are the first affected. . . . (Gaub, 1965/1763, p. 147)

References

Arno JN, Kumar ML, Edmonds K, Hayman T, Lindsay D, Schmidt D, Ellner JJ. Nonspecific adherent cell suppression of lymphocyte blastogenesis during periods of activity in humans with recurrent oral herpes simplex. Clinical Research 1983; 31:358A.

Ballow M, Seeley J, Purtillo DT, St. Onge S, Sakamoto K, Rickles FR. Familial chronic mononucleosis. Annals of Internal Medicine 1982; 97:821–825.

Boyce WT, Jensen EW, Cassel JC, Collier AM, Smith AH, Ramey CT. Influence of life events and family routines on childhood respiratory tract illness. Pediatrics 1977; 60(4):609–615.

Cornfeld D, Hubbard JP. A four year study of the occurrence of beta-hemolytic streptococci in 64 school children. New England Journal of Medicine 1961; 264:211–215.

Crary B, Hauser SL, Borysenko M, Kutz I, Hoban C, Ault KA, Weiner HL, Benson H. Epinephrine-induced changes in the distribution of lymphocyte subsets in peripheral blood of humans. Journal of Immunology 1983; 131(3):1178–1181.

Dubos R. Man adapting. New Haven: Yale University Press, 1980.

Dubos R. Unsolved problems in the study and control of microbial diseases. Journal of the American Medical Association 1955; 157(17):1477–1479.

Elliot GR, Eisdorfer C, eds. Stress and human health: a study by the Institute of Medicine/National Academy of Sciences. New York: Springer, 1982:372.

Gaub J. Gaub's essay of 1763 and commentary. In: Rather LJ, ed. Mind and body in eighteenth century medicine. Berkeley and Los Angeles: University of California Press, 1965: 144–147.

Glassroth J, Robins AG, Snider DE. Tuberculosis in the 1980s. New England Journal of Medicine 1980; 302(26):1441–1450.

Hamburg D. Biobehavioral sciences: an emerging research agenda. Psychiatric Clinics of North America 1981; 4:407–421.

Henle G, Henle W. Immunology of Epstein-Barr virus. In: Roizman B, ed. The herpes virus. New York: Plenum Press, 1982: 209–252.

Henle G, Henle W. The virus as the etiologic agent of infectious mononucleosis. In: Epstein MA, Achong BG, eds. The Epstein-Barr virus. New York: Springer-Verlag, 1979:297–320.

Holmes TH, Hawkins NG, Bowerman CE, Clarke ER Jr, Joffe JR. Psychosocial and psychophysiologic studies of tuberculosis. Psychomsomatic Medicine 1957; 19(2):134–143.

Kasl SV, Evans AS, Niederman JC. Psychosocial risk factors in the development of infectious mononucleosis. Psychosomatic Medicine 1979; 41:445–465.

Kraus A. Lilienfeld A. Some epidemiologic aspects of the high mortality rates in the young widowed group. Journal of Chronic Diseases 1959; 10:207–217.

Landmann RM, Muller FB, Perini C, Wesp M, Erne P, Buhler FR. Changes of immunoregulatory cells induced by psychological and physical stress: relationship to plasma catecholamines. Clinical and Experimental Immunology 1984; 58(1):127–135.

Mason JW, Buescher EL, Belfer ML, Artenstein MS, Mongey EH. A prospective study of corticosteroid and catecholamine levels in relation to viral respiratory illness. Journal of Human Stress 1979; 5(3):18–28.

McClelland DC, Floor E, Davidson RJ, Saron C. Stress and power motivation, sympathetic activation, immune function, and illness. Journal of Human Stress 1980; 6(2):11–19.

Meyer RJ, Haggerty RJ. Streptococcal infections in families: factors altering individual susceptibility. Pediatrics 1962; 29:539–549.

Reinherz LL, O'Brien C, Rosenthal P, Schlossman SF. The cellular basis for viral-induced immunodeficiency: analysis by monoclonal antibodies. Journal of Immunology 1980; 125(3):1269–1273.

Schmidt DD, Zyzanski S, Ellner J, Kumar ML, Arno J. Stress as a precipitating factor in subjects with recurrent herpes labialis. Journal of Family Practice 1985; 20(4):359–366.

Selye H. General adaptation syndrome and diseases of adaptation. Journal of Clinical Endocrinology 1946; 6:117–230.

Stein M, Keller SE, Schleifer SJ. Stress and immunomodulation: the role of depression and neuroendocrine function. Journal of Immunology 1985; 135(2):827s–833s.

Voors AW, Steward GT, Gutekunst PR, Moldow CF, Jenkins CD. Respiratory infection in marine recruits: influence of personal characteristics. American Review of Respiratory Disease 1968; 98(5):801–809.

18

Cancer Survival and the Family

BERNARD H. FOX
Boston University School of Medicine

The main question to be addressed in this chapter is whether the family, acting in any of its several roles, affects cancer survival. Very few studies can support firm conclusions about the family itself and cancer in general (Thomas, Duszynski, & Shaffer, 1979), let alone about cancer survival in particular. The answer to the question is at present speculative and hinges on inferential connection.

The determinants of cancer survival in general are very poorly understood. The known biologic determinants of survival include, among others, tumor site, stage, size, rate of growth, cytology, and vascularity; number of lymphocytes infiltrating positive lymph nodes; probability of metastasis; early or late metastasis; whether the tumor has metastasized to a vital organ; and iatrogenic dispersal of cancer cells or inadequate tumor extirpation. Among the demographic factors associated with cancer survival (e.g., age, race, country, and region) the determinants are not known (Morrison, Lowe, MacMahon, Warram, & Yuasa, 1972).

BEHAVIORAL DETERMINANTS

Behavioral determinants are mostly speculative and inferential, since we are sure of only a few, such as poor diet, which is often a consequence of a biologic condition—anorexia; therapeutic compliance (which is being questioned); smoking—melanoma or lung cancer patients who continue to smoke after surgery have shorter survival times than those who quit. Some behaviors are known to be associated with increased incidence of cancer. For example, men who do not exercise regularly are 1.6 times more likely to get colon cancer than men who get regular exercise (OT Briefs, 1985). Whether such behaviors are also associated with length of survival is not known. Certainly, we do not know whether these behaviors are merely epiphenomena or are actual determinants of survival length, and, if the latter, their mechanisms of effect.

PSYCHOLOGIC PHENOMENA

There is even less confidence in the role of psychologic phenomena in cancer survival. Scattered findings suggest that some psychologic conditions are indeed associated with duration of survival. Others refute such hypotheses. Rogentine and colleagues (1979) asked melanoma patients how much their surgery affected their lives. The authors compared the relapse status of those reporting that surgery had little effect (A) and those saying it had substantial effect (B). They found that more members of the A group relapsed during the first year after surgery than did B group members. In a follow-up of the same patients for an additional 2 years, Temoshok and Fox (1984) reported on both relapse and survival during the whole 3-year period. The difference in survival between groups A and B for year 1 was significant *(p < .05)*, just as it was for relapse, but a nonsignificant difference between the two groups was reported for the cumulative 3-year experience (.20 < *p* < .30). The first year's result for survival was predictable, since relapse almost always precedes mortality. But the findings suggest no relationship between the particular psychologic variable studied and survival over the 3 years.

Several studies have reported that breast cancer patients with a "fighting spirit" survive longer than those who react with a hopeless-helpless attitude or with resigned acceptance (Derogatis, Abeloff, & Melisaratos, 1979; Greer, Morris, & Pettingale, 1979; Pettingale, 1984). "Fighting spirit" implies resistance to fate, expression of anger, complaints to nurses and doctors, and denial.

The implication of these studies is that whatever psychologic effects exist outside the family can also be found within the family—perhaps in different proportions. On theoretic grounds, one particular aspect of the family that, if present, might contribute to increased survival and, if absent, might contribute to earlier relapse and death is social support. Social support, like family effect, is a multidimensional concept (Murawski, Penman, & Schmitt, 1978). Among the things the family can provide are maintenance of social identity, emotional support, tangible or environmental support, information, and social affiliation (Bloom, 1982). If it can be shown that social support affects cancer survival, it might be inferred that similar support within the family could do the same, but there are no data to show this to be the case. A further connection must enter the picture.

LOSS OF FAMILY SUPPORT:
BEREAVEMENT AND REJECTION

Perhaps *loss* of social or family support can be shown to affect cancer survival. There do exist some results of interest in this regard. Studies on bereavement would, if conclusive, provide a firmer empiric foundation for statements about cancer survival. A number of attempts to follow the survival experience of bereaved spouses have been made. In an excellent review, Jacobs and Ostfeld (1977) have analyzed most of those studies. They conclude that most of the elevation in risk of death following bereavement takes place during the first 6 months after death of spouse in widowers, and during the second 6 months after death of spouse in widows. In only a few of these studies, however, was cancer mortality found to be among the causes of excess death risk; heart and vascular disease were the predominant sources of excess risk. In an excellent study, Helsing, Comstock, and Szklo (1982) found no excess cancer risk as long as 12 years after bereavement, even though there was a clear risk for noncancer causes of death.

A theoretic issue bears on any suggestion from these findings that loss of a family member, especially a spouse, is associated with and might even contribute to increased incidence of cancer and deaths consequent on such new tumors. Such an inference is very questionable, since the implication in such a view is that the cancer cases were initiated at about the time of, or shortly after, the death in the family. In almost all cases this cannot be true. Almost always it takes years, not months, for a cancer to grow from a single transformed malignant cell into a tumor large enough to be discovered clinically. Very few breast tumors, for example, are less than 1 cm in diameter at diagnosis, and most are larger. To achieve a size of 1 cm, the originally transformed cell must have doubled in volume about 30 times. Although doubling time for most tumors is highly variable, in the average case it has been estimated that it takes 6 or 7 years for a breast tumor to reach a clinically diagnosable size (Fox, 1978); for lung cancer, the time is estimated to be about the same (Steel, 1977). The interval from time of diagnosis to death is also variable, but exceeds 7 years in the average breast cancer patient, and is about 7 months in the average lung cancer patient (National Cancer Institute, 1976). Though not extremes, these two do represent fast- and slow-growing tumors. If one conceives that death from cancer among those showing excess mortality comes about through the association of the bereavement event and the *initiation* of a new tumor, then the sum of the two periods—time to diagnosis and survival after diagnosis—is much too long to make such a notion reasonable on the basis of the studies of bereavement.

Nevertheless, we cannot deny the fact that excess cancer death among surviving spouses not long after the death of the index spouse was reported in some studies. [In many studies this was not the case, however, and in one study by McNeill (1973), the relative risk for cancer death was close to 1 among those less than 60 years of age *(N = 31)* and clearly *less* than 1 among the bereaved persons older than 60 years of age *(N = 83).*] Various factors are proposed to explain, at least in part, the excess relative risk: (1) common environment of spouses leading to similar causes of death; (2) poor life-style and emotional state of the survivor leading to neglect of health problems; and (3) reduced resistance to disease stemming from emotional disturbance, particularly depression.

The first two explanations are unlikely (see the analysis by Kraus & Lilienfield, 1959), but there are data tending to support the third. With respect to the time issue, heart attacks and vascular deaths do not pose a problem; that is, they tend to occur soon after the onset of bereavement. The cancer time problem, however, might have an explanation something like this: The distress or stress associated with emotional traumata like persistent depression or grief often produces hormonal changes, such as an increase in adrenocorticotropic hormone (ACTH) or corticosteroids (Hofer, Wolff, Friedman, & Mason, 1972). If a tumor already exists, but is being held in check or is growing very slowly by virtue of the controlling effect of the immune system, then abrogation of that control can be brought about if the immune system is compromised. Emotional distress and stress in general are known to affect immunity adversely. In such cases, a tumor that had been held in check at a size not too much smaller than the size that produces symptoms could grow to diagnosable size and activity in a short time.

Among the bereaved who die of cancer, it is not known what cancer sites were involved. For the suppressed immunity theory just outlined to be valid, the tumors would have to be fast-growing, like certain rapid lymphomas, or lung, pancreas, or liver cancers; or they would have to be the very fast growing among the group whose average growth speed is moderate or slow (e.g., colon cancer or melanoma). A study examining tumor sites and, if possible, tumor growth rates (such as the study done by Mizuno *et al.,* 1984) among the bereaved experiencing excess cancer deaths would be extremely interesting. Nevertheless, such studies may not be easy to carry out because the phenomenon of excess cancer risk seems to have appeared in relatively few studies (Helsing *et al.,* 1982, found none). Greenwald, Kirmss, and Burnett (1979) reported that relative risk of cancer death among widowers compared to married men is 1.8 for lung, 1.5 for prostate, 1.5 for colon, 1.1 for pancreatic, and 1.1 for stomach cancer. Their analysis of prostate cases, however, led to the following conclusion:

> Thus on the question of misclassification in widowers, three lines of evidence indicate that the high widower rates may be explained by artifacts. . . . These artifacts are: (1) Representation of some nonwidowers as widowers for both prostate cancer patients and controls; (2) if the

high mortality among widowers is real, we thought it likely that we would find an associated change in duration of widowhood—either shorter or longer—which was not found; and (3) the prostate cancer mortality ratios among widowers compared to married men became closer to 1 as the number of years of age included in each group was smaller. Therefore, we believe artifacts of classification may fully account for the high rates in vital records of prostate cancer and of other cancers among widowers. (p. 1135)

One might attempt to establish a connection between family support and survival by looking at different cultures. By and large, certain cultures (e.g., Middle Eastern, Japanese, and Italian) have been noted to have particularly close family relationships—protectiveness, rejection of outsider intrusion, interdependency. Cancer survival patterns have not been studied well in the Middle East except in Israel; unfortunately, those studies mixed Eastern European and Middle Eastern cultures. The Italian data are not readily available, but survival for breast cancer among the Japanese has been studied and compared with U.S. survival. For breast cancer, Japanese survival rates differ little from those of U.S. breast cancer patients, and, if anything, are lower. Unfortunately, two conditions make it hard to draw even suggestive inferences. First, the incidence of breast cancer among Japanese women is quite low—perhaps one-fifth that of Americans (Fujimoto, Hanai, & Oshima, 1979). The data of Morrison and colleagues (1972), based on U.S. statistics, also suggest that factors such as age at first pregnancy, schooling level, and cancer incidence rates are *not* related to survival in such a comparison. It is still possible that other biologic factors contribute to cancer incidence and survival, but there are not many biologic studies of incidence compared with survival.

The second condition making it hard to draw conclusions is that in those cultures mentioned above, the cancer patient is regarded with more rejection, fear, and disgust than in the United States. Thus, people having the disease are subjected to the reverse of the family support they had been used to, and hence might be predicted to have *shorter* survival, if indeed family support is a factor. An example of such rejection is reported by Baider and Abromovitch (1985) in a Kurdish family from Iraq.

Rejection is, of course, present in many U.S. families as well. Theoretically, such a family behavior can have a distinct effect on cancer survival. The paradigm of immune suppression is quite similar to that discussed for bereavement, but is more general in respect to time; that is, hormonal and immune effects could theoretically exist not only for the first few months after bereavement, but as long as the family's rejection or withdrawal lasts. Such effects are a function of the patient's makeup as well. How much is a person affected by such withdrawal? Does it produce anger or depression, some other emotion, or no overt emotion at all? If it produces depression or resignation or withdrawal, then an increase in corticosteroids, with associated immune suppresion, can well be an accompanying response.

Although we assume that a lowered immune capability is associated with shortened time to relapse or shortened survival, in fact very few studies examining this association exist. One such study is reported in a paper by Mandeville, Lamoureux, Legault-Poisson, and Poisson (1982), who showed shortened survival in breast cancer patients who had depressed response to phytohemagglutinin (PHA) when compared to those with normal response. Also, breast cancer patients with lowered responses to recall antigens, when compared with those having normal responses, showed the following pattern of survival after 5 years: 61% with low response were dead by 5 years versus 30% with normal response; 16% with low response showed progressive disease versus 18% with normal response; and 22% with low response were disease-free versus 52% with normal response.

The patients also showed lowered response to concanavalin A (ConA) and pokeweed mitogen (PWM), but neither of these was related to duration of survival. Apropos of these results, an interesting report by Kiecolt-Glaser and colleagues (1984) showed a relationship between loneliness in psychiatric patients on the one hand and their level of natural killer (NK) cells and PHA response on the other. PWM response did not show such a relationship. We cannot draw a conclusion from this result, which parallels that of Mandeville and colleagues (1982), but it points to an obvious need for research that would test similar hypotheses in normals. Kiecolt-Glaser and colleagues (1985) tested similar responses when they tried to improve immune status by relaxation and social support. Relaxation yielded significant improvement, but social support did not.

In view of the foregoing, it would be of interest to explore support and rejection by the family and, at the same time, to measure mitogen response and NK level.

Very few studies exist that directly relate family support or lack of it to cancer survival. Three such studies should be mentioned. Thomas and colleagues (1979) reported low levels of closeness to parents as a better-than-chance predictor of those who later died of cancer. In accordance with the foregoing discussion a distinction should be made between the factors contributing to the transformation of a cell to a malignant state, and the changes aiding or preventing the immune system from eliminating a newly transformed cell or the clone of daughter cells. The former deals with cancer initiation and the latter with survival. A certain amount of the protection against cancer appearance derives from such immune system action. Hence, studies on incidence are relevant to the present issue of survival, since the incidence report follows diagnosis, showing that the tumor has escaped immune system control. For that reason, the studies by Thomas and colleagues (1979) are relevant. Kerr (1981) discusses cognate concepts involving both hormones leading to increased risk of cancer and disturbing family interactions stimulating such hormonal secretion.

The second important study is that by Weisman and Worden (1975), who reported that patients with poor social relationships, as determined from interviews and psychologic autopsy and including closeness and mutual supportiveness of family members, had a smaller survival quotient (SQ) than did those with constructive interpersonal relationships. SQ, the ratio of the observed survival of a patient to his or her expected survival, is a rough measure having a monotonic correspondence with a more precise measure. SQ is based on observation of a truncated population throughout its survival period, and hence yields higher values than it should, since it omits the longer survivors in its denominator. Weisman and Worden's (1975) finding is consistent with that of Thomas and colleagues (1979).

The third study, now ongoing at the University of Maryland (Aisner, 1984), is examining the role of social support, including family support, in survival among patients with small-cell lung cancer and with leukemia. No data are yet available from this study.

Oddly enough, there are no studies of relative survival of bereaved cancer patients.

ROLE OF THE FAMILY: A BROADER VIEW

The family might be viewed in broader terms than those who are directly related or married to a person. Nonrelated significant others living with the person have roles similar to those of formal family. There are good reasons for including pets in the family structure, as family system theorists would attest. Although there seem to be no data on the effect of cancer broken down by particular family member other than by spouse and parents, there does exist information on pets. They can, in a real sense, be regarded as family members, playing the role of children or grandchildren to parents, of siblings to children, or of children to children. It is relevant that elderly persons who acquired pets showed improved activity, interest, and the like, compared to those who didn't have pets.

Further, one would hypothesize that among people at high risk (e.g., the elderly), stress might be mitigated somewhat by the presence of a pet. In people not particularly subject to stress, a pet might not be expected to affect the picture very much (the ceiling effect). Two studies are of interest here. In the first, Bross and Gibson (1970) examined the relative risks of leukemia in children who did and who did not at any time in their lives have (a) a childhood virus infection, (b) exposure to a well cat, (c) exposure to a sick or dead cat. The risk among those children who were exposed to none of the above is defined as 1.0. Children who were exposed to (a) childhood virus but not to (b) well cat, or (c) dead or sick cat, showed an increased but nonsignificant risk of leukemia. Children who were not exposed to (a) or (c), but who had been exposed to (b), well cat, showed a still greater but still nonsignificant risk. Those exposed to (a) and (b) but not (c), that is exposed to the virus and well cats only, showed a still greater risk, marginally nonsignificant. Finally, children who either were or were not exposed to (a) virus or (b) well cat but were exposed to (c), that is exposure to a sick or dead cat, whether or not there was childhood virus or well cat, showed a highly significant relative risk of leukemia (RR = 2.24, $p < .01$). The data, however, are probably only of theoretic interest for the relationship of stress to cancer, first because the child was probably stressed only a short time during the animal's illness, although there might have been an extended period of bereavement in some children whose cat died. Second, human leukemia, now suggested as being related to the virus causing feline leukemia, seemed to be more related to the biology of the sick cat than to its stress-reducing or supportive role as a family member. In a similar study, Bross, Bertell, and Gibson (1972) found confirming data for adults.

RESPONSE TO STRESS

A comparison of severity of children's and adults' responses to stress seems never to have been made. Adults are likely to assume that children's traumata are less severe than those of adults. On the other hand, children's reactivity to certain sensory stimuli is far stronger than that of adults. How much that extends to emotionality and steroidal output is unknown. Therefore, it is uncertain whether the findings of Bross and colleagues are a blow to the hypothesis that social support reduces stress, in turn reducing immune suppression. In fact, there are fewer studies (*ca.* 40%) showing that stress *is* related to cancer than those showing that it is *not*. This percentage is significantly more than the 2.5% to be expected by chance if there were truly no relationship, but many of the positive studies suffer from sampling and bias problems. Thus, from these data there seems to be little confirmation that social support decreases cancer risk or extends survival, or that its loss produces the reverse effect. Note that exposure to well cats and virus yielded an almost significant effect, tending to refute the possible stressful bereavement effect on the child by the cat's sickness or death.

Finally, it can be hypothesized that as age increases, greater stresses affect the person. If this is so, it may be relevant to the interesting observation that the older the patient is at the time of cancer diagnosis, beyond the 30s and 40s, the shorter the relative survival (National Cancer Institute, 1976). Such stressers might be the empty-nest syndrome, an increase in family deaths in older age groups, or perhaps retirement. As to the last, however, Eckerdt, Bosse, and Goldie (1983) have shown that for 3 to 5 years after retirement, no differences were found in health status when comparing retired and nonretired individuals from the same company, matched for marital status and age. Also, among the few studies relating life stress to cancer survival among cancer patients, no relationship was found in breast cancer patients (Greer *et al.,* 1979).

One could speculate that such a relationship of shortened survival with age could be due to the age-related appearance of faster growing tumors like lung cancer or pancreatic cancer. But that cannot be true, since the shortened survival phenomenon occurs *within* tumor types as well as for all types combined.

Is it possible that delay in going to the doctor among the older group causes cancer to be discovered at a more advanced stage in that group? Although this could occur to a mild degree, it cannot possibly be an important part of the survival picture because it would hardly apply to the slow-growing tumors like breast, since delays in going to the physician have been shown to be a matter of months, whereas survival for slow tumors is in years.

It might appear obvious that a slow tumor will be diagnosed later in life than a fast one if both transform at the same time. If so, older people should survive longer, since they would have more slow tumors than younger people. However, this is contrary to the actual state of affairs, therefore the putative excess of slow-growing tumors in the elderly can have only a small role in predicting cancer survival.

Although genetics is relevant to our general topic of the family, there is little information on genetics and survival, and increased relative risk of incidence within families which seems not to be based on intrafamily relationships; genetic susceptibility contributed only a limited amount.

A brief mention of animal studies is appropriate. Males and females living together and females living together have been observed, but the results differ according to strain. Some show an effect, others do not. It is dangerous to extrapolate to the human species from crowding data in animals. For some strains, 5 in a cage is optimal; for some, 10 is optimal; and for still others, 1 is optimal. Optimal number differs by sex of the animals involved as well. The data on control of stressors and perception of stressors is interesting, but at this point is mostly heuristic. It would be desirable to initiate studies on humans, but conclusions about humans cannot be drawn from animal work at this time.

CONCLUSION

In conclusion, very few studies have been done on the role of positive family support, and none could be discovered on negative support. The one or two that have been done on positive support point either to a slight increase in survival or to no clear-cut results. Of the studies looking at loss of family support, several studies show a short-term increase in cancer rates, and a few no such increase and even a decrease. Firm conclusions cannot be drawn from either set of findings. It is likely that if shortened survival does exist with bereavement, it is restricted to those people with already existing, subclinical tumors who are especially susceptible to stress.

References

Aisner J. Psychosocial support and intensive treatment in the elderly. National Institutes of Health Grant #NCI 1R01 AGO 05253, 1984.

Baider L, Abramovitch H. The Dybbuk, cultural context of a cancer patient. Hospice Journal 1985; 1(2):13–19.

Bloom JR. Social support systems and cancer: a conceptual view. In: Cohen J, Cullen JW, Martin LR, eds. Psychosocial aspects of cancer. New York: Raven Press, 1982:129–149.

Bross IDJ, Bertell R, Gibson R. Pets and adult leukemia. American Journal of Public Health 1972; 62:1520–2531.

Bross IDJ, Gibson R. Cats and childhood leukemia. Journal of Medicine 1970; 1:180–187.

Derogatis L, Abeloff M, Melisaratos N. Psychological coping mechanisms and survival time in metastatic breast cancer. Journal of the American Medical Association 1979; 242:1504–1508.

Eckerdt DJ, Bosse R, Goldie C. The effect of retirement on somatic complaints. Journal of Psychosomatic Research 1983; 27:61–67.

Fox BH. Premorbid psychological factors as related to cancer incidence. Journal of Behavioral Medicine 1978; 1:45–117.

Fujimoto I, Hanai A, Oshima A. Descriptive epidemiology of cancer in Japan: current cancer incidence and survival data. National Cancer Institute Monograph 1979; 53:5–15.

Greenwald P, Kirmss V, Burnett WS. Prostate cancer epidemiology: widowerhood and cancer in spouses. Journal of the National Cancer Institute 1979; 62:1131–1136.

Greer S, Morris T, Pettingale KW. Psychological response to breast cancer: effect on outcome. Lancet 1979; 2:785–787.

Helsing KJ, Comstock GW, Szklo M. Causes of death in a widowed population. American Journal of Epidemiology 1982; 116:524–532.

Hofer MA, Wolff CT, Friedman SB, Mason JW. A psychoendocrine study of bereavement: II. Observations on the process of mourning in relation to adrenocortical function. Psychosomatic Medicine 1972; 34:492–504.

Jacobs S, Ostfeld A. An epidemiological review of the mortality of bereavement. Psychosomatic Medicine 1977; 39:344–357.

Kerr M. Cancer and the family emotional system. In: Goldberg J, ed. Psychotherapeutic treatment of cancer. New York: Free Press, 1981.

Kiecolt-Glaser JD, Glaser R, Williger D, Stout J, Messick G, Sheppard S, Ricker D, Romisher SC, Briner W, Bonnell G, Donnerberg R. Psychosocial enhancement of immunocompetence in a geriatric population. Health Psychology 1985; 4:25–41.

Kiecolt-Glaser JC, Ricker D, George J, Messick G, Speicher CE, Garner W, Glaser R. Urinary cortisol levels, cellular immunocompetency, and loneliness in psychiatric inpatients. Psychosomatic Medicine 1984; 46:15–23.

Kraus AS, Lilienfeld AM. Some epidemiological aspects of the high mortality rates in the young widowed group. Journal of Chronic Diseases 1959; 10:207–217.

Mandeville R, Lamoureux G, Legault-Poisson S, Poisson R. Biological markers and breast cancer: a multiparametric study: II. Depressed immune competence. Cancer 1982; 50:1280–1288.

NcNeill DN. Mortality among the widowed in Connecticut, 1965–1968. Unpublished master's thesis, Yale University, New Haven, Conn., 1973.

Mizuno T, Masaoka A, Ichimura H, Shibata K, Tanaka H, Niwa H. Comparison of actual survivorship after treatment with survivorship predicted by tumor-volume doubling time from tumor diameter at first observation. Cancer 1984; 53:2716–2720.

Morrison AS, Lowe CR, MacMahon B, Warram JH Jr, Yuasa S. Survival of breast cancer patients related to incidence risk factors. International Journal of Cancer 1972; 9:470–476.

Murawski BJ, Penman D, Schmitt M. Social support in health and illness: the concept of its measurement. Cancer Nursing 1978; 1:365–371.

National Cancer Institute. Cancer patient survival. Report no. 5 (DHEW Publication no. NIH 77–992). Washington, D.C.: U.S. Government Printing Office, 1976.

OT Briefs. Oncology Times 1985; 7(1):23.

Pettingale KW. Coping and cancer prognosis. Journal of Psychosomatic Research 1984; 5:363–364.

Rogentine GN Jr, van Kammen DP, Fox BH, Docherty J, Rosenblatt J, Boyd SC, Bunney WE Jr. Psychological factors in the prognosis of malignant melanoma: a prospective study. Psychosomatic Medicine 1979; 41:647–654.

Steel GG. Growth kinetics of tumors. Oxford: Clarendon Press, 1977.

Temoshok L, Fox BH. Coping styles and other psychosocial factors related to medical status and to prognosis in patients with cutaneous malignant melanoma. In: Fox BH, Newberry BH, eds. Impact of psychoendocrine systems on cancer and immunity. Lewiston, N.Y.: C. J. Hogrefe, 1984: 258–287.

Thomas CB, Duszynski KR, Shaffer JW. Family attitudes reported in youth as potential predictors of cancer. Psychosomatic Medicine 1979; 41:287–302.

Weisman AD, Worden JW. Psychosocial analysis of cancer deaths. Omega 1975; 6:61–75.

PART FIVE

Family Systems Endocrinology

19

Family Systems, Stress, the Endocrine System, and the Heart

ROBERT S. ELIOT
The Institute of Stress Medicine, Denver, Colorado

ROLE OF STRESS

Stress can take two forms. The first of these is vigilance, a long-term softening-up process that occurs over a period of days, weeks, months, or years, The other is short-term stress— the fight-or-flight response.

Long term stress is mainly interpreted through the central nervous system (CNS) via the pituitary–adrenocortical axis. The end result of long-standing vigilance frequently includes excess cortisol activity. An experiment of nature that illustrates the extreme case of cortisol effects is Cushing syndrome. In this setting, the three major causes of death are hypertension, atherosclerosis, and suicide. Cortisol is involved with effective CNS derangements (e.g., depression) as well as with significant cardiovascular disorders. The long-term effects of excess cortisol include elevated cholesterol and triglyceride levels, sodium retention, increased blood volume, reduced total body potassium stores (especially myocardial potassium), reduced ventricular ectopic thresholds, and increased sensitivity of arterioles to catecholamines.

The *short-term,* acute stress response of "fight or flight" is predominantly mediated by the CNS through the limbic system, the hypothalamus, and the adrenal medulla. This response raises catecholamine levels. The effects of increased catecholamines include elevated levels of cholesterol and free fatty acids, reduced ventricular fibrillatory thresholds, elevated blood pressure, destruction of muscle fiber cells (contraction band necrosis), and increased platelet adhesiveness, among others. The "experiment of nature" that illustrates the consequences of excessive catecholamine production is pheochromocytoma, a tumor of the adrenal medulla that frequently results in death due to "catecholamine myocarditis," ventricular arrhythmias, myocardial infarction, hypertensive crises, or sudden cardiac arrest.

ANIMAL STUDIES

Although animal models are cognitively less complex than their human counterparts, they leave little doubt that emotional stress can induce changes in cardiovascular physiology and promote pathophysiologic mechanisms. Work summarized by Mason (1968) has clearly demonstrated that psychosocial stimuli in animals can elicit at least two distinct neuroendocrine responses. Again, one major pathway involves arousal of the pituitary adrenal cortical system, and the other that of the sympathetic adrenal medullary system. Such arousals occur during confrontations between various members of the social group as they seek food, territory, and mates. Social interactions resulting in downward displacement in the hierarchy lead to stimulation of the pituitary–adrenocortical system, accompanied by mental depression, decreased gonadotropin levels, enhanced vagal activity, gluconeogenesis, and pepsin production (vigilance or playing-dead reaction). The sympathetic adrenal medullary system is called into play by more active competitive behavior (alarm reaction). Either response, when it is of sufficient magnitude and duration, can elicit pathophysiologic consequences.

For example, Henry and Ely (1979) have demonstrated that socially deprived mice, when introduced into a colony with an established hierarchy, develop a significant incidence of hypertension, myocardial hypertrophy, progressive arteriosclerosis, myocardial fibrosis, and renal failure. Aggressive and submissive behavior is attended, respectively, by distinct urinary excretion patterns of catecholamine or corticosteroid precursors and metabolites until social roles are firmly established. Once roles are established and accepted within the social hierarchy, excessive neuroendocrine activity ceases.

In a classic demonstration of sympathetic arousal, Von Holst (1972) introduced a subordinate male tree shrew into a cage with a dominant one. In every such pair the dominant animal immediately attacked, while the subordinate one submitted. Each subordinate was removed before he was injured and then placed so that he could see and hear the dominant animal without being attacked again. The emotionally aroused subordinate shrew invariably lay still, watching the dominant animal's every move 90% of the time. His tail hair remained erect, indicating sustained arousal. Within 2 to 16 days, all subordinate animals died of hypertension and renal failure, despite adequate food and water.

A study by Lapin and Cherkovich (1971) utilized Hamadryas baboons, which mate for life and form very strong attachments to their mates. After the original male was removed from the cage and placed in another cage in full view of his original habitat, a new male of the same age was moved into the original cage with the original female. Although neither the diet nor any other component of the experiment was changed, the original males developed hypertension, coronary insufficiency, or myocardial infarction within 6 months to a year.

Investigators have also separated swine from their littermates after primary social bonds were formed and subsequently demonstrated that the separated and isolated animals had a significantly greater incidence, extent, and severity of coronary atherosclerosis. During life, the isolated swine manifested obviously depressed behavior (Ratcliffe, Luginbuhl, Schnarr, & Chacko, 1969). New Zealand rabbits housed singly and later moved into crowded settings died prematurely with severe myocardial hypertrophy, suggesting the development of a catecholamine-induced cardiomyopathy (Weber & VanderWalt, 1973).

During avoidance conditioning, the animal is trained to avoid a punishing stimulus by making a designated response. Dogs have been trained to diminish coronary blood flow without alterations in systemic hemodynamics, demonstrating that coronary circulation can be controlled independently by the CNS during stressful behavioral contingencies (Ernst, Kordenat, & Sandman, 1979). In avoidance yoke procedures, both animals receive shocks at the same time, but only the avoidance animal has control over whether the shock will occur. Yoked helpless monkeys tend to show physical deterioration with severe bradycardia and ventricular arrest (playing-dead reaction), whereas the avoidance monkey develops ECG abnormalities and myocardial degenerative lesions (fight-or-flight reaction). Here it appears that the perceived element of control is the key difference leading to divergent pathologies (Corley, Mauck, & Shiel, 1975).

Animal experimentation indicates that environmental manipulations and circumstances can elicit physiologic responses, and that the nature of the responses is determined by the animal's perception of the social environment rather than by direct action of the stimulus on the individual. If emotional arousal is avoided, physical stressors, such as fasting, fail to elicit notable neuroendocrine responses (Mason *et al.,* 1976). For instance, fasted monkeys exposed to the sights and sounds of feeding by their cohorts develop marked increases in urinary cortisol excretion, whereas isolated monkeys provided non-nourishing fruit-flavored pellets show no increased cortisol excretion at all (Mason *et al.,* 1976). Thus, personal assessment of the social environment arouses emotions that produce physiologic consequences.

The fact that the same experimental design may produce different results in different species or, by altering time frames or options, produce different results in the same species indicates that the impact and countenance of psychologic stress is highly individual. Whether an event is stressful depends on a complex amalgam of variables, including genetic predisposition, early social experience, and a lifelong process of conditioning and inculturation. Considering the disproportionate size of neocortical structures in humans and the nearly limitless variety of human perspectives and behaviors, it is hardly surprising that clinical investigations linking emotional stress and cardiovascular disease have produced less conclusive results than animal studies. It is interesting that the prevalence of coronary heart disease and hypertension generally parallels the increasing complexity and ambiguities of social systems and hierarchies, whether we speak of animals or humans. Socioeconomic status, local crime rate, relocation, and overcrowding have all been linked with hypertension and heart disease.

MECHANISMS OF PATHOGENESIS

Hypertension

The cause of hypertension is identifiable in less than 10% of cases. Although many factors have been noted to elevate blood pressure experimentally, the precise etiology of essential hypertension is undefined. There is strong evidence of hereditary susceptibility, which is manifested only in combination with sustained stress, high salt load, or other factors (Falkner, Onesti, & Angelakos, 1981). Studies have indicated that 25% to 40% of patients with essential hypertension are characterized by higher basal circulating catecholamine levels and by higher sympathetic activity in response to postural changes. Work by Alexander (1950) suggests that the hypertensive personality may be described as an individual who frequently manifests inhibited and poorly expressed rage and anger. This inhibited rage turned inward may result in stimulation of the autonomic nervous system, with the subsequent release of significant amounts of norepinephrine. Esler and colleagues (1977) have reported that in psychometric testing, patients with high-renin hypertension exhibited suppressed hostility linked to increased sympathetic activity.

Coronary Atherosclerosis

At the present state of our understanding, it appears that the atherosclerotic process involves injury and proliferation of intimal smooth muscle cells, attachment of platelets, invasion of monocytes, and alterations in permeability and/or metabolism. Subsequent deposition of lipid material and fibrin reduces the arterial lumen and diminishes the flow. It tends to occur at points of turbulence, and the site of lesion formation suggests that hydrodynamic stress and shear forces participate in the process; the greater and more frequent the forces, the more rapid the evolution of the lesion. These findings are consistent with hypertension as a risk factor, and it is generally accepted that elevated blood pressure and increased shearing forces aggravate the development of atherosclerosis.

A second factor obviously aiding the atherosclerotic process is enhanced lipid availability. Stress is a factor in increasing both cholesterol and low-density lipoprotein levels. As early as the 1950s, Friedman, Rosenman, and Carroll (1958) demonstrated that certified public accountants who were followed from January 1 to April 15 had as much as a 100-mg/dl rise in serum cholesterol without a change in diet. Francis (1979) has shown that high-density lipoprotein (HDL) and low-density lipoprotein (LDL) ratios are consistently altered 10 days after stress. He found that cortisol levels in students peaked shortly after taking examinations, and that soon afterward LDL rose, while HDL fell. The flip side of the cholesterol picture also may be related to psychologic factors: Nerem, Levesque, and Cornhill (1980) showed that rabbits that were fondled and petted while on a high-cholesterol diet had a markedly lower rate of plaque formation than a matched group that was not fondled or petted.

There is additional evidence that cortisol could play a role in atherogenesis (Starkman, Schteingart, & Schork, 1981). Cortisol has been shown to increase the activity of catecholamines and synthesizing enzymes in the adrenal medulla, while inhibiting the activity of enzymes that break down catecholamines. Patients with more severe coronary atherosclerosis have been observed to have higher morning cortisol levels than patients with minimal or no disease. Ross and Harker (1976), as well as other investigators, have suggested that increased platelet adhesiveness such as that associated with stress and catecholamines, may be a factor in atherosclerotic sequelae.

Platelets are also suspected of playing a role in the pathophysiologic process. The growth factor identified in the alpha granules of platelets is a potent stimulator of smooth muscle proliferation (Kaplan, Chao, Stiles, Antoniades, & Scher, 1979). Although it cannot act while confined to the granules, the arrangement provides a specific delivery system and suggests the possibility of platelet involvement in intimal smooth muscle proliferation at sites of endothelial injury.

Arrhythmias and Sudden Death

A large number of experimental animal studies have strongly implicated psychologic stress in the precipitation of arrhythmias and sudden death. Human studies and clinical reports have also demonstrated that psychologic stress can precipitate significant rhythm disturbances (Buell & Eliot, 1981; Donlon, Meadow, & Amsterdam, 1979; Taggart, Carruthers, & Somerville, 1973; Taggart, Gibbons, & Somerville, 1969). Several reports have documented the effects of psychologic stress in lowering the threshold for ventricular fibrillation and sudden death both in animals and in humans (Engel, 1978; Lynch, Paskewitz, Gimbel, & Thomas, 1977).

By monitoring dogs in stressful and unstressful environments, Corbalan, Verrier, and Lown (1974) demonstrated that psychologic stress lowered the vulnerable period threshold for repetitive ventricular responses by 82%. After myocardial infarctions had been induced in these dogs, the stressful environment also provoked adverse ventricular arrhythmias, including ventricular tachycardia and early extrasystoles with T-wave interruption.

Since liberation of catecholamines appears to be a common phenomenon in stress situations, the administration of catecholamines has been utilized to duplicate the effects of stress seen in experimental animals. In dogs, the intravenous administration of catecholamines results in histopathologic features of myocardial necrosis that are similar, if not identical, to those observed in 82% of cases of sudden cardiac death in humans (Eliot, Clayton, Pieper, & Todd, 1977; Eliot, Todd, Clayton, & Pieper, 1978). This type of myocardial necrosis, termed *coagulative myocytolysis*, is characterized by the presence of anomalous contraction bands visible under ordinary staining techniques. Calcium overload of the myocardium is apparently a factor. In animal experiments, pretreatment with calcium channel blockers, particularly diltiazem, reduced the cardiotoxicity of noradrenaline infusion (Todd *et al.*, 1986).

Many years ago, Raab (1966) demonstrated that corticosteroid administration potentiated and augmented the myocardial degenerative influences of catecholamine administration in animals. These results strongly suggest that the combination of heightened sympathetic arousal following a protracted period of hopelessness and helplessness is a particularly lethal combination (Engel, 1978). The ability of psychologic stress to elicit such responses leading to sudden death has been documented in a variety of studies.

Myocardial Infarction

Myocardial infarction (MI) and ischemic heart disease are known to occur in the absence of any significant coronary atherosclerosis (Chahine, Zacca, & Verani, 1979; Likoff, Segal, & Kasparian, 1967). Currently the suspected mechanisms under discussion emphasize spasm. Evidence that ergonovine, methylcholine, or epinephrine plus propranolol can induce spasm in suspectible patients suggests that the neuroendocrine system may be involved in this instance. Chahine and colleagues (1979) and Oliva and Breckenridge (1977) have also demonstrated the presence of spasm during acute myocardial infarction.

The importance of coronary thrombosis as an initiating mechanism in myocardial infarction has been widely discussed and remains controversial. Whether thrombosis is a primary or secondary event is of less importance for this discussion than understanding the potential role the neuroendocrine system may play in increasing platelet adhesiveness. Various studies have demonstrated the ability of stress and the catecholamines to enhance platelet stickiness and aggregation. When vascular damage leads to platelet deposition in the endothelial wall, the vasoconstrictor thromboxane A2 is liberated and perhaps contributes to the development of coronary spasm. The studies of DeWood and colleagues (1980) showed that total coronary occlusion seen in the early hours of acute MI is less evident 12 to 24 hours after the onset of symptoms, suggesting that coronary spasm or thrombus formation or both may be important in the evolution of infarction.

ROLE OF BEHAVIOR

Type A behavior has been correlated with a significant increase in the incidence of coronary heart disease (CHD) and was accepted as a risk factor in the epidemiologic sense by the Coronary Prone Behavior Review Panel (Weiss, 1981). Lately its acceptance has met with considerable controversy as various studies (e.g., Haynes & Feinleib, 1982; Shekelle *et al.*, 1985) employing a variety of methods have failed to corroborate the original Western Collaborative Group Study (WCGS) report (Rosenman *et al.*, 1964). Dimsdale (1985) has reviewed the literature on this rather extensively.

Type A behavior may be described as an aroused state superimposed on a complex substrate of interrelated factors. Its identification is usually based on a structured interview and the evaluation of 22 stylistics of behavior and speech, and it is characterized by hostility, impatience, time urgency, and other characteristics. Some studies have reported that certain biochemical and physiologic phenomena are highly associated with fully developed type A behavior. These include elevated serum cholesterol levels; elevated preprandial and postprandial triglycerides; enhanced platelet aggregation; faster clotting time; higher excretion of norepinephrine, particularly when provoked by emotional challenge; a higher average serum level of corticotropin; a greater insulinemic response to glucose; a decreased growth hormone response to arginine; and greater lability and magnitude of blood pressure response under time-demand tasks (Friedman, Byers, Diamant, & Rosenman, 1975).

It is important to distinguish between type A behavior and the constantly evolving concept of coronary-prone behavior. For example, cultural determinants are likely to be important modifiers. The cross-cultural study of the type A–CHD relationship among Japanese Americans living in Hawaii (Cohen, Syme, Jenkins, Kagan, & Zyzanski, 1979) demonstrated that men who were culturally mobile and also type A had a two or three times greater risk of CHD than men with either characteristic alone. Of course, genetic, perceptive, and coping factors likely operate to counterbalance predisposing behavioral effects in many individuals. Furthermore, recent information suggests that only certain components of type A behavior, such as anger turned inward, correlate with coronary heart disease (Williams *et al.*, 1982).

If by "behavior" one means the actions or reactions of humans or animals under specified circumstances, the study by Dembroski, MacDougall, and Lushene (1979) illustrates one distinction between behavior in coronary patients and in noncoronary controls. During the type A structured interviews and a U.S. history quiz, the investigators noted increases in systolic blood pressure during the history quiz in type B coronary patients but not in type B controls. Indeed, the greatest increment of blood pressure change in either type A or type B groups was evoked in type B myocardial infarction patients during the U.S. history quiz. Such observations suggest the need to integrate the multifaceted aspects of overt behavior with those of cognition and physiologic behavior if we are to gain further understanding of how behavioral facets translate into coronary proneness.

Vaillant (1979) has published a 40-year prospective study of 95 healthy young men, which examined their modes of adaptation. He found that maturity of defensive style was powerfully protective against somatic illness. He described immature defenses as those that put responsibility for feelings, conflicts, and cognitive dissonance outside the user (e.g., paranoia, prejudice, hypochondria). He listed the most mature defenses as humor, altruism, sublimation, and suppression. Of 25 men who deployed predominantly mature defenses before age 47, 80% remained in excellent health after age 55. In contrast, only a third of the 31 men who characteristically deployed immature defenses before age 47 were still in excellent health at age 55: 11 had died or become disabled by chronic illness (e.g., congestive heart failure and multiple sclerosis). Even when the contributions of smoking, suicide, alcohol use, obesity, and age at death of parents and grandparents have been controlled for, correlations between the mode of psychologic defense and physical health remain significant.

In discussing his findings, Vaillant (1979) noted that mature defense mechanisms still distort and alter feelings, conscious relationships, and reality when confronted with stressful stimuli, but they perform this task gracefully and flexibly. "Perhaps mature defenses like humor and art, while defending against stress, more closely approximate reality than do projection and fantasy" (p. 2). He added that mature defenses are more socially acceptable and tend to bind people together, thereby reinforcing social supports, which, he pointed out, are correlated in important ways with health.

STRESS TESTING

To elucidate the relationship of stress and physiologic reactivity, it is necessary to define the somewhat ambiguous term "stress" and to use objective measurements. We define stress as a cause of emotional or physiologic strain, often resulting from a mismatch between what one would like to have happen and what the world delivers. It may become manifest as overt behavior (e.g., anger, hostility, or impatience), or it may be expressed only as covert endocrine, metabolic, and other physiologic reactions in a person who outwardly remains calm.

We have developed a system of testing that is designed to measure physiologic response to a variety of objective and standardized mental tasks that are similar to the mild stresses encountered in daily activities (McKinney *et al.*, 1985). The subject's hemodynamic responses are monitored via an oscillometric blood pressure unit, an impedance cardiographic system, and electrocardiography. Technicians in another room observe the patient on closed-circuit television and monitor his or her physiologic responses, while a computer calculates hemodynamic values.

The most fundamental of these tests is a modified tilt test during which ventricular function is examined. Hemodynamics, including stroke volume and total systemic resistance, are calculated during greater (supine) and lesser (erect) amounts of preload. The patient is studied in a reclining chair and is tilted progressively from supine to 45 degrees, to seated, and then to standing.

With the electronic video game "Breakout" by Atari, subjects are challenged to better their performance in each successive game. Other tests involve mental arithmetic (serially subtracting 7 from 777 as fast as possible in 3 minutes), and the cold pressor test in which the patient puts his hand into ice water for about 60 seconds.

The hemodynamic results indicate that serial subtraction and the video game tend to be beta-mediated tasks. We normally anticipate that patients will vasodilate or show no change in total systemic resistance during these tests. If blood pressure rises, it is primarily via cardiac output mechanisms.

The cold pressor test appears to be a vasoconstrictive or alpha-mediated task (Buhler, Bolli, Hulthen, Amann, & Kiowski, 1983), and has been proposed by Keys and his associates (1971) as predictive of coronary heart disease. The cold pressor test induces rather remarkable drops in cardiac output in some subjects through depression of stroke volume index. Although the cold pressor reflex is alpha-adrenergic-mediated and is a spinal reflex, higher cortical functions and emotions, such as fear or pain, may activate beta-adrenergic pathways as well, resulting in a decreased or absent vasoconstrictive response. Such subjects may actually show an increase in their cardiac output, primarily through tachycardia and beta-adrenergic influences. However, the usual cold pressor response demonstrates vasoconstriction and no change in heart rate, or a slight drop due to baroreceptor activation from increased pressure.

THREE TYPES OF REACTIVITY

Obviously, blood pressure and heart rate are not the only cardiovascular indicators of stress; cardiac output, stroke volume, and total systemic resistance must also be evaluated. Our testing, which addresses all these factors, has established three basic mechanisms of reactivity. Since BP = Flow × resistance, there are only three possible combinations of flow and resistance that can yield an increase in blood pressure.

Blood pressure can be elevated exclusively by cardiac output while total systemic resistance remains unchanged or even drops slightly ("output" reactors). At the other end of the spectrum, "vasoconstrictive" reactors experience increased blood pressure exclusively through vasoconstriction; with increased resistance and unchanged cardiac output, blood pressure goes up. The third type ("combined") results from contributions of both output and resistance.

We have found that some individuals are cool reactors (i.e., they have a normal cardiovascular response to stress); others—about 1 in 5 apparently healthy individuals—are hot reactors, with an abnormally increased cardiovascular response. It is impossible to determine who is a hot or cool reactor simply by observing the behavioral façade. With some people their surface behavior reflects their internal physiologic state; with others, it does not. These findings have important implications for the so-called type A and type B behavior patterns. In our experience, both type As and type Bs have been found to be hot reactors, and either type may be cool reactors. Indeed, type A behavior correlates with hot reacting on a .1-to-.3 basis, which at the most is unremarkable (Ruddel *et al.*, 1986).

Hot reacting does generally correlate, however, with elevated LDL cholesterol, with elevated triglycerides, and with a positive family history for hypertension or cardiovascular disease. Family history, of course, is known to be an important predictor of cardiovascular disorders. Whether the connection is nature or nurture is still unclear. Even those with good genetic backgrounds can develop heart problems (as I know from personal experience). Hot reacting also appears to predict elevated blood pressure in the workplace.

ROLE OF THE FAMILY

The life-style set by the family involves diet, coping strategies, self-esteem, hygiene, drug habits, and many other factors that can impinge on family members' health. Family effects on chronic illness, with special emphasis on cardiovascular disease, are discussed in detail in a later chapter in this section (see Venters, Chapter 21, this volume).

But one of the most important impacts of family life seems to be as provider of social support. Many studies have confirmed the protective effect of strong family ties on the health of members even when other risk factors are controlled. Conversely, the breakup of the family by death or divorce is often associated with increased occurrence of illness (Jacobs & Ostfeld, 1979).

In a review of the effects of social support, Broadhead *et. al.* (1983) conclude that neuropeptides, such as beta-endorphin, can act as stress buffers, and that these may be the biochemical mediators for the positive health attributes of social support.

Because of the interactions within a family, stress management for any member necessarily involves all family members. In counseling, it is helpful to identify the sources of stress for each member. These may have to do with work, with conflicting roles, or with unrealistic expectations. Behavioral modifications may require increased cooperation and support as well as attitude changes and new coping strategies. Certainly, if any member is already having health problems (such as recovering from a heart attack), family involvement is necessary to institute the necessary modifications in diet, stress reduction, and exercise. Indeed, in light of the familial susceptibility to many conditions, it would be in the self-interest of the whole family to adopt more healthful behavior. Books like *Is It Worth Dying For?* (Eliot & Breo, 1984) can be used by a family as a source of information for achieving a healthful life-style. From the point of view of primary prevention, imprinting of healthful habits in the young by family education is the best medicine. As Ben Franklin said, "The best sermon is example."

Acknowledgment

The author gratefully acknowledges the editorial assistance of Esther Adler, and the support of the International Stress Foundation and the Monsour Medical Foundation.

References

Alexander FW. Psychosomatic medicine, its principles and applications. New York: Norton, 1950.

Broadhead WE, Kaplan BH, James SA, Wagner EH, Schoenbach VJ, Grimson R, Heyden S, Tibblin G, Gehlbach SH. The epidemiologic evidence for a relationship between social support and health. American Journal of Epidemiology 1983; 117:521–537.

Buell, JC, Eliot RS. The clinical and pathological syndromes of sudden cardiac death. In: Solomon F, Parron DL, Dews PB, eds. Institute of Medicine Report, Biobehavioral factors in sudden cardiac death. Washington, D.C.: National Academy Press, 1981:13–28.

Buhler FR, Bolli P, Hulthen UL, Amann FW, Kiowski W. Alpha-adrenoreceptors, adrenaline, and exaggerated vasoconstrictor response to stress in essential hypertension. Chest 1983; 83:304–306.

Chahine RA, Zacca, N. Verani MS. Update on coronary artery spasm. Practical Cardiology 1979; 5:27–32.

Cohen JB, Syme SL, Jenkins CD, Kagan A, Zyzanski SJ. The cultural context of type A behavior and the risk of coronary heart disease: a study of Japanese American males. Journal of Behavioral Medicine 1979; 2:375–384.

Corbalan R, Verrier R, Lown B. Psychological stress and arrhythmias during myocardial infarction in the conscious dog. American Journal of Cardiology 1974; 34:692–696.

Corley KC, Mauck HP, Shiel F O'M. Cardiac responses associated with "yoked-chair" shock avoidance in squirrel monkeys. Psychophysiology 1975; 12:439–444.

Dembroski, TM, MacDougall JM, Lushene R. Interpersonal interaction and cardiovascular response in type A subjects and coronary patients. Journal of Human Stress 1979; 5:28–36.

DeWood MA, Spores J, Notske R, Mouser LT, Burroughs R, Golden MS, Lang HT. Prevalence of total coronary occlusion during the early hours of transmural myocardial infarction. New England Journal of Medicine 1980; 303:897–902.

Dimsdale JE. Controversies regarding type A behavior and coronary heart disease. Cardiology Clinics 1985; 3:259–268.

Donlon PT, Meadow A, Amsterdam E. Emotional stress as a factor in ventricular arrhythmias. Psychosomatics 1979; 20:233–240.

Eliot RS, Breo DL. Is it worth dying for? New York: Bantam Books, 1984.

Eliot RS, Clayton FC, Pieper GM, Todd GL. Influence of environmental stress on the pathogenesis of sudden cardiac death. Federation Proceedings 1977; 36:1719–1724.

Eliot RS, Todd GL, Clayton FC, Pieper GM. Experimental catecholamine-induced acute myocardial necrosis. In: Manninen V, Halonen PI, eds. Advances in cardiology, Vol. 25. Basel: S. Karger, 1978:107–118.

Engel GL. Psychologic stress, vasodepressor (vasovagal) syncope and sudden death. Annals of Internal Medicine 1978; 89:403–412.

Ernst FA, Kordenat, RK, Sandman CA. Learned control of coronary blood flow. Psychosomatic Medicine 1979; 41:79–85.

Esler M, Julius S, Zweifler A, Randall O, Harburg E, Gardiner H, DeQuattro V. Mild high-renin essential hypertension: neurogenic human hypertension? New England Journal of Medicine 1977; 296:405–411.

Falkner B, Onesti G, Angelakos E. Effect of salt loading on the cardiovascular response to stress in adolescents. Proceedings of the Interamerican Society: Suppl. II. Hypertension, 1981; 3:II-195–199.

Francis KT. Psychologic correlates of serum indicators of stress in man: a longitudinal study. Psychosomatic Medicine 1979; 41:617–628.

Friedman M, Byers SO, Diamant J, Rosenman RH. Plasma catecholamine response of coronary-prone subjects (type A) to a specific challenge. Metabolism 1975; 24:205–210.

Friedman M, Rosenman RH, Carroll V. Changes in the serum cholesterol and blood clotting time in men subjected to cyclic variation of occupational stress. Circulation 1958; 17:852–861.

Haynes SG, Feinleib M. Type A behavior and the incidence of coronary heart disease in the Framingham Heart Study. Cardiology (Switzerland) 1982; 29:85–94.

Henry JP, Ely DL. Physiology of emotional stress: specific responses. Journal of the South Carolina Medical Association 1979; 75:501–509.

Jacobs S, Ostfeld A. An epidemiological review of the mortality of bereavement. Psychosomatic Medicine 1979; 39:344–357.

Kaplan DR, Chao FC, Stiles CD, Antoniades HN, Scher CD. Platelet alpha granules contain a growth factor for fibroblasts. Blood 1979; 53:1043–1052.

Keys A, Taylor HL, Blackburn HW, Brozek J, Anderson J, Simonson E. Mortality and coronary heart disease among men studied for 23 years. Archives of Internal Medicine 1971; 128:201–214.

Lapin BA, Cherkovich GM. Environmental changes causing the development of neuroses and corticovisceral pathology in monkeys. In: Levi L, ed. Society, stress and disease: the psychosocial environment and psychosomatic diseases, Vol. I. London: Oxford University Press, 1971:266–279.

Likoff W, Segal BL, Kasparian H. Paradox of normal selective coronary arteriograms in patients considered to have unmistakable coronary heart disease. New England Journal of Medicine 1967; 276:1063–1066.

Lynch JJ, Paskewitz DA, Gimbel KS, Thomas SA. Psychological aspects of cardiac arrhythmia. American Heart Journal 1977; 93:645–657.

Mason JW. A review of psychoendocrine research on the pituitary adrenal cortical system. Psychosomatic Medicine 1968; 30:576–607.

Mason JW, Mather JT, Hartley LH, Mougey EH, Perlow MJ, Jones LG. Selectivity of corticosteroid and catecholamine responses to various natural stimuli. In: Serban G, ed. Psychopathology of human adaptation. New York: Plenum, 1976:147–171.

McKinney ME, Miner MH, Ruddel H, McIlvain HE, Witte H, Buell JC, Eliot RS. The standardized mental stress test protocol: test–retest reliability and comparison with ambulatory blood pressure monitoring. Psychophysiology 1985; 22(4):453–463.

Nerem RM, Levesque MJ, Cornhill JF. Social environment as a factor in diet-induced aortic atherosclerosis in rabbits. Science 1980; 208:1475–1476.

Oliva PB, Breckenridge JC. Acute myocardial infarction with normal and near normal coronary arteries. American Journal of Cardiology 1977; 40:1000–1007.

Raab, W. Emotional and sensory stress factors in myocardial pathology. American Heart Journal 1966; 72:538–564.

Ratcliffe HL, Luginbuhl H, Schnarr WR, Chacko K. Coronary arteriosclerosis in swine: evidence of a relation to behavior. Journal of Comparative and Physiological Psychology 1969; 68:385–392.

Rosenman RH, Friedman M, Straus R, Wurm M, Kositchek R, Hahn W, Werthessen NT. A predictive study of coronary heart disease: The Western Collaborative Group Study. Journal of the American Medical Association 1964; 189:15–22.

Ross, R, Harker L. Hyperlipidemia and atherosclerosis. Science 1976; 193:1094–1100.

Ruddel H, Langewitz W, McKinney ME, Todd GL, Buell JC, Eliot RS. Hemodynamic responses during the type A interview: a comparison with mental challenge and a clinical interview. Journal of the Autonomic Nervous System (Suppl.) 1986; 685–688.

Shekelle RB, Hulley SB, Neaton JD, Billings JH, Borhani NO, Gerace TA, Jacobs DR, Lasser NL, Mittlemark MB, Stamler J. The MRFIT behavior pattern study: II. Type A behavior and incidence of coronary heart disease. American Journal of Epidemiology 1985; 122:559–570.

Starkman MN, Schteingart DE, Schork MA. Depressed mood and other psychiatric manifestations of Cushing's syndrome: relationship to hormone levels. Psychosomatic Medicine 1981; 43:3–18.

Taggart P, Carruthers M, Somerville W. EKG, plasma, catecholamines and lipids and their modification by oxprenolol when speaking before an audience. Lancet 1973; 2:341–346.

Taggart P, Gibbons, D. Somerville W. Some effects of motor car driving on the normal and abnormal heart. British Medical Journal 1969; 4:130–134.

Todd GL, Sterns DA, Plambeck RD, Joekel CS, Eliot RS. Protective effects of slow channel calcium antagonists on noradrenaline induced myocardial necrosis. Cardiovascular Research 1986; 20:645–651.

Vaillant GE. Natural history of male psychologic health: effect of mental health on physical health. New England Journal of Medicine 1979; 301:1249–1254.

Von Holst D. Renal failure as the cause of death in Tupaia belangeri (tree shrews) exposed to persistent social stress. Journal of Comparative and Physiological Psychology 1972; 78: 236–273.

Weber HW, VanderWalt JJ. Cardiomyopathy in crowded rabbits: a preliminary report. South African Medical Journal 1973; 47:1591–1595.

Weiss S. Coronary-prone behavior and coronary heart disease: a critical review. Proceedings of a panel sponsored by the National Heart, Lung, and Blood Institute. Circulation 1981; 63:1199–1215.

Williams RB Jr, Lane JD, Kuhn CM, Melosh W, White AD, Schanberg SM. Type A behavior and elevated physiological and neuroendocrine responses to cognitive tasks. Science 1982; 218:483–485.

20

Insulin-Dependent Diabetes Mellitus

MARK B. MENGEL
University of Oklahoma

WHO'S IN CONTROL?

The title of this section of the chapter represents the central question of diabetes management. Previous biomedical research has shown that it is clearly not the pancreas that is in control. Insulin-dependent diabetes mellitus (IDDM) is a chronic disease in which the pancreas no longer responds to physiologic stimuli, such as hyperglycemia, by secreting insulin (Gerich, 1986). The pancreas, probably because of autoimmune destruction of islet cells (Eisenbarth, 1986), no longer performs this crucial homeostatic role with regard to carbohydrate and fat metabolism. With the pancreas out of the control picture, it falls to the patient to provide the necessary mechanisms to regulate carbohydrate and fat metabolism.

Unfortunately, the patient is often a poor pancreas. Despite physicians' warnings that poor diabetic control may lead to more complications (Pirart, 1978), and despite instructions on proper diet, exercise, and monitoring behavior, only a minority of patients with IDDM can maintain excellent control (Goldstein *et al.*, 1980). Physicians have responded to this distressing circumstance by developing even more intensive methods of therapy and by continually emphasizing strict adherence to the treatment regimen (Mecklenberg *et al.*, 1982; Sulway, Tupling, Webb, & Harris, 1980). Yet, even these additional measures have not been fully successful in achieving better control (Daneman *et al.*, 1982; Mecklenberg *et al.*, 1985). Clearly, the patient–physician pair, though a slightly better pancreas than the patient alone, is still not totally satisfactory.

In an attempt to find the best substitute pancreas, diabetes researchers have been gradually expanding the context of their studies. Numerous early studies in what is a deep and rich literature postulated a relationship between control and various individual factors, such as knowledge of diabetes, various personality factors, and compliance behavior (Greydanus & Hoffman, 1979; Johnson *et al.*, 1982; Menninger, 1935). Later studies have dispelled the myth of the diabetic personality and have not shown a relationship between personality factors, knowledge of diabetes, or compliance and diabetic control (Etzwiler & Robb, 1972; Hamburg & Inoff, 1982; Johnson, 1980; Schafer, Glasgow, McCaul, & Dreher, 1983; Simonds, Goldstein, Walker, & Rawlings, 1981). Given these conflicting results and the growing sentiment among diabetes researchers that patients are not out of control solely because they are ignorant, uncooperative, or immature, studies examining the role the diabetic patient's family plays in control issues have appeared (Anderson & Auslander, 1980).

Because of this wider context, research paydirt has been struck. Viewing patients in the context of their families does seem to give us a better understanding of diabetic control. Insight has been gained into the mechanisms through which family factors may affect diabetic control. It is our purpose to review the literature that supports the foregoing claim and to propose areas for future study. As this literature contains studies that usually include only children and adolescents with diabetes, this review will be restricted to that age group. Space requirements preclude what might prove a fruitful expansion of the context of this discussion. Thus, the effects of the doctor–patient relationship, the patient's social/cultural system, and the overall health care system on diabetic control will not be discussed. The reader is referred to recent reviews that discuss those issues (Hanson & Henggeler, 1984; Holmes, 1986).

Literature Review

Research on the family of the diabetic is best viewed from a systemic perspective. Like the role of the pancreas in carbohydrate metabolism, the role of the diabetic's family can be viewed as homeostatic in terms of the functioning of the diabetic patient. Like the pancreas, which secretes insulin in response to hyperglycemia and stops when blood glucose has returned to normal, the diabetic's family, in response to stimuli that indicate that the individual diabetic is acting abnormally, can change its pattern of behavior in an attempt to normalize the diabetic member's behavior (Watzlawick, Beavin, & Jackson, 1968). Unfortunately, sometimes such interaction patterns become rigidified and only perpetuate the problem rather than leading to normalization of behavior (Watzlawick, Weakland, & Fisch, 1974). When such rigidification occurs, the family as a homeostatic mechanism breaks down, and the patient's behavior—and his or her diabetes, as we shall see from the literature—can spiral out of control.

Viewed systematically, the family functions best as a homeostatic mechanism under the following circumstances:

1. The boundary between the family and the outside world is semipermeable, meaning that information passes freely but selectively between the family and its community.
2. Parents form a family subsystem in which adult needs are fulfilled, agreement on child-rearing functions is mutual, both parents take an active and cooperative role in child rearing, and children are not involved in parental conflict.
3. Children form a family subsystem in which they are not forced to behave inappropriately given their developmental stage, and in which they receive an appropriate amount of parental support to ensure adequate growth and development.
4. Interactions both among and within subsystems are flexible and involve communication patterns that are clear and direct (Lewis, Beavers, Gossett, & Phillips, 1976; Minuchin, 1974).

From this theoretical base, researchers have attempted to measure the aforementioned family dynamics to see if impairment in any of these dynamics is associated with poor diabetic control.

It seems that is is. Diabetic patients from families with abnormal family dynamics do seem to be in poorer control than diabetics from families with more normal dynamics. Anderson, Miller, Auslander, and Santiago (1981) divided 58 adolescent diabetics into groups with "good," "fair," or "poor" control, based on levels of glycosylated hemoglobin, and noted an association between good control and less family conflict, greater family cohesion, more encouragement of adolescent independence, and greater parental involvement. Shouval, Ber, and Galatzer (1982) conducted a similar study on 97 diabetics

Table 20-1. Family Factors Associated with Good Diabetic Control

First author	Family factors
Anderson (1981)	Less family conflict, greater family cohesion, more encouragement of adolescent independence, greater parental involvement
Shouval (1982)	Clear family organization, good father support
Grey (1980)	Better family functioning
Cedarblad (1982)	Better adaptability and less anxiety in mother
Marrero (1982)	Less controlling father
White (1984)	Better family functioning
Koski (1977)	Healthier families
Minuchin (1978)	Not psychosomatic

Source: Adapted from Campbell (1986).

and noted an association between good control and two factors: clear family organization and good father support. Grey, Genel, and Tamborlane (1980) studied 20 preadolescent diabetics and noted an association between good control and on overall measure of family functioning. Others less well designed cross-sectional studies have noted similar associations (see Table 20-1) (Cedarblad, Helgesson, Larsson, & Ludvigsson, 1982; Marrero, Lau, Golden, Kershnar, & Myers, 1982; White, Kolman, Wexler, Polin, & Winter, 1984). Unfortunately, as Campbell (1986) has noted in his recent review of the literature on this subject, causality cannot be inferred from such cross-sectional work.

The only cohort study of diabetic control in adolescents and their families was done by Koski and Kumento (1977). Although they did note an initial association between diabetic control and family functioning, unfortunately they did not study the change in control over their 5-year follow-up period as it related to baseline family functioning. They did note an anecdotal association between a decrease in control and stressful life events in the family.

Additional evidence comes from nonrandomized treatment trials. Minuchin, Rosman, and Baker (1978) treated 15 adolescent diabetics from psychosomatic families with family therapy for 4 to 12 months. Psychosomatic families, as defined by Minuchin and colleagues (1975), exhibit five salient characteristics: (1) enmeshment, (2) overprotectiveness, (3) rigidity, (4) lack of conflict resolution, and (5) involvement of the child in parental conflict via triangulation. As the dysfunctional aspects of family life were corrected, chronic ketonuria, hospitalizations for ketoacidosis, and insulin dosages were reduced or ceased. Orr, Golden, Myers, and Marrero (1983) treated 8 out of 15 adolescent diabetics in poor control, who were referred to a tertiary-care center, with individual, group, or family therapy. He stated that family emotional factors accounted for poor control in half of his patients. After treatment, hospitalizations for ketoacidosis were reduced and psychosocial functioning improved, but levels of glycosylated hemoglobin were unchanged.

Although numerous review articles have concluded that, given the above evidence (Anderson & Auslander, 1980; Hanson & Henggeler, 1984; Holmes, 1986), a relationship exists between family dynamics and diabetic control, the lack of well-designed cohort studies and randomized, controlled trials of the effect of family therapy on diabetic control leaves others in doubt (Campbell, 1986). In addition, exactly *how* poor family functioning leads to poor diabetic control is unknown. Currently, two theories have been developed to explain the relationship between family functioning and diabetic control. The first theory states that family dysfunction adversely affects diabetic control via a hyper-responsive neuroendocrine system that develops as a result of the chronic effects of family stress (Minuchin *et al.*, 1975; Tarnow & Silverman, 1981–1982). The second theory states that family factors affect diabetic control via their effect on compliance behavior (Schafer *et al.*, 1983).

Evidence for the first theory comes from the physiology of the human neuroendocrine system and from several research reports. The sympathoadrenal system, through secretion of epinephrine by the adrenal gland, is the one neuroendocrine system thought to be hyper-responsive in out-of-control diabetes (Christensen, 1974; Cryer, 1980). Epinephrine, which is secreted in response to stress, not only has hemodynamic effects but also results in lipolysis, ketogenesis, gluconeogenesis, and reduced glucose clearance from the circulation, all effects antagonist to insulin (Cryer, White, & Santiago, 1986). High levels of epinephrine have been found in diabetic patients in ketoacidosis, and several case reports have linked psychosocial stress with increased epinephrine secretion and ketoacidosis (MacGillivray, Bruck, & Voorhess, 1981; Schade & Eaton, 1980; Schless & Von Laveran-Stiebar, 1964). Minuchin and colleagues (1978) have examined the physiologic responsiveness of the neuroendocrine system in three different groups of diabetics when exposed to a stressful family interview. Diabetic adolescents from enmeshed families experienced a marked rise in free fatty acid levels in response to family stress, an effect not observed in diabetics from normal or other types of families. They concluded that these adolescent diabetic patients, who had become overinvolved in their parents' problems, subsequently developed a hyper-responsive neuroendocrine system, which led to frequent attacks of ketoacidosis. By involving the child in their conflicts, parents were able to reduce their own anxiety and levels of free fatty acids.

The work of Minuchin, Rosman, and Baker (1978) has been criticized because it has never been formally published, involved small numbers of patients (fewer than 10 subjects in each group), and used no statistical analysis (Campbell, 1986). Additional contradictory evidence emerged from a well-designed study by Kemmer and colleagues (1986). They studied the response of the neuroendocrine system to acute psychologic stress (mental arithmetic and public speaking) in 9 normal subjects, 9 type 1 diabetic patients with normoglycemia, and 9 diabetic patients with hyperglycemia. They found that short-term stress, although it causes a marked cardiovascular response and elevation in levels of plasma epinephrine, norepinephrine, and cortisol, is unlikely to disturb metabolic control. Unfortunately, they did not study the possible effects of a more chronic stressor, such as abnormal family dynamics, on physiologic responsiveness and metabolic control in those diabetic patients.

As previously stated, the diabetic's family may affect diabetic control via an effect on diabetic adherence behavior. The fact that treatment of diabetes may disrupt family routines and that other family members (usually parents) are often asked to supervise treatment are two theoretical reasons that family dynamics may affect diabetic compliance (Doherty & Baird, 1983; see also Becker, Chapter 29, this volume).

Unfortunately, even though studies in adults with other diseases show a positive and strong relationship between supportive family behaviors and adherence to medical treatment (Campbell, 1986; Doherty & Baird, 1983), the few studies examining the relationship between family factors, adherence, and metabolic control in adolescent diabetics show inconclusive results (Drash, 1981; Schafer *et al.*, 1983; Wishner & O'Brien, 1978). A recent study of this issue, by Schafer, McCaul, and Glasgow (1986), reveals the problems in this research. These investigators studied 54 adults and 18 adolescents with IDDM. Adherence was assessed by self-report, as no laboratory measures of diabetic compliance exist. Supportive family behaviors were also assessed by self-report questionnaire at the time of induction into the study, and again 6 months later. Adolescents were in poorer control than adults by glycosylated hemoglobin measures; adolescents also reported more negative family interactions than did adults, but this was not linked to adherence behavior or control 6 months later. In adults, negative family interactions were associated with poor adherence behavior, but that was only weakly associated with poorer control.

Theoretical Speculations and Suggestions for Future Research

An understanding of the family as a homeostatic organization (i.e., playing a role similar to that of the pancreas in carbohydrate metabolism), which regulates the behaviors of its members and affects diabetic control either through its effects on the diabetic patient's neuroendocrine system or through compliance behavior, or both, is supported by the reviewed empiric studies. Flaws and criticisms of these studies preclude stronger causal statements and should encourage all those interested in this field to continue their research. Well-designed prospective cohort studies examining the effects of changes in family dynamics on diabetic control are definitely needed. In addition, randomized, controlled trials of family therapy in families with a diabetic member are needed, and would provide the strongest causal links if it could be shown that normalization of family dynamics led to improved diabetes control in the family therapy group while no such change occurred in a group that did not receive the family therapy interventions.

These encouragements aside, how can the results of these empiric studies be blended with current family systems concepts to yield a stronger theory of how family factors affect diabetic control? Such a blend seems possible using Bowen's (1978) family systems theory, developmental theory, and the concept of triangulation.

Bowen's theory postulates that a family's interaction patterns have a profound effect on the emotional state, behavior, and maturity (or differentiation) of its members. Normal interaction patterns (those described under the second paragraph of the literature review section) lead to psychologic stability (and probably to physiologic stability as well) and to the maturity of the family member. Bowen and others have identified one abnormal family interaction pattern—the pathologic triangle—that has been linked with emotional distress; with symptom formation; and, in diabetic patients, with being out of control (Haley, 1977; Hoffman, 1981; Vogel & Bell, 1968; Weakland, 1976). Minuchin and colleagues (1975) demonstrated that psychosomatic families often participated in triangular interaction patterns that included detouring, coalitions, and scapegoating.

Triangular interaction patterns can develop in family system when any two members (dyad) become conflicted (Hoffman, 1981). A natural responses in such a conflicted, dyadic emotional system is for one member, usually the weaker, to seek an ally. With the addition of this ally to the dyad, a triangle (triadic emotional system) is formed. Upon resolution of the conflict, often because the ally maintains good relations with both warring members, the triangle dissolves. However, if the conflict continues, or becomes submerged, this triadic emotional system becomes stabilized and rigid. If such an unresolved conflict develops between two parents, with the child becoming involved as an ally of one parent, or as a scapegoat of both, devastating psychologic and physiologic consequences for the child can result.

These consequences result because triangulation (1) retards the child's developmental process and precludes identity formation (differentiation) (Bell & Bell, 1982), and (2) results in the child becoming involved in parental conflict (Minuchin *et al.*, 1978). Minuchin and colleagues have shown that the anxiety of the parental conflict literally gets transferred to the child, with the child's sympathetic nervous system hyper-reacting and poor diabetic control developing.

Although the second consequence of triangulation seems to have more "stress" implications, the first has more compliance implications. Child development progresses on a continuum from totally dependent and enmeshed with parents to more independent, but still connected to parents (Erikson, 1963). As children progress along this continuum, they are expected to assume more and more responsibility for their actions. For diabetic children, this naturally includes assuming more responsibility for the management of their diabetes (Newbrough, Simpkins, & Mauver, 1985). Should this natural development process be stopped or impeded, as it might be if an unresolved conflict developed between parents, noncompliance under the guise of acting out or behavior difficulties may result (Henggeler, 1982; Sullivan, 1979). This is particularly noticeable in adolescents, as issues of impulse control and independence are paramount during that stage of development (Conger, 1973). Diabetic adolescents who are involved in a triangular interaction pattern can use their diabetes to gain independence denied them by failing to inject their insulin or by eating high-carbohydrate foods, an activity often supported by peers or even, covertly, by the family members themselves (Stein, 1985).

It may be, as Sargent (1985) has noted in his longitudinal study of 50 newly diagnosed diabetics at the Philadelphia Child Guidance Clinic, that the development of poor control in diabetic children is also on a developmental continuum depending on the strength of triangulation. Stronger triangulation—true psychosomatic families—results in poor control due to the transfer of stress phenomena, and seems to freeze the child at a mid-childhood level of development. Weaker triangulation—families with the psychosomatic family characteristics of rigidity, parental conflict, and either overprotectiveness or abandonment—results in poor control due to compliance problems and freezes the child at an early adolescent stage of development. Weaker triangulation (14 of 50) was more common than stronger triangulation (1 to 50) in his prospective study of newly diagnosed diabetic children, but both seemed amenable to family therapy. His indication for family therapy with diabetic patients are as follows: (1) poor compliance, (2) poor control, (3) poor physical functioning, (4) poor psychosocial adjustment, and (5) marked family strife.

In conclusion, widening the context in which we view diabetic control to include the family as a homeostatic organization to improve our understanding of the control issue. Correcting abnormal patterns of family dynamics that prevent normal family interactions, particularly triangulation, has great potential for lessening diabetic stress and improving compliance behavior. Clearly, the patient–family unit is still not quite as good as a healthy pancreas, but with future research focusing in more depth on family factors and treatment issues in well-designed longitudinal cohort and randomized, controlled trials, the answer to our first question—"Who's in control?"—should become clearer and the search for an even better substitute pancreas should be advanced.

THE INSULIN PUMP

Just as the first major section of this chapter expanded the context of control, this section will broaden the scope of studied outcome measures from a strictly biomedical perspective. Specifically, multiple areas of patient functioning will be defined, examined, and discussed with regard to a study of insulin-dependent diabetic patients' adaptation to the insulin pump in adults. These patients' adaptation to the insulin pump will then be related to their family system.

Quality of Life

Tarlow (1983) has suggested that medicine is moving into an era when the prevention of death or the correlation of physiologic abnormalities will not be the principal medical challenge. Rather, the new challenge for medicine in the coming years will be to maintain or improve the ability of the patient to function. This emphasis on quality-of-life issues has arisen because of the increasing costs of health care and the increasingly technical nature of medical practice, which, although it has produced spectacular biomedical successes, often serves to increase the emotional distance between doctor and patient (Reiser, 1984) and may adversely affect other areas of patient functioning or their overall quality of life (Anbar, 1984; Croog *et al.*, 1986).

Recently, Ware (1984) proposed to untangle the quality-of-life thicket by conceptualizing five areas of patient functioning—areas chosen because previous research has indicated their independence from one another. These are: (1) disease-specific functioning, (2) personal functioning, (3) psychologic distress/well-being, (4) general health perceptions, and (5) social role functioning. Disease-specific functioning is defined as those measurable physiologic parameters associated with the disease in question, such as blood glucose values in diabetes. Personal functioning is defined as the performance or capacity to perform the kinds of tasks that most people do every day, including self-care, mobility, and physical activities, as well as sexual function and cognitive function. Psychologic functioning refers to the feeling states of the individual patient and is divided into two concepts: psychologic distress (such as depression or anxiety) and well-being. General health perceptions are the individual's perception of his or her health based on the previous three areas: disease-specific, personal, and psychologic functioning. Even though they were associated with the previous three areas of patient functioning, Ware felt that general health perceptions were sufficiently independent to justify a separate category. Social and role functioning is defined as the person's ability to perform activities associated with an individual's usual roles in society, including formal employment, schoolwork, or homemaking. A person's role within the family would fall into this category. Thanks to Ware and many other researchers in the field, valid and reliable instruments are available to measure patient functioning in each of these five areas (Berke, Connis, Gordon, & Taylor, 1983).

Characteristics of the Insulin Pump

As noted in the first part of this chapter, one way physicians have responded to the difficulty experienced by some diabetic patients as they attempt to normalize carbohydrate and fat metabolism is to develop ever more intensive methods of therapy. One such method, the insulin pump, has been shown to improve glucose control (Felig & Bergman, 1982; Mecklenberg *et al.*, 1982), yet the long-term dropout rate among pump users is unusually high (20% to 80%) (Deeb & Williams, 1982; Dupre, Champion, & Rodger, 1982). It is hypothesized that the demands of such an intensive insulin regimen (frequent blood glucose monitoring; management of pump problems such as skin infections, tube blockages, and pump malfunction; and vigilance over diet and exercise) so impair the patient's functioning

Table 20-2. Patient Functioning Instruments

Level	Instrument	Measurement interval
1	Glycosylated Hemoglobin (Berke, Connis, Gordon, & Taylor, 1983)	Quarterly
	Fasting Blood Glucose (Berke, Connis, Gordon, & Taylor, 1983)	Monthly
2	Duke–UNC Health Profile (Parkerson *et al.*, 1981)	Biannually
	Pump Problem Checklist (Berke, Connis, Gordon, & Taylor, 1983)	Monthly
3	Spielberger State–Trait Anxiety (Spielberger, Gorsuch, & Lushene, 1970)	Biannually
	Rand Mental Health Inventory (Ware, Johnston, Davies-Avery, & Brook 1979)	Monthly
4	Rand General Health Perceptions Index (Ware, Davies-Avery, & Donald, 1978)	Quarterly
	DCCT Quality of Life (Diabetes Control and Complications Trial Research Group, 1985)	Biannually
	Health Locus of Control (Wallston, Wallston, & DeVellis, 1978)	Annually
5	Health and Daily Living Form (Moos, Cronkite, Billings, & Finney, 1983)	Biannually

in other areas that he or she will choose to sacrifice diabetic control in order to regain functioning in previously impaired areas.

Adaptation to the Insulin Pump

In an effort to investigate the foregoing hypothesis, a long-term prospective study of diabetic patients on the insulin pump was initiated by investigators in the Department of Family Medicine at the University of Washington (Gordon & Taylor, 1986). Patient functioning was measured over one year using previously validated and reliable instruments (Table 20-2). Although the final results of that study are not fully known, preliminary results indicated wide variability in measures of patient functioning over time (Elford *et al.*, 1986). Because of those results, a subset of that study was formed in which functioning over 6 months was assessed in patients beginning pump therapy. A group of diabetic patients on conventional insulin therapy, matched on age, sex, duration of diabetes, and complications of diabetes, was used as a control group. Following the assessment of patient functioning, family dynamics and social support were measured using Olson, Portner, and Lavee's (1985) Family Adaptability and Cohesion Evaluation Scales III (FACES III) and Cooke, Rossman, McCubbin, and Patterson's (1984) Social Support Inventory (SSI). This retrospective cohort study was supported by literature that has linked family systems concepts and social support with multiple areas of patient functioning (Ahlfield, Soler, & Marcus, 1985; Anderson & Auslander, 1980; Billings & Moos, 1982; Broadhead *et al.*, 1983; Hanson & Henggeler, 1984; Hauser, Herskowitz, Jacobson, & Wolfsdorf, Chapter 33, this volume; Schafer *et al.*, 1986; Stone, Bluhm, & White, 1984; Vallient, 1977).

This study showed that personal functioning improved in diabetic patients initiating pump therapy (as did glycemic control), but family social activities declined (Mengel, Connis, Gordon, & Taylor, 1988). This decline among pump patients was mediated by more balanced family dynamics. In other words, patients in the midranges of the cohesion and adaptability scales of FACES III lost less in terms of family social activities than did patients from the extremes of the cohesion (enmeshed, disengaged) and adaptability (rigid, chaotic) scales. It appears that initiating pump therapy, though resulting in improvement in the patient's biomedical and personal functioning, is associated with the patient's withdrawal from family social life in order to cope with the demands of pump use.

This study also showed that initiating pump therapy did not impair psychologic functioning; but changes in psychologic functioning that occurred among all diabetic patients in this sample were associated with measures of social support (more social support was linked with better 6-month psychologic functioning). This association was consistent with our hypotheses. However, the association of family dynamics with psychologic functioning in all diabetic patients in this sample was not in a direction consistent with theory. Specifically, more balanced family dynamics were associated with a deterioration in psychologic functioning, whereas patients whose families had more extreme family dynamics remained stable or improved.

In order to explain this surprising finding, the authors turned to the work of Reiss, Gonzalez, and Kramer (1986) and family systems theory (Hoffman, 1981). Reiss and colleagues found that adult patients with chronic renal failure died sooner after the start of renal dialysis if they were from families with more resources than did similar patients who were from families with fewer resources. Reiss and colleagues postulated that the patients from these relatively wealthier families saw the drain on family resources caused by their conditions, became distressed at this, and withdrew from family life, dying earlier to prevent further family losses, whereas patients from poorer families did not see such a drain, as few resources existed anyway, and so lived a more natural life span given their disease.

Likewise, diabetic patients from families that are more balanced dynamically may perceive the loss of family social activities that occurs with pump use and become distressed, whereas diabetic patients from families that are less well balanced dynamically may not notice the loss, either because of the denial that is known to exist in such families (Minuchin *et al.,* 1978) or because family social activities are already so poor. Thus, as Reiss and colleagues 1986 concluded, it is not so much the absolute structure, resources, or dynamics of the family alone that determine outcome, but, rather, the fit between the challenges and demands facing the family and the resources and dynamics the family has available with which to cope. Perceived losses in family social life thus appear to be relative. If a well-balanced family becomes overloaded, it appears that the individual will sacrifice him- or herself to preserve family resources, rather than risk destruction of the family. This may explain the high dropout rate associated with pump use.

Should this finding and the hypothesized link with dropout rate prove true in future studies, it has profound treatment implications for diabetic patients beginning insulin pump therapy. It appears that regardless of resources, and dynamics, if the diabetic's family is overwhelmed by the demands of this intensive therapy, supportive therapy is in order. The family must be taught how to find additional resources and new ways to cope with this crisis of adaptation. This substantially widens the context of therapy to include not only those families with poor resources and less well balanced dynamics, but also those families with more balanced dynamics who are facing challenges that outstrip their resources.

It is also interesting to speculate on why individuals from relatively "rich" families would sacrifice their own health in an attempt to preserve family resources. It may be something as simple as postulating a hierarchy of satisfactions, in which the rewards of family life so outweigh the rewards of good health that the individual's choice becomes obvious. A recent survey of where people obtained the most satisfaction in life concluded that the family was the primary source, just before television and friends (American Family

Physicians, 1986). On the other hand, the explanation may be as complex and strange to the notion of American individuality as the theory of "kin selection" in which the individual sacrifices him- or herself for the good of the family and society if such a sacrifice significantly increases the chance of a successful transmission of his or her genetic material into future generations (Hamilton, 1964; Wilson, 1980). Sacrificing health in order to maintain family resources may be one way that an ill member can increase the chances of successful genetic propagation.

In conclusion, this section has demonstrated the importance of widening the context of outcome measures to include nonbiomedical measures of patient functioning. Such a widened context will help us, as practitioners of the art of family systems medicine, to understand the competing and difficult choices our patients must make and how the patient's family and sources of social support affect those decisions. In the example cited, after 6 months of insulin pump therapy diabetic patients had a choice between family social activities versus continued improved control over their diabetes. Viewing such a choice through narrow biomedical glasses may result in the dismissal of the patient as noncompliant if the patient chooses the family over diabetic control. On the other hand, widening the context allows us to see and respect the difficult balancing act our patients often must negotiate to improve their health, and may enable us as practitioners to respect that choice and support them in their decision.

CONCLUSION

An attempt was made in this chapter to expand the narrow biomedical framework within which we often view diabetic patients to include family systems concepts. Such concepts not only improve our understanding of what affects diabetic control, but also illuminate the wider area of patient functioning. Even though detractors of this wider context can justly criticize the infantile state of this research, enough promising results have been generated to encourage investigators to design the prospective cohort studies and randomized trials of family therapy needed to convince the wider medical community. If earlier results are replicated, the potential benefit to diabetic patients could be enormous, not only in terms of a lower diabetic complication rate resulting from improved glycemic control, but in terms of improved patient functioning as well.

References

Ahlfield, JE, Soler NG, Marcus, SD. The young adult with diabetes: impact of the disease on marriage and having children. Diabetes Care 1985; 8(1):52–56.

American Family Physician. Quantum sufficit. American Family Physician 1986; 34(5):23.

Anbar M. Biological bullets: side effects of health care technology. In: Reiser SJ, Nabar M, eds. The machine at bedside: strategies for using technology in patient care. New York: Cambridge University Press, 1984:35–45.

Anderson BJ, Auslander WF. Research on diabetes management and the family: a critique. Diabetes Care 1980; 3(6):696–702.

Anderson BJ, Miller JP, Auslander WF, Santiago J. Family characteristics of diabetic adolescents: relationship to metabolic control. Diabetes Care 1981; 4:586–594.

Bell LG, Bell DC. Family climate and the role of the female adolescent: determinants of adolescent functioning. Family Relations 1982; 31:519–527.

Berks PA, Connis RT, Gordon MJ, Taylor TR. Selection of instruments for measuring patient functioning (Technical Report no. 1). Seattle: Department of Family Medicine, University of Washington, 1983.

Billings, AG, Moos RH. Social support and functioning among community and clinical groups: a panel model. Journal of Behavioral Medicine 1982; 5(3):295–305.

Bowen M. Family therapy in clinical practice. New York: Jason Aronson, 1978.

Broadhead WE, Kaplan BH, James SA, Wagner EH, Schoenback VJ, Grimson R, Heyden S, Tibblin G, Gehlbach SH. The epidemiologic evidence for a relationship between social support and health. American Journal of Epidemiology 1983; 117(5):521–536.

Campbell TL. Family's impact on health: a critical review. Family Systems Medicine 1986; 4:135–328.

Cedarblad M, Helgesson M, Larsson Y, Ludvigsson J. Family structure and diabetes in children. Pediatric Adolescent Endocrinology 1982; 10:94–98.

Christensen NJ. Plasma norepinephrine and epinephrine in untreated diabetics, during fasting and after insulin administration. Diabetes 1974; 23:1–8.

Conger JJ. Adolescence and youth: psychological development in a changing world. New York: Harper & Row, 1973.

Cooke BD, Rossman MM, McCubbin HI, Patterson JM. Measuring social support: application to parenthood. Unpublished manuscript, 1984.

Croog SH, Levine S, Testa MA, Brown B, Bulpitt CJ, Jenkins D, Klerman GL, Williams GH. The effects of antihypertensive therapy on the quality of life. New England Journal of Medicine 1986; 314(26):1657–1664.

Cryer PE. Physiology and pathophysiology of the human sympathroadrenal neuroendocrine system. New England Journal of Medicine 1980; 303:436–444.

Cryer PE, White NH, Santiago JV. The relevance of glucose counter-regulatory systems to patients with IDDM. Endocrine Reviews 1986; 7:131–139.

Daneman D, Epstein L, Siminerio L, Beck S, Farkas G, Figueroa J, Becker DJ, Drash AL. Effects of enhanced conventional therapy on metabolic control in children with insulin-dependent diabetes mellitus. Diabetes Care 1982; 5:472–478.

Deeb LC, Williams PE. Premature mortality from diabetes. Journal of Florida Medical Association 1982; 69(2):1004–1008.

Diabetes Control and Complications Trial Research Group. The DCCT quality of life measure: a preliminary study of reliability and validity. Unpublished manuscript, The DCCT Coordinating Center, Bethesda, Md., 1985.

Doherty WJ, Baird MA. Family therapy and family medicine. New York: Guilford Press, 1983.

Drash AL. Psychological and behavioral aspects of diabetes mellitus in the child. Behavioral Medicine Update 1981; 2:18–20.

Dupre J, Champion M, Rodger NW. Advances in insulin delivery in the management of diabetes mellitus. Clinics in Endocrinology and Metabolism 1982; 11(2):525–548.

Eisenbarth GS. Type I diabetes mellitus—a chronic autoimmune condition. New England Journal of Medicine 1986; 314:1360–1368.

Elford RW, Connis RT, Taylor TR, Gordon MJ, Liljenquist JE, Mecklenberg RS, Stephens JW, Baker M. Assessment of the impact of new medical technologies on patients (the insulin pump experience). Unpublished manuscript, Department of Family Medicine, University of Washington, Seattle, 1986.

Erikson EH. Childhood and society. New York: Norton, 1963.

Etzwiler DD, Robb JR. Evaluation of programmed education among juvenile diabetics and their family. Diabetes 1972; 21:967–971.

Felig P, Bergman M. Intensive ambulatory treatment of insulin dependent diabetes. Annals of Internal Medicine 1982; 97:225–230.

Gerich J. Insulin-dependent diabetes mellitus: pathophysiology. Mayo Clinic Process 1986; 61:787–791.

Goldstein DE, Walker B, Rawlings SS, Hess RL, England JD, Peth SB, Hewett JE. Hemoglobin A1C levels in children and adolescents with diabetes mellitus. Diabetes Care 1980; 3:503–507.

Gordon MJ, Taylor TR. Patient adaptation to insulin therapy in the first twelve months. Seattle: Department of Family Medicine, University of Washington, July 1986.

Grey MJ, Genel M, Tamborlane WV. Psychosocial adjustment of latency-age diabetes: determinants and relationship to control. Pediatrics 1980; 65:69–73.

Greydanus DE, Hoffmann AD. Psychological factors in diabetes mellitus. American Journal of Diseases of Children 1979; 133:1061–1066.

Haley J. Toward a theory of pathological systems. In: Watzlawick P, Weakland J, eds. The interactional view. New York: Norton, 1977:31–49.

Hamburg BA, Inoff GE. Relationship between behavioral factors and diabetic control in children and adolescents: a camp study. Psychosomatic Medicine 1982; 44:321–339.

Hamilton WD. The genetic theory of social behavior. Journal of Theoretical Biology 1964; 7:1–52.

Hanson CL, Henggeler SW. Metabolic control in adolescents with diabetes: an examination of systemic variables. Family Systems Medicine 1984; 2:5–16.

Henggeler SW, ed. Delinquency and adolescent psychopathology: a family–ecological systems approach. Littleton, Mass.: John Wright–PSG, 1982.

Hoffman L. Foundations of family therapy. New York: Basic Books, 1981.

Holmes DM. The person and diabetes in psychosocial context. Diabetes Care 1986; 9:194–206.

Johnson SB. Psychosocial factors in juvenile diabetes: a review. Journal of Behavioral Medicine 1980; 3:95–116.

Johnson SB, Pollak RT, Silverstein JH, Rosenbloom AL, Spillar R. McCallum M, Harkavy J. Cognitive and behavioral knowledge about insulin-dependent diabetes among children and parents. Pediatrics 1982; 69:708–713.

Kemmer FW, Bisping R. Steingruber JH, Baar H, Hardtmann F, Schlaghecke R, Berger M. Psychological stress and metabolic control in patients with type 1 diabetes mellitus. New England Journal of Medicine 1986; 314:1078–1084.

Koski ML, Kumento A. The interrelationship between diabetic control and family life. Pediatric Adolescent Endocrinology 1977; 3:41–45.

Lewis JW, Beavers R, Gossett JT, Phillips VA. No single thread. New York: Brunner/Mazel, 1976.

MacGillivray MH, Bruck E, Voorhess ML. Acute diabetic ketoacidosis in children: role of the stress hormones. Pediatric Research 1981; 15:99–106.

Marrero DG, Lau N, Golden MP, Kershnar A, Myers GC. Family dynamics in adolescent diabetics mellitus: parental behavior and metabolic control. Pediatric Adolescent Endocrinology 1982; 10:77–82.

Mecklenberg RS, Benson EA, Benson JW, Blumenstein BA, Fredlund PN, Guinn TS, Metz RJ, Nielsen RL. Long-term metabolic control with insulin pump therapy: report of experience with 127 patients. New England Journal of Medicine 1985; 313:465–468.

Mecklenberg RS, Benson JQ, Becker NM, Brazel PL, Fredlund PN, Metz RJ, Nielsen RL, Sannar CA, Steenrod WJ. Clinical use of the insulin infusion pump in 100 patients with type 1 diabetes. New England Journal of Medicine 1982; 307(9):513–518.

Mengel MB, Connis RT, Gordon MJ, Taylor TR. The relationship of family dynamics and social support to personal, emotional, and social functioning in diabetic patients on the insulin pump. Family Systems Medicine 1988; 6(3):317–334.

Menninger WC. Psychological factors in the etiology of diabetes. Journal of Nervous Mental Disease 1935; 8:1–13.

Minuchin S. Family and family therapy. Cambridge, Mass.: Harvard University Press, 1974.

Minuchin S, Baker L, Rosman BL, Liebman R, Milman L, Todd TC. A conceptual model of psychosomatic illness in children: family organization and family therapy. Archives of General Psychiatry 1975; 32:1031–1038.

Minuchin S, Rosman BL, Baker L. Psychosomatic families. Cambridge, Mass.: Harvard University Press, 1978.

Moos RH, Cronkite RC, Billings AG, Finney JW. Health and Daily Living Form manual. Palo Alto, Calif.: Social Ecology Laboratory, 1983.

Newbrough JR, Simpkins CG, Mauver H. A family development approach to studying factors in the management and control of childhood diabetes. Diabetes Care 1985; 8:83–92.

Olson DH, Portner J, Lavee Y. Family Adaptability and Cohesion Scales (FACES) III. Department of Family Social Science, University of Minnesota, St. Paul, 1985.

Orr DP, Golden MP, Myers G, Marrero DG. Characteristics of adolescents with poorly controlled diabetes referred to a tertiary care center. Diabetes Care 1983; 6:170–175.

Parkerson GR, Gehlbach SH, Wagner EH, James SH, Clapp NE, Muhlbaier LH. The Duke–UNC Health Profile: an adult health status instrument for primary care. Medical Care 1981; 19(8):806–828.

Pirart J. Diabetes mellitus and its degenerative complications: a prospective study of 4,400 patients observed between 1947 and 1973. Diabetes Care 1978; 1:168–188; 252–263.

Reiser SJ. The machine at the bedside: technological transformation of practice and values. In: Reiser SJ, Anbar M, eds. The machine at the bedside: strategies for using technology in patient care. New York: Cambridge University Press, 1984:3–19.

Reiss D. Gonzalez S, Kramer N. Family process, chronic illness and death: on the weakness of strong bonds. Archives of General Psychiatry 1986; 43:795–804.

Sargent J. Journal of Juvenile Diabetes Mellitus: Control, development, and the family. Presented at the Conference on Research on the Family System in Family Medicine, San Antonio, Texas, January 13–16, 1985.

Schade DA, Eaton RP. The temporal relationship between endogenously secreted stress hormones and metabolic decompensation in diabetic man. Journal of Clinical Endocrinology Metabolism 1980; 50:131–136.

Schafer LC, Glasgow RE, McCaul KD, Dreher M. Adherence to IDDM regimes: relationship to psychological variables and metabolic control. Diabetes Care 1983; 6:493–498.

Schafer LC, McCaul KD, Glasgow RE. Supportive and nonsupportive family behaviors: relationship to adherence and metabolic control in persons with type 1 diabetes. Diabetes Care 1986; 9(2):179–185.

Schless GL, Von Laveran-Stiebar R. Recurrent episodes of diabetic acidosis precipitated by emotional stress. Diabetes 1964; 13:419–420.

Shouval R, Ber R, Galatzer A. Family social climate and the health status and social adaption of diabetic youth. Pediatric Adolescent Endocrinology 1982; 10:89–93.

Simonds J, Goldstein D, Walker B, Rawlings S. The relationship between psychological factors and blood glucose regulation in insulin-dependent diabetic adolescents. Diabetes Care 1981; 4:610–646.

Spielberger CD, Gorsuch RL, Lushene RE. Manual for the State–Trait Anxiety Inventory. Palo Alto, Calif.: Consulting Psychologists Press, 1970.

Stein HF. The contest of control: a case of diabetes mellitus in multiple context. In: The psychodynamics of medical practice. Berkeley: University of California Press, 1985:113–142.

Stone JB, Bluhm HP, White MI. Correlates of depression among long-term insulin-dependent diabetics. Rehabilitation Psychology 1984; 29(2):85–93.

Sullivan BJ. Adjustment in diabetic adolescent girls: II. Adjustment, self-esteem, and depression in diabetic adolescent girls. Psychosomatic Medicine 1979; 41:127–138.

Sulway M, Tupling H, Webb K, Harris G. New techniques for changing compliance in diabetes. Diabetes Care 1980; 3:108–111.

Tarlov AR. Shattuck lecture—the increasing supply of physicians, the changing structure of the health-services system, and the future practice of medicine. New England Journal of Medicine 1983; 308:1235–1244.

Tarnow JD, Silverman SW. The psychophysiologic aspects of stress in juvenile diabetes mellitus. International Psychiatry in Medicine 1981–1982; 11:25–44.

Vallient GE. Adaptation to life. Boston: Little, Brown, 1977.

Vogel EF, Bell NW. The emotionally disturbed child as the family scapegoat. In: Bell NW, Vogel EF, eds. The family. New York: Free Press, 1968:382–397.

Wallston KA, Wallston BS, DeVellis R. Development of the multidimensional health locus of control scales. Health Education Monographs 1978; 6(2):160–170.

Ware JE. Conceptualizing disease impact and treatment outcome. Cancer 1984; 53(Suppl.):2316–2322.

Ware JE, Davies-Avery A, Donald CA. Conceptualization and measurement of health for adults in the health insurance study: Vol. V. General health perceptions (R-1987/5-HEW), Santa Monica, Calif.: Rand Corporation, 1978.

Ware JE, Johnston SA, Davies-Avery A, Brook RH. Conceptualization and measurement of health for adults in the health insurance study: Vol. III. Mental health (R-1987/3-HEW). Santa Monica, Calif. Rand Corporation, 1979.

Watzlawick P, Beavin J, Jackson D. Pragmatics of human communication. New York: Norton, 1968.

Watzlawick P, Weakland J, Fisch R. Change: principles of problem formation and problem resolution. New York: Norton, 1974.

Weakland J. The double bind hypothesis of schizophrenia and three-party interactions. In: Sluzki C, Ransom D, eds. Double bind: the foundation of the communicational approach to the family. New York: Grune & Stratton, 1976:23–37.

White K, Kolman ML, Wexler P, Polin G, Winter RJ. Unstable diabetes and unstable families: a psychosocial evaluation of diabetic children with recurrent ketoacidosis. Pediatrics 1984; 73:749–755.

Wilson EO. Sociobiology. Cambridge, Mass.: Harvard University Press, 1980.

Wishner WJ, O'Brien MD. Diabetes and the family. Medical Clinics of North America 1978; 62:849–856.

21

Chronic Illness and the Family:
The Example of Cardiovascular Disease

MAURINE VENTERS
University of Minnesota

> The modern family lives in a greater state of tension precisely because it is the great burden carrier of the social order. In a society of rapid social change, problems outnumber solutions, and the resulting uncertainties are absorbed by the members of society, who are for the most part also members of families. Because the family is the bottleneck through which all troubles pass, no other association so reflects the strains and stresses of life. With few exceptions persons in work-a-day America return to rehearse their daily frustrations within the family, and hope to get the necessary understanding and resilience to return the morrow to the fray. Thus, the good family today is not only the focal point of frustrations, but also the source for resolving frustrations and releasing tensions. (Hill, 1949, p. i)

Clinicians, behavioral scientists, epidemiologists, and others have explored the role of the family in relation to health and illness (Litman, 1974; Schmidt, 1978). Characteristics of the family unit have been considered in relation to the etiology, care, and treatment of cystic fibrosis (McCollum & Gibson, 1970; Turk, 1964; Venters, 1981; Wood, Boat, & Doershuk, 1976), arthritis (Ferguson & Bole, 1979; Oakes, Word, Gray, Klauber, & Moody, 1970), asthma (Dubo *et al.*, 1961; Purcell *et al.*, 1969), diabetes (Anderson & Auslander, 1980; Crain, Sussman, & Weil, 1966; Johnson, 1980), spina bifida (Freeston, 1971), myelomeningocele (Hunt, 1973), and other chronic physical conditions. Relatively few studies have considered the dynamics of family life-style in relation to the development of chronic physical disease, which is the focus of this review. Pertinent information, however, is available from investigations with other aims.

Today, chronic disease is the greatest contributor to adult morbidity and mortality rates in the industrial world. Development of chronic disease is frequently gradual, over several years, with the physiologic effects not appearing until middle age (Lilienfeld, 1980). This is true of cardiovascular disease (CVD); the leading cause of death and disability in the United States (Blackburn & Gillum, 1980). Family clusters of CVD suggest that etiology may be related to genetic factors, environmental factors common to family members, or the interaction of genetic factors with environmental factors (tenKate, Boman, Daiger, & Motulsky, 1982). Environmental factors that increase risk for CVD also cluster within certain families. Some families are better able than others, for example, to absorb stress experienced by individual members (Venters, 1981). This is as true today as it was when Reuben Hill (1949) first published the preceding quote. Researchers have shown a significant association between elevated levels of stress and certain types and indicators of CVD, such as hypertension (Cobb & Rose, 1973; D'Atri & Ostfeld, 1975; Harburg, Schull, Erfurt, & Schork, 1970; Kasl & Cobb, 1970; Scotch, 1960; Winkelstein, Kagan, Kato, & Sacks, 1975; Worth, Kato, Rhoads, Kagan, & Syme 1975), catecholamine elevations, hyperlipidemia, and hyperglycemia (Cryer, 1980; Dimsdale & Moss, 1980; Eliot & Forker, 1976; Fitzgerald, Hossmann, & Dollery, 1981; Goldstein, 1981). This review uses a family systems approach to explore family environmental factors as they relate to cardiovascular risk in light of the potential for prevention of CVD.

Broderick and Smith (1979) have noted that the development of family systems theory (Hill, 1971) is still in its infancy in its ability to predict and explain empirical issues. Concepts derived from a family systems approach, however, can be used to organize information for "grounded mid-range hypothesizing." Family systems concepts arise from viewing the family as a social system—a system whose members continually interact to maintain family boundaries, work toward goals, and maintain a functional equilibrium between stability and growth (Hill, 1971). In order to generate hypotheses for future testing and suggest preventive strategies, this chapter will examine findings from behavioral, clinical, and epidemiologic studies that suggest a relationship between family environmental factors and levels of cardiovascular risk characteristics.

The following interrelated propositions will serve as a guide to organize this review:

1. Cardiovascular risk factor status is influenced by life-style practices, demographic characteristics, and behavioral factors that reflect the family environment.
2. Information about family characteristics can be used to promote the effectiveness of strategies to prevent CVD.

THE FAMILY ENVIRONMENT AND CARDIOVASCULAR RISK

Viewing the family as a social system directs attention to the interdependence of family members: The behavior of one family member influences the behavior of other family members. As a result, family members are interdependent in their daily life-style practices and behaviors. This interdependence is further reinforced by the "boundary maintenance" characteristic of families. Over time, families maintain semiclosed boundaries, which unite individual members and differentiate the family environment from the broader cultural environment. As a result, members share similar demographic characteristics and a similar family history (Hill, 1971).

Family Life-style Practices: Eating, Physical Activity, and Smoking

Congruent evidence from clinical and experimental disciplines has shown that such factors as elevated blood pressure, elevated serum cholesterol, cigarette smoking, obesity, and family history of CVD are predictors of elevated risk of incidence of CVD (Blackburn & Gillum, 1980). Several of these risk factors are influenced by eating, physical activity, and smoking practices, all that occur in the family environment. Dietary intake of sodium and potassium, for example, has been related to levels of blood pressure (MacGregor, 1983). Dietary intake of saturated fat has been associated with levels of serum cholesterol and lipoprotein (Glueck & Connor, 1978), blood pressure (Puska *et al.*, 1983), and obesity (Stunkard, 1980). Regular physical activity has been related to changes in serum lipoproteins (Haskell, 1984), reduced body fat (Thompson, Jarvie, Lahey, & Cureton, 1982), and prevention of hypertension (Paffenbarger, Wing, Hyde, & Jung, 1983). Similarity among family members in terms of these life-style practices is suggested by studies that show that initiation of adolescent smoking is significantly related to parental smoking patterns (U.S.

Public Health Service [USPHS], 1982). Childhood overeating and obesity are related to biologic- and adopted-parent overeating and obesity (Garn & Clark, 1976). Finally, matched married couples are more likely than chance to share similar smoking patterns (Venters, Jacobs, Luepker, Maiman, & Gillum, 1984). Thus, effective individual strategies to prevent CVD necessitate consideration of the individual's family life-style.

Family Psychosocial Factors: Demographic and Behavioral Characteristics

Less conclusive but possibly equally important is the relationship of family psychosocial factors and CVD. Practitioners have observed a significant association between individual psychosocial factors and the development of cardiovascular disease. Researchers, however, have been more skeptical of this association because of the difficulty of measuring non-biological variables. This methodologic weakness has delayed rigorous research that could account for at least part of the cause of CVD that still remains unexplained (Jenkins, 1976a, 1976b, 1978). Behavioral variables may themselves be risk factors. Type A behavior, for example, has been shown to be significantly associated with CVD incidence, prevalence, recurrence, and underlying atherosclerotic pathology (Jenkins, Rosenman, & Zyzanski, 1974; Review Panel on Coronary-Prone Behavior and Coronary Heart Disease, 1981). Behavioral variables may also act synergistically with physiologic risk factors. Such potentially stressful situations as culture change (Scotch, 1960; Winkelstein *et al.*, 1975; Worth *et al.*, 1975), job loss (Kasl & Cobb, 1970), pressures faced by air traffic controllers (Cobb & Rose, 1973), living in crowded penal institutions (D'Atri & Ostfeld, 1975), and living in high-crime neighborhoods (Harburg *et al.*, 1970) have been shown to have a significant association with hypertension. Sustained emotional stress has also been associated with catecholamine elevations, hyperlipidemia, and hyperglycemia (Cryer, 1980; Dimsdale & Moss, 1980; Eliot & Forker, 1976; Fitzgerald *et al.*, 1981; Goldstein, 1981).

Research identifying type A behavior as a cardiovascular risk factor represents an advanced form of behavioral research (Jenkins, 1978). Research identifying stress as a cardiovascular risk factor is less methodologically sound in terms of determining general validity and causal implications (Jenkins, 1978). Although a number of adequately controlled studies support the notion that painful life events increase risk for cardiovascular morbidity and mortality (Jenkins, 1971), most studies of life stress in relation to CVD have been retrospective, and, therefore, little can be said about strength of association and time sequence (Jenkins, 1978). Social support research has not been explored in relation to cardiovascular risk. Future studies exploring this relationship may provide insights into determinants of risk factor levels. Previous findings show a significant relationship between social support and all cause mortality rates (Berkman & Syme, 1979). Findings showed that the larger the number of social ties, the lower the mortality rates. Social support research, however, has been burdened by a lack of clarity of definitions used for social support, as well as problems in conceptualizing its effects on health outcomes (Schaefer, Coyne, & Lazarus, 1981).

FAMILY DEMOGRAPHIC CHARACTERISTICS
Marital status (Venters, *et al.*, 1986), socioeconomic status (Khoury *et al.*, 1981; Liu *et al.*, 1982), and family size (Jenkins, 1976b) are shared family demographic variables that have been associated with cardiovascular risk. The health-related aspects of life-style to which these demographic indicators point may be the actual determinants of cardiovascular

risk. Stress, for example, may be one health-related aspect of family life that is associated with each of these family demographic variables. Stress could be expected to affect all family members. When individuals experience stress, their family, willing or not, shares their experience. A stressful situation could increase individual as well as family risk for CVD. Haynes, Eaker, and Feinleib (1983) provide evidence that family members do share stress by showing that married persons are more likely than chance to share their spouse's level of stress. Personal and situational stressors, such as worries about sex, change of life, money, family success problems, and marital disharmony, were shown to be highly correlated among matched husbands and wives. This spouse concordance was unaffected by husband's age or number of years married. These levels of stress were not analyzed by CVD rates or other indicators of long-term response.

Social support may be another aspect of family life that is associated with marital status as well as with family size. Married persons have been reported as receiving the most social support, never married and widowed persons as receiving less, and divorced individuals as receiving the least social support (Stephens, Blau, & Osler, 1978). Recent analysis of age/sex-adjusted data exploring a broad range of cardiovascular risk factors showed that separated/divorced men and women of all ages were more likely to smoke and less likely to quit than were married, never married, or widowed individuals of the same age and sex group (Venters et al., 1986). Social support has been identified as an aid in smoking cessation and maintenance of nonsmoking behavior (USPHS, 1982).

Studies of family size in relation to general health outcomes of individual family members show that for working mothers, rates of physical illness increase as the number of children in the family increases (Hare & Shaw, 1965; Kozlov, 1969). For all family members, Anderson and Kasper (1973) showed an inverse relationship between family size and use of health services. This relationship was independent of socioeconomic status, race, and geographic location.

Although large family size may not benefit the mother's health status, there may be some benefit for children's mental health status. Hare and Shaw (1965) showed that for children, rates of behavioral disorders increase steadily with family size up to 3 children, then decrease as the number of children continues to exceed 3 children. These findings suggest that working mothers with large families may lack access to emotional and practical support needed to manage child care tasks, and that members of large families may lack access to resources needed to utilize health care services. Children of large families, however, may benefit from a built-in network of social support within the family unit. This network may act as a buffer in dealing with daily stress-producing situations.

BEHAVIORAL FACTORS

Family Systems Theory (Hill, 1971) assumes that the behavior of one family member influences the behavior of other family members, an assumption that has not been studied fully in relation to cardiovascular risk behavior. One of the few existing studies is by Waldron and colleagues, (1980), who considered the possible effects of a shared family history by correlating type A scores of college students and parental behavioral characteristics. Type A college men were more likely than type B men to recall their fathers as having been more severe, having punished them more physically, and having made them feel resentful rather than guilty when punished. Type A women recalled their mothers as having punished them more often physically. These findings suggest that parental behaviors contribute to the development of anger and aggression, two important components of the type A behavior pattern.

INTERACTION EFFECTS OF PSYCHOSOCIAL FACTORS

The interaction effects of certain demographic and behavioral characteristics within the family setting may also influence risk for cardiovascular disease. Haynes and colleagues (1983), for example, explored the effect of spouse behavior on the development of coronary heart disease in men. Findings suggested that wives' educational level, employment status, and personal stress are associated with their partner's cardiovascular risk status. Using a select population in terms of age (45 to 64 years) and duration of marriage (90% married over 20 years), this study showed that men married to women with certain characteristics (e.g., high social and educational status, and employment in jobs with a nonsupportive boss) were significantly more likely to develop coronary heart disease. Eaker, Haynes, and Feinleib (1983) explored the possible mediating effects of spouse psychosocial characteristics on their husband's at-risk behavior. Findings showed a significant relationship between the educational level of wives and the behavior type of husbands. Type A men were more likely than type B to be married to women with 13 or more years of education.

In summary, this exploration of psychosocial factors in relation to cardiovascular risk factors provides further support for implementing prevention efforts within the context of family life-style.

IMPLICATIONS FOR PREVENTION OF CVD

The family systems approach directs attention to two interrelated family variables that could influence the effectiveness of efforts to prevent CVD: family life cycle stage and the degree of permeability of family boundaries.

Family Life Cycle Stage and Cardiovascular Health Education

The family life cycle has proved to be one of the most fruitful variables in explaining and predicting variation in families over time (Aldous, 1972; Burr, 1973; Hill & Rodgers, 1964; Straus, 1964). Family life cycle has been used to describe change in family structure (Duvall, 1971); occurrence of mental disorders (Belknap & Friedson, 1949); why families move (Rossi, 1955); change in family leisure activities (Cunningham & Johannis, 1960); family patterns of income, savings, and consumer behavior (Lydall, 1955); and family patterns of utilization of health care services (Anderson, 1968).

This conceptual approach expresses the family life span in eight distinctive life cycle stages, beginning with the coming together of the marital dyad, continuing through expanding family size through birth or adoption, then drawing apart as children leave home, and ending with divorce or the death of one parent and no remaining dependent children. Thus, the family is viewed as a system of developing and interacting personalities with a predictable history of normal growth and development. The family life cycle is further characterized by periods of transition accompanied by stress, as well as certain tasks and functions that must be accomplished successfully if the family is to survive and continue to be of benefit to its members (Hill & Rodgers, 1964).

Three basic family functions are of central concern to this discussion: the physical and emotional maintenance of family members, and the socialization of members for eventual placement in society. These three processes are most intense in the early stages of the family's life cycle, because of the demands of rearing young children (Aldous, 1972). The manner in which these functions are carried out could influence future development of cardiovascular risk factors. Adequate physical maintenance of family members, for example, could promote healthful patterns of eating and physical activity. Proper emotional maintenance could encourage the use of effective coping strategies to manage daily stress so that, for example, cigarette smoking or overeating need not be used as a means to deal with daily anxiety or tension. Conversely, since children's behavior is learned and reinforced by imitating their parents through the socialization process, the damaging parental modeling effects of a smoking parent, or of one who is sedentary or who indulges in an inappropriate diet, could be expected to increase the children's probability of eventually developing their own unhealthful life-style. Researchers, in fact, have expressed concern that continually eating high-fat convenience foods, smoking cigarettes, maintaining sedentary physical behavior, and engaging in a time-pressured life-style are patterns into which certain segments of the population are socialized at very young ages, even though the physiologic effects may not occur until middle age (Blackburn & Gillum; 1980).

Although family life cycle stage has not been specifically studied in relation to cardiovascular health education efforts, insights into family health promotion behavior are provided by family studies exploring decision-making behavior by life cycle stage. For families (Pratt, 1976) as well as individuals (Becker, 1974; Rosenstock, 1960), health promotion behavior has been associated with planful behavior and future orientation. Hill (1965) related planning and future orientation of families to family life cycle stage by comparing the economic decision making of three generations of related family units; the adult-child generation, their middle-aged parents, and their grandparents. Findings showed that of the three generations, newly formed families were most likely to plan before taking action, a process that resulted from decision making based on a systematic search for new information. Families in the stage of rearing school-age and adolescent children were more focused on meeting present needs, whereas families whose children had left home made the fewest attempts to structure the future. Thus, it could be expected that families in the early years of family life would be more likely than those in the later years to accept new health information. This acceptance might be directed toward developing tastes and preferences for foods included in a prudent diet, as well as integrating into daily life physical activities that would benefit their present and future health status.

The early years of marriage have also been characterized as a time of mutual participation in household tasks and egalitarian decision making. As time passes, segregation of household jobs occurs, and wives gain in decision-making power concerning family matters (Hill, 1958). Health information accepted in the early years of marriage would therefore be more likely to represent shared decisions and practices. Later in the marriage life cycle, one spouse alone might decide and attempt to implement a more healthful diet or exercise regime. The early years of family life have also been typified as a time of shared activities and interests, especially in the form of mutual participation in recreation outside the home. At this time, attempts to establish a pattern of physical activity would be most likely to be enjoyed by the whole family. As each child is added to the family unit, there is a decrease in joint recreational participation and family members' activities become more sharply differentiated. After children have left home, couples do not return to the extensive joint organization of the earlier phase, even when the need for differentiation produced by the presence of young children is no longer so great (Bott, 1957). Thus, it would appear that certain characteristics of young families establish this period as an ideal time for promoting the effectiveness of health education efforts intended to prevent development of cardiovascular risk factors.

This hypothesis is further supported by a growing body of evidence showing that primary prevention efforts are most effective for children when begun in the preschool years of life within the context of the child's family (Berenson *et al.*, 1976; Venters & Mullis, 1984). Strategies to promote healthful life-styles for this age group have been limited in number and effectiveness (Coates & Thoresen, 1978). Only a few programs, for example, have attempted to modify obesity in young children by altering family life-style. These attempts yielded limited success (Aragona, Cassady, & Drabman, 1975; Wheeler & Hess, 1976), possibly as a result of lack of consideration of family eating and exercise patterns, as well as family values and beliefs (Venters & Mullis, 1984). The family determines its members' health practices and beliefs (Litman, 1974). One effective prevention strategy, suggested for future testing, is to direct health education efforts toward the family life-styles of preschool children and newly formed families.

Family Boundaries and Cardiovascular Health Education

A second effective prevention strategy suggested for future study is for health educators to assess the degree of permeability of family boundaries (Broderick & Smith, 1979; Hill, 1971), and to use a compatible approach in relating to the family. Since families select information and ideas that are permitted entry into the family circle for processing and action, measuring the degree of openness of family boundaries to new health information and ideas could serve as a partial predictor of response to health education efforts. Health educators could promote their effectiveness by using different approaches based on the degree of permeability of family boundaries.

Families who frequently interact with their community are more likely than socially isolated families already to function effectively in the use of medical care and preventive services and to encourage health promotion behavior in their children (Pratt, 1976). Health educators could be most helpful to these families by acknowledging their attempts to work toward the goal of promoting health and by directing them to appropriate community resources. Health educators could then be helpful by guiding the transformation of new information within the family circle into appropriate family life-styles.

A more challenging situation for health educators is that of the socially isolated family. For continued growth and viability of the family unit, as well as the psychologic health of individual members, there must be continuing outside involvement with the broader community, involvement that promotes growth and change (Beavers, 1976; Miller, 1978). Families whose boundaries are closed to outside influence are more resistant to change (e.g., to promoting new and more healthful life-styles). Living in isolation for many years with other family members who share certain eating, physical activity, and smoking practices, as well as interdependent emotional responses, provides support for continuing the damaging behaviors and acts as a buffer against change. Health educators could be most helpful to such isolated families by encouraging increased contact with outside sources of health information, which would provide support for changes toward more healthful life-styles. Informational support (defined as access to helpful information or advice by Schaefer, Coyne, & Lazarus, 1981) is one dimension of social support. Social support research suggests that the type and amount of support derived form social contacts may vary for each family member. Men are most likely to benefit from support found in the workplace; women are most likely to benefit from support provided by relatives (Holahan & Moos, 1981). Women, however, are more likely than men to benefit from social support (Berkman & Syme, 1979; Billings & Moos, 1981; Holahan & Moos, 1981; Miller & Ingham, 1976). Health educators relating to socially isolated families could be expected to maximize their effectiveness by working with female family members as the family representative and by using the health resources of employment contacts and extended family members.

CONCLUSION

Results of previous studies have suggested that family environmental factors influence the development of CVD. However, the degree of certainty with which casual association can be inferred is not the same for all such factors. The evidence that family practices of eating, physical activity, and smoking contribute to the development of CVD is strong. Less clear, but possibly equally important, is the role of family demographic and behavioral factors, which may serve as indicators of level of family stress and social support. It is hypothesized for future study that the effectiveness of prevention efforts could be enhanced by two strategies—first, by focusing efforts on the family life style of preschool children and newly formed families, and, second, by considering the degree of permeability of the family boundary and using an appropriate approach to increase family access to community resources and information that provide support for healthful family life-styles.

Acknowledgment

This chapter is dedicated to the memory of Reuben Hill, who first introduced the preceding family concepts to the author.

References

Aldous J. The developmental approach to family analysis: the conceptual framework. Mimeographed. Minneapolis: Department of Sociology, University of Minnesota, 1972:90–152.

Anderson BJ, Auslander WF. Research on diabetes management and the family: a critique. Diabetes Care 1980; 3:696–702.

Anderson R. A behavioral model of families' use of health services. Research Series #25, Chicago Center for Health Administration Studies, University of Chicago, 1968.

Anderson R, Kasper JD. The structural influence of family size on children's use of physician services. Journal of Comparative Family Studies 1973; 4(1):116–130.

Aragona J, Cassady J, Drabman R. Teaching overweight children through contingency contracting. Journal of Applied Behavior Analysis 1975; 8:269–280.

Beavers WR. A theoretical basis for family evaluation. In: Lewis JM, Beavers WR, Gossett Jr, Phillips VA, eds. No single thread: psychological health in family systems. New York: Brunner/Mazel 1976:46–82.

Becker MH. The health belief model and personal health behavior. Thorofore, N.J.: Chas. B. Slack, Inc., 1974:27–59.

Belknap I, Friedson H. Age and sex categories as sociological variables in the mental disorders of later maturity. American Sociological Review 1949; 14:367–376.

Berenson GS, Frank GC, Hunter SM, Srinivansan SR, Voors AW, Webber LS. Cardiovascular risk factors in children: should they concern the pediatrician? American Journal of Diseases of Children 1976; 136:855–886.

Berkman LF, Syme SL. Social networks, host resistance and mortality: a nine-year follow-up study of Alameda County residents. American Journal of Epidemiology 1979; 109:186–204.

Billings, AG, Moos RH. The role of coping responses and social resources in attenuating the stress of life events. Journal of Behavior Medicine 1981; 4:139–157

Blackburn H, Gillum R. Heart disease. In: Last JM, ed. Maxcy-Rosenau public health and preventive medicine. New York: Appleton-Century Crofts, 1980:1168–1201.

Bott E. Family and social network. London: Tavistock, 1957.

Broderick C. Smith J. The general systems approach to the family. In: Burr W, Hill R, Nye F. Reiss I, eds. Contemporary theories about the family, Vol. II. New York: Free Press, 1979:112–129.

Burr W. Theory construction and the sociology of the family. New York: Wiley, 1973:218–233.

Coates, T, Thoresen C. Treating obesity in children and adolescents: a review. American Journal of Public Health 1978; 68:143–151.

Cobb S, Rose RM. Hypertension, peptic ulcer and diabetes in air traffic controllers. Journal of the American Medical Association 1973; 224:489–492.

Crain JA, Sussman MB, Weil WB. Effects of a diabetic child on marital integrations and related measures of family functioning. Journal of Health Behavior 1966; 7:122–127.

Cryer PE. Physiology and pathophysiology of the human sympathoadrenal neuroendocrine system. New England Journal of Medicine 1980; 303:436–444.

Cunningham K, Johannis T. Research on the family and leisure: a review and critique of selected studies. Coordinator 1960; 9:25–32.

D'Atri DA, Ostfeld AM. Crowding: its effects on the elevation of blood pressure in a prison setting. Preventive Medicine 1975; 4:550–556.

Dimsdale J, Moss J. Plasma catecholamines in stress and exercise. Journal of the American Medical Association 1980; 243:340–342.

Dubo S. McLean JA, Ching AYT, Wright HL, Kaufman PE, Sheldon JM. A study of relationships between family situation, bronchial asthma, and personal adjustment in children. Journal of Pediatrics 1961; 59:402–414.

Duvall E. Family development, 4th ed. Philadelphia: Lippincott, 1971:106–132.

Eaker, E. Haynes S, Feinleib M. Spouse behavior and coronary heart disease in men: prospective results from the Framingham Heart Study, Part II. American Journal of Epidemiology 1983; 118:23–41.

Eliot R, Forker AD. Emotional stress and cardiac disease. Journal of the American Medical Association 1976; 236(20):2325–2326.

Ferguson K, Bole GG. Family support, health beliefs, and therapeutic compliance in patients with rheumatoid arthritis. Patient Counseling and Health Behaviors 1979; 16:101–105.

Fitzgerald GA, Hossmann V, Dollery CT. Norepinephrine release in essential hypertension. Clinical Pharmacology Therapy 1981; 30:164–171.

Freeston BM. An inquiry into the effect of a spina bifida child upon family life. Developmental Medicine and Child Neurology 1971; 13:456–461.

Garn, SM, Clark DC. Trends in fatness and the origins of obesity. Pediatrics 1976; 57:443–456.

Glueck CJ, Connor WE. Diet–coronary heart disease relationships reconnoitered. American Journal of Clinical Nutrition 1978; 31:727–737.

Goldstein DS. Plasma norepinephrine in essential hypertension. Hypertension 1981; 3:48–52.

Harburg E. Schull WJ, Erfurt JC, Schork MA. A family-set method for estimating heredity and stress: a pilot survey of blood pressure among Negroes in high and low stress areas, Detroit, 1966–67. Journal of Chronic Disease 1970; 23:69–81.

Hare, EH, Shaw GK. A study in family health: health in relation to family size. British Journal of Psychiatry 1965; 111:461–466.

Haskell WL. Exercise-induced changes in plasma lipids and lipoproteins. Preventive Medicine 1984; 13:23–36.

Haynes S, Eaker E, Feinleib M. Spouse behavior and coronary heart disease in men: prospective results from the Framingham Heart Study, Part I. American Journal of Epidemiology 1983: 118(1):1–23.

Hill R. Families under stress: adjustment to crisis. New York: Harper & Row, 1949:i.

Hill R. Sociology of marriage and family behavior: a trend report. Current sociology 1958; 2:1–98.

Hill R. Decision making and the family life cycle. In: Shanes E, Streib G, eds. Social structure and the family: generational relations. Englewood Cliffs, N.J.: Prentice Hall, 1965:113–139.

Hill R. Modern systems theory and the family: a confrontation. Social Science Information 1971; October:7–26.

Hill R, Rodgers R. The developmental approach. In: Christensen HT, ed. Handbook of marriage and the family. Chicago: Rand McNally, 1964:171–211.

Holahan CJ, Moos RH. Social support and psychological distress: a longitudinal analysis. Journal of Abnormal Psychology 1981; 49:365–370.

Hunt G. Implications of the treatment of myelomeningocele for the child and family. Lancet 1973; 2:1308–1310.

Jenkins CD. Psychologic and social pressures of coronary disease. New England Journal of Medicine 1971; 284:244–255.

Jenkins CD. Recent evidence supporting psychologic and social risk factors for coronary disease, Part 1. New England Journal of Medicine 1976a; 294:987–994.

Jenkins CD. Recent evidence supporting psychologic and social risk factors for coronary disease, Part 2. New England Journal of Medicine 1976b; 294:1033–1038.

Jenkins CD. Behavioral risk factors in coronary artery disease. Annual Review of Medicine 1978; 29:543–562.

Jenkins CD, Rosenman RH, Zyzanski SJ. Prediction of clinical coronary heart disease by a test for the coronary-prone behavior pattern. New England Journal of Medicine 1974; 290:1271–1275.

Johnson SB. Psychosocial factors in juvenile diabetes: a review. Journal of Behavioral Medicine 1980; 3:95–116.

Kasl SV, Cobb S. Blood pressure changes in men undergoing job loss: a preliminary report. Psychosomatic Medicine 1970; 32:19–38.

Khoury PR, Morrison JA, Laskarzewski P, Kelly K, Mellies MJ, King P, Larsen R, Glueck CF. Relationships of education and occupation to coronary heart disease risk factors in school children and adults: the Princeton School District Study. American Journal of Epidemiology 1981; 113:378–395.

Kozlov AA. The effect of certain domestic factors on morbidity with temporary disability of female employees of an industrial plant. Sovetskoe Zdravoohranenie 1969; 28:14–19.

Lilienfeld A. Chronic disease. In: Last JM, ed. Maxcy-Rosenau public health and preventive medicine. New York: Appleton-Century-Crofts, 1980:1135–1146.

Litman TJ. The family as a basic unit in health and medical care: a social–behavioral overview. Social Science and Medicine 1974; 8:495–519.

Liu K, Cedres L, Stamler J, Dyer A, Stamler R, Nanas S, Berkson D, Paul O, Lepper M, Lindberg H, Marquardt J, Stevens E, Schoenberger J, Shekelle R, Collette P, Shekelle S, Garside D. Relationship of education to major risk factors and death from coronary heart disease, cardiovascular disease, and all causes. Circulation 1982; 66:1308–1314.

Lydall H. The life cycle income, savings, and asset ownership. Econometrica 1955; 23:131–150.

MacGregor GA. Dietary sodium and potassium intake and blood pressure. Lancet 1983; 1:750–752.

McCollum AT, Gibson LE. Family adaptation to the child with cystic fibrosis. Journal of Pediatrics 1970; 77:571–578.

Miller JG. Living systems. New York: McGraw-Hill, 1978.

Miller PM, Ingham JG. Friends, confidants and symptoms. Social Psychiatry 1976; 11:51–58.

Oakes TW, Word JR, Gray RM, Klauber MR, Moody PM. Family expectation and arthritis patient compliance to a hand resting splint regimen. Journal of Chronic Diseases 1970; 22:757–764.

Paffenbarger RS, Wing AL, Hyde RT, Jung DL. Physical activity and incidence of hypertension in college alumni. American Journal of Epidemiology 1983; 117:245–257.

Pratt L. Family structure and effective health behavior: the energized family. Boston: Houghton-Mifflin, 1976.

Purcell K, Brady K, Chai H, Muser J, Molk L, Gordon N, Means J. The effects of asthma in children of experimental separation from the family. Psychosomatic Medicine 1969; 31:144–163.

Puska P, Nissinen A, Vartainen E, Dougherty R, Mutanen M, Iacono JM, Korhonen HJ, Pietinen P, Leino U, Moisio S, Huggunen J. Controlled randomized trial of the effect of dietary fat on blood pressure. Lancet 1983; 1:1–9.

Review Panel on Coronary-Prone Behavior and Coronary Heart Disease. Coronary-prone behavior and coronary heart disease: a critical review. Circulation 1981; 63:119–215.

Rosenstock I. What research in motivation suggests for public health. American Journal of Public Health 1960; 50:295–302.

Rossi PH. Why families move: a study in the social pscyhology of urban mobility. Glencoe, Ill.: Free Press, 1955.

Schaefer C, Coyne JC, Lazarus RS. The health-related functions of social support. Journal of Behavioral Medicine 1981; 4(4):381–405.

Schmidt DD. The family as the unit of medical care. Journal of Family Practice 1978; 7:303–313.

Scotch NA. A preliminary report on the relation of sociocultural factors to hypertension among the Zulu. Annals of the New York Academy of Science 1960; 84:1000–1009.

Stephens RC, Blau ZS, Osler GT. Aging, social support systems and social policy. Journal of Gerontology and Social Work 1978; 1:33–45.

Straus M. Measuring families. In: Christensen HT, ed. Handbook of marriage and the family. Chicago: Rand McNally, 1964:335–400.

Stunkard AJ. Obesity. Philadelphia: Saunders, 1980.

tenKate LP, Boman H, Daiger P, Motulsky AG. Familial aggregation of coronary heart disease and its relation to known genetic risk factors. American Journal of Cardiology 1982; 5:945–953.

Thompson JK, Jarvie GF, Lahey BB, Cureton KJ. Exercise and obesity: etiology, physiology, and intervention. Psychological Bulletin 1982; 91:55–79.

Turk J. Impact of cystic fibrosis on family functioning. Pediatrics 1964; 34:67–71.

U.S. Public Health Service. Smoking and health: a report of the Surgeon General. U.S. Department of Health and Human Services, Washington, D.C.: U.S. Government Printing Office, 1982.

Venters M. Familial coping with chronic and severe childhood illness: the case of cystic fibrosis. Social Science and Medicine 1981; 15A:289–297.

Venters M, Jacobs D, Luepker R, Maiman L, Gillum R. Spouse concordance of smoking patterns: the Minnesota Heart Survey. American Journal of Epidemiology 1984; 120:608–616.

Venters M, Jacobs D, Pirie P, Luepker R, Folsom A, Gillum R. Marital status and cardiovascular risk: the Minnsota Heart Survey and the Minnesota Heart Health Program. Preventive Medicine 1986; 15:591–606.

Venters M, Mullis R. Family-oriented nutrition education and pre-school obesity. Journal of Nutrition Education 1984; 16:159–161.

Waldron I, Hickey A, McPherson C, Butensky A, Gruss L, Overall K, Schmader A, Wohlmuth D. Type A behavior pattern: relationship to variation in blood pressure, parental characteristics, and academic and social activities of students. Journal of Human Stress 1980; 17:16–26.

Wheeler M, Hess K. Treatment of juvenile obesity by successive approximation control of eating. Journal of Behavioral Therapy and Experimental Psychology 1976; 7:235–241.

Winkelstein WA, Kagan A, Kato H, Sacks ST. Epidemiologic studies of coronary heart disease and stroke in Japanese men living in Japan, Hawaii, and California: blood pressure distributions. American Journal of Epidemiology 1975; 102:502–513.

Wood R, Boat T, Doershuk C. State of the art, cystic fibrosis. American Review of Respiratory Diseases 1976; 113:833–878.

Worth RM, Kato H, Rhoads G, Kagan A, Syme SL. Epidemiologic studies of coronary heart disease and stroke in Japanese men living in Japan, Hawaii, and California: mortality. American Journal of Epidemiology 1975; 102:481–490.

PART SIX

Family Systems and Biologic Processes

22

Illness and Family Systems: A Coevolutionary Model

DONALD A. BLOCH
The Ackerman Institute for Family Therapy, New York

> . . . this paper is not an attack on medical science but a demonstration of an inevitable fact: that mere purposive rationality unaided by such phenomena as art, religion, dream, and the like, is necessarily pathogenic and destructive of life; and that its virulence springs specifically from the circumstance that life depends upon interlocking *circuits* of contingency, while consciousness can only see such short arcs of such circuits as human purpose may direct. (Bateson, 1972, p. 146)

This chapter grows out of an effort to develop a model for relating two classes of events: illness events and family systems events. The focus of the chapter is on the coevolution of disease pattern and family pattern.

This focus has involved, for one thing, an exploration of the concept of environment or context, as well as what we mean by the term "family," leading ultimately to a consideration of an entity that has been called the problem-generated or problem-defined system. This concept goes beyond family to include all elements that are involved in equilibrating or disequilibrating the entity under consideration—in this instance a disease or family pattern.

The main concern of this chapter is to present the coevolutionary perspective: how an entity and its context evolve together, shaping and stabilizing each other. Throughout, medical and psychiatric conditions are used as case examples. We will consider a wide variety of such conditions: the abdominal pain syndrome in children, postpartum depression, drug addiction, organ transplant, cervical cancer, nonorganic paralysis in children. The systemic perspective of the chapter should make clear that in none of these instances are we talking about the cause or etiology of any of these syndromes.

The connections between etiology, illness, and treatment appear to be self-evident, but only when *punctuated* in a very special fashion. The essential features of that punctuation are: (1) the restriction of contextual information, (2) the ordering of relational (causal) sequences in linear fashion over short time periods, and (3) the elimination of the observer or the observing system from the field of inquiry.

For four hundred years, this has been the ruling scientific paradigm, the road to "truth." From around the turn of the century, first in physics and more recently in biology and elsewhere in science, this governing paradigm has been challenged. As with the Copernican revolution, the adaptation to and incorporation of the systemic paradigm has been difficult and uneven. Nor is it suitable for all purposes—far from it. Family therapy, of all the clinical specialties, has been most hospitable to and intrigued by the possibilities associated with these newer paradigms. This has been forced on us from the very beginning of the field by our concern with the family as a system. When Jackson (1957) and Ackerman (1958), among others, turned their attention to the intriguing question, "How would the rules, roles, structures and functions, history, and organization of the family explain the

321

observable behavior of its members without recourse to individual pyschologic or motivational explanations?'' they looked to the systems theorists to provide paradigms.

The most influential metatheorists in the early days of the development of the family therapy field were the cybernetician Norbert Wiener (1948), the theoretic biologist Ludwig von Bertalanffy (e.g., 1969), who founded general systems theory, and the anthropologist Gregory Bateson (e.g., 1972, 1979). Our present interest is in physical medicine, where the great complexities of events, their multilevel nature—from molecular through cell, tissue, organ, organ system, organism, interpersonal field, family, community, and society—calls for new paradigms other than those of classsical Newtonian science. This chapter is an attempt to describe disease as a *microevolutionary* event drawing principally on cybernetics and general systems theory for its language.

We will consider an illness event to be any physical or behavioral pattern taken by the person exhibiting it, or by others, to be a sign of sickness or disease. As the lawyers would have it, we stipulate the existence of a large number of personal and cultural conditions under which such a judgment is made, and identify them as the proper subject for empiric research; such research is not our concern at present.

''What is the illness?'' is a question that often appears simple to answer but at times can be bewilderingly complex. The knife slips, there is a small cut, the bandage is applied, healing takes place. All is as it was before. Or is it? Is there a tiny scar? No matter. But it's on the face. Still, no matter. But she's a young girl. Ah! Well, then. Too little context has been provided for the story to be satisfying.

On occasion, we sense that something is wrong with the story: The wound fails to heal, or we hear that this is the third accident she has had this month. In these instances, we might have the disturbing feeling that the boundaries of the phenomenon were incorrectly drawn, not sufficiently inclusive. The correct boundaries in time and space do not inhere in the events, which after all are chosen (languaged) by the storyteller; rather, we choose what story to tell by our purposes and our relation to it. The emergency room team, the police investigators, and the psychiatrist all elicit and thereby tell different stories about a stab wound. More elegantly, it can be said that they construct different realities.

The terms ''family'' and ''family system'' are used to denote many different things. In the early days of family therapy, a common language definition was considered acceptable, although the difficulty in knowing the *time frame* being used was disturbing. When one spoke of ''family,'' for example, was it the family-of-origin as it had formerly existed, or the current representation of the family-of-origin, or the current actuality of the family-of-origin that was being alluded to?

That difficulty was complicated in different ways in speaking of the current or contemporary family. Whom to include was unclear here. According to what rules did one construct something called ''the family''? Did one speak of biologic, legal, or emotional definitions? How were partial units, such as sibling subsets or a marital pair, to be spoken of? What about kin extensions and multigenerational units, to say nothing of lovers, ex-mates, and children of new mates?

In addition, it has been necessary over the last decade at least to take into account other clearly nonfamily social structures in regard to the development and maintenance of less-than-optimally functioning (i.e., problematic) patterns. For example, it is a part of conventional systemic wisdom that the health care system is not infrequently an active stabilizer of malfunctional patterns; sophisticated psychotherapists routinely consider the ''iatrogenic'' effects of their own interventions. Several examples of this will be provided, ranging from the simple instance of pediatric involvement in the development of the abdominal pain syndrome in children to the picture of clinic involvement in maintaining heroin addition in its clients.

All the elements that make up the story can be thought of as making up what we might call the *problem-generated system,* which includes those elements ordinarily conceived to be part of the context of the target event as well as the describing observer.

Clearly, we have gone way beyond the standard definition of family here, yet some version of family is, I believe, central. In regard to what is specifically "human" functioning, "family" (i.e., some version of the intimate networks of past and present alluded to above) is first among equals among the social systems. There is a tendency among some current theorists to minimize or discard family entirely. An interesting and important presentation of this and associated concepts can be found in Anderson, Goolishian, and Winderman (1986): ". . . there are no set facts about family, family theory, or family therapy that are independent of our observations or our mode of engagement. There is no single objective reality about a family and its problem waiting to be discovered. There are multiverses, each valid in its own right," (p. 4) a point of view with which I agree, although I would point out that a shared language about "our observations [and] our mode of engagement" is what we mean by "family" and is our ticket of admission to the human race.

Peggy Penn (1983) said on this subject:

> I understand the epistemology of the organization we call "family" as closely following Bateson's construct of a "pattern through time," meaning that members of a family form relationships with one another over the generations and these relationships are specific patterns indentifiable to that family . . . if we regard time as ongoing process, then each pattern is known to its members as a sum of the past in the present, and that sum amounts to an identifiable stance in their social realm: we are, we did, we show, we felt, we know, etc. Continuation, perseverance, and familiarity of their pattern are the expectations families hold of their future together. . . . (p. 16)

Which elements of family belong in the problem-generated system, and the part the family plays in the relation of those elements to each other, are decisions to be made at the particular story (case) level. It is a function of the particular problem and the particular treatment theory and techniques in use: the *purposes* of the storyteller. As Bateson (1979) put it:

> The question, "What am I trying to discover?" is not as unanswerable as mystics would have us believe. From the manner of the search, we can read what sort of discovery the searcher may thereby reach; and knowing this, we may suspect that such a discovery is what the searcher secretly and unconsciously desires. . . . But epistemology is always and inevitably *personal.* The point of the probe is always in the heart of the explorer. [One wonders, is the double entendre intended?] What is *my* answer to the nature of knowing? I surrender to the belief that my knowing is a small part of a wider integrated knowing that knits the entire biosphere or creation. (p. 86–87)

Once again, what is illness? How are we to define its extensions in space and time? From the perspective of this chapter we would, in the words of Auerswald (1985), take the "initial role of a non-blaming ecological detective. The initial task, in this context, is to seek out and identify the *ecological event shape* [emphasis added] in time/space that includes the situation that led the family to issue a distress call" (p. 6).

The term "ecological event shape" is taken by me to describe a virtual space that is the universe of all possible elements that could be included in the problem-generated system. It is infinite and unknowable—out there, as it were, where mystery resides. Partial knowing, through language, is the activity of the nonblaming, ecologic detective leading to the construction of one among many possible realities.

The problem-generated system (corresponding to the term "situation" in the Auerswald definition above) is a language event. It lies within the space of the event/shape, always includes the observing system, and is to be parsimoniously defined.

Our general approach is to include in the story only (all of) those elements that (1) stabilize the problem-generated system or (2) disequilibrate its predecessor systems. This requires that we include in the story only (all of) those elements that are involved in observing and changing (disequilibrating) it, for example, treatment format, techniques, and theory.

FAMILY SYSTEMS AND ILLNESS SYSTEMS

In the accounts of clinical syndromes that follow, one may differ with interpretations of details; the reader is urged to (mostly) listen to the music rather than the words.

Abdominal Pain Syndrome

Let me begin with a tale that is familiar in many of its elements to all pediatricians and some family therapists as well: the abdominal pain syndrome in children. This physical syndrome is a chronic condition of obscure etiology, characterized by recurrent episodes of abdominal pain, flatulence, and mild diarrhea for which no organic cause can be found. These youngsters are frequently seized with abdominal pain that is serious enough for them to stay out of school and not uncommonly requires visits to the pediatrician. Often extensive diagnostic procedures are carried out, including endoscopy and even surgical exploration. Diet and medication are tried, often with ambiguous results.

The story can be told this way: It begins with a *random* disequilibrating event. There is some gas in the child's gut, and there is a relationship configuration in the child's family for which this random event has *meaning*. Consider as an oversimplified example, a family where the parents are covertly at war, and the mother, in the context of this undeclared war, moves closer to a potential ally, the child, around the issue of the moment of abdominal pain.

Over time, in many of these situations, a physician, in the effort to assist the overinvolved parent (more commonly the mother) with the worrisome problem of her child's gut, will become increasingly involved and increasingly frustrated. Out of the physician's desire to help, another shift in the relational geometry will take place, bringing the physician closer to the mother, and this may further stabilize this particular system. The relational geometry of the family *and* the health care system is further changed.

We may imagine that the distance between mother and father increases as the father attacks the increasingly closer alliance between mother and child ("All you do is baby him for every little ache and pain"). As part of this process, the father withdraws further, perhaps making a tie to an ally, such as work or a woman friend, outside the family ("I'll be at the office working late tonight"), or perhaps teaming up with a second sibling inside the family. The *relational geometry* of the family—of the mother–father–child triangle—is changed.

Clearly, it is inappropriate to talk about "cause" or "etiology" using this model. Indeed, the random event of the moment of colic might be considered, via the loops indicated here, to be the cause of its own existence (a tautology).

In the language of biologic evolution, we could say that the organism (in this case the illness pattern) modifies its context (in this case the family–physician relational pattern) so as to create an ecologic niche that supports it. Elsewhere, I have referred to this as *portable reality* (Bloch, 1967). It is, of course, equally true to say that the family–physician relational pattern modifies the illness pattern. The choice of which pattern is to be considered the target and which is to be considered context rests with the *purposes* of the observing system.

The loop whereby a pattern modifies its surroundings to produce the conditions for maintaining its own existence obviously need not involve the psychosocial level at all. The purposes and available language of the observer will determine the level at which the target phenomena are to be described.

An example from virology will illustrate. In a recent review article, the following thesis is developed:

> [T]he future of medical virology will probably relate far more to persistent viral infections and the diseases associated with them. Included within this group are many of the herpes viruses . . . hepatitis B virus, human T-cell lymphotropic virus (HTLV) Types I, II, and III . . . Such viruses may not kill the host cell in which they replicate . . . and may not generate immune responses that are effective in clearing the viruses. (Southern & Oldstone, 1986, p. 359)

These authors note that the host immune response acts by the route of antiviral antibodies and cytotoxic lymphocytes that act by "directly injuring cells displaying viral antibodies." This process, which is characteristic of *acute* infections, does not operate in the same way in persistent infections. The viral infection need not kill the host cell but, rather, can transform it by a number of mechanisms so that the host cell survives (indeed, can be induced to reproduce the viral DNA along with its own) but has an altered function, whence comes the disease associated with that particular virus. "Viruses can also change the differentiated functions of immunocompetent cells required for viral elimination, and this may be of major importance to the establishment of persistent infections" (p. 363).

In the language being used in this chapter, these persistent viruses persist by changing the characteristics of their contexts: Thus, the acute becomes chronic.

A second example at the physiologic level can be found in the following discussion:

> An appreciation of tumor stroma [the connective tissue and blood vessel supporting structures] is essential to the understanding of the biology of tumor growth; all solid tumors, regardless of their site of origin, require stroma if they are to grow beyond a minimal size of one to two millimeters . . . [Stroma] provides the vascular supply that tumors require for nourishment, gas exchange and waste disposal [as well as being able] to limit the influx of inflammatory cells, thus providing a barrier to immunological rejection. (Dvorak, 1986, p. 1650)

The author goes on to "present evidence that tumors behave in the body like wounds, and, in fact, *induce their stroma by activating the host wound-healing response*" (emphasis added) (p. 1050). This suggests that tumor stroma generation is wound healing gone awry.

"Viewing wound healing as a paradigm for the generation of tumor stroma makes considerable biologic sense. Without linking tumor stroma generation to *some fundamental host process* [emphasis added], one is forced to assume that the body responds to tumors with a unique mechanism, some deus ex machina whose sole function is to generate tumor stroma. . . ." (p. 1650). Further:

> They have developed the capacity to preempt and subvert the wound healing response of the host as a means to acquire the stroma they need to grow and expand. . . . Thus, tumors appear to the host in the guise of wounds, or more correctly, as an unending series of wounds that continually initiate healing but never heal completely. (p. 1657)

The reader's attention is drawn to the dramatic terms the author uses: "preempt," "subvert," "acquire," "in the guise of." In this example, we are confronted with the fashion in which a "normal" reparative process—wound healing—is recruited into providing the supportive structures without which the cancer could not survive.

Postpartum Depression

Kraus and Redman (1986) offer a strikingly similar view of postpartum depression:

> The new mother and others have inadvertently co-evolved a social system which neither desired. . . . These stages in the evolution of postpartum depression . . . are based on a deviation amplifying feedback model in which serious problems develop from well intended attempts at solving normal, everyday difficulties. . . . [P]ostpartum depression begins with the developmental crisis of pregnancy and childbirth. . . . [Further changes] occur when the husband and others switch from empathy for the new mother to frustration and irritation . . . and try to avoid aversive complaining by offering false reassurances. . . . [A full-scale depressive system evolves] when the husband and other family members can no longer tolerate the new mother's immutable depression and so exclude her from meaningful relations. (p. 68)

The "normal," short-lived postpartum depression that, in all likelihood, is hormonally induced can blossom in the favorable environment of certain family structures by inducing changes in those structures. These induced changes support the continued coevolution and change both of the structures *and* of the depressive behavioral pattern. The acute becomes chronic. Kraus and Redman (1986) note how a set of therapeutic interventions can be designed that depend on interrupting these circularities.

The clinical story by its very nature involves more than one systems level (e.g., the biopsychosocial model; Engel, 1982). We assume that the distinction of a systems level is a languaging event. The language in use will have its (more or less) consistent rules; between languages (i.e., levels), however, this consistency breaks down.

Time boundaries of the clinical story must be decided on as well. The decision about the time frame to be used is a crucial factor in story construction. The rate of change at a systems level is also a significant factor and must be taken into account. For example, slow-moving, biologic events (e.g., genetic disorders) introduce a fateful warp to the family destiny and provide the (relatively) immutable backdrop against which other dramas play themselves out.

In language we shall use later in this chapter, the stored experience of relationship becomes the template on which future experience is modeled. Repetition over time is essential to this process of replication; the earlier and more frequently a pattern occurs, the greater the chance that it will be replicated in the future. The stored pattern organizes the meaning of new experience on a moment-by-moment basis.

Drug Addiction

The next subject touches on the description of phenomena at different systems levels. At issue here is the isomorphism of patterns at two different systems levels. In this instance, an entire drug treatment social system comes to take on the characteristic pattern of the addict's family, thereby stabilizing the addictive pattern, and the institutional relational pattern as well. This issue is central to the notion of coevolution. Here is the problem: If we track events at two or more different levels of organization—say, a tissue level and a family level, or a family level and a social organization level—and those events seem to have patterns that are congruent with each other, have the same shape, are isomorphic, then how are we to interpret our observations? It is up to us how we define the system boundary, and we are free to regard an organized pattern at one level as a system. If we do so, we can think of a pattern at one level providing a template, a guide to the replication of a pattern, to the organization at another level. On the road to stabilizing, we would think of the pattern at each level as determining and being determined by the pattern at the other. In other words, as they become isomorphic, the patterns coevolve.

The example concerns the treatment of heroin addiction (Schwartzman, 1986). Three different system levels are involved in this story: the addict's family, the treating health care system, and the community. Of particular interest to us at this point is the isomorphism of the addict's family and the treating agencies. Schwartzman, a consultant to a network of centers treating heroin addicts, delineated the following pattern.

The typical addiction treatment center (part of a network of three) is staffed by paraprofessional counselors, most often former addicts who are considered to be street- and drug-wise, by nonaddict nurses who dispense medication, and by physician directors. To simplify Schwartzman's detailed account, there is always the potential for conflict between these groups. At stake is the control over availability and dosage of methadone, the addictive but noneuphoric medication which is dispensed to prevent withdrawal symptoms and is highly desired by the addicts. The counselors are in the position of having to demonstrate their superior knowledge of addict life by maintaining close ties with the patients. This involves condoning "cheating" when urine tests are not "clean," that is, when they reveal drug use. This puts the counselors at odds with the "straight" physicians, with whom they are already in a class- and ethnicity-driven conflict, since the counselors are most often black and lower-class. The different economic situation of the two groups fuels the fire, as does administrative confusion. For example, career lines for counselors are relatively unavailable, so their upward mobility is restricted.

Of principal importance is the fact that it is impossible under these conditions to develop the consistent limit-setting stance required for treatment. Excuses are constantly being made, agreements breached, the laws of the therapeutic community violated. The division and conflict of those in authority is reflected in continued drug use by the addicts.

The pattern is isomorphic with that of the typical addict family, where one parent is seductively enmeshed with the patient and the other is isolated or rendered powerless by the dyad. It is as difficult to develop a consistent pattern of limit setting in the family as it is in the treatment setting. As noted by Schwartzman (1986):

> The basic premises of those involved create and maintain social systems which are analogues to the families of clients and to the individual methadone clinics. The dissonances in ideology,

status of paraprofessionals, clinic professionals, medical personnel, and beliefs about addiction create more and more inclusive analogues to the addict's family: intrusive, pseudoconstraining, covertly conflictual, and lacking clear transitions. This system is maintained by a flow of clients and staff among clinics, and makes treatment primarily a function of the contingencies of the more inclusive social system. (p. 354)

Organ Transplant

Next, I will describe an investigation that looked at a sequence of events where two quite different variations on this theme were possible. In this situation, changes at one systems level could or could not exceed the available contingencies at another, depending on circumstances. Thus, in some instances the smooth development of isomorphism of levels would occur, in others not. The pilot study reported here is elegant in that it is prospective. It is presented, among other reasons, to illustrate the research possibilities inherent in this point of view.

Velasco de Parra (1982) studied families in which one member was a candidate for a kidney transplant. Before knowledge of the results of immunologic studies done to determine tissue compatibility, the investigator did structural studies of the family in the manner of Minuchin, Rosman, and Baker (1978). The family coalitions, splits, and subsystems were determined. Did mother and child/patient have a close or a distant relationship? How was the sibling group organized? What dyads were too close or too distant?

The reasoning of the researcher was that the psychosocial effect of an organ donation, a kidney in this instance, was to bring the two family members involved closer together. On the basis of this reasoning, predictions were made that depended on which dyad would be so involved. This dyadic change could be or not be isomorphic with the preexisting structures, and this was consequential. If two people were brought closer together who had already been quite close, there were no problems. But if the two who were brought closer together had been quite distant from each other, or were thereby pulled out of another close dyadic tie, there was an increase in distress and symptomatic behavior.

Cervical Cancer

In family therapy, the multigenerational family has, more often than not, been the unit of study; it is as close to routine as this maverick field is likely to get to do a *genogram*—that is, a family tree—as a regular clinical procedure. Yet, it is difficult to know what elements to include and how to relate them to each other. Let me illustrate.

Writing on gynecologic cancer, Labrum (1976) presents a vivid description relevant to our thesis. Recent demonstrations of the neuroendocrine and immunologic links to cancer make his writings seem even more prescient. I will abstract one section of his paper.

Labrum states that factors other than some coitally transmitted agent must determine which women develop cancer. The epidemiologic associations of early onset, multiple sex partners, and separation or divorce need to be reinterpreted. He notes the various studies indicating the connection between hopelessness and certain life patterns and cervical cancer. In a comparison of 100 women with cervical cancer and 100 women with other forms of cancer, it was noted that those with cervical cancer showed a dislike of sexual intercourse, reduced frequency of orgasm, a history of leukorrhea, a tendency to marry alcoholics, and a high incidence of divorce.

Finally, in a passage that exemplifies Auerswald's (1985) injunction to be a "non-blaming ecological detective," Labrum (1976) takes us to the heart of the matter:

> The woman most at risk grows up in a home with parental unemployment, poverty, absent parent(s), parental abuse, and inadequate love . . . the occurrence of sexual intercourse as a young teenager is the price she is willing to pay for a "loving" relationship. She usually does not enjoy the physical aspects of sex . . . and often has a series of brief sexual relationships in which she is looking, with increasing despair, for someone who will provide for her own (often enormous) needs. At some point she gives up . . . [and] as a teenager or young adult she finds herself separated or divorced (sometimes several times) and in a state of hopelessness. She will almost certainly have become infected with herpes virus II, possibly with other transmissible oncogenic factors or co-factors such as chronic trichomonal infections and, I believe, in this setting cervical changes occur, which progress if untreated through the dysplasias to carcinoma *in situ* and then to invasive cancer. *It is possible that in such high risk women changes occur very rapidly.* (p. 818; emphasis added)

Further, "To fit the theory being developed, immunologic variations would necessarily have to be under central control," a view, we may add, with much stronger support at this date than when initially proposed by Labrum (1976, p. 819).

If the full play of imagination is brought to bear on this story, we are led onto truly uncharted plains. It is not that we are hard pressed to answer such questions as, "What is the etiology of cervical cancer?" Rather, they are seen to be questions from another paradigmatic world. Instead, we peer through the mists and address ourselves to strange new questions, such as, "What elements should be included in the problem-generated system, one element of which is cervical cancer? And how do these elements coevolve?"

Nonorganic Paralysis in Children

The next example deals with a quite different clinical syndrome, but both accounts are strikingly similar in that a multigenerational structure and a particular relation to the larger culture is necessary for the final clinical picture to evolve. The Norwegian clinician/researcher Wencke Seltzer (1985), in an effort to understand and develop a rational treatment approach to certain highly resistant conversion disorders in children, extends her perspective to include the national culture as well as the changing multigenerational culture in the families in which these children are to be found.

The children came to clinical attention with crippling sensory motor disorders for which no organic problem could be found despite extensive and repeated investigations. Milder psychosomatic conditions, such as abdominal pain, backache, headache, and muscle/joint pain, were excluded. To oversimplify the author's elegant conceptual structure is distressing but necessitated by space limitations. These children grow up in low-status families that have been scorned and isolated by Norwegian society in the past. The grand parental families were commonly of the rural lumpen proletariat, although with mothers of slightly higher status than the fathers. The parental generation have valiantly struggled against the oppressive and stigmatizing past by self discipline, religious fundamentalism, sports involvement, physical action and exertion.

These are families with "a heritage of damaged goods"; conformity both within and outside the family is their protective watchword. A feature of this evolving pattern over the generations has consisted in overestimating the essentially mediocre intellectual capabilities of the child who is to become physically ill. ". . . when the time approached for the children—particularly—the youngest—to leave, the spousal unit was severely threatened. The question as to its future survival abruptly arose. Alternative solutions, such as work or other engagements outside the home for the mother, had been too long associated with negative mortality to appear workable.'' (p. 278). At this point symptoms began to appear in the child.

DISCUSSION

At this point we will attempt to identify some of the concepts that make for the ''goodness'' of these stories. They represent dimensions of the co-evolutionary model; it should be possible to describe each illness/treatment situation in regard to these dimensions.

How shall a system and its context be demarcated from all else, as well as from each other, and how shall they be connected to each other? This is, in fact, a single question that acknowledges two kinds of distinctions: between what is within a system and outside of it, and between the components that make up a system. ''Environment,'' ''context,'' ''surround'' are expressions of a particular location from which a scene is viewed. Gertrude Stein, 20th-century feminist, philosopher, and author, was asked on the occasion of viewing a distant California scene whether she was ''born over there.'' Her reply: ''There is no 'there' over there.'' What we choose to call context is arbitrary. The disease in the body-as-context reflects our viewing stance: A virus-eyed view would be quite different.

We may, at this point, set forth the coevolutionary perspective in the form of an axiom: To the extent that an illness system is chronic, it must change elements of its context in the direction that will reduce discrepancy (improve the fit) between the illness behavior (target system) and the context. The possibilities for improved fit must be (1) latent in the surround, or (2) achieved by changes in the surround induced by the target system. As noted earlier, the distinction between target system and surround depends on the purposes of the clinician/intervener.

''Random'' signifies that the incident at the outset of the sequence we are tracking has (comparatively) little meaning for the family system. Initially, it is relatively uncoupled, and makes only a minimal fit with elements in the surround. With the passage of time and the repetition of the pattern, the fit (i.e., the meaning) improves; the ease with which the component subsystems codetermine each other increases. In other words, the larger system coevolves; a self-maintaining (chronic) pattern comes into being.

''Fit,'' as we are using the term, can be thought of in this way: Gas bubble and pain (and associated behaviors) derive their meaning from analogic congruence with the family relationship configuration, a congruence most often expressed in language as metaphor.

Since the concept of fit is so central to the perspective of this chapter, I wish to quote at length from Steier and Smith's 1985 paper, ''Organizations and Second Order Cybernetics.'' They say:

> Von Glasersfeld (1984), building on the foundations Bateson's critique offered, points out that many of the key misconceptions about adaptation arose because of how Darwin's famous dictum, ''the survival of the *fit*,'' became interpreted. This has, over the years, been translated into the ''survival of the fittest,'' implying that it is the strong that survive. Von Glasersfeld discusses the inappropriateness of this view and adds to Bateson's notion that adaptation, without a concomitant shift in an entire distribution, can be a process through which variety becomes ''eaten up'' or reduced and thereby, flexibility is lost.
>
> Von Glasersfeld argues that a fruitful way to think about fit is in the metaphor of a key fitting into a lock. He notes that any particular lock may be opened by numerous keys, a

dubious awareness we have due to the contribution of the professional burglar. If we discover a particular key opens the lock, we don't describe it as the fittest; we merely say it fits. In fact, no key that opens the door is any more or less fit than any other. What we do discover is that some keys will not open the lock no matter how much we pull and twist. (pp. 58–59)

"Evolution" is a term used to describe the process whereby a durable pattern of organization changes over time in such a fashion that distinguishably new forms are stabilized. It was Darwin's gift to see that this entire process—the change and the stabilization—was a function of the fit of the system and its environment (i.e., adaptation).

"Fit" describes the key–lock congruence of system and context. Quoting again from Von Glasersfeld (cited in Steier & Smith, 1985), "Darwin's dictum might be better expressed as the elimination of the *nonfitting* (or un-fit)" (p. 59). This switch in understanding makes the whole subject of adaptation one where evolution is primarily a process of elimination rather than of survival. The mere fact that an organization has not yet had its contours so constrained that it doesn't "fit into the lock" is no guarantee that this possibility isn't just around the corner. Hence, a more modest slogan for those surviving entities, and one that is congruent with this evolutionary perspective, would be "not yet extinguished" rather than "survival of the fit." It is the viability of the system, rather than its adaptability, that is crucial.

The question then becomes: Why do so *few* cancer cells survive (see Labrum, 1976)?

In the preceding quotation, it appears as if fit is being thought of as unidirectional (i.e., from target pattern to surround). As Bateson (1972) tells us, the horse and the grassy plain coevolve; organism and context codetermine each other. "Surely the grassy plains were evolved *pari passu* with the evolution of the teeth and hooves of the horses and other ungulates. Turf was the evolving response of the vegetation to the evolution of the horse. It is the *context* which evolves" (p. 155).

Family appropriately enters into our considerations when the relationship configuration in the family is *what the fit is with*. But it obviously is not necessary for the interface between illness pattern and *family* to be the location for the fitting. When system A and system B make an interface, any information in system A that is new, or dissonant, for system B creates the conditions for such a coevolutionary realignment (see the example from virology quoted earlier).

Repetition and meaning are closely interrelated. Over time, as the *biopsychosocial* pattern takes on meaning for the family–health care configuration, it is repeated; as it is repeated, it takes on meaning. Repetition, and the frequency with which it occurs, is of course crucial for establishing a stable (i.e., chronic) pattern. Nothing is exactly repeated, *pace Heraclitus;* there is always some degree of changing fit between the elements of a pattern under consideration.[1] But it is in precisely this regard that an important additional element of chronicity enters: The target pattern (abdominal pain in one of our examples we are using here) is recruited into maintaining the stability of other systems or subsystems.[2]

For example, the structure/function of the child's gut may be changed; a kind of "gut learning" takes place, mediated by the autonomic nervous system. In the absence of irreversible tissue changes, the pattern is maintained and stabilized by changes in the psychology of the child *and* the relational geometry of the family *and* the child's gastrointestinal physiology.

Mediation concerns us where events occur at two or more levels of complexity. The term is used here in the general systems sense; as noted earlier in this chapter, theorists have tended to take the idea of "level" for granted without paying much attention to the place of language in establishing the concept. This leads to a reification of the notion of levels as if they existed in nature. It is more useful to think of a "level" as a convention of constructed realities, but it is difficult to write about them that way—in English at least. Within a particular language system, such as that of physiology and biomedicine, it is necessary to be able to demonstrate the neuroendocrine mediating links connecting psychosocial systems to organ systems.

As for mediation, it seems to refer to the process whereby change at one level is information about a difference for another; subsystems at that point are discrepant contexts for each other, and dissonance reduction takes place.[3]

Reversible changes can become (comparatively) irreversible at any level, for example by the death and disappearance of a cell line or by some process that radically distorts the normal tissue architecture. We say "comparatively irreversible" to indicate that suprasystems may come into play to reverse the irreversible: The stored frozen sperm of a man long dead may fertilize the ova of a woman as yet unborn.

As time passes, a metastable (chronic) system comes into being. The elements or components of the system *coevolve;* that is, they improve their mutual fit. The entire entity with which we are concerned includes, at a minimum, the biology, psychology, and physiology of the patient; the relational structure of the multigenerational family, and relevant aspects of the health care system and of the larger society.

Notes

1. The failure to recognize that fit is always partial and changing and that some degree of asynchronicity is always present has embroiled family therapists in endless and unproductive arguments about homeostasis. It is unfortunate that Ackerman (1958) never had any luck with his effort to promote the term "homeodynamic." A look at the evolving galaxies might be salutary.

2. As for the relation of the random to meaning, Oliver Sacks, the neurologist essayist, is worth quoting. He notes first the random event occurring at one systems level that then has meaning ("elaboration and accretion of meaning"; Sacks, 1983), that is, *fit* with another. He describes a patient, Miriam H, a postencephalitic woman who had developed Tourette-like tics with treatment by L-dopa:

> An entirely novel symptom which had developed on the increased dose of L-dopa was a *tic,* a lightning-quick movement of the right hand to the face, occuring about 20 times an hour. When I questioned Miss H. about this symptom, shortly after its inauguration, she replied that it was a "nonsense-movement." . . . Within 3 days of its appearance, however, this tic had become associated with an intention and a use; it had become a mannerism, and was now used by Miss H. to adjust the position of her spectacles. (Sacks, 1983, pp. 124–125)

3. "Enzymes are generally thought to speed up chemical reactions by stabilizing the transitional state, the most unstable and therefore the highest energy intermediate formed by the reactants during the conversion to products. Enzymes, by stabilizing the transition state, lower the energy needed for the conversion and consequently increase the rate of the reaction" (Marx, 1986, p. 1497).

References

Ackerman NW. The psychodynamics of family life. In: The homeostasis of behavior. New York: Basic Books, 1958:68–79.

Anderson H, Goolishian H, Winderman L. Problem determined systems: transformation in family therapy. Journal of Strategic and Systemic Therapies 1986; 5(4).

Auerswald EH. Thinking about thinking in family therapy. Family Process 1985; 24:1–12.

Bateson G. Steps to an ecology of mind. New York: Ballantine Books, 1972.

Bateson G. Mind and nature. New York: Dutton, 1979.

Bloch DA. Psychosocial replication. Unpublished manuscript, 1967.

Dvorak HF. Tumors: wounds that do not heal. New England Journal of Medicine 1986; 315(26):1650–1659.

Engel GL. The biopsychosocial model and medical education: who are to be the teachers? 1982; 20:211–221.

Jackson DD. The question of family homeostasis. Psychiatric Quarterly 1957; 31(Suppl.).

Kraus MA, Redman RS. Postpartum depression: an interactional view. Journal of Marital and Family Therapy 1986; 12(1):63–74.

Labrum AH. Psychological factors in gynecological cancer. Primary Care 1976; 3(4):811–823.

Marx, JL. Making antibodies work like enzymes. Science 1986; 234:1497.

Minuchin S, Rosman BL, Baker L. Psychosomatic families: anorexia nervosa in context. Cambridge, Mass.: Harvard University Press, 1978.

Penn P. Coalitions and binding interactions in families with chronic illness. Family Systems Medicine 1983; 2:16–25.

Sacks O. Awakenings. New York: Dutton, 1983:124–125.

Schwartzman J. The natural history of a drug treatment system. Family Systems Medicine 1986; 4(4):344–357.

Seltzer, WJ. Conversion disorder in childhood and adolescence: a familial/cultural approach: Part I. Family Systems Medicine 1985; 3(3):261–280.

Steier F, Smith KK. Organizations and second order cybernetics. Journal of Strategic and Systemic Therapies, 1985; 4(4):53–65.

Velasco de Parra ML. Changes in family structure after a renal transplant. Family Process 1982; 21(2):195–201.

von Bertalanffy L. General systems theory—an overview. In: Gray W, Duhl FJ, Rizzo ND, eds. General systems theory and psychiatry. Boston: Little, Brown, 1969:92.

Wiener N. Cybernetics, or control and communication in the animal and the machine. Cambridge, Mass.: Technology Press, 1948.

23

The Family System's Influence on Reproduction

CHRISTIAN N. RAMSEY, JR.
University of Oklahoma

Reproduction is a biologic process. It is also a primary function of the family, along with protection and nourishment of individual family members. Aberrancy of the reproductive process causes substantial impact on the quality of life. In fact, the World Health Organization (1980) has identified low birth weight as the single most important determinant of chances for a newborn to survive, and to begin the process of healthy growth and development. From a clinical standpoint, 70% of all perinatal deaths that are not caused by congenital malformations are related to low birth weight. There is strong evidence that low birth weight infants are at considerably higher risk of morbidity and mortality during the first year of life, and that they are at increased risk for a number of congenital malformations, mental retardation, neurologic impairments, and a variety of other abnormalities.

This chapter begins with a review of what is known about the biologic and behavioral/ psychosocial determinants of low birth weight. Then, the results of research looking specifically at the effect of family functioning on birth weight will be described. Finally, the chapter will conclude with several hypotheses about how the family system might interact with the mother and fetus to produce adverse pregnancy outcome.

Table 23-1 lists the factors that have been shown to influence birth weight. As can be seen, biologic, anthropometric, behavioral, nutritional, psychosocial, and family factors have all been reported to influence birth weight.

BIOLOGIC DETERMINANTS OF ADVERSE PREGNANCY OUTCOME

Two groups of biologic determinants are of particular interest because they may play a role in explaining the biologic mechanisms through which the family system influences birth weight: (1) hypertension/preeclampsia and (2) maternal infection and immunoincompetence.

The Role of Hypertension/Preeclampsia in Intrauterine Growth Retardation

Beginning with McBurney's work in 1947 and in a number of subsequent studies (Baird, Thompson, & Billewics, 1957; Low & Galbraith, 1974; Morris, Osborn, & Wright, 1955), there is very strong evidence that intrauterine growth retardation (IUGR) and hypertension are associated. It is generally believed that uteroplacental physiology plays a major role in hypertension/preeclampsia. Changes in three areas of uteroplacental structure and functioning have been shown to relate to IUGR. First, examination of significant numbers of pla-

Table 23-1. Determinants of Low Birth Weight

Biologic/medical factors:	*Nutritional factors:*
Parity	Maternal–fetal
Anemia	Fetal immunity
Hypertension/preeclampsia	*Psychosocial factors:*
Renal disease	Anxiety
Genital infections	Pregnancy planning
Maternal immunoincompetence	Social support
Anthropometric factors:	Maternal attitude
Height	*Family factors:*
Body habitus	Couvade syndrome
Weight gain	Dyadic relationships
Maternal birth weight	Children/sibling relationships
Behavioral factors:	Role expectations
Smoking	
Alcohol	
Work	

centas in IUGR have revealed substantial changes in placental weight in women with chronic hypertension, but intermittent hypertension showed no effect (Bjoro, 1981; Fox, 1978). In other words, women who experienced transient preeclampsia at some point during pregnancy did not exhibit the same degree of inhibited placental growth as did women with prolonged hypertension.

Second, from the standpoint of placental ultrastructure, studies by DeWolf, DeWolf-Peeters, Brosens, and Robertson (1980) have shown that there is intimal thickening and atheromatous change within the vessels in placentas from women with hypertension. Sheppard and Bonnar (1980) noted spiral artery occlusion and necrosis.

Third, a number of workers have studied changes in uteroplacental blood flow (Lunell, Sarby, Lewander, & Nylund, 1979; Nylund, Lunnell, Lewander, & Sarby, 1983). Blood flow changes have been studied in a number of ways, but most recently using radioactive isotopes. Although the study populations tend to be rather small, workers have demonstrated a substantial decrease in uterine artery blood flow in IUGR, particularly in cases associated with hypertensive disease.

Changes in uteroplacental blood flow also influence stress in the fetus. By measuring either fetal plasma catecholamines or amniotic fluid catecholamines in women with hypertensive or eclamptic pregnancies, a number of workers have demonstrated a stress response in the fetus that is associated with IUGR (Divers, Wilkes, Babaknia, Hill, Quilligan, & Yen, 1981; Divers, Wilkes, Babaknia, & Yen, 1981; Jones & Robinson, 1975; Lagercrantz, Sjoquist, Bremme, Lunell, & Somell, 1980; Zuspan *et al.*, 1975).

In summary, hypertension is associated with changes in the placenta's size and architecture, in the blood vessels, and in placental blood flow; it is also associated with fetal changes, as it appears that maternal hypertension activates the adrenergic nervous system.

The Role of Maternal Infection/Immunoincompetence in IUGR

The second group of biologic determinants of low birth weight that may be important in understanding family system influences involves the effects of maternal genitourinary infection and maternal immune status on birth weight and pregnancy outcome. Studies of maternal genitourinary infection have demonstrated that a wide variety of genitourinary infections caused by bacteria and viruses cause IUGR. Although the exact mechanism is not known, it is felt that infection causes chorioamnionitis, which interferes with maternal–fetal diffusion processes. Several investigators have related various forms of maternal infection to adverse outcome or low birth weight (Baker, 1977, 1979; Braun *et al.*, 1971; Elder, Santamarina, Smith, & Kass, 1971; Frommell, Rothenberg, Wang, & McIntosh, 1979; Kass, 1970; Klein, Buckland, & Finland, 1969; Regan, Chao, & James, 1981; Shurin, Alpert, & Rosner, 1975; Stagno, Pass, Dworsky, & Alford, 1983; Sweet, Schachter, & Landers, 1983; Thompson & Dretler, 1982; Whitley, Nahmias, Visintine, Fleming, & Alford, 1980).

In addition to maternal infection, some workers have studied the impact of direct suppression of the maternal immune system. Several investigators have shown that immunosuppression of the mother causes IUGR. This phenomenon has been studied on a worldwide basis in women who have received organ transplants and been given immunosuppressive drugs, and who have subsequently become pregnant (Rifle & Traeger, 1975; Sciara, Toledo-Pereyra, Bendel, & Simmons, 1975; Scott, 1977).

BEHAVIORAL DETERMINANTS OF ADVERSE PREGNANCY OUTCOME

Nilsen and co-workers (Nilsen, Sagen, Kim, & Bergsjo, 1984) reported that smoking one-half pack of cigarettes per day increased the risk of low birth weight. Another study by Sexton and Hebel (1984) reported a mean increase of 92 grams (about one-quarter pound) in birth weight for babies born to women who were smokers but did not smoke throughout pregnancy.

With reference to alcohol effects on the fetus, fetal alcohol syndrome has been studied extensively. A study by Mills, Graubard, Harley, Rhoads, and Berendes (1984) showed that even very moderate use of alcohol (one drink per day) causes some decrease in fetal birth weight. Fetal birth weight, then, continues to decrease as the amount of alcohol consumed increases. Other workers have reported that drinking doubles the risk of congenital abnormalities (Ouellette, Rosett, Rosman, & Weiner, 1977).

Two studies investigating the effects of work on birth weight have been reported in the recent literature. The first study surveyed over 20,000 working women and concluded there was no difference in birth weight, mortality, or morbidity between working and nonworking women (Murphy, Dauncey, Newcombe, Garcia, & Elbourne, 1984). Another study looked at a particular type of work-related stress—occupational fatigue—and the outcome of pregnancy (Mamelle, Laumon, & Lazar, 1984). This study concluded that there is a substantial relationship between occupational fatigue and prematurity. Of the 3,500 women surveyed, however, fewer than 20 made up the subset in question.

IMPACT OF NUTRITION ON PREGNANCY OUTCOME

There are conflicting reports in the literature on the magnitude of nutritional influences on pregnancy outcome. A number of workers have measured nutritional influences on pregnancy outcome. Metcoff and co-workers have done several studies (Metcoff, 1980, 1981a,

1981b; Metcoff *et al.*, 1973) in which individual amino acid concentrations, metabolic rates within the mother, and leukocyte metabolic rates were measured with very sophisticated biochemical techniques. Metcoff and colleagues are convinced that birth weight is related to maternal nutrition and nutritional processes. Other workers (Picone, Allen, Olsen, & Ferris, 1982; Picone, Allen, Schramm, & Olsen, 1982) have reported that low maternal weight gain (<15 pounds) results in longer gestation (0.5 weeks), smaller infants, and smaller placentas. However, the studies of several workers (Mora *et al.*, 1979; Stein, Susser, & Rush, 1978) involving administration of nutritional supplements have resulted in only modest gains in birth weight. Clearly, much work needs to be done to confirm and elucidate the ways in which maternal nutrition affects birth weight.

In a related area, work has been done in the United States, Scandinavia, and elsewhere in Europe to demonstrate the impact of maternal nutrition on the newborn immune system, including some studies of circulating antibodies in children (Chandra, 1979, 1983; Ferguson, Lawlor, Neumann, Oh, & Stiehm, 1974; Sirisinha, Suskind, Edelman, Asvapaka, & Olson, 1975; Watson, Reyes, & McMurray, 1978). Thus, there is an association between nutrition and fetal immune system development and reactivity.

PSYCHOSOCIAL FACTORS AND PREGNANCY OUTCOME

One of the more difficult areas of study involves assessing the effects of psychosocial factors on the outcome of pregnancy. The types of factors (e.g., maternal anxiety, pregnancy planning, stress, and social supports) that have been studied are as diverse as the outcomes reported. However, most workers believe that psychosocial factors can have an adverse impact on pregnancy outcome.

One of the most frequently studied psychosocial effects is maternal anxiety (Crandon, 1979a, 1979b; Gorsuch & Key, 1974; Laukaran & van den Berg, 1980; McDonald, Gynther, & Christakos, 1963; Newton & Hunt, 1984; Norbeck & Tilden, 1983). Postpartum hemorrhage, labor time, and difficulty of labor have been shown to be related to maternal anxiety, although there are no direct reports of maternal anxiety being associated with low birth weight.

One psychosocial factor that has been investigated recently is whether or not the pregnancy was planned. Berkowitz and Kasl (1983) studied the desirability of pregnancy (whether or not the pregnancy was wanted) versus life events to determine if there was a correlation with preterm delivery. They found that unwanted pregnancies combined with high life events scores resulted in prematurity in a large number of women in their sample.

Our group (Baker, Abell, & Ramsey, 1984) found that pregnancy planning was more likely to take place in families that had moderate adaptability and cohesion as measured by the FACES. Conversely, planning was less likely to occur in families scoring at the extremes of adaptability or cohesion. Laukaran and van den Berg (1980) found an association between unwanted pregnancy and perinatal death, congenital malformation, or postpartum infection. Another study reported a correlation between length of labor and conflict over acceptance of pregnancy as measured in a Family APGAR (Lederman, Lederman, Work, & McCann, 1984).

The effect of stress and social support on pregnancy outcome has been studied by many workers. Sosa, Kennell, Klaus, Robertson, and Urrutia (1980) reported the effects on the length of labor of placing a doula, or lay support person, into the labor room with the mother. They found that there was a 50% reduction in labor time and increased mother–infant interaction following birth, as measured by smiling, stroking, and other types of maternal interaction.

Nuckolls, Cassel, and Kaplan (1972) performed a frequently cited study in which women with low psychosocial assets and high life events had a much higher complication rate than other women. Data from this study are summarized. Complications included: hospital admission for preeclampsia or hyperemesis; threatened abortion; premature rupture; prolonged labor; APGAR rating of less than 7; systolic blood pressure of over 139 mm and/or diastolic blood pressure of over 89 mm during both labor and postpartum recovery; birth weight of less than 2,500 grams; abortion, stillbirth, or neonatal death within the first 3 days. The sample in this study was a group of 200 military wives whose husbands were preparing to go to Vietnam. The effects occurred in a small subsample of the study population tested. Several other studies have demonstrated a general relationship between social support and pregnancy outcome (Mercer, Harkley, & Bostrom, 1983; Smilkstein, Helsper-Lucas, Ashworth, Montano, & Pagel, 1984).

FAMILY IMPACTS ON PREGNANCY OUTCOME

There are a few studies of family effects on pregnancy and of pregnancy impacts on the family. Workers studying the impact of pregnancy on the family have reported that fathers in some families develop physical and biologic symptomatology of pregnancy (couvade syndrome) and seek medical care much more often than is their normal pattern (Lipkin & Lamp, 1982; Quill, Lipkin, & Lamb, 1984). This phenomenon has been observed principally in clinics and health maintenance organizations, where detailed records of pre- and postpregnancy behavior of husbands are available. Other factors studied include role expectations (Fishbein, 1984), family subsystem relations (Olson, Bell, & Portner, 1978; Olson, Sprenkle, & Russell, 1979; Richardson, 1981, 1983a, 1983b), and family functioning (Smilkstein, 1978). Smilkstein and co-workers (1984) used the Family APGAR (Smilkstein, 1978) to study postpartum complications. He found that women with APGAR scores below a perfect 10 suffered more from postpartum complications than did women with APGAR scores of 10.

Fishbein studied role expectations and found that paternal anxiety varied with congruity of maternal/paternal role projections. Additionally, the degree to which the father was projected to be involved in child care did not relate to paternal anxiety.

Richardson's work (1981, 1983a, 1983b) has focused on describing the changes in significant relationships and their impact on pregnancy. She has concluded that the effects of early childhood relationships with parents and subsequent relationships with others are of major significance. She believes that the mother's relationships shape the mother's perception of her own adequacy or inadequacy as a mother.

FAMILY STRUCTURE AND FUNCTIONING: IMPACT ON BIRTH WEIGHT

On the basis of this background, our group asked: "Do family structure and functioning relate to birth weight?" (Ramsey, Abell, & Baker, 1986). We developed a project to measure the impact of several aspects of family functioning on birth weight.

Figure 23-1 summarizes the study design. The sample was drawn from two sources:

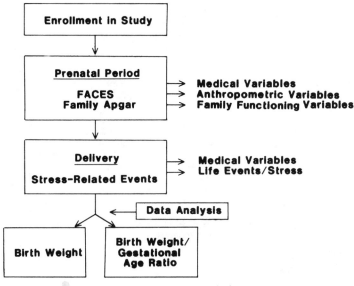

Figure 23-1. Study design.

(1) women who were seen at the Family Practice Center in Waco, Texas, and (2) women who went to the McLennan County, Texas, Health Department. Standard medical and anthropometric data were collected, and FACES (Olson *et al.*, 1978) and the Family APGAR (Smilkstein, 1978) were administered at the first visit, before the 25th week of pregnancy. At subsequent prenatal visits and at the time of delivery, additional medical variables were measured. Life events were measured just following delivery. The data were analyzed using birth weight and birth weight/gestational age ratio as the dependent variables. The original sample size was 132 women. Seven of the 132 mother–infant pairs were outliers, so data for them was not analyzed, yielding a revised study population of 125. Further review of the data base revealed 23 mother–infant pairs for which there were incomplete data. This reduced the sample to 102 mother–infant pairs. There is not a significant difference in the variables between the original and the final sample.

The curvilinear scales of FACES were transformed into linear scales called enmeshed, disengaged, rigid, and chaotic. Life events were grouped into four categories.

The model used for data analysis regresses birth weight and birth weight/gestational age first on the anthropometric and medical variables known to influence birth weight. After running variables shown to influence birth weight, family variables were added in. In other words, a hierarchic inclusion of variables was used rather than a stepwise inclusion.

Table 23-2 shows the overall result of regressing infant birth weight with medical variables, then with anthropometric variables, then family structure, life events, and family scales. As can be seen, it is possible to explain approximately 30% of the variation in birth weight on the basis of traditional medical and anthropometric variables, which agrees with what has been reported in the literature on pregnancy outcome. With reference to family effects, there is a positive contribution if the woman is married. In fact, marital status alone explains about 5% of the variance. Enmeshed family explains approximately 7% of the variance (adjusted R^2 .425 to R^2 .495). Table 23-3 shows similar effects by regressing the variables on infant birth weight/gestational age as the dependent variable.

Table 23-2. Determinants of Infant Birth Weight

Characteristic	B	Beta[a]	R^2	Adjusted R^2
Intercept	(84.797)			
Gestational age	0.273[b]	0.346	0.096	0.087
Emergency caesarian section	10.859[c]	0.208	0.134	0.117
Maternal age >30	−16.590[d]	−0.199	0.135	0.108
Parity	3.497[c]	0.262	0.160	0.125
Maternal height	−1.045	−0.166	0.203	0.162
Highest diastolic blood pressure	0.654[b]	0.302	0.288	0.243
Third trimester bleeding	−16.948[b]	−0.293	0.340	0.291
Maternal smoking	−4.424	−0.115	0.358	0.303
Hispanic	5.891	0.148	0.392	0.332
Married	8.662[c]	0.241	0.439	0.378
Living alone	−6.611	−0.123	0.444	0.376
Prepregnancy money-related stress	−11.011[b]	−0.281	0.493	0.425
Enmeshed family	−0.828[b]	−0.291	0.560	0.495

Note: $n = 102$. Dependent variable: infant birth weight (ounces).

[a] Standardized regression coefficients.

[b] $p < .001$.

[c] $p < .01$.

[d] $p < .05$.

Next, birth weight and birth weight/gestational age were regressed on only those variables that were statistically relevant. Deleting some variables caused the amount of variance explained to be lower (R^2 .495 to R^2 .415). However, enmeshed family system still had an effect, contributing approximately 4% to the variance.

The data generally confirm the work of others with regard to the contribution of medical and anthropometric factors to birth weight. Taken together, medical and anthropome-

Table 23-3. Determinants of Infant Birth Weight/Gestational Age Ratio

Characteristic	B	Beta[a]	R^2	Adjusted R^2
Intercept	(0.513)			
Emergency caesarian section	0.044[b]	0.240	0.052	0.043
Maternal age > 30	−0.067[c]	−0.232	0.054	0.035
Parity	0.013[b]	0.287	0.082	0.053
Maternal height	−0.003	−0.121	0.114	0.078
Highest diastolic blood pressure	0.002[d]	0.310	0.210	0.169
Third trimester bleeding	−0.061[d]	−0.303	0.264	0.218
Maternal smoking	−0.022	−0.166	0.297	0.245
Hispanic	0.023	0.168	0.333	0.276
Married	0.026[c]	0.204	0.364	0.301
Living alone	−0.026	−0.137	0.370	0.301
Prepregnancy money-related stress	−0.044[d]	−0.321	0.440	0.371
Enmeshed family	−0.003[d]	−0.297	0.509	0.443

Note: $n = 102$. Dependent variable: infant birth weight/gestational age ratio (ounces/days).

[a] Standardized regression coefficients.

[b] $p < .01$.

[c] $p < .05$.

[d] $p < .001$.

tric variables account for approximately one-third of the observed variation. More important, even the most conservative statistical analysis of the data shows that family structure and family functioning are powerful predictors of variation in birth weight.

BIOLOGIC PATHWAYS FOR FAMILY SYSTEM IMPACT ON BIRTH WEIGHT

In this section, two pathways will be elaborated in which it is possible to explain how functioning of the family system achieves an impact on birth weight through interaction with biologic systems. As described elsewhere in this book, the science of family medicine involves the study of how the family system interacts with the three major regulatory networks of the body—the nervous, immune, and endocrine systems. We have hypothesized two possible pathways by which the family system has an impact on birth weight: one that is predominantly immune and one that is predominantly endocrine. In reality, the pure form of either may be rare, but for demonstration purposes it is helpful to report the description of each.

A number of studies have demonstrated the relationship between family and social systems and the immune system. There are three major lines of work that involve the impact of the family system on immune status: (1) work relating the incidence of infection to family life events, status, and functioning; (2) work showing that circulating antibodies are sensitive to stress; and (3) work showing that IgA levels in a variety of body fluids are related to infection.

The evidence for a relationship between immune status and infection comes first from Meyer and Haggerty's (1962) study of families in Baltimore, in which they found that "high-stress" families had a higher incidence of streptococcal infection. We have studied influenza and family functioning and found that with reference to type B influenza, dysfunctional families have a much higher rate of infection than do normal families, as measured by FACES (Ramsey, Baker, & Campbell, 1983).

With reference to stress and onset of infection, Kraus and Lilienfeld (1959) studied the impact of the stress of widowhood on death rates in young males. They found a strikingly higher morbidity and mortality for infectious disease—tuberculosis and pneumonia—in the widower population as compared to a nonwidower cohort. David Schmidt and colleagues (1982) have shown that there is a significant association between stress and strain (daily hassles) and recurrence of herpes simplex infections.

A number of studies of the effects on stress on circulating antibody levels have shown that IgA is sensitive to stressful events (Fubara & Freter, 1973; Jemmott *et al.*, 1983). It is also important to note that a major role of secretory IgA is to guard the body orifices, one of which is the opening of the uterus (Brunham, Kuo, Cles, & Holmes, 1983).

With this background, it is possible to consider the question of how the family system might interact with the immune system to cause low birth weight. Figure 23-2 will present a formulation of such a pathway. As conceived, functioning of the family system, either through enmeshment or social isolation (in the case of a mother living alone) or through mechanisms yet to be identified, produces stress, which is transmitted to the maternal CNS, which then has an impact on the cellular and/or the humoral arm of the immune system to produce maternal immunoincompetence.

If immunoincompetence occurs through the humoral arm, for instance, one might speculate that cervical IgA levels would be lowered. Studies have shown that cervical IgA levels are related to the shedding of organisms in certain kinds of viral cervicitis. Within this context, it is possible to postulate that genitourinary infection would occur, and genitourinary infection is related to low birth weight.

Construction of such a hypothetical pathway is possible through a series of associations linking the family system to the creation of stress, relating immune status to stress, relating genitourinary infections to the immune system, and relating low birth weight to genitourinary infections (see Figure 23-2). Such a pathway, though still hypothetical, serves as a useful framework for observation and as a guide to the design of more complex experiments.

The second pathway involves the vascular and endocrine systems. A number of fascinating studies, many of which have used animal models, form the basis for projecting such a pathway. There is a great deal of evidence to suggest that with hypertensive disease there are uterine vascular abnormalities and abnormalities of catecholamine production. For instance, a number of studies have shown differences in the size and architecture of the placenta in caged versus free-ranging rhesus monkeys (Koford, 1965). He also showed that there is a significant difference in birth weight between caged and free-ranging monkeys. In another study, Valerio and co-workers (Valerio, Courtney, Miller, & Palotta, 1968) related caging stress and stillbirths, and showed that the stillbirth rate was substantially higher in the socially isolated rhesus monkeys than it was in those in free-ranging herds. Caging stress has thus been shown to have a substantial impact on birth weight and status.

Environmental stress, such as noise, has been shown to cause decreased birth weight in rats and rabbits (Geber & Anderson, 1967). Psychologic stress appears to activate the catecholamine, or bioamine, pathway and to cause IUGR and complication of pregnancy (Myers, 1975).

There have been a number of studies evaluating the indirect impact of catecholamines on pregnancy outcome. Greiss and Gobble (1967), among others, have studied the impact

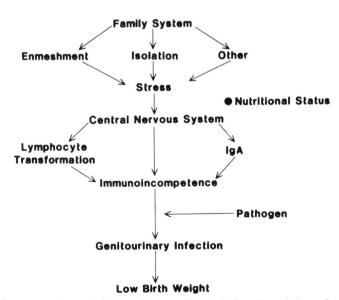

Figure 23-2. Immune pathway in intrauterine growth retardation. Associations: family system and stress; immune status and stress; genitourinary infection and immune system; low birth weight and genitourinary infection.

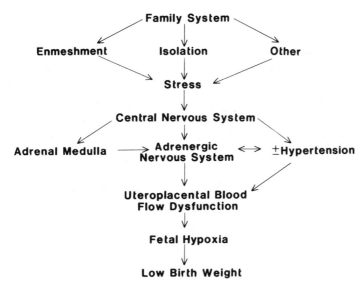

Figure 23-3. Adrenergic nervous system/vascular/endocrine pathway in intrauterine growth retardation. Associations: family system and stress; stress and adrenergic nervous system; hypertension and uteroplacental blood flow; hypertension and low birth weight; stress and low birth weight.

of infusion of epinephrine on uterine blood flow in sheep. They have done studies in which uterine and placental vessels in live preparations were cannulated. Blood flow was decreased by as much as one-third in response to epinephrine infusion.

To hypothesize an endocrine/vascular pathway, one would postulate that dysfunction of the family system causes stress, which activates the catecholamine system. Activation of the catecholamine system in turn causes uteroplacental blood flow decrease and chronic fetal hypoxia, and ultimately leads to low birth weight. Such a pathway is depicted in Figure 23-3.

CONCLUSIONS

The work presented in this chapter reviews data that show that family structure and functioning are powerful determinants of infant birth weight. It appears that the family system may interact with either the immune or the endocrine system (or both) to affect birth weight. In the case of the immune system, the effect would be through maternal immunoincompetence. In the case of the endocrine system, the effect would be through vascular inefficiency.

Much work is needed to improve our understanding of the relationships between family systems and biologic systems in order to prove the specific biologic pathways by which family functioning affects birth weight. From a clinical standpoint, when it is possible to better understand the precise mechanisms by which family dysfunction causes adverse pregnancy outcome, it should be possible to design family system interventions that will improve the outcome of the reproductive process.

References

Baird D, Thompson AM, Billewics WZ. Birth weights and placental weights in pre-eclampsia. Journal of Obstetrics and Gynecology of the British Empire 1957; 64(3):370–372.

Baker CJ. Summary of the workshop on perinatal infections due to group B streptococcus. Journal of Infectious Disease 1977; 136:137–152.

Baker CJ. Group B streptococcal infections in neonates. Pediatric Review 1979; 1:5.

Baker L, Abell TD, Ramsey CN Jr. The interaction of family structure and function in a study of pregnancy planning. Presented at the 12th annual meeting of the North American Primary Care Research Group, Orlando, Florida, May 2–9, 1984.

Berkowitz GS, Kasl SV. The role of psychosocial factors in spontaneous preterm delivery. Journal of Psychosomatic Research 1983; 27(4):283–310.

Bjoro K Jr. Gross pathology of the placenta in intrauterine growth retardation. Annales Chirurgiae et Gynaecologiae 1981; 70:316–322.

Braun P, Lee Y-H, Klein JO, Marcy SM, Klein TA, Charles D, Levy P, Kass EH. Birth weight and genital mycoplasmas in pregnancy. New England Journal of Medicine 1971; 284(4)167–171.

Brunham RC, Kuo C-C, Cles L, Holmes KK. Correlation of host immune response with quantitative recovery of *Chlamydia trachomatis* from the human endocervix. Infection and Immunity 1983; 39(3):1491–1494.

Chandra RK. Interactions of nutrition, infection and immune response. Acta Paediatrica Scandinavica 1979; 68:137.

Chandra RK. Numerical and functional deficiency in T helper cells in protein energy malnutrition. Clinical and Experimental Immunology 1983; 51:126–132.

Crandon AJ. Maternal anxiety and neonatal wellbeing. Journal of Psychosomatic Research 1979a; 23:113–115.

Crandon AJ. Maternal anxiety and obstetric complications. Journal of Psychosomatic Research 1979b; 23:109–111.

DeWolf F, DeWolf-Peeters C, Brosens I, Robertson WB. The human placental bed: electron microscopic study of trophoblastic invasion of spiral arteries. American Journal of Obstetrics and Gynecology 1980; 137(1):58–70.

Divers WA, Wilkes MM, Babaknia A, Hill LM, Quilligan EJ, Yen SSC. Amniotic fluid catecholamines and metabolites in intrauterine growth retardation. American Journal of Obstetrics and Gynecology 1981; 141:608.

Divers WA, Wilkes MM, Babaknia A, Yen SSC. An increase in catecholamines and metabolites in the amniotic fluid compartment from middle to late gestation. American Journal of Obstetrics and Gynecology 1981; 139:483.

Elder HA, Santamarina BAG, Smith S, Kass EH. The natural history of asymptomatic bacteriuria during pregnancy: the effect of tetracycline on the clinical course and the outcome of pregnancy. American Journal of Obstetrics and Gynecology 1971; 111:141.

Ferguson AC, Lawlor GJ Jr, Neumann CG, Oh W, Stiehm ER, Decreased rosette-forming lymphocytes in malnutrition and intrauterine growth retardation. Journal of Pediatrics 1974; 85(5):717–723.

Fishbein EG. Expectant father's stress—due to the mother's expectations? Journal of Gynecological Nursing 1984; September–October: 325.

Fox H. Pathology of the placenta. London: W. B. Saunders, 1978.

Frommell GT, Rothenberg R, Wang S-P, McIntosh K. Chlamydial infection of mothers and their infants. Journal of Pediatrics 1979; 95:28.

Fubara ES, Freter R. Protection against enteric bacterial infection by secretory IgA antibodies. Journal of Immunology 1973; 111(2):395.

Geber WF, Anderson TA. Abnormal fetal growth in the albino rat and rabbit induced by maternal stress. Biology of the Neonate 1967; 11:209.

Gorsuch RL, Key MK. Abnormalities of pregnancy as a function of anxiety and life stress. Psychosomatic Medicine 1974; 36(4):352.

Greiss FC Jr., Gobble FL Jr. Effect of sympathetic nerve stimulation on the uterine vascular bed. American Journal of Obstetrics and Gynecology 1967; 97:962.

Jemmott JB III, Borysenko M, Chapman R, Borysenko JZ, McClelland DC, Meyer D, Benson H. Academic stress, power motivation, and decrease in secretion rate of salivary secretory immunoglobulin A. Lancet 1983; 2:1400.

Jones CT, Robinson RO. Plasma catecholamines in foetal and adult sheep. Journal of Physiology 1975; 248:15–33.

Kass EH. Pregnancy, pyelonephritis and prematurity. Clinical Obstetrics and Gynecology 1970; 13:239.

Klein JO, Buckland D, Finland M. Colonization of newborn infants by mycoplasmas. New England Journal of Medicine 1969; 280:1025.

Koford CB. Population dynamics of rhesus monkeys on Cayo Santiago. In: DeVore I, ed. Primate behavior: field studies of monkeys and apes. New York: Hold, Rinehart & Winston, 1965: 160–174.

Kraus A, Lilienfield LS. Some epidemiologic aspects of the high mortality rate in the young widowed group. Journal of Chronic Disease 1959; 10: 207–217.

Lagercrantz H, Sjoquist B, Bremme K, Lunell N-O, Somell C. Catecholamine metabolites in amniotic fluid as indicators of intrauterine stress. American Journal of Obstetrics and Gynecology 1980; 136:1067.

Laukaran VH, van den Berg BJ. The relationship of maternal attitude to pregnancy outcomes and obstetric complications: a cohort study of unwanted pregnancy. American Journal of Obstetrics and Gynecology 1980; 136:374–379.

Lederman RP, Lederman E, Work BA Jr, McCann DS. The relationship of maternal prenatal development to progress in labor and fetal–newborn health. In: Birth defects: original article series, Vol. XVII, No. 6, 1984: 5–28.

Lipkin M, Lamb G. The couvade syndrome: an epidemiologic study. Annals of Internal Medicine 1982; 96:509.

Low JA, Galbraith RS. Pregnancy characteristics of intrauterine growth retardation. Obstetrics and Gynecology 1974; 44:122.

Lunell NO, Sarby B, Lewander R, Nylund L. Comparison of uteroplacental blood flow in normal and in intrauterine growth-related pregnancy; measurements with Indium-113m and a computer-linked gammacamera. Gynecologic and Obstetric Investigation 1979; 10:106–118.

Mamelle N, Laumon B, Lazar P. Prematurity and occupational activity during pregnancy. American Journal of Epidemiology 1984; 119:309–322.

McBurney RD. The undernourished full term infant. West German Surgery, Obstetrics and Gynecology 1947; 55:363.

McDonald RL, Gynther MD, Christakos AC. Relations between maternal anxiety and obstetric complications. Psychosomatic Medicine 1963; 357–363.

Mercer RT, Hackley KC, Bostrom AG. Relationship of psychosocial and perinatal variables to perception of childbirth. Nursing Research 1983; 32(4):262–267.

Metcoff J. Maternal nutrition and fetal development. Early Human Development 1980; 4(2):99–120.

Metcoff J. Association between fetal growth and maternal nutrition. In: Harper A, Davis C, eds. Nutrition in health and disease and international development. New York: Alan R. Liss, 1981a:629–641.

Metcoff J. Fetal growth regulated by maternal nutrients. In: Monset-Couchard M, Minkowski A, eds. Physiological and biochemical basis for perinatal medicine. Basel: S. Karger, 1981b:108–124.

Metcoff J, Wikman-Coffelt J, Yoshida T, Bernal A, Rosado A, Yoshida P, Urrusti J, Frenk S, Madrazo R, Velasco L, Morales M. Energy metabolism and protein synthesis in human leukocytes during pregnancy and in placenta related to fetal growth. Pediatrics 1973; 51:866–877.

Meyer RJ, Haggerty RJ. Streptococcal infections in families: factors altering individual susceptibility. Pediatrics 1962; April:539–549.

Mills JL, Graubard BI, Harley EE, Rhoads GG, Berendes HW. Maternal alcohol consumption and birth weight. Journal of the American Medical Association 1984; 252:1875–1879.

Mora JO, deParedes B, Wagner M, DeNavarro L, Suescun J, Christiansen N. Nutritional supplementation and the outcome of pregnancy: I. Birth weight. American Journal of Clinical Nutrition 1979; 32(2):455–462.

Morris W, Osborn SB, Wright HP. Effective circulation of uterine wall in late pregnancy measured with ^{24}NaCl. Lancet 1955; 1:323–325.

Murphy JF, Dauncey M, Newcombe R, Garcia J, Elbourne D. Employment in pregnancy: prevalence, maternal characteristics, perinatal outcome. Lancet 1984; 1:1163.

Myers RE. Maternal psychological stress and fetal asphyxia: a study in the monkey. American Journal of Obstetrics and Gynecology 1975; 122:47.

Newton RW, Hunt LP. Psychosocial stress in pregnancy and its relation to low birth weight. British Medical Journal 1984; 288:1191.

Nilson ST, Sagen N, Kim HC, Bergsjo P. Smoking, hemoglobin levels, and birth weights in normal pregnancies. American Journal of Obstetrics and Gynecology 1984; 148:752–758.

Norbeck JS, Tilden VP. Life stress, social support, and emotional disequilibrium in complications of pregnancy: a prospective, multivariate study. Journal of Health and Social Behavior 1983; 24:30–46.

Nuckolls KB, Cassel J, Kaplan BH. Psychosocial assets, life crisis and the prognosis of pregnancy. American Journal of Epidemiology 1972; 95(5):431.

Nylund L, Lunell N-O, Lewander R, Sarby B. Uteroplacental blood flow index in intrauterine growth retardation of fetal or maternal origin. British Journal of Obstetrics Gynecology 1983; 90:16–20.

Olson DH, Bell R, Portner J. FACES: Family Adaptability and Cohesion Evaluation Scales. Department of Family Social Science, University of Minnesota, St. Paul, 1978.

Olson DH, Sprenkle DH, Russell C. Circumplex model of marital and family systems; I. Cohesion and adaptability dimensions, family types, and clinical applications. Family Process 1979; 18(1):3–28.

Ouellette EM, Rosett HL, Rosman P, Weiner L. Adverse effects on offspring of maternal alcohol abuse during pregnancy. New England Journal of Medicine 1977; 297:528.

Picone TA, Allen LH, Olsen PN, Ferris ME. Pregnancy outcome in North American women: II. Effects of diet, cigarette smoking, stress, and weight gain on placentas, and on neonatal physical and behavioral characteristics. American Journal of Clinical Nutrition 1982; 36:1214–1224.

Picone TA, Allen LH, Schramm MM, Olsen PN. Pregnancy outcome in North American women: I. Effects of diet, cigarette smoking, and psychological stress on maternal weight gain. American Journal of Clinical Nutrition 1982; 36:1205–1213.

Quill TE, Lipkin M, Lamb GS. Health-care seeking by men in their spouse's pregnancy. Psychosomatic Medicine 1984; 46(3):277.

Ramsey CN Jr, Abell TD, Baker LC. The relationship between family functioning, life events, family structure, and the outcome of pregnancy. Journal of Family Practice 1986; 22: 521–527.

Ramsey CN Jr, Baker LC, Campbell J. Family functioning and stress as predictors of influenza infection. Presented at the 11th annual meeting of the North American Primary Care Research Group, Banff, Alberta, April 17–20, 1983.

Regan JA, Chao S, James LS. Premature rupture of membranes, preterm delivery, and group B streptococcal colonization of mothers. American Journal of Obstetrics and Gynecology 1981; 141:184–186.

Richardson P. Women's perceptions of their important dyadic relationships during pregnancy. Maternal–Child Nursing Journal 1981; 10(3):159–174.

Richardson P. Women's perceptions of change in relationships shared with children during pregnancy. Maternal–Child Nursing Journal 1983a; 12(2):75–88.

Richardson P. Women's perceptions of change in relationships shared with husbands during pregnancy. Maternal–Child Nursing Journal 1983b; 12(1):1–19.

Rifle G, Traeger J. Pregnancy after renal transplantation: an international survey. Transplantation Proceedings 1975; 7(1), Suppl. 1:723.

Schmidt DD, Zyzanski S, Ellner J, Kumar ML. Schacter B, Arno J, Heyman T, Grava I. The integration of behavioral and biologic research: the model of stress induced disease. Early results from a study of herpes simplex type I. Presented at the Northeast Regional Meeting of the Society of Teachers of Family Medicine, Providence, Rhode Island, November 19, 1982.

Sciara JJ, Toledo-Pereyra LH, Bendel RP, Simmons RL. Pregnancy following renal transplantation. American Journal of Obstetrics and Gynecology 1975; 123(4):411.

Scott JR. Fetal growth retardation associated with maternal administration of immunosuppressive drugs. American Journal of Obstetrics and Gynecology 1977; 128(6):668.

Sexton M, Hebel JR. A clinical trial of change in maternal smoking and its effect on birth weight. Journal of the American Medical Association 1984; 251:911–915.

Sheppard BL, Bonnar J. Ultrastructural abnormalities of placental villi in placentae from pregnancies complicated by intrauterine fetal growth retardation: their relationship to decidual spiral arterial lesions. Placenta 1980; 1:145–156.

Shurin PA, Alpert S, Rosner B. Chorioamnionitis and colonization of the newborn infant with genital mycoplasmas. New England Journal of Medicine 1975; 293:5.

Sirisinha S, Suskind R, Edelman R, Asvapaka C, Olson RE. Secretory and serum IgA in children with protein-calorie malnutrition. Pediatrics 1975; 55(2):166.

Smilkstein G. The Family APGAR: a proposal for a family function test and its use by physicians. Journal of Family Practice 1978; 6:1231.

Smilkstein G, Helsper-Lucas A, Ashworth C, Montano D, Pagel M. Prediction of pregnancy complications: an application of the biopsychosocial model. Social Science Medicine (England) 1984; 18(4):315–321.

Sosa R, Kennell J, Klaus M, Robertson S, Urrutia J. The effect of a supportive companion on perinatal problems, length of labor, and mother–infant interaction. New England Journal of Medicine 1980; 303:597–600.

Stagno S, Pass RF, Dworsky ME, Alford CA. Congenital and perinatal cytomegalovirus infections. Seminars in Perinatology 1983; 7(1):31.

Stein Z, Susser M, Rush D. Prenatal nutrition and birth weight: experiments and quasi-experiments in the past decade. Journal of Reproductive Medicine 1978; 21(5):287.

Sweet RL, Schachter J, Landers DV. Chlamydial infections in obstetrics and gynecology. Clinical Obstetrics and Gynecology 1983; 26:143.

Thompson SE III, Dretler RH. Epidemiology and treatment of chlamydial infections in pregnant women and infants. Review of Infectious Disease 1982; 4:S747.

Valerio DA, Courtney KD, Miller RL, Palotta AJ. The establishment of a Macaca mulatta breeding colony. Laboratory Animal Care 1968; 18:589–595.

Watson RR, Reyes MA, McMurray DN. Influence of malnutrition on the concentration of IgA, lysozyme, amylase, and aminopeptidase in children's tears. Proceedings of the Society of Experimental Biological Medicine 1978; 157:215–219.

Whitley RJ, Nahmias AJ, Visintine AM, Fleming CL, Alford CA. The natural history of herpes simplex virus infection of mother and newborn. Pediatrics 1980; 66(4):489–494.

World Health Organization. The incidence of low birth weight: a critical review of available information. Geneva, Switzerland: WHO Division of Family Health, 1980.

Zuspan FP, Gumpel JA, Mejia-Zelaya A, Madden J, Davis D, Filer M, Tiamson A. Fetal stress from methadone withdrawal. American Journal of Obstetrics and Gynecology 1975; 122(1):43–46.

24

The Family System and Failure to Thrive

PATRICK H. CASEY
University of Arkansas for Medical Sciences;
Arkansas Children's Hospital, Little Rock

Failure to thrive (FTT) is a model condition in the study of causal links of disease development between a host organism and the organism's environment, which includes parents, family, and society. In this chapter, I will define these links as they relate to failure to thrive at the theoretic level, and defend the theory with empirical research.

For too long, failure to thrive has been dichotomized by medical clinicians into organic and nonorganic causes, the latter usually referring to a vague concept of "maternal deprivation." During the last decade, significant contributions in the broad area of child abuse and neglect have been provided by multiple disciplines including pediatrics, psychiatry, pediatric psychology, family sociology, and developmental psychology. Unfortunately, there has been inadequate integration of the theories and empirical data bases developed within these various disciplines. Only recently have integrated theoretic constructs been developed that overlap these multiple perspectives. The focus of this chapter is to present an interactional model of failure to thrive that integrates medical and social variables.

First I will review the definition and prevalence of failure to thrive. I will then present the more traditional medical perspective and terminology regarding failure to thrive, followed by a description of a model of parental competence, which was recently presented in the developmental psychology literature, with adaptation to an interactional model of casuality of failure to thrive. Next an overview of the controlled empirical research relating this model to failure to thrive will be presented. The chapter will end with a discussion of the research and diagnostic implications of this model.

FAILURE-TO-THRIVE OVERVIEW

"Failure to thrive" is a descriptive term used for babies who are not growing at an expected rate in comparison to children of similar age and sex. This growth problem is often associated with delayed achievement in developmental skills. The term is most commonly used in infants under the age of 36 months; after this age, the term "deprivation dwarf" is commonly used. FTT describes children whose weight is abnormally below the 3rd percentile for gestation-corrected age, where birth weight was normal for gestational age. The term is also used for children whose weight fails to proceed according to expected growth patterns, demonstrating an increasing deviation from the established growth curves (i.e., crossing two major percentile lines over time). For example, a premature infant whose birth weight, corrected for gestational age, is below the 5th percentile may be considered a FTT infant if weight growth progressively falls away from the expected pattern. On the other hand, a child who is in the 95th percentile at birth whose weight crosses to the 10th percentile at the age of 6 months may also be considered a failure-to-thrive infant.

Although population-based data are not available, FTT occurs frequently, with an estimated 10% prevalence in both rural and urban ambulatory care settings. The problem is common in pediatric practices, accounting for as many as 10% of children evaluated in outpatient settings, and for 1% to 5% of pediatric hospitalizations (Bithoney & Rathbun, 1983). It is likely that many children with the condition are not recognized. Most pediatricians dichotomize the cause of FTT into organic versus nonorganic, or environmental, causes. Organic FTT includes any biomedical condition that is severe enough to result independently in the child's growth problem. Any disease in every organ system can cause FTT, and pediatric textbooks provide long lists of such organic causes. Typically, organic diseases are sought by the traditional medical approach of history, physical examination, and thorough laboratory evaluation. When all medical diagnoses are excluded, the typical pediatrician then attributes the child's FTT to nonorganic causes, such as maternal deprivation. Recently, a third category of mixed-etiology FTT has been described for children whose growth problems result from a combination of organic and environmental etiologies (Homer & Ludwig, 1981). Many publications over the last decade have demonstrated that the vast majority of children with FTT suffer from nonorganic FTT (Holmes, 1979; Homer & Ludwig, 1981; Sills, 1978). No more than 30% of children with FTT suffer from organic illness alone. Our recent experience confirms this finding. Of 131 children seen in our FTT secondary-level referral clinic, 17% suffered from organic disease only, 45% suffered from nonorganic FTT, and 35% suffered from a mixed etiology (Casey, Wortham, & Nelson, 1984).

The exclusionary diagnostic approach, as described above, presents several problems. The symptoms of the child with FTT at the time of presentation, such as persistent vomiting or diarrhea, are often not clearly attributable to either organic or nonorganic causes, and concerns persist regarding the nature of FTT. Second, few features other than overt parental poverty or psychoemotional lability are used to make a positive diagnosis of nonorganic FTT. Although observation for weight gain during a hospital stay is the most concrete positive clinical feature used to diagnose nonorganic FTT, this approach is subject to error. Some children with nonorganic FTT require many weeks to begin to gain weight. Likewise, some children with growth problems due primarily to physical disease may demonstrate rapid growth when hospitalized. Thus, diagnostic decisions using this criterion after short-term observation may be incorrect. On occasion, pressure for diagnosis can result in premature or counterproductive labeling. For example, the awareness of family stress may bias diagnostic opinion toward environmental causes and limit data gathering regarding organic disease. At the other extreme, some clinicians hesitate to accept the importance of environmental factors, which can lead to an uncritical acceptance of borderline physical abnormalities as proof of an organic cause. These concerns will be discussed further at the end of the chapter, when we discuss clinical implications.

PROCESS MODEL OF PARENTAL COMPETENCE

Failure to thrive may be viewed as a clinical manifestation of parenting incompetence or failure. Fortunately, models of parenting success and failure have evolved significantly beyond the simplistic and judgmental "maternal deprivation" terminology of years ago. Increasingly sophisticated theoretic perspectives on the determinants of parenting have evolved, taking into account recent empirical data developed from several disciplines. One integrated theoretic perspective I believe to be particularly germane has been described by Belsky (1984); I will attempt to review this model as a starting point from which to begin our overview of failure to thrive. It is now agreed that healthy socioemotional development and cognitive–motivational competence during infancy and the preschool years are most effectively promoted by sensitive, attentive, warm, stimulating, responsive, and moderately nonrestrictive caregiving. But why are some individual parents and sets of parents successful in this regard, while others fail to such an extent that their children grow and develop abnormally?

Without question, parenting competence is determined by multiple factors. Characteristics of the parents, their children, and the broader environmental context in which the parent–child relationship is embedded all combine to affect the parental role. Characteristics of children that may affect parents include the child's health and nutritional status, physical appearance, temperament, and neurodevelopmental status. These characteristics, whether positive or negative, may make the parenting task relatively more difficult or easier to accomplish. I will return to these characteristics as the interactional model of failure to thrive is presented.

Parent characteristics that may have an impact on competency of parenting include education, health, personality traits, and experience as parents. The parents' developmental experiences as children with their own parents is viewed as particularly important in the development of parenting competency. The clinical literature in child abuse suggests an increased likelihood of traumatic childhood experiences in parents who demonstrate parenting deficiencies. The parents' developmental experience provides a background that may have negative impact on their adult personality traits and experience in parenting.

Although specific parent and child characteristics affect the effectiveness of parenting, a broader perspective of parenting requires that the parent–child relationship be evaluated in the context of environment. Stress and support in a parent's environment interact, and the relative strengths and weaknesses in these areas have a significant impact on overall parenting effectiveness. It is suggested that support functions in three ways: first, by providing emotional support; second, by providing instrumental–physical assistance; and third, by providing social expectations and advice. Within the microenvironment of a family's home, the areas of strengths and weakness that may have an impact on parenting competence include the quality of the marital relationship; the physical quality of the home and economic resources available; the physical organization of the home; and, finally, the stability of the living situation itself. Outside the immediate home, the broader family, the neighborhood, and work situations provide potential support in all these areas, but they may likewise promote stress.

In the center of Belsky's model is the focus of interest—parenting. This is affected by the child's characteristics and by traits of the individual parents, both inborn and learned during developmental experience. The environment is represented by the marital relationship, by social networks, and by the work situation. Clearly, there are multiple interacting links between personality, marital relations, social network, and work on parenting. A parent's developmental history and personality shape parenting directly, but also indirectly by helping to shape and influence the broader context of marital relations, social network, and occupational experience. Thus, the choice of spouse, the living situation selected, and occupational choices are affected by the parent's personality and developmental experience, which affect the context of parenting.

Finally, while noting that parenting is multiply determined by infant, parent, and environmental characteristics, Belsky suggests that these three areas are not equally influential in promoting or undermining parenting. When two of the three areas of determinants of parenting competence are problematic, he suggests that parent competence is most protected when the parents' developmental history and personality traits continue to promote attentive and sensitive parenting, and least protected when it is the child's characteristics that are positive.

INTERACTIONAL MODEL OF FAILURE TO THRIVE

We have developed an interactional model as a clinical and research approach to FTT that predates the Belsky model of parenting competence (Casey, 1983). We believe that this model, which fits neatly in Belsky's scheme, provides an effective overview to understand the clinical development of FTT, as well as a research approach to this condition.

The model (Figure 24-1) conceptualizes interaction at several levels. First, the central cause of FTT is viewed as a breakdown in the parent–infant (usually mother–infant) interaction. In the maladapted parent–infant interaction, the parent does not "read" and respond to the infant appropriately, and the infant has difficulty in eliciting attention and appropriate care from the parent. This bidirectional problem ultimately results in nutritional and nurturing deficiencies that then result in deviation from normal growth and development. Clearly, certain physical, emotional, or social problems of the parent, when severe enough, cause *unidirectional* effects that may result in FTT in any child. This parent-to-child effect has dominated the literature on nonorganic FTT with labels such as "maternal deprivation" and "psychosocial deprivation." We believe that in most situations abnormalities, often minor and subtle in physical, temperamental, and/or psychoattitudinal aspects of the parent, combine with real or perceived abnormalities of the infant to result in interactional FTT.

The next level of interactional FTT is the interaction between the abnormalities of the parents and those of the child. For example, infants who present problems in the basic caregiving requirements, such as ease of feeding and soothing, place stress on the parent–infant interaction. Similarly, infants who are unpredictable and have difficulty signaling their needs can impede a mutually rewarding relationship. These problems occur more

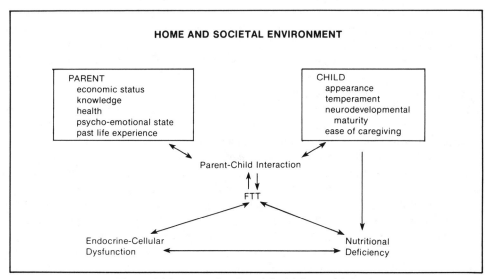

Figure 24-1. Interactional model of failure to thrive.

commonly in premature infants, children with difficult temperaments, and children with both major and minor neurologic dysfunction.

Recent data suggest that undernutrition has an independent detrimental affect on parent–infant interaction as early as the first 6 months of life. Undernutrition increases the difficulty of caring for the infant and thus has a compounding negative impact on the parent–infant interaction.

The final level of interactional FTT is the interaction between the parent–child pair and aspects of the micro- and macroenvironment in which the pair exist. The physical home provides the milieu in which the parent–infant interaction occurs. The number of people present in the house, the adequacy of the physical home, the home's organization, and the adequacy of cognitive support available all affect parent–infant interaction and the parents' ability to meet their infants' needs. In sum, this interactional model of FTT implies a multifactorial causation mediated by the maladapted parent–child interaction. The maladapted interaction results in nutritional and, ultimately, endocrine-cellular abnormalities, which in turn lead to problems in growth and development.

EMPIRICAL RESEARCH REGARDING THE INTERACTIONAL MODEL OF FTT

I will now present the empirical research that examines various aspects of the theoretic model of parent–infant causality of FTT. Until the last decade, the literature in these areas was anecdoctal and clinically based, and much of this information has not held up with controlled research. Selected relevant, controlled research that evaluates aspects of the interactional model in the areas of parent–child interaction, child characteristics, parent characteristics, and finally environmental characteristics will be described.

Mother–Child Interaction

There has been one published report that prospectively assessed interactional styles between mother and infant prior to the time of the development of FTT (Vietze *et al.*, 1980). Four hundred ninety-eight urban poor mothers and their infants were followed from the time of pregnancy forward, and 35 children were ultimately identified as suffering from FTT prior to the age of 18 months. These FTT infants were compared during a feeding event at 2 weeks of age to a matched group of children who ultimately grew normally. There was a greater probability that mothers of male infants later diagnosed as nonorganic FTT would prematurely terminate their response to the infant than for mothers of male infants who had normal growth. Also, mothers of male infants who later developed nonorganic FTT had a greater probability of discontinuing an active interaction between mother and infant during the feeding event as compared to mothers of male infants in the comparison group. This study of specific abnormal social interaction patterns prior to the time of development of FTT is original and requires duplication and further delineation.

There have been several controlled studies that assessed the parent–child interaction after the time of diagnosis of FTT. We prospectively identified 23 infants with nonorganic FTT, and individually matched them to a normally grown control subject by infant age, sex, and race as well as family income, maternal education, and number of people living in the household (Casey, Bradley, & Wortham, 1984). Maternal age and education were nearly identical in both groups, and the economic status of all of these families was extremely low. An assistant unaware of infant growth rate visited their homes within 3 weeks after diagnosis and performed the Home Observation for Measurement of the Environment Inventory, known as the HOME. This research instrument requires a one-hour visit at home and attempts to assess different aspects of the mother–infant interaction and the quality of the cognitive and emotional support available to the infant's home. The version of the HOME used in infants up to age 3 includes 45 items clustered into 6 subscales: Emotional and Verbal Responsivity of Mother, Acceptance of Child, Organization of the Physical and Temporal Environment, Provision of Appropriate Play Materials, Maternal Involvement with Child, and Opportunity and Variety in Daily Stimulation. The assistant also completed the Coddington Life Events Record, an interview-based inventory that attempts to quantify the amount of psychosocial readjustment required to cope with events occurring in the family during the preceding year. Significant differences in social and nonsocial aspects of the children's homes were found. The total HOME Inventory and the subscales entitled Maternal Responsivity, Maternal Acceptance, and Organization of the Physical Environment were significantly lower for the FTT group than for the control group. A multiple discriminant analysis was performed using the six HOME subscales and the Coddington Life Events Record in an attempt to differentiate between infants with FTT and control infants. Using the discriminant function coefficient generated in the analysis, it was possible to place correctly 32 of the 46 children into FTT or control groups, with an overall correct prediction rate of 70%. This set of environmental variables significantly separated the two groups.

It is premature in the understanding of the abnormalities in parent–child interactions in FTT to generalize the characteristic patterns of abnormal social relations between parents and FTT infants. Our research, along with that of others, suggests a less vocally responsive and less nurturing environment. Further research in this area is required.

Child Characteristics

Let us now focus on the child to examine which characteristics have been demonstrated to contribute to the problem of FTT. It makes theoretic sense that the problems listed in the interactional model—infant appearance, temperament, neurodevelopmental maturity, and ease of caregiving—might contribute to the interactional problems that result in FTT. Unfortunately, controlled empirical research has not been performed to confirm these associations. There is, however, indirect evidence to support their relevance. In samples of normal children, many of these characteristics that are hypothesized to make children more or less easy to care for have been shown to affect the quality of parent–child interaction (Crockenberg & Smith, 1982; Goldberg, 1977). Second, these characteristics are more likely to be found in premature infants (Field, 1980) and neurologically impaired infants, both of which categories are overrepresented in FTT populations. In at least two studies, including the prospective controlled study of FTT described earlier (Vietze *et al.*, 1980), the birth weights of FTT infants matched to controls were significantly lower. In summary, although more prospective research is required to confirm the characteristics of the child that contribute to parent–infant interactional difficulties resulting in FTT, there is a sound theoretic rationale and adequate empirical evidence in children of normal populations to support the notion that specific characteristics of infants may contribute to interactional difficulties.

One characteristic of the child that has been adequately evaluated is the child's health. Children who develop failure to thrive are viewed as being more sickly by their parents and have more episodes of illness both before and after the onset of failure to thrive when compared to normal children. Kotelchuk and Newberger (1983) reported a sample of 42 children hospitalized with FTT and compared them to a group of children hospitalized for acute short-term medical illnesses. During the time of the childrens' hospitalization, the mothers were interviewed using a standardized interview schedule. FTT infants were perceived by their mothers as substantially more sickly than controls: 38% of FTT children were seen as being in poor health compared to 7% of controls, and 64% of controls were seen as healthy compared to only 14% of the FTT children. This variable was the strongest differentiator of the two groups among the 50 variables evaluated during the study.

A more objective and careful design was used by the group that performed the prospective study described earlier. Health data were collected on a sample of 80 children, 11 abused children, 31 children with nonorganic failure to thrive, 14 children from neglectful families, and 24 children from control families. Data collectors who were unaware of group status reviewed the hospital records for all clinic visits, emergency room visits, and inpatient admissions. These records were evaluated from birth until 36 months after birth. There was a significant difference between the children with FTT and those in the control group in the number of illnesses during the first year and over the 3-year period. The nonorganic failure-to-thrive group showed significant differences from controls during the first 3 months of life prior to the onset of FTT. There were no group differences in the frequency of accidents. The nonorganic FTT group had more hospitalizations when compared to the control group. Finally, only the nonorganic FTT group demonstrated more anatomic anomalies, usually minor in degree, when compared to the control group. This finding is of interest since children with serious anomalies were considered to have organic FTT and were not included in the nonorganic group. This study, in summary, determined that children with nonorganic failure to thrive were ill more often than control children, particularly in the first 3 to 6 months of life (Sherrod, O'Connor, Vietze, & Altemeier, 1984).

I will digress briefly here to describe the effect of malnutrition on a child's behavior, and to comment on how this might affect the quality of parent–child interaction. Although there is surprisingly little systematic information concerning the nature and severity of nutritional deficits associated with children with FTT, most clinicians agree that some degree of undernutrition is ubiquitous by the time of diagnosis of FTT. Several studies suggest that undernutrition has an independent negative effect on infant behavior and mother–infant interaction. A cross-sectional study of 74 well-nourished and undernourished 12-month-old infants in Nepal found significantly greater activity levels, distance interactions, and interactions in general for the well-nourished group (Graves, 1978). In a prospective intervention study performed in rural Mexico, 17 infants were supplemented with formula from birth and compared with 17 matched infants who were not supplemented (Chavez, Martinez, & Yaschine, 1975). By 24 weeks of age there were differences in infant behaviors and activity, as well as differences in the parent–child interaction. The nonsupplemented infants were more passive and dependent on their mothers. The parents of the supplemented infants provided more stimulating behaviors, such as smiling, playing, and talking. In summary, these reports suggest that malnourished infants are less active and demonstrate more dependency in clinging behaviors, and that their parents are less responsive and stimulating.

Parent Characteristics

Let us now focus our attention on characteristics of the parents that may contribute to the child's FTT. The early clinical literature focused on specific deficits of the parents, usually the mother, that were considered causes of the failure to thrive. These noncontrolled reports suggested that the problem resulted from specific personality defects, socioeconomic stress, or parental demographic characteristics, such as relative youthfulness or single marital status. For example, a clinical report of FTT children in 1971 found that 11 of the 12 mothers of these children were depressed (Fischoff, Whitten, & Pettit, 1971). On the other hand, controlled studies published over the last decade have found no differences between study and control group mothers in maternal age, marital status, maternal knowledge, stress, mental health, or attitudes. The largest of these studies was the prospective study of 498 urban mothers and their infants followed from the prenatal period until the age of 18 months (Vietze *et al.*, 1980). The workers found no differences in maternal age, education, number of siblings, race, or marital status when comparing 35 of these children, who ultimately developed nonorganic FFT, to 50 randomly selected normal infants from the larger group. In a separate study of 19 nonorganic failure-to-thrive children who were matched to a control group for child age, race, and sex, there were again no differences noted in the aforementioned demographic and attitudinal data (Pollitt, Eichler, & Chee-Khoon, 1975).

The interactional model of FTT described earlier included other maternal characteristics, such as health and previous experience as children and as parents. Unfortunately, however, there is no research that has evaluated a possible association between these areas. One of the more important gaps in the study of child maltreatment, particularly failure to thrive, is the role of the father in the development of this clinical problem. I am aware of no studies that attempt to assess characteristics of the father in the study of FTT. In fact, both in clinical practice and in research, it is often difficult to obtain adequate information concerning the role of the father.

Environmental Characteristics

Let us now focus our attention to the characteristics of the child's home environment as they relate to FTT. Characteristics of the environment that may be of significance include structural and resource aspects of the home, such as income, family size, spacing of the children, and adequacy of the household and its organization, as well as stresses and supports provided by the broader family, neighborhood, and work environment. Multiple environmental characteristics described in the earlier clinical literature as being etiologically related to FTT, such as large family size, closely spaced children, and multiple financial difficulties and stress, have not held up under controlled research. Two controlled reports described earlier failed to note differences between families with FTT children and control families in number of family members, birth order of index child, number of rooms in the house, or other global measures of environmental stress (Kotelchuk & Newburger, 1983; Vietze *et al.*, 1980). Clearly, we must look more closely at the home environment rather than just using these crude environmental markers, as most infants living in stressed situations do not develop FTT. In our controlled research described earlier, the homes of the children with FTT were more disorganized, although there were no differences in the quality of play materials available or the opportunity for exploration (Casey, Bradley, & Wortham, 1984). Finally, when Kotelchuk and Newburger (1983) compared families of 42 infants with FTT to families of 42 infants hospitalized for acute illness, there was less perceived positive support from family and neighbors available to the mothers of FTT children than to the control mothers. The mothers of FTT children differed significantly from the control mothers in the perception that their neighborhood was unfriendly, that they did not like their neighborhood, and that they were visited less often by family members.

Despite the dearth of adequate empirical data with families of FTT children, it is clear from research with normal and high-risk samples that the availability and quality of support received from relatives and friends exerts a positive impact on the parent–child relation. Further, the role of adequate social support is viewed as a major protective factor in the presence of negative stress factors. Crnic, Greenberg, Ragozin, Robinson, and Basham (1983) reported a prospective study of a group of 105 full-term and premature infants. Mother's life stress and social supports were assessed at a home visit 1 month postpartum using standardized research instruments. Mothers who reported greater life stress at 1 month were less positive in their attitudes and in the sensitivity of their interactive behavior with their infants when assessed again at 4 months, whereas mothers with greater support were significantly more positive at the same visit. In addition, social support noted by the mothers at 1 month postpartum had a moderating beneficial impact on the adverse effects of stress on multiple mother behaviors in interaction with infants at the 4-month evaluation.

In summary, research has determined that the homes of children with FTT are less organized, and that children with FTT are more likely to live in families with less social support. Further controlled research is required to replicate these findings and to assess other aspects of the environment. As has been done in other risk populations, the interaction between environmental stress and support needs to be examined more carefully in studies using failing-to-thrive children.

RESEARCH AND CLINICAL IMPLICATIONS

Research regarding children with FTT is moving beyond the simplistic unicausal models of the past into a much more sophisticated perception of the child in the context of the family and living environment. To review briefly, we believe that there may be mild or subtle problems in both parent and child that in variable combination result in interactional difficulties that ultimately lead to failure to thrive. The parents' experiences as children, household disorganization and crowdedness, economic and interpersonal stress, and social networks and support all may interact to contribute to the pathogenesis of FTT. Strengths and weaknesses in each of these areas, as well as the children's characteristics, may be protective or promotive. Further research using controlled designs will be required. The following are some of the questions that will require answers:

1. Is it possible to identify characteristics of the parent–child interaction that are maladaptive in FTT children and their parents, and to understand the relative contribution of infant, parent, and environmental characteristics to this maladaptive interaction?
2. Is it possible to identify subgroups of FTT children, based on infant, parent, environmental, nutritional, and interactional data, that have different growth, development, and behavioral outcomes?
3. Is it possible to identify subtypes of FTT children who respond differently to various types of clinical management? For example, certain children may require inpatient versus outpatient management; some may require foster care placement immediately; some may require psychiatric care while others need only supportive and nutritional care.

Finally, it is of interest to place these considerations of an interactional model of FTT in a clinical perspective. As described earlier, the typical medical diagnostic process is focused only on the child, so that the diagnosis of nonorganic FTT is made from a negative perspective by a process of elimination of medical diagnosis. A more positive diagnostic process would account for the three categories of influence on parenting as delineated by Belsky (1984): (1) the child's temperamental and developmental characteristics, (2) the parents interactional style and psychologic resources derived from their own developmental experience, and (3) the multiple sources of stress and support in the environment. A careful history should be obtained concerning the infant's early behavioral and feeding style, soothing, crying, and other clinical situations that result in mild developmental–behavioral deviations. Subtle neurodevelopmental and behavioral problems should be assessed during the physical examination.

A diagnostic evaluation that focuses on the parent or the child independently may miss the etiologic basis for the FTT when the pathophysiologic process exists in the interaction between the two individuals. The diagnostic evaluation should include an assessment of the parent–infant interaction, with particular emphasis on verbal and affective responsivity between parent and infant. Although there are several research methodologies for this purpose, clinical research is ongoing to develop useful standardized clinical assessments for office or hospital use by medical clinicians. Related methods include rating the quality and appropriateness of parent–child interaction in structured stressful events, such as the physical examination or free play, or natural events such as feeding or clothing. Next, an assessment of the physical organization of the home environment may contribute to the positive diagnosis of FFT. Rather than relying on nonspecific sociodemographic data, such as educational level or family income, clinicians may find information obtained on a home visit by a social worker or a visiting nurse to be of positive value in the diagnostic evaluation. Finally, management plans for infants with FTT should deal with weaknesses in the parent–infant interaction and the home environment. Counseling to enhance the parents' awareness and understanding of normal developmental skills and to improve the quality and appropriateness of their interaction with the child may be provided by a physician, nurse, or social worker. This approach must accommodate for the broader family and social context in which the parent–child interaction exists.

In summary, the research and clinical perceptions of children with failure to thrive and the families that foster this condition are evolving. In this chapter we have described research questions and clinical approaches that transcend the traditional medical approach, which evaluates the child for the presence of organic diseases. The interactional family system model, which accounts for problems in children, families, and environment, is more likely to yield accurate diagnostic results and management plans that have a better chance of success. Thoughtful collaboration between physicians, nurses, and developmental psychologists will be required for research planning to assess this approach.

References

Belsky J. The determinants of parenting: a process model. Child Development 1984; 55:83–96.

Bithoney WG, Rathbun JM. Failure to thrive. In: Levine WB, Carey AC, Crocker AD, Gross RJ, eds. Developmental behavioral pediatrics. Philadelphia: Saunders, 1983:557–572.

Casey PH. Failure to thrive, a reconceptualization. Developmental and Behavioral Pediatrics 1983; 4:63–66.

Casey PH, Bradley RH, Wortham B. Social and nonsocial environments of children with nonorganic failure to thrive. Pediatrics 1984; 73:348–353.

Casey PH, Wortham B, Nelson JY. Managment of children with failure to thrive in a rural ambulatory setting. Clinical Pediatrics 1984; 23:325–330.

Chavez A, Martinez C, Yaschine T. Nutrition, behavioral development and mother–child interaction in young rural children. Federation Proceedings 1975; 35:1574–1582.

Crockenberg SB, Smith P. Antecedents of mother–infant interaction and infant irritability in the first three months of life. Infant Behavior and Development 1982; 5:105–110.

Crnic KA, Greenberg MT, Ragozin AS, Robinson NM, Basham RB. Effects of stress and social supports on mothers and premature and full-term infants. Child Development 1983; 54:209–217.

Field TM. Interactions of preterm and term infants with their lower and middle-class teenage and adult mothers. In: Field TM, Goldberg S, Stern D, Sostek AM, eds. High-risk infants and children: adult and peer interactions. New York: Academic Press, 1980:113–132.

Fischoff J, Whitten CF, Pettit MG. A psychiatric study of mothers of infants with growth failure secondary to maternal deprivation. Journal of Pediatrics 1971; 79:209–215.

Goldberg S. Social competence in infancy: a model of parent–infant interaction. Merrill-Palmer Quarterly 1977; 23:163–177.

Graves PL. Nutrition and infant behavior: a replication study in the Katmandu Valley, Nepal. American Journal of Clinical Nutrition 1978; 31:541–551.

Holmes GL. Evaluation and prognosis in nonorganic failure to thrive. Southern Medical Journal 1979; 72:693–698.

Homer C, Ludwig S. Categorization of etiology of failure to thrive. American Journal of Diseases of Children 1981; 135:848–851.

Kotelchuk M, Newburger EH. Failure to thrive: a controlled study of familial characteristics. Journal of the American Academy of Child Psychology 1983; 22:322–328.

Pollitt E, Eichler AW, Chee-Khoon Chan. Psychosocial development and behavior of mothers of failure to thrive children. American Journal of Orthopsychiatry 1975; 45:525–537.

Sherrod KB, O'Connor S, Vietze PM, Altemeier WA. Child health and maltreatment. Child Development 1984; 55:1174–1183.

Sills RH. Failure to thrive—the role of clinical and laboratory evaluation. American Journal of Diseases of Children 1978; 132:967–969.

Vietze PM, Falsey S, O'Connor S, Sandler H, Sherrod K, Altemeier WA. Newborn and interactional characteristics of non-organic failure to thrive infants. In: Field TM, Goldberg S, Stern D, Sostek AM, eds: High-risk infants and children: adult and peer interactions. New York: Academic Press, 1980:5–23.

25

Family Medicine and Family Gerontology

JAY A. MANCINI
Virginia Polytechnic Institute and State University

Several years ago *Time* magazine titled one of its cover stories ''The Graying of America'' and alerted the general populace to the changing characteristics of Americans as they related to chronologic age. The United States is an aging society, with half of its population now over 30 years old. By the year 2000, approximately 13% or about 35 million people, will be over 65 years of age (U.S. Bureau of the Census, 1982). The life cycle phase called ''adulthood'' has lengthened significantly. Whereas in 1900 a young couple could expect to survive together for another 25 or so years, the young married couple by the 1980s can expect, barring separation by choice, to have 50 or more years of married life (Perlmutter & Hall, 1985).

Although we may be most aware of chronologic age and how it is changing, of greater importance is biologic, psychologic, social, and functional age (Birren & Renner, 1977). ''Biologic age'' involves one's physical health; ''psychologic age'' refers to cognitive, emotional, and personality domains of adulthood; ''social age'' pertains to roles associated with being in the position of adult or older adult; ''functional age'' is the term that represents one's general ability to function effectively in the society, and is said to reflect biologic, psychologic, and social age (Perlmutter & Hall, 1985). The study of age is the systematic examination of all these facets of aging and, appropriately, a mode of study that accounts for the interplay among them.

The awareness of age as a multifaceted adult characteristic is relevant to the current discussion of the family system and its relationship to aging in this regard: To know where any particular older adult fits in the family system, one must understand his or her level of development as it involves the five dimensions of aging. For example, an older person's *biological age* may limit the level of involvement he or she may have in family life. The dimension of *psychological age* will indicate how able the older adult is to communicate and solve problems with family members. *Functional age* will provide insight into how dependent he or she is on family support and will contribute to understanding stress in the family. *Chronological age* often determines what the family expects of an older person, and *social age* will tell exactly what one does in the position of older adult. Research on the older adult in the family should account for aging in more than chronologic terms because these other dimensions of age are most informative regarding quality of life and family life quality.

It appears that many professionals are now interested in family gerontology, that is, the study of aging as it interfaces with family life. A great deal of social science research in this area has been published; in fact, several hundred articles, book chapters, and books have reported on some aspect of aging and family life. After reviewing much of this research and conceptual writing, I recently concluded that ''the research frontier about families in later life is broad and multidimensional. For the researcher this situation is advantageous because there are few definitive answers to the important questions on generational relationships; however, it is equally disadvantageous because explorations of a frontier often lack the guideposts needed for fruitful discovery'' (Mancini, 1984b, p, 282). The field of family gerontology is frontier-like in that there is considerable opportunity for addressing the significant questions related to the family's role in successful aging. The primary goal of this chapter is to suggest where research on family gerontology needs to be strengthened; the lens I will use focuses on family relationships and the family as a system. Therefore, in this chapter I will delineate those research questions that are of an applied nature and that are relevant for family medicine and for those providing therapeutic services to the family system. It is hoped that these ideas will be of interest to family physicians and social scientists, as well as to family life educators and family therapists. To accomplish these goals, I will address several questions:

1. What are the trends in social science research on the family system and its relationship to aging?
2. What is the nature of family medicine research?
3. What are the relevant domains of research regarding the aged and the family?
4. What guidelines should be utilized in conducting this research?

Although it is beyond the scope of this chapter to report what is currently known about families in later life, some of this knowledge will be presented in the course of specifying research needs.

BRIEF SUMMARY OF TYPICAL FAMILY GERONTOLOGY RESEARCH

So that the function of the present discussion can be better understood, an attempt will be made to note the history of social science research on the family and aging. Troll, Miller, and Atchley (1979) said that until about 1970 gerontologists and family social scientists were not especially aware of what each were doing in family gerontology. An important literature review by Troll (1971) represented a bridge between the disciplines and was the first widely read attempt at such an integration. Since that time, several other publications have appeared that update the literature and continue that integrative work (Bengtson & DeTerre, 1980; Blieszner, 1986; Brubaker, 1983; Fogel, Hatfield, Kiesler, & Shanas, 1981; Mancini, 1980, 1984b; Quinn & Hughston, 1984; Troll, Miller, & Atchley, 1979).

I stated previously that a substantial portion of family gerontology research has addressed the alienation, enrichment, and empty-nest hypotheses (Mancini, 1984b). The correlative research questions are:

1. Do families neglect their elderly?
2. Do family relations enhance successful aging?
3. Are there deleterious effects on older parents when children establish a separate residence?

Answers to these questions, respectively, are "No," "It's difficult to say," and "Usually not." Most of the literature concurs that families generally do not neglect their elderly members and are in regular contact with them (Shanas, 1979). The data also suggest, however, that spending time with one's family does not necessarily promote successful aging (Mancini & Blieszner, 1986). Troll (1971) said, "There is little evidence of the empty-nest crisis accompanied by great distress and massive readjustment" (p. 198). The research in family gerontology has mushroomed and is now reaching voluminous proportions when compared to the whole of studies on adult relationships. Most books include several chapters on the marriage relationship, parent–child relations, grandparenthood, separation and divorce, family stress, minority families, and the single life-style. There is now often a chapter on elder abuse, long-term care, and policy implications. But there are few treatments that integrate the family and health issues as they pertain to aging (Streib & Beck, 1980), nor are there many interdisciplinary studies of any kind. Butler (1981) noted the necessity of integrating biology and behavior, the physical and the social dimensions of aging. He stated that, "Solving the problems of old age requires the concurrent application of the latest and best information available from the biological sciences, clinical medicine, and studies of personal and social behavior" (p. 7). Unfortunately, family gerontology receives low marks for interdisciplinary research and theorizing.

FUTURE RESEARCH NEEDS IN FAMILY GERONTOLOGY

Research conducted in the 1960s, 1970s, and 1980s on the family and its relationship to aging has been critically reviewed by several social scientists, and suggestions for subsequent research have been delineated (Bengtson & DeTerre, 1980; Blieszner, 1986; Mancini, 1980; Mancini, 1984b; Mancini & Blieszner, in press; Streib & Beck, 1980; Troll, 1971; Troll, Miller, & Atchley, 1979). Altogether these scientists have listed well over fifty avenues that future research ought to take. Several years ago I summarized these reviews in detail, but for the present I will paint a broader picture of research needs (Mancini, 1984b). Most of these critical reviews point to the need for research on the internal workings of the family that take into account such dimensions as feelings, conflict, negotiation, and cooperation—in effect, the qualitative aspects of family life. It is agreed that the intricacies of family support patterns deserve more study, as does the issue of the family's specific role in the physical and emotional well-being of an aged person. The reviews also point to the need for more sophisticated research designs, including longitudinal and cross-sequential approaches, and to deficits in the actual measurement of family dynamics. Specific suggestions from these critical reviews germane to the family gerontology–family medicine interface will be touched upon later in this chapter.

FAMILY MEDICINE RESEARCH

The family practice discipline is multidisciplinary in intent and scope. Geyman (1980) has noted that family practice "is the specialty in breadth which builds upon a core of knowledge derived from other disciplines and which establishes a cohesive unit, combining the behavioral sciences with the traditional biological and clinical sciences" (p. 19). Rosen and Arsht (1979) add that "The conceptual framework of family practice further expands the locus of disease to encompass the contribution of familial and social factors" (p. 2). They affirm their position by stating, "It can be safely inferred that every disease has its psychological aspect, and every psychological state has its bodily expression, although one may be dominant and the other not essentially significant" (p. 3). Hoffmaster (1981) makes a case for family medicine being considered a social science. He suggests that it can be considered a social science because knowledge from the social sciences is accessed, because in some manner the physician functions as a social scientist, and because the discipline itself parallels social science. Wood (1983) classified family medicine research into five categories: patient care or clinical research; epidemiologic research; behavioral, psychologic, and social research; operational and organizational research; and educational research. Perkoff (1981) also delineates five research domains: (1) research on the content of family practice; (2) research on the delivery of family medical care; (3) research on the family aspects of family medicine; (4) research external to personal health services; and (5) cross-cultural studies relevant to family medicine. Parkerson and The Study Group on Family Medicine Research (1982) name health and disturbed health, health care delivery, and medical education as research categories. They note that

> the involvement of family medicine with people in the context of their personal social support groups within their own communities is an excellent base for research on individual and group behavioral factors. The "family" component of family medicine is used as an indicator for social groups, which include, but by no means are confined to, the traditional nuclear family. The interactions between individuals and members of their own families or other social support groups have important but poorly understood relationships to health and disease that need to be elucidated. (Parkerson *et al.*, 1982, p. 107)

Perkoff (1981), in discussing dimensions of family medicine research, states that "The present surge of interest in studies of aging includes family and social factors affecting the aging process and the handling of problems of the aged in various social and medical settings" (p. 556). Geyman (1980) similarly suggests that the domain of behavioral research in family medicine should include family dynamics, changing patterns, and developmental aspects of the family life cycle. And Redman, Everett, and Wallace (1984) discuss aspects of behavior and the family that are appropriate avenues of family medicine research: normal/abnormal, changing patterns of the household unit, and the family life cycle (teenage problems and the social problems of aging).

Authorities in the family medicine field concur that behavioral and social research is significant for an effective understanding of the individual and the family system. They also recommend that the family medicine field focus more on the process of aging (Gelbart & Bono, 1982) and, in particular, on family gerontology (Perkoff, 1981). It is in this context that the following research issues are discussed. The issues cut across research involving patient care, program evaluation, and social-psychologic factors in adult development. These issues/research questions are applied in nature; that is, the data designed to address them can be applied to the everyday life of older adults and their families.

RESEARCH ON THE FAMILY SYSTEM IN LATER LIFE

Farley and Farley (1983) state that

> all care providers, particularly family doctors, must recognize and deal with the reality and impact of the intergenerational family with its strengths, weaknesses, and associated problems. If the provider is unaware of the context of the individual within the family and community, he cannot identify or respond adequately to the problems of the individual seeking comprehensive care. (p. 1713)

Several assumptions underlie the present discussion on research needs in family gerontology that are of relevance to the family medicine field:

1. The family is a complex system.
2. The older person is a component in a family system whose role is not very well understood.
3. Quality of life should be a context for discussing research needs.

For some years now, "quality of life" has received a great deal of attention from social scientists. George and Bearon (1980) described the conceptual and measurement problems of quality of life; they also suggest that quality of life has two dimensions: (1) subjective evaluations (life satisfaction and self-esteem) and (2) objective conditions (health and functional status and socioeconomic status). The following suggestions for research are felt to interface with the notion of quality of life; that is, they are seen as having some impact on the aging experience. Although research has been conducted to some degree in all of these areas, there are few answers that we can accept with confidence.

Negotiating Relationship Change

If any one term characterizes adult development and aging, it is "change." Families experience difficulty when changing relationships are not understood and are not mutually accepted. For the family in later life, a significant research question involves how parents' and children's roles change over time; of even greater importance is research on the place that negotiation has in these changes. Is there conflict, and if so, to what degree? Under what conditions does conflict *not* develop? What happens in families where change is difficult and painful? Kuypers and Bengtson (1984) suggest that "Families continuously struggle as they try to let go of old patterns of interaction" (p. 4). The outcome of such change may affect the type and extent of family support that is given and received. The identification of how change is negotiated so that both aged parents and adult children benefit has implications for those who are called on to counsel. A model of conflict negotiation and resolution that accounts for aging and family interaction is as yet undeveloped.

Aging as a Roleless Role

Almost thirty years ago, Burgess (1960) discussed aging as a "roleless role," that is, one where there are either minimal expectations or where the expectation is a role devoid of content. The following questions regarding the roleless role of the older adult in family relationships should be asked: What is the substance of being an aged family member? What effects are there when the older adult desires a more significant, instrumental role in family life but is not given such an opportunity by other family members? Does this situation have a substantial impact on self-esteem, and does it create relationship tension? In the larger scheme of the aging experience, any ill effects may be negligible. A researchable question that is linked to health is: How does one's involvement in the family relate to positive health behavior and the will to live a vital life-style?

Individual Vulnerability

What combination of physical and emotional conditions leaves the older adult vulnerable to low quality of life, more disease, and more mental anguish? To date there is relatively little formal investigation linking the various dimensions of age: chronologic, biologic, psychologic, social, and functional (Birren & Renner, 1977). Perlmutter and Hall (1985, p. 68) distinguish between normal physical aging and secondary physical aging, the latter being a result of disease, disuse, or abuse. The former includes graying or thinning hair, impaired vision and hearing, slowed response to temperature change, slower recovery from physical exertion, and impaired DNA functioning. These two categories of age are often confused, and relevant therapies may be misapplied. The nature of aging and research on the integration of its many facets has importance for the family because family cohesion may be altered when there is marginal understanding of the complexities of social, personal, and physical life. For example, we may attribute a person's objectionable behavior to his or her will rather than to a physical condition or biologic change.

Realistic Burden of Care

Even though most older adults are in reasonably good health (Kart, Metress, & Metress, 1978), a number of families will have older members who must live with two or more chronic diseases (Hickey, 1980; U.S. Senate Special Committee on Aging, 1985–1986). The major health problems of the aged are cardiovascular disease, cancer, osteoarthritis, and osteoporosis (Wantz & Gay, 1981); the major causes of death are cardiovascular disease, cancer, respiratory disease, and diabetes. This raises the question of what amount of burden families can realistically bear in the course of caring for a frail, aged family member. Research can explore the question of what determines family vitality when ongoing, intense family support is required. It is already known that some adult children are ambiguous and ambivalent in regard to their responsibilities to their aged parents (Hausman, 1979). A recent report from Cantor (1983) states that only 48% of adult child caregivers felt that they understood their sick parent well, and only 28% felt that their sick parent understood them. These data seem to point toward the need to investigate family dynamics in such potentially burdensome situations.

Independence versus Learned Helplessness

A major interest in social gerontology is the promotion of independence (see Quinn & Hughston, 1984). It has been suggested that "the core of well-being includes independent aging—general self-care, facility in making decisions that influence one's own welfare, accessing support systems as required, and maintaining reasonable continuity with one's life-style in earlier years" (Mancini, 1984a, p. 70). Older adults value their independence, as do their families. Yet there are family systems in which a family's best intentions encourage an elder to be dependent and to learn the sick role; the cycle of learned helplessness becomes a drain on family resources due in part to increasing demands of the sick role occupant. A viable research question involves the point and level at which family support promotes dependency and is not in the best interests of families or their aged members.

Salience of Grandparenthood

As researchers, we often focus on the roles that end as a result of chronological aging. One role that emerges as we age is that of grandparent (Troll, 1983), but very little research has examined the family system as it includes grandparents. If we are interested in how the aged are integrated with all facets of the family system, then a likely role to explore is that of grandparent. A prime area of investigation is the grandparents' role in child development and socialization. For those professionals whose agenda includes adequate interpersonal role involvement for the aged, the question of how the oldest contribute to the well-being of the youngest, and vice versa, is significant.

The Family as Mediator and Navigator

A principal service the family can provide to its older members is assistance with accessing formal support. This dimension of family support has recently been discussed by Seelbach (1984) and Brubaker and Brubaker (1984). Older adults in need can benefit from various support sources, but unraveling the bureaucracy involved to get that support can be difficult; families who try to act on behalf of older members are also frustrated in trying to find out about such services and how to access them. As yet, there are insufficient data on how families receive information about programs and services for the aged, how they enter the formal support network, and the barriers they face in doing so. More needs to be known also about families who are so frustrated by bureaucracies that they no longer seek assistance. For families to be adequate mediators and navigators for their aged, there must be support for their endeavors.

Aged Parents and Aged Children

One reality of the lengthening life span is that both parents and children may be chronologically old (Pifer & Bronte, 1986). The fastest growing group of aged people is the very old, those who are 80 years of age and older. Quite a number will have children who are in their 60s and older. What are the implications for family support? Empirical information on these old generations could indicate how their needs differ from those of other adult generations and how the fact that all are old influences quality of life. Treas (1977, p. 490) states that "the extreme aged now pose an impediment to their aging offspring's aspirations for a retirement free of financial cares or demands on their time."

The Use of Time

It has been said that "one's satisfaction with existence is closely dependent on whether he feels he is getting what he wants out of life, a goal irrevocably connected with the utilization of time" (Kantor & Lehr, 1975, p. 89). In my own research, I assumed that

> Determinants of whether spending time together is beneficial include whether the older adult is invited to be a full participant in family life, as opposed to being defined as a bystander; the past history of family relationships (i.e., what conflict patterns have existed over the years); whether the generations feel obligated to spend time together and do so with reluctance; whether cooperative decisions are made about the nature of leisure experiences and not mandated by a particular individual; and the quality of current interaction that may leave family members feeling motivated to spend either more or less time in shared leisure. (Mancini, 1984a, p. 69))

In reality, research has not adequately tested these assumptions.

Motivating Use of Formal Support

Total personal independence is not a reasonable or a desirable goal for those elderly who are experiencing a health or mental deficit (Arling & McAuley, 1984). Yet, a proportion of those family elders who used outside assistance will not take advantage of formal support because of pride, values, or fear of stigma. An important applied research question concerns the predictors of formal support use, as well as the testing of strategies to promote service use.

Program and Service Coordination

In most communities, programs and services for the older adult are disorganized and not adequately coordinated (Brubaker & Brubaker, 1984). Evaluation research methodologies have not been sufficiently applied to the network of aging-related services. If families are to interface effectively with formal support sources, then there must be easier avenues of entry into the system.

Functions of Relationships

Robert Weiss (1969), as a result of his work with Parents Without Partners groups, has discussed the various functions of relationships, including intimacy/attachment, social integration, nurturance, worth, assistance/alliance, and guidance. Weiss feels that a psychologically healthy individual has a set of relationships that provides for these functions as specific needs arise. To what degree does the family system (or particular components of the family system) provide for these functions? At present, we are testing the relationship between these functional provisions and psychologic well-being (Mancini & Blieszner, 1985). A basic question involves the relative significance of these provisions, and the results may imply a variety of directions that service delivery and therapeutic intervention may take. Correlative to focusing on family functions is the examination of friend relations. In some domains of life, elders' expectations of friends and family are remarkably similar (Mancini & Simon, 1984); it would seem logical to examine functions of friend and family systems concurrently.

Ongoing Long-Term Care

Kalchthaler (1983) discusses the many service aspects of long-term care, including homemaker services, home health aides, hot meal programs, meals-on-wheels programs, transportation, community mental health programs, social services, nursing, physical therapy, occupational therapy, and domiciliary care (adult homes, foster care, and nursing home care). We also should include in our research efforts those older adults who live in their own homes or in the home of family members. Masciocchi, Thomas, and Moeller (1984) have said that there is very little information on families who care for the frail, impaired aged over time. What are their special strains? What is the nature of stress, disorganization, and crisis? What coping methods develop over time? In particular, the role and effects of respite care should be examined (e.g., relief provided by day care centers and other centers designed for the care of the frail elderly). Streib (1983) also notes the lack of social-psychologic research on the frail, homebound elderly; at the same time he criticizes research for focusing too much on the rational, functioning aged person. It is only now that social scientists are systematically addressing these issues (Mancini, in press).

Health Care Education

An area of much needed research and program development involves education about health, health care, and aging. Barbaro and Noyes (1984) report that those older people who were given knowledge about the aging process tended to behave in a way that would mitigate the effects of aging. All too often elders, their families, and helping professionals are not aggressive when it comes to addressing the unwanted aspects of aging. When someone speaks of an older person's life-style or health, the phrases we often hear are "Oh well, you're getting older" or "I guess it's just because I'm getting old." There is a need for applied research that is oriented toward examining effects of positive health behaviors on quality of life and quality of family life in the later years.

Midlife Squeeze

As a period of development, middle age has not been adequately investigated. One aspect of midlife as it relates to the family system has been called the "midlife squeeze." It describes those adults who are called on to provide considerable care for their aged parents and their dependent children at the same time (Hagestad, 1981, 1986).

It is these midlife people who mediate the social system for young and old, who navigate on their behalf, and who may be their first choice or last resort of support. In any case, they are pivotal in the family system. Therefore, research needs to address how they orchestrate the demands that other generations may place on them while at the same time managing their own adult development.

CONCLUSIONS AND CAVEATS

Walsh (1980) has said that the family system with aged members is a system of change and adaptational challenges. Much of what I have suggested is related to changing roles, statuses, and circumstances in the family. This chapter, like other reviews published earlier, indicates that there remains a significant amount of research to be conducted on the family system and its relationship to aging. This is especially true if we are to have a positive influence on the quality of life and the quality of family life. The family medicine field and its goals for effective patient care are amenable to the kinds of research needs discussed herein. There are, however, several research guidelines that I would like to discuss which will improve the quality of research in family gerontology.

First, the traditional approaches to the alienation, enrichment, and empty-nest hypotheses should be discarded. Instead of asking if families neglect their older members, we should examine specific areas of neglect and support and the conditions under which neglect or support occur. Rather than asking if spending time with one's family covaries with psychologic well-being, we should investigate the circumstances under which family contact is conducive to well-being and those conditions under which it is not. Rather than asking whether parents experience stress when there are no longer children in the home, we should inquire about the relationship transitions that occur as parents and children age.

Second, theory-based research should be encouraged. It is rare for a study of the family system and aging to be grounded in theory. As a field of study, social gerontology has been fixated with the activity, disengagement, and continuity theories of successful aging. Worse yet, the application of these and other, less commonly utilized social science theories has been sporadic and has not supported the integration of the many findings in family gerontology.

Third, researchers on families in later life should be aware of the need for designs that integrate structured and unstructured measures. To date, the meaning that older people attach to their superficial description of family life is largely unknown. This means that investigators will have to rely less on readily quantifiable, structured questionnaires and more on open-ended interviewing.

Fourth, effective family gerontology research should use a systematic approach to understanding quality of life in old age. As with any stage of development, the past and present, the macroscopic and microscopic must be acknowledged and assessed. For example, the understanding of aging in a family context must address the varying dimensions of individual aging, the family group's developmental phase, relationships in the family, and the societal events that have been the content of aged adults' life experience as well as of their families' life experience.

In conclusion, the family gerontology area is ripe for research by professionals in family medicine, family therapy, and general social science. For family therapy, the major interest may be in the shift in generational roles (Doherty & Baird, 1983, p. 52). For family physicians, the major interest may be in updating the knowledge base in order to deal with an expanding population of aging patients (see Eckert, Galazka, & Carroll, 1983; Reichel & Barnett, 1978). Herr and Weakland (1979) state that "until gerontologists begin to view many of the problems associated with aging in an interactional manner, the myth that success can be achieved by the patient application of cures aimed at correcting deficits within the aging individual will be perpetuated" (p. 152). Their advice is consistent with the framework of family medicine and with the spirit of the present discussion. Some years ago, it was suggested that the goal of adding years to life was more realizable than that of "adding life to years." This latter goal is where family gerontology research should be directed, and where its most direct interface with family medicine is evident.

References

Arling G, McAuley WJ. The family, public policy, and long-term care. In: Quinn WH, Hughston GA, eds. Independent aging: family and social systems perspectives. Rockville, Md: Aspen, 1984:133–148.

Barbaro EL, Noyes LE. A wellness program for a lifecare community. The Gerontologist 1984; 24:568–571.

Bengtson V, DeTerre E. Aging and family relations. Marriage and Family Review 1980; 3:51–76.

Birren JE, Renner VJ. Research on the psychology of aging: principles and experimentation. In: Birren JE, Schaie KW, eds. Handbook of the psychology of aging. New York: Van Nostrand Reinhold, 1977:3–38.

Blieszner R. Trends in family gerontology research. Family Relations 1986; 35:555–562.

Brubaker TH, ed. Family relationships in later life. Beverly Hills, Calif.: Sage Publications, 1983.

Brubaker TH, Brubaker E. Family support of older persons in the long-term care setting: recommendations for practice. In: Quinn WH, Hughston GA, eds. Independent aging: family and social systems perspectives. Rockville, Md: Aspen, 1984:106–114.

Burgess EW. Aging in western societies. Chicago: University of Chicago Press, 1960.

Butler RN. Overview on aging: some biomedical, social, and behavioral perspectives. In: Fogel RW, Hatfield E, Kiesler SB, Shanas E, eds. Aging: stability and change in the family. New York: Academic Press, 1981: 1–8.

Cantor MH. Strain among caregivers: a study of experience in the United States. The Gerontologist 1983; 23:597–604.

Doherty WJ, Baird MA. Family therapy and family medicine: toward the primary care of families. New York: Guilford Press, 1983.

Eckert JK, Galazka JJ, Carroll J. The geriatric patient in ecological perspective. Journal of Family Practice 1983; 16:757–761.

Farley LF, Farley ES. Intergenerational family problems. In: Taylor RB, ed. Family medicine: principles and practice. New York: Springer-Verlag, 1983:1713–1725.

Fogel RW, Hatfield E, Kiesler JB, Shanas E, eds. Aging: stability and change in the family. New York: Academic Press, 1981.

Gelbart AO, Bono SF. Geriatrics: significance for family physicians. Geriatrics 1982; 37:145–146.

George LK, Bearon LB. Quality of life in older persons: meaning and measurement. New York: Human Sciences Press, 1980.

Geyman JP. Family practice: foundation of changing health care. New York: Appleton-Century-Crofts, 1980.

Hagestad GO. Problems and promises in the social psychology of intergenerational relations. In: Fogel RW, Hatfield E, Kiesler JB, Shanas E, eds. Aging: stability and change in the family. New York: Academic Press, 1981:11–46.

Hagestad GO. The family: women and grandparents as kin-keepers. In: Pifer A, Bronte L, eds: Our aging society. New York: Norton, 1986:141–160.

Hausman, CP. Short-term counseling groups for people with elderly parents. The Gerontologist 1979; 19:102–107.

Herr JJ, Weakland JH. Communications within family systems: growing older within and with the double bind. In: Ragan PK, ed. Aging parents. Los Angeles: University of Southern California Press, 1979:144–153.

Hickey T. Health and aging. Monterey, Calif.: Brooks/Cole, 1980.

Hoffmaster B. Family medicine as a social science. Journal of Medicine and Philosophy 1981; 6:387–410.

Kalchthaler T. Long-term care. In: Taylor RB, ed. Family medicine: principles and practice. New York: Springer-Verlag, 1983:1849–1855.

Kantor D, Lehr W. Inside the family: toward a theory of family process. New York: Harper, 1975.

Kart CS, Metress ES, Metress JF. Aging and health: biologic and social perspectives. Reading, Mass. Addison-Wesley, 1978.

Kuypers JA, Bengtson VL. Perspectives on the older family. In: Quinn WH, Hughston GA, eds. Independent aging: family and social systems perspectives. Rockville, Md.: Aspen, 1984:2–20.

Mancini JA. Strengthening the family life of older adults: myth-conceptions and investigative needs. In: Stinnett N, ed. Family strengths: positive models for family life. Lincoln: University of Nebraska Press, 1980: 333–343.

Mancini JA. Leisure lifestyles and family dynamics in old age. In Quinn WH, Hughston GA, eds. Independent aging: family and social systems perspectives. Rockville, Md.: Aspen, 1984a:58–71.

Mancini JA. Research on family life in old age: exploring the frontiers. In: Quinn WH, Hughston GA, eds. Independent aging: family and social systems perspectives. Rockville, Md.: Aspen, 1984b:265–284.

Mancini JA, ed. Aged parents and adult children. Lexington, Mass.: Lexington Books, in press.

Mancini JA, Blieszner R. The social provisions scale. Presented at the annual meeting of the Gerontological Society of America, New Orleans, Louisiana, 1985.

Mancini JA, Blieszner R. Successful aging and family life. Presented at the annual meeting of the Gerontological Society of America, Chicago, 1986.

Mancini JA, Blieszner R. Research themes on intergenerational relationships in later life. Journal of Marriage and the Family, in press.

Mancini JA, Simon J. Older Adults' expectations of support from family and friends. Journal of Applied Gerontology 1984; 3:150–160.

Masciocchi C, Thomas A, Moeller T. Support for the impaired elderly: a challenge for family care-givers. In: Quinn WH, Hughston GA, eds. Independent aging: family and social systems perspectives. Rockville, Md.: Aspen, 1984:115–132.

Parkerson GR, The Study Group on Family Medicine Research. Meeting the challenge of research in family medicine. Journal of Family Practice 1982; 14:105–113.

Perkoff GT. Research in family medicine: classification, directions, and costs. Journal of Family Practice 1981; 13:553–557.

Perlmutter M, Hall E. Adult development and aging. New York: Wiley, 1985.

Pifer A, Bronte L, eds. Our aging society. New York: Norton, 1986.

Quinn WH, Hughston GA. Independent aging: family and social systems perspectives. Rockville, Md.: Aspen, 1984.

Redman RW, Everett GD, Wallace RB. Research in family medicine. In: Rakel RE, ed. Textbook of family practice, 3rd ed. Philadelphia: Saunders, 1984:285–294.

Reichel W, Barnett BL. Care of the geriatric patient. In: Rakel RB, Conn HF, eds. Family practice, 2nd. ed. Philadelphia: Saunders, 1978: 222–238.

Rosen M, Arsht ED. Psychological approaches to family practice: a primary care manual. Baltimore, Md.: University Park Press, 1979.

Seelbach W. Filial responsibility and the care of aging family members. In: Quinn WH, Hughston GA, eds. Independent aging: family and social systems perspectives. Rockville, Md.: Aspen, 1984:92–105.

Shanas E. Social myth as hypothesis: the case of the family relations of old people. The Gerontologist 1979; 19:3–9.

Streib GF. The frail elderly: research dilemmas and research opportunities. The Gerontologist 1983; 23:40–44.

Streib GF, Beck RW. Older families: a decade review. Journal of Marriage and the Family 1980; 42:937–956.

Treas J. Family support systems for the aged: some social and demographic considerations. The Gerontologist 1977; 17:486–491.

Troll LE. The family in later life: a decade review. Journal of Marriage and the Family 1971; 33:263–290.

Troll L. Grandparents: the family watchdogs. In: Brubaker TH, ed. Family relationships in later life. Beverly Hills, Calif.: Sage Publications, 1983:63–74.

Troll LE, Miller SJ, Atchley RC. Families in later life. Belmont, Calif.: Wadsworth, 1979.

U.S. Bureau of the Census. Statistical abstract of the United States, 1982–1983 (103rd ed.). Washington, D.C.: U.S. Government Printing Office, 1982.

U.S. Senate Special Committee on Aging. Aging America: trends and projections. Washington, D.C.: American Association of Retired Persons, 1985–1986.

Walsh F. The family in later life. In: Carter EA, McGoldrick M, eds. The family life cycle: a framework for family therapy. New York: Gardner Press, 1980:197–220.

Wantz MS, Gay JE. The aging process: a health perspective. Cambridge, Mass.: Winthrop, 1981.

Weiss RS. The fund of sociability. Trans Action 1969; 6:36–43.

Wood M. Research in family medicine. In: Taylor RB, ed. Family medicine: principles and practice. New York: Springer-Verlag, 1983:1927–1942.

PART SEVEN

Family Health and the Process of Medical Care

26

Family Influences on Health Behavior: An Ethnographic Approach

HOWARD F. STEIN
University of Oklahoma

We all grow up in families. It is in families that we learn how to be sick. We carry those families—both internally as amalgams of identifications and as relationships in which we currently live—into the doctor's office and the hospital. From these families we bring to clinical encounters readily conscious and deeply unconscious premises, values, attitudes, beliefs, explanations, expectations—all of which have been patterned in our formative relationships. In many respects, social institutions such as medicine are heir to the early family world. This chapter offers an approach to understanding sickness and disability from the family point of view.

This chapter also makes a plea for the ethnographic—which is to say the longitudinal, naturalistic, participatory, observational, intensive, open-ended, and serendipitous—study of health-related decision-making and illness behavior in families. Such an approach gives us access to uncover the family story that confers on an illness episode its timing and timeliness, its meaning, its organization and direction, if not its outcome. In modern America, without the family story, we have only biomedical fragments that, when taken alone, trivialize the lives in which they occur in the guise of explaining them.

The trouble is that in eliciting others' stories we, in all likelihood, encounter our own. At issue, then, is what we do with that unwelcome autobiographic fact. If we dared admit it, it is often terrifying to study or treat families. We will do almost anything—including go to war—to avoid encountering and reviving those meanings and feelings and situations we experienced in our families of origin. We certainly do not want to rehash all that again when, as physicians or behavioral scientists, we study or treat families. That is why we invent, perfect, and defend, as if our very well-being depended on it, that secular religion called methodology. What we cannot remember we can only repeat (Freud, 1914/1958). And what we cannot tolerate to remember we will not observe, let alone understand.

If, in this ethnographic odyssey I am about to describe, I am harsh on the use of behavioral science and clinical method to implement our scotomata rather than our insight, it is because I know how anxiety-evoking it is to work with families in *any* capacity. In observing, interpreting, and supervising the treatment of families, I must keep asking myself, "What *mustn't* I see? What don't I want to learn about myself that I *already* secretly know? What am I employing a particular method, or asking a particular question, for?" For with methodology at our side, we can rationalize distancing ourselves from our human subject matter, self-protectively keeping painful aspects of our own families at bay. Used this way, methodology is a compromise between looking and not seeing, the goal of which is observing without feeling.

If we are to be scientific, our methods must follow our subject, not lead it, whatever the name of our diverse disciplines, for the issue is the same everywhere. They must help us to face, understand, and resolve those anxieties the subject awakens. Our methods must include, not exclude, the part we ourselves play in that subject. We must be capable of being moved by that subject—and know how we are moved so that we may clinically better understand, observe, and intervene. We are capable of having insight into others—persons, families, groups—only in terms of acknowledging and understanding how they affect us.

In 1967 anthropologist Jules Henry wrote, "Direct observation of families in their native habitats should be the microscope that reveals new phenomena of family existence and so provides the possibilities of new theory" (p. 31). Anthropologist Oscar Lewis (1967) called for "intensive individual family case studies in cultures all over the world" (p. 140):

> . . . because individual families can be described without recourse to abstractions and stereotypes, the publication of case studies would provide us with some basis for judging the generalizations made by anthropologists and others concerning the total culture patterns of any community. The implication of the family case study for anthropological research is clear. It means that we have to go more slowly, that we have to spend more time doing careful and detailed studies of units smaller than the entire culture before we can be ready to make valid generalizations for the entire culture.

This is to impugn neither strictly biomedical nor epidemiologic research. Rather, it is to argue that our methods must be commensurate with what we are purporting to observe. Even the best microscope will tell us nothing about the planets at their current distance. A strictly biomedical focus and epidemiologic method will tell us nothing about a family's lived reality, which is, after all, what we purport to measure (see Devereux, 1967; La Barre, 1978; Schwartz & Breunlin, 1983; Stein, 1979, 1982b). McClain (1983) argues that "The anthropological approach [to studying decision making] is that of naturalistic or descriptive decision making, which uses elicited verbal data to develop predictive models of decision principles and behavior of people making real-life choices" (p. 26).

After a brief literature review and a discussion of methodologic issues in the ethnographic approach to family studies, I describe a graduate and faculty seminar in which this approach is used. In the following sections, I offer a number of detailed illustrations of the virtues of this approach in eliciting, describing, and explaining family-based health behavior. In a later section, I venture beyond accounts of individual families and offer a portrait of a culture area-shared system of health beliefs and behavior among midwestern United States white farming families. My purpose is not only to share the findings from a decade and a half of clinical teaching with family medicine residents, but also to demonstrate that the astute, community-based or academic family physician can acquire insight into the culture(s) of his or her practice population. In the final section of this chapter, I briefly inquire into the wider national and international picture in which the resurgent interest in the family takes place, and which context stalks our work in family studies and family medicine alike.

BRIEF REVIEW OF PERTINENT LITERATURE

In recent decades, clinical researchers have increasingly taken into account the patient's perceptions of reality as a determinant of illness behavior. Lipowski (1969), for instance, draws attention to such personal meanings of illness as loss and gain. In his classic text *Medical Sociology: A Selective View,* Mechanic (1968) explores how social role, attitudes, values, and the like, mediate health action. In *People in Pain,* Zborowski (1969), on the basis of interviews with and observation of patients in a Veterans Administration hospital, compares the health beliefs and attitudes of four Euro-American ethnic groups (Yankees [Anglo-Americans], Irish Catholics, Italians, and East European Jews). Papers by Stein explore how the Slovak-American ethos of suffering and toughening is expressed in health behavior (1976) and examine the relationship between the annual wheat-farming cycle and health action among Oklahoma farming families (1982a).

An influential school within medical anthropology, co-founded by Leon Eisenberg and Arthur Kleinman, attempts to determine the "explanatory model" constructed by patients and how in clinical relationships it interacts with the biomedical explanatory model constructed by the medical profession (Chrisman & Maretzki, 1982; Eisenberg & Kleinman, 1981; Good, 1977; Kleinman, 1980). Chrisman (1977) cautioned researchers not to assume homogeneity among ethnic groups, but instead to document actual natural histories. He identified five components of health seeking: symptom definition, illness-related shifts in behavior, lay consultation and referral, treatment actions, and adherence. Trostle, Hauser, and Susser recently (1983) studied the management of epilepsy from the patient's point of view. This study involved long-term participant observation with seven patients over 10 months in a variety of contexts.

In all these studies, and others of their genre, vignettes of family process were included to illustrate how the family participates in decision making. Nevertheless, in none of these studies is the family the explicit focus of analysis. Rather, the patient is followed within a variety of decision-making contexts. Summarizing Suchman (1965), Pratt (1976), for instance, writes that

> The definition of a state of illness, preliminary evaluation of symptoms, and decisions about what action should be taken are, in many important respects, family transactions. Initial discussion of symptoms with family members plays an important part in providing a person with provisional validation that she or he is sick and should prepare to take appropriate action. (p. 24).

Gerber and Sluzki (1978) argue that illnesses are family events and not exclusively personal events. They propose that we view illness in two ways: in terms of its impact on family functioning, and in terms of "how the family's dynamics influence the expression of symptoms and affect the course of the illness in the individual family member" (p. 216). Moreover, "Any symptom may help regulate or unbalance the family's interpersonal processes, generate or modify family rules, and establish or break family boundaries" (p. 217).

METHODOLOGICAL ISSUES

Self-medication and family-based health care are the rule rather than the exception. Before we go to the doctor (or to some alternative health provider, from chiropractor to medicine man) and after we return home, we consult with family members and friends about what the problem is to be called, whether it is serious enough (or at an appropriate enough time) to warrant outside attention, what accounts for it, its likely outcome, what ought to be done about it, and who ought to be included in the remedy (Chrisman, 1977; Kleinman, 1980; Suchman, 1965). A motley network of family, friends, and work associates is involved in assessment, etiologic speculation or explanation, diagnosis, some notion of treatment plan, and some combination of speculation and expectation about prognosis. When we are sick, we engage in precisely the same *types* of decision-making activities in our families that physicians do when we, as patients, present ourselves to them. It is the *premises* of the thinking (emotional as well as cognitive), not the *process or sequence* of thought, that distinguishes the clinician's from the patient's and family's clinical decision making. All symptom evaluation or assessment consists of interpretation within some framework. It thus behooves students of family-based health behavior to elicit the patient's and family's "explanatory model," to become acquainted with the logic of their illness behavior (Trostle, Hauser, & Susser, 1983).

Let me now briefly outline the methodologic, theoretic, and clinical assumptions that underlie this chapter. Methodologically, the approach consists of an ethnographic framework for understanding any symptom from the patient's and family's viewpoint, and subsequently for recommending, planning, and evaluating clinical intervention based on knowledge of that viewpoint. The ethnographic method, which is the foundation of anthropologic field work, is quintessentially contextual and open-ended (Kuzel, 1986; Snider & Stein, 1987; Stein & Pontious, 1985). In observing, one never knows quite what to look for, and can therefore discover what others may have overlooked. This chapter explores, within a family context, what people do, what they claim to do, why people do so (from both their own interpretive framework and that of the trained observer), and how they go about deciding what course(s) of action to take. Preordained questions and structured questionnaires are, for this type of study, inappropriate, since they would initially reflect the researcher's own priorities rather than elicit those of the families themselves.

This chapter approaches health care utilization/nonutilization using the intensive case study method of participant observation (ethnography); the researchers work with individuals in their various contexts (family, lay network, occupational, etc.) to discover the process by which health-related decisions are actually made (as contrasted with our assumptions about how they should be made). Through immersion in the group on its own "home ground," often over long periods of time, one learns how that system and its many subsystems are organized (Geertz, 1973; La Barre, 1978; Spiro, 1982, p. xv; Stein, 1982b, 1983a). In a paper on primary care theory and research, Kleinman (1983) advocates the ethnographic method as a means of eliciting meanings associated with illness and treatment.

> Qualitative description, taken together with various quantitative measures, can be a standardized research method for assessing validity. It is especially valuable in studying social and cultural significance, e.g., illness beliefs, interaction norms, social gain, ethnic help seeking, and treatment responses, and it is the appropriate method to describe the work of doctoring. . . . If the ethnography of meaning is not legitimated in primary care research, even though it is legitimated in anthropology, sociology, and social psychology, then meaning will not receive a scientifically appropriate assessment in primary care. (Kleinman, 1983, p. 543)

In recent years, family studies researchers have, in my view, largely recapitulated the identical methodologic pitfalls that occurred within anthropology in its quest for heuristic precision and cultural high status during the past several decades. Based on the wider cultural model of exclusively quantitative empiricism and the isolation of discrete entities, many family studies researchers now commonly isolate specific content from the contextual gestalt and then proceed to act as though the resulting encapsulation is inherent "in nature" (or in "the family") instead of being an artifact of the instrument and the defense structure of the instrument maker. A quarter century ago the late Margaret Mead decried many scientists' "insistence on measurement as a substitute for commensurability" (1962, p. 134). In cross-cultural studies of infant swaddling, for instance, she urged that we encompass the "affect-laden" and "emphathic" system of parent–child communication as part of the swaddling, and not restrict our investigations of the meaning and effect of swaddling to the formal child care routines themselves (see Benedict, 1967, p. 350; Hartmann, Kris, & Loewenstein, 1970, pp. 265–267; Stein, 1978). To do so is to impose our cultural blinders (in the guise of observation) on others' experience and to organize their experience in terms of our own cognitive style and defenses, which it implements.

Further, rigidity (methodologic orthodoxy) is commonly mistaken for rigor. Much biomedical research has an implicitly homeostatic quality, one built into the very research design. One seeks what one wishes to find, and finds that which one seeks—and is capable of observing. The defensive and consensus-maintaining function of prevailing theoretic and research paradigms is a little-discussed factor in scientific method (see Devereux, 1967; La Barre, 1978).

Consider as a *cultural artifact,* for instance, the additive channel model of affective communication in social interaction (Notarius, Markman, & Gottman, 1983), based on an electronics metaphor of communication in multiple, separate channels: " . . . the dominant view is that emotion resides in the so-called nonverbal channels. To study emotion in a purely scientific manner it thus becomes necessary to filter out the verbal content and focus on the nonverbal. This has led to a technology of electronic filtering, random splicing, spectral analysis of voices, and stop-frame video analysis" (p. 133). However, "These so-called channels of emotional communication cannot be isolated, separately investigated, and then later reintegrated" (p. 133). They illustrate the limitations of the additive model with an example about the vocal channel.

> Various strategies have been developed to remove the content from speech so as to isolate the vocal components of emotion. One strategy to accomplish this is by random splicing; another is by electronic filtering of high-frequency cycles. A problem with random splicing is the loss of temporal form, so that an angry moment, precisely defined by steadily rising volume, will be chopped up and randomly spliced together so that its temporal form is unrecognizable and the anger is lost. A problem with electronic filtering is that we may be filtering out precisely the emotional cues of interest. (pp. 133–134)

They then cite Gottman (1982): "The point is that an additive model of communication is not tenable: *Emotion is communicated by a nonadditive gestalt of channels"* (p. 949, emphasis in original). The authors call for a "gestalt" or "cultural informants" approach instead of one that artificially isolates specific cues. "The cultural informants approach thus has abandoned the notion of the complete catalogue of physical features" (Notarius, Markman, & Gottman, 1983, p. 134).

My point in citing this recent study at length is that it can be seen as a metaphor for how many in family studies, and, more broadly, how we in American culture prefer to define and study human behavior. Why, one might ask, do we have such difficulty accepting and examining human behavior in temporal form? Could it be that chopping it up serves as a defense against the acknowledgment of time in human life and relationships? Might we recognize some of our proudest methodologies to be our shared symptoms? Systematic observation based on participant observation within a group leads to the uncovering of patterns and levels of meanings and relationships that are often not discernible by standard cultural techniques of data collection and analysis. Considering several of our cultural rules in scientific investigation, La Barre (1977) writes that:

Compulsive quantification does not make the communication of an anthropological complex more exact; on the contrary, it crowds out of observation numerous subtle qualitative contexts and ingredients that alone give the real event its coherence and meaning. Numbers denude contexts of their significant meanings. Hence cross-cultural and other techniques become more meaningless as they become more exact. The contextual is the essence of the ethnographic. . . .[D]iscovery itself is always high-contextual serendipity. Hence in the hungry pursuit of intellectual veridity and Truth, we sacrifice the validity of fact, by a kind of Heisenberg Principle, and we can only prove what we already believe. (p. 784)

The ethnographic method used here in the study of family-based health care decision making is introduced as a potential corrective in clinical research. That is, it supplements rather than supplants biomedical research designs. Ideally, at least, each helps the other to become more rigorous. There is no necessary antipathy between researchers or clinicians who focus on different parts or levels of a problem. The antipathy enters only when researchers or clinicians act or claim that their ''part'' is in fact the ''whole,'' or the part that matters most. Devereux (1967) writes that the use of scientific methodology to reduce anxiety is itself not illegitimate, but rather becomes so only when methodology is ''used *primarily* as an ataractic—as an anxiety-numbing device'' (p. 97). Good methodology ''does not empty reality of its anxiety-arousing content, but 'domesticates' it, by proving that it, too, can be understood and processed by the conscious ego. . . . What matters, therefore, is not whether one *uses* methodology *also* as an anxiety-reducing device, but whether one does so *knowingly*, in a sublimatory manner, or unconsciously, in a defensive manner *only*'' (p. 97).

THE ETHNOGRAPHIC APPROACH AS A TRAINING AND FACULTY DEVELOPMENT MODEL

As a medical anthropologist, psychoanalytic anthropologist, and psychohistorian, I take a psychodynamically oriented approach to the clinical teaching of medical students, physician's associate students, physicians and graduate physician's associates in occupational medicine, and family medicine residents in community practice (see Stein, 1982b). In this section, I briefly outline how I have employed this approach in an ongoing monthly family medicine faculty development seminar in the ethnography of family health behavior, and in an annual graduate seminar called ''Behavioral Sciences in Occupational Medicine'' for occupational medicine physicians and physician's associates, most of whom become middle-level administrators. In both groups, time is spent discussing such issues as family assessment and definition of symptoms, negotiation of sick role and caretaker role, identifying the types and timing of search for treatment, family response to practitioner-prescribed regimens, family and clinician definitions of success and failure, and so forth. We try to construct and reconstruct in detail entire illness episodes and their management from the point of view of the family. For both faculty and graduate students, the goal of this approach is to help them acquire the ability to (1) elicit family patterns, sequences, and meanings in one's practice and/or research population; (2) improve observational, assessment, and psychosocial interpretive skills; and (3) improve psychosocial interventions and prediction of family (and occupational relationship) patterns, thereby enhancing clinical outcomes (for practitioners) by knowing the context in which they are working.

One technique I have used is to ask each seminar participant to reconstruct in as great detail as possible a recent illness episode in his or her own family (e.g., how symptoms were identified, with whom a course of action was negotiated, how family members re-sponded to the symptoms, how family members explained what was taking place, and so forth). The seminar participant is not only asked to do this at first himself or herself alone, but also expected to ask other family members to do likewise separately—and then to compare each member's perceptions, explanations, feelings, and actions with those of other family members. This exercise not only allows the participant to begin to formulate some family-level patterns, expectations, beliefs, values, sequences of behavior, and the like, but also permits participants to recognize significant differences in perception and interpre-tation among family members of the same event, and prompts further inquiry into the individual and family meaning of these differences. We begin to discover—and test—patterns of family meaning and response that recur in different illness episodes, those that are specific to a particular family member's role, and so on.

I then introduce the familiar genogram, a tool of multigeneration family assessment, but with a slight variation on conventional use. I ask seminar participants to prepare it along several parameters (relatives by blood and marriage, terminal diseases and other causes of death, occupation, religion, ethnicity, mobility, etc.) but first without consulting other family members to fill in the facts the participant cannot remember. At this point in the exercise, I am as much interested in conveying to seminar participants the importance of *construction* in family life as I am in obtaining a complete factual picture of the multi-generation family. What, and whom, people remember, what and whom they forget or omit, is a crucial statement about their inner representation of the family and a part of the reality of each person's family. Whatever the outer reality of these self-reports, I empha-size the importance of perception, selection, affectively based emphasis and omission—in short, the narrative or storylike quality that emerges. What seem like facts remembered and forgotten are, in fact, symbols and meanings.

The emotional significance of those who are remembered and omitted, and the asso-ciations about those who are remembered, are explored within the group. The seminar participant then may contact other family members to complete the picture, to construct their own genograms and compare the two. The participants' (and family members') free associations while constructing the genogram are considered crucial rather than incidental or epiphenomenal or gratuitous data. My own questions largely follow upon participants' associations, omissions, and interpretations, rather than preceding them. This approach to the genogram—and to family history—allows me to elicit the participants' construction of the family story and to help participants recognize the process by which this construction unfolds. The ethnographer–informant relationship I develop with seminar participants is explicitly designed to help prepare them to become competent ethnographers of families to be studied and/or treated. I devote as much attention to teaching participants about the process by which this knowledge is obtained as I do to the content or product itself.

Further, I try to avert imposing my own culture-bound assumptions about who should be included in or excluded from a subject's, informant's, or patient's genogram. Empha-sizing the subject's construction—and the importance of eliciting that construction—I ask such questions as: "Whom all do you consider as being members of your family?" "What all people, whether or not related by blood or marriage, do you consider to be 'significant others' in your current personal network and in your childhood?" I likewise emphasize the importance not only of asking questions that elicit the informant's or patient's perception and definition of family and network, but also of becoming sufficiently familiar with the informant's or patient's lived world that one can infer (and then further ask the informant or patient about) crucial relationships from participant observation. When constructing his genogram in class, one married but childless family medicine resident included his two pet dogs in his nuclear family. Many patients incorporate neighbors, pastors, pharmacists, and even physicians into their familial world. Roman Catholic residents and patients tend to include godparents as kinfolk (what anthropologists call "fictive kinship"). The fact that all these depart from the official cultural and genetic construction of the genogram does not vitiate the necessity of obtaining an accurate picture of the social world from the patient's or subject's point of view.

Once, while working with a graduate student to construct a genogram with a woman in her late 30s, I discovered that while I had wished to trace her religious and ethnic ancestry many generations removed, she only vaguely recalled data I was interested in obtaining. She adamantly insisted that her family literally began when her maternal grandfather moved from Kentucky to Missouri and then to Oklahoma. He was the founder of *her* family. Like many white Americans in the Great Plains, who pride themselves on their resolute self-reliance, on what they have done and initiated for themselves, she was far more interested in the future and the present than in the past; the remote historical past of her vaguely recollected Irish-German-Protestant family roots held no interest for her. We discovered that, not coincidentally, when someone was ill in her family world, he or she tried to "tough it out" and maintain autonomy as long as possible.

An approach that I have developed to complement the genogram is that of the home floor plan of one's family of origin (and, in the occupational medicine seminar, the spatial layout of an earlier or current occupational setting). The genogram enables one to tap family health behavior over generational time; the floor plan enables one to view how a family is organized over space (shorter-duration time). I ask seminar participants to prepare a sketch of their home of origin—since many participants grew up in several homes, this elicits additional data on the stability and change in family organization. The initial sketch consists exclusively of things: rooms, doors, windows, appliances—artifacts. I then ask participants to tell me about their home: who did what, where; who spent time with whom; when additions were made onto the home, and the like. The focus of attention is thus far on the conduct of a family life in a meaningful space called "home." Then I ask them to describe what people did—where they went—when someone was ill. Were there any general patterns? The result is often a fascinating story about the use of space during illness, which yields an understanding of how family patterns taken for granted decisively influence patterns of health care utilization, outcome, and so forth. And just as we employ the genogram as a tool of rapport building and free association in the seminar, we do this likewise with the floor plan.

Let me illustrate this process with an example from a seminar of several years ago. One graduate student in occupational health not only complied with the assignment to draw a floor plan of his childhood home, but drew adjacent to it a smaller sketch of the home enclosed *within* his church, with a short line extending from the church to work (a cotton mill in which his father worked). This subsidiary representation was, of course, a truer experiential representation of his home than the larger sketch, which was based on strict compliance with the assignment. To understand his experienced and constructed world, I had to be able to follow his lead rather than discount his embellishment on the assignment. I invited him to discuss *both* portraits of his home and, in turn, what he defined as home and household.

He spoke of how religion regulated every aspect of home life, the utter absence of boundary between home and church, and virtual lack of consequence that the world of work had for that inner sanctum, even though the father toiled long hours in the company town cotton mill. A more stark delineation between inside and outside, the next world and this world, could scarcely be made. Despite the value placed upon work (the fact that the father worked at three jobs to support his family) and the sheer amount of time and frustration spent on the job, its emotional significance was devalued if not wholly discounted. One could invoke Bowen's (1978) term ''emotional cutoff'' to describe the force of excising work from the inner world.

Let me turn to a consideration of the implications of this family's themes (as revealed in spatial utilization and representation) for health-related decision making. It is already clear that an ethic of binding togetherness links the nuclear family, the extended family, the church family, and the relative continuity between this world and the next. (Ideally, at least, there is greater ease of communion between humans and the supernatural than between the church and the secular, profane world of the flesh.) It thus comes as little surprise to learn that a similar togetherness and blurring of boundaries come actively into play during illness episodes. When everyone was healthy, the parents' room was off limits to the children. When the children were sick, they were able to luxuriate in the parents' bed during the day. The graduate student glowingly described the large, comfortable bed; the chest at the bottom of the bed; and the care that his mother took of them when they were sick. He recalled that, because his father worked at so many jobs and for such long hours, he was rarely home, and that his mother was the devoted caretaker during health and sickness.

Let me contrast this sickness *style* with that of a second graduate student who went through the same exercise. If togetherness is an organizing theme in the family just described, separateness might well describe an overarching theme in the second. The first family was from the deep South; the second family from the Midwest. In response to illness in the family, the second student described a process of lying down on couches at progressively greater distances from the center of family activity. If one felt a little ill, one lay down on the couch in the living den; if one felt a little more ill, he or she would lie down on the couch in the small study (a room on the same level, but separated from the living den by the kitchen); if one felt even worse, he or she would move to the couch in the formal living room; and if one felt *really* sick (high fever, nausea, something for which physician consultation was sought, etc.), one went upstairs to his or her bedroom, closed the door, and went to bed. So far, these data describe behavioral sequences and patterns. However, in a series of free associations, which we explored, he made an intriguing analogy when asked to describe his and his family's response to being ill:

> When you're sick, you withdraw. You go away like a dog retreats into the bushes when he's sick or wounded, to be by yourself. When you're better, you come back in circulation. You come back out of hiding. Nobody wants to see somebody when they're sick. You're weak, of little use to anybody. You don't want to be around and be seen. It's not that they didn't care about you. They made sure you got the care you needed, but you didn't get babied. You tried to get better on your own, not to be in anyone's way.

Yet another boundary issue is illustrated by a comparison between these two families: the relationship between family and work or occupation. In the first family, the husband toiled endlessly to be a good provider: The haunting ballad ''Sixteen Tons'' applies to the provider's sense of futility in any hope to effect change in this world. Owing his body to the company store (company town, in fact), he and his family made certain that they would *not* owe their *soul* to that company store. The locus of control, perceived to be wholly external in this world, was likewise perceived to be wholly outside their influence in the next. Hopelessness and helplessness were associated with the cotton mill, hope and help—salvation—with church and home. An emotional chasm separated family and work, while family and church were fused.

In the second family, on the other hand, although some members were in fact church-goers, the graduate student described himself and his family as nominally Protestant. They were, in fact, exemplars of Weber's *Protestant Ethic and the Spirit of Capitalism* (1904/1930). Work was their religion. With rare exception, they worked for companies, were not chance-takers, were more security-oriented than wealth-oriented (examples of jobs held in this second family are postal worker, college teacher, worker in international exchange, salesman/saleswoman, chemist, insurance agent, engineer). Educational achievement, middle-level jobs, and this-worldly security characterize their dominant values. Family visits are often characterized by work-oriented conversations, discussions about who is achieving what and where. In this family, religious fervor is applied to education and to work, which in turn are inseparable from the family itself. As a social institution, however, religion plays a subordinate role; in many cases, it plays absolutely none.

I now turn to an illustration of how inadvertently family social science concepts blur into facts, become accepted as entities instead of ideas, and become projectively and matter-of-factly introduced as part of the data. The illustration shows, I believe, how ethnography can correct this universal propensity in all forms of interpretation. Within our own departmental and faculty seminar discussions over the past years, I noticed that the concept of "family health expert," introduced by two faculty members, had gained widespread currency and was used routinely in clinical case conferences (see discussion of family health authority, Doherty & Baird, 1983, p. 42). The assumption was that every family possessed one such health authority, and that it was advisable for family medicine residents to incorporate the concept into his or her repertoire so as to be able to identify that family member and thereby enhance patient/family care.

At one faculty family ethnography seminar in 1984, the group self-ethnography that ensued suggested that the global term "family health expert" might be premature, that it might inadvertently blur significant family role distinctions in health care decision making. One participant spoke of the "worrier" role of his mother-in-law, one to whom family members brought their sore throats and allergies, and who made the emotional diagnosis "Cancer?" or "Asthma?" For one participant's family, the source of health decisions came from a primary member who herself sought further consultants. For another, autonomy and privacy were prized, so that health decisions were derived from a nonhierarchical pooling of information, with final authority resting on the initiator of such discussions. Some families mobilized around symptoms; others responded to symptoms by reaffirming distinct personal boundaries.

Discussing patterns in their own families, then, seminar participants discovered the value of a thorough *description* of family health behavior during illness episodes, one that also enabled us to test the applicability of the concept of family health expert for particular families and to develop further concepts that were more in keeping with some family's lived reality. My point in this brief illustration is not to advocate theoretic nihilism. Narrative ethnography can meander endlessly at times. Yet such excess is not inevitable. Careful attention to people's expressed purposes and observed behavior can improve our inferences about their deduced purposes (Richards, 1956), that is, their implicit rules and roles.

There is, apparently, no shortcut around becoming familiar with a family's organization through open inquiry (and errors) rather than by formulas arrived at beforehand. One can, for a start, inquire over time with a patient and/or family, "How do you make your health care decisions?"—a naturalistic, inquisitive perspective. An inquiry into how families think, feel, and decide helps practitioners and students of the family to know others' frameworks within which they are always (if unwittingly) working. Moreover, as these illustrations suggest, the group or seminar format itself can be used as an ethnographic field in which participants are at once informants or subjects *and* interpreters of the data.

Various family rules and roles are brought to bear upon members' health behavior. Such rules as "The kids always come first," "Mom always comes first," "Dad is never sick," "Don't think about it and maybe it will go away," and "Every symptom might be serious" influence the choice of what to treat, whom to treat, and when. Such explicit family rules, however, are often not the only ones in place. What the family (or specific family members) identify as the only rule might in fact be observed by the physician to coexist, if not conflict, with other rules that the family may not acknowledge. Instrumental or practical roles may often conflict with or serve unstated expressive or emotional roles. If "the kids always come first," then perhaps "Mom is never sick" (Mom, the emotional bulwark, must never be sick)—even when she is! Mom, in turn, might resort to the ruse of bringing a child to the doctor in order to justify voicing some complaint of her own— or hope that the doctor will notice that she is not all well and treat her rather than wait for her to seek treatment. If "Dad is always strong," his alcohol consumption and alcoholic behavior may be denied and supported. Knowledge of a family's officially prescribed health-related rules, together with its members' account of what they do, constitutes the family's self-portrait to the world, and must always be compared with the observer's careful description of the family's actual behavior (and the implicit rules inferred from it).

Health roles follow closely from and are defined by conscious and unconscious family roles. Let me cite a personal example to convey the importance of including *unconscious* determinants of family role in our understanding of health-related decision making (see also Stein, 1986). Pratt (1976) sensibly argues that "a person's distinctive role obligations within the family are reflected in his or her behavior concerning sickness" (p. 21). Sometimes those obligations are internal debts to the dead, so much so that one who cannot let go of the dead must almost literally embody them in word and deed, even as they also condemn them for such bondage (Volkan, 1981). My maternal grandmother died of kidney disease in her 50s, when my mother was in her 30s and I was 3. The entire family reveres this grandmother as a self-sacrificial angel. When she died, my mother "fell apart" (her words). Among my mother's physical symptoms—all in the absence of diagnosed biomedical disease—is an inability to control her urine, first showing itself some years ago, and now controlled only by a Foley catheter.

Not only has my mother profoundly identified with her mother, but, furthermore, in facies, gesture, attitude, and posture, she has noticeably "become" my deceased maternal grandfather. In 1983, while my wife and I were visiting my parents in Pennsylvania, we brought my mother home from the nursing home to try to include her in family holiday celebrations during the spring Passover. Once, while we sat in the living room, she expressed the need to empty her urine bag, but declined to go to the bathroom (at that time, she still could walk, though only with assistance). I remembered that my grandfather had died alone on the toilet on Christmas Eve, 1963. I said to her: "I know you're afraid of dying in the bathroom like Grandfather. You won't, Mom. We'll be with you." A minute or two later, she said, "I have to go to the bathroom." We went with her, and emptied the bag uneventfully.

To understand such a family-based health care decision as elemental as elimination, one must understand meanings that infuse family roles. And these meanings are by no means always easily evident. Universal issues of oedipal and pre-oedipal patterns of conflict and identification are, I believe, the uncharted emotional topography of family health care decision making.

Families identify, define, and negotiate what is and what constitutes a symptom, what kind of symptom it is (disease, sin, possession, crime, etc.), who the bearer of the symptom is, and what should be done about it. In some families, one is regarded as normal only if one never takes medicine, no matter how sick one is; in other families, one is accepted as normal only if one is sick like everyone else and takes—even flaunts—multiple medications. Minimizing and maximizing symptoms themselves serve as family norms of behavior. For still other families, noncompliance with physician-prescribed behavior (including the taking of oral medication) may serve as a heroic attempt at self-control or the preservation of self-sufficiency in the face of the specter of dependency. A family whose child neglect or abuse is virtually infanticidal (deMause, 1974) may not bring the child for medical treatment, because the family does not identify its family dynamics to be a problem (for them, it is a solution). Indeed, it may utilize religious belief and ritual to rationalize clinical inaction.

The following case discusses the family dynamics that underlie the timing of one woman's refusing and accepting the sick role during a single illness episode. Nancy N is a 36-year-old divorcee living in the Midwest with two teenage children. She supports her family by working as an enterprising business executive. She prides herself on her self-reliance and self-sufficiency. Recently, undergoing a hysterectomy, she amazed physicians and hospital staff alike by her ability to withstand considerable pain without calling for medication, and by her resilience. Her expected period of 6 to 8 weeks for recovery was cut in half. She was eager to return to work, and worried that responsibilities would pile up and that money to run the household would be depleted.

Her parents, retired out of state, insisted on coming to spend a few weeks with her to help her recuperate from surgery. Arriving a week before surgery, they stayed until about a week afterwards. The day before their arrival, she thoroughly cleaned the house for fear her mother would criticize her housekeeping ("Mother would be sure to notice crumbs or dirt under the toaster and proceed to clean the house if I didn't.") While her parents were in her home, she was cheerful, talkative, and active around the house. Although her parents had come to take care of her, she refused to allow them to do so, but instead took care of herself *and* them. She later explained, "I don't act sick so they won't worry." They left satisfied that she was recovering well. Only after they had gone did she allow herself to feel and act sick at home (i.e., take on the sick role). She looked tired and pale. Her energy level, though still surprisingly high, was not sustained for hours as it had been in the presence of her parents. Only when she had reclaimed her home and her independence could she allow herself to rest and sleep. From the perspective of most physicians I know, this woman would be regarded as a good, if not ideal, patient. But familiarity with her world, through open-ended interview and participant observation in her home environment, gave a far different significance to her illness behavior.

The following case (developed with J. M. Pontious, MD) shows the complex choreography of family relationships and meanings that influence the decision to have surgery. Mrs. Jane C is a 36-year-old white female with scoliosis. She is the eldest daughter in a midwestern wheat-farming family. She is married and has two children, ages 3 and 9. She and her husband live and work on the family farm.

She had been in fairly good health during her childhood and early adulthood. In high school, she had been noted as having minimal scoliosis, but no intervention had been advised. Recently, Mrs. C had had several episodes of bronchitis and pneumonias with persistent fever and dehydration. On one occasion she required hospitalization during which her scoliosis was once again noted. This resulted in a referral to the orthopedist in a nearby city. Over several visits, it was noted that her scoliosis had advanced a total of 30 degrees in 2 years. She was advised that this was also probably the etiology of her recurrent back pain and played a role in her recurrent pneumonias. Further, the orthopedic surgeon advised that she consider surgical correction of the scoliosis and the placement of Harrington rods. He suggested several distant regional centers where this expensive and delicate surgery could be performed. He also gave her several names of patients who had had this surgery, for her to contact for further information.

Mrs. C called a brother-in-law who was a primary care physician to ask for further information about scoliosis and the recommended surgery, its implications and problems. She asked if there were any physicians whom he would recommend to do the surgery. She expressed anxiety about the timing of the surgery and the distance from home that she would have to travel to get to the regional center. Because the recovery would involve 8 to 9 months in a body cast, timing was important so as not to interfere with the work load on the family farm.

The physician brother-in-law recommended a colleague at the regional medical center, and an appointment was made for Mrs. C's evaluation. Meanwhile, Mrs. C contacted several patients who had had previous scoliosis surgery. One of these patients was particularly jubilant about her experience and her surgeon, who practiced at a location even farther away than the regional medical center. Family involvement in Mrs. C's decision for surgery was ambivalent. Their several messages were, "You need to be careful about when or where you have surgery, so as not to interfere with the farm work," and, "Of course you would want the most experienced surgeons doing the procedure." Also, surgery would spoil the family togetherness during the approaching Christmas holidays. Finally, Mrs. C canceled all other appointments and arranged to be evaluated for surgery after the holidays at the farthest medical center recommended by its satisfied patient. Her logic was that she had been impressed by the patient's outcome and wanted a similar outcome for herself.

In January 1984 the surgery was performed with no complications. After a 2-week hospital stay, Mrs. C was released to convalesce at home. She tolerated the body cast without difficulty, although she continued to worry about what effect her relative disability would have on the farming activities of the family, especially as the wheat harvest would be accomplished without her.

Mrs. C's position in the sibling order figured prominantly in her family's mixed feelings and messages toward her regarding her decisions about surgery. Although the eldest of the three sisters, she has an older brother. Among midwestern farming families, the eldest son is ideally groomed to inherit and manage the family farm. In this family, however, the eldest son had been scalded as a child, an event to which his mother responded by overly protecting him. As a teenager, he had sustained foot and back injuries from an automobile accident. Although as an adult he successfully holds a job, has married, and has children, he was never reared to manage the farm. This role of successor fell early upon the future Mrs. C, a sturdy, decisive woman.

In this family, Mrs. C was invested with the family responsibilities associated with being the eldest son. The family inadvertently pressured her to continue in her role at the same time that the disease process made that role increasingly difficult to uphold. In a sense, for her to have the surgery and not to have the surgery equally posed threats to her and to her family's concern for their joint future.

This ethnographic case explored medical decision making in a Baptist Scotch-English wheat-farming family from northern Oklahoma. It revealed how family roles, priorities, values, and expectations affect health care choices and timing; the paramount value of work in the family structure; the virtually indistinguishable domains of family and work; the utilization of multiple health care providers as part of the patient's and family's decision-making strategy; the influence of family and lay referral networks on health care decisions and the management of illness episodes; and the process of choice between locally based treatment and treatment at a regional health care center. As the case unfolded over many months, it became evident that what physicians often regard as background in fact occupies the foreground of a family's health-related perceptions, decisions, and actions. This case examined the unseen context in which biomedical intervention occurred.

TOWARD ELICITING, DESCRIBING, AND EXPLAINING CULTURALLY SHARED FAMILY PATTERNS OF HEALTH MEANING AND BEHAVIOR: THE EXAMPLE OF THE MIDWEST

In this section, I wish to go beyond—in the sense of transcending, yet never leaving—the individual family case descriptions and paint a portrait of culturally shared midwestern family patterns of health meaning and behavior. The purpose of this section is to suggest to the reader that clinically useful and intellectually tenable interfamily patterns of health belief and action can be identified, patterns that—carefully elicited by long-term participation and open-ended interview in clinic and home, and corrected and/or confirmed through feedback from reflecting one's descriptions and interpretations to one's informants or patients—are accurate impressions of the culture rather than stereotypes about it.

While I have elsewhere at length discussed midwestern farmer/cowboy personality, family, culture, and patterns of health behavior (Stein, 1982a, 1983b, 1984b, 1987a), I wish here to identify briefly the conceptual framework for this *type* of interpretation in any research setting or practice population. It helps the observer take account of commonalities and differences (and the level at which these occur) and thereby avoid glib generalization and cultural stereotyping. Although it is essential that we recognize deep-seated ethnic personality and family patterns, we must also recognize that those with their cultural personalities (Hippler, 1974) from diverse ethnic backgrounds have, over many generations, forged a supraethnic cultural areal ethos and areal personality (Devereux, 1951), such as can be identified in the Great Plains region.

This regional ethos mobilizes, organizes, overrides, and in a sense supersedes the deep-seated, unconscious diversity of individuals within their original groups. Such an areal personality trend comes to be expressed and institutionalized in political, religious, health, and other social patterns that have a distinctly regional flavor while being simultaneously available for use or integration into the unconscious division of labor or identity of the larger nation (Stein, 1981). The fact that members of such diverse cultures as Irish, German, Czech (Bohemian), Polish, and English, and of such varied religious denominations as Lutheran, Baptist, Roman Catholic, Disciples of Christ, and Church of Christ can trace ancestry to family members who sought freedom from family, neighborhood, ethnic, and religious constraints only to contend slightly with the problem of control through a variety of fundamentalisms, suggests the type of shared dynamic we need to look at in order to understand how a culture area's common denominator is forged. Such an approach allows us to examine both the earlier familial cultural roots and the later migration and socialization through which the next generations reworked those roots into a new system of ego defenses, family structure and function, social symbols and institutions, and health behavior.

Having worked in rural Oklahoma for over 10 years (since 1978) with family medicine residents supervising the behavioral science component of their care of largely Caucasian families who are wheat and cattle farmers, I soon became familiar with what might be called a family mandate of secrecy and protective insularity from such diverse ancestries as Irish, Czech, English, and German. Especially in the face of family conflict or emotional distress, families strive to maintain a tidy exterior and devote much social energy to shoring up an elaborate façade that "all is well." Such self-protection leads families to hold onto the underlying pain for years and even decades. Family doctors and therapists sometimes discover it only generations later.

Within these midwestern families, open controversy is often avoided. A show of anger within the family is virtually intolerable; in the face of conflict, one withdraws, uses self-effacing humor, disavows any aggressive intent—all to avoid confrontation and preserve "peace at any price." Feelings cannot be trusted because they cannot be controlled. The only officially permissible display of open anger is from the church pulpit.

In the Midwest, indirectness of communication assures that one will save face, that one will maintain a safe distance from another. One goes to considerable lengths to avoid making direct demands upon another, or doing anything that would appear to create conflict or threaten the delicately choreographed harmony. For instance, when I was at a friend's home some months ago, the wife had cooked an elaborate meal of egg casserole, bacon, sausage, biscuits, and gravy. The gravy was near the end of the table at which I was seated. I had just spooned some onto my biscuits. Her husband said with something of a sparkle, "The gravy sure goes good with the biscuits, don't it?" I replied a complimentary "Yes" and started eating. He then said with a smile, but now with more animation in his voice, "You mind sharin' some and passin' it down this way?" I passed the gravy, only then realizing the implicit request in the earlier seemingly rhetorical question. One values indirectness and understatement as a way of asking for something without ever appearing to request it. One thereby protects oneself from the possibility of being misunderstood, and creating or losing control. "Peace at any price" is a widely held family value, the purpose of which is to foster family harmony—and its myth—and to prevent the surfacing of aggression.

In this region, it is often insuperably difficult for a family member to come to the doctor over family or emotional difficulties. The fear of public exposure, of being found out, of ridicule and censure are often far greater than the pain or conflict over which one would seek help and endanger the integrity of the family name. Moreover, for many midwesterners the specter of mental illness is steeped in the dread of irreversible sin and loss of control over their minds and lives. Not to treat it is to be able to deny, if only for a while, that it is there at all. And to have it treated is to chance condemnation from a doctor whose medical authority and expected rebuke often blurs with that of a preacher. In the family and in the clinical relationship, a conspiracy of silence often results in an obsession with somatic complaints and biomedical tests and intervention. (For example, Richtsmeier and Waters, 1984, discuss more generally how physical symptoms and individual family members serve as foci for family myths that displace attention from deeper, more painful issues in the family.) The language of somaticization and the fact of having an organic lesion diagnosed (which relieves the fear of being crazy) enables family members to save face in the presence of the family and physicians alike.

In this familial and cultural atmosphere of health-related decision making, I have found that family members feel relatively safe in going to primary care physicians, osteopaths, and chiropractors, who are not seen as possessing the stigma associated with physicians and non-MD practitioners in mental health, family therapy, and the like. Moreover, somatic symptoms and the language of physical pain are acceptable forms of discourse with the doctor (mechanical failure is acceptable, whereas personal or emotional failure is often seen as moral weakness or divine punishment). The physician in this region who is accepting of the patient's physical complaints (often somaticization) and who does not peremptorily challenge them or translate them into emotional or family ones paradoxically has the greater chance of helping the patient to save face with the doctor and slowly to recognize their emotional and situational dimensions without offending or frightening the patient. In this way, the physician not only expresses an interest in the family dynamics, but uses knowledge gained from that interest to address the family in its own cultural language.

Let me offer a brief example. A 30-year-old married professional woman has been diagnosed by her family physician as having anorexia nervosa. Supplementing treatment by him, she was treated by a female family therapist. The patient began increasing her weight through work with the family physician and family therapist working in concert. Both therapists likewise encouraged the husband to involve himself more in the marriage, and the wife to separate from her own overinvolved mother.

The patient began speaking of wanting to have menstrual periods again, perhaps to become pregnant. The family therapist changed the focus of therapy from eating issues to those of body image and sexual functioning with the husband. She became more direct, confrontive, and concrete. The patient felt very uncomfortable with this approach, and shortly terminated therapy with the family therapist. She nonetheless continues to work closely with her family physician (who, like her and the family therapist, are midwesterners).

I remarked to the family physician that the family therapist's inadvertent error, in my opinion, was not that she took an interest in the patient's sexuality, but that she was direct, confrontive, far too quickly intimate about it, almost intrusive—as the patient experienced her mother. Such identification or transference might have been anticipated and dealt with, say interpretively rather than by unwittingly acting the situation out in taking the role of the dominating mother. The family physician commented to me that when he talks regularly with the patient about sexual issues, he always hints at them rather than dealing directly with them. In this case, euphemism and understatement are less a matter of masking and colluding with the obscurity than a culturally appropriate clinical strategy that simultaneously acknowledges the subject together with its sensitivity to the patient.

Patients, clients, or families will often rank values differently from the way physicians, counselors, or therapists do. In the wheat belt of the U.S. Midwest, for instance, families will almost invariably choose completion of the harvest over jeopardizing harvest by taking time off to seek medical care—even in life-endangering situations. In this respect at least, farming families tend to value the continuity and integrity of the family and farm over the survival or health of the individual family member (Stein, 1982a). Where health practitioners may rank-order health in the ordinal position, and family or occupation lower in priority, many wheat-farming families do precisely the reverse. Where there is a conflict of values, explanations, and expectations between practitioners and the culture(s) of the practice population, the practitioner can devise creative strategies for working within that cultural context (see Maranhão, 1984).

CONCLUSION

In this chapter, I have argued that the use of the ethnographic method in family medicine teaching, research, and patient care is not only intrinsically worthwhile and methodologically sound, but practical as well. It helps us to "flesh out" the data we seek. For family medicine, or any other discipline or profession, to be a science—in contrast to an ideology—we must remain true to our subject matter, that is, the lived reality of people in sickness and health. Truth is to be found in painstaking details, not in broad and magical brushstrokes that make fact the handmaiden of belief. Yet the latter is a strong temptation within family medicine as a discipline still struggling to find, assert, claim, and safeguard its place in the ideologic as well as political and clinical sun.

The philosopher Whitehead (1926/1954) wrote that "a one-sided formulation may be true, but may have the effect of a lie by its distortion of emphasis" (p. 123). Moreover,

> Progress in truth—truth of science and truth of religion—is mainly a progress in the framing of concepts, in discarding artificial abstractions or partial metaphors, and in evolving notions which strike more deeply into the root of reality. (p. 127)

I would like, in this concluding section, to turn my ethnographic eye to the larger national and international context, for it is the larger polemical and political environment in which we are conducting our family studies and family therapies, and designing our future science of family medicine. It is fruitful to explore the concept of family systems as a central organizing dogma (in the sense of ideology rather than the original meaning of philosophic opinion) within the discipline of family medicine borrowed or culturally diffused from the disciplines of family studies and family therapy (Stein, 1987b). Stated differently, the concept of family systems can, I believe, tell us more about the viscissitudes of professional and cultural identity in American medicine and culture than it reveals about the nature of persons and their families.

We might ask, as a beginning of a corrective to such a tendency in family studies and family medicine, "Why are we interested in 'the family' at this particular time in family medicine's and the United States' history?" We might ask, further, "What is it that we wish to find, that we feel especially urgent to confirm?" Is it mere coincidence, in an era of great national and international upheaval and disorder, that much of family social science and therapy should be devoted to discovering if not creating order and structure in family life? Here, cross-cultural studies of the family, on the one hand, and evolutionary perspectives on contemporary family forms and problems, on the other hand, can help protect us from taking an overly nostalgic or rigid view of current models of family life cycles or of goals and brevity of therapy.

Further, much of cultural and intercultural (international) life is a playing out and replaying of family themes in the group arena of unconscious issues, especially surrounding feelings of love and hate, safety and danger. This is an area that colleagues in psychohistory and psychoanthropology have been examining for a decade (e.g., Binion, 1981; deMause, 1974, 1982, 1984; Stein, 1984a; Stierlin, 1976; Volkan & Itzkowitz, 1984). Such studies persuade me that although international diplomacy and war are not isomorphic with family relations, they feel to their participants like family conflicts among the "family of nations," and national groups take various family roles in the destructive drama of warfare. What makes these international object relations so fragile and volatile is the fact that the participants, the more frightened and regressed they become (and this now includes ourselves), the less they perceive each other as real, complex, whole persons. Instead, they perceive one another as parts of persons that are dealt with as if they were embodiments of all-good or all-bad.

It is not enough for us in family medicine to take an interest in what people do in the microcosms of families. We must also take a vital interest in what people do in their groups heir to family life: in occupational, community, cultural, and intercultural contexts. The pall that the prospect of nuclear war casts over the human species, and perhaps all higher forms of life on this planet, is thus not an intrinsic or alien subject matter to the science and future of family medicine. The problem of human aggression and its sanctioning in groups is part of our very subject matter. It has been the vision of many in family medicine that the future of medical science and practice lies in a systems view of health, illness, and healing. That systems vision must now, in turn, widen its parallax of interest and responsibility with the realization that the future of family medicine—indeed, all medicine—is bound up with the fate of the earth.

The promise of the ethnographic method in family medicine as practiced both by behavioral scientists and family physicians is that, as a way of thinking as well as a way of doing research and patient care (see Stein, 1982b, 1983a, 1985; Stein & Apprey, 1985), it keeps us close to the everyday world of our patients and families. In American culture, we are predisposed to look for explanations of human behavior in terms of major, dramatic outer events (e.g., military victories and defeats, epidemics, research breakthroughs, and the like). The quest for the big picture is often a disguised effort to avoid seeing the painful details of the small world of intimate, daily life. The Annales school of French historiography (of which Philippe Ariès is a well-known exemplar), the applied psychoanalytic research in psychohistory (of which Lloyd deMause, David Beisel, Casper Schmidt, Helm Stierlin, Rudolf Binion, and Henry Ebel are perhaps the best known practitioners), and the ethnographic tradition of anthropology in studies of everything from medical to political decision making (e.g., Lloyd Fallers's 1974 classic study of the social anthropology of the state) all argue that only by careful attention to the minutiae of people's everyday lives can we come to explain those "big pictures" that we thought accounted for everything else.

To one knowledgeable of the history of medicine, however, this *naturalistic* approach to the psychosocial and historic realm would be congruent with if not simply an extension of the inquisitive naturalism we associate in biomedicine with such luminaries as Hippocrates, Leonardo da Vinci, Sir William Harvey, Sir Alexander Fleming, Louis Pasteur, and Robert Koch. The promise of family medicine lies in the fact that many of its members have all along questioned what the subject matter of medicine ought to be, and have opened themselves to the study and treatment of context in family medicine undergraduate and residency training. The use of the ethnographic method to describe and explain the family dynamics of health behavior (and the group dynamics of medical practice as well) will be a valuable tool for practitioners, teachers, and researchers who wish to help family medicine go further in that new direction.

At this point the reader—perhaps a busy practicing physician, or a researcher interested in achieving results—may object to this chapter saying, "It is all very interesting, but it is a time-consuming, labor-intensive way of gathering data, one that is certainly not cost-effective, especially in these spartan times." While I wish that there were an easier, quicker, and less anxiety-arousing way to gain access to our subject—human beings suffering their afflictions and seeking respite if not cure for them—I must insist that our methods be true to our subject matter. That is my point of departure. I see no shortcuts in data gathering and data reporting that do not falsify the elusive reality we are trying to chronicle and explain.

Whether we like it or not, there is no way to read others' minds or lives. To pursue what Maranhão (1984) wryly calls a "snapshot anthropology" (p. 270), as if it offered accurate portraits of people's lives in sickness and health, is to confuse the pursuit of convenience with the nature of the subject we are trying to comprehend. Context-denuded behavioral science questionnaires and interview protocols may reveal more about the culturally shared fantasies and myths of researchers themselves than about the subjects of the study. Such instruments might inadvertently reveal superficialities that people will publicly acknowledge, but such revelations should not be confused with a comprehension of what truly organizes people's lives and thereby their health behavior.

The practice of medicine in the United States is being increasingly subjected to simplification and regimentation of clinical thought, standardization, centralized outside control, mechanization, and a minimalist philosophy of responsibility (Kormos, 1984; Stein & Hill, 1984; Stephens, 1984a, 1984b, 1984c). In our increasingly bureaucratized medical world (Ritzer & Walczak, 1986), the family could readily come to be yet another "organ system" to be controlled and "efficiently" managed—but rarely understood. The sound exercise of clinical judgment depends on *context-embedded thinking and planning* on the part of the clinician. The practitioner's interest in the family dynamics of his or her patient is not an academic frill superfluous in hard times. It is indispensable to good patient care irrespective of the official political-medical climate.

Acknowledgments

This chapter benefited from long discussions with Lisa C. Baker, PhD, James Michael Pontious, MD, Stephen Spann, MD, and Paul E. Tietze, MD, on the subject of clinical and family ethnography. The illusion of a self-made manuscript is one way we disguise our indebtedness to others. I do not wish to traffic in such an illusion. This chapter is a testimony to that indebtedness instead. Margaret A. Stein, MA, painstakingly edited and typed this manuscript.

References

Benedict R. Child rearing in eastern European countries. In: Hunt R, ed. Personalities and cultures: readings in psychological anthropology. New York: Natural History Press, 1967: 340–351.
Binion R. Soundings: psychohistorical and psycholiterary. New York: Psychohistory Press, 1981.
Bowen M. Family therapy in clinical practice. New York: Jason Aronson, 1978.
Chrisman NJ. The health seeking process: an approach to the natural history of illness. Culture, Medicine and Psychiatry 1977; 1:351–377.
Chrisman NJ, Maretzki TW, eds. Clinically applied anthropology: anthropologists in health science settings. Boston: D. Reidel, 1982.
deMause L. The history of childhood. New York: Psychohistory Press, 1974.
deMause L. Foundations of psychohistory. New York: Creative Roots, 1982.
deMause L. Reagan's America. New York: Creative Roots, 1984.
Devereux G. Reality and dream: psychotherapy of a Plains Indian. New York: New York University Press, 1951.
Devereux G. From anxiety to method in the behavioral sciences. The Hague: Mouton, 1967.
Doherty WJ, Baird MA. Family therapy and family medicine: toward the primary care of families. New York: Guilford Press, 1983.
Eisenberg L, Kleinman A, eds. The relevance of social science for medicine. Boston: D. Reidel, 1981.
Fallers LA. The social anthropology of the nation-state. Chicago: Aldine, 1974.
Freud S. Papers on technique: Remembering, repeating and working-through, 1914. In: The standard edition of the complete psychological works of Sigmund Freud, Vol. 12. London: Hogarth Press, 1958.
Geertz C. The interpretation of cultures: selected essays. New York: Basic Books, 1973.
Gerber WG, Sluzki CE. The physician–family relationship. In: Taylor R, ed. Family medicine principles and practice. New York: Springer-Verlag, 1978: 216–220.
Good B. The heart of what's the matter: semantics and illness in Iran. Culture, Medicine and Psychiatry 1977; 1:108–138.
Gottman J. Temporal form: toward a new language for describing relationships. Journal of Marriage and the Family 1982; 44:943–962.
Hartman H, Kris E, Loewenstein RM. Some psychoanalytic comments on "culture and personality." In: Muensterberger W, ed. Man and his culture: psychoanalytic anthropology after Totem and Taboo. New York: Taplinger, 1970: 239–270.

Henry J. My life with the families of psychotic children. In: Handel G, ed. The psychosocial interior of the family: a sourcebook for the study of whole families. Chicago: Aldine, 1967: 30–46.

Hippler AE. The North Alaska Eskimo: a culture and personality perspective. American Ethnologist 1974; 1:449–469.

Kleinman A. Patients and healers in the context of culture: an exploration of the borderland between anthropology, medicine, and psychiatry. Los Angeles: University of California Press, 1980.

Kleinman A. The cultural meanings and social uses of illness: a role for medical anthropology and clinically oriented social science in the development of primary care theory and research. Journal of Family Practice 1983; 16:539–545.

Kormos HR. The industrialization of medicine. In: Ruffini JL, ed. Advances in medical social science, Vol. 2. New York: Gordon & Breach, 1984: 323–339.

Kuzel AJ. Naturalistic inquiry: an appropriate model for family medicine. Family Medicine 1986; 18:369–374

La Barre W. Review of: Hall E. Beyond culture. Garden City, N.Y.: Anchor Books, 1977. American Ethnologist 1977; 4:783–784.

La Barre W. The clinic and the field. In: Spindler GD. ed. The making of psychological anthropology. Los Angeles: University of California Press, 1978: 258–299.

Lewis O. An anthropological approach to family studies. In: Handel G, ed. The psychosocial interior of the family: a sourcebook for the study of whole families. Chicago: Aldine, 1967: 131–140.

Lipowski ZJ Psychosocial aspects of disease. Annals of Internal Medicine 1969; 71:1197–1206.

Maranhão T. Family therapy and anthropology. Culture, Medicine and Psychiatry 1984; 8:255–279.

McClain CS. Review essay on: Sargent CF. The cultural context of therapeutic choice: obstetrical care decisions among the Bariba of Benin. Hingham, Mass.: D. Reidel, 1982; and Garro LY, guest ed. The ethnography of health care decisions [special issue]. Social Science and Medicine 1982; 16:1451–1530. Medical Anthropology Quarterly 1983; 15:25–27.

Mead M. Retrospects and prospects. In: Anthropology and human behavior. Washington, D.C.: Anthropological Society of Washington, 1962: 115–149.

Mechanic D. Medical sociology: a selective view. New York: Free Press, 1968.

Notarius C, Markman H, Gottman J. Couples interaction scoring system: clinical implications. In: Filsinger EE, ed. Marriage and family assessment. Beverly Hills, Calif.: Sage Publications, 1983: 117–136.

Pratt L. Family structure and effective health behavior: the energized family. Boston: Houghton Mifflin, 1976.

Richards A. Chisungu. London: Faber & Faber, 1956.

Richtsmeier AJ Jr, Waters DB. Somatic symptoms as family myth. American Journal of Diseases of Children 1984; 138:855–857.

Ritzer G, Walczak D. The changing nature of American medicine. Journal of American Culture 1986; 9:43–51.

Schwartz RC, Breunlin D. Research: why clinicians should bother with it. Family Therapy Networker 1983; July–August: 23–59.

Snider G, Stein HF. An approach to community assessment in medical practice. Family Medicine 1987; 19:213–219.

Spiro ME. Oedipus in the Trobriands. Chicago: University of Chicago Press, 1982.

Stein HF. A dialectical model of health and illness attitudes and behavior among Slovak-Americans. International Journal of Mental Health 1976; 5:117–137.

Stein HF. The Slovak-American "swaddling ethos": homeostat for family dynamics and cultural continuity. Family Process 1978; 17:31–45.

Stein HF. The salience of ethno-psychology for medical education and practice. Social Science and Medicine 1979; 13B:199–210.

Stein HF. Trumpets and drums: some issues in fantasy-analysis methodology. Journal of Psychohistory 1981; 9:199–236.

Stein HF. The annual cycle and the cultural nexus of health care behavior among Oklahoma wheat farming families. Culture, Medicine and Psychiatry 1982a; 6:81–99.

Stein HF. The ethnographic mode of teaching clinical behavioral science. In: Chrisman N, Maretzki T, eds. Clinically applied anthropology: anthropologists in health science settings. Boston: D. Reidel, 1982b: 61–82.

Stein HF. The case study method as a means of teaching significant context in family medicine. Family Medicine 1983a; 15:163–167.

Stein HF. Investing psyche and capital: farming and its hidden meanings. Review essay on: Bennet JW with Kohl SB, Binion G. Of time and the enterprise: North American family farm management in a context of resource marginality. Minneapolis: University of Minnesota Press, 1982. Journal of Psychoanalytic Anthropology 1983b; 6:91–98.

Stein HF. The scope of psycho-geography: the psychoanalytic study of spatial representation. Journal of Psycho-analytic Anthropology 1984a; 7:23–73.

Stein HF. Sittin' tight and bustin' loose: contradiction and conflict in midwestern masculinity and the psychohistory of America. Journal of Psychohistory 1984b; 11:501–512.

Stein HF. The psychodynamics of medical practice. Los Angeles and Berkeley: University of California Press, 1985.

Stein HF. Social role and unconscious complementarity. Journal of Psychoanalytic Anthropology 1986; 9:235–268.

Stein HF. Farmer and cowboy: the duality of the midwestern male ethos—a study in ethnicity, regionalism, and national identity. In: Stein HF, Apprey M. From metaphor to meaning: papers in psychoanalytic anthropology, Monograph Vol. 2. Charlottesville: University Press of Virginia, 1987a.

Stein HF. Polarities in the identity of family medicine: a psychocultural analysis. In: Doherty W, Christianson CE, Sussman MB, eds. Family medicine: the maturing of a discipline. New York: Haworth Press, 1987b: 211–233.

Stein HF, Apprey M. Context and dynamics in clinical knowledge, Monograph Vol. 1. Stein HF, Apprey M. eds. Series in ethnicity, medicine and psychoanalysis. Charlottesville: University Press of Virginia, 1985.

Stein HF, Hill RF. American medicine and the enchanted machine. Continuing Education for the Family Physician 1984; 19:428–430.

Stein HF, Pontious JM. Family and beyond: The larger context of non-compliance. Family Systems Medicine 1985; 3:179–189.

Stephens GG. Five aspects of the healer. Continuing Education for the Family Physician 1984a; 19:663–666.

Stephens GG. The medical supermarket: futuristic or decadent? Continuing Education for the Family Physician 1984b; 19:243, 245.

Stephens GG. The medical supermarket: futuristic or decadent? Part II. Continuing Education for the Family Physician 1984c; 19:600–610.

Stierlin H. Adolf Hitler: a family perspective. New York: Psychohistory Press, 1976.

Suchman EA. Stages of illness and medical care. Journal of Health and Human Behavior 1965; 6:114–128.

Trostle JA, Hauser WA, Susser IS. The logic of noncompliance: management of epilepsy from the patient's point of view. Culture, Medicine and Psychiatry 1983; 7:35–56.

Volkan VD. Linking objects and linking phenomena: a study of the forms, symptoms, metapsychology, and therapy of complicated mourning. New York: International Universities Press, 1981.

Volkan VD, Itzkowitz N. The immortal Atatürk: a psychobiography. Chicago: University of Chicago Press, 1984.

Weber M. The Protestant ethic and the spirit of capitalism. London: Allen & Unwin, 1904/1930.

Whitehead AN. Religion in the making. New York: World Publishing, 1926/1954.

Zborowski M. People in pain. San Francisco: Jossey-Bass, 1969.

27

The Family and Health Promotion among the Elderly

LOIS PRATT
Jersey City State College

This chapter examines the extent and mode of the family's influence on the health practices of older people. It begins with a review of research literature that compares the health practices of older people with practices of younger adults to assess how great the problem of defective health practices is among the elderly, and to document the extent and nature of the health promotion efforts that are needed. The chapter focuses on three types of health practices: diet, exercise, and obtaining needed professional health care.

Then, using evidence from a 1984 study conducted in New Jersey among a sample of approximately 400 persons aged 60 and older, the chapter addresses the following questions concerning the current involvement of older people's families in health promotion:

1. Are the health practices of older people who live in families superior to the practices of those who live alone?
2. Does household composition make a difference in the quality of health practices of older members? Specifically, are there advantages in one household form as compared to another (e.g., husband–wife or living with adult children) and in certain marital statuses (i.e., married, divorced, single, or widowed)?
3. Does the family provide some unique form of support for health behavior, or can other groups and relationships provide health-promoting forms of support equally well for older persons living alone and for those living in family households?

Finally, the chapter offers some limited formulations concerning the dynamics through which families function to influence the health practices of older people for better or worse.

Both the independent and the dependent variables examined in the present study differ from those used in most of the previous research on the family and on the functioning of older people. Research on the family has tended to focus on a constricted segment of the family lifetime—the young adult child-rearing stage. When older people have been included in family research, it has generally been the families of adult children in their roles as caregivers to the elderly parents that have been of concern. Yet 20% of all families, 16 million households, are headed by persons aged 65 and older. Over half of all persons 65 and older are married and live together in two-person households, and 72% of elderly people live in their own homes. The present study focuses on families and households composed of older people.

Previous research on the effects of family support in the lives of older people has concentrated on their physical and mental well-being. The studies have yielded inconsistent results and low correlations, and the goal of identifying the mechanisms and processes through which family support functions to influence health and well-being has been elusive (Ward, 1985). This should not be surprising, since the outcome measures are diffuse and subject to lifelong modification by a complex and changing constellation of factors and processes, and health and well-being are in themselves a potent influence on the hypothe-sized causal factors.

Health behavior was chosen as the outcome variable in the present study for the fol-lowing reasons. First, health practices of older people are in themselves useful indicators of the extent to which older people are coping effectively. Second, knowledge of social factors that influence particular health practices may have considerable practical utility for health professionals; such knowledge can assist health care providers who want to help patients and families, for example, to modify an irregular eating pattern or a failure to exercise by prescribing specific regimens and obtaining family support for the regimens. Third, it may be more feasible scientifically to identify antecedent factors that are directly linked to health behaviors than to account for well-being by factors that may be several causal steps removed from the outcome. For example, the tendency to get needed medical care might be linked to practical instrumental supports provided by the family, such as a car or an escort.

HEALTH PRACTICES OF OLDER PEOPLE

We need to review research literature that compares the nutrition, exercise, and use of professional services among the elderly and younger adults in order to assess how serious and widespread the problem of defective health practices is among the elderly, and to document the extent and nature of the health promotion efforts that are needed.

Eating Practices of the Elderly

The available evidence indicates there are some differences between the dietary practices of the elderly and younger adults, such as low consumption of protein and milk, and higher consumption of fresh fruits and vegetables, and of breads and cereals, among the elderly; the elderly also have a lower tendency to snack and a greater tendency to eat full break-fasts. Overconsumption of calories is a much more widespread problem than undercon-sumption, for the elderly as well as for other age groups.

MEAL REGULARITY

According to the National Health Interview Survey (National Center for Health Statistics [NCHS], 1980a), 58% of Americans reported eating breakfast every day. The proportion increased steadily with advancing age, from 42% of those 20 to 34 years of age to 86% of those aged 65 and older. Only about 8% of elderly people never ate breakfast, compared to 36% of persons aged 20 to 34. A Milwaukee study reported that the breakfasts of the elderly tended to be more adequate meals than the breakfasts eaten by the young (Slesin-ger, McDivitt, & O'Donnell, 1980).

About 38% of American adults ate snacks every day, a practice that was also related to age, declining from about 43% of those aged 20 to 34 to 28% of those 65 and older (NCHS, 1980a). The Milwaukee study found that the elderly reported fewer eating epi-sodes per day and also tended to skip fewer meals. The young had the highest incidence of meal skipping (especially of skipped breakfasts) and the largest number of eating epi-sodes, which were occasioned by snacking.

Together, the data on breakfast eating and snacking indicate that regular eating habits are positively associated with age. Eating patterns of persons 55 to 64 and of those 65 and older were found to be similar, and contrasted with habits of persons younger than 55.

UNDER- AND OVERCONSUMPTION

There has been considerable concern about possible undernutrition among the elderly. The "tea-and-toast" syndrome is often cited by health and social workers. The mean daily caloric intake was found to be 1,307 for elderly women and 1,805 for men. Some have interpreted this as constituting only about three-quarters of the Recommended Daily Allowances of calories, which are 1,800 for women and 2,400 for men aged 51 and older (NCHS, 1977). The difficulty in concluding that this represents a generally inadequate caloric intake among the elderly is that intake may decline with age parallel to the decrease in basal oxygen consumption and reduction in physical activity.

When actual height/weight ratios were compared with desirable height/weight ratios, it was found that 16% of persons 65 and older were underweight by 5% or more of their optimal weight. The youngest adults, those aged 20 to 34, were even more likely than the elderly to be underweight (26%) (NCHS, 1980a).

The much more widespread weight tendency was overweight. Only 24% of American adults were found to be within 5% of their desirable weight, with 58% above and only 18% below optimal weight. Almost 15% of the adult population were 30% or more overweight. Persons 65 and older were more likely than the youngest adults, those aged 20 to 34, to be above optimal weight, as well as grossly overweight; but persons 65 and older were *less* likely to be either moderately or grossly overweight than were those aged 45 to 64.

The most significant pattern concerning the weight of the elderly is that it resembles the general pattern for U.S. adults, among whom a majority are overweight, and only a small minority underweight.

COMPOSITION AND QUALITY OF THE DIET

Kim, Caldwell, and Snyder, (1984) asked older people to make checklists of food items kept in storage, and then compared foods on hand with a list of foods recommended for an adequate diet. They found that these older people tended to have an adequate supply of meat, dairy foods, fruits, vegetables, bread, and cereal to supply the recommended servings per day, and this was true in the winter as well as the summer.

According to a national dietary intake study, the elderly population tended to meet or exceed the recommended intake of protein (NCHS, 1977). Women aged 65 and older averaged 53 grams of protein, or 115% of the recommended protein intake, and men averaged 72 grams, or 129% of the recommended intake.

All age groups consumed inadequate amounts of milk and milk products, but the elderly were significantly more deficient than younger age groups. The 65 and over group averaged less than one-half of the recommended two servings, and one-third reported no milk intake on the day of the study. All age groups fell below the recommended four servings of fruits and vegetables, and of breads and cereals, but the elderly came closer to meeting the recommended levels of these two food groups than did younger people (Slesinger *et al.*, 1980).

CAUSES OF AGE DIFFERENCES IN EATING HABITS

We are faced with a crucial question concerning how—by what dynamics—these age differences in eating habits come about. There are several possibilities. An *aging* effect is at work if a difference between age groups was caused by the aging process, that is, if people changed their diets as they grew older. A second possibility is a *cohort* effect, whereby persons born in different historical periods started out in different circumstances that so shaped their lives that they remained different from other cohorts throughout their lives. A *time* effect is a third possible dynamic. A widespread social change can affect all age groups, so that members of each age group behave differently in old age than when they were young because events have so altered their lives. The development of contraception, Social Security, and refrigeration, for example, have modified the lives of all age groups.

There is no way to determine from cross-section surveys whether differences between age groups are due to aging or to cohort effects. For example, the fact that older people eat fewer snacks and eat breakfast more regularly may have come about because these people developed more regular eating habits as they grew old, or because they were born early in this century when people established more regular eating patterns, which they carried throughout their lives.

An elegant study has been conducted at the National Institute on Aging (Elahi *et al.*, 1983) that attempted to untangle and identify aging, cohort, and time effects on the nutritional intake of men. These authors obtained 7-day dietary diaries from 180 men, who were aged 35 to 74 at the outset of the study, during each of three time periods: 1961–1965, 1966–1970, and 1971–1975.

They found that *in each cohort* caloric intake decreased with increasing age; that is, caloric intake declined *as a result* of the aging process and paralleled the decrease in basal oxygen consumption and the reduction in physical activity that occur with advancing age.

Carbohydrate and cholesterol consumption also declined, but the dynamics were quite different from those involved in the decrease in total calories. There was a *time* effect on carbohydrate and cholesterol consumption; that is, all age groups showed a reduction in carbohydrates and cholesterol between the three study periods: 1961, 1966, and 1971. Thus, reduction in these nutrients was *not* a response to growing old, but was a general response in the population—by all ages—to public health efforts to modify dietary practices.

Notably, no cohort effects were found in that study. None of the age differences in dietary patterns were due to the particular period in which the various age groups were born.

Exercise Practices

A national survey conducted by Louis Harris and Associates (1979) among 1,510 adults showed that 59% of the total sample, but only 29% of persons aged 65 or older, were currently involved in regular physical activity. About half of the 65-and-older group who were physically active were involved only at a low level of activity. When asked, "If older people have their doctor's permission, is it a good idea for older people to be involved in sports and athletic activities?" almost three-fourths said it was a good idea, but 57% said, "I don't need more exercise because I get enough as it is."

The Harris survey indicates that the family is extremely important in promoting physical exercise, at least when the child is growing up. Subjects who said their mother was interested in participating in sports and athletics when the subjects were growing up were significantly more likely to be active currently in sports themselves than were those whose mothers were not interested in sports when the subjects were growing up—80% compared to 55%. The findings were similar for fathers' interest in sports participation.

Evidence from the Harris survey indicates that there has been an increase over the years in the degree of exposure to and encouragement about exercise offered by the family, particularly by fathers. Forty-six percent of the youngest age groups (18–24) reported that their fathers had encouraged them to participate in sports, compared to only 13% of the oldest group. This appears to be a cohort effect. Thus, if today's elderly have a very low level of physical activity, it may be due to the low level of support given when they were young; hence it may not be possible to stimulate many of these persons to revise a lifelong pattern. On the other hand, an increasing proportion of successive cohorts may reach old age with well-established patterns of physical activity. The elderly of the future and their families may be highly receptive to encouragement and advice regarding appropriate exercise.

Obtaining Needed Professional Health Care

Persons aged 65 and older make proportionately more visits to physicians than do members of younger age groups (4.3 visits per person per year compared to 2.6 per person for the population as a whole; NCHS, 1983). The sheer volume does not indicate whether the care they obtained was sufficient or appropriate.

CANCER DETECTION
There is some evidence that older people may not act as judiciously regarding the risk of cancer as is warranted or to the degree that younger persons do. Since the risk of developing cancer increases rapidly with age, it is of concern that older women were less likely to participate in available screening programs (Hobbs, Smith, George, & Sellwood, 1980) and to practice breast self-examination than younger women (Foster *et al.,* 1978; Reeder, Berkanovic, & Marcus, 1980). Elderly patients were also less likely to present at an early stage of the disease (Holmes & Hearne, 1981).

DENTAL CARE
The National Health Interview Survey (NCHS, 1980b) indicated that about half the population aged 65 and older had not been to a dentist for 5 years or more, and only 30% had visited a dentist within the last year.

MEDICAL CARE ENCOUNTERS
Older patients may tend to cope less effectively with professional encounters than younger patients. Only 2% to 4% of persons in an American Association of Retired Persons (AARP) survey said they asked questions about their prescriptions; asked their pharmacists how much medicine to take or when to take it; or asked for information on refills, precautions, or side-effects (AARP, 1984). These specific behaviors may be rooted in a more basic pattern of dealing with professional encounters. Patients 60 and older were more likely to accept physician authority, in terms of both attitudes and behaviors, than were younger patients (Haug, 1979). Older patients have been found to prefer a low information/high affect strategy by physicians, whereas younger patients preferred a high degree of both information and affect (O'Hair, Behnke, & King, 1983).

Summary

This review of health habits has documented some health behaviors of older people that fall short of those of younger people—in particular, lower consumption of milk, significantly less regular exercise, a greater tendency to delay in obtaining dental care and cancer screening, and less resourceful use of medical care visits. Overall, however, the health practices of older people were found to be quite adequate. In some respects, older people's practices surpassed those of younger people, most notably in the eating of regular meals.

Implications for Health Professionals

There is a fairly pervasive tendency to attribute any distinctive behavior pattern of older people to the aging process. We say, for example, "People tend to become picky eaters as they get old." The judgment that aging causes pickiness leads us to make different decisions about whether and how to intervene than would an assessment that events of the current time period are inducing older people as well as people of all ages to modify their diets, or a judgment that this cohort of older people has always been careful about food wastage because they were raised in comparative scarcity.

Consider how differently health professionals might approach the problem of regular eating habits depending on what we interpret to be the cause of the distinctive practices of older people. If eating habits tend to *become* regular in old age, then all we have to do is wait until people reach 55, or perhaps try to speed up the onset of the pattern of regularity. On the other hand, if today's elderly have always had regular eating habits, there is little need to intervene with this cohort, but we can expect a major nutrition problem when the later cohorts carry their lifelong habits of snacking and skipping meals into old age.

What we can realistically enlist families to do about dietary and exercise practices depends in large measure on whether the change we seek to foster is one that is supported by strong societal trends that are affecting all age groups—such as the movement to lower dietary cholesterol and to undertake regular exercise—or whether it is a movement that is mainly affecting young people—such as breast self-examination—or a temporary fad. Knowledge that the elderly as well as the young are responding to the movement to reduce dietary cholesterol offers encouragement to health professionals that their efforts to get older patients and their families to modify their diets have substantially greater prospects of success than they did before this social movement developed.

The tendency for older people to be somewhat less assertive than younger people in obtaining needed health care may represent, in part, an increasing dependency that comes with advancing age. However, it also may be more characteristic of the present cohort of elderly, who were born early in this century and tended to obtain less formal education and to acquire less knowledge of medical care than did cohorts born later. If so, we might anticipate that forthcoming cohorts of old people would show greater readiness to persevere in obtaining needed care.

RESEARCH FINDINGS

Research findings concerning the influence of family life on the health habits of older people will be presented. The data are based on interviews conducted in 1984 with a representative sample of 396 noninstitutionalized men and women aged 60 and older living in the 12 municipalities of Hudson County, New Jersey. This is an ethnically mixed and densely populated county of just over one-half million people, among whom 18% are 60 or older. Using directories listing households in the county, we contacted every 75th household (2,474), determined that 1 out of every 4 (740) of the contacted households contained a person aged 60 or older, and interviewed 54% (396) of eligible households.

Three household forms in which older people may live are compared: living with husband or wife, living with adult children, and living alone. Four family statuses are also compared: married, widowed, divorced, and single.

For the purposes of this analysis, one measure of eating habits was selected. This was the question, "How many meals do you usually eat in a day?" An answer of three meals a day was defined as regular eating habits. The measure of exercise was the question, "In good weather, how often do you take a walk?" A daily walk was defined as regular exercise. The measure chosen to represent the practice of obtaining needed professional health care were the questions, "Do you have any health problems that need care that you have not gotten?" and "Do you have any dental (teeth) problems that need care that you have not gotten?"

In the sample as a whole, 3 in 10 did not eat three meals a day, 6 in 10 did not walk daily, 1 in 20 had not obtained needed medical care, and 1 in 10 had not gotten needed dental care.

Eating Habits

Does family life confer an advantage on older people in sustaining regular eating habits? The findings point to regular companionship as a key to eating regularly, and family and friends can both provide such companionship.

Persons who lived with their husband or wife or with their adult children were somewhat more likely to eat three meals a day than were persons who lived alone or were divorced or single, as shown in Table 27-1. Those living with husband or wife and those living with adult children were equally likely to eat regularly. The pattern was weak for women but strong for men, with 51% of men who lived alone eating regular meals, compared to 80% of men with wives. The pattern persisted under control for age and level of health.

It turned out that having an available meal partner was the factor largely responsible

Table 27-1. Percentage of Older Persons Who Ate Regular Meals, Exercised, and Needed Medical and Dental Care, Classified by Household Form and Family Status

Household form and family status	Number of cases	Percentage			
		Ate regular meals	Exercised regularly	Needed medical care	Needed dental care
Household form					
Lived alone	165	64[a]	47[a]	5	9
Lived with spouse	148	73[a]	39	4	10
Lived with child	90	72	39	6	11
Family status					
Married	151	73	38[a]	4	11
Divorced	23	57	52	9	13
Widowed	178	69	44	6	10
Single	43	63	44	2	12
Total sample	396	69	42	5	10

Note: The three household forms total more than the sample of 396 because 7 persons who lived with both spouse and child have been reported twice.

[a]$p \leq .05$.

Table 27-2. Relationship of Eating Meals with Someone to Eating Regular Meals, by Household Form

Household form	Percentage who ate regular meals	
	Ate alone	Ate with someone
Lived alone	60	80[b]
Lived with spouse	67	75[a]
Lived with child	56	77[a]
Total		
Percentage	60	76
Number	129	198

[a]Comparison of "ate alone" with "with someone ": $p \leqslant .05$.

[b]$p \leqslant .01$.

for the more regular eating habits of those living in families. Persons who said they usually ate their meals with someone were significantly more likely to eat three meals a day than were those who generally ate alone. Persons living in families were much more likely to eat with someone than were persons not living in families. When we controlled for this factor and considered those people who said they regularly ate their meals with someone, we found that those who lived alone, or were divorced, widowed, or single, were just as likely to eat three meals as were those who lived in families, either with husband or wife or with grown children. The data are summarized in Table 27-2.

Having friends whom they visited with or went out with regularly was also associated with eating regular meals. Having regular visits with friends was more commonly found among older persons who lived alone, especially single persons, than among those living in families. As shown in Table 27-3, when we controlled for this factor and examined the group who regularly visited with friends, we found that both divorced and single adults had a rate of regular eating that compared favorably with the rate for all married persons. Regular friendship visiting, then, can serve as an alternative to the family as a source of companionship that promotes regular eating habits among those who are not married.

Table 27-3. Relationship of Visiting with Friends to Eating Regular Meals, by Household Form and Family Status

Household form and family status	Percentage who ate regular meals		
	Visited with friends regularly	Visited with friends occasionally	Visited with friends not at all
Household form			
Lived alone	66[a]	66	50
Lived with spouse	81[b]	72	55
Lived with child	74	74	63
Family status			
Married	81	72	55
Divorced	89	40	25
Widowed	65	73	68
Single	75	46	50
Total			
Percentage	73	68	59
Number	163	165	58

[a]Comparison of "visited with friends regularly" and "not at all": $p \leqslant .05$.

[b]$p \leqslant .01$.

Among married people, visiting with friends contributed additional support to regular mealtime eating beyond the major support provided by the spouse. Although fewer married than nonmarried older people maintained regular visiting with friends, when the married did have such friendships they were significantly more likely to eat regular meals than the married who lacked regular visiting with friends.

Availability of companionship appears to be an operative force that sustains regular eating habits. Family life confers an advantage because most family households provide mealtime companions, whereas single-person households do not. Older people who do not live in families but who visit regularly with friends achieve comparable support for regular eating. Married persons who have been able to maintain regular visiting with friends are doubly advantaged. Another study (McIntosh & Shifflett, 1983) also found that having many friends was the single most important form of social support that influenced dietary adequacy of elderly persons who attended a congregate meal site.

Exercise Habits

Older people who lived in families tended to incur a disadvantage, compared to those who did not live in families with respect to regular walking exercise. Older persons who lived with husband or wife or with adult children were somewhat less likely to take regular walks than were persons who lived alone or who were divorced, widowed, or single (see Table 27-1). The pattern was especially strong among women, with 46% of women who lived alone walking daily compared to only 26% of women with husbands.

It was contacts that drew older people *outside* the home that promoted regular walking. Those whose relationships were circumscribed by the family (i.e., those who did not visit regularly with friends, said they did not see people as much as they would like, and said they would like help in meeting people) were significantly less likely to go out to walk. Since family life appears to inhibit relationships beyond the home that foster regular walking, whereas living alone encourages them, those living in families tended to walk less than those who lived alone. Notably, when older people who lived in families did maintain visiting relationships with friends and telephoned regularly to friends and relatives, they were as likely to walk regularly as persons who did not live in families. Thus, families of older people *can* foster exercise by linking the members to a network beyond the family. Illustrative data are given in Table 27-4.

Table 27-4. Relationship of Visiting with Friends to Regular Exercise, by Household Form

Household form	Percentage who exercised regularly		
	Visited with friends regularly	Visited with friends occasionally	Visited with friends not at all
Lived alone	52[a]	46	29
Lived with spouse	50[a]	31	36
Lived with child	57[a]	36	13
Total			
Percentage	52	38	31
Number	167	170	59

[a]Comparison of ''visited with friends regularly'' and ''not at all'': $p \leq .01$.

Table 27-5. Relationship of Having Someone to Help in Case of Sickness to Being in Need of Medical and Dental Care, by Household Form

Household form	Percentage who needed medical care		Percentage who needed dental care	
	Someone to help if sick	No one to help if sick	Someone to help if sick	No one to help if sick
Lived alone	3[b]	17	9	13
Lived with spouse	2[b]	18	10	12
Lived with child	3[a]	14	8[b]	29
Total				
Percentage	3	17	10	15
Number	318	47	317	47

[a] Comparison of "someone" and "no one to help if sick": $p \leq .05$.
[b] $p < .01$.

Obtaining Needed Professional Health Care

Family life did not provide an advantage to older people in obtaining needed professional care for health and dental problems. As shown in Table 27-1, the proportions who failed to obtain needed medical or dental care were veritably the same regardless of whether older people lived in families (either with husband or wife or with adult children), lived alone, or were widowed or single. Only the divorced had a slightly larger proportion with unmet needs for professional care. Findings for the divorced group should be accepted cautiously, however, because of the small number of cases.

This pattern (of no difference among household forms) persisted among various age levels, sexes, and health levels, with one exception. Among persons who were in *poor health,* more of those who lived alone than of those who lived in families had failed to obtain needed medical care.

The factors that were found to be associated with getting needed professional care are measures of the types of support that are commonly regarded as the special contribution of the family to personal well-being. The most significant contributors to getting needed care were having someone to call in an emergency, someone to help if one got sick, and someone to help if one needed money. These are forms of instrumental support. Companionship types of support, such as visiting with friends and relatives, which were influential in fostering regular eating and exercise habits, also contributed some influence on getting needed health care, but their influence was not as important as that of instrumental supports.

This pattern held true for all family status groups. Lack of instrumental support was strongly associated, and lack of companionship support was associated to a lesser degree, with failure to get needed medical and dental care. Data in Table 27-5 exemplify the pattern.

Among the divorced, who were the only family status group with a higher than average level of unmet needs, those who did have someone to help them if they were sick and those who visited regularly with friends and relatives had no unmet needs for care. The lack of support relationships among the divorced as compared to all other marital status groups accounted for a large amount of the higher level of unmet needs for professional care that was found among the divorced.

Among single and widowed persons, who generally had extensive contacts outside the home, those who did not have anyone to call in an emergency or to help if they were sick were significantly more likely to have unmet medical and dental needs than were those who had instrumental support.

Clearly, it was appropriate forms of support, rather than a marital partner per se, that contributed to getting needed professional care. Among married persons, there were some who said they did not have someone to call in an emergency or to help when they were sick, and these married persons were much more likely to have unmet medical care needs than were married persons who did have these instrumental supports. In addition, among those married persons who were confined to the family—who did not visit relatives or friends—the rate of unmet needs was high. And among those for whom marriage did not provide adequate companionship—who said they ate their meals alone—the rate of unmet needs was high. This is not to say that the married had a high rate of unmet needs, but that when instrumental and companionate supports were lacking, the married, like the unmarried, were less likely to obtain needed medical and dental care.

CONCLUSIONS

The evidence from this study warrants the following general conclusions:

1. The family's influence differs for various health practices.
2. The family does not provide some unique form of support for health protective practices of older people that cannot be supplied by other social relationships.
3. Health protective practices tend to be more strongly fostered when older people participate in diversified groups and relationships, rather than when their relationships are narrowly circumscribed by the household.

Family Influence on Various Health Practices

The influence of the family on health practices of older people is complex, and is not the same for all health practices. Elderly persons living in family households tended to have more regular eating habits than did persons living alone, but less regular exercise practices, and just about the same rate of obtaining needed medical and dental care.

Family Support Is Not Unique

When the health practices of older people living in family households were compared to the practices of older persons with nonfamily face-to-face relationships, it was found that the supportive influence of the family was not unique. Availability of companions was found to foster regular eating practices, and when older people who lived alone had well-developed friendship bonds, they had as regular eating habits as did persons in families. Availability of instrumental support was found to be a significant force in getting older people to obtain needed medical and dental care, and its effect was substantially the same whether supplied by family or nonfamily relationships.

Diversified Groups and Relationships

The pattern of groups and relationships to which a person belongs can range from narrow and homogeneous to broad and heterogeneous: family relationships only or friends only; family and relatives; or family, relatives, and friends. The pattern of relationships that appears to function most effectively in fostering older people's health practices is a broad and heterogenous pattern. Elderly persons whose relationships were restricted to the household, whether the household was a family or a single-person domicile, were disadvantaged in all three health protective practices compared to persons with complex patterns of relationships.

Morgan, Patrick, and Charlton (1984) and Hammer (1983) have reported the importance of relationships outside the family as supports for health and have cautioned against using the family as a proxy measure of social support. In a previous study of families with young children (Pratt, 1976), the concept "energized family" was proposed to characterize the type of family that was found to function most effectively in promoting the personal health practices and use of medical services by the parents and children. A central feature of energized families was that they maintained varied contacts with persons, groups, and resources beyond the family. These contacts helped them to obtain information, cope effectively with health matters, and negotiate effectively for professional care. The findings of the present study concerning the importance of bonds beyond the family in promoting the health practices of older people are consistent with those earlier conclusions concerning young families.

A Needed Revision in Conceptual Framework

A conceptual framework regulates what we examine and how we interpret what we see. A family systems framework channels attention toward relationships within the family as a bounded system and leads us either to ignore relationships "outside" the system or to evaluate them in terms of their impact on the system; it further constrains us to regard maintenance of the family unit, rather than support of individual members, as the goal of intervention. When we are concerned with understanding social influences on the health behavior of older persons or with designing interventions to foster health protective behavior among older persons, we require a conceptual approach that orients us toward all patterns of social relationships that function to influence and support older people's health behavior. The data from the present study "make sense" when cast in the framework of social relationship patterns that vary in scope and complexity.

Implications for Intervention

The evidence suggests that in planning interventions to foster health-promoting behavior among older persons, the availability to the older person of various types of social relationships should be considered rather than regarding the family as the only or most important social resource. Older people living alone may have networks available to them that are as supportive of health practices as those available to elderly persons living in families.

Acknowledgment

This study was supported by a grant from the Hudson County (New Jersey) Office on Aging.

References

American Association of Retired Persons. Lack of post-marketing checks for risky medication is decried. AARP News Bulletin 1984; June:6.

Elahi VK, Elahi D, Andres R, Tobin JD, Butler MG, Norris AH. A longitudinal study of nutrition intake in men. Journal of Gerontology 1983; 38:162–180.

Foster RS, Lang SP, Castasz MC, Worden J, Haines CR, Watts J. Breast self-examination practices and breast cancer stage. New England Journal of Medicine 1978; 299:265–270.

Hammer M. "Core" and "extended" social networks in relation to health and illness. Social Science and Medicine 1983; 17:405–411.

Harris, Louis, and Associates, Inc. The Perrier study: fitness in America. New York: Great Waters of France, Inc., 1979.

Haug M. Doctor–patient relationships and the older patient. Journal of Gerontology 1979; 34:852–860.

Hobbs P, Smith A, George WD, Sellwood RA. Acceptors and rejectors of an invitation to undergo breast cancer screening compared to those who referred themselves. Journal of Epidemiology and Community Health 1980; 34:19–22.

Holmes F, Hearne E. Cancer stage to age relationships: implications for cancer screening in the elderly. Journal of the American Geriatrics Society 1981; 29:55–57.

Kim SK, Caldwell NR, Snyder E. Seasonal changes related to food choice practices of independent living elderly. Journal of Nutrition for the Elderly 1984; 4:47–64.

McIntosh WA, Shifflett PA. Social support, stress, and diet among the elderly. Presented at the annual meeting of the American Sociological Association, Detroit, 1983.

Morgan M, Patrick DL, Charlton JR. Social networks and psychosocial support among disabled people. Social Science and Medicine 1984; 19:489–497.

National Center for Health Statistics, U.S. Department of Health, Education and Welfare. Dietary intake finding, United States, 1971–1974, No. 77-1647. Washington, D.C.: U.S. Government Printing Office, 1977.

National Center for Health Statistics, U.S. Department of Health and Human Services. Health practices among adults: United States: 1977, No. 64. Washington, D.C.: U.S. Government Printing Office, 1980a.

National Center for Health Statistics, U.S. Department of Health and Human Services. Health United States, 1980, Number 81-1232. Washington, D.C.: U.S. Government Printing Office, 1980b.

National Center for Health Statistics, U.S. Department of Health and Human Services. 1981 summary: national ambulatory medical care survey, No. 88. Washington, D.C.: U.S. Government Printing Office, 1983.

O'Hair HD, Behnke RR, King, PE. Age-related patient preferences for physician communication styles. Educational Gerontology 1983; 9:147–158.

Pratt L. Family structure and effective health behavior: the energized family. Boston: Houghton Mifflin, 1976.

Reeder S, Berkanovic E, Marcus AC. Breast cancer detection behavior among urban women. Public Health Reports 1980; 95:276–281.

Slesinger DP, McDivitt M, O'Donnell M. Food patterns in an urban population: age and sociodemographic correlates. Journal of Gerontology 1980; 35:432–441.

Ward RA. Informal networks and well-being in later life: research agenda. The Gerontologist 1985; 25:55–61.

28

Family Factors in the Decision to Seek Medical Care

JOHNYE BALLENGER
JOEL J. ALPERT
Boston City Hospital and Boston University School of Medicine

Despite changes in the composition of families over the past 40 years, the family continues to be the primary unit of living as well as the primary unit of illness. The view that family factors play a major role in the decision to seek medical care is as relevant today as it was when advanced by Richardson (1945). The application of systems theory to the study of the family, along with family therapy models, has furthered our understanding of the family unit (Sargent, 1984a, 1984b). We are now in a position to increase our understanding of how the interactions and behavior that occur within families affects individual members' decision-making behavior, as well as how they affect the family unit as a whole. The ordering of complex family interactional patterns and behaviors that systems analysis provides makes expansion of Richardson's ideas possible. For the purposes of this chapter, it is just as important to examine the family as the unit of living and health as it is to examine the family as the unit of illness.

Socialization is a basic task of the family, and by accomplishing this task the family becomes the carrier of cultural as well as biologic inheritance (Miller & Janorik, 1980). Many definitions of health and illness and the sanctioned responses to alterations in these states have their basis within the family. For example, Zborowski's study (1969) of reaction to pain by ethnic groups is regarded as a classic example of social learning influencing a response to illness. Social attributes such as sex, birth order, age, social class, and race are frequently associated with an individual's or a family's behavior in response to an illness (Andersen & Kasper, 1973; Mechanic, 1964; Prugh, 1983).

Considerable work has been accomplished in the field of medical sociology examining the decision to seek medical care. Parsons's (1951) sick role theory offered a pioneering framework for understanding why and how people react to illness. Modification of the sick role concept has led to the development of additional illness behavior theories. Notable are Mechanic's general theory of help seeking (1968) and Suchman's stages of illness and medical care (1965). These theories provide a basis for the development of health service utilization models.

From the work of these medical sociologists, we can expand a commonsense view and conclude that the expectation of a healthy family is its continued good health. When that state of good health is lost, the family's expectations shift to one of ready access to medical care that provides not only swift and technically competent evaluation and treatment of the physiological derangements, but also care that is responsive to their psychosocial needs, both as individuals and as family members. In common terms, the family's expectation is that they will receive care that is affordable and personal; care that fosters and promotes preventive health measures; and, when needed, care that will provide rehabilitative services and follow-up. Finally, there is the expectation of a relationship between the family and their physician that is supportive of the family's efforts to maximize and ensure the personal, emotional, and physical development of each of its members.

Despite the importance of the family, little recent work has focused on family determinants of health care-seeking behavior. Weyrauch's (1984) article, reviewing 150 consecutive patient visits to a family medicine program, stands out. Underscoring the deficiency of work in the field is the fact that the most recent reference in his article is 10 years old.

This chapter relies, to a considerable degree, on our experiences as pediatricians (Haggerty & Alpert, 1963). A number of child health studies provide helpful information (Blaxter, 1981; Gallagher, 1978; Haggerty, Roghmann, & Pless, 1975; Harvard Child Health Project, 1977; Robertson, Kosa, Haggerty, Heagarty, & Alpert, 1974). As we consider the role of the family in the decision to seek medical care, we must first consider the changing nature of the family, of pediatric illness, and of the organization of medical services. With that background, we will describe a list of family factors that have been shown to influence the decision to seek medical care.

THE CHANGING NATURE OF THE FAMILY

During the 1980s, the structural profiles of families have become more diverse. We now have more unmarried couples with children, older parents with young children, single-parent households, divorced parents with shared custody, gay couples, and lesbian couples. Notwithstanding this greater diversity, the standard profile of the typical family unit continues to consist of husband, wife, and children living together.

There are several aspects of this new diversity that warrant special note. First is the increase in the rate of first births to older women. In 1981, the rate increased by 8% in the 35- to 39-year-old group. The increase was 33% in the 40- to 44-year-old group, although this represented less than 1% of births that year. Factors contributing to the trend of the first births to older women include: deliberate delay after marriage before having children; a rise in age at marriage; and an increase in the general educational level of women, contributing to the postponement of childbearing among these more educated women until their 30s (Wegman, 1984).

Second is the continued high rate of divorce. Although as of 1987 divorce rates have decreased for the second consecutive year, the divorce rate is still nearly twice the 1950 rate, and equals nearly half the number of marriages in this country (Wegman, 1984). In 1981, almost 1.2 million children were involved in new divorces. It is estimated that more than 9% of all children less than 18 years old live with a divorced parent (Better Health for Our Children, 1981). This number is likely to increase. Third, it is projected that, by 1990, 25% of all children will live with only one parent. The majority of these single-parent families will be headed by women. Concomitant with this rise will be an increase in the number of children living below the poverty line. In 1978, 16% of all children lived below the poverty line: 41% of black children, 27% of Hispanic children, and 11% of white children. The overall figure currently is 22% (Miller, 1984).

Fourth, changes have occurred in the American family as a result of increased numbers of women entering the work force. Currently, 60% of U.S. women work, including 55% of all mothers with children less than 18 years old and 45% of mothers with preschool children (Heins, Stillman, Sabers, & Mazzeo, 1983). Despite their presence in the workplace and increased paternal participation in child bearing, working mothers generally continue to assume primary responsibility for child care and household duties. All these factors directly influence the decision to seek medical care.

THE CHANGING NATURE OF PEDIATRIC ILLNESS

The nature of illness in the pediatric age range has changed and continues to change, altering the reasons for which care is sought. The most notable changes have occurred in the area of communicable diseases. Improvement in sanitary conditions, immunization and screening programs, better quality and less crowded housing, improved nutrition, and the decline in virulence of some organisms contribute to this phenomenon. Antibiotic use has also contributed substantially to the sharp decline in mortality and morbidity due to infectious diseases, as has improvement in the management of the fluid and electrolyte imbalances that often accompany the gastroenteriditis.

However, there are new areas of infectious disease that are now of concern. For example, diseases behave differently within the day care setting (Goodman, Osterholm Granoff, & Pickering, 1984). Pass, Hutto, Reynolds, and Polhill (1984) reported that in a group day care setting, the acquisition of cytomegalovirus is facilitated, and its prevalence is especially high among toddlers 12 to 18 months of age. The attendant viral shedding and excretion poses a potentially serious threat to susceptible women of childbearing age, often including the child's own mother. Other infectious diseases that require study include invasive *Haemophilus influenzae* type B, organisms responsible for infectious diarrhea, and hepatitis A; these diseases highlight the continued interplay between illness, the child, and the family. Fear of previously innocuous diseases, such as herpes simplex, has made what had been for many a simple cold sore into a perceived threat of a serious sexually transmitted disease. Awareness of rare but real events, such as sudden infant death and the possible association of Reye syndrome with aspirin, make parents respond differently to common events like upper respiratory infections, influenza, and chicken pox.

The changing nature of pediatric illness has been referred to as the new morbidity, of which social and behavioral disorders are a large component. The exact prevalence of behavioral disorders has not been determined. Starfield (1982) reports studies where the prevalence of specific disorders is consistently 10%. One in seven mothers of preschool children reported a problem in growth or development, and 1 in 10 mothers reported difficulty in behavior or discipline. Fifteen percent of children aged 5 to 14 years were reported to have a problem of behavior or discipline, and 10% a problem in social relationships.

The determination of the precise prevalence of behavioral disorders in the general population is hampered by the lack of agreement on a single definition of what constitutes a behavioral disorder. The overlaps between the psychologic and social contributors to behavioral problems makes formulation of a single definition difficult. However, problems of conduct, learning and developmental maturation, exposure to environmental hazards and their consequences, and violence and substance abuse are increasingly the focus of study for both specialists and primary care physicians.

The new morbidity includes traumatic injury and violence. Injuries continue to be the leading cause of death and disability among children and adolescents. Motor vehicle injuries account for more than 20% of child deaths each year. In 1978, one-fifth of all motor vehicle deaths were among teenagers. This was the highest motor vehicle death rate of any age group. Increases in the number of deaths due to suicide and homicide have contributed to the rise in the mortality rate in 15- to 24-year-olds. Suicide is the third leading cause of death in this group, with white males having three times the risk of all others. Homicide is the cause of death in just over 10% of all deaths among adolescents and young adults: 7% for whites, but an alarming 30% for blacks (Better Health for Our Children, 1981). There seems to be a clear association between violent events and substance abuse. In the period between 1972 and 1979, illicit substance use by youths 12 to 17 years of age more than doubled for marijuana, and increased more than fourfold for cocaine. Eleven percent of high school seniors report themselves as daily marijuana smokers, smoking an average of three and a half marijuana cigarettes per day. Alcohol continues to be the most commonly used intoxicant in our society. As we know, alcohol abuse often begins in early adolescence. Nearly half of all 9th-graders have had at least one episode of drinking, and 95% of teenagers graduating from high school have used alcohol (Better Health for Our Children, 1981; Dupont, 1984).

Acute and chronic stress also contribute to the morbidity picture within families and can be associated with physical illness in children. Absence of social support, lack of a sense of predictability and stability, and a view of life events as uncontrollable predispose to stress and tension, and predict increased susceptibility to disease and, as a result, to medical visits. Increased reporting of injuries, abuse, and infections has been documented in families who have experienced recent social or personal stress (Haggerty, Roghmann, & Pless, 1975; Meyer & Haggerty, 1962). When Haggerty and co-workers (1975) examined the influence of stress on health care utilization behavior, they found a positive correlation. Looking at two sets of data, their 1971 survey reported that the presence of stress leads to increased utilization of health services. Children with "unhappily married parents" showed the highest utilization rates for sick care. Utilization rates for preventive care were highest among children with "happily married parents." There was also a positive correlation between mothers' perceptions of difficulty in coping, feelings of confusion, stressful living, and seeking of sick care. When these investigators looked at data from daily health diaries, they again found that stress increased medical contact; this was true even in the absence of illness. The probability of telephone calls, visits to emergency rooms, and outpatient department visits doubled during identified periods of stress. They postulated that this occurred because of the easier access to services using the above routes. They implied that walk-in visits, emergency room visits, and patient telephone calls were "stress-sensitive" contacts within the medical care system. Significant stress may lead a parent to bring an infant to the physician because of fears that the infant will be neglected or abused. Experience has shown that vaguely stated reasons for coming to the physician may actually represent a parental cry for help.

The idea of "stress-sensitive" contact is not new. In 1961, Yudkin published his classic article "Six Children with Coughs: The Second Diagnosis." In it, he illustrated that underlying family stresses, pressures, and fears often dictate the time at which parents may seek medical attention for their children.

THE FAMILY AS A SOURCE OF ILLNESS

Family factors influencing the decision to seek medical care include the family both as a source of disease and as a factor influencing outcome. These influences may be viewed as classical in the sense of the long-term recognition of their contribution.

Consideration of the family as a source of pediatric illness includes genetic factors.

Genetic disorders occur 3 to 4 times in every 100 births, accounting for significant morbidity and mortality. Genetic disorders account for 25% to 30% of all hospital admissions to major children's hospitals (Milunsky, 1977). In addition, advanced maternal age and exposure to environmental agents, such as drugs, infectious agents, and toxic chemicals, increase the risk of genetic disorders. These disorders tax the family's emotional and financial resources.

Another easily recognizable example of the family as a source of illness comes from the literature describing the intrafamily spread of infectious diseases. For example, studies by Dingle, Badger, and Jordon (1964) contributed to our knowledge about the spread of viral illness. Miller, Covit, Walton, and Know (1960), in Newcastle-upon-Tyne, described streptococcal families and staphylococcal families, as well as families with recurrent intestinal disease. Meyer and Haggerty (1962) described the contribution of stress to the development of clinical disease using streptococcal disease as a model.

Finally, cultural beliefs greatly influence the extent to which families may generate or perpetuate illness. The degree of ethnic identification influences beliefs and behavior. For example, very traditional Hispanic American families may first seek the advice of a folk practitioner, and *espiritista* or *curandera;* only if symptoms persist, or if the outcome is unsatisfactory, do they consult a physician. Beliefs also influence responses to advice. For Hispanic Americans who adhere to the hot-and-cold theory of disease, a prescription for penicillin, a "hot" medicine, may be rejected if the disease is also considered hot (Spector, 1979).

FAMILY DEMOGRAPHICS

Socioeconomic and family resource variables can predict health care utilization (Haggerty *et al.*, 1975). Younger children are seen more often than older ones. There is an inverse relationship between the number of children in the family unit and visits to physicians. Maternal education and parental occupation predict utilization in the same direction (i.e., increased education and higher work status are associated with increased utilization rates).

FAMILY REACTION TO A CHILD'S ILLNESS

Experienced pediatricians and primary care practitioners are aware that the child may represent a parental ticket of admission. Bass and Cohen (1982) found that in their pediatric practice, one-third of the time, the reason for seeking care was associated with a previous family event. Parents had linked the child's symptoms to similar symptoms in other family members or in friends, or to a previous event in the child's past that made the child seem particularly vulnerable. Parents' unverbalized fears in these circumstances can take the form of anxiety that appears excessive when compared with the child's chief complaint of physical findings. Parental anxiety may also manifest itself by lack of closure or satisfaction at the end of a visit.

Families sometimes decide to seek care depending on the child who is ill. The vulnerable child, so labeled because of premature birth, a previous accident or illness, an associated chronic disease, or a significant event in another child, may be treated differently. Care may be sought sooner or later depending on the family's response to the vulnerability.

SERVICE FACTORS AFFECTING UTILIZATION

Obvious fractures, deep lacerations, or dramatic changes in mental status generally prompt families to seek medical attention quickly. Chronic problems and less concrete or acute symptoms, however, bring into play a complex process of decision making. A family's reaction to a high fever in an 18-month-old who has had two previous febrile seizures, or to the development of a cold in the case of a well-known asthmatic, is based on their previous experience. This experience or knowledge can be either firsthand, obtained from friends or other family members, or called to attention by the mass media. It is the change in the usual that prompts action. The action taken is, in turn, dependent on the outcome of those earlier, often initial, experiences and episodes, and on whether the previous recommendations and treatments brought about satisfactory results and relief of anxiety.

Another factor influencing the family's decision making is the family's established pattern of health utilization. There are two extremes of care with episodic, symptomatic care at one end, and comprehensive primary care at the other. Robertson and colleagues (1974) examined the effect of comprehensive care on a population of clinic patients. In their study, the morbidity was primarily nonserious acute illness. When they examined the effect of comprehensive care on symptoms and action in a randomized trial, the experimental groups had fewer physician visits for illness and more for prevention. They concluded that, with comprehensive care available, more of the perceived symptoms (the less serious symptoms, to be sure) were handled by mothers, frequently with the reassurance of telephone consultation. In general, the experimental families also had fewer and shorter hospitalizations, more visits for health maintenance, lower medical expenses, and greater patient satisfaction. Patient satisfaction, like patient education, is a goal worthy of pursuit in its own right. It has a positive influence on patient compliance and appointment keeping.

Availability of services is yet another factor influencing patient decision making. Proximity of services, convenience of transportation to health centers, and location of the services can be either barriers or incentives to care seeking. In addition to concerns about travel time, the character of the neighborhood and the type of facility can also play a role. Families may bypass a physician's office or neighborhood health clinic for a hospital's outpatient department or emergency ward, depending on the family's perception of the seriousness of the symptoms or illness. Conversely, a family particularly attached to a primary care provider may bypass a hospital in an emergency, not realizing the limitation of an office facility.

Clinic and office hours may facilitate or, often, may work counter to patients' needs and can have a significant impact on utilization. For working parents, visits to see the doctor can pose a challenge when the physician's office hours are inconvenient and inflexible. Time off from work for routine health care maintenance in a seemingly healthy child becomes a low priority. The prospect of loss of pay may even force acute conditions to wait until after work hours, resulting in a visit to an emergency room with loss of the benefits of primary care or, more seriously, with increased morbidity. The expansion to evening office hours or Saturday hours helps to avoid the pitfalls of episodic care and fosters patient–physician bonds.

Along with physical access to services, financial barriers affect increasing numbers of children and their families. We have already noted that the number of children living below the poverty line is rising. Government entitlement funds are being reduced. We have observed that concomitant with the decrease in eligibility for aid to families with dependent children is a decrease in utilization of prenatal services and an increase in infant mortality. What we can anticipate are increasing numbers of families and their children existing without financial access to even minimum, essential health services and care. The problem is compounded by rising hospital and medical costs, decreased sources of subsidized care, and the decreasing number of physicians accepting Medicaid. As a consequence, we once again have a pattern of utilization based on income, where only the very poor and the very rich can afford to be ill. Families in the low-to-moderate income range are often forced to postpone care until it is absolutely critical, and preventive care becomes a luxury.

The practitioner's response to the family at the time of illness influences subsequent behavior. Families that have been positively reinforced for their actions are more likely to comply with medical recommendations and less likely to reject them than families that have been made to feel incompetent or irresponsible. At the time an acute illness presents itself, a family's behavior is most likely to be open to modification through positive reinforcement and through direct education. The family praised for bringing a sick child to medical attention, or with whom time has been spent exploring concerns about a minor symptom, is more likely to return at appropriate times than is the family made to feel inadequate about its child care abilities. The responsibility to educate and to reinforce are important duties for the primary care practitioner and may be even more important in the setting of poverty, where stress is high and a family's threshold for coping may be low, or in any situation where family members' cognitive ability may be limited by lack of education.

The organization of medical services influences the decision to seek care in a number of ways. There is no question, for example, that the case management approach best exemplified in health maintenance organizations (HMOs) influences family and physician behavior. The understandable emphasis on decreased hosptialization (because of its contribution to increased costs) must have an accompanying emphasis on ambulatory services, with or without financial deductibles. Moreover, many HMOs concentrating on young and essentially healthy individuals may not do as well as smaller groups of physicians when it comes to providing family services. What is acceptable for the parent may not be acceptable for the children. These parameters will require ongoing examination.

CONCLUSION

How does the information we have provided help the practitioner deliver medical care? We have deliberately avoided an approach that makes use of highly valuable but more theoretic approaches to the decision to seek medical care. Though theoretically useful, such constructs as health belief models are utilized little by the clinician. On the other hand, the recognition that the decision is to seek medical care is not straightforward and is multifactorial can be of great assistance to the practicing clinician. For example, learning to ask questions, such as why did the patient come now or what are the patient's expectations from the visit, can contribute to more effective care as well as to increased patient satisfaction and compliance.

As child advocates, we must do our part to see that financial barriers to care are minimized, and that services remain accessible. Unfortunately, in the mid-1980s, we must also be aware of the enormous financial pressures to keep patients away from us. We contribute to these financial pressures when we order or prescribe expensive services or drugs. The purpose of ambulatory deductibles in the HMO setting is not to minimize hospitalization, but to discourage physician visits. The tightening of medical eligibility and the increase in Medicare deductibles places a large financial burden on families and also influences their decisions to seek care by changing their financial resources. Low-income families are at particular risk. The utilization gap that has historically existed between poor and rich, black and white, was largely reversed by the entitlement programs of the 1960s. These accomplishments are now being eroded, and the situation may get worse before we again consider a program of national entitlements known in other countries as National Health Insurance.

It has been estimated that by the year 2000, 50% of Americans will be in some form of managed care, principally HMOs. They will be cared for, using present ratios, by 120,000 physicians. The other 120 million Americans will have 480,000 physicians available to care for them. We can only imagine the different utilization patterns that may emerge. One beneficial outcome may be that physicians will provide increasingly flexible and accessible services as they begin to compete with each other for patients.

Finally, our aim as physicians and practitioners should be understanding why our patients come to see us, seeking the second diagnosis where appropriate, and pursuing our goals of more successful management, less expensive services in any setting, decreased use of multiple resources, and increased patient satisfaction.

References

Andersen R, Kasper JD. The structural influence of family size on children's use of physician services, Journal of Comparative Family Studies 1973; 4:116–129.

Bass LW, Cohen R. Ostensible versus actual reasons for seeking pediatric attention: another look at the parental ticket of admission. Pediatrics 1982; 70:870–874.

Better health for our children: a national strategy. Report of the Select Panel for the Promotion of Child Health (DHHS Publication No. PHS 79-55071). Washington, D.C.: U.S. Government Printing Office, 1981.

Blaxter, M, Ed. The health of children. London: Heinemann Educational Books, 1981.

Dingle JH, Badger GF, Jordan WS. Illness in the home—a study of 25,000 illnesses in a group of Cleveland families. Cleveland, Ohio: Western Reserve University Press, 1964.

Dupont RL. Teen-age drug use: opportunities for the pediatrician. Journal of Pediatrics 1984; 102:1003–1007.

Gallagher EB. Infants, mothers and doctors. Lexington, Mass.: D.C. Heath, 1978.

Goodman RA, Osterholm MT, Granoff DM, Pickering LK. Infectious diseases and child day care. Pediatrics, 1984; 74:134–139.

Haggerty RJ, Alpert, JJ. The child, his family and illness. Postgraduate Medicine 1963; 34:228–233.

Haggerty RJ, Roghmann KJ, Pless IB. Child health and the community. New York: Wiley, 1975.

Harvard Child Health Project Task Force. Developing a better health care system for children. Cambridge, Mass.: Ballinger, 1977.

Heins M, Stillman P, Sabers D, Mazzeo J. Attitudes of pediatricians toward maternal employment. Pediatrics 1983; 72:283–290.

Mechanic D. The influence of mothers on their children's health attitudes and behavior. Pediatrics 1964; 3:444–453.

Mechanic D, ed. Medical sociology. New York: Free Press, 1968.

Meyer RJ, Haggerty RH. Streptococcal infections in families: factors altering individual susceptibility. Pediatrics 1962; 25:539–549.

Miller CA. The health of children: a crisis of ethics. Pediatrics 1984; 73:550–558.

Miller FJW, Court WDM, Walton WS, Know EG. Growing up in Newcastle upon Tyne. London: Oxford University Press, 1960.

Miller JR, Janorik ED. Family focused care. New York: McGraw-Hill, 1980.

Milunsky A. Know your genes. Boston: Houghton Mifflin, 1977.

Parsons T. The social system. New York: Free Press, 1951.

Pass RF, Hutto SC, Reynolds DW, Polhill RB. Increased frequency of cytomegalovirus infection in children in group day care. Pediatrics 1984; 74:121–126.

Prugh DC. The phsychosocial aspects of pediatrics. Philadelphia: Lea & Febiger, 1983.

Richardson HB. Patients have families. New York: Commonwealth Fund, 1945.

Robertson LS, Kosa J, Haggerty RJ, Heagarty MC, Alpert JJ. Changing the medical care system. New York: Praeger, 1974.

Sargent AJ. The family: a pediatric assessment. Journal of Pediatrics 1984a; 102:973–976.

Sargent AJ. The sick child and the family. Journal of Pediatrics 1984b; 102:982–987.

Spector RE. Cultural diversity in health and illness. New York: Appleton-Century-Crofts, 1979.

Starfield B. Behavioral pediatrics and primary health care. Pediatric Clinics of North America 1982; 29:377–390.

Suchman E. Stages of illness and medical care. Journal of Health and Human Behavior 1965; 6:114–128.

Wegman ME. Annual summary of vital statistics—1983. Pediatrics 1984; 74:981–990.

Weyrauch KF. The decision to see the physician: a clinical investigation. Journal of Family Practice 1984; 18:265–272.

Yudkin S. Six children with coughs: the second diagnosis. Lancet 1961; 9:561–563.

Zborowski M. People in pain. San Francisco: Jossey-Bass, 1969.

Suggested Readings

Clyne MB. Night calls. London: Tavistock, 1961.

Crawford C, ed. Health and the family. New York: Macmillan, 1971.

Kasi S. Health behavior, illness and sick role behavior. Archives of Environmental Health 1966; 12:246–266.

Larson L, Larsen D. Family, health and illness: a selected bibliography. Journal of Comparative Family Studies 1973; 4:143–158.

Lewis CE, Lewis MA, Lorimer A, Palmer BB. Child-initiated care: the use of school nursing services by children in an ''adult-free'' system. Pediatrics 1977; 60:499–507.

Litman T. The family as a basic unit in health and medical care: a social-behavioral overview. Social Science and Medicine 1974; 8:495–519.

McWhinney IR. Beyond diagnosis. New England Journal of Medicine 1972; 287:384–386.

McWhinney IR. An introduction to family medicine. New York: Oxford University Press, 1981.

Steward M, McWhinney IR, Buck C. How illness presents: a study of patient behavior. Journal of Family Practice 1975; 2:411–414.

Stoeckle J, Zola IK, Davidson G. On going to see the doctor: the contributions of the patient to the decision to seek medical care. Journal of Chronic Disease 1963; 16:975–989.

Twaddle AC. Health decision and sick role variation: an exploration. Journal of Health and Social Behavior 1969; 10:105–115.

Weyrauch KF. The decision to see a physician: differential diagnosis of the one am dilemma. Journal of Family Practice 1982; 15:237–245.

29

Family Systems and Compliance with Medical Regimen

LORNE A. BECKER
University of Toronto

Compliance is arguably the greatest contemporary challenge to those engaged in the clinical practice of medicine. In the past few decades, there has been an explosion in the number of effective drugs available for use in treatment or prevention of disease. In addition, physicians routinely recommend a number of nondrug interventions that require changes in personal habits such as diet, exercise, cigarette smoking, or alchohol use. Well-designed epidemiological studies have shown that these measures are indeed effective—if carried out as prescribed. Most people, however, find it difficult to make major life-style changes or to use medications consistently over long periods of time, and thus few patients are fully compliant with physicians' recommendations.

Noncompliance with antihypertensive therapy has been well studied and serves as an example of the magnitude and effect of this problem on the management of a chronic illness. It is estimated that only one-half of patients identified as hypertensive begin therapy for their disorder. Of those beginning treatment, one-half drop out of care within 1 year. Of those remaining in care, only two-thirds use enough of their medications to achieve adequate control of their blood pressure (National Heart, Lung, and Blood Institute [NHLBI] Working Group, 1982).

This chapter will review contemporary models of patient compliance behavior, examine the role assigned to family interactions in these models, and suggest a new formulation, in which the role of the family is seen as central in each of the major areas of the compliance model. Studies of compliance with medical recommendations that have examined the role of the family in compliance behavior or have attempted to improve compliance by involving family members will also be reviewed. The implications of this body of theory and research for clinical practice will be discussed and suggestions made for future research in this area.

DEFINITION OF COMPLIANCE

"Compliance," as defined by a political scientist, involves "a relationship consisting of the power employed by superiors to control subordinates and the orientation of the subordinates to this power" (Etzioni, 1961, p. xv). This definition, with its emphasis on power relationships and authority/dependency roles, makes it clear why some authors feel uncomfortable with the term "noncompliance." Other options have been suggested, most frequently "nonadherence" or "defaulting." But none of the alternatives offers any real improvement. The term "compliance" is now thoroughly embedded in the medical literature and has been given a definition that is much less judgmental and authoritarian than the one quoted above: "the extent to which a person's behavior (in terms of keeping appointments, taking medications, and executing life-style changes) coincides with medical ad-

416

vice'' (Haynes, 1979). Although this definition is very balanced and nonjudgmental, it must be pointed out that, in most articles on the topic, if a patient's behavior does not coincide with medical advice, it is usually assumed that it is the patient's behavior rather than the medical advice that needs changing. It is also interesting that ''cooperation,'' a term that suggests a much more balanced relationship, has not been seriously promoted as a replacement for ''compliance.''

MODELS OF COMPLIANCE BEHAVIOR

A number of different models have been proposed in an attempt to explain and predict compliance behavior. Early attempts, rather simplistically, portrayed the physician as an informed ''expert'' acting to benefit an uninformed help-seeking patient. The ''expert'' reviewed the patient's complaints, decided on the pathologic process involved, and prescribed some corrective measure. It was clearly in the best interest of the ''nonexpert'' patient to follow the prescription given, and any noncompliance was seen as deviant behavior. Attempts to identify characteristics of patients that could explain this deviance have been uniformly unsuccessful. No consistent relationship has emerged between compliance and age, sex, education, religion, marital status, socioeconomic status, or other patient characteristics (Stunkard,1979).

Motivational Models

A different approach to patient noncompliance has examined the motivation of individuals to change. Education and information are perceived to be important factors in patient mo-

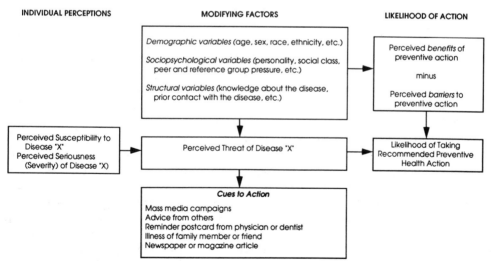

Figure 29-1. The health belief model as predictor of preventive health behavior. Reproduced with permission from ''Patient Perceptions and Compliance: Recent Studies of the Health Belief Model'' by M. H. Becker, L. A. Maiman, J. P. Kirscht, D. P. Haefner, R. H. Drachman, & D. W. Taylor, 1979, Chapter 6 in *Compliance in Health Care*, edited by R. B. Haynes, D. W. Taylor, & D. L. Sackett, Baltimore: Johns Hopkins University Press, p. 79.

tivation. Patient noncompliance has been attributed to a lack of sufficient knowledge of the disease process and its treatment. Educational interventions attempt either to arouse fear of the consequences of noncompliance, or to emphasize the benefits of compliance. Although they appear to lead to some improved compliance with short-term therapy, these educational interventions have been unsuccessful in promoting compliance with long-term regimens (Sackett, Gibson, Taylor, *et al.*, 1975).

A motivational model that has received a great deal of attention is the health belief model (Becker, Drachman, & Kirsch, 1974). As originally formulated (Figure 29-1), this model suggests that patient behaviors are determined by beliefs concerning susceptibility to disease, the seriousness of the disease, and the benefits to be derived from compliance. The model also includes consideration of environmental barriers to compliance and allows for the positive effects of cues to action. Although this approach has been successful in explaining compliance with some preventive and short-term treatments, the amount of variation explained has in most cases been quite small (Haynes, 1976; Sackett, 1976). Interventions designed to change health beliefs have been relatively ineffective in producing changes in compliance. Modification of barriers to compliance, for example, simplifying complex medication regimens (Blackwell, 1979) or instituting appointment schedules in previously inconvenient clinics) (Rockart & Hofmann, 1969), has been a slightly more fruitful approach. However, only relatively small differences in compliance may be attributed to regimen factors such as these.

Behavioral Learning Models

Behavioral learning models that have been applied to the understanding of compliance behavior include operant behaviorism, social learning, communication, and attitude change models. In operant behaviorism as originally developed by Skinner (1950), behavior is seen as solely the result of environmental cues and rewards. Behavior change can be achieved by manipulating the environment to deliver rewards or reinforcements for appropriate behaviors. Although operant techniques have been successfully employed to improve compliance in a few cases (Dapcich-Miura & Hovell, 1979; Lowe & Lutzker, 1979), the methods involved are very time-consuming, and the results appear to be short-lived. Once the rewards are withdrawn, the compliant behavior tends to disappear.

All of the foregoing formulations tend to treat the individual solely as a recipient of compliance interventions. The only differences lie in the interventions used: attempts to change knowledge, beliefs, or motivating factors, or to provide rewards from the environment. The cognitive–behavioral (or social learning) approach is more comprehensive and assigns an active role to the individual in behavior change. In this paradigm, the individual is seen as shaping the environment to provide reinforcement for behaviors consistent with personal goals. "Reciprocal determinism" is the term used in social learning theory to denote this circular relationship. "Efficacy expectation" (defined as the individual's subjective estimate of personal capacity to cope successfully with a given situation) is another important concept in the social learning approach (Bandura, 1977). A given compliance behavior is more likely to occur if the individual feels confident that the behavior is clearly possible. Of course, previous successes increase self-efficacy. An additional difference from operant behaviorism involves the use of techniques other than to promote new behaviors. Thus, a social learning approach could encompass techniques such as modeling, guided participation, rehearsals and education, and persuasion to change health attitudes and actions (Wilson, 1980).

Communication and Attitude Change Models

Other models of compliance behavior stress communication (Weiss, 1969) or the process of attitude change (Leventhal, 1973). This body of research has identified six discrete steps that lead from the sending of a message to action resulting from that message: (1) generating a message, (2) receiving the message, (3) comprehending the message, (4) retaining the message, (5) accepting the message, and (6) taking action on the message. Like the social learning approach, this perspective focuses more on the active role of the recipient of the message than on the sender or the environment. Reception (Step 2) may not occur if the patient is inattentive or resistant to what is being said. Comprehension (Step 3) requires not only understanding of the words being used, but also reconciliation of the information received with past experiences and preconceptions. For example, "hypertension" is often interpreted by patients to mean "high levels of nervous tension" (Blumhagen, 1980). Patients with this interpretation of their diagnosis may stop taking their medications when they perceive themselves to be less nervous. Acceptance is more likely if the message communicated is congruent with the person's own beliefs or with those of important significant others. Finally, no action will occur unless the individual knows what to do, understands how to do it, and believes himself or herself to be capable of acting.

The Self-Regulation Model of Compliance

The preceding formulations all represent a cross-sectional look at compliance behavior at a single point in time. Communication is attempted, behavior is or is not learned, and compliance (or noncompliance) results. Compliance with medical advice, however, does not usually involve only a single action, but, rather, requires behaviors to be repeated frequently over long periods of time. In order to maintain their health, patients are advised to take their antiepileptic medications daily, abstain from smoking forever, and stick to their diet for weeks, months, or an entire lifetime. Most compliance interventions are much more impressive in initially obtaining compliant behavior than they are in maintaining that behavior over time, suggesting that current models inadequately address this ongoing decision making process. The "self-regulation model," recently articulated by Leventhal, Zimmerman, and Gutmann (1984), provides a longitudinal perspective on complaince. In this formulation, the individual is seen as an information-processing system, regulating his or her own relationship to the environment on an ongoing basis using a cyclical process with the following components: (1) gathering data from the environment; (2) formulating a representation of the illness; (3) establishing behavioral goals and generating plans and responses to reach those goals; and (4) monitoring how one's coping reactions affect the problem and oneself. Thus, compliance behavior involves a cybernetic process, guided by the patient, with periodic modifications made as necessary.

The self-regulation model provides a way of integrating many of the concepts articulated in other compliance models. For example, models of communication and attitude change provide an elaboration of some of the processes involved in the first step of the self-regulation model. The health belief model deals in some depth with factors involved in formulating a representation of the illness (Step 2). "Efficacy expectation" and other concepts from social learning theory are useful in understanding how patients accomplish the third step of the model.

There are interesting parallels between the self-regulation model and the concept of "coping" with illness. Moos and Tsu (1977) describe seven coping skills used by patients with chronic illness: (1) seeking relevant information, (2) finding a general purpose or meaning to the illness, (3) denying or minimizing the seriousness of a crisis, (4) setting concrete limited goals, (5) learning specific illness-related procedures, (6) rehearsing alternative outcomes, and (7) requesting reassurance and emotional support. The first of these skills fits well with the first step off the self-regulation model. The second and third skills are aspects of forming a representation of the illness (Step 2), and the final five coping skills fit with the third step of the self-regulation model. Although the self-regulation model has not yet been subjected to empiric testing, its concepts are attractive because of their fit with clinical experience and with other theoretic formulations.

ROLE OF THE FAMILY IN COMPLIANCE MODELS

"Although families and social networks are the major social contexts where illness is interpreted, health care delivered, and utilization of professional services determined, this popular arena of care is commonly discounted by professional health planners and providers" (Chrisman & Kleinman, 1983, p. 571)

This has certainly been the case in conceptualizations of compliance behavior. The most recent review of the role of the family in compliance with medical regimens was published in 1975 by Becker and Green. They identified three major ways in which family–patient interactions were important to compliance. The first situation was the one in which the patient was elderly, a child, or disabled, and therefore dependent on other family members who assumed responsibility for compliance. The second factor they identified was the importance of specific roles of individual family members in compliance behavior (e.g., the individual with the role of food purchasing and preparation influences dietary compliance of other family members). Finally, they suggested that the family exerts a "normative influence" on the patient, which may have an enabling or an inhibiting effect on compliance.

Somewhat more has been written about the role of "social support" in compliance. However, this has been broadly defined as any "input directly provided by another person (or group) which moves the receiving person towards goals which the receiver desires" (Levy, 1980). Although this definition clearly encompasses family interactions related to compliance, it is so broad that it also includes compliance-related interactions with friends, acquaintances, health professionals, and even total strangers. Levy has reviewed compliance and social support using a narrower definition that includes only the "activities of persons in the patient's natural environment (e.g., family and friends)" (1980, p. 145). She suggests a number of ways in which support is related to compliance, but presents no unifying model for the compliance–social support relationship.

In general, a case can be made for social or family support as a factor in some area of each of the compliance models enumerated above, but it has not been seen as a central component in any of them. In terms of the health belief model, the family is important in the transmission of beliefs, motives, and behaviors. In the language of operant conditioning, family members can create adherence by rewarding appropriate behaviors and extinguishing inappropriate ones. This is particularly important in the maintenance of behaviors that have been initially produced by operant techniques. From a social learning perspective, the family can be called on to provide reinforcing and discriminative cues and to serve as resources in the development of self-control strategies. Family support could lead as well to increased feelings of self-efficacy, and thus to successful change. The difficulty in finding a specific place for family or social support in compliance models is illustrated in Figure 29-2. The diagram represents the most recent formulation of the health belief model

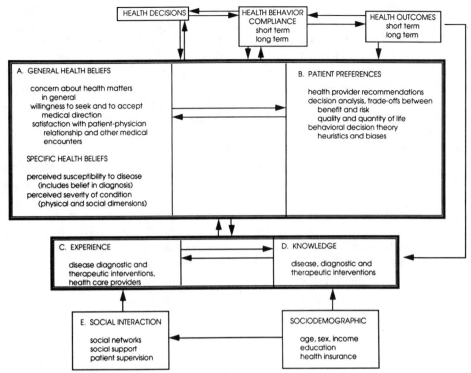

Figure 29-2. The health decision model, combining the health belief model and patient preferences including decision analysis and behavioral decision theory. Reproduced with permission from "Understanding and Improving Patient Compliance" by M. D. Eraker, J. P. Kirscht, & M. H. Becker, 1984, *Annals of Internal Medicine,* Vol. 100, p. 261.

(now called the "health decision model") (Eraker, Kirscht, & Becker, 1984). "Social interaction" occupies a peripheral spot on the bottom left corner and is directly related to patients' experience and knowledge, but only indirectly related to health beliefs and the decision process.

The Family and the Self-Regulation Model of Compliance

Family support has not been considered as one of the components of the self-regulation model. In my opinion, however, this model could provide the clearest perspective on the role of the family in compliance. Family interaction, rather than being seen as merely another factor to be added to the model somewhere, can be shown to play an important role at each step in the self-regulation process. The following section examines this contention in some detail.

Gathering Data from the Environment

Contrary to popular medical opinion, physicians and other health professionals are not the major source of health information for most people. Only one illness episode in three results in a visit to a physician (White, Williams, & Greenberg, 1961). Six of every seven symptoms experienced by individuals are handled without consulting a physician (Alpert, Kosa, & Haggerty, 1967). On the other hand, a family member is consulted about what to do for one-half of all illness episodes (Richardson, 1970). Individuals turn to family members and friends for information about home remedies and self-medication more often than to physicians or pharmacists (Knapp, Knapp, & Engle, 1966). Even the decision to seek professional health care is influenced by discussion with family members (Antonovsky & Kats, 1970), and patients frequently consult a "family health expert" before deciding to accept or reject the information received from health professionals (Doherty & Baird, 1983).

Berkanovic the and Telesky (1982), in their analysis of data from the Los Angeles Health Survey, clearly showed the interaction between personal health beliefs and advice from family members and close friends in the decision to seek physicians' advice. As predicted from the health belief model, respondents were more likely to visit a physician when they had a symptom if they believed either that the symptom was serious, or that care for the symptom was highly likely to be efficacious. Regardless of their health beliefs, however, respondents were more likely to visit a physician if they received such advice from one or more members of their social network. The differences were greatest among respondents who believed either that their symptoms were not very serious, or that medical attention was unlikely to help (Table 29-1).

Forming a Representation of the Illness

People appear to represent illness on two different levels simultaneously—a concrete level, which deals with symptom experience, and an abstract level, which involves finding a diagnostic label and constructing a satisfactory explanatory model of the disease. The process is reciprocal: Individuals who experience specific symptoms will attempt to explain them, and individuals who receive a diagnosis will watch carefully for the appearance of symptoms compatible with that diagnosis. Physicians are often unaware of the degree to which their pronouncements are reinterpreted by this process. For example, Blumhagen (1980) has shown that "hypertension"—a term intended by physicians simply to imply

Table 29-1. Percentage of Respondents Initiating a First Doctor Visit for a Symptom by Network Advice and Perceived Seriousness of Symptom

Proportion of network members advising respondent to see doctor for symptom	Symptom serious	Symptom not serious
Some or all	85.6% (259)	49.3% (74)
None	65.2% (383)	13.4% (446)

n = number of respondents in each category. From "Social Networks, Beliefs, and the Decision to Seek Medical Care: An Analysis of Congruent and Incongruent Patterns" by Emil Berkanovic & Carol Telesky, 1982, *Medical Care,* Vol. 20, No. 10, p. 1021. Reprinted with permission of the authors and Lippincott/Harper & Row.

elevation of blood pressure—is usually interpreted by patients as "hyper-tension," that is, an increased level of perceived stress and nervous tension. Thus, both doctor and patient can discuss the illness using identical words without ever realizing that their explanatory models are totally incompatible. When the culturally accepted explanation for an illness differs from the one approved by current medical science, it is the medical explanation that is usually rejected. We all know, for example, that the common cold is caused by sitting in a draft or going out in cold weather with wet hair, regardless of the insistence of medical science that no such relationship exists.

Interactions with family members and other social contacts play an important role in the process of constructing a representation of the illness. Symptoms, illness patterns, and diagnoses are discussed with family members and compared with past experiences. Expectations about the seriousness or possible outcome of the illness are frequently based on the observation of a similar illness in a family member. According to Ringler (1978), this is a major reason for the widespread image of cancer as a highly malevolent disease. A shared "family construct" (Reiss, 1981) shapes the individual's perception of illness and reactions to it.

Several studies have shown that the health beliefs of family members are as important as those of the identified patient in determining compliance. The mother's beliefs about a child's susceptibility to and the severity of illness, concerns in general about the child's health, concerns about the health threats of obesity, and beliefs about probable difficulty in following a diet all have been shown to correlate with weight control in obese children (Kirscht, Becker, Haefner, & Maiman, 1978). Similarly, health beliefs of the wives of participants in the coronary primary prevention trial were related to the degree to which they supported their husband's participation and compliance in the project. This support, in turn, was related to the degree to which their husbands adhered to the medication prescriptions they had been given (Doherty, Schrott, Metcalf, & Iasiello-Vailas, 1983). Thus, the family "defines whether or not a member is sick, validates the sick role, and is often instrumental in the decision process that may or may not lead to contact with the health care system" (Gorton, Doerfler, Hulka, & Tyroler, 1979 p. 37).

Determining Goals and Plans for Action

Although the formulation of goals and plans is usually considered to be an individual activity, there is good evidence for powerful family influences in this phase of self-regulation as well. Family members resemble one another in their use of medication and in their personal health habits. Osterweis, Bush, and Zuckerman (1979), in a survey of Baltimore households, found that the use of medications by an individual family member was more closely related to medication used by other family members than to the individual's morbidity. Similar concordance between family members has been found for the number and timing of visits to physicians (Gorton *et al.*, 1979) and for several aspects of lifestyle, such as diet, exercise, smoking, alcohol use, and seatbelt use (Baranowski, Nader, Dunn, & Vanderpool, 1982). Venters, Jacobs, Luepker, Maiman, and Gillum (1984), in a study of 560 married couples, found significant concordance between spouses in smoking, alcohol intake, and salt use when compared with matched surrogate couples. Ex-smokers were not only likely to be married to ex-smokers, but were found to have quit at about the same time as their spouse. Expectations of compliance or noncompliance on the part of other family members have also been shown to be an important factor. Patients who felt that their family expected them to wear a splint (prescribed for treatment of rheumatoid arthritis) spent twice or three times as long wearing the splint as did patients who perceived no such expectation from their family members (Oakes, Ward, & Gray, 1970).

If goals and plans for action are indeed formulated on a family level, one would expect that effective family problem-solving skills would be associated with better compliance. This has been found to be true for families with a member suffering from cystic fibrosis or chronic renal disease. Compliance with therapy for cystic fibrosis was better in families characterized by joint efforts on the part of both parents to maintain family integration, cooperation, and optimism (Patterson, 1985). Pentecost, Zwerenz, and Manuel (1976) found that good communication within the family was correlated with compliance by patients with chronic renal disease requiring dialysis. Steidl and colleagues (1980) assessed renal dialysis patients and their families using the Beavers-Timberlawn scales. Compliance was correlated with high scores on the "executive" functions of the family—problem solving, coalitions, intergenerational boundaries, leadership and control, and responsibility. Use of alcohol, marijuana, and tobacco among adolescents is also related to family problem-solving skills (McCubbin, Needle, & Wilson, 1985). Adolescents who participate in direct efforts to work out difficult issues with family members and to reduce tension in the home environment are less likely to use any of these three substances.

Monitoring, Appraisal, and Reassessment

In addition to monitoring the effects of their personal behavior on their illness and on themselves, patients monitor the effects on other family members and the reactions of other family members to these new behaviors. Several studies have investigated the relationship between the perception of support by family members and compliant behavior. A group of men enrolled in a program of physical exercise listed the desire to please their wives as least among their reasons for entering the program. However, the wife's attitude about the program was found to be a significant factor in predicting the husband's continued participation (Heinzelmann & Bagley, 1970). Support by spouse, relatives, and friends was found by Kar (1977) to be the most powerful variable for explaining variance in fertility behavior. Women whose partners value family planning are less likely to drop out of family planning programs than are those who report less support (Bracken, 1977), and those who drop out early are likely to give the objection of their partner as a major reason (Bracken & Kasl, 1973). Success in losing weight (Jeffery, Bjornson-Benson, Rosenthal, *et al.*, 1984; Streja, Boyko, & Rabkin, 1982) and cigarette smoking cessation (Mermelstein, Lichtenstein, & McIntyre, 1983; Ockene, Benfari, Nuttall, Hurwitz, & Ockene, 1982; West, Graham, Swanson, & Wilkinson, 1977) have also been shown to be associated with perception of spouse support for the changes being undertaken.

Of course, appraisals by family members are not always positive, and, when negative, may lead to noncompliance. Strickland, Alston, and Davidson (1981) present two case reports in which family members became upset by the changing family dynamics as a depressed patient improved with antidepressant therapy and promoted noncompliance. In one case, family therapy led to improved compliance. Stuart and Davis (1972) observed 14 overweight women and their husbands at mealtimes. Husbands were 7 times more likely to proffer food to their spouse, and were 12 times as likely to criticize eating behavior as to praise it. Their conclusion was that some husbands "are not only not contributors to their wives' efforts to lose weight, but they may actually exert a negative influence."

A few studies have looked at specific behaviors by other family members that tend either to promote or to inhibit compliance. Mermelstein and colleagues (1983), in a study of participants in a smoking cessation program, found that smokers whose spouses talked them out of smoking cigarettes during the program, or expressed pleasure at the their efforts to quit, were more successful at achieving and maintaining abstinence. On the other hand, smokers whose spouses nagged, complained abut the irritability resulting from abstinence, or kept track of the number of cigarettes smoked had less success in the program. A study of men taking lipid-lowering agents in the Coronary Primary Prevention Trial showed similar results (Doherty *et al.*, 1983). Men whose wives showed an interest in the program or provided reminders to take medications were more compliant; men whose wives nagged about medications or diet were less compliant.

At times, the family's appraisal of the course of events differs radically from that of the physician, often because the family chooses different indicators of success or failure from those used by the physician. Allen, Tennen, McGrade, Affleck, and Ratzan (1983) found no correlation between the physician's index of diabetes control and parents' index. Parents tended to use the child's symptoms and urine testing results. Only 2 of 34 parents suggested that "blood test results" were important in monitoring control. Physicians rejected urine results as unreliable, weighted symptoms only very lightly, and gave a very high weight to blood sugar levels.

EXPERIMENTAL STUDIES OF THE FAMILY AND COMPLIANCE

If, as I have suggested, the family has a vital role at every stage in the self-regulation of compliance, family interventions should be effective in improving compliance. All the studies quoted herein have been observational and thus can only suggest the potential fruitfulness of a family approach to compliance. A few experimental trials have been done in which some intervention was directed at one or more family members in an attempt to change compliance or to change disease outcome that was thought to be related to compliance behavior. These studies have been done primarily in two areas—weight reduction and hypertension therapy—and have produced mixed results.

Saccone and Israel (1978) randomized obese patients to a number of different weight reduction interventions. Reinforcement by a family member for changes in eating behavior was more effective in promoting weight loss over a 9-week period, than was reinforcement by the therapist for the same behavior. Both types of reinforcement were more effective than the basic weight reduction program with no reinforcements provided (Table 29-2). Brownell, Heckerman, Westlake, Hayes, and Monti (1978) invited spouse participation in a weight reduction program. Patients whose spouses agreed to participate were randomized into two groups. In one, the spouse attended all meetings and was trained in modeling, monitoring, and reinforcement. In the other, the subject attended the meeting alone. Both groups were compared with patients whose spouses had refused to participate. There were

Table 29-2. Mean Weight Pre- and Posttreatment for All Groups

Groups	Pre-treatment	Post-treatment	Change score	Change score S.D.
No treatment	182.6	186.6	+4.0	6.5
Program only	185.6	181.9	−3.7	7.4
Therapist reinforcement	170.9	163.3	−7.6	6.2
Significant other reinforcement	175.4	162.4	−13.0	5.7

few differences immediately after the program. At both 3- and 6-month follow-up, however, the spouse training group had the greatest amount of weight loss (Figure 29-3). Weight loss in this group was greater than that reported in any other controlled study of obesity intervention. No significant differences in weight loss were noted in patients whose spouse refused to cooperate and those whose spouse agreed to attend, but was randomized to the individual-only group. In a similar study (Pearce, LeBow, & Orchard, 1981), education of the spouse led to no significant posttreatment difference, but contributed to superior maintenance of weight loss in obese patients at 3-, 6-, 9-, and 12-month follow-ups. Similar results have been found for children when their mothers were invited to attend weight loss sessions (Brownell, Kelman, & Stunkard, 1983). Children whose group met separately from their mother's group had a greater weight loss than those meeting together with their mothers.

Not all studies have shown positive results. Wilson and Brownell (1978) reported no benefits from family involvement in a weight reduction program. They suggested that simply asking the spouse to attend meetings and to receive instructions may be an insufficiently intense intervention. The numbers of patients involved were small, however, and, even with this minimal intervention, the data reported showed a consistent trend for better weight loss in the group whose families were involved.

Morisky, Bowler, and Finlay (1982) tested three different interventions, alone or in

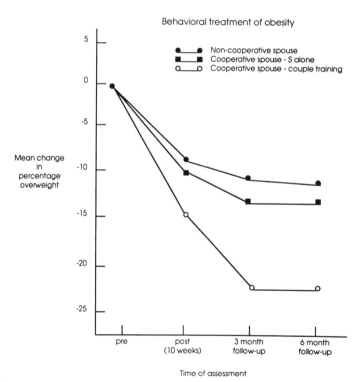

Figure 29-3. Mean changes in percentage overweight for all experimental conditions at posttreatment and the 3-month and 6-month follow-ups. Reproduced with permission from "The Effect of Couples Training and Partner Cooperativeness in the Behavioral Treatment of Obesity" by K. D. Brownell, C. L. Heckerman, R. J. Westlake, S. C. Hayes, & P. M. Monti, 1978, *Behaviour Research and Therapy*, Vol. 16, p. 326. Copyright 1978, Pergamon Journals, Ltd.

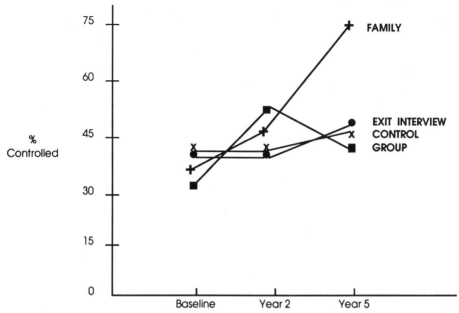

Figure 29-4. Effects of three different interventions on blood pressure control. Redrawn from ''Five Year Blood Pressure Control and Mortality Following Health Education for Hypertensive Patients'' by D. E. Morisky, D. M. Levine, L. W. Green, S. Shapiro, R. P. Russell, & C. R. Smith, 1983, *American Journal of Public Health,* Vol. 73, No. 2, pp. 153–162.

combination, on a group of hypertensive patients. Patients were followed for 5 years, and blood pressure control and mortality end points were used. The first intervention involved an exit interview by a health educator immediately after the physician visit. At this interview, the practitioner's instructions were explained and reinforced, and the regimen was adapted to the patient's individual schedule and daily activities. The second intervention involved a single instructional session in the patient's home, with an adult identified by the patient as being the relative or household member to whom he or she felt closest. This session stressed the ways in which the household member could help the patient adhere to the regimen. The third intervention was a series of three 1-hour group sessions in which hypertensive patients met to provide group support and strength self-confidence while discussing hypertension management and compliance. At 2-year follow-up, the third intervention (group support) appeared to be superior in promoting hypertension control (Figure 29-4). At the end of 5 years, however, 75% of patients receiving the family member intervention alone were in good control, compared to only 54% receiving the exit interview, and 46% receiving the group intervention alone. Combinations of the family intervention with the other two interventions led to even higher rates of blood pressure control. Patients receiving one or more of the three interventions in any combination had a 57% decrease in all-cause mortality when compared to the control group.

In a second study of hypertension control, Earp, Ory and Strogatz (1982) compared two different interventions. In the first, a pharmacist or nurse made three to five home visits per year over an 18-month period. During these visits, patients were taught to take their own blood pressure, and compliance was encouraged. In the second group, an attempt was made to involve one or more significant others (usually family members) in the home visits and blood pressure monitoring activities. Six months after the intervention ceased, both groups had significantly better blood pressure control than did the control group who received no intervention. However, the differences between the two groups were not significant. The authors suggest that the home visit alone intervention may not have been "pure." In many cases, family members involved themselves during home visits and became more active in the care of the hypertensive patients following the visit, even though this involvement was not solicited. The authors suggest that their intervention may have tested the difference between "formal" involvement of family members and "informal" involvement. Both appear to be effective.

DIRECTIONS FOR FUTURE RESEARCH

Results of these clinical trials suggest that involvement of family members may be effective in improving weight loss and maintenance of weight loss in obesity programs and in promoting long-term blood pressure control. It is interesting that in many of the studies the immediate effects of family member involvement are not as impressive as the effects noted months or years later. This is not surprising since an intervention that changes the way in which family members interact should be expected to have long-term effects. However, this represents a distinct difference from other studies of compliance intervention. For example, Glanz and Scholl (1983), in reviewing compliance interventions for hypertension, were able to find no intervention that continued to be effective after the active phase was discontinued. They conclude that "it appears that behavior changes cannot be sustained without continued intervention." The studies cited above suggest that family interventions may represent an exception to this rule. It is clear, however, that any future studies of family interventions for compliance must include long-term follow-up, even if the immediate effects of the intervention are not impressive (as in the study by Morisky *et al.*, 1983).

Additional randomized control trials of family interventions of various types should be done for conditions other than hypertension and obesity. This could include participating in other health-promoting activities, such as exercise programs or smoking cessation programs, or might including compliance with medication taken for disorders other than hypertension. There is also a great need to determine the specific components of family interventions that are effective or ineffective. Some hints that these differences exist are available from the literature. For example, Jeffrey and colleagues (1984) found that men whose wives attended obesity classes actually had less weight loss than did those whose wives did not attend. Similarly, Brownell and colleagues (1983) found better weight loss in children whose mothers attended a separate group than in children whose mothers attended the same group with them.

In addition to finding which types of interventions are effective, it will be important to tailor specific family interventions to specific patients or specific families. For example, in reanalyzing Morisky's data, Estaugh and Hatcher (1982) found that for patients who were depressed, a family intervention was particularly effective. In fact, for this group, the family intervention when used alone was more effective than when used in combination with an intervention of another type.

Family interventions are no panacea. Perhaps there are some families for whom this type of intervention should not be tried. Barbarin and Tirado (1985), for example, found that family support was a relatively unimportant factor in weight loss for members of disengaged families. Similarly, McIntyre (1985) found that involvement of a spouse in a smoking cessation program was effective only if the spouse was a nonsmoker.

CONCLUSION

Compliance (or noncompliance) can be best understood when viewed as only one of a number of possible options that a patient can choose in dealing with an illness or a threat to health. The self-regulation model provides a cybernetic description of the process by which patients arrive at such decisions. The family can be seen to be important at every step of this process. The few experimental trials of intervention with family members show promising results and suggest that long-term effects may be even greater than those seen over the short term. Only a few interventions have been tested, however, and we still have much to learn about exactly how and when to use family-level interventions in our attempts to improve compliance.

References

Allen DA, Tennen H, McGrade BJ, Affleck G, Ratzan S. Parent and child perceptions of the management of juvenile diabetes. Journal of Pediatric Psychology 1983; 8:129–141.

Alpert JJ, Kosa J, Haggerty RJ. A month of illness and health care among low income families. Public Health Report 1967; 82:705.

Antonovsky A, Kats R. The model dental patient: an empirical study of preventive health behavior. Social Science of Medicine 1970; 4:367–380.

Bandura A. Self-efficacy: toward a unifying theory of behavioral change. Psychological Review 1977; 84:191–215.

Baranowski T, Nader PR, Dunn D, Vanderpool NA. Family self-help: promoting changes in health behavior. Journal of Communication 1982; Summer:161–172.

Barbarin D, Tirado M. Enmeshment, family processes, and successful treatment of obesity. Family Relations 1985; 34(1):115–122.

Becker MH, Drachman RH, Kirsch JP. A new approach to explaining sick-role behavior in low-income populations. American Journal of Public Health 1974; 64(3):205–216.

Becker MH, Green LW. A family approach to compliance with medical treatment. International Journal of Health Education 1975; 18(3):173–182.

Becker MH, Maiman LA, Kirscht JP, Haefner DP, Drachman RH, Taylor DW. Patient perceptions and compliance: recent studies of the health belief model. In: Haynes RB, Taylor DW, Sackett DL, eds. Compliance in health care. Baltimore: Johns Hopkins University Press, 1979.

Berkanovic E, Telesky C. Social networks, beliefs, and the decision to seek medical care: an analysis of congruent and incongruent patterns. Medical Care 1982; 10:1018–1026.

Blackwell, B. The drug regimen and treatment compliance. In: Haynes RB, Taylor DW, Sackett DL, eds. Compliance in health care. Baltimore: Johns Hopkins University Press, 1979:144–156.

Blumhagen D. Hyper-tension: a folk illness with a medical name. Culture Medicine and Psychiatry 1980; 4:197–227.

Bracken MB. The Jamaican family planning program: clinical services and social support. International Journal of Health Education 1977; 20:126–135.

Bracken MB, Kasl SV. Factors associated with dropping out of family planning clinics in Jamaica. American Journal of Public Health 1973; 63:262–271.

Brownell KD, Heckerman CL, Westlake RJ, Hayes SC, Monti PM. The effect of couples training and partner cooperativeness in the behavioral treatment of obesity. Behaviour Research and Therapy 1978; 16:323–333.

Brownell KD, Kelman JH, Stunkard AD. Treatment of obese children with and without their mothers: changes in weight and blood pressure. Pediatrics 1983; 71:515–523.

Chrisman NJ, Kleinman A. Popular health care, social networks, and cultural meanings: the orientation of medical anthropology. In: Mechanic D, ed. Handbook of health, health care and health professions. New York: Macmillan, 1983:569–589.

Dapcich-Miura E, Hovell MF. Contingency management of adherence to a complex medical regimen in an elderly heart patient. Behavioral Therapy 1979; 10:193–201.

Doherty WJ, Baird MA. Family therapy and family medicine. New York: Guilford Press, 1983:42.

Doherty WJ, Schrott HG, Metcalf L, Iasiello-Vailas L. Effect of spouse support and health beliefs on medication adherence. Journal of Family Practice 1983; 17(5):837–841.

Earp JA, Ory MG, Strogatz DS. The effects of family involvement and practitioner home visits on the control of hypertension. American Journal of Public Health 1982; 72(10):1146–1152.

Eraker MD, Kirscht JP, Becker MH. Understanding and improving patient compliance. Annals of Internal Medicine 1984; 100:258–268.

Estaugh SR, Hatcher ME. Improving compliance among hypertensives: a triage criterion with cost-benefit implications. Medical Care 1982; 20(10):1001–1017.

Etzioni A. A comparative analysis of complex organizations. New York: Free Press, 1961:xv.

Glanz K, Scholl T. Intervention strategies to improve adherence among hypertensives: review and recommendations. Patient counseling and Health Education 1983; 1(4):14–28.

Gorton TA, Doerfler DL, Hulka BS, Tyroler HA. Intrafamilial patterns of illness reports and physician visits in a community sample. Journal of Health and Social Behavior 1979; 20:37–44.

Haynes RB. Strategies for improving compliance: a methodologic analysis and review. In: Sackett DL, Haynes RB, eds. Compliance with therapeutic regimens. Baltimore: Johns Hopkins University Press, 1976:69.

Haynes RB. Introduction. In: Haynes RB, Taylor DW, Sackett DL, eds. Compliance in health care. Baltimore: Johns Hopkins University Press, 1979.

Heinzelmann F, Bagley RW. Response to physical activity programs and their effects on human behavior. Public Health Reports 1970; 85:905–911.

Jeffery RW, Bjornson-Benson WM, Rosenthal BS, Lindquist RA, Kurth CL, Johnson SL. Correlates of weight loss and its maintenance over two years of follow-up among middle-aged men. Preventive Medicine 1984; 13:155–168.

Kar SB. Community interventions in health and family planning programs. International Journal of Health and Education 1977; 20:2–15.

Kirscht JP, Becker MH, Haefner DP, Maiman LA. Effects of threatening communications and mothers' health beliefs on weight change in obese children. Journal of Behavioral Medicine 1978; 1(2):147–157.

Knapp DA, Knapp DE, Engle J. The public, the pharmacist and self medication. Journal of the American Pharmaceutical Association 1966; 56(9):460–462.

Leventhal H. Changing attitudes and habits to reduce risk factors in chronic disease. American Journal of Cardiology 1973; 31:571–580.

Leventhal H, Zimmerman R, Gutmann M. Compliance: a self-regulation perspective. In: Gentry WD, ed. Handbook of behavioral medicine. New York: Guilford Press, 1984:369–436.

Levy RL. The role of social support in patient compliance: a selective review. U.S. Department of Health, Education and Welfare, U.S. Public Health Service, NIH Publication No. 81-2102, 1980:139–163.

Lowe K, Lutzker JR. Increasing compliance to a medical regimen with a juvenile diabetic. Behavior Therapy 1979; 10:57–64.

McCubbin H, Needle R, Wilson M. Adolescent health risk behaviors: family stress and adolescent coping as critical factors. Family Relations 1985; 34(1):51–62.

McIntyre K. Spouse training in a multicomponent smoking cessation program. Presented at the Conference on Research on the Family System in Family Medicine, San Antonio, Texas, January 1985.

Mermelstein R, Lichtenstein E, McIntyre K. Partner support and relapses in smoking-cessation programs. Journal of Consulting and Clinical Psychology 1983; 51(3):465–466.

Moos RH, Tsu VD. The crisis of physical illness: an overview. In: Moos RH, ed. Coping with physical illness. New York: Plenum Medical Book Company, 1977:3–21.

Morisky DE, Bowler MH, Finlay JS. An educational approach toward increasing patient activation in hypertension management. Journal of Community Health 1982; 7(3):171–182.

Morisky DE, Levine DM, Green LW, Shapiro S, Russell RP, Smith CR. Five year blood pressure control and mortality following health education for hypertensive patients. American Journal of Public Health 1983; 73(2):153–162.

NHLBI Working Group. Management of patient compliance in the treatment of hypertension, Haynes RB, Working Group Chair. Hypertension 1982; 4:415–423.

Oakes MA, Ward JR, Gray RM. Family expectations and arthritis patient compliance to a hand resting splint regimen. Journal of Chronic Disease 1970; 22:757–764.

Ockene JK, Benfari RC, Nuttall RL, Hurwitz I, Ockene IS. Relationship of psychosocial factors to smoking behavior change in an intervention program. Preventive Medicine 1982; 11:13–28.

Osterweis M, Bush PJ, Zuckerman AE. Family context as a predictor of individual medicine use. Social Science Medicine 1979; 13a:287–291.

Patterson J. Critical factors affecting family compliance with home treatment for children with cystic fibrosis. Family Relations 1985; 34(1):79–90.

Pearce JW, LeBow MD, Orchard J. The role of spouse involvement in the behavioral treatment of overweight women. Journal of Consulting and Clinical Psychology 1981; 49:236–244.

Pentecost RL, Zwerenz B, Manuel J. Intrafamily identity and home dialysis success. Nephron 1976; 17:88–103.

Reiss D. The family's construction of reality. Cambridge, Mass.: Harvard University Press, 1981.

Richardson W. Measuring the urban poor's use of physicians' services in response to illness episodes. Medical Care 1970; 8:132–142.

Ringler K. Process of coping with cancer chemotherapy. Unpublished doctoral dissertation, University of Wisconsin–Madison, 1978.

Rockart JF, Hofmann PB. Physician and patient behavior under different scheduling systems in a hospital outpatient department. Medical Care 1969; 7:463–470.

Saccone AJ, Israel AC. Effects of experimenter versus significant other controlled reinforcement and choice of target behavior on weight loss. Behavior Therapy 1978; 9:271–278.

Sackett DL. Priorities and methods for research. In: Sackett DL, Haynes RB, eds. Compliance with therapeutic regimens. Baltimore: Johns Hopkins University Press, 1976:169.

Sackett DL, Gibson ES, Taylor DW, Haynes RB, Hackett BC, Roberts RS, Johnson AL. Randomized clinical trial of strategies for improving medication compliance in primary hypertension. Lancet 1975; 1:1205–1207.

Skinner BF. Are theories of learning necessary? Psychological Review 1950; 57:193.

Steidl JH, Findelstein FO, Wexler JP, Feigenbaum H, Kitsen J, Kliger AS, Quinlan DM. Medical condition adherence to treatment regimens and family functioning. Archives of General Psychiatry 1980; 37(9):1025–1027.

Streja DA, Boyko E, Rabkin SW. Predictors of outcome in a risk factor intervention trial using behavior modification. Preventive Medicine 1982; 11:291–303.

Strickland R, Alston F, Davidson J. The negative influence of families on compliance. Hospital Community Psychiatry 1981; 32(5):349–350.

Stuart RB, Davis B. Slim chance in a fat world: behavioral control of obesity. Champaign, Ill.: Research, 1972.

Stunkard AJ. Behavioral medicine and beyond: the example of obesity. In: Pomerleau OF, Brady JP, eds. Behavioral medicine: theory and practice. Baltimore: Williams & Wilkins, 1979: 279–298.

Venters MH, Jacobs DR, Luepker RV, Maiman LA, Gillum RF. Spouse concordance of smoking patterns: the Minnesota Heart Survey. American Journal of Epidemiology 1984; 120(4):608–616.

Weiss W. Effects of the mass medial of communication. In: Lindzey G, Aronson E, eds. The handbook of social psychology, Vol 5. Reading, Mass.: Addison-Wesley, 1969:77–195.

West DW, Graham S, Swanson M, Wilkinson G. Five year follow-up of a smoking withdrawal clinic population. American Journal of Public Health 1977; 67:536–544.

White KL, Williams TF, Greenberg BG. The ecology of medical care. New England Journal of Medicine 1961; 265:885–892.

Wilson GT. Cognitive factors in lifestyle changes: a social learning perspective. In: Davidson PO, Davidson SM, eds. Behavioral medicine: changing health lifestyles. New York: Brunner/Mazel, 1980:3–37.

Wilson GT, Brownell K. Behavior therapy for obesity: including family members in the treatment process. Behavior Therapy 1978; 9:943–945.

PART EIGHT

Family Systems and Chronic Illness

30

The Family and Medical Team in Chronic Illness: A Transactional and Developmental Perspective

DAVID REISS
George Washington University Medical Center

ATARA KAPLAN DE-NOUR
Hadassah University Hospital, Jerusalem

From a human perspective, the central experience of chronic illness is discomfort or constraint from which there is no escape. Some chronic illnesses come on rapidly and then remain the same; others come on slowly and insidiously worsen; still others come and go with near normal periods of remission followed by severe exacerbations. In all cases, chronic illness is a major ongoing challenge to the skills and endurance of patients, families, and the medical staff. As we learn more about the nature of this challenge, and the responses to which it gives rise, three aspects seem most important. First, characteristics of the medical staff, the family, and the patient can have a major impact on the course of chronic illness itself, its severity, the complications that arise, and the duration of the patient's survival. It is likely that these separate factors interweave in patterns of influence across the course of illness. Second, the characteristics of the illness itself have a major impact on the patient's family and the medical staff. Third, different factors—family, staff, patient, and illness—play different roles in optimal adjustment across the course of illness from the acute phases, through chronicity, and, in many illnesses, the terminal phase.

As a stimulus for systematic thinking about the unfolding of chronic illness in the family, we will sketch a transactional and developmental model based on these three aspects of chronic illness. The model is *transactional* in that it centers on the interlinking of patient, family, and medical system and the mutual influences these three have on each other. It is *developmental* in that it focuses on a series of stages of chronic illness. We propose that staff, family, and patient go through at least three specifiable stages of development in an epigenetic sequence; each phase has its central task that must be accomplished, at least in part, in order to move into the next phase with some success, courage, or resolve.

The concept of epigenetic phase of development in individual psychology is a familiar one; it is a perspective that was enriched by Erikson's (1959) work, from which we borrow freely here. More recently, the concept of development has been applied to families. Here the concepts are less well developed and usually not epigenetic; developmental phases are not seen, strictly speaking, as sequentially dependent (i.e., the latter depending on successful resolution of the former). Still, recent work is beginning to clarify precisely how such development might go forward in families. In this chapter, we are introducing a concept of even broader scope. We suggest that medical staff, family, and patient are linked together in a social system that also develops through recognizable phases, each with its own task, and that the phases are epigenetically arranged, with competence in the latter depending on accomplishment in the former. These phases are partially driven by the biology of the chronic illness itself—but not entirely. The phases themselves, as we will explain, are at their core psychosocial and are shaped substantially by the staff–family–patient system itself; indeed, it is conceivable that the biology of the illness may be partially responsive to the psychosocial forces inherent in this developing transactional system (see Table 30-1).

Preparatory to our model, we propose three psychosocial phases in the development of the staff–family–patient system response to chronic illness (see Table 30-1). For simplicity, we will focus on the attending physician as a key member of the staff (a more fully realized model would embrace the greater subtlety and complexity of social process among all relevant professional caretakers).

First is the *acute phase,* with the central task being analysis and, in many cases, life support. Second is the *chronic phase.* The doctor–family–patient system has clarified diagnosis, prognosis, and life support. The task here is vigilance and maintenance. The doctor–family–patient system must remain alert and engaged to assure participation in complex medical and rehabilitative regimens while minimizing discouragement and despair. The next phase (in many chronic illnesses) is the terminal period, ushered in, in most cases, by a downward turn in the illness itself. Entry into this phase, however, also requires an implicit orientation by the doctor–family–patient system that the illness is beyond retrieval. In many instances a true terminal phase never occurs or is very transitory. In some cases, this is because the doctor, patient, or family—and sometimes all three—cannot recognize or accept that the illness is beyond retrieval, and that death impends. In other instances, such as chronic coronary artery disease, death may occur suddenly in the chronic phase. We believe, however, that it is well to draw attention to the time at the close of a chronic illness because, whether or not there is a clear experience of impending death, there is enormous developmental significance to events and transactions in this period. Whatever the mode of death and the level of acceptance of dying in the whole system, the family—and in many cases the doctor—must reorganize, without the patient,

Table 30-1. A Summary of the Three Phases of the Chronic Illness Caregiving System

	Phase		
	Acute	Chronic/maintenance	Terminal/bereavement
	Facets		
Biosocial marker	Variations in the experience of illness onset	Routinization of medical care in the family and in the medical practice	Construction of death as inevitable and realignment in the family and in the medical practice
Task	Assessment and life support	Vigilance versus burnout; maintenance of morale, development, and rehabilitation	Comfort and composure
Regnant experience	Centrality of technical priorities	Compromise of needs, obligations, and debts	Inevitability
	Roles		
Patient	Passive; providing information and following orders	Active and collaborative	Acquiescent and gradually excluded from the future
Family	Reinforcing the doctor and supporting the patient	Compromising between support of patient and development of the group	Conservation of the family
Doctor	Technical director; a succession of different individuals is tolerated and expected.	Collaborator, facilitator; different individuals in this role are not well tolerated.	Authoritative; emotionally available but self-protected

during and after this period. The processes entailed here are suggested by the term "bereavement," and so we refer to this last phase in the development of the caregiving staff–patient–family system as the *terminal and bereavement stage.*

Our model of the phases and their tasks is designed to clarify the interdependency of doctor, family, and patient. Thus, we outline the primary job of the system considered as a whole. We will usually refer to this social grouping as the *caregiving system.* A focus on the system as a whole enables us to define separate roles that maximize accomplishment of the common task. Intrinsic here is the accurate definition of "success" or "accomplishment." We wish to avoid sentimentalizing, intellectualizing, or trivializing chronic illness, so the concept of task must embrace a full range of strong and painful feelings and still allow that success, even in the best of cases, will be only partial.

We want, as well, to indicate the range of variation allowed by our developmental and transactional mode. We do not want to shrink from the simple dichotomy of success and failure. We believe that many doctor–family–patient systems fail in their management of one or even all phases of chronic illness; this produces needless anguish and despair as well as poor adaptation, untimely death, and emotional scars in the survivors that last long after death. Indeed, it is the purpose of this model to clarify factors that can prevent these morbid consequences. It is important to emphasize, however, that many different configurations of the doctor–family–patient system, within each phase, can be relatively successful. We will be attentive to this difference in three ways, First, we will outline differences that may exist among illnesses themselves. Second, we will indicate some differences among the caregiving systems. Third, and most pertinent to the joint authorship of this chapter, we will suggest certain cultural differences. Indeed, as we elaborate each phase we will do our best to clarify, on the basis of our own experience, some differences in the transactional and developmental forms between the United States and Israel. Although both countries, on the surface, are technically advanced and "Westernized," there are important differences, we believe, in social process in both the medical system and families.

THE ACUTE PHASE

Almost all chronic illness begins in ambiguity. From a psychosocial perspective, we can recognize four modes of illness onset by which this phase is initiated. (Some of these variations among illnesses were described by Rolland, 1984.) The first is the "medical thunderbolt." Pain or disability strikes without warning; moreover, it is clear at once, or almost so, that a medical emergency has occurred. The most frequent examples are myocardial infarction; stroke; and severe, permanently disabling injury. Unanticipated and severe congenital anomalies should also be grouped here. However, careful psychosocial analysis often reveals a chronic backdrop to the apparent thunderbolt. An injury in an auto accident may occur against the backdrop of chronic alcoholism. Heart disease or stroke may have had prodromal warnings in the individual affected, or, along with some congenital anomalies, may occur against the backdrop of conspicuous family history of disorder.

A second mode of onset reflects a "crescendo of symptoms." Weakness, fatigue, irritability, coughing, bleeding, skin rashes, pain, depression, psychosis may exist for days, weeks, and even months. Suchman's (1965) data suggest that families may most often attribute these to emotional causes or even the weather; doctors may have a variety of explanations. Gradually it becomes clear that there is a medical condition underlying the symptoms; then, as a precise diagnosis is made, it become apparent what the condition is: diabetes, renal failure, cancer.

A third mode of onset might be termed "incidental." The doctor discovers severe, chronic illness as part of a routine survey where there have been no symptoms whatsoever: Positive stool guaiac, routine X-rays, positive Pap tests, tuberculin reactions can all be the initial indicators of severe underlying illness.

A fourth mode of onset might be termed a "chronic aftermath." A number if illnesses (e.g., hepatitis, mumps, and pyelonephritis) typically have acute and limited courses from which complete recovery can be expected. A small percentage of cases, however, go on to severe and disabling chronicity; this aftermath usually is not heralded by any clinical feature in the acute illness.

Strictly speaking, there is no easily definable acute phase in the last two modes of onset. Where the discovery of illness is incidental, the caregiving system passes into a chronic phase almost immediately. Where chronic illness is the infrequent aftermath of a relatively benign acute phase, the acute phase itself lacks the urgency it has in other illnesses. For simplicity's sake, we will concentrate on the first two modes of onset. There are three major challenges that the caregiving system must confront. First, accurate medical assessment is of abiding importance even though there may be uncertainty—at least for a short period—about the diagnosis. "Diagnosis," as used here, is meant broadly: the precise etiology, severity, location, and, where possible, complications and prognosis of the illness. Second, patients in this phase are in danger. In many instances, their lives hang in the balance. In others, the amount and degree of their recovery is critically dependent on care provided during the acute phase. This is clearly true of major vascular disorders (e.g., myocardial infarction and stroke), of a broad range of traumatic injuries, of severe congenital anomalies and aquired neonatal illness, and of cancers that require major surgery (brain tumors, cancers of the gastrointestinal and genitourinary tract, and lung cancers). Third, both diagnosis and treatment require major changes in routine behavior patterns and transaction of both patient and family. The patient is usually hospitalized, must passively submit to a variety of diagnostic procedures, may often be fully anesthetized for surgery, and must follow a detailed, closely supervised medical regimen allowing little latitude. At a minimum, the family must be available for support to both doctor and patient; if the patient played a critical role in the family, his or her functions must be taken over temporarily by other family members.

In summary, the acute phase is ushered in by arrant symptoms or signs of illness whose cause may be far from obvious. It closes when the immediate threat to life has abated, and (usually) with a clear diagnosis and an approximate prognosis. Its central task is diagnosis or *assessment* and *life support*.

Our central interest here, as in later phases, is the variation in the organization of the patient–family–doctor or caregiving system. Within Western medicine, we suggest, this social organization is shaped—during the acute phase—by a shared experience of the *technical priorities* of this phase. By this we mean that the well-functioning caregiving system shares a conviction that despite severe and at times overwhelming feelings of panic, patient, family, and doctor become linked by a common perception that both assessment and life support are essentially technical efforts that depend on expert information gathering, interpretation, and technically expert administration of treatment.

The distinction is between two fundamentally different modes by which human relationships can be ordered (see Redfield, 1953). In the *technical mode,* the rules and values by which transactions are ordered are determined primarily by the shared technical tasks that a group must perform. This is a contrast to the *moral order,* where people have an intrinsic value to one another. Relationships in the moral order are ordered by abiding sentiments. We do not deny there are strong feelings of anxiety, panic, love, support, and the like that permeate many of the relationships in the caregiving system during the acute phase. Rather, these feelings are subordinate to the immediate technical requirements of assessment and life support.

If effectively linked by this shared, though anxiety-ridden, percept, an orderly differentiation of roles within the system is possible. The doctor assumes immediate and authoritative leadership by virtue of his or her technical knowledge. The importance of technical mastery for the differentiation of the doctor's role often means that it can be filled by many doctors in quick succession: emergency room physician, radiologist, surgeon, surgical resident, and so on. Any occupant of this role, however, must assume quick, unquestioned, though time-limited authority. Correspondingly, the patient's role is restricted and fundamentally passive: to provide information and follow orders. The family has an intermediate role: to reinforce the doctor's authority, to provide rapid emotional and practical support to the patient, and to fill in for the roles and duties that the patient cannot perform during this period.

The three facets of the caregiving system—physician, patient, and family—must function in specific ways in order to ensure success during the acute phase. First, the physician must combine the technical skills of diagnosis and treatment with the ability to be comforting yet authoritative and decisive in order to command immediate response from patient, family, and medical staff. The patient must be able to tolerate the passivity of his or her role during the acute phase; often this depends on summoning sufficient basic trust in the caregiving system. Finally, the family—to carry out its role successfully—must show reasonable flexibility. Flexibility is important because the family actually has to fulfill two quite contradictory roles. In its relationship with the physician the family is mostly passive; it receives information, supports (agrees with) the physician's interventions, and so forth. At the same time, the family's relationship with the patient is mostly active; it relays medical information from the physician to the patient, fulfills roles the patient cannot maintain, and the like.

Most important is the family's ability to demonstrate high levels of what previous research has termed "coordination." Coordination (Reiss, 1981) refers to an underlying readiness of the family to experience themselves as a single unit, particularly in times of stress. When disaster strikes, these families are primed to exchange information about the circumstances rapidly and effectively and quickly assume roles that promote the welfare of the group and its individuals. Families of this kind stand in marked contrast to low-coordination families, where each individual functions as an isolate in his or her own world. When disaster strikes these families, there are no built-in mechanisms for mobilization. When the alarm sounds for "all hands on deck," members show up late, if at all.

The immediate culture shapes these transactions among patient, family, and doctor. Indeed, successful mastery of the basic tasks of this phase may require from the caregiving system one form of organization in one particular culture, and a different form in another. For example, Israeli medical practice typically has an authoritarian and paternalistic caste inherited almost intact from the classic academic clinics of Western and Middle Europe. Within this tradition, now fully transplanted to Israel's soil, doctors arrogate to themselves even more authority than our foregoing model depicts. This is most clearly illustrated in how doctors share or do not share information about the illness. For example, cancer patients are rarely, if ever, told by their doctor the truth about their diagnosis. In a similar vein, the family is told the bare essentials, not with the aim of fully informing them about the road that lies ahead, but with the much narrower objective of making sure the doctor is not held accountable by the family for failing to cure an incurable illness. The patient is supposed to be extremely passive. Thus, the roles within Israeli caregiving systems are more extreme than in American ones. The physician is in complete authority. The sharing role of the family, both with the physician and with the patient, does not exist. The family consults with neither physician nor patient, but obeys the physician and tells the patient what is "good for him."

These cultural differences in caregiving systems raise a number of questions. The two most important questions, we believe, are which of the two systems is more effective in handling the acute phase, and which system, following the resolution of acute into chronic phase, adapts better to the required role changes.

THE CHRONIC PHASE

As in the acute phase, the underlying nature of the medical illness strongly colors the chronic phase. In general, we can recognize three different forms of illness in this phase. The first can be called "stable without life shortening." The best example is traumatic spinal cord injury. A permanent disability, say paraplegia, becomes stable after the acute phase is over and remains for life with little impact on longevity. A second form is "progressive deterioration." Certain cancers, neurologic illnesses, and the muscular dystrophies show an unremitting deterioration leading to death. Cystic fibrosis probably belongs in this group as well. Other chronic illnesses, such as retinitis pigmentosa, cause deterioration but do not lead to early death. A third form of chronicity is "irregular episodicity." Epilepsy in adolescence is an interesting case in point. Some adolescents, despite adequate medication, have seizures quite regularly—weekly or more often. These patients, along with their families and doctors, belong to the first category—stable without life shortening. Other adolescents, however, also following medical regimens quite closely, have intermittent epilepsy that strikes without warning after a lapse of months or even years. It is our impression that the adjustment of both adolescent and family may be poorer in this group. Other conditions in which relapses strike suddenly, and with little or no warning, are multiple sclerosis, some forms of cancer, coronary artery diseases, and sickle cell anemia.

The beginning of the chronic phase is marked by completion of the assessment of the nature, extent, severity, and prognosis of the illness, as well as the most dramatic life-supporting treatment. The boundary here, however, like the boundary between health and the acute phase, is *fundamentally psychosocial*. It is marked by the routinization of medical care: the establishment of a persistent medical regimen, often involving the doctor, patient, and family; the routinized integration of medical care within a regular diurnal framework for all members of the caregiving system; a shift in focus away from the anxious uncertainties of diagnosis and immediate survival to the maintenance of morale, rehabilitation, and vigilance for medical and psychologic complications of illness.

The fundamental tasks of the acute phase were assessment and life support. The major tasks of the chronic phase can be summarized in a one-word epigram: *maintenance*— maintenance of morale (patient, family, and doctor); maintenance of maximum competence in the entire system; maintenance—again by the whole system—of vigilance for complications or conditions that are dangerous to physical or psychologic health. Doctor "burnout" and depression, loss of morale in the patient, and withdrawal and stunted development in the family are all signs of failure of the caregiving system in this phase.

A different mode of shared experience organizes roles within the caregiver system in the chronic phase. In the acute phase, the shared preception was technical: At its core, the caregiving system was organized to achieve technical mastery over the illness. To be sure, technical issues persist in the chronic phase, but they become subordinate to moral issues, particularly ones of *compromise*. Individuals' experience of one another within the caregiving system becomes organized by mutually perceived obligations and perceived interpersonal debts. For example, in the acute phase the doctor's role is shaped quite precisely by the technical conception of the requirements of the illness itself. Over the long haul of the chronic phase the doctor attempts to shape his or her role by fashioning a compromise among a set of perceived obligations: obligations to the patient and family as well as obligations to other patients, to the doctor's staff, to his or her own family, and to himself or herself. Within any caregiving system the doctor's role is also determined by the obligations he or she is made to feel by the patient and the family. There are wide variations, but almost universally patient and family will not tolerate a procession of different persons filling the doctor role during the chronic phase, as was possible in the acute phase. More than technical expertise is required now, and the doctor as an engaged person is demanded.

Within the family itself, the obligations of family members to one another must be balanced. A particularly poignant example, in our experience, is to watch the painful balancing of obligations by parents of chronically ill children. Very often these parents speak of "shortchanging our healthy ones." They know that all their children need support, attention, and emotional involvement, which the demands of the chronically ill child compromise. This balance of obligations is particularly difficult in single-parent families.

It is in the demands of these balanced obligations that we can define doctors, patients, and families that may be at high risk during this phase. Paradoxically, where certain characteristics may lead to success in the acute phase, they may bode difficulty in the chronic phase. Consider the family with high coordination built out of a sense of group loyalty. When the emergency alarm sounds in the acute phase, these families can mobilize support to the patient and, where necessary, to the doctor. These same families, however, may have more difficulty in the chronic phase. For example, preliminary data from a study of families of chronic renal patients suggest that highly coordinated families endure more stress during the chronic phase and may not be able to rebalance obligations; they may very well remain centered on the patient without allowing the developmental needs of the family as a whole to receive adequate attention (Reiss, Gonzalez, & Kramer, 1986). Likewise, a doctor who remains riveted to the patient and the family—as is appropriate for the acute phase—may be most vulnerable to burnout.

A new balance must be achieved within the caregiver system. The physician must step back from his or her authoritative, dominant role of the acute phase and take up a more consultative role. Yet he must continuously remain alert for possible complications. The patient must relinquish the passive role and take a more active and responsible role for his or her own health–disease balance, and for the health of the family. The family must allow the patient this partial independence so that both patient and family can continue the process of growth and development. Even when/if this new balance is achieved, it is, at best, a temporary one. Changes in the course of the illness can often call for a shift back to the "acute phase." The most extreme example of this is probably chronic hemodialysis, especially center dialysis: For three half-days a week the situation reverts to the acute phase, with all the earmarks of life-sustaining interventions. For the rest of the week, however, it is back to the chronic phase (Kaplan De-Nour, 1983).

There is no doubt that intrapsychic forces play a major role in whether the delicate balance of the chronic phase is achieved and maintained. There are, however, also strong cultural influences. In Israeli society, contrary to that of the United States, the physician is much more likely to maintain a dominant role and the patient a passive role; the family often reinforces these two roles. It remains to be studied which caregiving system is better, and better for whom—patient, family, or physician. Does the difference influence the burnout of physician or family, does it affect the quality of life of the three partners, or does it modify the patient's survival?

THE TERMINAL/BEREAVEMENT PHASE

In theory, this phase begins when the caregiving system as a whole recognizes that the illness is beyond retrieval, when the routines of care shift from warding off complications and maximizing rehabilitation to maintaining comfort and composure in the system as death impends. We think this version of the closing phase of a chronic illness are infrequent. By implications, we suggest Kübler-Ross's (1969) influential concepts may be more ideal than typical. Our own experience is that physicians or patients or families are slow to recognize the imminence of death, and struggle, often to the last moments, to maintain the ordinary routines of the chronic phase, or, failing these, search valiantly for new, potentially effective treatments. To be sure, a "final hospitalization" when the disease has become overwhelming may signal to the whole system that death is near. But, equally often, caregiving systems have experienced several "final hospitalizations," and no event serves as a clear signal that the terminal phase has begun.

We are suggesting instead that this phase may be ushered in by a more subtle process, harder to detect than the demarcations of the previous two phases. One change occurs when the caregiving system comes to recognize not the *certainty* of impending death, but its *inevitability*. For example, our experience suggests that many cancer patients—while not accepting that death itself is imminent—can imagine the likelihood that they will, sooner or later, die of their disease. Quite frequently, a similar image develops in both doctor and family. There is, then, an ineffable awareness and anticipation that the patient's life is circumscribed. We have observed, for example, that at about this time the transactions of the caregiving system no longer include long-range planning. Indeed, we think it a critical shift when the family and doctor may begin transactions around medical information, particularly its implications for the long-term future, that do not fully include the patient. In Israeli caregiving systems, these transactions are frequent from the outset, but may become more intense. In American caregiving systems—where open exchange of information throughout the system is more typical—exclusive doctor–family transactions may occur for the first time early in this phase. Likewise, the family may begin subtly to exclude the patient from long-term planning—certain financial decisions, for example, or major family events that are planned for some months in the future. It does not necessarily follow that the patient becomes more emotionally isolated in the system. Indeed, doctor and family, dimly perceiving the inevitability of death, may become more attentive. It is our impression that in some families during this phase years of inhibitions and taboos may partially melt, and long-standing problems may be confronted more openly. Where the patient becomes isolated is in the forward flow of time: The patient becomes the specialist within the caregiving system of living on a day-to-day basis. Correspondingly, the doctors and particularly the family focus more intently on the long-term future.

These early processes set in motion a series of changes that continue through death to the period of explicit bereavement. From a transactional and development point of view, we wish to emphasize that the patient's death itself does not constitute the end of the terminal phase, but occurs midway in the transitional process. In most instances, before the patient's actual death both doctor and family (and often the patient, too) prepare for the patient's final departure and the reorganization of the survivors that, to some degree, must occur. The old clinical concept of "anticipatory grief" has not received much empiric support and, like Kübler-Ross's concepts of the stages of dying, may be more ideal than typical. Data strongly suggest, however, that the way caregiving systems function as death impends determines the success of the transition (Lopata, 1979; Vachon, 1976). The data suggest that the central task of the caregiving system in this phase is one of *maintaining composure* and *comfort*. Composure is not an end in itself but, according to recent observations, may facilitate bereavement (Weisman, 1979). For the survivors' welfare—for the family as well as for the physician—the feeling that all that could and should have been done was indeed done is of utmost importance. The physician must withstand the tendency to withdraw and resume the authoritative, emotionally remote leadership role of the acute phase.

In some cultures (e.g., Israel), the family's behavior often makes it harder for the physician. As the terminal stage approaches, the tendency increases to go for unofficial second opinions to other doctors or religious figures. The social expectation is very strong that the family demonstrate it has done everything possible for the patient. The physician must understand this "treason" and at times even encourage it without withdrawing from his or her leadership role. Doctor and family, thus, are strengthened during the period after death by the sense that all that could have been done for the patient was done. The family's grief and reorganization are not significantly hindered by feelings of guilt and recrimination.

SUMMARY

We have presented a scheme for understanding the role of the family in chronic illness. It is intended to highlight three concepts derived both from research and from our own clinical experience. First, the role of the family shifts in the course of the development of the illness. Characteristics of the family that may be adaptive in one phase may not be in another. Second, the role of the family cannot be fully understood unless it is conceived as a component of a larger caregiving system. Here, for simplicity's sake, we have discussed only the physician, but other health professionals are also critical parts of this system. Moreover, the nature of the clinical course of the illness itself must be understood as an integral part of this caregiving system. Third, we have rendered a very preliminary sketch of how this system may be organized in different cultural settings.

From a research perspective, we hope this model serves as a more comprehensive summary of existing data and, more important, serves as a stimulus for future research. We believe it indicates three priorities for research in this area. First, it emphasizes the need for research designs that compare caregiving systems in different illness conditions. Second, it emphasizes the need to include the doctor and other health care professionals as part of programmatic research efforts to explore the specific role of the family. Third, and most important, it emphasizes the need for longitudinal studies that conceive of the family's response to chronic illness as a crucial form of psychosocial development. The family, we have argued, does not simply "react" to the unique stress of chronic illness. Indeed, the increased prevalence of chronic illness—a paradoxical result of improved medical care—makes this experience a standard and almost expectable one. Thus, there is a pressing need, through strategically designed longitudinal studies, to understand how families develop and transform themselves in response to the demands of chronic illness.

References

Erikson E. Identity and the life cycle. Psychological Issues 1959; 1:1–171.

Kaplan De-Nour A. An overview of psychological problems in hemodialysis patients. In: Levy NB, ed. Psycho-nephrology, Vol. 2. New York: Plenum Press, 1983.

Kübler-Ross E. On death and dying. New York: Macmillan, 1969.

Lopata HZ. Women as widows. New York: Elsevier, 1979.

Redfield R. The primitive world and its transformations. Ithaca, N.Y.: Cornell University Press, 1953.

Reiss D. The family's construction of reality. Cambridge, Mass.: Harvard University Press, 1981.

Reiss D, Gonzalez S, Kramer N. Family process, chronic illness and death. Archives of General Psychiatry 1986; 43:795–804.

Rolland J. Toward a psychosocial typology of chronic and life-threatening illness. Family Systems Medicine 1984; 2:245–262.

Suchman EA. Social patterns of illness and medical care. Journal of Health and Social Behavior 1965; 6:2–16.

Vachon MLS. Grief and bereavement following the death of a spouse. Canadian Psychiatric Association 1976; 21:35–44.

Weisman AD. Coping with cancer. New York: McGraw-Hill, 1979.

31

Family Functioning and End-Stage Renal Disease

JOHN H. STEIDL
The Institute of Pennsylvania Hospital, Philadelphia;
Yale University School of Medicine

FAMILY FUNCTIONING AND END-STAGE
RENAL DISEASE: THE CONTEXT

I will begin by describing end-stage renal disease (ESRD), its various treatments, and the current political and economic situation that surrounds it. I think this will be a helpful context within which to review the research on family functioning and ESRD, and to suggest directions for the future of family research with this illness.

United States Data on End-Stage Renal Disease

By the end of 1987, there were 98,420 end-stage renal disease patients on some form of dialysis in the United States, nearly double the figure at the beginning of the decade. In addition to these dialysis patients, there were almost 9,300 end-stage renal disease patients who received kidney transplants during 1987, also an increase of 100% during the decade, although the rate of increase in transplants patients is greater than the rate of increase in dialysis patients by a factor of 3 to 2. Not only is this patient population growing, but the age statistics are also shifting: 72% are over the age of 50, an increase of nearly 50% in the last 4 years, and the average age of patients beginning treatment is now 55, an increase of 5 years between 1983 and 1987. Partly, this is because the U.S. population as a whole is older; but to a significant extent it is because the criteria for selecting patients for treatment have changed dramatically over the last 15 years. We are now willing to take high-risk patients, such as those with diabetes, hypertension, cancer, and psychiatric illness, who would not have been accepted for treatment 15 years ago because of scarce resources and more primitive technology, and who are still not widely treated outside the United States, except in a palliative sense.

End-stage renal disease (ESRD) is a chronic illness in which the kidneys stop functioning enough to maintain bodily equilibrium. This may happen as the end product of another chronic illness, such as hypertension or diabetes, which was not initially related to the kidneys; it may happen as the result of a long and chronic renal condition, such as polycystic disease or glomerulonephritis; or it may happen acutely, as in the case of an acute toxic or allergic injury. Once the kidneys have ceased to function enough to maintain bodily equilibrium, the patient and his or her family are faced with three options: death, transplantation of a new kidney from a living relative or from the body of someone who has just died, or dialysis. Dialysis is a repetitive medical intervention that serves to remove toxins from the blood as the kidneys would have, had they been functioning. Today, for those patients who elect dialysis or are forced to use it for lack of an acceptable donor kidney, there are three options, using one of two technologies. The patient can choose hemodialysis, a procedure that requires being attached to a machine three times a week for 4 or 5 hours each episode, during which time the buildup of toxins is removed as the patient's blood passes through an artificial kidney. This procedure can be done in a center for dialysis to which the patient goes three times a week on a regular schedule. Centers are located both in community hospitals and in free-standing satellites. Or the patient can be trained to do the hemodialysis procedure at home with the aide of a significant other as the assistant, again three times a week. The third option for dialysis, which involves a different and newer technology, is continuous ambulatory peritoneal dialysis (CAPD), a procedure that is performed by patients themselves four times a day, 7 days a week. The dialyzing solution is passed in and out of the abdominal cavity via a more or less permanent tube that has been surgically inserted through the abdominal wall. This procedure requires about 30 minutes each time and can be performed almost anywhere, although it is usually referred to as a home dialysis.

The vast majority of ESRD patients end up on dialysis for one reason or another, at a ratio of 11 dialysis patients to one transplant patient. In this group of 98,420 dialysis patients, less than 20% were on home dialysis, including both home hemodialysis and CAPD. However, the number of patients using home dialysis grew nearly 80% during this decade, a figure that is accounted for by the very large increase in CAPD. The number of patients choosing CAPD more than tripled from 1980 to 1987, while home hemodialysis declined. This shift from hemodialysis to CAPD in the home dialysis population is the result of a number of factors: Home hemodialysis is more intimidating; it takes longer and is more difficult to learn; it is a procedure that requires a partner; and it is more disruptive of family life. The ESRD population electing transplantation has also increased, though more modestly; and—although both cadaver and living, related donor transplants increased—living, related donor transplants increased over 40% during this period, a trend that is accounted for in part by the better prognosis attached to this option (Vollmer, Wahl, & Blagg, 1983).

The Political and Economic Context of ESRD

Much of this information, which is substantial, must be seen in a political and economic context. In 1973, the U.S. government decided to make life-sustaining treatment available to patients with ESRD, regardless of ability to pay (Public Law 92-603). Since then, the number of patients requiring such treatment in order to live has vastly exceeded the original projections, and the cost for the medical care of these patients in 1985 was projected at $1.5 billion. This is the cost to Medicare, not for dialysis treatment alone but for the total care of these patients, many of whom have serious co-morbidity and require periodic hospitalization.

Because of the increased costs for this and other medical therapies, Congress turned its attention to cost containment. In 1983, Public Law 97-35 was passed changing reimbursement to a prospective system. The intent of this law is to encourage the least costly medical care, which for ESRD was thought to be home dialysis and transplantation. The cost of caring for ESRD patients on center hemodialysis is about $20,000 to $25,000 per year, whereas the cost of the medical care for patients on home dialysis, either CAPD or hemodialysis, is about $14,000 to $18,000 per year. This difference largely reflects the fact that patients selected for home dialysis have fewer serious concurrent illnesses, requiring less additional medical care and fewer days in the hospital (Plough, Salem, Shwartz, Weller, & Ferguson, 1984). It is estimated that the group receiving the less expensive home dialysis can be increased to perhaps 30% of the dialysis population without altering this financial picture. If it is to be increased beyond that, however, it is likely that current criteria for home dialysis will have to be altered to include patients who are more disabled, thus moving the per-patient cost of total medical care for those on home dialysis into the range of center hemodialysis. Furthermore, as pressure to reduce costs escalates and reimbursement figures are ratcheted down, the free-standing proprietary dialysis centers will be forced to develop even more stringent criteria for accepting patients for whom they can provide adequate care within the Medicare dollars provided (i.e., the healthier patients). Nonproprietary hospitals will then be left with the most seriously ill patients, on whom they will lose money. At that point, we will likely be back to the situation of nearly 20 years ago when patients with serious co-morbidity were reviewed by committees and deemed unacceptable for life-sustaining therapy. Increasingly, as long as our current national priorities hold, patients with severe end-stage chronic illness requiring expensive care may receive only palliative care.

The Family Studies Context of ESRD

Before moving to current and future research efforts in the field, it is important to remind ourselves of the family studies context within which we work. Over forty years ago, Henry Richardson (1945), then associate professor of clinical medicine at Cornell University, published a book entitled *Patients Have Families,* in which he vividly described the powerful interaction between family life and medical illness. It is sad that this wonderful book had so little impact on physicians and family researchers that 30 years later, John Weakland (1977) was led to deliver a paper entitled ''Family Somatics—A Neglected Edge.'' In that paper, he lamented the comparative inattention to physical problems from a family interaction viewpoint. I don't wish to suggest that nothing happened during the intervening years. In 1974, Theodor Litman published a lucid review of the considerable literature written during those intervening years, entitled ''The Family as a Basic Unit in Health and Medical Care: A Social-Behavioral Overview.'' However, he placed this review in the context of a 1971 World Health Organization report, which noted that ''In spite of its central position in society, the family has been infrequently studied from the public health point of view. The complex interrelationships between health and the family virtually constitute terra incognita'' (World Health Organization, 1971, cited in Litman, 1974).

By the time of the Weakland and Litman papers, Minuchin and colleagues at the University of Pennsylvania were already very productively at work investigating the interaction between medical illness and family dysfunction in children (Liebman, Minuchin, & Baker, 1974; Minuchin *et al.,* 1975; Minuchin, Rosman, & Baker, 1978). However, it is mostly in the exceptions that we have progressed beyond Richardson's work of 40 years ago, and by and large ESRD is not one of the exceptions. As I will review in a moment, the literature on psychosocial functioning and ESRD is weighted toward case reports and studies dealing with individual variables, even though references are made to the family. There is a comparatively smaller number of family research studies that are systemic in nature; and, to my knowledge, there are no studies investigating the impact of a family intervention in ESRD. This is the situation with many diseases and is not peculiar to ESRD. Much of medicine has not arrived at Dr. Richardson's (1945) position in accepting the interaction between illness and family functioning as significant, perhaps because the majority of patients with chronic illnesses (including ESRD) have remarkably effective psychologic adaptation, similar to that reported for the general public (Cassileth *et al.,*

1984). But even if medicine were enthusiastic about looking at that subpopulation of patients who were not adapting well and willing to consider that family dysfunction might be interacting with poor medical condition among these "outliers," family research as a field is only beginning to be ready for the challenge. The task of investigating the relationship between such multivariate realities as family functioning and chronic medical illness is immensely complicated; there is very little consensus in our field when it comes to models for thinking about families, and there are as many assessment devices as we have models.

LITERATURE REVIEW, 1975–1984

Having described the context as I see it, let me highlight the current literature, also as I see it. There are a variety of legitimate ways one could choose to provide an orientation to the literature. One could organize the literature by outcome variables: findings affecting medical condition, adherence to treatment, adjustment, rehabilitation, and so on. Alternatively, one could organize it into groups of studies and articles that share the same theoretic orientation to family interaction. Or one could organize it into clusters of studies sharing the same research methodology. I have chosen to organize the literature in a way that, while presenting current findings, underlies important gaps and thereby implies directions for future research. There are a number of studies that, although they make some references to the family, are looking primarily at the interaction between ESRD and individual functioning. In addition, a number of articles having to do with families are case reports, not research studies. Happily, there are an increasing number of research studies that investigate correlations between medical condition, adherence to treatment, and family functioning, although not all of these have a systemic orientation and only a handful deal explicitly with the question of how family variables mediate medical condition. Finally, there are no studies that investigate the results of a family system intervention on medical condition, adherence to treatment, or various adjustment mechanisms such as rehabilitation. Let me illustrate each of these points.

ESRD and Individual Functioning

Family interaction is still peripheral to much of the literature that deals with psychosocial factors in relation to ESRD. Many of the studies look primarily at interaction between ESRD and individual functioning, even though they may make reference to the family, have "family" in the title, or call for family intervention (Anderson, 1975; Atcherson, 1981; De-Nour, 1982; Greenberg, Weltz, Spitz, & Bizzozero, 1975; Hagberg & Malmquist, 1974; Kirilloff, 1981; Lowry & Atcherson, 1980; Procci, 1980, 1981; Stewart, 1983). Let me indicate two of these by way of example. De-Nour (1982) published a study of the psychosocial adjustment of a large number of hemodialysis patients using the self-report version of the Psychological Adjustment to Illness Scale (PAIS), the Multiple Affect Adjective Check List (MAACL), and physician rating. This study was oriented to the impact of the illness on adjustment, and focused on the individual, noting that 15 years of research had failed to provide a consistent picture of individual adjustment to chronic hemodialysis. The author, in a manner reminiscent of previous studies (Finkelstein, Finkelstein, & Steele, 1976; Hagberg & Malmquist, 1974), noted that half of the patients in the study reported moderate to severe domestic impairment, and 60% reported severe sexual impairment, even though they denied that such impairment had an effect on their intrafamily relationships. De-Nour also noted that PAIS is not as adequate in gathering information about relationships as it is in other areas of adjustment. Atcherson (1981) reported on a prospective study of spouse assistants in home hemodialysis. The focus here was on the psychologic well-being of the partner as a deciding factor in the success of home dialysis: support for the spouse assistant, not work with the couple, was suggested as a treatment intervention.

Case Reports or Suggestions for Intervention

Much of the literature is essentially case reports or suggestions for clinical intervention (Armstrong & Weiner, 1981–1982; HIll, 1981; Levenberg, Jenkins, & Wendorf, 1978–1979; Palmer, Canzona, & Wai, 1982; Scheinberg, 1983; Wheeler, 1977; Winkes, 1983), only a few of which indicate a sytemic family orientation. Again, let me indicate two of these, by way of example. Levenberg and colleagues (1978–1979), describing a family-oriented crisis intervention approach to home hemodialysis families, noted that "a couple whose premorbid relationship is dysfunctional will soon manifest this under the stress of home dialysis." Palmer and co-workers (1982) described the functioning pattern of 20 families with a member on home hemodialysis and concluded with a hypothesis, consistent with the theoretic framework of Robert Beavers (1976), that "families with more flexible, open patterns of interaction will be more successful with home dialysis."

Correlations between Medical Conditions and Family Functioning

Happily, there are an increasing number of studies investigating and reporting significant correlations between medical condition and family functioning (Finkelstein *et al.*, 1976; Goldman, Cohn, & Longnecker, 1980–1981; Marshall & Rice, 1975; Maurin & Schenkel, 1976; McGee, 1981; Pentecost, 1970; Reiss, Gonzales, & Kramer, 1986; Sherwood, 1983; Steidl *et al.*, 1980), although not all are systemic in their orientation. Let me indicate three by way of example. Steidl and his colleagues (1980) published a study of 23 hemodialysis patients in which they investigated the relationship between family functioning, medical condition, and adherence to treatment. They found significant correlations between ratings of family functioning and medical condition using the Beavers-Timberlawn methodology with videotaped family interaction (Beavers, 1976). They also noted a nearly significant relationship between adherence to treatment and family functioning. Furthermore, specific family variables that correlated significantly with either medical condition or adherence to treatment were identified, and these were similar to those noted by Minuchin and co-workers in pediatric populations (Liebman *et al.*, 1974; Minuchin *et al.*, 1975; Minuchin, Rosman, & Baker, 1978). Steidl and co-workers (1980) concluded by saying that "while we do not believe that poor family functioning is responsible for poor medical condition or the lack of adherence to treatment regimens, we recognize that medical condition and family functioning influence each other in a circular fashion."

We did not do a follow-up on this group of patients, and, having read a recent study by Reiss *et al.* (1986), I wish we had. In a careful study of 23 hemodialysis patients, using laboratory techniques for measuring family problem-solving strategies, and following their medical complications and survival over a period of 3 years, Reiss and his colleagues arrived at two very surprising and unexpected conclusions. "In sharp contrast to expectations based on previous data, high scores on the problem solving variables—as well as [family] measures of accomplishment and intactness—predicted early death rather than survival. Equally surprising was the finding that noncompliance accounted for most of the association between family variables and survival.''

Another very good paper, both from the standpoint of systemic thinking and from that of good research, is Sherwood's (1983) ''Compliance Behavior of Hemodialysis Patients and the Role of the Family.'' While the data are elicited from standardized patient interviews and should be augmented by family interactional data, a recommendation also made by the author, he reports significant interactions between compliance and family variables, and effectively raises questions about the meaning of support–nonsupport, enmeshment–disengagement, organization–disorganization. One of his findings appears connected to those of Reiss *et al.* (1986) that patients who reported their families worked together during crisis periods were less compliant with potassium control, one of the five dependent variables. Sherwood then shifts to Minuchin *et al.*'s (1978) conceptual framework of enmeshment and disengagement, and wonders if ''noncompliant patients' families may become so overly involved during crisis periods that patients may feel incompetent to deal with the situation. The patient may seek a sense of autonomy and competence by being noncompliant.'' These papers lead directly into the question of family influences mediating medical condition.

Family Influence Mediating Medical Condition

To my knowledge, there are no studies investigating the results of a family system intervention on medical condition, adherence to treatment, or various other adjustment measures such as rehabilitation in ESRD. If we could demonstrate that intervention at the level of family variables leads to significant changes in medical condition, we might then be closer to understanding the mechanism by which family variables have such an influence. In the published ESRD literature, there is to my knowledge only one article that explicitly addresses the question of mediating mechanisms. Chowanec and Binik (1982), in their review, espouse a circular, systemic model in which ESRD has an impact on marital adjustment and that adjustment in turn affects physical health. Recognizing the enormous problem of quantification when operating from a broad general systems theory framework, they suggest limiting family investigation to marital roles as a relevant, measurable subset within which to investigate how marital interaction translates into patient adjustment. Although I agree with this systemic, circular way of approaching the complexities, I also see the need to narrow the field. However, it is not as clear to me that marital roles are a sufficient focus for viewing family interaction.

David Reiss and his colleagues (1986) have also clearly addressed the issue. He thoughtfully suggests several mechanisms by which family and medical variables may interact. For example, he points out that recent studies suggest that most families dealing with the first phase of severe illness tend to coalesce around the illness and become more closely integrated. However, high coordination—while an effective response to an acute medical emergency—if it persists—may make the family more vulnerable in the long run. The idea of a persistent and inflexible response beyond the time when it is appropriate is quite consistent with the entropy–negentropy model of Beavers (1976), in which either a chaotic or a too rigidly structured family system will have difficulty dealing with the ongoing changes required by a severe, chronic, end-stage illness, and this will have a negative impact on the patient. A healthier family system, with structure and flexibility, will have the necessary adaptive capability, and the patient will tend to do well. Although Reiss addresses a variety of mechanisms, they are all presented within the context of a family exclusionary process, which excludes the patient out of a drive for the survival of the vulnerable unit.

It is interesting that 15 years ago, Litman (1974), reporting on a study of his, commented that "whereas the cohesion of an extremely close, well-integrated and maritally happy family may be severely strained as a result of a member's illness, such an event may serve to bring those with more disparate family ties closer together. Why this should be so remains unclear and in need of further study."

Another well-known model for mediation, outside the ESRD literature but still within the chronic illness literature, is that of Minuchin and his colleagues (Leibman *et al.,* 1974; Minuchin *et al.,* 1975, 1978), in which structural variables exert a mediating influence on medical condition. Here, the more dysfunctional the structure, the more likely the system is to need a stabilizing or detouring focus in order for the system to survive. In such a case, the family can make use of a patient in a less than optimal medical condition in order to provide a focus that enhances survival, although with ESRD, as with brittle diabetics and severe anorectics, the family is playing Russian roulette. For example, Plough and Salem (1982) reported on a review of the medical records of deceased ESRD patients, and noted that the primary underlying cause of death was dietary indiscretion (27%), followed by preventable treatment accidents (17%), findings that one could hypothesize having something to do with family interaction.

One further model, again outside the ESRD literature, is of interest. Ramsey, Abell, and Baker (1986), working from a stress model (Coyne & Holroyd, 1982), looked at the interaction between family variables and pregnancy outcome, and hypothesized an interaction between family functioning, the immune system, and low birth weight. Here, dysfunctional families contribute through the mechanism of stress to compromise immunologic functioning, thereby causing fetal growth retardation.

In other fields, there has been much interest of late in the possible mediating impact of psychosocial factors on basic biology: the contribution of stress, type A behavior, and diet to cardiovascular disease; the impact of depression and stress on the immune system in a variety of diseases, including cancer; and so on. This raises the question of whether there are significant family interactions with some of the basic biologic processes in ESRD. Although this is likely for some patients, it is virtually impossible to research. For example, it is reported that over time, a very large number of ESRD patients develop atherosclerotic lesions (Cramp, Moorhead, & Willis, 1975; Lindner, Charra, Sherrard, & Scribner, 1974; Mordasini, Frey, Flury, Klose, & Greten, 1977; Nicholls, Catto, Edward, Engeset, & MacLeod, 1980; Rapaport, Aviram, Chaimovitz, & Brook, 1978). Given this fact, it is certainly prudent to pay attention to such family-mediated risk factors as diet, hypertension control, and exercise. However, atherosclerotic disease is so pervasive and severe in this patient population for many other reasons that research on family interaction as a mediating variable is not a productive use of energy. Similarly, one can also look at cellular immunity in ESRD and raise the question of the interaction between family stress and the functioning of the immune system. Ten years ago, the increased incidence of malignancy during chronic renal failure was noted (Matas, Simmons, Kjellstrand, Buselmeier, & Majarian, 1975). However, we would expect that there would be a loss of immunosurveillance in transplant patients on immunosuppressive therapy that would account for much of the increased incidence, even when controlled for family variables. Since there is also a relationship between uremia and immunocompetence, predialysis and dialysis patients would also be at risk; and, in fact, a sevenfold increase in the incidence of malignancy over the age-matched general population has been reported (Matas *et al.,* 1975; Raska *et al.,* 1983). Again, although successful intervention to decrease stress, depression, or other variables associated with immunocompetence is certainly warranted, as with cardiovascular disease it seems most unlikely that we can demonstrate family-mediated variables in such a multifactorial situation.

The Meta-Analysis of Variables Related to Adjustment

In summary, one way to highlight the literature on psychosocial factors in ESRD is to say that over the last 10 years, there have been a number of studies looking at variables related to adjustment to ESRD that reported conflicting results, lacked consistency in measuring variables, and used different statistical analyses. In 1983, Carol Olsen published a meta-analysis of 40 studies reporting variables predictive of adjustment in hemodialysis patients. Demographic variables, time on dialysis, and health belief were not predictive of adjustment in this meta-analysis. What she found to be statistically significant were predialysis functioning (accounting for 28% of the variance), individual personality (accounting for 18% of the variance), and family relations (accounting for 20% of the variance). It is interesting to note that the family variables measured in the majority of the studies were those of support, closeness, and cohesion.

FUTURE RESEARCH ON FAMILY FUNCTIONING AND ESRD

Methodologic Concerns

Let me begin a look to the future by very briefly identifying several methodologic concerns. First are the associated problems of sample size and multiple variables. Most of the studies are too small to be more than suggestive. When one begins to look at several aspects of medical condition and family functioning, it is not hard to have more variables than patients, making even expected results a bit suspect. Research that is going to be most helpful to the field will need to increase dramatically the number of subjects and controls, as well as limit the variables under investigation. To accomplish this probably means targeting our efforts on communities or centers with a large number of ESRD patients, since going the route of the multicity, multicenter design introduces many more complications around standardization, especially when it comes to intervention studies.

Second, there is the problem of multiple family assessment devices: patient self-report measures, clinician ratings of family interviews, video recordings of family interaction scored by experienced raters, and the performing in a controlled setting of family tasks that can be analyzed along a variety of dimensions. Further complicating the situation, these various devices are based on various theoretic orientations. Some, such as FACES II (Olson, Russell, & Sprenkle, 1983) or the Beavers-Timberlawn methodology, (Beavers, 1976) are more widely known than others. Most of the studies reviewed here, however, use different protocols. A large variety of assessment devices based on different theoretic models makes it hard to compare and interpret results across studies. Again, it would be more helpful if we could select a standardized assessment device that is reliable and valid and is fairly uncomplicated to administer to a large sample of patients.

At this point in history, I would be inclined to use FACES III with a sample of several hundred ESRD patients, for the following reasons (Olson, Portner, & Lavee, 1985). It may well be the best and most widely used self-report device. Its predecessor (FACES II) is widely used with a variety of medical populations, and it is likely that FACES III will be used similarly. FACES II is inexpensive to administer and will not need the tremendous grant support necessitated by a complex protocol assessing and scoring family interaction in a large sample. I would, in addition, use the Beavers-Timberlawn (Beavers, 1976) assessment of interaction with a subset of the larger group, in order to establish and compare the distinctive data elicited by each methodology.

Third, there are several kinds of family interventions represented in the current family literature: single-family therapy, marital therapy, multiple family or couples groups, psychoeducational approaches to the family, and family-oriented individual therapy. There are also multiple models or theoretic orientations for doing whatever kind of intervention one chooses: psychodynamic, structural, strategic, psychoeducational, behavior, and so forth. For a major intervention study, it would be extremely useful if we could develop a standardized intervention protocol that is based on a widely accepted model and is theoretically consistent with our choice of assessment device, perhaps using one of our national professional organizations to sponsor such an effort.

In short, all of this indicates a major effort at collaboration beyond what we are now doing. Without it, we will continue to have a variety of small studies, with all the aforementioned drawbacks, which will no doubt increase our list of publications but, except for the rare watershed study, not advance the field very much.

Priorities for Research

If we can deal adequately with these methodologic concerns, there are several areas I would suggest as priorities. Among the most important questions for future research is: Can we identify the mechanisms by which family interaction mediates medical condition?

As I have indicated, there are several such mechanisms stated in the chronic illness literature. If one were to investigate mechanisms within the framework of stress, as Ramsey and his co-workers (1986), one would need to follow patients over time, beginning preferably with renal diagnosis and looking at multiple measures. For example, we would need operational definitions of family dysfunction, individual stress, and medical condition. We would then follow these factors over time so that we could begin to define how event A (family dysfunction) is involved in event B (the individual's assessment of that dysfunction and consequent stress reaction), and how each of these events are involved in event C (medical condition), and vice versa. This takes us out of any rigid notion of dependent and independent variables and looks at each component of the hypothesized equation as potentially a dependent as well as an independent variable.

Minuchin and his colleagues (Liebman *et al.*, 1974; Minuchin *et al.*, 1975, 1978) provide a somewhat different approach to the question of mechanism. Although they have demonstrated the impact of stressful family dysfunction on biologic mechanisms, they appear to view poor medical condition more in relation to the stabilization of a dysfunctional structure than as the fallout of stress. If one were to investigate this mechanism by which family variables have mediating influence on medical condition, it would be important to assess family structure as close as possible to renal diagnosis and to follow it over time, noting the ways in which family structure does or does not adapt to the developmental stages of the illness (Rolland, 1984), identifying dysfunctional areas of structure and the interaction of the patient's illness with that dysfunction, while at the same time following the patient's medical condition. In short, in order to shed light on the question of mediating mechanisms, one would need to start with an interactive model or hypothesis and examine concurrent data over time.

A second priority for future research is investigating the impact of a family intervention on medical condition, a task that could be linked with that of identifying the mechanisms by which family variables mediate medical condition. To some extent, the correlation between family functioning and medical condition has been shown by earlier studies; and Minuchin and co-workers at the University of Pennsylvania have established the positive effect of a family intervention on medical condition in a number of pediatric populations, and have suggested a model for the interaction between family and medical condition (1975, 1978). Therefore, one might ask: Why bother to investigate the obvious in ESRD? To some degree this is a legitimate basis for moving on to other priorities. However, there is little in the way of intervention studies with adult patients, and I am convinced that very little routine family assessment and treatment will be utilized by nephrologists, much less be reimbursed, until it is firmly established not only that ESRD patients from dysfunctional families are likely to do worse medically and cost more to treat, but also that medical condition can be improved and the cost of treatment reduced by such intervention. Of course, there are other appropriate outcome measures, such as compliance (Hoebel, 1976), rehabilitation (Hughson, Collier, Johnston, & Tiller, 1974; Procci, 1980; Rennie, 1981), and sick role behavior (Kasl & Cobb, 1966), all of which have implications for medical condition and some of which may represent mechanisms by which family interaction has a mediating influence on medical condition. However, since both the medical profession and the reimbursement system will evaluate any procedure in terms of its contribution to the efficient improvement of medical condition, it would be well to investigate these other related outcomes only if we think we can demonstrate how they affect medical condition.

A third area for research addresses a question that is partly political, partly financial, and partly clinical: What is the medical treatment of choice for ESRD? As noted in the introductory comments, there is pressure from reimbursement sources as well as from the clinical side to emphasize home dialysis and transplantation, particularly living, related donor transplantation. For various reasons, these procedures are more stressful on many families than center dialysis, and consequently some patients from dysfunctional families may do worse on these protocols. This leads to the question of whether we can identify the interaction between a particular treatment procedure and family functioning, and develop a profile of which families will do well or poorly on a particular protocol. There are already partial definitions in the literature (Marshall & Rice, 1975; McGee, 1981; Speidel, Koch, Black, & Kniess, 1979; Stewart, 1983).

Finally, a fascinating area for family investigation is that of the longitudinal effect of severe chronic illness on the future medical and family behavior of children. Although not as much a priority as interventions, mediating mechanisms, or choice of medical treatment, this area could shed light on mechanisms and allow us to intervene more effectively in the future. Clinically, one sees cases where a physically healthy person chooses a medically ill spouse, often in an attempt to work out old conflicts around illness derived from childhood experiences. One also sees patients who have adopted a repertoire of illness behaviors, which have been developed in direct relation to their experience growing up in a family with severe chronic illness. By following a large sample of chronic illness families with children over time, one might be able to identify the sequelae of growing up in a family with chronic illness. One might also identify which family variables contribute to poor outcomes in the children. Finally, with a large enough population, one could experiment with interventions that would ameliorate those outcomes.

CONCLUSIONS

Certainly ESRD is one of the most complex of chronic illnesses, both clinically and from a research standpoint. It is a multisystem disease with many variables, and there are perhaps not as clear biologic markers for medical condition and compliance as there are with other illnesses. This is a very complex reality to interface with the even more complex and diverse realities of family assessment and treatment. Given the high degree of complexity in both areas, can we justify the family research energies of either family systems or medical professionals with this particular illness? I think there are important reasons to make ESRD an area of investigation. It is a catastrophic illness affecting the family in which the promise of unlimited and expensive treatment comes up against unexpected needs and costs. Given these facts, as well as the English and European practice of much more limited treatment for ESRD, there will be increased consideration of limiting treatment. In this climate, and with a push toward the less expensive treatments that involve families more, it is important to learn as much as we can about the mechanisms or ways by which family interaction influences the patient's condition for health as well as for illness. It is important to try to establish the differential demands of the various treatment protocols on patients and their families so that treatment choices can include family factors along with cost considerations and medical data, and to make as much progress as possible in the efficient intervention with families to improve or stabilize medical condition.

References

Anderson K. The psychological aspects of chronic hemodialysis. Canadian Psychiatric Association Journal 1975; 20:385–391.

Armstrong SH, Weiner MF. Noncompliance with post-transplant immunosuppression. International Journal of Psychiatry in Medicine 1981–1982; 1:89–94.

Atcherson E. Home hemodialysis and the spouse assistant. Journal of the American Association of Nephrology Nurses and Technicians 1981; August:29–34.

Beavers WR. A theoretical basis for family evaluation. In: Lewis JM, Beavers WR, Gossett JT, Phillips VA, eds. No single thread: psychological health in family systems. New York: Brunner/Mazel, 1976:46–82.

Cassileth BR, Luch EJ, Strouse TB, Miller DS, Brown LL, Cross P, Teneglia AN. Psychosocial status in chronic illness: a comparative analysis of six diagnostic groups. New England Journal of Medicine 1984; 311:506–511.

Chowanec GD, Binik YM. End-stage renal disease (ESRD) and the marital dyad: a literature review and critique. Social Science Medicine 1982; 16:1551–1558.

Coyne JC, Holroyd K. Stress, coping and illness: a transactional perspective. In: Millon T, Green C, Meagher R, eds. Handbook of clinical health psychology. New York: Plenum Press, 1982.

Cramp DG, Moorhead JF, Wills MR. Disorders of blood-lipids in renal disease. Lancet 1975; March:672–673.

De-Nour AK. Psychosocial adjustment to illness scale (PAIS): a study of chronic hemodialysis patients. Journal of Psychosomatic Research 1982; 26:11–22.

Finkelstein OF, Finkelstein SH, Steele TE. Assessment of marital relationships of hemodialysis patients. American Journal of the Medical Sciences 1976; 271:21–28.

Goldman RH, Cohn Gl, Longnecker RE. The family and home hemodialysis: adolescents' reactions to a father on home dialysis. International Journal of Psychiatry in Medicine 1980–1981; 10:235–254.

Greenberg IM, Weltz S, Spitz C, Bizzozero JO. Factors of adjustment in chronic hemodialysis. Psychosomatics 1975; 16:178–184.

Hagberg B, Malmquist A. A prospective study of patients in chronic hemodialysis: IV. Pretreatment psychiatric and psychological variables predicting outcome. Journal of Psychosomatic Research 1984; 18:315–319.

Hill MN. When the patient is the family. American Journal of Nursing 1981; March:536–538.

Hoebel FC. Brief family-interactional therapy in the management of cardiac-related high risk behaviors. Journal of Family Practice 1976; 3:613–618.

Hughson BJ, Collier AE, Johnston J, Tiller DJ. Rehabilitation after renal transplant. Medical Journal of Australia 1974;2:732–735.

Kasl SV, Cobb, S. Health behavior, illness behavior, and sick-role behavior. Archives of Environmental Health 1966; 12:531–541.

Kirilloff LH. Factors influencing the compliance of hemodialysis patients with therapeutic regimen. Journal of the American Association of Nephrology Nurses and Technicians 1981; August:15–20.

Levenberg SB, Jenkins C, Wendorf DJ. Studies in family-oriented crisis intervention with hemodialysis patients. International Journal of Psychiatry in Medicine 1978–1979; 9:83–92.

Liebman R, Minuchin S, Baker L. The use of structural family therapy in the treatment of intractable asthma. American Journal of Psychiatry 1974; 131:535–540.

Lindner A, Charra B, Sherrard DJ, Scribner B. Accelerated atherosclerosis in prolonged maintenance hemodialysis. New England Journal of Medicine 1974; 290:697–738.

Litman TJ. The family as a basic unit in health and medical care: a social-behavioral overview. Social Science and Medicine 1974; 8:495–519.

Lowry M, Atcherson E. Home dialysis dropouts. Journal of Psychosomatic Research 1980; 24:173–178.

Marshall JR, Rice, DG. Characteristics of couples with poor outcome in dialysis home training. Journal of Chronic Diseases 1975; 28:375–381.

Matas AJ, Simmons RL, Kjellstrand CM, Buselmeier TJ, Majarian JS. Increased incidence of malignancy during chronic renal failure. Lancet 1975; April:883–886.

Maurin J, Schenkel J, A study of the family unit's response to hemodialysis. Journal of Psychosomatic Research 1976 20(3):163–8.

McGee MG. Familial response to chronic illness: the impact of home versus hospital dialysis. Journal of the American Association of Nephrology Nurses and Technicians 1981; August:9–12.

Minuchin S, Baker L, Rosman BL, Liebman R, Milman L, Todd TC. A conceptual model of psychosomatic illness in children. Archives of General Psychiatry 1975; 32:1031–1038.

Minuchin S, Rosman BL, Baker L. Psychosomatic families. Cambridge, Mass.: Harvard University Press, 1978.

Mordasini R, Frey F, Flury W, Klose G, Greten H. Selective deficiency of hepatic triglyceride lipase in uremic patients. New England Journal of Medicine 1977; 297:1362–1366.

Network Coordinating Council of Connecticut 1983 Annual Report. (Network-27). New Haven, Conn.: Author, 1983.

Nicholls AJ, Catto GRD, Edward N, Engeset J, MacLeod M. Accelerated atherosclerosis in long-term dialysis and renal transplant patients: fact or fiction? Lancet 1980; February:276–278.

Olsen CA. A statistical review of variables predictive of adjustment in hemodialysis patients. Nephrology Nursing 1983; November–December:16–27.

Olson DH, Portner J, Lavee Y. FACES III. Department of Family Social Science, University of Minnesota, St. Paul, 1985.

Olson DH, Russell CS, Sprenkle DH. Circumplex model of marital and family systems: VI. Theoretical update. Family Process 1983; 22:69–84.

Palmer SE, Canzona L, Wai L. Helping families respond effectively to chronic illness: home dialysis as a case example. Social Work in Health Care 1982; 8:1–14.

Pentecost RJ. Family study in home dialysis. Archives of General Psychiatry 1970; 22:538–546.

Plough AL, Salem SR. Social and contextual factors in the analysis of mortality in ESRD patients: implications for health policy. American Journal of Public Health 1982; 11:1293–1295.

Plough AL, Salem SR, Shwartz M, Weller JM, Ferguson CW. Case mix in end-stage renal disease. New England Journal of Medicine 1984; 310:1432–1436.

Procci WR. A comparison of psychosocial disability in males undergoing maintenance hemodialysis or following cadaver transplantation. General Hospital Psychiatry 1980; 2:255–261.

Procci WR. Psychosocial disability during maintenance hemodialysis. General Hospital Psychiatry 1981; 3:24–31.

Ramsey CN, Abell TD, Baker LC. The relationship between family functions, life events, family structure, and the outcome of pregnancy. Journal of Family Practice 1986; 22(6):521–7.

Rapoport J, Aviram M, Chaimovitz C, Brook GJ. Defective high-density lipoprotein composition in patients on chronic hemodialysis: a possible mechanism for accelerated atherosclerosis. New England Journal of Medicine 1978; 299:1151–1326.

Raska K Jr, Raskova J, Shea SM, Frankel RM, Wood RH, Lifter J, Ghobrial I, Eisinger RP, Homer L, T cell subsets and cellular immunity in end-stage renal disease. American Journal of Medicine 1983; 75(5):734–40.

Reiss D, Gonzales S, Kramer N. Family process, chronic illness and death: on the weakness of strong bonds. Archives of General Psychiatry 1986; 43:795–804.

Rennie D. Renal rehabilitation—where are the data? New England Journal of Medicine 1981; 304:351–352.

Richardson HB. Patients have families. New York: Commonwealth Fund, 1945.

Rolland JS. Toward a psychosocial typology of chronic and life-threatening illness. Family Systems Medicine 1984; 3:245–262.

Sheinberg M. The family and chronic illness: a treatment diary. Family Systems Medicine 1983; 2:26–36.

Sherwood RJ. Compliance behavior of hemodialysis patients and the role of the family. Family Systems Medicine 1983; 1:60–73.

Speidel H, Koch U, Black F, Kneiss J. Problems in interaction between patients undergoing long-term hemodialysis and their partners. Psychotherapy and Psychosomatics 1979; 31:235–242.

Steidl JH, Finkelstein FO, Wexler JP, Feigenbaum H, Kitsen J, Kliger AS, Quinlan DM. Medical condition, adherence to treatment regimens, and family functioning. Archives of General Psychiatry 1980; 27:1025–1027.

Stewart RS. Psychiatric issues in renal dialysis and transplantation. Hospital and Community Psychiatry 1983; 34:623–627.

Vollmer Wm, Wahl PW, Blagg C. Survival with dialysis and transplantation in patients with end-stage renal disease. New England Journal of Medicine 1983; 308:1553–1580.

Weakland JH. ''Family somatics''—a neglected edge. Family Process 1977; 16:263–272.

Wheeler D. Teaching home dialysis for an 8-year-old-boy. American Journal of Nursing 1977; February:273–274.

Winkes AL. The promotion of adaptation to end-stage renal disease: implications for clients and their families. Nephrology Nursing 1983; January–February:17–19.

32

Spinal Injury: Impact and Implications for Family Medicine Research

JEFFREY R. STEINBAUER
University of Oklahoma

INTRODUCTION

The purpose of this chapter is threefold. First, the literature regarding adaptation to spinal cord injury will be reviewed. Second, the potential impact of family dynamics on outcome of spinal cord injury will be examined, utilizing observations from other research on family–disease interaction. Finally, questions for future research will be suggested. Two questions will be addressed before beginning the review: 1. Why study spinal cord injury in family medicine? 2. What is the syndrome of spinal cord injury?

Why Study Spinal Cord Injury in Family Medicine?

Spinal cord injury with resultant quadriplegia or paraplegia is a devastating but low-incidence injury that, at first glance, has little applicability to the pragmatic world of family medicine. In the strictest sense of its clinical applicability, spinal cord injury research would assume a position of low priority due mainly to the low prevalence of the syndrome. However, the adaptive responses of the patient and his or her family are similar to those described for other diseases. In a broader sense, spinal cord injury offers some unique opportunities for research on the relationship between patient, family, and disease or, as in this case, disability. Research on spinal cord injury is also important for what it can teach us about the effects of family dynamics on physical health. The importance of this relationship has profound implications in family medicine and is the basis of a new wave of family medicine research. Therefore, spinal cord injury is a topic worthy of clinical investigation by family practitioners.

What Is the Syndrome of Spinal Cord Injury?

Data regarding spinal cord injury have been gathered by regional spinal cord injury centers since the early 1970s. In a 1982 report from the Good Samaritan Hospital in Phoenix, Arizona (Young, Burns, Bowen, & McCutchen, 1982), the incidence of spinal cord injury was reported to be 52 cases per million. Many of these patients die early in the course of their disability from the spinal injury or associated injuries. The incidence of people surviving the initial injury and coming to rehabilitation is 32 per million. The prevalence in the United States is estimated to be 200,000. Some patients are cared for outside regional reporting centers, and the exact prevalence is therefore uncertain. Spinal cord injury affects males four times more commonly than females. It occurs in a young population, with the mean age being 29 years, and 80% of spinal cord injuries occur prior to age 40.

Fifty-five percent of spinal cord patients have a high school education or more at the time of their injury, and 50% are working at the time of their injury, whereas 21% are students and 11% unemployed. Marital status data revealed that 53% of spinally injured adults are single; 33% are married; and 14% are divorced, separated, or widowed. Racial distribution is also random, with the injury affecting different racial groups with equal frequency. Therefore, spinal cord injury affects primarily a young, otherwise healthy population of mostly male adults who, prior to their injury, have a history of productivity in work or education.

Damage to the spinal cord is largely irreversible. Therefore, some degree of neurologic impairment is unfortunately permanent for spinal cord-injured patients. The degree of impairment depends on the level at which the spinal cord is injured and the parts of the cord damaged. Patients may exhibit varying degrees of paralysis and spasticity as a result of damage to motor fibers. Anesthesia, dysesthesia, and pain syndromes may be the outcomes of sensory nerve involvement. Disruption of autonomic nervous fibers can result in sexual dysfunction, bladder and bowel incontinence, trouble with temperature regulation (dysthermia), erratic blood pressure control with extremes of low blood pressure (postural hypotension), and high blood pressure (autonomic dysreflexia) depending on the level and extent of injury.

Data from the Good Samaritan Hospital (Young *et al.*, 1982) found 15 common complications of spinal cord injury in the outpatient setting. In order of occurrence, these are: (1) urinary complications, (2) pressure sores, (3) spasms, (4) pain, (5) pulmonary complications, (6) neuroses, (7) burns, (8) heterotopic ossification, (9) dysreflexia, (10) curvature of the spine, (11) fractures, (12) obesity, (13) phlebitis, (14) anemia, and (15) septicemia. These complications, in many cases, are reduced by fastidious attention to self-care, which is taught in the rehabilitation setting.

Lists of neurologic effects and medical complications of spinal cord injury, though scientifically accurate, paint a sterile picture of life after spinal cord injury. To begin to appreciate how the medical problems translate into daily life-style, one must understand the concept of functional ability. Functional assessment is the cornerstone of rehabilitation, since rehabilitation is the process of maximizing independent function through restoration or adaptation. Functional assessment in spinal cord injury includes evaluation of activities of daily living, ambulation, elimination, and transfer skills. Activities of daily living (ADLs) include evaluation of the patient's ability to dress, groom, bathe, feed, cook, do housework; to operate devices such as light switches, door knobs, and telephones; or to drive a vehicle. Ambulation for spinal cord patients is usually via wheelchair, but there are great differences in patients' levels of skill, endurance, and mobility with a manual wheelchair. Some patients lack the strength to push a manual wheelchair and must use an electric wheelchair. Elimination refers to management of the bowel and bladder. Most spinal cord patients are taught to empty their bladders periodically by self-catheterization. Bowel management is done by reflex training and use of a suppository on a regular basis to stimulate bowel movements. Transfer skills refer to the patient's ability to move from the wheelchair to the car seat, bed, toilet, or bathtub. Patients vary in their abilities to perform all of these functional tasks. When a patient is not fully independent in self-care, responsibility for helping the patient frequently falls on family members.

From the functional perspective, spinal cord injury is a devastating disability. Healthy, independent, young adults are suddenly reverted to a stage of physiologic dependence similar to early childhood. Rehabilitation from this injury requires that patients learn new survival skills, new ways of dressing, bathing, eating, ambulating, and eliminating. The end result of spinal cord injury is that an otherwise healthy young adult, who is grappling with the life issues of an adult, suddenly finds himself transplanted into a life stage that requires his full attention to relearn basic survival techniques. This challenge constitutes an enormous adaptive task for the patient and his family. The goal of rehabilitation is to return the patient to the extent allowed by his neurologic injury.

The degree to which patients are successful at adjusting to this disability is extremely variable. It is not unusual to see two patients with the same neurologic deficit who are polar opposites with regard to outcome. One patient may live alone, drive, work, return to school, pursue friendships, engage in sexual relationships, and in every way manifest the outward signs of adjustment to the disability. Another patient, *with the same lesion* and therefore the same functional potential, may be totally *dependent* in self-care, reside in a nursing home, and be socially isolated. This striking contrast has prompted research aimed at understanding the forces that are at work in determining these outcomes. We know that purely medical, socioeconomic, or demographic data do not explain the different outcomes in spinal cord injury.

ADAPTATION FROM THE PERSPECTIVE OF THE INDIVIDUAL

Several authors, in an effort to explain differences in adjustment to spinal cord injury, have looked primarily at characteristics of the injured individual. Work from this perspective may be categorized into three broad areas: (1) stages of coping, (2) developmental task analysis, and (3) trait analysis. The first two are largely descriptive of the adaptation process, while the last one looks at predictors of outcome.

Work on the stages of coping originated from the writings of Kübler-Ross (1969). These concepts have been applied to spinal cord injury to explain the process of individual adaptation. The most commonly described stages for adaptation are: (1) shock and fear, (2) grief and mourning, (3) denial, (4) anger, and (5) acceptance and adjustment. Stage theory argues that patients pass through each stage on the way to final adjustment to the disability. Failure to complete a stage may result in failure to achieve final adjustment. Research has not supported a universal coping style in spinal cord injury (SCI). In fact, some authors have concluded that depression is not a universal experience of spinal cord patients and that absence of depression may, in fact, portend a better outcome for long-term adjustment (Cook, 1976). Caywood (1974) has argued against the stage theory citing his own experience in adapting to SCI. He outlines several tasks that face spinal cord patients, including: (1) resocialization, which includes putting friends at ease and dealing with uncomfortable situations; (2) frustration with difficult tasks, with rehabilitation staff, and the like; (3) physical fatigue in learning rehabilitation skills. He suggests that the rehabilitation team's expectation that patients will become depressed may result in some increase in that diagnosis, but that depression is not a universal experience for SCI patients. Still others have concluded that psychologic reactions are dependent on the premorbid personality type and not on the injury itself (Cook, 1976). Therefore, a universal progression of stages in adaptation to spinal cord injuries seems unlikely. Although there may be universal problems and frustrations that face spinal cord patients, the process of adjustment probably varies from person to person.

Another group of authors has described developmental tasks facing the young adult and applied these to the spinal cord patient trying to cope with disability (Glueckauf & Quittner, 1984). The major task of the young adult is to form mature interpersonal relationships, including vocational, social, and sexual relationships. The process of adaptation to spinal cord injury must address each of these areas. Other studies (Kleck, 1966; Kleck *et al.*, 1968) have shown differences in affect and length of social encounters when non-injured subjects interact with the disabled. These studies, which document a measurable change in social interactions, lend support to the contention that patients must cope with changes in social relationships as a part of the adjustment process in SCI. Other workers have described situations that are universally stressful for spinal cord patients, including accidental bowel movement, catheter leakage, and falling out of a wheelchair (Dunn, 1975). Problems in vocational areas have been extensively studied as well. Several studies have shown decreased ranges of vocational choices available to disabled patients (Bors, 1956; Brown, 1974; Frank, 1969). Other barriers to achieving vocational goals include transportation difficulties (Crewe, Athelstan, & Meadows, 1975; Dvonch, Kaplan, Grynbaum, & Rusk, 1965) and financial disincentives (Crew *et al.*, 1975). Sexual consequences of SCI include physiologic changes, such as the possibility of impotence and/or infertility, and changes in body image. Although developmental analysis gives us descriptions of difficulties encountered by spinal cord patients, it does not provide an explanation of why some patients adjust and others do not.

The third area of the literature examining adjustment to SCI from the individual perspective explains outcome on the basis of trait analysis. Kemp and Vash (1971) studied 50 spinal cord patients who had been injured for more than 5 years. They looked at 16 predictor variables, and categorized outcome in five groups based on measures of employment, income, a vocational activity, participation in organizations, place of residence, and responsibilities in the home. The most important predictors of outcome were: (1) the number and types of goals expressed; (2) the perceived greatest loss—that is, less successful people focused on lost movement of their limbs, whereas more successful people focused on the loss of activities; (3) a creative thinking style; and (4) the degree of interpersonal support perceived by the patient. Trieschmann (1980), in a lengthy review of the psychologic literature, found the following variables to be associated with good adjustment to SCI: (1) youth, (2) a good background of social adjustment, (3) interpersonal support, (4) financial security, (5) independence, (6) aggressiveness, and (7) creativity.

In a similar review, Cook (1976) examined data regarding outcome in SCI. His findings were that psychologic response to the injury was determined by premorbid personality and that there was no consistent personality type or universal coping mechanism in SCI patients. He also concluded that adjustment depended on resocialization. This suggests that adjustment is not a process purely internal to the individual, and that a quest for determinants of adjustment must be expanded to examine a broader scope. Research efforts aimed at describing a pattern that all patients follow in coping with SCI, or at describing a personality type consistent with spinal cord injury, ignore the fact that people with SCI cope with this problem the same way they cope with premorbid problems. Several of the studies presented above suggest that interpersonal support and resocialization are important parts of adjustment. That is, a part of adjustment to SCI will depend on forces external to the individual. Therefore, this chapter will also address the interaction between the family in SCI.

CHALLENGES TO FAMILIES OF PATIENTS WITH SPINAL CORD INJURY

A systems approach to understanding adjustment to SCI requires an understanding of how the injury effects the family. Spinal cord injury is a disability that has changed in the last

20 years. There have been changes in medical expectation, changes in functional expectation, and changing family demographics, all of which have had an impact on the outcome of the disability.

Prior to World War II, most patients did nor survive SCI. Many died within 2 years secondary to urinary tract infections or decubiti. With the advent of better nursing care, the development of antibiotics, and the emergence of organized rehabilitation centers, the life expectancy for spinal cord patients has increased. Minaire and co-workers (1983), in a 10-year follow-up of spinal cord patients, found that, after the first postinjury year, life expectancy for their sample was the same as that of the noninjured population. Although not all data support such a good long-term prognosis (Young *et al.*, 1982), survival following SCI has increased. Therefore, SCI has become a long-term disability, placing long-term demands on patients, families, and medical systems.

At the same time that medical outcome has changed, functional expectations have changed as well. Studies describing the long-term living arrangements of spinal patients are scarce, but a review of our patients and patients injured for more than 10 years reveals a change in the length and the quality of life that spinal cord-injured patients can expect to live. For example, prior to 1970 many spinal cord patients were institutionalized. Most were advised that their life span would be severely shortened; many were told they should not expect to marry, have a family, or return to productive employment. The expectation now is that most patients should return to the community and be independent in all living skills. At least 80% of our patients with at least a C6 or lower cervical injury do live in the community. Therefore, increasing life expectancy and changing functional expectations have loaded families with the responsibility for long-term care in many cases and confront the family with many challenges. Few other disease models have the potential for such long-term impact on the family.

While medical and functional expectations have been changing, family demographics are also changing. Ireys and Burr (1984), describe four major trends in American families that have had an effect on the family's resources in responding to SCI. First, children are moving away from their family of origin at an earlier age. Therefore, more injured young adults have already left home at the time of their injury. Second, there is a trend toward young adults marrying later in life. Therefore, chronically injured adults are more likely to be single. Third, there are growing numbers of one- and two-person households, with increased numbers of single adults living with one dependent. Therefore, single, injured adults may be more likely to have dependents who may or may not be able to help provide care. Fourth, married young adults have smaller families. Therefore, there will be fewer hands to help with the care of the disabled member. The overall effect of changing medical outcome, changing functional expectations, and changing family demographics is to increase the burden of responsibility placed on the family while decreasing the size of the family available to respond to those demands.

When a family member sustains a spinal cord injury, several predictable burdens will come to bear on the family. First is the financial burden. Medical expenses of the spinal cord patient are estimated to average at least $20,000 per year after the initial cost of acute care and,rehabilitation. This must be added to the loss of income caused by unemployment or underemployment. Families may need to respond by changing life-style or returning a previously unemployed member of the household to the work force.

Second, the physical dependency needs of the patient must be met. Depending on the functional ability of the individual patient, the patient may require help with weight shifting, bowel care, bladder catheterization, transfers, dressing, and even feeding. Obviously, these needs can place a great burden on the family member designated as the caretaker.

Third, the family must reallocate resources. This includes reallotment of living space within the home, changes in time commitments, and renegotiation of career options as the family begins to cope with caring for its injured member.

Fourth, roles within the family must be renegotiated. For example, siblings may be required to help with dependent care, wives may become family providers, and the injured member may become more dependent than has previously been the case. The family must also cope with the changing social support structure. Friendships likely will change during the phase of adjustment, and community reaction toward the family members may change as earlier described in reaction toward the patient.

Several studies have examined the responses of families with a chronically ill member. Grolnick (1971) and Bruhn (1977) both have written review articles on the effects of chronic illnesses on the family. They drew four conclusions:

1. Families act or re-act to chronic disease. There are feedback mechanisms in the family that respond to chronic disease and may perpetuate the disease state.
2. Some types of family interaction, especially rigidity within the family, result in poor health outcome in chronic illness.
3. Much adaptation is required by the family in response to chronic illness. Failure to change will usually result in breakdown of the family systems.
4. Role expectations offered by the family may affect the adjustment to chronic disease; that is, continuation of the disease may be dictated by family rules.

The assumption that these observations should also apply in a family with a spinally injured member is upheld by two case studies (Steinglass, Temple, Lisman, & Reiss, 1983). The first case was a 58-year-old, T12 paraplegic who died from physiologic suicide. The family interaction style in this case was one of overinvestment, with all activities being centered on the care of the patient. The time of the family members was prioritized to care for the patient; space reallocation in the home resulted in the patient monopolizing home space. Other warning signs of trouble included problems with the two sons: One began receiving bad grades at school, and the other, who was diabetic, began having trouble with control of his diabetes. A fatal depression in the patient was triggered 6 years after his injury, when his wife and one son took their first vacation. Prior to this time, the family appeared to do well and was felt to represent the model of adjustment. However, old methods of coping finally broke down many years after the injury, and in retrospect this family appears to have been quite rigid.

In the second case, a 52-year-old computer operator became quadriplegic. Preexisting coping patterns for the family were used, but these were not effective in helping them face the SCI. The family became organized around a single issue and developed what Steinglass and colleagues refer to as "developmental paralysis." This was also a very rigid family. The family was overattentive to the patient's needs and, in coping with the injury, continually invoked an old family rule. No member should become upset, especially the injured on. The patient was uncooperative with therapy and did not live up to her functional expectations. The end result was that, with family therapy, the patient was able to do better in rehabilitation and became less depressed. Families may be tempted to swap long-term development for short-term stability, but Steinglass and colleagues concluded that developmental tasks arise in families with a spinal cord-injured member that are long-term in nature and are not amenable to crisis-oriented problem solving. Family coping will follow preset rules, and more flexible families tend to do better by learning new coping methods, whereas more rigid families get stuck and begin to break down.

Some long-term effects of SCI on family dynamics have been described. Cleveland (1979) investigated changes in family dynamics wrought by SCI by studying 19 families of injured children at the beginning of rehabilitation and 6 months after release from the rehabilitation center. The following changes in family structure were described:

1. Tasks were reallocated within families. Some families occasionally brought in a surrogate mother, usually a female relative. At the 6-month follow-up, the only person in the family with increased tasks was the mother, who had begun to show role strain between mother and wife roles.
2. Affection structure changed within the family, with initial feelings of increased closeness followed by increased dyadic relationships at the 6-month follow-up.
3. Communications tended to be centered on the injured person, with the mother frequently taking the role of the interpreter. There was less communication between noninjured siblings and parents, and growing closeness between the mother and the injured person, with growing distance between the mother and father.
4. Power structure within the family changed over time. Initially, the mother and father in these families were equally powerful, but at the 6-month follow-up, there was a growing struggle between the father and the injured person for power within the family.
5. Initially, family unity was viewed as not being a problem. However, at the 6-month follow-up, "holding the family together" became more of a problem.
6. Siblings frequently turned to the community for the relief of tension and pressure, but the mother and father remained somewhat isolated.

This study concluded that spinal cord injury has a long-term impact on the structure of the family. A tantalizing question arises as a result of the report by Steinglass *et al.* (1983) from the study by Cleveland (1979): Does the family's ability to meet these challenges affect the ability of the individual to adjust to the disability?

THE EFFECT OF THE FAMILY ON ADJUSTMENT TO SPINAL CORD INJURY

There are few studies that specifically address the impact of family dynamics on outcome in SCI. However, the interrelationship between family and disease has been studied in other settings. These studies will be briefly reviewed and inferences made for outcome in spinal cord injury.

Several studies have looked at the impact of the family on adjustment to chronic renal disease. Reiss, Gonzalez, Wolin, Steinglass, and Kramer (1983) did a longitudinal prospective pilot study of patients with end-stage renal disease. The dependent variable in this study was medical complications, with the independent variable being family processes measured by a card-sort technique. A positive relationship was found between family flexibility and openness and the patient's freedom from serious complications. However, a surprising negative relationship existed between family coordination (a sense of being partners in task solving) and patient survival. Accomplishment variables were also negative predictors for survival. In effect, some patients may die so that the family may survive.

Steidl, Finkelstein, and Wexler (1979) did a prospective study of 21 adult dialysis patients using the Beavers-Timberlawn assessment of family function (see Chapter 5, this volume) and a medical assessment based on evaluations of three internists. This study showed good medical outcomes in families with (1) a strong parental coalition (instead of a parent–child coalition); (2) close family relationships, with individuality respected (midpoint on the cohesion scale); and (3) a warm, affectionate, humorous, and optimistic mood, as opposed to hostile, depressed, cynical, pessimistic, or hopeless outlooks in the family. The authors also found that compliance with treatment was not related to global family function but was related to specific characteristics of the family, including: (1) ability to negotiate and solve problems; (2) strong parental coalitions; (3) openness and respect for others' feelings; (4) leadership and control shared by spouses; and (5) an individual sense of responsibility for actions rather than avoidance of responsibility. They concluded that certain types of family interaction, relationships, and affective patterns predicted better medical outcome and adherence to medical regimens in adults with chronic renal disease.

Dimond (1979) studied 36 adult dialysis patients. Social support was measured on three axes, including family environment, level of spouse support, and presence of a confidant. Adaptation to the disease was measured in terms of the Behavioral Moral Scale and the Sickness Impact Profile. The results of the study indicted that some relationship between medical outcome and specific social support did exist. Greater expressiveness, the presence of a confidant, and higher morale were associated with fewer medical problems. As one might expect, greater changes in social functioning were associated with more medical problems.

Minuchin *et al.* (1975) wrote about psychosomatic illnesses in children. He argued that the child is not viewed as a "passive reactor" to noxious stimuli. Certain types of family organization, especially enmeshment, overprotectiveness, rigidity, and lack of conflict resolution, are closely related to psychosomatic symptoms. An important conclusion from this study is that in some cases poor outcome for the patient may protect the family.

These studies all illustrate that certain patterns of family interaction have measurable effects on the patient's health in chronic disease. They also suggest that in some cases the patient's well-being or health may be sacrificed in order to save the family. Applying these principles to SCI, we can speculate that poor adjustment and adaptation to SCI may serve to stabilize the family.

There is a smaller body of research regarding the effect of family on rehabilitation from disability. A number of studies have suggested that social support is an important predictor of adjustment to disability (Cook, 1976; Davidson, Bowden, & Feller, 1981; Hyman, 1972).

Litman (1966), in an early study of rehabilitation patients, proposed that family "solidarity" could enhance outcome. He also hypothesized that therapeutic performance could be heightened by a positive supportive relationship, and that performance would be maximized if the patient reenters a supportive family constellation. (The study looked at 100 orthopedically disabled patients, including paraplegics, quadriplegics, and patients with myelitis and peripheral neuropathies.) These patients were evaluated only in the rehabilitation setting. Patient cooperation and motivation were rated by the rehabilitation staff, and family solidarity was rated by the Jansen-Hill scale. The study found that the family plays an indirect role in supporting convalescence, but family solidarity did not affect rehabilitation outcome or performance measurably. However, 75% of the patients in the Litman study reported that the family was the main source of support and encouragement.

One of the problems with the Litman study may have been that it used a rather narrow definition of outcome, defining "outcome" as compliance with rehabilitation schedules. Other authors have identified aggressiveness and creative thinking as positive predictors of good adjustment, although these two qualifications may not result in good compliance in the rehabilitation setting. We must also question whether high degrees of family "solidarity'' would be equal to high degrees of rigidity and cohesiveness, the two terms currently used to describe family interactions. If a family with high solidarity is the same as a highly rigid and cohesive family, the negative outcome in this study may actually support the findings of Reiss and co-workers (1983) and Steidl *et al.* (1979).

Despite the questions raised by Litman (1966), there seems to be ample support for the contention that family dynamics and interaction patterns do affect the health of chronically ill members. We speculate that this effect holds true in cases of the chronically disabled as well.

CONCLUSIONS

In light of the data presented, the following conclusions may be drawn:

1. Good outcome in chronic illness is associated with certain family patterns (e.g., coalition between parents, close but not enmeshed relationships, and a warm and affectionate family mood).
2. Rigidity in families leads to poorer outcome in chronic disease. This trait is associated with increased chronicity in psychosomatic illness.
3. ''Bad'' family types may do better in adjusting to chronic disability. Our notions of ''normal'' and ''abnormal'' with regard to family dynamics may need redefinition, at least in the area of chronic disease.
4. Families respond to predictable stresses during the course of adapting to SCI. The success with which they respond to these stresses may affect the outcome for the injured member. However, coping mechanisms are premorbidly learned for both the patient and the family. The family thus faces new challenges with old adaptive tools.
5. Family coping mechanisms in some chronic illness models may work because the patient either gets better or dies. In SCI, however, long-term disability may heighten the impression that families ''freeze''—that is, that they continue to use the same short-term coping mechanisms for what is in fact a very long-term problem. Our interventions, therefore, need to be directed toward long-term follow-up in the care of SCI patients and their families. The problems encountered by families of spinal cord patients, at least in some reports, have occurred many years after the injury.
6. Continued dependency by some patients with chronic illness may, in some cases, meet a family's need. In similar fashion, continued disability and poor adjustment to SCI may serve a function in some family systems to help defuse conflict and maintain a family stability. A pattern of poor adjustment for a spinal cord patient may not be totally understood by assessing level of injury, personality traits, or individual coping mechanism. In general, in cases of chronic disability, of issues of social support from the family may be better predictors of outcome than individual psychologic measures.

A number of research questions are stimulated by these observations. Additional descriptive research regarding adaptive mechanisms in families of patients with SCI will help delineate how families respond to this stress. It may become possible to determine what family types are associated with positive long-term adjustment by the spinal cord patient, and to design an intervention during rehabilitation to enhance those behaviors in the family.

Research in this area is complicated. Outcomes need to be measured at multiple levels—medical, functional, and psychosocial—for both the patient and the family. This requires collaborative research teams including medical personnel, rehabilitation personnel, and social scientists. Long-term follow-up seems especially important. An additional research problem is that SCI is a low-incidence injury and therefore, sample sizes will be small. Research designs must be appropriate for smaller sample sizes.

Much is yet to be learned about SCI in the family. Family models in SCI may be different than in other areas of family research because this is largely a population of young people who have a profound disability with a normal life span. Therefore, complicating factors, such as continued physiologic decline as a result of progression of disease, will be minimized. This is one intriguing aspect of using SCI as a model for the study of the interaction between family dynamics and medical illness.

SCI offers a unique opportunity for physicians and social scientists to collaborate in further understanding the interplay between family systems and health. Even though SCI represents a low-prevalence syndrome in the average family medical practice, other characteristics make this disability relevant to family medicine research.

References

Bors E. Challenge of quadriplegia: some personal observations in a series of 233 cases. Bulletin of Los Angeles Neurological Society 1956; 21:105–123.

Brown B, Chanin I. Patterns of education and employment: rehabilitants from severe spinal cord injury. Rehabilitation Research Reports FY 1972–3; Number 30. Sacramento, Calif.: Department of Rehabilitation, June 1, 1974.

Bruhn J. Effects of chronic illness on the family. Journal of Family Practice 1977;4:1057–1060.

Caywood T. A quadriplegic young man looks at treatment. Journal of Rehabilitation 1974; 40:22–25.

Cleveland M. Family adaptation to the traumatic spinal cord injury of a son or daughter. Social Work in Health Care 1979; 4:459–471.

Cook DW. Psychological aspects of spinal cord injury. Rehabilitation Counseling Bulletin 1976; 19:535–543.

Crewe NM, Athelstan GT, Meadows GK. Vocational diagnosis through assessment of functional limitations. Archives of Physical Medicine and Rehabilitation 1975; 56:513–516.

Davidson T, Bowden ML, Feller I. Social support and post burn adjustment. Archives of Physical Medicine and Rehabilitation 1981; 62:274–278.

Dimond M. Social support and adaptation to chronic illness: the case of maintenance hemodialysis. Research in Nursing Health 1979;2:101–108.

Dunn ME. Psychological intervention in a spinal cord injury center: an introduction. Rehabilitation Psychology 1975; 22:165–178.

Dvonch P, Kaplan LI, Grynbaum BB, Rusk HA. Vocational findings in postdisability employment of patients with spinal cord dysfunction. Archives of Physical Medicine and Rehabilitation 1965; 46:761–766.

Frank DS. The multitroubled jobseeker: the case of the jobless worker with a convulsive disorder. Washington, D.C.: Three Cities Employment, Training, Counseling Program and the Epilepsy Foundation of America, 1969.

Glueckauf R, Quittner A. Facing disability as a young adult: psychological issues and approaches. In: Eisenberg M, Sutkin L, Jansen M, eds. Chronic illness and disability through the lifespan. New York: Springer, 1984:167–183.

Grolnick L. A family perspective of psychosomatic factors in illness: a review of the literature. Family Process 1971; 11:457–486.

Hyman M. Social isolation and performance in rehabilitation. Journal of Chronic Disease 1972; 25:85–97.

Ireys HT, Burr CK. Apart and a part: family issues for young adults with chronic illness and disability. In: Eisenberg M, Sutkin L, Jansen M, eds. Chronic illness and disability through the lifespan. New York: Springer, 1984:184–206.

Kemp B, Vash C. Productivity after injury in a sample of spinal cord injured persons: a pilot study. Journal of Chronic Disease 1971; 24:259–275.

Kleck R. Emotional arousal in interactions with stigmatized persons. Psychological Reports 1966; 19:1226.

Kleck R, Buck PL, Goller WL, London RS, Pfeiffer JR, Vukcevic DP. Effect of stigmatizing conditions on the use of personal space. Psycological Reports 1968; 23:111–118.

Kübler-Ross E. On death and dying. New York: Macmillan, 1969.

Litman T. The family and physical rehabilitation. Journal of Chronic Disease 1966; 19:211–217.

Minaire P, Demolin P, Bourret J, Girard R, Berard E, Deidier C, Eyssette M, Biron A. Life expectancy following spinal cord injury: a ten-years survey in the Rhone-Alpes Region, France 1969–1980. Paraplegia 1983; 21(1):11–15.

Minuchin S, Baker L, Rosman B, Liebman R, Milman L, Todd T. A conceptual model of psychosomatic illness in children. Family Organization Psychiatry 1975; 32:1031–1038.

Reiss D, Gonzalez S, Wolin S, Steinglass P, Kramer H. Family process, chronic illness and death. Presented at the annual meeting of the American Psychiatric Association, May 1983.

Steidl J, Finkelstein F, Wexler J. Medical condition, adherence to treatment regimens and family functioning. Archives of General Psychiatry 1979; 37:1025–1027.

Steinglass P, Temple S. Lisman S, Reiss D. Coping with spinal cord injury: the family perspective. Unpublished manuscript, 1982.

Trieschmann R. Spinal cord injuries: psychological, social and vocational adjustment. New York: Pergamon Press, 1980.

Young J, Burns P, Bowen AM, McCutchen R. Spinal cord injury statistics: experience of the regional spinal cord injury systems. Phoenix, Ariz.: Good Samaritan Medical Center, 1982.

33

Family Contexts of Self-Esteem and Illness Adjustment in Diabetic and Acutely Ill Children

STUART T. HAUSER
ALAN M. JACOBSON
Joslin Diabetes Center and Harvard Medical School, Boston

DONALD WERTLIEB
Institute for Health Research and Tufts University, Boston

JOSEPH I. WOLFSDORF
RAYMONDE D. HERSKOWITZ
Joslin Diabetes Center and Harvard Medical School, Boston

MARIE ANNE VIEYRA
University of Connecticut

JENNIFER ORLEANS
University of Kansas

OVERVIEW

Many forces influence a child's initial adjustment to an unexpected chronic illness such as diabetes. Among the most powerful are those within his or her family. Clinical observations and empirical studies highlight the importance of the family environment in the clinical course of child and adolescent diabetic patients (Anderson & Auslander, 1980; Anderson, Miller, Auslander, & Santiago, 1981; Hanson & Henggeler, 1984; Koski, Ahlas, & Kumento, 1976; Marrero, Lau, Goldern, Kershnar, & Myers, 1982; Minuchin *et al.*, 1975; Shouval, Ber, & Galatzer 1982; Wishner & O'Brien, 1978). Building upon many of these contributions, we have emphasized the numerous considerations that apply when thinking about the interplay of the family and the diabetic child (Hauser, Jacobson, Wertlieb, Brink, & Wentworth, 1985; Hauser & Solomon, 1985). Evidence suggests that family factors are influential in several different ways. For instance, there is the role of the family in the short-term guidance of the newly diagnosed diabetic child. From a longer term perspective, the family is a major context for the early and continuing socialization of the chronically ill child or adolescent.

Besides the influences that go from family to child, it is essential to recognize that the presence of a chronically ill child in the family can exert important effects on the family's overall atmosphere and values as well as on the daily experience of individual family members. One obvious impact of the illness on the family is through the greater attention required to care for the newly diagnosed child, shifting attention from both younger and older siblings, as well as within the marital pair. In more tangible terms, there must be changes in (and possibly conflicts over) previously established mealtime routines, as well as emphases on new matters such as injections and monitoring of body fluids, urine, or blood. In short, the family unit experiences both disruptions of ongoing patterns and the advent of new and often highly charged issues.

In light of the enormous complexity of the family environment, it is not possible simply to study "the family" of the diabetic child. One must specifically choose, on conceptual and clinical grounds, those family dimensions likely to be most relevant to the functioning of the diabetic child or adolescent. In addition, it is important to select carefully the individual child's characteristics that are thought to be theoretically and clinically linked to family dimensions. This is the strategy that guides our Health and Illness longitudinal project (Hauser *et al.*, 1985) and underlies the work that is presented in this chapter, the second in a series of reports on family aspects of child and adolescent diabetes.

In a previous report (Hauser *et al.*, 1985), we presented results from preliminary analyses of diabetic child and adolescent patients revealing that family emphases on independence, participation in social and recreational activities, and organization were strongly associated with the young patients' perceived competence. These relationships were *not* found in a comparison group of acutely ill adolescents. Fewer, and different, family dimensions were linked with the comparison patients' perceived competence. A second set of analyses described numerous and substantial links between family orientations and aspects of adjustment to diabetes. This new work represents an extension of our probes into family aspects of the diabetic child's development and adjustment. We have now extended this investigation in several ways:

1. The sample of families and children analyzed in considerably larger than the one originally studied.
2. We follow parent perspectives separately from those of the child.
3. We include additional individual indices of self-esteem, thereby broadening our assessment of this aspect of the child's personality.
4. We perform new analyses (multiple regression) designed to identify the *special contribution* of family orientation to individual patient characteristics.

The realm of family dimensions that we explore here are those of family values and assumptions, characterized as "orientations" by Moos (1974) or as "constructs" by Reiss (1982). On the basis of clinical and personal observations, we know that these factors are salient ones in families, influencing such patterns as members' response to new stressors and children's orientations to themselves and the surrounding world. These orientations do not simply flow from family to passive child. Rather, family values and emphases may be modified by new events (such as the advent of diabetes in a child). Our general hypothesis is that family orientations and assumptions will play a key role in the child's psychologic and medical functioning. A second hypothesis is that the diabetic child has powerful impacts on family orientations, values, and ways of coping with new strains. With the exception of the contributions of Anderson and Auslander (1980) and of Minuchin (Minuchin *et al.*, 1975; Minuchin, Rosman, & Baker, 1978), studies of diabetic families have most often assumed that the influences flow from the family to the child. The most extreme expression of this reasoning is that the child is in some way a "victim" of the family, or a "scapegoat." Our theoretic and empirical strategy has been to expect that the form of influence (e. g., unidirectional or bidirectional) will vary with the particular variables under scrutiny. Dimensions such as fundamental family values regarding cohesiveness or conflict are likely to be powerful determinants of a child's or adolescent's personality characteristics, as well as of how the child adjusts to a new illness. Other values, less deeply held by the family, may be modified or questioned when a powerful event, such as a chronic illness, enters the family life. (To be sure, other family dimensions—coping strategies, actual interactions—are involved with how a child or a family responds to a new and important illness. These realms are followed in our observations, and will be reported in subsequent papers.)

In this chapter, then, we present findings referring to these orientations, assumptions, and values. We explore differences between the families of diabetic and acutely ill children in terms of the strength of these factors. In addition, a second set of questions focuses on relationships between family perceptions and child functioning. Since these these analyses are cross-sectional, there is no empirical way to disentangle direction of influence. Given the variables under examination, our assumption guiding the analyses is that the influences flow *from* family to child. As already suggested, besides expecting "traitlike" family constructs, there are probably ones that are more responsive to new forces (such as a chronic illness) impinging upon the family. These reactive changes can be shaped by (1) the nature of the event, (2) the developmental levels of individual family members, (3) the developmental level of the family, and (4) the family's appraisal of the event and ways of coping with it. An important purpose of our overall longitudinal project is to discern those family dimensions that function as significant determinants of the individual child's adjustment to his or her diabetes, and those family dimensions that are significantly changed by the presence of the illness.

METHODS

Research Design

The Health and Illness Project is a multimethod prospective study of newly diagnosed preadolescent and early adolescent diabetes patients and their families. A second sample, used as a comparison group, consists of patients with a newly diagnosed acute illness, which is neither trivial nor life-threatening. This second sample, matched for age, sex, and socioeconomic status, also includes the families of the acutely ill children. All available patients are invited to participate in the study. For the diabetic sample, this means that all newly diagnosed insulin-dependent diabetics admitted to the Joslin Diabetes Center are approached. In return for joining the study, they receive free outpatient care and routine laboratory testing over a 4-year period. Similarly, all eligible, acutely ill patients from a local health maintenance organization (HMO) are approached immediately after their illness has subsided. This group of patients and families are given $40 each year of their participation. This different mode of payment for participation was chosen because free medical care for the acutely ill patients over time would not have the same meaning or inducement as for the chronically ill patient. Nonetheless, we wished to indicate, both materially and symbolically, our appreciation for the time and effort required by the study.

The adolescent subjects and their parents respond to a range of measures designed to tap individual variables (psychosocial and medical) and conceptually relevant family processes. The following analyses deal with assessments of self-esteem, diabetes adjustment, and family orientations (assumptions and values).

Table 33-1. Demographic Characteristics

	Diabetes	Acute illness
Age (S.D.)[a]	12.82 (1.91)	12.83 (1.89)
Sex		
Male	24	27
Female	28	15
Family type[b]		
Two-parent	41	34
One-parent	8	5
Socioeconomic status[c]		
Upper-middle and middle	26	26
Lower-middle	12	13
Working and lower class	12	3

[a] Average age (S.D. in parentheses).

[b] Five families could not be classified here because of more unusual arrangements (e.g., mother with other adult).

[c] SES is based on Hollingshead's (1957) two-factor indexes; missing data on two families did not permit their classification here.

Sample

Ninety-four patients and their families are investigated in the following analyses. The sample includes preadolescent and early adolescent boys and girls who have either newly diagnosed insulin-dependent diabetes ($n = 52$) or are acutely ill ($n = 42$). Both sets of families were primarily upper-middle and middle class. They did not differ significantly either for this dimension or in terms of one- versus two-parent families. The average age for the diabetic patients was 12.82 years, and the average age for the acutely ill patients was 12.83 years. In terms of sex, there were 24 boys and 28 girls in the diabetic sample, and 27 boys and 15 girls in the acutely ill group. There were no significant differences between the two samples for these demographic characteristics. Table 33-1 presents the demographic properties of the sample in more detail.

Measures

THE FAMILY ENVIRONMENT SCALE

The Family Environment Scale (FES) is an instrument that is used to assess family members' perceptions of basic orientations and values along 10 salient dimensions (Billings & Moos, 1982; Moos, 1974; Moos & Moos, 1976, 1983). The scale focuses on description of such orientations as those involving personal growth within the family, interpersonal relationships among family members, and the basic structure or "system" of the family. The FES has been shown to significantly differentiate various groups of families, such as those of psychiatrically disturbed versus matched nonpatient families (Moos & Moos, 1976, 1983). In addition, a new index has been formed from several conceptually relevant scales of the instrument, namely the Family Relationships Index (FRI) (Barerra, Sandler, & Ramsey 1981; Holohan & Moos, 1981). Finally, the instrument has been used to differentiate between families of adolescents functioning at varying levels of psychosocial competence or maturity (Bell & Bell, 1982).

Recently, investigators of diabetic families have applied this instrument in their studies. Among the investigations using the FES are those reported by Anderson and colleagues (1981); Schafer, Glasgow, McCaul, and Dreher (1983); and Shouval and colleagues (1982). The first two studies found specific patterns of perceived family environment present for diabetic adolescents in good metabolic control and adherent to the treatment regimen. For instance, parents of diabetics in this group described their families as placing a high value on independence and expressiveness, more so than did parents of poorly controlled diabetic adolescents. Comparisons of adolescent perceptions also revealed different family patterns. Patients whose metabolic control was rated as "good" described their families as being high in cohesion and low in conflict. The third study, that by Schafer and colleagues (1983), found meager to no relationship between perceived family environment and the child's reported adherence to treatment regimen. Until now, investigations of the family environment of diabetic children have not looked into how these family environments differ from those of nondiabetic children; nor have they looked into *relationships* between these family factors and the child's self-reported or observed psychologic functioning.

The Family Environment Scale consists of 90 true–false items that are divided into 10 subscales. As described above, each of these subscales measures emphases on specific aspects of the family environment (Moos, 1974). These specific aspects can be grouped in terms of three conceptual domains. The *personal development* or personal growth dimensions are assessed by five scales: (1) independence, (2) achievement, (3) intellectual–cultural orientation, (4) activity–recreational orientation, and (5) moral–religious orientation.

The cohesiveness, expressiveness, and conflict subscales assess *relationship* dimensions in families. These subscales measure the extent to which family members feel that they "belong to" and are "proud of" their family, the extent of open expression within the family, and the degree to which conflict expression is a family characteristic. As noted above, these three scales have been shown to have strong degrees of coherence and, when the direction of the conflict scale is reversed, the reflect an index of family relationships. The last two subscales refer to organization and control. They focus on members perceptions of the family *system*, its structure or organization, and the degree of control that is usually perceived as being exerted by members on one another.

The 10 subscales show adequate internal consistency and favorable test–retest reliability, and have average subscale intercorrelations of approximately .20 (Moos, 1974). These intercorrelations are important because they reveal that the scales are measuring distinct though somewhat related facets of the family's social environment.

All parents and adolescent patients respond to the 90 FES items each year. Two scores are used in the following analyses: (1) a score consisting of both parents' view of the family, or the view of an individual parent if only he or she responded to the scale, and (2) a second score consisting of the child's or adolescent's perceptions of the family's environment. In the following analyses, we report separate results for differences between the diabetic and acutely ill families, looking at (1) parental perceptions and (2) child perceptions. The remaining analyses, those exploring correlations between family environment and child functioning, use *only* parental perceptions of the family so as to avoid any confounding of the child's perception of his family and his or her self-perception. Contrasts of one-and two-parent reports on the FES revealed that of the 13 comparisons made, only one showed a significant difference. The one showing a significant difference was that for "moral" orientations, which reveal that the one-parent responders had higher values for this particular orientation. In light of the high degree of similarity between the one-and two-parent results, these scores are pooled in all of the analyses for parent scores.

SELF-ESTEEM

We assessed self-esteem through two different instruments: the Perceived Competence Scale (PCS) (Harter, 1982) and the Self-Esteem Inventory (SEI) (Coopersmith, 1967). The PCS assesses competence perceptions in three domains: cognitive (school competence), social (peer-related), and physical (skills at sports and outdoor games). A fourth subscale refers to the patient's view of his or her self-worth as a person over and above specific competence judgments. Factor-analytic studies of 341 students have shown that scale items have moderate to high loadings on designated factors and do not load on other factors. Moreover, this factor pattern has been replicated in five additional samples (Harter, 1982).

The Perceived Competence Scale is composed of 28 items. The formatting of this instrument is specially designed to offset the tendency for socially desirable responses. In fact, Harter notes that the instrument has shown extremely low correlation with children's social desirability scores.

The second assessment of self-esteem was based on the procedure development by Coopersmith (1960, 1964, 1967; Self-Esteem Institute, 1974). This is a 50-term questionnaire in which subjects are asked to judge whether a statement is "like me" or "unlike me." Items include "I'm pretty sure of myself" and "I'm proud of my schoolwork." The instrument has four conceptually derived subscales: general, school, social, and home. Although Coopersmith did not fully explore dimensions inherent in the SEI and accepted the conceptually derived subscales, work by Kokenes (1974, 1978) has suggested that there are multiple dimensions of self-esteem found in the SEI that, in part, reflect the subscales developed by Coopersmith.

In addition to the subscales, there is an eight-item scale that consists of improbable but personally and socially desirable statements such as "I am never unhappy" and "I like everyone I know." This scale detects response patterns in which the subject minimizes problems and seeks social approval. Assessment of both split-half and retest reliability has indicated acceptable reliability levels (Coopersmith, 1967). All diabetic and acutely ill patients respond to the PCS and SEI each year.

Our strategy in the following analyses of self-esteem and family environment has been to draw upon the strengths of both instruments. Consequently, we rely on the PCS for general and several domain-specific scales (general, social, cognitive, physical, and total). An additional domain is tapped by our other instrument, namely "home self-esteem." The results for this dimension are included in the following analyses as well. Support for using either of these assessment procedures (but *not* both), with the exception of home self-esteem, comes from our own correlation analyses of 128 subjects responding to both instruments. Other than the "physical" and "home" scales, the scales for the two instruments correlated at high levels (e.g., .744 for total, .679 for general, .698 for social). In light of our previous experience with the Perceived Competence Scale (Hauser *et al.*, 1985) and the persuasive arguments for its psychometric strengths (Harter, 1982; Hauser *et al.*, 1985), we have opted to rely primarily on the results of this instrument. In future ventures, we plan to form composite scores (Epstein, 1983) from both instruments and thereby maximize our assessment of self-esteem through reliance on multiple indicators. For each illness group, we will investigate correlations between self-esteem indices and family orientations, and the extent that family orientations can predict self-esteem, after controlling for key demographic variables.

THE DIABETIC ADJUSTMENT SCALE

The Diabetic Adjustment Scale (DAS) was originally devised to assess aspects of diabetic adolescent girls' attitudes toward their diabetes (Sullivan, 1979a, 1979b). The scale was developed as a means of empirically describing individuals' views of juvenile diabetes, its treatment, and its influence on their daily functioning. The DAS subscales tap adolescents' attitudes toward diabetes and body functioning, peer adjustment, school adjustment, dependence–independence issues, and family relationships. A pool of items was originally gathered from interviews with adolescents, their parents, their clinicians, and other family members. The interviews focused on ways in which diabetes affects the lives of people who have insulin-dependent diabetes. Additional items were then drawn from literature dealing with adolescent development and psychosocial aspects of diabetes. The current revised version consists of 68 items that were assembled using a team of clinicians who judged the items as best reflecting how diabetes influences life-styles. Eighteen of these items are informational ones that are not used in the adjustment scoring.

The five adjustment areas are based on factor analyses of items that the patient responded to in terms of extent of agreement. Specific items indexing these adjustment areas include: "I think I have too many dents and bumps on my body" (attitudes toward diabetes and bodily functioning); "I tell my friends at home that I have diabetes" (peer adjustment); I think I would enjoy school more if I didn't have diabetes" (school adjustment); "I control my diabetes myself" (dependence–independence issues); and "My brothers and sisters tease me about having diabetes" (family relationships).

Sullivan (1979a, 1979b) reports clinically meaningful intercorrelations among the adjustment areas (e.g., attitudes toward diabetes and dependence–independence issues). In addition, a second study of 105 girls revealed significant correlations with measures of self-esteem (Rosenberg, 1965) and depression (Beck, 1967). Both sets of findings lend support to the validity of the DAS.

All diabetic patients respond to the DAS annually. In this chapter, we present the correlations between aspects of diabetes adjustment and family environment indices, as well as the extent to which family environment can predict diabetes adjustment when key demographic variables have been taken into account. Finally, and most stringently, we investigate how well family orientations can predict diabetes adjustment *after* the child's self-esteem has been taken into account.

RESULTS

Differences between Illness Groups in Family Perceptions

In terms of *parents' views* of the family, ANCOVA technique (controlling for social class) revealed that the diabetic families placed greater emphases on *achievement* ($F = 3.77$; $p < .06$) and *moral* orientation ($F = 6.50$; $p < .01$). Both scales refer to "personal growth" dimensions. In addition, the parents describe greater family emphases on *organization* ($F = 3.67$; $p < .06$), *control* ($F = 4.08$; $p < .05$), and the overall index of *system maintenance* ($F = 5.83$; $p < .05$). These clinical group factors did not interact with patient age, sex, or family type (one- or two-parent), which were also included in the ANCOVA procedures. Figure 33-1 presents these findings.

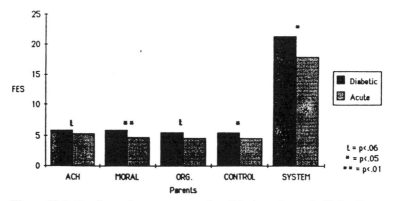

Figure 33-1. Family environment scores for diabetic and acutely ill families.

Children's Perceptions

Using the same ANCOVA design as for the parent comparisons, a second contrast involved the children's views of their families. In contrast to the *parent* findings, the diabetic adolescents differed in terms of only *two* aspects of family environment: *organization* ($F = 4.39$; $p < .05$) and *activity* ($F = 3.52$; $p < .06$). The diabetic children described more intense family emphases on both orientations. Figure 33-2 presents these findings for the children's views of their families.

Contributions of Family Orientations to Child and Adolescent Self-Esteem

These analyses consider the question of how family orientations *differentially* influence the self-esteem of diabetic and acutely ill children. To avoid confounding children's views of family with their self-perceptions, these analyses are based on *parents'* family constructs.

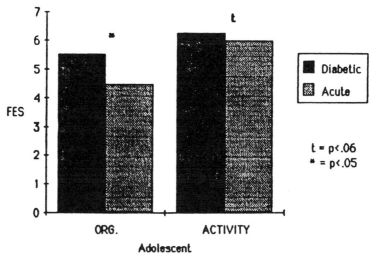

Figure 33-2. Family environment scores for diabetic and acutely ill adolescents.

Table 33-2. Correlations between Family Environment Orientations and Self-Esteem: Diabetic and Acutely Ill Children

Self-esteem aspects	Family environment orientation												
	Cohesion	Expressions	Conflict	Independence	Achievement	Intellectual	Activity	Morality	Organization	Control	Family relations index	Growth index	Systems index
Diabetic patients and their families													
Cognitive	.027	−.136	.115	−.042	.143	.123	.035	−.044	.226*	−.144	.005	.049	.070
Social	−.023	−.072	−.044	.311**	.136	−.087	−.066	−.124	−.050	−.131	−.059	−.022	−.107
Home	.171	.008	.228*	.108	−.108	.257*	.236*	.091	.103	−.121	.173	.239*	.001
Physical	.105	.070	.108	.035	.033	—	.165	.073	.056	.051	.120	.009	.066
General	.061	.024	.179'	.074	.264*	.071	.253*	.137	.331***	.024	.113	.258*	.235*
Total	.059	−.052	.129	.134	.210'	.032	.102	.007	.206'	−.083	.059	.109	.091
Acutely ill patients and their families													
Cognitive	.035	.197	−.028	.025	.169	.192	−.081	.084	−.176	−.231'	.081	.177	.245'
Social	−.072	−.204'	.034	−.081	.395***	−.300*	−.065	.213'	−.077	.206'	−.096	.072	.070
Home	.273*	.262*	.145	−.080	.245'	.163	.096	.190	−.038	−.089	.288*	.273*	−.076
Physical	.044	−.223'	.106	.022	.341*	−.220'	−.278*	−.089	−.060	−.092	−.023	−.140	.015
General	.090	.195	.080	.149	.229	−.004	−.057	.182	−.148	−.074	.152	.216'	−.137
Total	.025	−.049	.065	.027	.372***	−.137	.163	.113	−.136	.025	.020	.078	−.072

Note: All self-esteem scores are based on the Perceived Competence Scale (Harter, 1982), except for "home self-esteem," drawn from the Self-Esteem Inventory (Coopersmith, 1967).

'$p < .10$.
* $p < .05$.
** $p < .01$.
*** $p < .005$.

We proceeded through two stages. First, separate correlation matrices were generated for each illness group. Inspection of these correlations reveals a pattern emphasizing *organization* and selected growth dimensions as salient for the diabetic children. In contrast, the nondiabetic families show strong links between relationship and multiple growth dimensions (especially *achievement*) with self-esteem. Table 33-2 presents the matrices of Pearson correlations between family environment and self-esteem for each illness group.

At the next stage of analysis, we investigated these significant correlations more rigorously. Since it is possible that the child's social class, age, or sex may shape his or her self-esteem, we analyzed the extent to which the significant family–self-esteem linkage in each sample continued to be significant *after* these key demographic variables were accounted for by entering them as earlier terms in hierarchic multiple regressions. *Organization* and *independence* orientations continued to predict self-esteem for the diabetic children. On the other hand, only *achievement* orientations remained as a significant predictor for the acutely ill group. Table 33-3 summarizes these predictive results.

Contribution of Family Orientations/Values to Diabetic Adjustment

This set of analyses logically was restricted to the diabetic children and their families. We first examined the simple correlations between family environment dimensions and aspects of diabetes adjustment. As can be seen from Table 33-4, there were many significant correlations between family dimensions and diabetic adjustment.

Again, we proceeded to identify the *unique* contribution of family orientations to aspects of the child's diabetic adjustment. The relevant question here was: What are the influences of family environment dimensions, after accounting for demographic characteristics such as social class, age, and sex? Numerous family perceptions explained significant proportions of diabetes adjustment variance, even after controlling for these other dimensions. Particularily prominent were *cohesion* and *intellectual/cultural* orientation dimen-

Table 33-3. Contributions of Family Environment Orientations to Self-Esteem: Hierarchic Regression Analyses

	R^2 with age	R^2 with SES	R^2 with sex	R^2 with FES[a]	Increment[b] in R^2	β[c]	r[d]
			Diabetic families				
General esteem				Organization			
	.001	.004	.004	.106	.102*	.329	.331
Social competence				Independence			
	.000	.000	.001	.133	.132*	.361	.311
			Acutely ill families				
Social competence				Achievement			
	.008	.020	.020	.182	.162*	.407	.395

[a]The specific orientation scale or index is given below.

[b]Significance of *change* is R^2 when FES is entered (*F*-test).

[c]β is for FES variable following age, sex, and social class.

[d]r is the Pearson correlation between the given diabetes adjustment scale and family orientation.

*$p \leq .05$.

Table 33-4. Correlations between Family Environment Orientations and Diabetic Adjustment

Diabetes adjustment scale	Family environment orientation												
	Cohesion	Expressions	Conflict	Independence	Achievement	Intellectual	Activity	Morality	Organization	Control	Family relations index	Growth index	Systems index
Dependence–independence	.203'	.101	.174	.195	.191'	.245*	.201'	.192'	.247*	-.016	.202'	.349***	.170
School	.294	.160	.155	.095	.091	.330**	.303*	.264*	.407***	.070	.257*	.404****	.307*
Family relations	.364***	.215'	.140	.213'	.019	.345***	.322**	.023	.139	-.057	.303*	.346***	.058
Peer	.338**	.246*	.284*	.116	-.016	.266*	.223'	.218	.307*	-.066	.367****	.308*	.162
Attitude towards diabetes	.221'	.020	.196	-.023	-.130	.312**	.184'	.104	.182	-.098	.186	.212'	.062
Overall	.349***	.173	.238*	.135	.020	.376****	.302*	.192	.316**	-.050	.321**	.392****	.178

'$p < .10$.
*$p < .05$.
**$p < .01$.
***$p < .007$.
****$p < .004$.

sions, explaining as much as 12% of the variance for diabetes adjustment. Table 33-5 summarizes these results.

The most stringent test of the family environment's significance is carried out in the next set of analyses. We investigated how important these family factors were *in addition to* the child's self-esteem. In other words, how would our prediction of a child's adjustment to diabetes be strengthened by knowledge of aspects of his or her family environment *after* we already knew the level of his or her self-esteem? For these analyses, the general self-esteem scale from Harter's Perceived Competence Scale (1982) was entered immediately prior to the given DAS variable. Family relationships (particularly *cohesion*) and numerous *growth* factors continue to explain significant amounts of diabetes adjustment. These results are presented in Table 33-6.

Table 33-5. Diabetes Adjustment: Relationships to Family Orientations; Hierarchic Regressions and Correlations

Diabetes adjustment scale	R^2 with age	R^2 with SES	R^2 with sex	R^2 with FES[a]	Increment[b] in R^2	β[c]	r[d]
				Cohesion			
Peer	.022	.087	.106	.183	.076*	.296	.340
Family relations	.000	.004	.021	.142	.121*	.373	.364
Overall	.000	.012	.061	.159	.098*	.335	.355
				Activities			
School	.046	.072	.092	.168	.076*	.289	.309
Family	.000	.004	.021	.116	.095*	.322	.322
Overall	.000	.012	.061	.131	.070'	.276	.302
Attention to				*Intellectual*			
diabetes	.016	.018	.044	.159	.115*	.420	.318
Family relations	.000	.044	.021	.133	.111*	.413	.344
Overall	.000	.012	.061	.162	.101*	.393	.377
				Moral			
School	.046	.072	.092	.186	.095*	.313	.278
				Organization			
Peer	.022	.087	.106	.165	.059'	.250	.312
Independence	.090	.095	.210	.261	.051'	.233	.306
School	.046	.072	.092	.220	.129**	.371	.388
Overall	.000	.012	.061	.137	.076'	.285	.325
				Family relations index			
Peer	.022	.087	.106	.183	.076'	.296	.340
Family relations	.000	.004	.021	.102	.080*	.307	.302
Overall	.000	.012	.061	.168	.107*	.368	.392
				Growth			
School	.046	.072	.092	.229	.138***	.418	.408
Family relations	.000	.004	.021	.126	.105*	.364	.345
Overall	.000	.012	.061	.168	.107*	.368	.392
				Systems maintenance			
School	.046	.072	.092	.158	.066'	.262	.283

[a] The specific orientation scale or index is given below.

[b] Significance of *change* is R^2 when FES is entered (*F*-test).

[c] β is for FES variable following age, sex, and social class.

[d] r is the Pearson correlation between the given diabetes adjustment scale and family orientation.

' $p \le .10$.

* $p \le .05$.

** $p \le .01$.

*** $p \le .005$.

Table 33-6. Relationship of Diabetes Adjustment to Family Environment, *after* Accounting for Self-Esteem: Hierarchic Multiple Regressions

Diabetes adjustment scale	R^2 with age	R^2 with SES	R^2 with sex	R^2 with general self-esteem[a]	R^2 with FES[b]	Increment[c] in R^2	β^d
					Cohesion		
Overall	.000	.010	.047	.342	.453	.087*	.318
Family relations	.003	.006	.013	.148	.281	.104**	.358
Peer	.017	.078	.092	.281	.371	.068*	.279
Attention to diabetes	.027	.032	.046	.217	.286	.069	.284
					Achievement		
Attention to diabetes	.027	.032	.046	.217	.289	.072*	−.287
					Intellectual		
Overall	.000	.010	.047	.342	.439	.098**	.383
Family relations	.003	.006	.013	.148	.284	.136***	.465
Attention to diabetes	.027	.032	.046	.217	.350	.133***	.459
					Activities		
Family relations	.003	.006	.013	.148	.220	.072'	.291
					Moral		
School	.044	.071	.093	.422	.481	.059*	.248
					Organization		
School	.044	.071	.093	.422	.437	.044'	.214
					Family relations index		
Overall	.000	.010	.047	.342	.410	.069*	.287
Peer	.017	.078	.092	.281	.347	.066*	.281
Family relations	.003	.006	.013	.148	.240	.093*	.334
					Growth index		
Family relations	.003	.006	.013	.148	.236	.088*	.355

[a] R^2 when Harter General Perceived Competence Scale is entered.

[b] The specific orientation scale or index is given below.

[c] Significance of increment is R^2 when FES is entered (*F*-test).

[d] β is for FES variable following age, demographic, and self-esteem variables.

'$p \leqslant .07$.

*$p \leqslant .05$.

**$p \leqslant .01$.

***$p \leqslant .005$.

DISCUSSION

These analyses of the first year of our longitudinal data point to the importance of family perceptions or orientations in terms of their likely impact on the preadolescent's and adolescent's self-perceptions. This implication was clearly embedded in our earlier analyses (Hauser *et al.*, 1985). Now, however, the idea is given considerably more support because these new results are based on larger samples and a clear separation of any confounding influences that might come from the child's own perceptions as well as from demographic variables. Obviously, not all aspects of the family's orientations are of equivalent importance to the family of the diabetic or acutely ill child. With respect to the diabetic child, when we look at the linkage between the parents' descriptions of the family and the child's own perceptions of competence, the family elements that come through as most important have to do with orientations toward *organization* of the family and *independence*. Explorations in the acutely ill group revealed that achievement orientations were most closely linked to the acutely ill child's self-esteem.

In another set of analyses, we found that several aspects of diabetes adjustment could be predicted by family orientations. Consistent with our previous results (Hauser *et al.*, 1985), we once again found many significant associations between family orientations and the child's diabetes adjustment. What is impressive, and important, is that these associations were found between *parent* perceptions of the family's and the *child's* adjustment to diabetes. Moreover, these linkages continued to be significant after controlling for possible confounding factors of age, sex, social class, *and* self-esteem. We can regard these analyses as delineating a substantial link between these family orientations and the adolescent's perceived adjustment to his or her diabetes. Most prominent among the family orientation predictors of diabetes adjustment were those that pertained to family relationships and personal growth.

In terms of the different self-esteem–family correlation patterns between the two illness groups, one way to interpret these results is to speculate that the diabetic children may be especially sensitive to such emphases as independence and the family's organization. In light of predictable preadolescent and adolescent conflicts over independence, exacerbated by the onset of diabetes, it not surprising that family emphases on autonomy would be associated with enhanced self-esteem on the part of the child. Another aspect of the onset of diabetes, as remarked on earlier, is the necessity for rearranging as well as employing many new routines within the family. Family emphases on organizational aspects may serve to alleviate some of the confusion and fears that come with the many new issues of self-management (body management) that accompany the onset of diabetes. The importance of this "organizational" orientation is further underlined by the fact that we discovered that diabetic families expressed significantly higher emphases on this particular facet of the family than did the parents of the acutely ill children. The fact that these family orientations were not significantly associated with self-esteem for the nondiabetic children certainly suggests that the diabetic children were differentially receptive to particular aspects (namely organization and independence) of the family environment. On the other hand, the nondiabetic children showed numerous significant correlations between aspects of self-esteem and family achievement orientations. Given that the two groups of families were middle- and upper-middle-class ones, it is not surprising that achievement orientations within the family might be tied to self-esteem perceptions. The fact that this significant linkage could be found only for the acutely ill group can be understood in terms of the possibly greater distraction experienced by the diabetic families as a result of the new illness and its special demands, which shifts their focus from "achievement" within the social context. It will be of interest to see whether in later years, with possibly increasing adaptation to the illness, the diabetic families begin to resemble those of our contrast group in their emphasis on such matters of achievement.

Our second important individual variable, diabetes adjustment, was linked to many aspects of the family environment. Especially noteworthy is the fact that this linkage remained even after numerous demographic and other self-perceptions (self-esteem) were accounted for. Clearly, then, the families' emphases on certain values and assumptions is of great importance in shaping the child's attitude toward his or her new and complex illness. Not surprisingly, such matters as family relationships and family emphases on personal growth had especially prominent linkages with aspects of diabetes adjustment.

It is important to remember that these results are based on self-reports from preadolescent and adolescent patients and their parents. Thus, we do not know how much the obtained relationships are the result of perceptions shared by the children and their parents, as opposed to associations between individual child perceptions and *actual* family behaviors. Responding to this important issue requires family assessment methods that are not dependent on self-report data. Such procedures are built into our project, and analyses of the data derived from these observational procedures will lead to more thorough investigation of such questions of whether and how family encouragement of independence may enhance the diabetic child's self-esteem and/or adjustment to diabetes. Ongoing analyses are taking up this very question of the relationship between family interaction patterns and child adjustment to diabetes.

Analyses carried out for this report and our previous work (Hauser *et al.*, 1985) continue to emphasize that diabetic children do *not* have lower self-esteem than nondiabetic children (Hauser & Pollets, 1979; Turtle & Dunn, 1981). In contrast to our previous findings, however, we now do have indications that the two groups of families differ in terms of some of their orientations within the family. At this point, then, we have intriguing suggestions of links between the family and individual self-esteem as well as overall adjustment. But we do not know the extent to which the family environment patterns are *determined by* individual adjustment and personality characteristics. Our assumption in the current study has been that these individual characteristics are more likely consequences of the surrounding, ongoing family environment. This view is based on logical or conceptual grounds and cannot yet be empirically defended. As we analyze the data collected from these groups of families and children over the ensuing three years following this first diagnostic year, we will be in an excellent position to understand how individual forces may shape the family environment, as well as the converse.

There have been increasing numbers of studies of individual psychosocial aspects of diabetes (e.g., Kovacs *et al.*, 1985). These understandings are extremely important in terms of better grasping ways to work with and comprehend the situation of diabetic children. We see our work as connected with and complimenting this emphasis on individual variables. In our perspective, we consider that both individual and family dimensions are important in determining the course of diabetes and the impact of this course on the life of the child and that of the family. Such understandings have many potential benefits for health care providers working with these patients and their families. We anticipate that, through results such as ours, health care providers can generate imaginative, empirically grounded, new ways of teaching families how their espoused (and latent) values may be most conducive to the patient's experience of competence and illness adjustment.

Acknowledgment

Supported by Grant AM 27845 from the National Institute of Arthritis, Diabetes, and Digestive and Kidney Diseases, and by a Research Scientist Award (Dr. Hauser) MH 70178 from the National Institute of Mental Health.

References

Anderson B, Auslander W. Research on diabetes management and the family. Diabetes Care 1980; 3:696–702.

Anderson B, Miller JP, Auslander W, Santiago J. Family characteristic of diabetic adolescents: relations to metabolic control. Diabetes Care 1981; 4:586–594.

Barerra M, Sandler IN, Ramsey TB. Preliminary development of a scale of social support: studies of college students. American Journal of Community Psychology 1981; 9:435–447.

Beck A. Depression—cause and treatment. Philadelphia: University of Pennsylvania Press, 1967.

Bell LG, Bell DC. Family climate and the role of the female adolescent: determinants of adolescent functioning. Family Relations 1982; 31:519–527.

Billings AG, Moos RH. Family environments and adaptation: a clinically applicable typology. American Journal of Family Therapy 1982; 10:26–38.

Coopersmith S. Self-esteem and need achievement as determinants of selective recall and repetition. Journal of Abnormal Social Psychology 1960; 60:310–317.

Coopersmith S. Relationship between self-esteem and sensory (perceptual) constancy. Journal of Abnormal Social Psychology 1964; 68:217–221.

Coopersmith S. The antecedents of self-esteem. San Francisco: Freeman, 1967.

Epstein S. Aggregation and beyond: some issues on the prediction of behavior. Journal of Personality 1983; 51:360–392.

Hanson CL, Henggeler SW. Metabolic control in adolescents with diabetes: an examination of systemic variables. Family Systems Medicine 1984; 2:5–16.

Harter S. The Perceived Competence Scale for children. Child Development 1982; 53:87–97.

Hauser ST, Jacobson AM, Wertlieb D, Brink S, Wentworth S. The contribution of family environment to perceived competence and illness adjustment in diabetic and acutely ill adolescents. Family Relations 1985; 34:99–108.

Hauser ST, Pollets D. Psychosocial aspects of diabetes: a critical review Diabetes Care 1979; 2:227–232.

Hauser ST, Solomon M. Coping with diabetes: views from the family. In: Ahmed P, ed. Coping with diabetes. Springfield, Ill.: Thomas, 1985:234–266.

Hollingshead A. Two factor index of social class. New Haven, Conn.: mimeo, 1957.

Holohan CJ, Moos RH. Social supports and psychological distress: a longitudinal analysis. Journal of Abnormal Psychology 1981; 90:365–370.

Kokenes B. Grade level differences in factors of self-esteem. Developmental Psychology 1974; 10:954–958.

Kokenes B. A factor analytic study of the Coopersmith Self-Esteem Inventory. Adolescence 1978; 13:149–155.

Koski ML, Ahlas A, Kumento A. A psychosomatic follow-up study of childhood diabetics. Acta Paedopsychiatrica 1976; 42:12–25.

Kovacs M, Feinberg TL, Paulauskas S, Finkelstein R, Pollock M, Crouse–Novak M. Initial coping response and psychological characteristics of children with insulin-dependent diabetes. Journal of Pediatrics 1985; 106:827–834.

Marrero DG, Lau N, Goldern M, Kershnar A, Myers G. Family dynamics in adolescents with diabetes mellitus: parental behavior and metabolic control. In: Laron Z, Galatzer A, eds. Psychosoical aspects of diabetes in children and adolescents. Basel: Karger, 1982: 72–82.

Minuchin S, Baker L, Rosman B, Liebman R, Milman L, Todd T. A conceptual model of psychosomatic illness in children. Archives of General Psychiatry 1975; 32:1031–1038.

Minuchin S, Rosman B, Baker L. Psychosomatic families. Cambridge, Mass.: Harvard University Press, 1978.

Moos R. Family Environment Scale. Palo Alto, Calif.: Consulting Psychologists Press, 1974.

Moos RH, Moos BS. A typology of family social environments. Family Process 1976; 15:357–371.

Moos RH, Moos BS. Clinical applications of the Family Environment Scale. In: Filsinger E, ed. Marriage and family assessment. Beverly Hills, Calif.: Sage Publications, 1983:253–273.

Reiss D. The family's construction of reality. Cambridge, Mass.: Harvard University Press, 1982.

Rosenberg M. Society and the adolescent self-image. Princeton, N.J.: Princeton University Press, 1965.

Schafer LC, Glasgow R, McCaul K, Dreher M. Adherence to IDDM regimens: relationship to psychosocial variables and metabolic control. Diabetes Care 1983; 6:493–500.

Self-Esteem Institute. Self-Esteem Institute norms for the Coopersmith Self-Esteem Inventory. San Fransisco, Calif.: Self-Esteem Institute, 1974.

Shouval R, Ber R, Galatzer A. Family social climate and the health status and social adaptation of diabetic youth. In: Laron Z, Galatzer A, eds. Psychosocial aspects of diabetes in children and adolescents. Basel: Karger, 1982:89–103.

Sullivan BJ. Adjustment in diabetic adolescent girls: I. Development of the Diabetic Adjustment Scale. Psychosomatic Medicine 1979a; 41:119–126.

Sullivan BJ. Adjustment in diabetic adolescent girls: II. Adjustment, self-esteem, and depression. Psychosomatic Medicine 1979b; 41:127–138.

Turtle J, Dunn S. The myth of the diabetic personality. Diabetes Care 1981 6:640–646.

Wishner WJ, O'Brien M. Diabetes and the family. Medical Clinics of North America 1978; 62:849–856.

PART NINE

Family Systems and Behavioral Disorders

34

Family Systems and Behavioral Disorders: Schizophrenia, Depression, and Alcoholism

CAROL M. ANDERSON
DIANE P. HOLDER
University of Pittsburgh

A few years ago, one of the authors (CMA) was asked to participate in a family practice program by spending an afternoon a week with a physician as he saw his patients. The plan was to discover how an increased awareness of family issues and family interviewing skills might be integrated productively into an everyday practice. After observation of a number of cases seen in a routine way, a decision was made to experiment by collecting more family information. The first case chosen was a single-parent mother bringing her two boys in for their camp physicals. The physician thought she would be an easy trial case, since he had seen her over a 2-year period during which time she had seemed reasonably well adjusted and healthy, with only a slight tendency to overuse the health center for minor somatic complaints.

The family-oriented interview produced the following information: The mother was the product of two alcoholic parents, who abused both her and her siblings. She was subsequently raised by her grandparents, who had died a few years earlier. Her brother had been schizophrenic for many years, and it had become her responsibility to support him and handle the many crises that arose as he went in and out of hospitals. She had never been married but had produced two male children out of wedlock, whom she had raised without much help from anyone. She did not date and had no close friends. Not surprisingly, she occasionally became quite depressed. When asked how she managed and who gave *her* support, she looked at her family practitioner and said, with an embarrassed smile, "He does." With an awareness of these difficult life circumstances, her "frequent" brief visits to the clinic seemed an entirely reasonable and almost insignificant means of support. Yet, these visits had an important impact on her quality of life.

Over time, this woman had been coping with alcoholism, depression, and schizophrenia, all three of the major behavioral disorders that will be addressed in this section. She derived significant support from her family doctor, even though her contacts with him were brief and never addressed her depression or family stress. She had chosen not to talk spontaneously about these family issues and would not have accepted a referral to a psychiatrist. Although the physician was not fully aware of his importance to her, his role was a vital and helpful one. An awareness of the problems in her life, however, along with some knowledge of what is helpful for patients and their family members as they attempt to cope with these disorders, could have made him even more useful.

This woman's story is an example of just one of the ways that behavioral disorders are a part of the complex picture presented regularly to family practitioners. In this case, the disorders themselves were only indirectly relevant to the presenting complaint and the ongoing care of the patient. Far more important was the chronic stress that they produced. This "indirect" presentation of behavioral disorders is quite a common one. Although patients themselves may ask family practitioners directly for help with schizophrenia, alcoholism, or depression, it is far more likely that sensitive practitioners will discover these disorders as contributing or confounding variables as they attempt to treat other problems in patients.

In some ways, there could not be three more diverse mental disorders than schizophrenia, depression, and alcoholism. The type and severity of symptoms differ; the incidence differs; even the age, sex, and marital status of patients tends to differ. Alcoholism, a progressive disease, is estimated to affect 5% to 7% of our adult population. Although traditionally rates have been higher in adult males, recently there has been a significant increase in addiction rates for women and adolescents. Depression, also a common disorder, affects at least 4% to 9% of adults, with estimates that 1 in 10 individuals will become clinically depressed at some point during his or her lifetime. For biologic, cultural, or social reasons, the rates are far higher for women than for men. Schizophrenia, on the other hand, tends to have much lower incidence, estimated at 1% of the population. However, since it is an illness that first occurs in adolescence or young adulthood and tends to become chronic, its prevalence is high, and its severity results in an overwhelming impact on both the overall functioning of patients and that of their families.

Despite these differences, there are some very important commonalities in these disorders. Each is an illness, probably with a biologic or genetic component; each has a high probability of chronicity; and each, at least at this point in time, is not curable in the usual sense of the word. These illnesses involve seriously dysfunctional family members who usually have a strong impact on the rest of the family. Other family members, temporarily or permanently, are required to take on extra tasks and duties, to play caretaking roles, and to overfunction for extended periods of time. In addition, these illnesses have an impact of family relationships and tend to induce a myriad of negative feelings. Often, these disorders so dominate the household that the family becomes increasingly isolated from extended family or friends. Thus, each disorder has the potential to distort the development, not only of the patient, but also of other family members and the family as a whole. On the other hand, families also influence illness. Evidence that might suggest that they play a causal role in the development of these disorders is inconclusive, but there is beginning evidence that families can have an important impact on course and on treatment compliance.

In recent years, a great deal has been learned about these problems and the way they interface with family processes, structure, and relationships. The other chapters in this section have been written by major contributors to the development of our knowledge about families and these illnesses, and each will give a detailed discussion of his or her work. Therefore, this introductory chapter will attempt to provide an overview that identifies key issues medical practitioners should be aware of in attempting to help patients and their families who are coping with these disorders. Using three case examples, three possible levels of intervention following a family assessment will be demonstrated: referral, crisis intervention, and ongoing family treatment.

KEY ISSUES FOR FAMILY PHYSICIANS

Before family practitioners can make a decision regarding the appropriate level of intervention, they must be able to assess patients and families in such a way that behavioral disorders can be identified. To be able to make such an assessment, a physician must possess six basic skills: (1) the ability to see the family as a system; (2) an acceptance of behavioral disorders as legitimate illnesses; (3) the ability to know when to convene a family session; (4) the ability to conduct a basic family assessment; (5) an awareness of techniques for engaging resistant patients and families; and (6) a knowledge of family and community resources.

Seeing the Family as a System

The patient is part of a family system, and change or stress in any family member will affect the lives of the rest of the family. An awareness of the interrelatedness of family members can help family practitioners understand the reciprocal impact of illness on family members and the reciprocal impact of family stress on the development or maintenance of illness. Furthermore, knowledge of the issues inherent in the normal family life cycle can help the family physician to predict times of greater vulnerability at stressful transition points and eventually to educate family members about the role of stress in their lives.

With this systems perspective, family practitioners are in a position to take advantage of their unique situation of having access to more people in the same family than do most service providers, having concern for "family health" rather than "individual health" as part of an overt definition of their role, and having the ability to observe family members over the family life cycle under a variety of conditions. In other words, they potentially have a broader and more useful definition of "patient" than does any other specialty in medicine.

Acceptance of These Problems as Legitimate Illnesses

In the past, and sometimes still today, schizophrenia was regarded as representing "problems in living," alcoholism was painted as a moral failing, and depression as a self-indulgent or even willful refusal to pull oneself up by one's bootstraps. Although each of these disorders involved entrenched problems that did not go away, they were not regarded as legitimate illnesses. Professionals were reluctant to get involved with these problems because they, too, were not sure the problems were indeed illnesses. They did not recognize their early warning signs, did not know their causes, and did not have effective treatments for them. Furthermore, the behavioral presentations of some of these illnesses (including lethargy, irritability, withdrawal, impulsivity, etc.) made patients seem uncooperative and unwilling to try to get better. As a result, family members and clinicians coping with these problems tended to feel impotent in their attempts to induce change, which resulted in increased anger, guilt, defensiveness, and hopelessness on everyone's part.

Fortunately, advances in neuropsychiatry and psychopharmacology are helping to identify these disorders as genuine ones. Although many of the problems they produce cannot be dealt with through medication alone, advances in pharmacologic treatment of these multifaceted illnesses may help to change negative and hopeless attitudes both within and outside the medical profession. Family practice physicians can use their increased awareness of the legitimacy of these disorders as illnesses rather than as vices to help patients and families accept this fact. This may enable families to accept treatment and learn to cope more effectively.

Recognizing When a Family Session Should Be Scheduled

Doherty and Baird (1983) suggest that physicians should be prepared to ''assemble a family'' for at least one joint session using the following guidelines:

1. When there is a new diagnosis of serious, acute, or chronic illness.
2. When there is no response to or noncompliance with treatment.
3. When there is the presence of psychosocial problems.
4. When there is need to make a life-style change (e.g., drinking, weight loss).

There are many reasons to schedule family sessions when the above situations are present. The initial diagnosis of a serious illness is usually very upsetting to the rest of the patient's family. Illness in one member often means a change in his or her capacity to function in his or her usual roles and means that other family members must shift responsibilities. Noncompliance or lack of treatment response can often be handled successfully by incorporating the family into the treatment team. Issues such as dietary alteration or medication regimes can easily be undermined by well-meaning family members who do not understand the treatment recommendations or by less functional family members who have personal needs that conflict with a patient's cooperation with medical treatments. The presence of a psychosocial problem or the need for a change in life-style requires a family meeting to clarify family relationships that are either adding stress or that might constitute untapped resources for support for the patient. Thus, these sessions can be used to assess the needs and responses of family members and to provide information. In all of these situations, the ability to hold family sessions that include providing information to families is an important intervention skill for family practitioners. The provision of information to patients and families is a powerful intervention. Furthermore, it is consistent with the physician's previous training, is less time-consuming than more traditional therapies, increases compliance, and allows the provision of concrete help. For instance, approximately 50% of schizophrenic patients either never make it to aftercare or drop out after one or two sessions. Among the families who attended the information-sharing workshop in our schizophrenia project, however, there were *no* treatment dropouts (Anderson, Reiss, & Hogarty, 1980, 1986). Information does not just encourage compliance, however, but also appears to decrease anxiety and increase receptivity to advice and change.

Assessment Skills: Ability to Conduct an Initial Family Session

As with most forms of treatment, family interventions are based on the data gathered and the assumptions the practitioner makes regarding what change is needed. Without adequate data, treatments often fail. Physicians who have developed a relationship with family members, and have become acquainted with the basic family structure and family stresses, will be better able to engage in the prevention or early identification of problems. Furthermore, they will have laid the groundwork for treatment or for a referral that otherwise would not be accepted. Although not all family assessments and interventions require seeing the family as a group, this technique is so powerful and so frightening to professionals who have been trained using an individual model that special attention must be paid to learning the skills of family group interviewing.

To be able to conduct a systems assessment, family practitioners must be able to ask the right people the right questions and have a conceptual framework to organize the data collected. By doing so, family physicians can conduct a solid assessment of these behavioral disorders in the context of their ongoing relationship with the individual patient and/or the family as a whole, which could constitute an invaluable aid in the early identification of problems and would lay the groundwork for treatment or referral.

It is beyond the scope of this chapter to provide a detailed and comprehensive outline of all the skills needed to conduct an initial family meeting. However, a few guidelines may be helpful.

First, the practitioner should assume that the family members want to help a patient get better and will contribute to solving their own problems. It is important not to assume there is significant pathology in families until there is evidence that this is the case. All families have problems and conflicts. Families rightly become resistant and defensive when professionals make the implicit assumption that they are to blame for the patient's problems. Thus, at least equal attention to family strengths and respect for their priorities is crucial during the assessment phase.

Second, it is important to know who is involved in the family (even those who may now live away from home). Very often crucial supports or crucial stresses are more related to the extended family network than to the nuclear family unit. A genogram (a pictorial representation of the family) can provide an immediate and graphic depiction of a family and its issues over time. This tool also will highlight recent events (deaths, emancipations, marriages) and patterns of alliance and support.

Third, the physician should try to include each member of the family in the discussion and obtain everyone's perspective on the problem(s). It is important not to lean too heavily on the information from one very verbal spokesperson, both because the ideas revealed in this way are only one person's view and because less verbal members are more likely to feel uninvolved or uncommitted to the treatment process.

Fourth, physicians should be aware of family communication patterns, since they will provide a sense of family structure, alliances, power, and the coping mechanisms that have worked over time. In particular, these patterns will help the family practitioner to know who must be included in treatment decisions to ensure that the decisions will be put into practice.

Finally, physicians must have an understanding of the constellation of symptons that are early warning signs of each of these disorders. For each of these illnesses, such signs may first be exhibited in problematic family and social functioning. Withdrawal from normal family activity, excessive absence from school or work, lack of interest in previously enjoyed activity, repeated complaints of physical distress in the patient or other family members, increased agitation or irritability, or unremitting conflict with family members can all signal the early stages of a behavioral disorder in the family. Physicians who learn possible symptom profiles of each of these disorders are able to offer patients and families support, early intervention, and educational interventions that separate fact from fiction.

Techniques for Engaging Patients and Families Resistant to Discussing Personal Issues and/or Accepting Referrals

As we have mentioned, although patients may come with these disorders as their presenting complaints, it is more likely that they will present with some other medical problem for which a behavioral disorder complicates the possibility of treatment, or that family members will present asking how to get help for a recalcitrant, behaviorally disturbed patient. In all of these instances, treatment, engagement, and compliance are likely to be problems.

Thus, it is crucial that physicians learn to present treatment suggestions in ways that address the needs of the individuals involved without increasing defensiveness and, particularly, to use the energy of other family members, who are often more uncomfortable than the individual with a behavioral disorder, to insure follow-through on recommendations.

Three factors greatly influence the family's level of cooperation with both assessment and treatment. Compliance will be greater if physicians (1) can communicate a genuine belief in the importance of family issues in individual health care; (2) can learn to use the energy of family members other than the patient to accomplish change; and (3) can learn to connect with patients and families using the presenting complaint and the family's own style. Most families asked directly to participate in a meeting will do so, but some are reluctant, and in these cases the manner in which the session is presented is important. Emphasizing the routine nature of convening such sessions, as well as the value of involving those people who know the patient best and who might offer information, suggestions, or support, will help to minimize a family's fear of being blamed. It is also advisable to avoid terms like "family therapy session" or "counseling session." The use of the term "family meeting' is such less threatening. Finally, emphazing the need to find "solutions" rather than to identify "problems" may increase motivation, reinforce the family's sense of power and responsibility, and reduce their initial anxiety enough to get them involved.

Knowledge of Resources

Resources include an awareness of family strengths, community resources, and most effective treatments for the disorders involved. A complete understanding of the etiology of disorders is not a prerequisite to helping patients and families who are coping with a behavior disorder. The most cherished belief in medicine in general, and in psychiatry in particular, that an understanding of etiology generates treatment is simply not true. Mastectomy is not related to the *cause* of cancer, nor is insulin related to the *cause* of diabetes. Neither do most treatments cure illnesses. Treatments, in general, attempt to alter the *course* of illnesses, bringing them under reasonable control and enhancing the quality of life of patients and those who love them.

Given the complex relationship between these behavioral problems and family life, it is important that physicians develop a realistic acceptance of the benefits and limitations of our current knowledge and treatments. Physicians must be aware, however, that there is clear beginning evidence of the development of effective treatments for these illnesses that appear to help both patient and family (Anderson *et al.*, 1980; Anderson, Griffin, Rossi, Pagonis, Holder, & Treiber, 1986; Falloon *et al.*, 1982; Friedman, 1975; Kovacs, 1980; Stanton, Todd, & Associates, 1982; Weissman & Paykel, 1974). In other words, family practitioners can legitimately communicate to their patients that there is reason for hope and optimism in the treatment of behavioral disorders. Some treatment interventions have proved effective in controlled trials, and it is now possible to relieve many patients of debilitating symptoms, to improve their quality of life, and to decrease the number of crises to which the rest of the family must be exposed. The ability to offer hope, based on an awareness of family strengths and of available effective treatments and community resources, may be the most effective intervention for behavioral disorders.

Although some family practitioners may choose to go well beyond the development of these six basic skills, mastery of these skills can help physicians to deal effectively with most behavioral problems. The following discussions of schizophrenia, depression, and alcoholism, and their respective case examples, will illustrate three levels of involvement in the assessment and treatment of these disorders.

SCHIZOPHRENIA

Perhaps more research has been concentrated on the family issues of patients with schizophrenia than on the families of patients with any other disorder (see Hirsch & Leff, 1975, and Wynne, 1981, for good reviews of these efforts). One of the most interesting recent developments, however, involves the work of a group of British investigators who have looked at family variables as they related to the course of the disorder. As Wynne (Chapter 35, this volume) will discuss in more detail, these investigations found that the single most predictive factor of relapse in these patients was the amount of expressed emotion of the patient's relative(s) on admission. Those families who rated high in expressed emotion, especially the components of "critical comments" and "emotional overinvolvement," tended to have patient members who were more likely to relapse, with rates of relapse even higher with increased amounts of face-to-face contact between the patient and the "expressive" relative.

This work provided the cornerstone for the development and testing of several new clinical approaches to working with these patients and their families (Anderson *et al.,* 1980; Falloon *et al.,* 1982; Leff, Kuipers, Berkowitz, Eberlein-Vries, & Sturgeon, 1982). On the basis of the assumption that if family members could have an influence on the *course* of the disorder, they also were relevant to its treatment, treatment models were developed that bypassed the issue of etiology and concentrated on influencing the course and improving the quality of life for patient and family members as well. Our own particular model, one that we called "psychoeducational," provides family members with support, information, and specific suggestions for more effective coping with this devastating and chronic illness. This treatment is cost-effective and relatively simple to provide. Although the content of this model is specifically related to schizophrenia, the principles and structure of the treatment offered are relevant to most chronic mental and physical disorders. In fact, several projects have been initiated applying these principles to affective disorders and several childhood learning disabilities.

CASE EXAMPLE

A 6-year-old male patient was brought to the family practice center by his mother for regular health care. Because his behavior was extremely hyperactive in the waiting room and the office, the physician began to question his mother about his development. The mother's responses were bizarre, rambling, and often nonsensical. She did, however, manage to communicate that the child slept in the same bed with her and her husband even when they engaged in intercourse. She also mentioned that the child had eaten nothing but canned spaghetti and sauce for several months, and generally revealed that the amount of structure and child care in the home were substantially below standard. When the mother was asked about her own mental health, she admitted to having been hospitalized twice for "breakdowns," but said that she had not followed through on recommendations for ongoing medication maintainance through her local mental health center. This woman was sufficiently disturbed to require hospitalization, and a few years ago she would have been institutionalized. Now, however, the treatment of almost all patients with chronic illnesses occurs primarily in their homes. For this reason, families increasingly have become primary caretakers. Because most schizophrenic patients are likely to be impaired to greater or lesser degrees in their emotional and instrumental role functioning, other family members often are required to perform more than their fair share of roles, chores, and emotional need-meeting. Furthermore, other family members are often very upset about the patient's behaviors and feel guilty about their perceived role in the development or maintenance of the patient's problems.

Crucial in the ongoing management of all of these stresses is the support and information that could be provided by the family physician. Psychoeducational models of treatment for this illness have taught us that patients and family members are more likely to be anxious and fearful of what they do not understand. Information helps them to see not only the need for temporary or permanently diminished expectations, but also the need to avoid overfunctioning or helping patients so much that they become helpless.

Furthermore, since motivation and compliance are serious problems for patients with this disorder, the family physician can help by involving other family members, at least briefly, to ensure that acceptance of some sort of referral or treatment will occur. In this case, the family physician did not wish to assume responsibility for the care of this woman's schizophrenia. Nevertheless, using his awareness of the importance of psychotropic medication, he could make contact with the patient's husband directly, convening a ''couples session'' to involve the husband as an effective force in her treatment. Without undermining the strengths she still possessed (she did bring her child in for treatment), the physician could make practical suggestions that would ensure continuity of care. For instance, the physician could recommend that her husband accompany her to her first appointment at the mental health center, and could emphasize his vital role in supporting her subsequent treatment to prevent future crises and episodes. The physician's knowledge that family factors do have an influence on the course of the treatment, and even on compliance with it, put him in a unique position to offer hope and engage both the patient and her husband in the treatments that would be of use to them. Because the physician will have gained their trust over time on less highly charged issues, he already possesses an awareness of their responses to stress and their strengths and weaknesses, which will make his choice of a treatment or a referral more informed than that of a consultant. The physician is also in the best position to support and assure the success of his recommendations.

In terms of knowledge of treatment issues and resources generally, the physician should know and communicate that the disorder tends to recur and that there is no known cure. He should also know and communicate, however, that there exist psychologic treatments with demonstrated effectiveness in controlled trials.

A knowledge of community resources also is important in this regard. Although physicians must provide some support and information themselves, there are other resources to help on an ongoing basis once the patient and family have accepted the problem. Many communities now have psychoeducational, self-help, and/or advocacy programs. Self-help groups have the added advantage of giving patients and families the opportunity to be helpful to others, and altruism is truly therapeutic.

Immediate crisis intervention in this case should not only include facilitating the husband's involvement in his wife's care, and reconnecting the patient with mental health services, but also a referral of their 6-year-old child to a therapeutic day school and the mother to a parent education and support group, all of which were facilitated with the help of a family consultant.

Once the patient stabilizes on her medication, it is likely that she will gradually settle into a period of lethargy and amotivation. Like most relatives at this time, her husband is likely to become impatient and irritated by her inactivity and the slowness of change.

Because the symptoms of these illnesses are often just variations of more understandable behaviors ("the blues," etc.), many assume that patients could control their symptoms if only they tried harder. Further, many of these patients do not seem to be performing the one behavior required of patients in order to be allowed the sick role—*trying* to get better. In treating these individuals, it is important to remember that they are *not* in control of their symptoms. In these illnesses, the affected organ is the brain, making rational thought and motivation a problem. The negative symptoms that so often follow an acute episode of schizophrenia, including amotivation, lethargy, and apathy, cannot be overcome through sheer will. Furthermore, attempts to push past them tend to precipitate relapse. These disorders, like any other serious illness, have their sequelae. The physician can continue to be helpful at such times by providing support for the relative and pointing out that these "negative symptoms" represent another phase of the illness.

DEPRESSION

There are several types of depression likely to present to family physicians. Most patients with clinical depressions require sustained intervention rather than crisis intervention, usually at least partially pharmacologic in nature. Depressions tend to be of longer duration and are accompanied by changes in the patient's neurovegetative signs, including sleep disturbance, appetite disturbance, and sexual and role dysfunction. Reactive depressions (those occurring in response to life events) are less likely to respond to medication, and both families and physicians tend to become frustrated over time with the intractable nature of depressive symptoms. In any case, both usually are accompanied by family problems (Bothwell & Weissman, 1977) and thus might well be helped by attention to family issues.

Unfortunately, although depression is a pervasive problem in our culture, very little work has been done to investigate the reciprocal impact of the depressed patient and the family. Yet, the recurrent nature of this disorder when it is a clinical illness, along with the unresponsiveness of its psychosocial symptoms (whether or not it is clinical), clearly affects interpersonal functioning *and* the well-being of family members with whom the depressed individual lives. Since individuals who become depressed tend to suffer from chronic low self-esteem, hopelessness, and sensitivity to criticism, these traits cannot help but influence the entire family. When someone is depressed, it has a major impact on those around them. Some workers have reported that as little contact as a brief telephone conversation with depressed and nondepressed patients was sufficient to cause those who spoke to depressed patients to rate them as less "likeable." Even more strikingly, such brief conversations also cause those people who talked to depressed patients to rate themselves as more depressed (Coyne, 1976; Hammen & Peters, 1977).

On the other hand, depression can also be a response to other family problems. Wives may report depression when their husbands are alcoholic and unavailable; teenagers frequently display depressive behaviors or even make suicide attempts as a result of being caught up in the chronic marital struggles of their parents. Young housewives may become depressed by the isolation of their lives and the overwhelming nature of what it takes to care for small children.

Whether depression precedes family problems or vice versa, the family relations of depressed patients are problematic. Since depression is most prevalent among adult women, it tends to have its major impact on families through depressed mothers with dependent children. Research has clearly demonstrated that the marriages, spouses, and the children of these women are likely to be symptomatic (Beardslee, Bemporad, Keller, & Klerman,

1983; Orvaschel, 1983; Weissman & Paykel, 1974; Widmer, Cadoret, & North, 1980). In fact, one of the primary complaints listed by depressed women is that of marital problems (Weissman & Paykel, 1984). Direct observation studies comparing couples containing a depressed versus a physically ill spouse confirm that couples with a depressed member experience more tension, more negative expressions, more disruptions of each other's messages, more self-preoccupation, and diminished congruence between nonverbal and verbal communication (Hinchcliffe, Hooper, Roberts, & Pamela, 1975). Depressed mothers tend to have more problematic relationships with their children, to be less available and less nurturant than other mothers (Orvaschel, 1983; Weissman, 1972). The children of depressed women have been described as at some increased risk for psychologic problems and accidents (Brown, Harris, & Copeland, 1972), and both the children and the spouses of depressed patients have been reported to make more visits to their family doctor (Widmer *et al.*, 1980).

The main coping problems of families with a depressed member involve tendencies toward under- or overresponse. On the one hand, family members tend to ignore depression because the symptoms of the illness are less obvious and are more likely to be thought of as a part of the patient's personality. In fact, family members and health professionals may come to avoid or reject these patients because of a misinterpretation of the meaning of symptoms. Lowered vitality may be likened to laziness; feelings of worthlessness may appear to be self-indulgence; hopelessness and helplessness may be interpreted as unwarranted and excessive; requests for continuous reassurance and comfort may be seen as unreasonable; and increasing stridency may be viewed as just plain nastiness. Since attempts to help and reassure the patient tend to be ineffective or unaccepted, naturally many spouses and family members of depressed individuals become increasingly upset in the face of having to live with such behaviors over time.

At the other extreme, as in the case we are about to discuss, family members may become overinvolved and oversolicitous with depressed patients, taking on their chores, expecting too little, and in general, undermining whatever functional capabilities patients may have.

The following case of short-term depression provides an example of a less complicated and less entrenched family problem than schizophrenia. In this case, a basic awareness of family issues and skills in family engagement allowed the family practitioner to take immediate and helpful action, without spending much time and without making a referral for special care.

CASE EXAMPLE

A woman in her late 70s was being managed for multiple medical problems by her family physician. After being admitted to the hospital for a relatively minor brief procedure, she began to appear increasingly depressed. She refused to eat, told her physician that she wanted to die, and vehemently declared she did not want to go home *or* to a nursing home.

Her family consisted of a sister and brother-in-law with whom she lived, three children, and several grandchildren, all in the immediate area and all very concerned about her welfare. Over the past several months, their response to her failing health had been to help her in every way possible in order to protect her from strain or injury. Consequently, at the expense of their own time and convenience, they currently performed all the homemaking chores (meals, laundry, etc.), did all her errands, and helped with her personal hygiene. The entire family was completely bewildered by her current attitude. She was in good enough health to live for years, and, for them, her death was an unacceptable subject. They cared about her and were willing to be actively involved in her health care. Consequently, when she talked of wanting to die and not wanting to return home, they responded by saying such things as, "Don't talk that way"; "There is no reason for you to feel this way"; "We'll do everything for you, don't worry"; "You can manage with our help." This woman's very well meaning relatives were behaving in ways that not only were diminishing her quality of life, but also were exacerbating her depression and ultimately actually endangering her physical health. They were "overfunctioning," robbing this woman of a chance to function at all, and thereby perpetuating her depression. This problem was an ideal one for short-term educational interventions delivered by a family practitioner.

With an understanding of the need for all patients, even physically ill and depressed ones, to maintain as much control over their lives as possible, as well as the need to provide family members with support and guidance in this regard, the family physician was able to provide an enormously helpful service in one relatively brief family session. "Assembling the family," he prepared this woman's relatives for her very natural need to talk about her past, her awareness of her own diminishing capabilities, and her fears of death, explaining that this life review and illness focus was a natural component of the aging process. While rewarding them for their attempts at caretaking, he emphasized that she was not completely helpless and, in fact, needed to keep busy. He helped them to identify a few tasks she could handle, such as folding laundry or cutting up vegetables for supper, and emphasized the importance of their finding other such tasks that would occupy her and make her feel she was a useful member of the household. With this revised family organization, this woman was able to return home, her depression lifted without the use of drugs, and she returned to playing a role that was more central in her family. In other words, dysfunctional family behaviors were reduced by the provision of information and concrete guidance.

ALCOHOLISM

Alcoholism is often called a family illness. This usually refers to the United States' 9 million alcoholics and 36 million affected wives, husbands, parents, and children who live with the disorder. There is no shortage of negative psychosocial problems associated with alcoholism: marital conflict and divorce, spouse and child abuse, absenteeism and low productivity, illness and accidental death, suicide and homicide. Each of these problems intimately affects and reflects the course of family relationships (Doherty & Baird, 1983; Steinglass, 1976; Steinglass, Bennett, Wolin, & Reiss, 1987).

Physicians have had difficulty identifying alcohol problems in the early phase of the disorder, for several reasons. First, there is no monolithic structure that can be designated "alcoholism." Few aspects of medicine are as semantically, territorially, or emotionally confused (Freed, 1982). Second, the legacy of the 19th century, in which alcoholism was a "moral failing," has perpetuated negative, nontherapeutic attitudes toward people with alcohol addiction, in many ways recapitulating the history of the mentally ill. This prejudice has made families and alcoholics reluctant to discuss their problems. Third, once the shift from a moral to a medical definition of alcoholism occurred, attention was focused on the individual and the progressive nature of the disease. As Davis and colleagues have observed, the attention of researchers was riveted on the search for ultimate causes (Davis, Berenson, Steinglass, & David, 1974). Problems were undetected until late-stage alcoholism developed, and the prognosis then was poor.

The late-stage alcoholic diagnosed with serious physical complications usually had severe social, emotional, and financial problems, which had not begun 6 months earlier.

Long before a physical exam would show an enlarged liver, there was probably marital distress. Before cardiac arrhythmia is diagnosable, the 10-year-old son may have been "overly active" and missing school because of chronic sore throats. As Freed (1982) described, "one does not become a deviant drinker overnight. The course of alcoholism is not a two-stage process—sobriety to addiction" (p. 46). Familial, social, and work relationships usually deteriorate prior to the onset of any physical illness related to alcohol.

The families of alcoholics have not been ignored. But the clinical and research emphasis of the past 40 years, prior to 1970, focused on the negative emotional impact of alcohol abuse on children and spouses and on the analysis of personality factors of the patient and spouse (Jacob, Favorini, Meisel, & Anderson, 1978).

During the past decade, systems theory has been used to conceptualize the alcoholic family. Researchers have challenged the search for ultimate causes and postulate that alcoholic behavior is "more profitably thought of as a final common pathway and that excessive drinking can therefore be put to a wide variety of uses by a wide variety of types of people" (Davis *et al.*, 1974, p. 209). This group began to explore not only what was negative about abusive drinking, but also what was adaptive.

What are the implications of these data for the family practitioner? If the physician has decided to create a practice in which he or she will attempt to understand and discuss family relationships, then a way must be found to open discussion of these sensitive issues. A rapport must be developed that encourages drinkers, their spouses, or their children to discuss an enormously painful and shameful family secret that frequently they are busy hiding from themselves and everyone else.

CASE EXAMPLE

Linda B, a 15-year-old white, single female patient, presented for her first visit to the family medicine practice with throat pain of 3 days' duration, spitting thick mucus, running a low-grade temperature, with a weight loss of 17 pounds in a 3-week period, accompanied by general malaise and a frontal headache. At least two nearly identical episodes of varying degrees of severity had occurred each year since she was 8 years old, usually in the fall and the spring. Hospitalization was required on four occasions because of dehydration. Linda had a previous diagnosis of asthma but had no history of formal wheezing. Her mother had consulted numerous physicians during the past 7 years, and extensive testing had been negative. Her mother complained that the patient refused fluid intake at home, was lethargic, and often refused to speak. Furthermore, she had missed 15 of the first 40 days of school. Mrs. B was angry with her daughter because of both her refusal of fluids and the lack of communication between them.

Two days following the initial exam, Linda was admitted to the pediatric unit for a fifth hospitalization for rehydration and further testing, all of which was negative once rehydration was complete. Anorexia nervosa was ruled out. Psychosocial data at admission were unremarkable. When not ill, she was active in the school band and church activities.

A first-year family medicine resident was assigned primary responsibility for this case. This particular program maintained a systems orientation and employed a psychologist, who on advice from both her attending physician and the family consultant, decided to call a "family conference," certainly appropriate under the Doherty and Baird (1983) guidelines already mentioned. The possibility of depression was considered.

Everyone attended the initial session except Linda's 18-year-old brother. The resident chose not to make his absence an issue at that point. The following information emerged.

Linda's father had never finished high school; he was laid off permanently from his job 5 years previously, with virtually no chance of being called back to his former position in a local steel mill where he had worked 15 years. Since the layoff, his employment history had been an erratic one; he was now unemployed. Meanwhile, Linda's mother, who was very obese, worked two part-time jobs and attended college part-time, maintaining a straight A average.

The parental relationship had involved frequent arguments over the past 10 years, usually about money and, more recently, about the housework. Occasionally, these arguments escalated and divorce was threatened. In fact, when Linda was 8 years old, her mother tried very briefly to separate from her husband, taking the children with her. Linda's mother currently uses Linda as a confidant regarding family, school, and financial problems. Linda has been very upset about the family arguments and has tried to keep the house as orderly as possible to avoid her father's anger. She often cleans the house while her father "rests." Her greatest fear is that her parents will divorce.

All three children in the family have "learning problems," and all have received remedial coursework in their respective schools. In addition, Linda's younger brother has asthma, and her 18-year-old brother was caught shoplifting 2 years ago. He also refuses to attend church and family activities, and recently has begun to neglect his self-care. Currently, he even refuses to brush his teeth, and the father frequently "yells" at him about these behaviors. Everyone in the family is angry with Linda, who, they say, "won't help herself," and everyone seems to feel that her illness is her way of "avoiding unpleasant things in life."

Without a conceptual framework, all these family data are cumbersome and difficult to process. The resident, overwhelmed with the information she received, was in need of a hypotheses. It was unclear what it meant that Linda must stay home from school excessively to "work" while her father "rested." On the other hand, it was clear that Linda had a particularly difficult role in the family. She was required to placate her father while serving as both confidant and substitute for her mother in family functions and tasks.

A session with the psychologist raised two important question: Are there data missing? Is there any important family function served by Linda's illness? It was possible that Linda's behavior served to distract or protect the family from some more painful issue, and also possible that Linda's father suffered from depression and/or substance abuse. Since it seemed that Linda's symptoms began around the time her mother first attempted to leave her father, it also seemed possible that Linda's symptoms functioned as a way of stabilizing the family. It is not unusual for families with chronic conflict to focus on another major problem or issue to diffuse tension and unite warring factions rather than to find a way to deal more directly and effectively with their differences or the threat of separation.

Since it was obvious that further data would be needed to understand which hypothesis was most relevant for this particular family, the resident used the next session to explore the issues raised by the consultant. First, she obtained a family history by using the genogram format already mentioned. She discovered that father's father and father's younger brother were alcoholics. When she asked what role alcohol played in the father's life, he began to deny its significance, but Linda's 11-year-old brother immediately complained, "He drinks *a lot*." Eventually, the father acknowledged a drinking problem, and a clear picture of family functioning began to emerge. Consistent with cases described in the literature, their deteriorating relationships were in part a sign of "hidden" alcohol addiction. In this family, however, Linda's illness was an easier focus than her father's alcoholism.

There were sufficient data to indicate the possible usefulness of a trial of family therapy to attempt to diminish the family conflict and to influence Linda's recurrent illness. This particular resident was interested in family therapy and decided to attempt to provide ongoing treatment rather than referring the family elsewhere. The fact that this family practice program employed a staff family consultant who was able to serve as a co-therapist and supervisor in the ongoing treatment made the family treatment of a complicated case feasible. Once the family conflict and the father's alcoholism were out in the open, Linda's physical symptoms remitted. Her school attendance significantly improved, and Linda returned to normal social functioning.

CONCLUSIONS

Most of medicine requires physicians to deal with microscopes, not the wide-angle lens required to see things from a family systems perspective. In fact, medicine has become increasingly scientific and decreasingly humanistic. Today, as Lewis Thomas (1983) says, with a certain amount of nostalgia:

> The doctor can set himself, if he likes, at a distance remote from the patient and the family, never touching anyone beyond a perfunctory handshake as the first and only contact. Medicine is no longer the laying on of hands, it is more like the reading signals from machines.
> The mechanization of scientific medicine is here to stay. The new medicine works. (p. 58)

The question is: Does the new medicine preclude the kind of broad-based attention family practice proposes to give to the patient's social context, addressing the interrelatedness of biologic and social issues, the quality—not just the prolongation—of life? On the one hand, it is possible, and the role of family medicine in this regard could be a crucial one, not because family practitioners can or should learn to treat all disorders (not all medical disorders, much less all behavioral ones), but because they can, by maintaining a focus on patient and context, be in a unique position to further develop our understanding of the interrelationship between social and biologic forces.

Technology may be here to stay and may continue to develop, but it does not preclude the very special contribution of broadly trained professionals. It is very clear that the function of family practitioners is not simply one of triage, but one of playing a very special role in the development of a whole new science of interrelated factors: biology, psychology, and sociocultural forces. In a way, the unique and potentially creative contribution of the human factor in all this is illustrated in another Lewis Thomas (1983) quote:

> Computers are good at seeing patterns—better than we are. They can connect things that seem unrelated to each other, scanning the night sky or the strained blotches of 50,000 proteins on an electrophoretic gel or the numbers generated by all the world's stockmarkets, and find relationships that matter. We do something like this with our brains, but we do it differently, we get things wrong. We use information not so much for its own sake as for leading to thoughts that really are unrelated, unconnected, patternless, and something's therefore quite new. If the human brain had not possessed this special gift, we would still be sharpening bones, muttering to ourselves, unable to make a poem or even whistle.
> These two gifts, the ability to lose information unpredictably and to get relationships wrong, distinguish our brains from any computer I can imagine ever being manufactured. (p. 90)

On the other hand, maybe family practice shouldn't reach so high. Getting involved in patients' families is bound to go against the sanctity of the one-to-one relationship, with its comfort and confidentiality. It's bound to raise physician anxiety and lead into areas in which physicians will feel overwhelmed, underinformed, and incompetent. They will have to cooperate with family therapists who may be insensitive to the realities of a family practice. Understanding families, family dynamics, and the impact of these issues on the patient's illness and care causes information overload for which there is no provision in residency training. The kind of discussion of intimate issues and taboo topics inherent in exploring psychosocial issues will challenge the defenses of obsessive control and interpersonal distance so carefully instilled in medical school education. Humanizing medicine, much less really dealing with human systems, is probably no longer within the grasp of physicians who have so much science to learn.

Acknowledgment

Special thanks to Susan Erstling, family therapy consultant to the Shadyside Hospital Family Practice Residency, and Laurel Milberg, consultant to the Forbes Health System, for the provision of case material.

References

Anderson CM, Griffin S, Rossi A, Pagonis I, Holder DP, Treiber R. A comparative study of the impact of education vs. process groups for families of patients with affective disorders. Family Process 1986; 25:185–206.

Anderson CM, Reiss DJ, Hogarty GE. Family treatment of adult schizophrenic patients: a psycho-educational approach. Schizophrenia Bulletin 1980; 6(3):490–505.

Anderson CM, Reiss D, Hogarty G. Schizophrenia and the family. New York: Guilford Press, 1986.

Beardslee WR, Bemporad J, Keller MB, Klerman GL. Children of parents with major affective disorder: a review. American Journal of Psychiatry 1983; 140:825–832.

Bothwell S, Weissman M. Social impairments four years after an acute depressive episode. American Journal of Orthopsychiatry 1977; 47(2):231–237.

Brown GW, Harris T, Copeland JR. Depression and loss. British Journal of Psychiatry 1972; 130:1–18.

Coyne JD. Depression and the response of others. Journal of Abnormal Psychology 1976; 85:186–193.

Davis D, Berenson D, Steinglass P, Davis S. The adaptive consequences of drinking. Psychiatry 1974; 85:209–215.

Doherty WJ, Baird M. Family therapy and family medicine. New York: Guilford Press, 1983.

Falloon IRH, Boyd JL, McGill CW, Razoni J, Moss HB, Gilderman HA. Family management in the prevention of exacerbations of schizophrenia. New England Journal of Medicine 1982; 306:1437–1444.

Freed E, ed. Interfaces between alcoholism and mental health. New Brunswick, N.J.: Journal of Studies on Alcohol, 1982.

Friedman AS. Interaction of drug therapy with marital therapy in depressive patients. Archives of General Psychiatry 1975; 32.

Hammen CL, Peters DS: Differential response to male and female depressive reactions. Journal of Consulting and Clinical Psychology 1977; 45:994–1001.

Hinchcliffe M, Hooper D, Roberts FJ, Pamela WV. A study of the interaction between depressed patients and their spouses. British Journal of Psychiatry 1975; 126:164–172.

Hirsch SR, Leff JP. Abnormalities in parents of schizophrenics. London: Oxford University Press, 1975.

Jacob T, Favorini A, Meisel S, Anderson C. The alcoholic spouse, children and family interactions. Journal of Studies on Alcohol 1978; 39(7):1231–1251.

Kovac M. The efficacy of cognitive and behavior therapies for depression. American Journal of Psychiatry 1980; 137:1495–1501.

Leff J, Kuipers L, Berkowitz R, Eberlein-Vries R, Sturgeon D. A controlled trial of social intervention in the families of schizophrenic patients. British Journal of Psychiatry 1982; 141:121–134.

Orvaschel H. Maternal depression and child dysfunction: children at risk. In: Lahey B, Kazdin A, eds. Advances in clinical child psychology, Vol. 6. New York: Academic Press, 1983.

Stanton, MD, Todd TC, and Associates. The family therapy of drug abuse and addiction. New York: Guilford Press, 1982.

Steinglass P. Experimenting with family treatment approaches to alcohol, 1950–1975: a review. Family Process 1976; 16:97–123.

Steinglass P, Bennett L, Wolin S, Reiss, D. The alcoholic family. New York, Basic Books, 1987.

Thomas L. The youngest science: notes of a medicine watcher. New York: Viking Press, 1983.

Weissman M. The depressed woman: recent research. Social Work 1972; September:19–25.

Weissman M, Paykel ES. The depressed woman: a study of social relationships. Chicago: University of Chicago Press, 1974.

Widmer RB, Cadoret RJ, North CS. Depression in family practice: some effects on spouses and children. Journal of Family Practice 1980; 10(1):45–51.

Wynne L. Current concepts about schizophrenics and family relationships. Journal of Nervous and Mental Disorders 1981; 169(2):82–89.

35

Family Systems and Schizophrenia: Implications for Family Medicine

LYMAN C. WYNNE
University of Rochester School of Medicine and Dentistry

Schizophrenia often has been considered the prototype of those disorders that are under the exclusive care of mental health professionals, especially in an earlier era of custodial institutions. Increasingly, during the last 15 years, general physicians, community agencies, and the families of schizophrenics have shared in the care of this perplexing illness. The deinstitutionalization of chronic psychiatric patients, mainly schizophrenics, has occurred partly because of improved management of florid psychotic symptoms with psychotropic medications, partly because of rising costs of hospitalization, and partly because of ideologic and humanitarian objections to unnecessary incarceration. Public policies have strongly favored the release of schizophrenics into the community, but have generally failed to provide specialized community aftercare, even for continuing symptoms and serious social/occupational role dysfunction. Day treatment centers, halfway houses, and rehabilitation programs gradually have become more available, but are inadequate in most community settings.

All too frequently, the shift to "community care" has meant the transfer of caretaking responsibility from hospitals to families that are poorly informed, puzzled, conflicted, emotionally and financially burdened, and socially isolated. Lacking adequate public and professional assistance, families in many settings have organized themselves into self-help and consumer advocacy groups (Bernheim, Lewine, & Beale, 1982; Hatfield, 1981). Sometimes they have coped remarkably well, sometimes not. Belatedly and inadequately, mental health professionals have begun to recognize that comprehensive treatment of schizophrenic individuals in the community requires better understanding of both the healthy resources and the coping difficulties of families (Hatfield & Lefley, 1987).

With any chronically ill patient for whom the family bears major caretaking responsibility in the home or must participate in care planning elsewhere, the stress-related symptoms in the nonpatient family members commonly become the concern of the family physician. Currently, much public attention is being given to the burdens experienced by the spouses and families of Alzheimer patients. Unfortunately, many families of schizophrenics have been less ready to acknowledge their distress and despair, often because they have experienced or expected blame or lack of support from mental health professionals (Hatfield, 1979, 1983). In many instances, it is the alert and empathic family physician who is more likely to hear about the distress of relatives of schizophrenics. This distress in dealing with a chronically ill patient who all too often has been "dumped" into family care is apt to have long-term health consequences for the family members. Family physicians should be able to identify in the community both family support groups, such as affiliates of the National Alliance for the Mentally Ill (NAMI), and those local mental health professionals who are able and willing to collaborate in a supportive relationship with family members. In this strategic role, family physicians can serve as systems consultants (Wynne, Mc-

Daniel, & Weber, 1986) to assist families of schizophrenics in identifying their options. These options should include supportive and educational services.

Current "psychoeducational" approaches usually begin with a frank, open discussion of the concept of schizophrenia and related mental illness (Anderson, Hogarty, & Reiss, 1980). First, however, it is essential that the diagnosis of schizophrenia be confirmed by a qualified psychiatric consultant. Who has made the diagnosis? When and with what criteria was the diagnosis established? All too often, a suspected or provisional diagnosis is understood by family and patient as definitive. It is now widely recognized, within and beyond the psychiatric profession, that the label of "schizophrenia" was far too loosely and widely applied in the United States, especially before the narrower, present criteria of the *Diagnostic and Statistical Manual of Mental Disorders* (DSM-III) were introduced in 1980. The consequences of faulty diagnosis have often been appalling. For example, I was recently asked to consult with a family in which the patient had been provisionally diagnosed as "latent schizophrenic" in 1954. Careful review indicated that she had had a postpartum depression associated with an unhappy marriage at age 19. Nevertheless, for more than three decades she had been treated with maintenance neuroleptics on the assumption that she was "schizophrenic" and that relapse had to be forestalled, despite the complications of tardive dyskinesia and restricted psychosocial functioning. An all-too-casual diagnosis and iatrogenic impairment had had consequences for her and her family that now could only be partially corrected.

A CONCEPTUAL MODEL FOR SCHIZOPHRENIA

Even with a reasonably definitive diagnosis, the syndrome of schizophrenia encompasses a diversity of dysfunctions, with variable courses and outcomes that are not individually predictable. Therefore, the nature of the disorder must be explained in a way that is intelligible and clear, but that realistically takes into account the diversity and uncertainty of symptomatology and prognosis.

Vulnerability

In working with many troubled families of schizophrenics, I have found that predisposition or vulnerability is a central concept that is understandable by almost everyone. As with the predisposition to diabetes, hypertension, or peptic ulcer, "vulnerability" may or may not be transformed into overt, diagnosable, symptomatic illness. The concept of vulnerability is usually understood to imply inborn, genetic tendencies that may be modified by environmental factors, either biologic or psychologic (Wynne, 1978). The onset of schizophrenic symptoms usually comes unexpectedly. Only retrospectively can onset be linked to possible, precipitating, stressful events or circumstances. After an initial episode, however, the circumstances that are likely to precipitate subsequent exacerbations and relapses can be usefully considered, first, by identifying with the family the antecedent stressful situations and, second, by developing strategies for avoiding and coping with similar stressors (Goldstein & Kopeikin, 1981).

The similarity of vulnerability to schizophrenia and to well-known medical illnesses is both clarifying and reassuring, though sobering for most families. It correctly implies that the symptomatic illness is treatable but the vulnerability may not be curable, that the outlook is therefore serious but by no means hopeless, and that thoughtful interventions may provide useful but not guaranteed improvement.

Stimulus Overload

The vulnerability to schizophrenia is most easily and accurately described as an unusual, individualized sensitivity to stimulus overload. Almost everyone can relate personally to the experience of feeling swamped and potentially disorganized by events and other stimuli that are too intense, ambiguous, numerous, frequent, contradictory, or cumulative. Both clinical, phenomenologic evidence (Sullivan, 1956) and laboratory data (Nuechterlein & Dawson, 1984) support this interpretation of schizophrenic vulnerability as an impaired ability to focus attention and to process information. Less well understood is the schizophrenic's difficulty in establishing and maintaining interpersonal attachments and in sharing foci of attention with other persons—necessary for sustained communication and problem solving.

Joint Genetic and Environmental Effects

The psychiatric literature has been filled with ideologically polarized views about the importance of biologic versus psychosocial factors in the etiology and pathogenesis of schizophrenia. In the last 15 years, there has been a strongly dominant but poorly conceptualized tendency to regard positive data about biologic factors as meaning that psychosocial factors are not important. Actually, the more sophisticated geneticists agree that *joint* effects of genetic and environmental factors surely are operative (Kendler & Eaves, 1986). For schizophrenia, the most convincing, traditional evidence that the genetic contribution to vulnerability is not sufficient to account for the clinical picture derives from studies of genetically identical twins. According to the calculations of Gottesman and Shields (1982), the newer twin studies show that, with a diagnosis of schizophrenia in one of a pair of twins, a minority (46%) of monozygotic co-twins are concordant for schizophrenia. If only genetic factors were relevant, 100% would be concordant.

The nature of the nongenetic factors in schizophrenia is still hotly debated and under active investigation. Two recent studies are especially noteworthy in supporting the hypothesis that communicational and emotional family factors antedate the onset of schizophrenia and related "spectrum" disorders. Goldstein (1985) began with a sample of intact families that applied for help from a psychology clinic for their nonpsychotic, 15-year-old offspring. Initial family assessments using measures of communication deviance (Singer & Wynne, 1966), affective style (Doane, West, Goldstein, Rodnick, & Jones, 1981), and expressed emotion (Vaughn & Leff, 1976) successfully predicted the later onset of schizophrenia and spectrum disorders at 5- and 15-year follow-up.

The joint effects of environmental factors (in adoptive rearing families) and genetic factors (transmitted from adopting-away biologic schizophrenic mothers) are being studied in Finland by Tienari and co-workers (1985). When reared in a seriously disturbed adoptive family, 26 of 45 (57.8%) of the potentially vulnerable index adoptees with a biologic schizophrenic mother have thus far developed psychotic illness or a severe personality disorder. Even more interesting and important in its implications for prevention and treatment is the contrasting fact that of 50 index adoptees, also having schizophrenic mothers, there are no psychotic diagnoses and only two cases (4%) of severe personality disorder in the offspring reared in healthy or mildly disturbed adoptive families. This strongly suggests a protective function of these adoptive family rearing environments. Of nine adoptees who have become schizophrenic or paranoid psychotics, seven are in the subgroup that has the combination of genetic risk and a seriously disturbed adoptive family. This combination of findings supports, but does not yet confirm, the hypothesis that genetic vulnerability has interacted with the adoptive rearing environment. It should be kept in mind that this study is still in progress and will include a group of families that were first studied when the adoptees were nonsymptomatic youngsters who will be prospectively followed until they reach the age of risk for schizophrenia.

Communication Deviance

The family environmental variables studied in the Goldstein (1981) and Tienari *et al.* (1985) research, as well as in an earlier adoption study reported by Wynne, Singer, and Toohey (1976), emphasized the concept of communication deviance (CD) (Jones, 1977; Singer & Wynne, 1965, 1966; Singer, Wynne, & Toohey, 1978; Wynne, Singer, Bartko, & Toohey, 1977). Communication deviance is a research measure derived from the stimulus overload model of schizophrenia mentioned earlier. Following this model, it is hypothesized that ambiguous, confusing forms of family communication, if used with high frequency, will be associated with individual problems in focusing attention and communication that will have a greater likelihood of becoming symptomatically manifest in any individual who is already biologically vulnerable to schizophrenia. From a systems viewpoint, there is no implication that the hypothesized effects of CD are unidirectional. The designated patient may have an impact on parents and siblings, as well as the reverse. Differing family roles, differing extrafamilial supports and experiences for individual family members, and differing biologic vulnerability of the individuals contribute to expectably diverse outcomes for persons within the same family. There is no way that a genuine system orientation to families can justify the attribution of blame and intentionality to individual family members. As I stated years ago, "There are no one-way streets in family life" (Wynne, 1968, p. 186).

Healthy Communication

In a study of families with children at increased genetic risk because of hospitalized mental illness of a parent, Wynne and Cole (1983) applied a concept of the positive, health-enhancing counterpart of CD, namely, "healthy communication" (HC). Like CD, it can be reliably scored from protocols of family interaction. We found that parental CD and HC both predict highly significantly to the competence levels of children aged 7 to 13, as rated entirely independently by teachers and peers in the schools. Additionally, measures of positive and negative affect expressed during family interaction and the "structure" of family interaction (the balance between the relative amounts of participation and initiative by parents and children) also predict to child competence outside the family in the school setting. Importantly, positive HC and other forms of family interaction are associated with superior child functioning even when there has been a serious parental mental illness, such as schizophrenia (for further findings, see Baldwin, Baldwin, & Cole, 1982, and Chapters 23 through 31 in Watt, Anthony, Wynne, & Rolf, 1984).

Although CD and HC have not yet been studied as predictors of the course and outcome of schizophrenic illness, these concepts have been applied implicitly in several family treatment studies. The basic idea of psychoeducational family approaches (Anderson, *et al.*, 1980; Falloon, Boyd, & McGill, 1984) is that schizophrenics will benefit from clear, simple, consistent communication; this entails minimizing CD and promoting HC. Falloon and co-workers (1984) have made a distinction, similar to that of Wynne (1984), between problem solving and communication. Communicational skills can be viewed as a developmental precursor of the more sustained and elaborated skills necessary in sustained or renewed problem solving (Wynne, 1984). In the Falloon *et al.* (1984) approach to family intervention, assistance at the problem-solving level is provided first to families. If problem solving seems persistently undermined by confusing and ambiguous communication (that is, by CD), then sessions are introduced that are explicitly oriented to training in basic communication skills.

Expressed Emotion

In contrast to considerable research on CD as a factor in development and the lack of such research in relation to outcome and treatment, another family concept, expressed emotion (EE), has been extensively studied as a predictor of relapse of florid schizophrenia, but not as an antecedent of the initial episode (Leff & Vaughn, 1985). Two components of EE, critical comments and emotional overinvolvement, have been regarded as together constituting "the best single predictor of symptomatic relapse in the 9 months following discharge" from hospitalization for schizophrenia (Vaughn & Leff, 1976, p. 134).

The earlier predictive studies in the United Kingdom (Brown, Birley, & Wing, 1972; Vaughn & Leff, 1976) now have been replicated in California (Vaughn, Snyder, Jones, Freeman, & Falloon, 1984). On the other hand, a more recent British study of first-episode schizophrenics found that EE was not related either to outcome or to response to medication (MacMillan, Gold, Crow, Johnson, & Johnstone, 1986). This study also revealed a major problem with the EE research to date: The conditions under which EE is thought to be relevant were "present only in a minority of cases; many patients lived alone and of those that were with families, most were not in high face-to-face contact with other members" (p. 133). Other investigations suggest the importance of cultural differences; high EE, as measured with ratings of individual interviews with relatives, is infrequent in non-Anglo-American cultures, for example Hispanic and Indian. How extrafamilial factors may substitute for, augment, or protect against intrafamilial emotional expression needs much more study (Falloon *et al.*, 1985b; Leff & Vaughn, 1985). Also, the relationship of EE to relapse has been chiefly apparent in young males living with their parents and is much less (if at all) significant in older, married females. Still another issue is that EE is clearly nonspecific for schizophrenia and has been shown to be relevant to the course of other disorders such as depression, anorexia, and obesity (Leff & Vaughn, 1985; Szmulker, Eisler, Russell, & Dare, 1985).

A Developmental Process

These studies of CD, HC, and EE should be understood in the context of the principle that what we see clinically in schizophrenic illness is not the simple consequence of an ultimate "etiology" but, rather, that the precursors, onset, and later course are part of a complex developmental, epigenetic process (Wynne, 1968) that involves multiple system levels—genetic and nongenetic biologic factors; rearing and developmental variables, both intrafamilial and extrafamilial; variations in the fit, integration, and developmental timing of "intrapsychic" processes; and the responsiveness of the therapeutic systems that interface with the family system and the identified patient. Therapeutically, schizophrenia cannot be treated in an encapsulated way, unlike some psychiatric problems (e.g., phobias, which often are conceptualized and treated in a rather one-dimensional way with behavioral techniques). Schizophrenia typically involves a multiplicity of dysfunctions—in attachment and affect, in communication and cognition, in initiative and problem solving, in social and occupational skills, and in overall quality of life.

Treatment Issues

It is necessary from the very beginning of treatment to think in systems terms, to think of systems on multiple levels and not just in terms of relieving florid, psychotic symptoms. Treatment of such symptoms with neuroleptic medication is comparatively simple, but medication is much less effective for the more enduring problems—the residual or deficit symptoms, the possibility that familial and other stressors will precipitate florid relapse, the occupational impairment, the developmental and social dislocations of the patient, and the profound reverberations on the family and immediate social network. A phase-oriented approach to treatment of schizophrenia is essential to address properly the enormous changes over time in the needs of these patients, their families, and others who participate in their care (Wynne, 1983).

Especially during the acute florid and subacute stages, a clear, structured, predictable treatment environment is essential. Neuroleptic medication appears to help protect the patient against stimulus overload. The "negative," deficit symptoms of social withdrawal, lack of energy, interests, and initiative are nearly always distressing to families that need assistance in understanding the protective function that these distancing symptoms may have. At this stage, high environmental stimulation seems likely to precipitate relapse. Later, however, the deficit symptoms often can be relieved with a more active but still clear (CD-free), structured environment, usually with reduced or intermittent medication. In this phase, "low EE" may not be helpful if it implies remoteness or lack of interest by family members or other persons in the immediate environment. Because of the changing needs of schizophrenics over time, families understandably may become frustrated because what professionals advised and what "worked" earlier may become counterproductive later on.

Unfortunately, there still are too few mental health professionals who are able and willing to take a comprehensive view of the difficulties and resources of these families and patients. On the other hand, a considerable number of programs now provide clear models for how to work more effectively with schizophrenics and their families (Falloon *et al.*, 1984; Falloon *et al.* 1985a; Goldstein, 1981; McFarlane, 1983). The most widely adopted psychosocial approaches currently emphasize psychoeducational and behavioral methods, sometimes with training in communication and social skills added (Anderson, Reiss, & Hogarty, 1986; Falloon *et al.*, 1984). Furthermore, these programs now are reporting impressive research data that document the effectiveness as well as the limitations of family management in schizophrenia, with work still proceeding on the combined effects of medication and psychosocial intervention (Hogarty *et al.*, 1986; Falloon *et al.*, 1985b).

A related issue is that schizophrenia burns out professionals and families alike because of the protracted though variable course it takes. I am afraid that much of the psychiatric literature, including the DSM-III, has conveyed the erroneous impression, which recreates the initial error of Kraepelin (1896), that this illness shows an inevitably deteriorating, downhill course. To be sure, it is often "chronic," which by DSM-III criteria only means that with prodromal and/or residual symptoms included, it has lasted over 2 years. But if one looks at longer term outcome, over 10 or more years, even chronic patients make surprising degrees of recovery. There are several major studies, for example by Bleuler (1978) and, more recently, by Ciompi (1980) and Harding, Zubin, and Strauss (1987) that have shown the great variability of long-term outcome. Bleuler (1978) observed that after a 5-year duration, "tendencies for improvement prevail over tendencies for deterioration" (p. 497). The recovered patients may not be the most successful persons in the world, but they typically are functioning persons who can take their place in the community without public assistance and often without the need for further professional care. The past expectation that permanent custodial care was inevitably needed was not justified. Also unjustified is the too frequent, current belief that neuroleptic medication must routinely be maintained for a lifetime. Iatrogenic factors often have made schizophrenics more impaired than they need to be.

On the other hand, with overzealous deinstitutionalization and without adequate provision for community care, the complex problem of achieving maximal recovery has fallen excessively on families. In collaboration with knowledgeable and supportive mental health professionals and family support groups, the family physician can be a valuable resource both for the patient and for other family members.

References

Anderson CM, Hogarty GE, Reiss DJ. Family treatment of adult schizophrenia patients: a psychoeducational approach. Schizophrenia Bulletin 1980; 6:490–505.

Anderson CM, Reiss DJ, Hogarty GE. Schizophrenia and the family: a practitioner's guide to psychoeducation and management. New York: Guilford Press, 1986.

Baldwin AL, Baldwin CP, Cole RE. Family free-play interaction: setting and methods. In: Baldwin AL, Cole RE, Baldwin CP, eds. Parental pathology, family interaction, and the competence of the child in school. Monograph of the Society for Research in Child Development 1982; 47:36–44.

Bernheim KF, Lehman AF. Working with families of the mentally ill. New York: Norton, 1985.

Bernheim KF, Lewine RRJ, Beale CT. The caring family: living with chronic mental illness. New York: Random House, 1982.

Bleuler M. The schizophrenic disorders: long-term patient and family studies, SM Clemens, trans. New Haven: Yale University Press, 1978.

Brown GW, Birley JLT, Wing JK. Influence of family life on the course of schizophrenic disorders: a replication. British Journal of Psychiatry 1972; 121:241–258.

Ciompi L. Three lectures on schizophrenia: the natural history of schizophrenia in the long term. British Journal of Psychiatry 1980; 136:413–420.

Doane JA, West KL, Goldstein MJ, Rodnick EH, Jones JE. Parental communication deviance and affective style: predictors of subsequent schizophrenia spectrum disorders in vulnerable adolescents. Archives of General Psychiatry 1981; 38:679–685.

Falloon IRH, Boyd JL, McGill CW. Family care of schizophrenia: a problem-solving approach to the treatment of mental illness. New York: Guilford Press, 1984.

Falloon IRH, Boyd JL, McGill CW, Williamson M, Razani J, Moss HB, Gilderman AM, Simpson GM. Family management in the prevention of morbidity of schizophrenia: clinical outcome of a two-year longitudinal study. Archives of General Psychiatry 1985a; 42:887–896.

Falloon IRH, and Others. Family management of schizophrenia: a study of clinical, social, family, and economic benefits. Baltimore: Johns Hopkins University Press, 1985b.

Goldstein MJ, ed. New developments in interventions with families of schizophrenics. San Francisco: Jossey-Bass, 1981.

Goldstein MJ. Family factors that antedate the onset of schizophrenia and related disorders: the results of a fifteen year prospective longitudinal study. Acta Psychiatrica Scandinavica 1985; 71(Suppl. 319):7–18.

Goldstein MJ, Kopeikin HS. Short- and long-term effects of combining drug and family therapy. In: Goldstein MJ, ed. New developments in interventions with families of schizophrenics. San Francisco: Jossey-Bass, 1981:5–26.

Gottesman II, Shields J. Schizophrenia: the epigenetic puzzle. Cambridge: Cambridge University Press, 1982.

Harding C, Zubin J, Strauss J. Chronicity in schizophrenia: fact, partial fact, or artifact? Hospital and Community Psychiatry 1987; 38:477–486.

Hatfield AB. Help-seeking behavior in families of schizophrenics. American Journal of Community Psychology 1979; 7:563–569.

Hatfield AB. Self-help groups for families of the mentally ill. Social Work 1981; 26:408–413.

Hatfield AB. What families want of family therapists. In: McFarlane WR, ed. Family therapy in schizophrenia. New York: Guilford Press, 1983:41–65.

Hatfield AB, Lefley HP, eds. Families of the mentally ill: coping and adaptation. New York: Guilford Press, 1987.

Hogarty GE, Anderson CM, Reiss DJ, Kornblith SJ, Greenwald DP, Javna CD, Madonia BA, the EPICS Schizophrenia Research Group. Family psycho-education, social skills training and maintenance chemotherapy in the aftercare treatment of schizophrenia: I. One year effects of a controlled study on relapse and expressed emotion. Archives of General Psychiatry 1986; 43:633–642.

Jones JE. Patterns of transactional style deviance in the TATs of parents of schizophrenics. Family Process 1977; 16:327–337.

Kendler KS, Eaves LJ. Models for the joint effect of genotype and environment on liability to psychiatric illness. American Journal of Psychiatry 1986; 143:279–289.

Kraepelin E. Psychiatrie, 5th ed. Leipzig: Barth, 1896.

Leff J, Vaughn C. Expressed emotion in families: its significance for mental illness. New York: Guilford Press, 1985.

McFarlane, WR, ed. Family therapy in schizophrenia. New York: Guilford Press, 1983.

MacMillan JF, Gold A, Crow TJ, Johnson AL, Johnstone EC. The Northwick Park study of first episodes of schizophrenia: IV. Expressed emotion and relapse. British Journal of Psychiatry 1986; 148:133–143.

Nuechterlein KH, Dawson ME. Information processing and attentional functioning in the developmental course of schizophrenic disorders. Schizophrenia Bulletin 1984; 10:160–203.

Singer MT, Wynne LC. Thought disorder and family relations of schizophrenics: III. Methodology using projective techniques. Archives of General Psychiatry 1965; 12:187–200.

Singer MT, Wynne LC. Principles for scoring communication defects and deviances in parents of schizophrenics: Rorschach and TAT scoring manuals. Psychiatry 1966; 29:260–288.

Singer MT, Wynne LC, Toohey ML. Communication disorders and the families of schizophrenics. In: Wynne LC, Cromwell R, Matthysse S, eds. The nature of schizophrenia: new approaches to research and treatment. New York: Wiley, 1978:499–511.

Sullivan HS. Clinical studies in psychiatry. New York: Norton, 1956.

Szmulker GI, Eisler I, Russell GFM, Dare C. Anorexia nervosa, parental ''expressed emotion'' and dropping out of treatment. British Journal of Psychiatry 1985; 147:265–271.

Tienari P, Sorri A, Lahti I, Naarala M, Wahlberg K-E, Ronkko T, Pohjola J, Moring J. The Finnish adoptive family study of schizophrenia. Yale Journal of Biology and Medicine 1985; 58:227–237.

Vaughn CE, Leff JP. The influence of family and social factors on the course of psychiatric illness: a comparison of schizophrenic and depressed neurotic patients. British Journal of Psychiatry 1976; 129:125–137.

Vaughn CE, Snyder KS, Jones S, Freeman WB, Falloon IRH. Family factors in schizophrenic relapse: replication in California of British research on expressed emotion. Archives of General Psychiatry 1984; 41:1169–1177.

Watt NF, Anthony EJ, Wynne LC, Rolf JE, eds. Children at risk for schizophrenia: a longitudinal perspective. Cambridge: Cambridge University Press, 1984.

Wynne LC. Methodologic and conceptual issues in the study of schizophrenics and their families. Journal of Psychiatric Research 1968; 6(Suppl.):185–199.

Wynne LC. From symptoms to vulnerability and beyond: an overview. In: Wynne LC, Cromwell R, Matthysse S, eds. The nature of schizophrenia: new approaches to research and treatment. New York: Wiley, 1978:698–714.

Wynne LC. A phase-oriented approach with schizophrenics and their families. In: McFarlane WR, ed. Family therapy in schizophrenia. New York: Guilford Press, 1983:251–265.

Wynne LC. The epigenesis of relational systems: a model for understanding family development. Family Process 1984; 23:297–318.

Wynne LC, Cole RE. The Rochester risk research program: a new look at parental diagnoses and family relationships. In: Stierlin H, Wynne LC, Wirsching M, eds. Psychosocial intervention in schizophrenia: an international view. Berlin: Springer-Verlag, 1983:25–48.

Wynne LC, McDaniel SH, Weber TT, eds. Systems consultation: a new perspective for family therapy. New York: Guilford Press, 1986.

Wynne LC, Singer MT, Bartko JJ, Toohey ML. Schizophrenics and their families: recent research on parental communication. In: Tanner JM, ed. Developments in psychiatric research. London: Hodder & Stoughton, 1977:254–286.

Wynne LC, Singer MT, Toohey ML. Communication of the adoptive parents of schizophrenics. In: Jørstad J, Ugelstad E, eds. Schizophrenia 75: psychotherapy, family studies, research. Oslo: Universitetsforlaget, 1976:413–452.

36

Depression: The Family Systems Aspect

REUBEN B. WIDMER
University of Iowa

Incidence studies indicate that affective disorder is one of the top 10 diagnoses in primary care (Marsland, Wood, & Mayo, 1976). Depression is likely the most common psychiatric disease in the world and, when it results in suicide, is a terminal illness (Robins, Murphy, Wilkinson, Gassner, & Kayes, 1959).

Depressed patients are mentally and physically disabled because of their psychologic and somatic symptoms. They seek help for their complaints with frequent visits to the physician's office. Patients with an organic disease and a concurrent major depression may have a prolonged morbidity. This chapter is concerned with three aspects of depression: (1) the way in which depressed patients present to the family physician, (2) whether depression is the result of nature or of nurture, and (3) the relationship of depression to family dynamics.

Depressed patients usually present themselves to their family physician in ways unlike the textbook description and unlike the ways psychiatric outpatient clinics see them. These patients visit the family physician's office more frequently than nondepressed patients, with many somatic, pain, and anxiety complaints that frequently lead to increased diagnostic tests.

The records of 154 patients diagnosed as depressed and 154 controls matched for age, sex, and time of year seen were compared for number of office visits, number of hospitalizations, and type of complaints during the 6-month period before the date of diagnosis (Widmer & Cadoret, 1978). The records of 218 depressed patients were compared to those of 218 matched controls from two other family practices in the same manner (Cadoret, Widmer, & Troughton, 1980; Wilson, Widmer, Cadoret, & Judiesch, 1983). Compared to controls, the combined 372 depressed patients had significantly more office visits, hospital admissions, and somatic, pain, and anxiety complaints. One of these practices (117 patients and 117 controls) had family dysfunction data. Social complaints (primarily parent–child conflict, marital problems, and occupational difficulties) were significantly higher in the depressed group (Cadoret, Widmer, & Troughton, 1980).

It is of interest to note that the increased physician visits and hospital admissions, as well as the somatic, pain, and anxiety complaints, returned to premorbid levels and on a par with the controls within a year after treatment was initiated (Cadoret, Widmer, & North, 1980).

Twenty-three children who frequently visited a pediatric clinic with recurring functional abdominal pain all met the DSM-III criteria for a major depression when properly interviewed (Hughes, 1984). The author feels that "the depressive illness of these children is manifest in the interaction with their mothers and suggests that the children's depression may be a reflection of maternal issues of depression and loss" (p. 153). The young patients in the aforementioned family practices had similar presenting complaints that camouflaged their depressive illness.

In families, there are two main mechanisms for perpetuation of depression: the family environment and the genetic factors making for depression, which are passed from parent to child. A third mechanism is also possible—the interaction of the genetic propensity with factors in the family environment that might markedly increase or decrease the chance for depression in the offspring.

There is some evidence for a genetic factor in bipolar affective disorder (Cadoret & Winokur, 1982) and in unipolar depression (Cadoret, 1978), although evidence from adoption studies is weak (von Knorring, 1983).

Recent evidence from an adoption study (Cadoret, O'Gorman, Heywood, & Troughton, 1985) suggests that, despite a weak genetic effect, there is good evidence that family environment provides important predisposing factors making for increased major (unipolar) depression in adult life. These factors appear to act on the individual prior to 18 years of age. Figure 36-1 shows the relationship of major depression to other adult psychiatric conditions and to genetic and environmental antecedents for males. Figure 36-2 shows the same relationship for females.

At present there is one other adoption study that shows that depression in adoptees is increased by the presence of a depression in the male parent, a finding compatible with the idea of family environment influencing later depression (von Knorring, Bohman, & Sigvardsson, 1982). In none of the adoption studies cited was there evidence of the third mechanism, gene–environment interaction, increasing depression.

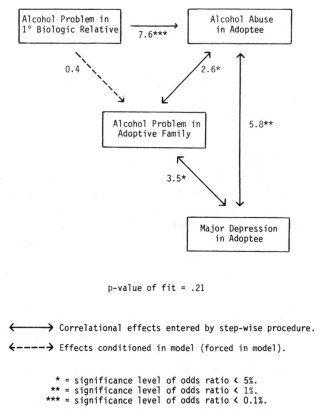

p-value of fit = .21

⟶ Correlational effects entered by step-wise procedure.

⟵- - - -⟶ Effects conditioned in model (forced in model).

* = significance level of odds ratio < 5%.
** = significance level of odds ratio < 1%.
*** = significance level of odds ratio < 0.1%.

Figure 36-1. Interaction diagram of major depression and alcohol abuse with genetic and environmental factors (male = 242). (Reproduced with permission from Cadoret *et al.*, 1985.)

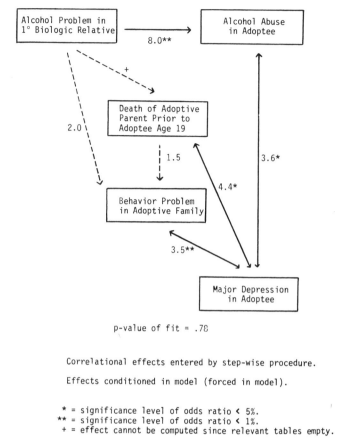

p-value of fit = .78

Correlational effects entered by step-wise procedure.

Effects conditioned in model (forced in model).

* = significance level of odds ratio < 5%.
** = significance level of odds ratio < 1%.
+ = effect cannot be computed since relevant tables empty.

Figure 36-2. Interaction diagram of major depression and alcohol abuse with genetic and environmental factors (female = 201). (Reproduced with permission from Cadoret *et al.,* 1985.)

Physicians who deal with the whole family have observed the effect of an illness of one member on the behavior of the family unit, and, in turn, the effect of the family's reaction to the illness of the patient. The dynamics will vary depending on who is ill and what the illness is. The family members of an alcoholic react differently from the family members of a depressed person. The primary purpose of this chapter is the observation of family interactions when a member of that family is depressed. From the literature and our own experience, there is considerable abnormal intrafamily reaction to the presence of a depressed member in the family unit. A number of studies seem to give variable results and conclusions.

We compared the records of spouses and children of the 154 depressed patients in a family practice to spouses and children of the 154 matched controls never diagnosed as depressed. The spouses of depressed patients when compared to spouses of controls had significantly more office visits and somatic, pain, and anxiety complaints during the 6-month period before depression was diagnosed. The children of depressed patients when compared to children of controls had significantly more somatic complaints, pain complaints, and infections during the 6 months before the parent was diagnosed as depressed. The spouses and children of the depressed patient frequently demonstrated abnormal behavior as early as the patient did and sometimes even before (Widmer, Cadoret, & North, 1980).

The visits and complaints of family members returned to control levels during the 6-month period between 12 and 18 months after treatment of the depressed individual was initiated. It is possible that the abnormal behavior of the spouse and children was secondary to their close relationship with the ill person. The data in the study do not tell us why they reacted as they did. Examining retrospectively the behavior of the family members and their feelings during the 6 months before the diagnosis of depression and then prospectively for 12 months after would shed some light on these relationships.

The depressed member and the nondepressed members of the same family see the family situation in a different light. The nondepressed members consider the family environment in as positive a way as do family members of a nondepressed person. The depressed member, however, sees the same situation negatively. A medical and psychiatric history given by depressed patients during their depression will be quite different from a history given after their recovery (Bromet, Ed, & May, 1984).

The presence of a manic-depressive parent has a deleterious effect on the affective and attachment behavior of the child at an early age; this effect increases in severity between 12 and 18 months of age (Gaensbauer, Harmon, Cytryn, & McKnew, 1984). Children of a depressed parent have a threefold higher risk of experiencing emotional disturbances. The risk of major depression increases linearly if both parents are psychiatrically ill. These children when compared with children of normal parents are more likely to suffer from (1) a major depression, (2) attention-deficit disorders, (3) separation anxiety, (4) conduct disorders, and (5) substance abuse (Weissman *et al.*, 1984).

There is an association between psychiatric illness and divorce. Three-fourths of a divorced female sample and two-thirds of a divorced male sample had a psychiatric disease, primarily depression and antisocial personality in men and women, and hysteria in women (Briscoe, Smith, Robins, Marten, & Gaskin, 1973). These investigators recommend that the clinician treat the depression first, regardless of the association between marital problems and depression. In a group of bipolar patients, 57% experienced marital failure, suggesting that manic symptoms are incompatible with a stable marriage (Brodie & Leff, 1971). Recurring flareups of marital conflict after apparently successful conjoint therapy should alert the therapist to a possible bipolar disorder (Lesser, 1983). Over a 2-year period, married depressed patients had a divorce rate 9 times the expected rate for the general population. The divorce rate was significantly higher when both partners had a psychiatric illness (Merikangas, 1984). These studies demonstrate how certain family events and behaviors predispose some members of the family to psychiatric illness in the months to years ahead. The mechanisms of this process are not clear. Perhaps further prospective studies would clarify the "why" and the "how" of these interactions.

Affectionless control, based on low parental care and overprotection of children, is an effective predictor of adult depression (Parker, 1983). The association of such parental representation with depression and anxiety traits in their adult children was as strong in the adoptive group (Parker, 1982) as in earlier studies (Parker, 1979a, 1979b) dealing with biologic parents. The author considered this indirect support for a causal rather than a hereditary process. Lack of care from father and/or stepmother increased the incidence of depression in a group of young women. The incidence of depression was higher among those women who were married to an unaffectionate husband. However, a caring, affectionate husband reduced the tendency to greater depression due to uncaring parenting (Parker & Hadzi-Pavlovic, 1984).

Parent–child separation due to parental illness and marital discord is associated with a later morbidity of anxiety and depression in 5- to 10-year-olds. Only separation due to parental illness has the same effect on 11- to 15-year-olds, and none of the above has any effect on newborn to 4-year-olds (Tennant, Hurry, & Bebbington, 1982).

Chronic depression lasting 4 years or longer occurred in 18% of the 154 depressed patients from a rural family practice. In this group, late onset of the first depressive episode in older women frequently led to chronic depression (Cadoret *et al.*, 1980). The following life events in the family system are associated with chronicity in primary depression: (1) positive family history of affective disorder, (2) multiple loss through death of family members, (3) disabled spouse, (4) concurrent incapacitating disease, and (5) secondary alcoholism and/or drug abuse (Akiskal, 1982).

Patients who have a high score in a self-administered depression scale questionnaire tend to have a low score on the Family APGAR, a self-administered test of the functional integrity of the family, as it measures an individual's ability to nurture and grow in the family. The greater the emotional disturbance of the individual, the more he perceives his family as being dysfunctional (McNabb, 1983). While depressed, a family member views the family environment negatively; after recovery, the same member's perception of the family becomes more positive (Bromet *et al.*, 1984). The question of which comes first, family malfunction or psychiatric disease, is unclear from existing studies. Longitudinal studies carried out in the family's physician's clinic would be the ideal method of resolving this dilemma.

The characteristic symptoms of depressed patients will impair their ability to interact with family members, co-workers, and friends. The spouse of the depressed individual will find it difficult to communicate in a loving way with a person who is irritable and uninterested in the activities he or she usually enjoyed. This relationship would deteriorate even more, with a loss in sexual interest, a pessimistic outlook, and a feeling of hopelessness with frequent death wishes. As the patient withdraws further, communication is almost nil. In the face of such symptoms, the significant other is hard pressed to maintain a civil, positive attitude. Paranoia with a low self-esteem causing unreasonable jealousy increases the pressure on the marriage. Unfortunately, employers, friends, and family may misinterpret the low energy, temper outbursts, and functional complaints, and thus regard the patient as an unreasonable, lazy person. It is not surprising that these misconceptions may result in marital discord and even divorce. Although treatment of the depression with antidepressants and appropriate family counseling may restore domestic tranquillity, a number of marriages go on to divorce months after the depressed member is well. The marital role impairment may persist an average of 4 years after symptomatic recovery (Bothwell & Weissman, 1971). This erosion of the relationship may be due to the inability of the couple to erase the memory of their suffering, or the marriage may have been unstable before the advent of the depressive illness. The couple may have developed certain patterns of handling their disagreements during the depressive illness that now may be a detriment to the marriage.

Family physicians, from their experience with families and from the literature, can understand how the divorce rate goes up when both partners in such a marriage have a psychiatric illness. This is particularly true when the wife of a depressive is an hysteric (somatization syndrome) or antisocial, and the husband of a depressive is antisocial or alcoholic.

These traits of depressed parents will have an adverse effect on the development of young children and their future health. The irritable, pessimistic parent with low self-esteem has been found to give poor care and then to compensate with overprotection. This affectionless control has been shown to result in a higher incidence of depression in children during their third and fourth decades of life. The psychomotor retardation and profound fatigue of a major depression would create serious obstacles to home management for the depressed homemaker. The result would resemble a chaotic family.

Data gathered on such families over a long time period by their family physicians could prove or disprove the first hypothesis—that psychiatric illness, particularly depression, may be the cause of marital problems and divorce. These same physicians would have available the data to prove or disprove the second hypothesis—that the children of one or both depressed parents may suffer attention-deficit disorders, separation anxiety, and conduct disorders, and at some future time may develop a major depression and/or substance abuse.

The close relationship of the interested family physician to all members of the family puts the practitioner in a good position to collect data for such research. The family system holds many secrets that affect the health and welfare of the family as a macro-organism as well as the well-being of the individual members.

References

Akiskal HS. Factors associated with incomplete recovery in primary depressive illness. Journal of Clinical Psychiatry 1982; 43:266–271.

Bothwell S, Weissman MM. Social impairment four years after an acute depressive episode. American Journal of Orthopsychiatry 1971; 47:231–237.

Briscoe W, Smith JB, Robins E, Marten S, Gaskin F. Divorce and psychiatric disease. Archives of General Psychiatry 1973; 29:119–125.

Brodie HK, Leff MJ. Bipolar depression: a comparative study of patient characteristics. American Journal of Psychiatry 1971; 127:126–130.

Bromet EJ, Ed V, May S. Family environments of depressed outpatients. Acta Psychiatrica Scandinavica 1984; 69:197–200.

Cadoret RJ. Evidence for genetic inheritance of primary affective disorder in adoptees. American Journal of Psychiatry 1978; 135:463–466.

Cadoret RJ, O'Gorman TW, Heywood E, Troughton E. Genetic and environmental factors in major depression. Journal of Affective Disorders 1985; 9:155–164.

Cadoret RJ, Widmer RB, North C. Depression in family practice: long-term prognosis and somatic complaints. Journal of Family Practice 1980; 10:625–629.

Cadoret RJ, Widmer RB, Troughton EP. Somatic complaints: harbinger of depression in primary care. Journal of Affective Disorders 1980; 2:61–70.

Cadoret RJ, Winokur G. Genetics and psychiatry. In: Spittell JA Jr, ed. Clinical medicine, Vol. 12. New York: Harper & Row, 1982.

Gaensbauer TJ, Harmon RJ, Cytryn L, McKnew DH. Social and affective development in infants with a manic-depressive parent. American Journal of Psychiatry 1984; 141:223–229.

Hughes MC. Recurrent abdominal pain and childhood depression: clinical observations of 23 children and their families. American Journal of Orthopsychiatry 1984; 54:146–155.

Lesser AL. Hypomania and marital conflict. Canadian Journal of Psychiatry 1983; 28:362–366.

Marsland DW, Wood M, Mayo F. Content of family practice: Part 1. Rank order of diagnosis by frequency. Journal of Family Practice 1976; 3:37.

McNabb R. Family function and depression. Journal of Family Practice 1983; 16:169–170.

Merikangas KR. Divorce and assortative mating among depressed patients. American Journal of Psychiatry 1984; 141:74–76.

Parker G. Parental characteristics in relation to depressive disorders. British Journal of Psychiatry 1979a; 52:1–10.

Parker G. Reported parental characteristics in relation to trait depression and anxiety levels in a non-clinical group. Australian and New Zealand Journal of Psychiatry 1979b; 13:260–264.

Parker G. Parental representations and affective symptoms: examination for an hereditary link. British Journal of Medical Psychology 1982; 55:57–61.

Parker G. Parental "affectionless control" as an antecedent to adult depression: a risk factor delineated. Archives of General Psychiatry 1983; 40:956–960.

Parker G, Hadzi-Pavlovic D. Modification of levels of depression in mother-bereaved women by parental and marital relationships. Psychological Medicine 1984; 14:125–135.

Robins E, Murphy GE, Wilkinson RH Jr, Gassner S, Kayes S. Some clinical considerations in the prevention of suicide based on a study of 134 successful suicides. American Journal of Public Health 1959; 49:888–899.

Tennant C, Hurry J, Bebbington P. The relation of childhood separation experiences to adult depressive and anxiety states. British Journal of Psychiatry 1982; 141:475–482.

von Knorring A-L. Adoption studies on psychiatric illness: epidemiological, environmental and genetic aspects. Umea University Medical Dissertations (New Series No. 101-ISSN0346-6612), Umea University, Umea, Sweden, 1983.

von Knorring A-L, Bohman M, Sigvardsson S. Early life experiences and psychiatric disorders: an adoptee study. Acta Psychiatrica Scandinavica 1982; 65:283–291.

Weissman MM, Prusoff BA, Gammon GD, Merikangas KR, Leckman JF, Kidd KK. Psychopathology in the children (ages 6–18) of depressed and normal parents. Journal of the American Academy of Child Psychiatry 1984; 23:78–84.

Widmer RB, Cadoret RJ. Depression in primary care: changes in pattern of patient visits and complaints during a developing depression. Journal of Family Practice 1978; 7:293–302.

Widmer RB, Cadoret RJ, North CS. Depression in family practice: some effects on spouses and children. Journal of Family Practice 1980; 10:45–51.

Wilson DR, Widmer RB, Cadoret RJ, Judiesch K. Somatic symptoms: a major feature of depression in a family practice. Journal of Affective Disorders 1983; 5:199–207.

37

Alcohol and the Family System

PETER STEINGLASS

George Washington University School of Medicine

Chronic alcoholism traditionally has been thought of as a condition of individuals. Although speculation about its etiology and factors accounting for its chronic course have ranged all the way from genetic hypotheses (Cloninger 1987; Goodwin, 1979; Reich, Cloninger, Lewis, & Rice 1981) to personality theories (Barnes, 1983) to theories of biochemical diatheses (Schuckit & Haglund, 1977; Schuckit, 1984), each of these perspectives assumes a defect of some sort in the *individual* who develops this condition. When family factors are brought into the picture, they typically are done so with two thoughts in mind: either that the presence in the family of an already alcoholic member genetically predisposes future generations to alcoholism—a genetic high-risk hypothesis supported by data from a growing body of adoption and twin studies (Cloninger, Bohman, & Sigvardsson, 1981; Goodwin, Schulsinger, Hermansen, Guze, & Winokur, 1973) or that factors within the family environment influence the overall course of alcoholism, especially response to treatment on the part of the alcoholic individual (Jacob, Dunn, & Leonard, 1983; Moos & Moos, 1984; Orford *et al.*, 1975).

The family systems approach to alcoholism takes a very different perspective vis-à-vis this problem. It proposes that independent of the influence of individual biologic and psychologic variables in predisposing someone to alcoholism, and despite the fact that this is a condition defined by the behavior (drinking) of one individual, it is nevertheless possible (and profitable) to conceptualize alcoholism as a family-level as well as an individual-level condition. Thus, the systems approach, though sensitive to the need to account for individual-level factors, nevertheless places primary attention on core systemic properties of family behavior and organizational characteristics as its special contribution to the understanding of alcoholism.

Further, because the systems approach is, at its core, an interactional one, it focuses attention not only on the relationships between family variables and the course of alcoholism, but also on the reciprocal impact of alcohol on family life. For example, if one of the core systemic properties of families is the nature of their organizational structures (hierarchic ordering of subsystems, boundary characteristics, etc.), then the family systems approach to alcoholism examines how different patterns of family organization either increase or decrease the likelihood that alcoholism will thrive in the family environment *and* how these properties are affected by the presence of a chronic behavioral disorder like alcoholism.

Take, for example, the following brief clinical vignette excerpted from a research interview: A woman in her 20s, attempting to describe to the interviewer what it was like for her growing up in an alcoholic family, said that when she was in high school, she would frequently come home on Friday afternoon and, on seeing an opened bottle of liquor on the kitchen table, would go on ''automatic pilot'' for the rest of the weekend. When asked what she meant by ''automatic pilot,'' she replied that she was referring to a set of preprogrammed behaviors that she would carry out for the rest of the weekend. In that she would do so in an unthinking fashion, the term "automatic pilot" seemed to her an appropriate one.

The behaviors included such things as breaking the usual mealtime routine and eating instead on an "as needed" schedule (because of her assumption that the family would not be convening for meals); not inviting any of her friends into the house for the weekend; and assuming that she would not be having any meaningful contacts with other family members over the course of the weekend—in other words, putting family life on ice for that weekend. Her father, who was the identified alcoholic and was a weekend drinker, would usually sober up in time to return to work on Monday. Having now returned to a state of sobriety, he (and other family members) would again participate actively in family life.

In this family, therefore, even though only the identified alcoholic was actively drinking during a particular weekend, the behavior of each and every family member changed as a result of his active drinking. Further, these behaviors were so familiar to the woman telling the story as to lead her to use the metaphor of an "automatic pilot" to describe her actions. Even more to the point, her behaviors were in many ways analogous to those we typically associate with alcohol intoxication: disruption of sleep and mealtime patterns, diminution of meaningful social interactions, and the like. Thus, it appears that in this family, *all* family members took on a style of interaction typically associated with intoxication, even though only one person was doing the active drinking. When systems-oriented clinicians have used the term "alcoholic system" in describing family behavior, they are referring to this type of behavior. That is, the on-again, off-again drinking pattern of an alcoholic member has become a *central organizing principle* around which whole programs of family behavior are built.

In this chapter, I will attempt to provide an overview of the family systems approach to alcoholism. I will do so, first, by outlining those characteristics of chronic alcoholism that are of greatest relevance to the systems perspective, and then by illustrating how these properties have been conceptualized, incorporated into theoretic models, and subjected to systematic study by systems-oriented family researchers. Thus, I will not attempt a comprehensive review of the family research literature into alcoholism, nor will I address questions of treatment (family therapy) as such. Instead, my goal is to convey, through selected examples, an accurate flavor of how the family systems approach to alcoholism has been conceptualized and operationalized. The reader is referred to several excellent reviews of the research and therapy literature for detailed overviews of these other topics (Ablon, 1984; el-Guebaly & Offord, 1977; Kaufman & Kaufman, 1979; Lawson, Peterson, & Lawson, 1983; Orford & Harwin, 1982; Paolino & McCrady, 1977; Steinglass & Robertson, 1983).

ALCOHOLISM AND THE FAMILY: UNIQUE ASPECTS

Of the many features of alcoholism that have attracted research and clinical interest, five aspects have particular relevance for a family systems approach to alcoholism. These aspects are that alcoholism (1) is a chronic condition, (2) entails the use of a psychobiologically active drug, (3) is cyclical in nature, (4) produces predictable behavioral responses, and (5) has a definable developmental course.

Chronicity

Although alcoholism is highly heterogeneous in presentation and course, its onset is typically an insidious one, and its course, chronic. Although this course may include periodic crises, often explosive in nature, alcoholism is by definition a chronic condition. Looked at from a systems perspective, therefore, the challenge is to understand how the family manages to maintain its long-term structural and functional stability in the face of what might be presumed to be a destabilizing condition. How is this long-term stability achieved, and what price does the family pay for incorporating a chronic condition as one of its life themes? The variable presentation of alcoholism and differences in drinking patterns also seem to place different degrees of stress on the family and to be associated with different family response patterns. Thus, our interest is focused not only on typologies of drinking patterns, but also on typologies of alcoholic families.

Use of a Psychobiologically Active Drug

Alcohol is a powerful drug whose psychopharmacologic properties include both transient stimulant and subsequent depressant qualities, as well as major disturbances of memory function, cognition, and verbal interactional behavior. Therefore, it can be assumed that introducing such a drug into a family system has an impact on multiple aspects of interactional behavior. For example, the depressant nature of alcohol presumably alters affective tone, sexual behavior, aggressive behavior, and the like. Further, long-term central nervous system depression produces lethargy, somnolence, and withdrawal. Cognitive disturbances make verbal communication unreliable. Nonverbal communication channels, such as physical communication, affective feeling tone, interaction rates, and the like, probably are therefore of heightened importance in these families.

Dual-State Pattern of Behavior: Off–On Cycling

Most alcoholic drinking patterns are cyclic in nature. Periods of intoxication ranging from several hours to several days are interspersed with periods of sobriety. The often sharp contrast between intoxicated and sober behavior is as striking in dealing with the individual alcoholic as the manic-depressive cycling of bipolar affective psychosis. Of all the clinical features of alcoholism, this is the most dramatic. Presumably, therefore, the family system must account for this cycling process if it is to maintain overall stability. Thus, different family-level patterns of behavior may be evident when alcohol is present versus when it is absent.

Predictability of Behavioral Responses

Individual alcoholics have been found to have remarkably consistent patterns of behavior during periods of intoxication (Tamerin & Mendelson, 1969). Behavior during one drinking episode can be predicted from a knowledge of prior responses to alcohol. Predictability of behavior implies a high degree of patterning. If this individual-level phenomenon is extended to the family, one would then expect to see predictable patterns of interactional behavior associated with alcohol use. In that families often use their most highly patterned behaviors as regulators of the family environment (i.e., such behaviors become incorporated in family homeostatic processes), alcoholic families may well wind up using alcohol-related behaviors to regulate the constancy of the family's internal environment. It has been proposed, therefore, that as alcoholism takes hold in the family, these aspects of behavior particularly are prone to being shaped by the impact of the highly predictable individual-level response of the family's identified alcoholic member once drinking has started (Steinglass, Bennett, Wolin, & Reiss, 1987). Examples of such behaviors are daily routines and family rituals. Hence, systems-oriented researchers have focused on these behaviors as convenient "windows" in studying the relationship between alcohol use and family behavior in the alcoholic family (Steinglass, 1981; Wolin, Bennett, Noonan, & Teitelbaum, 1980).

Life Course of Alcoholism

Alcoholism was long thought to be a condition with an insidious onset and a life course of steady, if somewhat variable, deterioration (Jellinek, 1960). Although a number of respected studies have tended to support this view (e.g., Vaillant, 1983), large-scale survey data have suggested that alcoholism is instead a heterogeneous condition with a variable long-term course. A compelling argument can therefore be made for a model of alcoholism that views it as a spectrum disorder rather than a unitary condition (Pattison, Sobell, & Sobell, 1977). At the most concrete level, alcoholic drinking patterns vary widely not only with regard to temporal patterning (steady state versus binge drinking, etc.) but also in their contextual variables (in-home versus out-of-home drinking, solo versus group drinking, etc.).

Although it is as yet unclear whether these different patterns reflect different "types" of alcoholism or are attributable to other factors, it stands to reason that different long-term patterns of drinking behavior should be associated with different life histories for alcoholic families (Steinglass, 1980). The family systems approach would perhaps phrase it in terms of the "goodness of fit" that exists between the drinking pattern of the alcoholic individual on the one hand and family organizational characteristics on the other hand. In the "stable" family situation, a reasonable and probably complementary fit exists between the characteristics of the alcoholism life course variable (steady-state drinking, versus alternating periods of months to years of sobriety and months to years of drinking, versus spontaneous remission, versus treatment-associated remission), and specific organizational characteristics of the family (patterns of daily routines, relative tolerance of uncertainty, family developmental characteristics, and the like).

REPRESENTATIVE STUDIES USING SYSTEMS APPROACHES

In this section, I will review a representative sample of family studies of alcoholism, focusing particular attention on those studies that have used systems concepts in formulating their research designs and/or interpreting research findings. Three groups of studies have been selected: first, the body of studies carried out by Steinglass and his colleagues, which represents the most extensive application to date of systems concepts to the exploration of alcoholism and the family; second, the work of Jacob and his colleagues, which focuses more explicitly on empirical investigations of the impact of alcohol on interactional behavior and emotional satisfaction in alcoholic families; and third, studies by Wolin and Bennett of family rituals in alcoholic families, which are illustrative of a concentrated look at one type of family regulatory behavior as it relates to alcoholism.

The Steinglass Studies

In that Steinglass and his colleagues have been the alcoholism researchers who have most explicitly adopted a family systems perspective in their model-building efforts and research designs, the overall development of this work will be discussed at some length. The work can be conveniently divided into three separate phases based on the different versions of the family systems model of alcoholism proposed by Steinglass.

PHASE I: A FAMILY SYSTEMS APPROACH TO ALCOHOLISM

The work of Steinglass and his colleagues dates back to a series of papers centering on reports of direct clinical observations of interactional behavior between family members observed during periods of "experimentally-induced intoxication" (Steinglass, Weiner, & Mendelson, 1971; Weiner, Tamerin, Steinglass, & Mendelson, 1971), observations that revealed dramatic changes in patterns of interactional behavior when alcohol was being consumed. Although this was hardly an unexpected finding, the direction these changes took was totally unanticipated. In contrast to the usual conceptions of intoxication as contributing to instability, violence, interference with stable interpersonal relationships, and disorganization of behavior, interactional behavior during intoxication, as observed in these familial dyads, appeared *more* patterned and organized than interactional behavior observed during sobriety.

A theoretic model developed in response to these clinical observations postulated that alcoholism served one of two very different functions in family systems. First, it could serve as a *signal* of major stress. Second, and perhaps of greater relevance, it could come to play a significant role in systems *maintenance*. Furthermore, alcohol abuse, by dint of its profound behavioral, cultural, societal, and physical consequences, might assume such a central position in the life of some families as to become an *organizing principle* for interactional life within these families. Steinglass called such families "alcoholic systems," a term that, it was argued, would also apply to such nonfamily social systems as the skid row drinking gang.

This model of alcoholism as an organizing principle for family life represented a radical departure from the customary view that saw alcoholism as a disruptive force in family life. However, a series of laboratory and naturalistic studies designed to explore the "systems approach" model generated data entirely consistent with the basic postulates of the alcoholic system concept described above (Steinglass, 1975; Wolin & Steinglass, 1974). These findings, many of which were counterintuitive, encouraged further development of systems-based theoretic models.

PHASE II: ALCOHOLIC MAINTENANCE MODEL

During Phase II, the findings and design strategies developed during Phase I were applied to a study of married couples (as opposed to homeless chronic alcoholics). Married couples were simultaneously admitted to an inpatient service for a 10-day stay as part of an experimental treatment program. During this period of conjoint hospitalization, direct observations were made of interactional behavior during states of intoxication as well as sobriety (Steinglass, Davis, & Berenson, 1977).

Two major conclusions emerged from these observations. First, it was found that intoxication in one spouse leads to a series of behaviors by *both* spouses that are repetitive, predictable, and different from sober behaviors; and, second, interactional behavior associated with intoxication seemed not only patterned and predictable, but also purposeful.

Clinical analyses of these data led to the conviction that not only were couples expressing novel behavior during intoxication, but also that this behavior was potentially functional in nature (Davis, Berenson, Steinglass, & Davis, 1974). For example, a sexually inhibited couple was more expressive and affectionate during periods of intoxication; a meek and ineffectual couple was able to assert itself more effectively during intoxication. In this sense, intoxicated interactional behavior seemed to solve a problem for the couple.

A second-generation model, the "alcohol maintenance model," was developed to incorporate these findings. Emphasis was placed on the repetitive cycling that occurs in alcoholic families between what was called the "sober family system" and the "intoxicated family system." Insofar as the family gradually but persistently would begin to use behaviors associated with intoxicated states to solve extant family problems, alcoholism inevitably would become enmeshed with ongoing family problem-solving strategies. It was proposed that this process is pushed along and heightened by the family's assumption (consciously or unconsciously) that alcohol, rather than the interactional behavior associated with the intoxicated state, is a crucial component of successful problem-solving (see Figure 37-1).

In the families studied, alcohol-induced behaviors seemed to provide the family with vehicles for rapidly stabilizing problematic situations in the family. This stabilizing effect of alcohol seemed to be made possible by two features of the behavior it induced. First, the new behavior patterns associated with intoxication immediately became available for

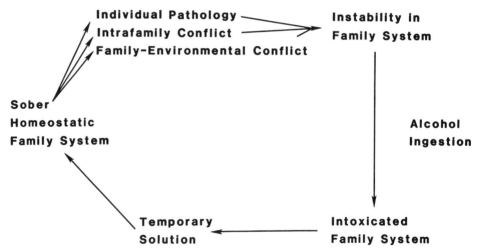

Figure 37-1. This graphic representation of the maintenance model illustrates not only the proposed relationship between the family's sober interactional state and its intoxicated interactional state, but also that the "problem," which destabilizes the family and initiates the cycling over to the intoxicated interactional states, can occur at any one of three different systemic levels within the family: at an individual level; at an intrafamilial level; or at the interface between the family and its outside environment. (Redrawn from Steinglass, Davis, & Berenson, 1977.)

stabilization related to the rapid change in behavior associated with the physiologic effect of alcohol. Second, the behavior appeared stylized and stereotyped; it held few surprises. This "surpriseless" quality, it was proposed, is especially useful for stabilization.

Observations made during the conjoint hospitalization study indicated that the actual direction of changes in family behavior for intoxicated as contrasted with sober states varied from family to family. For example, in some families, equilibrium might be restored by increasing interactional distance (drinker goes off to drink in the basement), or diminishing physical contact (no sex with someone who is drunk), or reducing tension in the family (familiar patterns of behavior are less tension-provoking than unique patterns); whereas in another family alcohol ingestion might be associated with closer interactional distance (making contact by fighting after the alcoholic spouse has been drinking), disinhibition (alcohol permits ritualized sexual behavior), or maintaining distance from the social environment (fights with neighbors when drunk).

This alcoholism maintenance model, supported by clinical data including direct observations of family interaction during states of intoxication, suggested a central role for alcohol-associated interactional behavior in family problem solving. By extension, it could also be hypothesized that families who have come to rely on intoxicated interactional behavior for problem solving would be disadvantaged in their efforts to convert from an active alcoholism state to a remission or a recovery state—disadvantaged, that is, when compared to families who are not alcohol-dependent problem solvers.

PHASE III: ALCOHOLISM LIFE HISTORY MODEL

Although no time frame was applied to the "maintenance model," the implication was that problems—whether related to intracouple interactional distance or to family–external environment conflict—emerge rapidly, create instability in short order, and are dealt with by rapid switches from sober to intoxicated interactional states. In addition to the rapid switches in interactional behavior associated with sobriety → intoxication cycling, Steinglass (1980) proposed that alcoholic families also evidence more macroscopic *developmental* patterns tied to important aspects of the drinking pattern of the identified alcoholic in the family.

Utilizing a family developmental perspective (Carter & McGoldrick, 1980; Hill & Rodgers, 1964), a model was designed to apply a family life cycle concept to the alcoholic family. Called the family life history model, it was originally based on the assumption that different phases in the drinking history of the family with identified alcoholics would also be associated with fundamentally different organizational patterns of behavior on the part of the family system. That is, as the identified alcoholic moved between phases of active drinking, phases of sobriety, and transitional phases between the two, systemic family behavior would also change in synchrony with this alcohol-related cycle.

This original version of the model (Steinglass, 1980) focused on three such alcohol-related phases—called respectively the "stable-wet," "stable-dry," and "transitional" phases of alcoholism. The assumption was that although some families might live through only one major transition from active drinking period to a period of permanent abstinence, other alcoholic families experienced multiple transitions between wet and dry phases. Thus, the model also included, as a core concept, the notion that the overall life cycle of the alcoholic family is to a large extent determined by the number and timing of such phasic switches.

To explore the concept of the life history model further, an ambitious study was designed that included extensive behavioral observations of families in three different settings—their homes, multiple family discussion groups, and the family interaction laboratory. The overall strategy of the study was to use a subgrouping of families based on the current drinking status of each family's identified alcoholic member as the independent variable, and then to attempt a statistical demonstration of consistencies in *family* interactional behavior (the dependent variable).

The most ambitious component of the study was the observations made of families in their homes (Steinglass, 1981). Behavioral data were collected during 9 observation sessions, each approximately 4 hours long, held in subject families' homes over a period of 6 months. Each family was observed by two behavior observers who were trained to use a structured observational technique called the Home Observation Assessment Method (HOAM) (Steinglass, 1979). The data generated by this method were thought to reflect underlying family regulatory processes as represented by family propensities in the organization and structuring of their home routines. A factor analysis of the HOAM data identified five major dimensions of home behavior (see Figure 37-2). These dimensions were then used as the dependent variables in a series of analyses of variance and discriminate function analysis procedures. The research demonstrated strong associations between alcoholic family subtype (stable-wet, stable-dry, transitional), and home behavior patterns. For example, the discriminate function analysis yielded two discriminate functions, one with a significant level of $p = .004$ (its level of power in discriminating the three families' subgroups based on different home behaviors), and another with a significant level of $p = .04$. The discriminate functions plot (Figure 37-3) graphically illustrates the differences found in the home behavior of the three types of alcoholic families.

Originally, Steinglass argued that these patterns of home behavior were most likely highly plastic. That is, these were patterns of behavior tied to the alcohol drinking phase, not necessarily behaviors reflective of inherent temperamental properties of the families themselves. At the same time, however, the cross-sectional nature of the data seemed to preclude an examination of this question. But a 2-year follow-up of this group of families suggested a very different conclusion (Steinglass, Tislenko, & Reiss, 1985). Family behavior patterns proved to be far more stable than originally appreciated. Further, it was found that those families who were originally labeled as "transitional" (that is, in a transitional developmental phase between wet and dry drinking periods) had, by history, already experienced many such episodes (of alternations between these two drinking phases). By way of contrast, families labeled as stable-wet in the first panel of data collection did not have this alternating history vis-à-vis drinking behavior.

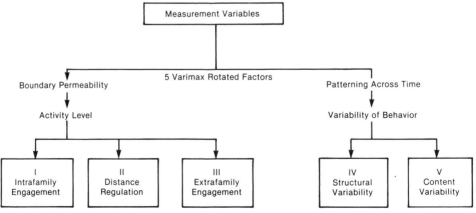

Figure 37-2. HOAM factor analysis.

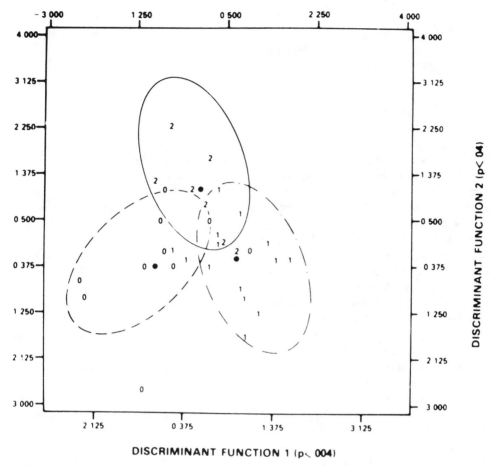

Figure 37-3. Discriminant analysis of in-home interactional behavior: comparison of stable-wet, stable-dry, and transitional families.

These follow-up data therefore suggested that the relationship between drinking pattern and family behavioral style could be best formulated as a *goodness of fit* between any individual-level characteristic (the type of drinking pattern) and a family-level behavioral characteristic (family temperament as reflected in patterns of daily routines). Such a goodness-of-fit hypothesis is, of course, entirely consistent with a family systems approach to alcoholism.

This changed perspective led to a revision of the family life history model (Steinglass, *et al.*, 1987). The emphasis in this revised model was not so much on the construct of the family alcohol phase, but rather on the notion of family *developmental distortions* associated with alcoholism. Steinglass and his colleagues argued that the fundamental impact of a chronic condition like alcoholism on family life is its ability to *invade* key family regulatory behaviors and, as a consequence, alter the normative developmental sequence of systemic maturation that occurs in the nonpathologic situation. "Developmental distortion" was the term used to identify this process of alteration.

The Jacob Studies

The studies of Jacob and his colleagues provide an interesting contrast to the work of the Steinglass group. Whereas Steinglass's major contribution has been his use of both research and clinical data about alcoholism and the family in the service of systems-oriented clinical model building, Jacob has argued for the value of carefully designed, empirical studies of family behavior of more narrow and explicit focus. In particular, Jacob's interest has focused on three issues of crucial importance to our better understanding of the relationships between alcoholism and family systems.

First, Jacob wants to know what aspects of behavior in alcoholic families are products of the presence of a chronic psychopathologic condition (any condition), and what aspects are unique to alcoholism. Thus, his studies have included, as a central design feature, matched samples of families with alcoholic members, families with chronically depressed members, and nonclinical families.

Second, Jacob wants to know if the changes that occur in family behavior when alcohol is introduced are fundamentally different for alcoholic families, or if they reflect instead just a more exaggerated version of a common family behavioral response to alcohol. Jacob argues that it is the contrast between alcohol-on and alcohol-off behavior that is the most crucial aspect of behavior to understand in these families. Hence, his studies have included extensive laboratory-based observations of family conflict resolution discussions during alcohol-present versus alcohol-absent testing sessions.

Third, Jacob is interested in the impact of alcoholism on psychologic adjustment of family members. He has attempted to explore further the hypotheses of Steinglass and others (Davis *et al.,* 1974) that alcohol-related behaviors may have adaptive as well as maladaptive features by empirically assessing the temporal relationships between alcohol use and reports of psychologic well-being on the part of both alcoholic and nonalcoholic spouses in alcoholic marriages.

Thus far, Jacob and his colleagues have reported only pilot data from their large-scale study of alcoholic versus depressed versus nonclinical families (Jacob & Seilhamer, 1987). These data, however, though based on observations of very small numbers of families, are nevertheless fascinating. In particular, because they draw on multiple observation points for each family, and because they focus so explicitly on the alcohol-on/alcohol-off contrast, they provide an important resource for current hypothesis generation about the alcoholic family system. A brief summary of the most important sets of findings follows.

The Jacob protocol included three laboratory observation sessions—the first geared to acclimate the family to the experiment setting, but the second and third sessions used to contrast family behavior during alcohol-on versus alcohol-off states (alcoholic beverages were made available to the spouses during one of these testing sessions, but not during the other). During each of these sessions family members were asked to engage each other in brief discussions of topics based on items derived from a "revealed difference" questionnaire and from Weiss's (1980) Areas of Change Questionnaire. These discussions were videotaped and subsequently coded using the Marital Interaction Coding System (MICS) (Weiss, 1976), a frequently used, empirical interaction coding system of established reliability.

According to Jacob and Seilhamer (1987), preliminary analyses of these data suggest that not only is marital interaction in alcoholic couples more negative and less constructive, but also that there is a marked increase in negative communication occurring during the alcohol-on session. This contrast between drinking and nondrinking testing sessions was not present for the two comparison groups of depressed and nonclinical families. These pilot data replicate earlier findings reported by Jacob and his colleagues (Jacob, Ritchey, Cvitkovic, & Blane, 1981) from a study of eight families containing an alcoholic father/ husband and eight normal control families who had undergone laboratory assessments comparable to the ones reported above.

Parenthetically, studies of alcoholic couples in drinking versus nondrinking laboratory sessions have not always demonstrated a finding of increased negative activity associated with drinking for the alcoholic couple group. For example, a study by Frankenstein, Hay, and Nathan (1985), a study that also utilized the MICS to examine aspects of verbal interaction during laboratory discussions of marital problems, although reporting statistically significant differences between drinking and nondrinking sessions, also indicated that the direction of the difference was a *positive* one.

Frankenstein and colleagues (1985) argued that the results of their study was supportive of a hypothesis of an adaptive or reinforcing role for alcohol use in alcoholic marriages (a hypothesis already discussed in our review of the Steinglass *et al.*, 1977, study). Jacob (1985), on the other hand, contends that his findings would support a very different conclusion. Yet if both sets of findings are examined from a systems perspective, the more important aspect of these studies is the consistent finding of differences in interactional behavior associated with alcohol use versus behavior during sobriety. It is the uniqueness of this finding to the alcoholic couple that is the most important clinical finding. That is, it is entirely possible that some alcoholic couples shift their behavior in a positive direction when alcohol is being used, whereas other couples shift in a negative direction. (The more common direction is most likely an increase in negative affect, but small sample studies may well yield a different set of findings, as in Frankenstein *et al.*, 1985).

But the fact that the actual direction of change being manifested may vary from couple to couple in no way undermines the importance of the finding that alcoholic couples do in fact have a dual-state system of interactional behaviors. Further, for our purposes it is important that we not confuse positivity/negativity of affect with the notion of adaptive consequences of alcoholism. The Steinglass *et al.* (1977) study of conjointly hospitalized couples suggests that for some couples an increase in negative affect might well have adaptive consequences, whereas for other couples it is the expression of positive feelings in association with alcohol use that solves an extant problem for the couple. The most important finding, therefore, is the uniform identification of a unique dual-state phenomenon in the alcoholic family, a property of interactional behavior not present when nonalcoholic families are examined in dry versus drinking behavioral contexts.

A second group of findings reported by Jacob and his colleagues addressed the relationship between alcohol consumption and marital satisfaction in the alcoholic couples studied. Here the focus was not so much on judgments made by outsiders (behavioral coders), but rather on subjective perceptions of alcoholic and nonalcoholic spouses about their own psychologic status and satisfaction with the marriage.

The initial findings were quite striking (Jacob *et al.*, 1983). The alcoholic husbands (all identified alcoholics in the study sample were male) who had been consuming the larger amounts of alcohol over the past month were at the same time reporting relatively high levels of marital satisfaction. This finding, by itself, might not seem surprising. But a comparable finding was obtained from nonalcoholic wives. That is, wives whose husbands fell into the heavier drinking category regarding alcohol consumption over the previous month were not only reporting relatively greater marital satisfaction (using the Locke-Wallace [1959] test and the Dyadic Adjustment Scale [Spanier, 1976]), but were also obtaining relatively lower scores on the Beck Depression Inventory (Beck, Ward, Mendelson, Mock, & Erbaugh, 1961). Here again, then, is another report that could be construed as evidence of a possible adaptive role for alcohol use in at least some alcoholic marriages.

Finally, a third group of findings from the Jacob studies deals with attempts to subgroup his alcoholic family sample based on drinking characteristics of the family's identified alcoholic member. The interest here is to see if subtypes of alcoholic families can be identified that have different behavior patterns in association with alcohol use. Two variables were used to divide the families into subgroups: steady versus binge drinking, and in-home versus out-of-home drinking. Examples of these analyses are as follows.

Comparisons of steady-drinker versus binge-drinker marital couples with regard to marital satisfaction indicated that most of the correlations noted above between alcohol consumption scores and marital satisfaction measures could be attributed to the steady drinker subgroup alone (Jacob *et al.,* 1983). That is, correlations for the binge-drinker subgroup proved nonsignificant, but correlations for the steady drinker subgroup were highly significant.

Further, an intriguing study of the temporal relationships (day-to-day covariations) between alcohol consumption and marital satisfaction carried out on eight families who had already participated in the aforementioned study, also pointed to major differences in the patterns of these variables for subgroups of families based on drinking type (this time, out-of-home versus in-home drinking subgroups). Wives in the out-of-home drinking subgroup (alcoholics in this group were primarily weekend drinkers) reported a negative relationship between alcohol consumption and marital satisfaction ratings. But, most important, the relationship was a lagged one (marital satisfaction ratings decreased 5 days after increase in alcohol consumption) leading the investigators to conclude that this drop in satisfaction was in fact an anticipatory response to the upcoming weekend drinking bout. For the in-home drinking subgroup, on the other hand, findings were more equivocal (in that there was much more heterogeneity of response patterns). For at least two of the four couples, however, an increase in drinking was associated with an *increase* in marital satisfaction scores.

These findings have led Jacob to reanalyze his laboratory interaction (MICS) data, taking into account the above drinking behavior contextual variables (drinking style and primary drinking location). In these new analyses, families were divided into three subgroups: out-of-home binge drinkers, out-of-home daily drinkers, and in-home steady drinkers. A preliminary report of these analyses indicated crucial differences in negativity, problem-solving scores, and positivity for the three subgroups of families (Jacob, 1985).

Jacob found that in binge-drinking families, communications appeared to be generally negative and aversive, with this negativity being expressed primarily by the identified alcoholic. This increased negativity is in turn associated with a decrease in couple-level problem-solving efforts, attributable largely to the nonalcoholic wife's reduction in task focus. In the in-home steady-drinker subgroup, on the other hand, communication is considerably less negative than for the binge-drinking subgroup, and problem-solving behavior appears actually to improve somewhat during the drinking session. But the most striking finding is a dramatic increase in positivity during the drinking session for this subgroup. Finally, the out-of-home steady-drinking subgroup was described as ''the least stable type examined so far, sometimes appearing more similar to the binge drinkers and at other times operating more like the steady in-home drinker.''

These reports from the Jacob group of striking differences in the relationship between alcohol use and interactional behavior tied to a subgrouping of families based on drinking pattern variables thus parallels the reports from the Steinglass group of differences in laboratory and in-home behavior for stable-wet versus alternator versus stable-dry subgroups. If there is not yet consistency in the directions of these findings, it is probably attributable at this point to the very different methods used by these two groups of investigators rather than to a fundamental flaw in the concept of subgroup typing of alcoholic families.

The Wolin and Bennett Studies

The studies of Wolin and Bennett (Bennett *et al.*, 1987; Wolin *et al.*, 1980) are distinctive in two regards. First, they have focused explicitly on factors contributing to intergenerational transmission of alcoholism. Second, they have developed an intriguing strategy for using family ritual behavior as a psychosocial marker of underlying, systemic, regulatory processes in the family environment, processes that in turn might contribute to or protect family members from transmission of alcoholism.

Wolin and Bennett start from the premise that the intergenerational transmission of alcoholism is a product of both genetic and environmental influences. The environmental component (especially those factors attributable to the family environment), to their way of thinking, is the major determinant of the *penetrance* of alcoholism, given a genetic predisposition to develop this condition.

Wolin and Bennett assume that the most powerful of these family systemic factors are the underlying regulatory mechanisms used by the family to organize its internal environment. Regulatory mechanisms, however, cannot be directly observed and measured. Instead, a better research strategy is to focus attention on one or more surface-level, observable behaviors that are assumed to be "markers" of underlying systemic regulatory processes.

The behavior they have chosen to focus on is the "family ritual," that is, a repetitive form of behavior acted out in a systemic fashion over time, which has become a "symbolic form of communication" in the family (Wolin & Bennett, 1984). Because of the central role of ritual behavior in family life, these investigators have hypothesized that the relationship between alcohol use and ritual behavior should be an excellent prognosticator of the variability of cross-generational transmission of alcoholism in families.

Wolin and Bennett also point out that cross-generational transmission of alcoholism in families is best conceptualized as a two-generational process. On one side is the "sender" generation—the parents—at least one of whom is alcoholic. For this generation, the issue is whether or not this condition will be passed on to the next generation. On the other side is the "receiver" generation—the children—who presumably play a role in determining whether or not they will "accept" this alcoholic legacy. Wolin and Bennett have argued that, by paying careful attention to the relationship between alcoholic behavior and ritual behavior in these families, the independent contributions of the parental and childhood generations to the outcome of the transmission issue can be tracked systematically and predicted.

In their first study, Wolin and Bennett focused on the parental generation and used a semistructured interview technique to reconstruct the nature of family ritual behavior during that period of time when the alcoholic spouse was engaged in his or her heaviest drinking and the children were still living at home (Wolin *et al.*, 1980). Careful analyses of the nature of ritual behaviors in a sample of 25 white, middle-class alcoholic families identified three different family types. The first group of families tended aggressively to protect their ritual behavior from the consequences of alcoholism. The investigators labeled these families "distinctive," in that ritual behavior was kept distinctive from alcoholic behavior. In a second group of families, ritual behavior was substantially altered to accommodate the needs or demands of the actively drinking alcoholic family member. This group of families was labeled "subsumptive," in that the ritual behavior was subsumed by alcoholic behavior. A third group of families seemed to fall in an intermediate range in that some ritual areas were protected and others were changed in the face of the demands of alcoholism.

After having classified families into one of these three groups, the investigators examined the relationship between ritual classification and alcohol transmission status. The transmitter families—that is, those families in which one or more of the children had become alcoholic—turned out to be subsumptive or intermediate families. The nontransmitter families, on the other hand, turned out to be predominantly distinctive families. In other words, the ability or willingness of the family to protect these family behavior patterns from accommodations to the needs of the alcoholic member seemed to have *protected* the children in the family from the subsequent development of alcoholism.

A second study carried out by these investigators examined the same question, but this time from the perspective of the "receiver" families. That is, the focus in this second study was on what happens when an adult child of an alcoholic parent marries and has to deal with the issue of what traditions from his or her family of origin will be perpetuated in the new family. The premise of this study was that a careful tracking of whether or not rituals from an alcoholic family of origin were perpetuated in the new family would be predictive of transmission of alcoholism as well.

To explore these intergenerational issues, Bennett, Wolin, Reiss, and Teitelbaum (1987) interviewed two or more grown siblings and their spouses from 30 families in which at least one parent was alcoholic (a total of 68 couples participated in this study). The same semistructured interview technique developed for the first study was used in this second study to generate detailed data about ritual behavior. Data were collected from each subject about family life when he or she was a child ("origin family interview") and present family life ("nuclear family interview"). Comparisons of data from these two interviews were used to determine, first, the extent of continuity of ritual behavior from each couple's family of origin versus the development of new ritual behaviors, and, second, how conscious a process this was for the couple.

These variables, along with demographic characteristics, were then introduced into a multiple regression analysis, and proved to be quite powerful predictors of transmission of alcoholism (alcoholism status was the criterion variable). In particular, the degree of *deliberateness* exercised by the couple in choosing *not* to replicate behavior patterns from the alcoholic family of origin proved to be a highly protective factor in diminishing the likelihood of alcoholism developing in this new generation.

Overall, therefore, the Wolin and Bennett studies provide strong evidence of the role of a family systemic property—in this case, the regulatory behavior they call family rituals—as a factor in the differential course of chronic alcoholism across generations.

CONCLUSION

Our understanding of the relationship between alcohol and the family system is still in its infancy. Only a handful of family systems-oriented researchers have thus far addressed this issue. Yet, as has been illustrated in the three groups of studies we have reviewed, the work in this area has been both exciting and rewarding. In particular, investigators have been able to identify specific aspects of family behavior that are linked to important clinical aspects of alcoholism.

For example, both the Steinglass and the Jacob studies have provided compelling data suggesting that behavior in alcoholic families varies dramatically depending on the drinking characteristics of the alcoholic family member. In particular, the family's use of alcohol-linked interactional behaviors for adaptive as well as maladaptive purposes (a phenomenon that has by now been repeatedly alluded to in the clinical and research literature) may be a phenomenon that applies only to a particular subset of alcoholic families—those in which the alcoholic member drinks at home and in a relatively predictable rather than an impulsive fashion.

As a second example, the Wolin and Bennett studies illustrate the feasibility of using a surface-level family behavioral characteristic to track the intergenerational course of alcoholism. The clinical extension of this work should be obvious. These findings clearly suggest that therapists should pay careful attention to such behaviors as family rituals, home routines, and family problem-solving strategies, as ways of assessing the extent to which alcoholism has invaded fundamental, systemic, regulatory processes within families.

The findings from these family interaction studies also point to the value of attending to differences in interactional behavior that emerge when alcohol is introduced into these families. After all, when all is said and done, the single most important distinguishing feature of alcoholism is the pathologic consumption of alcohol itself. Surely, therefore, it is crucial to our appreciation of the impact of alcoholism on families that we focus particular attention on the changes that occur in family behavior when drinking is going on. The fact that we now have ample data supporting the contention that the introduction of alcohol into family systems also induces substantial and predictable changes in family-level behavior is therefore an important advance. In light of these research findings, we can contend with considerable conviction that a clinical understanding of the impact of alcoholism on the family *must* include a thorough appreciation of this difference between the family's intoxicated interactional state and its sober interactional state.

Finally, we also have growing evidence of the value of using a developmental perspective in analyzing research findings. Presumably, such a perspective will prove equally valuable in the clinical setting. That is, our understanding of such important clinical issues as the timing of the initial presentation of alcoholism, the selection of treatment options, and the consequences of alcoholism for other family members will be considerably improved if approached from a *family* developmental perspective such as the life history model of alcoholism (Steinglass *et al.*, 1987).

Thus, alcoholism is clearly one of those conditions the understanding of which can be advanced very substantially by a family systems approach. We can most likely look forward to continuing progress not only in our elucidation of the behavioral consequences of alcohol use for the family but also in increasingly more specific clinical recommendations regarding family therapy techniques for the treatment of alcoholism.

References

Ablon J. Literature on alcoholism and the family. In: Galanter M, ed. Recent developments in alcoholism, Vol. 2. New York: Plenum Press, 1984: 383–396.

Barnes GE. Clinical and pre-alcoholic personality characteristics. In: Kissin B, Begleiter H, eds. The biology of alcoholism, Vol. 6. The pathogenesis of alcoholism: psychosocial factors. New York: Plenum Press, 1983:113–195.

Beck AT, Ward CH, Mendelson M, Mock J, Erbaugh J. An inventory for measuring depression. Archives of General Psychiatry 1961; 4:561–571.

Bennett LA, Wolin SJ, Reiss D, Teitelbaum MA. Couples at risk for alcoholism recurrence: protective influences. Family Process 1987; 26(1):111–129.

Carter EA, McGoldrick M, eds. The family life cycle: a framework for family therapy. New York: Gardner Press, 1980.

Cloninger, CR. Neurogenetic adaptive mechanisms in alcoholism. Science 1987; 236:410–416.

Cloninger CR, Bohman M, Sigvardsson S. Inheritance of alcohol abuse: cross fostering analysis of adopted men. Archives of General Psychiatry 1981; 38:861–868.

Davis DI, Berenson D, Steinglass P, Davis S. The adaptive consequences of drinking. Psychiatry 1974; 37:209–215.

el-Guebaly N, Offord DR. The offspring of alcoholics: a critical review. American Journal of Psychiatry 1977; 134:357–365.

Frankenstein W, Hay WM, Nathan PE. Effects of intoxication on alcoholics' marital communication and problem solving. Journal of Studies on Alcohol 1985; 46:1–6.

Goodwin DW. Alcoholism and heredity: a review and hypothesis. Archives of General Psychiatry 1979; 36:57–61.

Goodwin DW, Schulsinger F, Hermansen L, Guze SB, Winokur G. Alcohol problems in adoptees raised apart from alcoholic biological parents. Archives of General Psychiatry 1973; 28:238–243.

Hill R, Rodgers LRH. The developmental approach. In: Christensen HT, ed. Handbook of marriage and the family. Chicago: Rand-McNally, 1964:171–214.

Hops H, Wills T, Patterson G, Weiss R. Marital interaction coding system. Unpublished manuscript.

Jacob T. Alcoholism and family interaction: clarifications resulting from subgroup analyses and multi-method assessments. Presented at the International Conference on the Impact of Family Research on our Understanding of Psychopathology, Munich, Germany, September 2–5, 1985.

Jacob T, Dunn NJ, Leonard K. Patterns of alcoholic abuse and family stability. Alcoholism: Clinical and Experimental Research 1983; 7:382–385.

Jacob T, Ritchey D, Cvitkovic J, Blane H. Communication styles of alcoholic and non-alcoholic families while drinking and not drinking. Journal of Studies on Alcohol 1981; 42:466–482.

Jacob T, Seilhamer RA. Alcoholism and family interaction. In: Jacob T, ed. Family interaction and psychopathology: Theories, methods and findings. New York: Plenum Press, 1987.

Jellinek EM. The disease concept of alcoholism. New Brunswick, N.J.: Hillhouse Press, 1960.

Kaufman E, Kaufman PN. Family therapy of drug and alcohol abuse. New York: Gardner Press, 1979.

Lawson G, Peterson JS, Lawson A. Alcoholism and the family: a guide to treatment and prevention. Rockville, Md.: Aspen Publications, 1983.

Locke HJ, Wallace KM. Short. Marital adjustment and prediction tests: their reliability and validity. Marriage and Family Living 1959; 21:251–255.

Moos RA, Moos BS. The process of recovery from alcoholism: III. Comparing functioning in families of alcoholics and matched control families. Journal of Studies on Alcohol 1984; 45:111–118.

Orford J, Guthrie S, Nicholls P, Oppenheimer E, Egeit S, Hensman C. Self-reported coping behavior of wives of alcoholics and the association with drinking outcome. Journal of Studies on Alcohol 1975; 9:1254–1267.

Orford H, Harwin J, eds. Alcohol and the family. London: Croon Helm, 1982.

Paolino TJ, McCrady S. The alcoholic marriage: alternative perspectives. New York: Grune & Stratton, 1977.

Pattison EM, Sobell MB, Sobell LC. Emerging concepts of alcohol dependence. New York: Springer, 1977.

Reich T, Cloninger CR, Lewis C, Rice J. Some recent findings in the study of genotype–environment interaction in alcoholism. In: NIAAA Research Monograph No. 5. Rockville, Md.: NIAAA, 1981:145–165.

Schuckit MA. Generic and biochemical factors in the etiology of alcoholism. In: Grinspoon L, ed. Psychiatric update: the American Psychiatric Association annual review, Vol III. Washington, D.C.: American Psychiatric Press, 1984.

Schuckit MA, Haglund RMJ. An overview of the etiological theories on alcoholism. In: Estes N, Heinemann E, eds. Alcoholism: development, consequences and interventions. St. Louis: Mosby, 1977.

Spanier GD. Measuring dyadic adjustment: new scales for assessing the quality of marriage and similar dyads. Journal of Marriage and the Family 1976; 37:15–28.

Steinglass P. The simulated drinking gang: an experimental model for the study of a systems approach to alcoholism: I. Description of the model; II. Findings and implications. Journal of Nervous and Mental Disease 1975; 161:100–122.

Steinglass P. The home observation assessment method (HOAM): real-time observations of families in their homes. Family Process 1979; 18:337–354.

Steinglass P. A life history model of the alcoholic family. Family Process 1980; 19:211–227.

Steinglass P. The alcoholic family at home: patterns of interaction in dry, wet and transitional stages of alcoholism. Archives of General Psychiatry 1981; 38:578–584.

Steinglass P, Bennett LA, Wolin SJ, Reiss, D. The alcoholic family. New York: Basic Books, 1987.

Steinglass P, Davis D, Berenson D. Observations of conjointly hospitalized ''alcoholic couples'' during sobriety and intoxication: implications for theory and therapy. Family Process 1977; 16:1–16.

Steinglass P, Robertson A. The alcoholic family. In: Kissin B, Begleiter H, eds. The biology of alcoholism: Vol. 6. The pathogenesis of alcoholism: psychosocial factors. New York: Plenum Press, 1983:243–307.

Steinglass P, Tislenko L, Reiss D. Stability/instability in the alcoholic marriage: the interrelationship between course of alcoholism, family process and marital outcome. Family Process 1985; 24:265–376.

Steinglass P, Weiner S, Mendelson JH. A systems approach to alcoholism: a model and its clinical applications. Archives of General Psychiatry 1971; 24:401–408.

Tamerin JS, Mendelson JH. The psychodynamics of chronic inebriation: observations of alcoholics during the process of drinking in an experimental group setting. American Journal of Psychiatry 1969; 125:886–899.

Vaillant, GE. The natural history of alcoholism. Cambridge, MA: Harvard University Press, 1983.

Weiner S, Tamerin JS, Steinglass P, Mendelson JH. Familial patterns in chronic alcoholism: a study of a father and son during experimental intoxication. American Journal of Psychiatry 1971; 127:1659–1664.

Weiss R. The Areas of Change Questionnaire. Eugene: University of Oregon Department of Psychology, 1980.

Weiss R. Marital Interaction Coding System (MICS): training and reference manual for coders. University of Oregon Marital Studies Program, Eugene, Oregon, 1976.

Wolin SJ, Bennett LA. Family rituals. Family Process 1984; 23:401–420.

Wolin SJ, Bennett LA, Noonan DL, Teitelbaum MA. Disruptive family rituals: a factor in the intergenerational transmission of alcoholism. Journal of Studies on Alcohol 1980; 41:199–214.

Wolin SJ, Steinglass P. Interactional behavior in an alcoholic community. Medical Annals of D.C. 1974; 43:183–187.

PART TEN

Assessment and Future Directions

38

Description, Inference, Prescription: Data Analysis, Scientific Inference, and Epistemologic Reasoning in Clinical Research

TROY D. ABELL
University of Oklahoma

Why are we interested in formal research that goes beyond daily impressions, clinical or otherwise? One reason is that human health and disease are complex. There are too many variables on too many patients to keep in our memories. There is the tendency of the human memory, when presented with such complex interactions, to slide back to preexisting categories, to remain stereotypic in perspective (D'Andrade, 1974). Even though the cynics say that researchers only state the obvious, it is not so. The type of quantification of risk necessary for improved treatment or more efficacious screening is not self-evident. Many issues of human health or disease can be addressed only with explicitly designed observations, in-depth probing far beyond the normal patient–physician encounter, systematic analysis, and a sample large enough to overcome inconsistencies due to random fluctuation.

A telephone company advertisement proposes that "nobody goes into business to grow smaller." One assumption being made here is that nobody goes into research to explain zero percent of the variance. No family therapist or physician goes into a clinical encounter hoping that nothing learned from the past will be applicable in the present. If I say, "This case is useful," I am implicitly moving to a second case. Thus, there is comparison. Whether you are a therapist, a physician, a nurse, or a researcher using participant observation, in-depth interviewing, pencil-and-paper measures, clinical observations, or secondary data sources, you finally come to data analysis.

It is artificial in some ways to separate a discussion of the analysis of data from our thoughts about designing observations. One possible punctuation of the entire research process is that we (1) design observations, (2) describe our observations, (3) infer meaning to our observations, and (4) prescribe new behavior (whether that behavior be treatment, program changes, or additional research) on the basis of these observations.

This discussion of analysis will focus on the three elements of the research process that come into play once the data are collected: (1) description, (2) inference, and (3) prescription. The emphasis will be less on technique than on orientation, less on the latest analytic tool than on using our best logical and correlational abilities to make sense of the data at hand.

The epistemologic stance taken here is that we sculpt our data. We punctuate. We orchestrate. Our short- and long-term goals influence our orchestration. The data do not speak for themselves. We search hungrily for minute manifestations of associations for some factors and seemingly suppress rather powerful manifestations of association with others. What we tease out of our data is harmonious with our needs, or with those of the funding agencies, or of the editors of journals. Analysis of data takes place in a context— personal, scientific, and political—including the history of family-oriented research itself.

Family medicine and family-oriented health research are primarily human sciences. Humans are made up of fundamental particles—atoms, organs, and physiologic systems—and tend to live in social groups. Research is needed at all these levels. The overwhelming challenge for the family medicine researcher is at the comprehensive level where all of these levels interact. A woman's uterus is not pregnant, the woman is pregnant—all of her: her endocrine system, her cardiovascular system, her central nervous system. Not only is she pregnant, but so can be the biologic or nonbiologic father, her parents, and her extended family.

It is wonderful to chat over hot tea about holistic health, but it is a difficult task to face the scientific consequences of such holism. The enormous number of interactions contained in one human as we study a particular health or disease process has several ramifications for researchers. No one variable or conceptual framework is going to provide a breakthrough that will allow us to explain 100% of the variance in outcome. There will probably not be a psychosocial "double helix." Such wonderful breakthroughs tend to occur at more fundamental levels of analysis. The closer one comes to the totality of humanness, the more probabilistic interactions become pertinent. No matter how sophisticated our knowledge about genetic mutation, the type and timing of a specific mutation is randomly associated with its usefulness in the environment. We must face the possibility that randomness is ontologic in human affairs, and not just a result of error, in measurement or otherwise.

Thus, although we admire the economists who can explain 99% of the variance in total spending patterns using inflation rates, the gross national product, and other macroeconomic factors, we need to be reminded that these same economists can explain only a small proportion of the variance in a basic human research problem: Who gets what, and why, in the socioeconomic market? In family medicine research we attack problems similar to this latter question. Humans are too complex for the essentialist concept of causality: If E then D, if not E then not D. We live, as humans, in a probabilistic world.

As we search for family factors that will aid in our understanding of health and disease, we must be prepared for relatively low levels of association. We must face the possibility that another operationalization, from an entirely different conceptual framework, will explain just about the same amount of variance in outcome. Given this almost overwhelming problem, we must learn to *describe* our research results well if we are going to help each other synergistically.

DESCRIPTION

Given the epistemologic stance stated above, it seems naive to talk about *just* description, as though description is simple, noninformative, and only a stage or section of an article through which we must pass quickly. Before we ever began to analyze the data, we designed our observations. We decided on the focus. We attenuated to several sets of behaviors and not others. Blinders are useful and crucial to good research, but we must be aware that our first descriptive act is already highly analytic. For this reason, I prefer not to overemphasize the distinction between descriptive and analytic stages of analysis. Our description is already analytic, and our most sophisticated analytic attempt is still descriptive.

What seems mere univariate description is already multifactorial, given all the variables we exclude or hold constant. A description of the zero-order correlation between two factors allowed to vary in a laboratory is a special case of an extremely complex, multifactorial, interactional process.

Many researchers conceptualize the statistical process as consisting of (1) descriptive,

Table 38-1. Descriptive Statistics, Analytic Statistics, and Statistical Testing

	Descriptive statistics	Analytic statistics	Statistical testing
A			
B	Descriptive statistics		Statistical testing
C	Exploratory data analysis	Statistical modeling	
D	Probability-free statistics	Probability-based statistics	
E	μ　　σ　　ρ		Statistical testing

(2) analytic, and (3) significance testing components (see Table 38-1, row A). Although I have just stated my preference for avoiding a strict dichotomy between descriptive and analytic statistics (Table 38-1, Row B), it is evident that mathematicians and statisticians perceive different processes taking place. The distinction between exploratory data analysis (EDA) (Mosteller & Tukey, 1977) and statistical modeling (SM) manifests this perception (Table 38-1, row C). Another orientation has been to separate analyses based on probability distributions and analyses that use probability-free models (Table 38-1, row D).

Although these distinctions are not tapping necessarily identical phenomena, they are complementary on one key issue. There exist tests of statistical significance that evaluate the effects of random variation or chance on described relationships. These tests are distinct from the actual description and must be kept separate in our thinking and presentation (Table 38-1, Row E). What is it we want to describe? The sample. The variables. The association or difference between the variables. Thus the generic mathematic symbols μ σ ρ. We describe central tendency (μ), dispersion (σ), and association (ρ) in our sample.

The Sample

In describing the sample, we need to be explicit about who was included and who was excluded. We owe our colleagues and readers a detailed description of how our sample was chosen and who was lost to follow-up. It is crucial to gather as much information as is ethically and technically possible on those who refuse to participate, those who initially consent but subsequently decide to withdraw, and those who drop out for unknown reasons. For example, studies in perinatal mortality and infant birth weight show that missing data on birth certificates and other medical records are proportionately higher for infants who have died than for survivors (Combs-Orme & David, 1984). We should offer the biases we know or suspect are affecting our data, along with a quantitative estimate of these effects on our outcome. Many of us use convenience samples; let us say so, then, and describe them well.

The Variables

Not only are the appropriate measures of central tendency (mean, median, mode) and dispersion (standard deviation, variance, range, percentiles) important, but visual display allows others to study the outliers and their potential effects. The handling of outliers must be guided more by scientific content than statistical theory. Our colleagues need a careful description of our rationale in decisions concerning outliers. Especially with the small samples that, of necessity, many of us use, dispersion is a crucial factor. It is refreshing to hear a mathematical statistician say, in a conference on data analysis and inference, that 90% of any statistical analysis should involve careful examination of the data using, for example, scatter plots and cross-tabulation (Leonard, 1983). Box (1983) describes 95% of the data analysis as a "wandering journey" involving "heroic subjective choices." The antithesis of careful data description is "the bad practice of adopting a probability model, fitting it by some reasonably efficient procedure, reporting a few canned tests of adequacy, and never really thinking hard or exploring for failures of the model which could compromise ultimate findings" (Dempster, 1983, p. 121). We do not want to move so quickly into the use of probability models that we forgo the opportunity to "uncover unsuspected new forms of structure which could be crucial" (Dempster, 1983, p. 120).

Mallows (1983) suggests six criteria of a good descriptive technique: appropriateness, effectiveness, accuracy, completeness, resistance, and standardization (pp. 140–148). He makes explicit that data analysis is context-dependent: "It seems to me the fact that you are choosing to describe a batch of numbers as a whole, rather than to consider each of the elements of the batch separately, is connected with the basic nature of statistical reasoning" (p. 140). Given that we are assuming that summarizing a batch of numbers as a whole is worthwhile, it seems paramount that we carefully examine these numbers before submitting them to rather standard models of association and testing.

Data transformation often seems warranted before associations are measured. Z scores are sometimes preferred over raw data, because many measures of association are heavily affected by variables with the greatest variance.

The optimal use of discrete and continuous operationalizations of the same variable is a complex issue. For example, although years of education can be measured as a continuous variable—actual number of years of formal schooling completed—it becomes a more powerful predictor of behavior when the continuum is categorized into groups that theoretically make sense. Few educators would argue that the difference between 10 and 11 years of schooling is the same as that between 11 and 12 years. Although our mathematical notation treats these intervals as equal, we have learned from practical experience that a high school degree opens doors to occupational achievement. Thus, the credentialist approach to educational operationalization suggests that levels of educational attainment be lumped into discrete categories for optimal utilization.

In family medicine and family therapy, there are factors we desire to measure that simply cannot be operationalized as continuous variables. A patient may manifest tremendous improvement, slight improvement, no change, or a worsened state. It is impossible to transform such data into interval-level measurement. Moses, Emerson, and Hosseini (1984) clearly demonstrate, however, that we lose much information if we collapse rank-ordered data into binary categories; they present a convincing case for protecting the information inherent in the ordering of observations.

Some variables seem rather clearly nominal (female/male), binary (alive, dead), or interval (blood pressure). Other factors are more difficult to operationalize appropriately. As a general rule, we attempt not to throw away information. There are measures of association and tests of statistical significance for nominal, ordinal, and interval-level measurement. Ordinarily we protect the information inherent in each level of measurement. As alluded to before, however, there are times when collapsing data (years of education to discrete groupings) is appropriate. Such manipulation should be guided by scientific or content considerations; these decisions are crucial to the outcome of a study and should be clearly described.

Additional mathematic modeling or creative manipulating of the variables may be called for. For example, in research focusing on diabetes and cardiovascular disease, body mass indices are not interchangeable (Lee & Kolonel, 1984; Mueller, 1983). Thus, whether the issue is the appropriate level of measurement or more complex mathematical modeling, our sculpting of the individual variables is a meaningful component of analysis.

The Association

In describing the association or the difference between two variables, please do. It is still not uncommon to read an article or listen to a presentation and find no explicit estimate of effect; that is, there is no quantitative estimate of the magnitude of the association or of the difference. We read "the association was statistically significant at the .01 level" or "the new regimen was significant only at the .09 level." We hungrily wait for the proof in the pudding: What was the proportion of successes with the new regimen when compared with the old approach or with a placebo? What was the correlation between the two factors of interest? Some writers tend to put one, two, or three asterisks or other symbols in the table to symbolize somehow the size of the effect; these are, of course, misleading. Most of us are interested in practical relevance, whether clinical or programmatic. Colleagues cannot judge the clinical relevance of "a statistically significant relationship." Estimating the probability of ruling out random threats to validity is not the same as describing the effect size.

CONFUSION OF ESTIMATES OF EFFECTS AND TESTS OF STATISTICAL SIGNIFICANCE

Why is there a confusion between estimates of effect or measures of association and tests of statistical significance? Many of us were trained in a world highly influenced by Sir Ronald Fisher (1925), where the paramount goal was to test the consistency of the data with the null state. The null was zero—no association. No difference. Consequently, a victory was any association greater than zero. Decades (if not centuries) of research had been performed prior to Fisher without an appreciation for the capricious effects of random variation on estimated associations. Thus, Fisher's dictum was an appropriate stance.

Addressing random threats to validity, however, became such an overriding concern that an entire generation of researchers—of which I am a part—lost sight of the usefulness of describing the magnitude of the association. Many of us, when asked toward the completion of our graduate training, "What is the measure of association in a 2×2 contingency table?" answered, after much pondering, that it was either chi-square or a pattern reflected in the cell frequencies. It is still common to see a value for chi-square listed in an article, with an accompanying p value but no measure of association.

Chi-square is certainly an excellent measure of the significance of an association, that is, a test of the consistency of the data with the null. Chi-square is not, however, a measure of association, given that it is a function of both the proportions in the various cells and the sample size. As Fleiss (1981) puts it: "The degree of association is really only a function of the cell proportions. The number of subjects studied plays a role in the chances of finding significance if association exists, but should play no role in determining the extent of association" (p. 58).

A similar confusion of estimates of association and tests of statistical significance exists in analysis of variance with the use of eta-squared (η^2). Contrary to some texts, eta-squared cannot be interpreted as r^2 in regression. The magnitude of eta-squared is effected by (λ) lambda, the sample size, and the number of treatments (e.g., in a clinical trial). According to Murray and Dosser (1984), "values of η^2 from different experiments should be compared only if the experiments have exactly the same number of treatments and the same sample size" (p. 14).

These two examples point to one characteristic we desire in a measure of association. We need information that is independent of the sample size, information that can allow comparisons from one study to the next.

CHOICE OF A MEASURE OF ASSOCIATION

If we desire a single index to condense an association, we must accept the limitations of such a condensation, just as measures of central tendency are limited representations of the entire batch of numbers. Several criteria guide our choice of a measure of association: (1) the nature of the data (e.g., nominal, ordinal, and interval-level measurements), (2) patterns of the relationships (e.g., linearity), (3) the number of variables, and (4) the type of study (e.g., cross-sectional, case-reference, or cohort). Each measure brings with it a certain set of assumptions and limitations. For example, Pearson's product–moment correlation *(r)* assumes that the relation between the variables is linear and the data are normally distributed. Of course, neither nature nor our investigative perturbations conform perfectly to mathematical assumptions. We strive for as close of a match as is feasible.

We all are aware of some of the appropriate fits of levels of measurement with models of association. Nominal or categoric data can be evaluated using contingency table analysis. Ordinal or rank-order data use Spearman's rho and Kendall's tau, among others, as appropriate measures of association. The properties of interval level data allow such measures of association as Pearson's product-moment correlation *(r)* and regression.

An Example: Measures of Association and the 2 × 2 Table. I shall focus for a moment on categoric data in general and the 2 × 2 table specifically to illustrate certain issues pertinent to choosing a measure of association (Table 38-2). A review of six measures of association using the information from this seemingly simple table points to the inherent complexity of such a choice.

The magnitude of all six of the measures of association presented in Table 38-3 is not affected by sample size, meeting that criterion as an adequate measure. The two most common problems potentially effecting contingency table measures of association are skewed marginal distributions and unequal numbers of rows and columns. (Of course, the latter problem is not an issue for 2 × 2 tables.)

Of the six listed, phi is sensitive to marginal distributions. The greater the imbalance in the marginal distributions, the lower its value. Thus, phi can be said to underestimate an association when the margins are not equally distributed. Phi, not being invariant to the

Table 38-2. The 2 × 2 Contingency Table for Displaying the Relation between Exposure and Disease

	D	$\bar{D}$	
E	a	b	m_1
$\bar{E}$	c	d	m_0
	n_1	n_0	

Table 38-3. Six Commonly Used Measures of Association in 2×2 Contingency Tables

Measure	Formula	Range	Statistical independence
1. Phi (ϕ) coefficient	$\phi = \dfrac{ad - bc}{\sqrt{m_1 m_0 n_1 n_0}}$	-1.0 to 1.0	0.0
2. Yule's Q	$Q = \dfrac{ad - bc}{ad + bc}$	-1.0 to 1.0	0.0
3. Rate ratio (RR)	$RR = \dfrac{a/(a+b)}{c/(c+d)}$	0.0 to ∞	1.0
4. Odds ratio (OR)	$OR = ad/bc$	0.0 to ∞	1.0
5. Log odds ratio	$\text{Log } OR = \log a + \log d - \log b - \log c$	$-\infty$ to ∞	0.0
6. Rate difference (RD)	$RD = [a/(a+b)] - [c/(c+d)]$	-1.0 to 1.0	0.0

margins, is not comparable across a series of tables with varied margins. The advantage of phi is that it is, for dichotomous data, the mathematical equivalent to Pearson's product-moment correlation (r) and can be interpreted analogously. Phi attains its upper limit only under strict perfect association (see Reynolds, 1977, for a precise distinction between strict, implicit, and weak perfect correlation). Phi is not invariant over different types of study designs; it has been suggested that phi be restricted to cross-sectional studies (Kleinbaum, Kupper, & Morgenstern, 1982).

Yule's Q is one of the oldest and best known measures of association for a 2×2 table in the social sciences. Many researchers feel that it overstates the strength of an association, attaining its upper limit under strict, implicit, or weak perfect association. (Q is 1.0 whenever the b or c cell is zero and -1.0 whenever the a or d cell is zero.)

The rate ratio (RR) is a ratio of the proportion of disease among the exposed $[a/(a+b)]$ and the proportion of disease among the nonexposed $[c/(c+d)]$. This ratio measure of association has great intuitive appeal and can be approximated for rare diseases in case reference studies with the cross-product ratio, the odds ratio (OR). Unlike the case of phi or of Yule's Q, the range for the rate ratio and the odds ratio is not -1.0 to 1.0, but 0.0 to ∞, with 1.0 signifying statistical independence. Note that departures from 1.0 are not symmetric, with negative associations measured on the interval 0.0 to 1.0 and positive associations measured on the interval 1.0 to $+\infty$. This lack of symmetry in the odds ratio, for example, can be removed by calculating the natural logarithm of the odds ratio. This log odds varies from $-\infty$ to $+\infty$, with 0.0 satisfying independence. Both the odds ratio and the log odds are invariant to marginal distributions, whereas the rate ratio is not. The odds ratio (or its log odds equivalent) has gained popularity in epidemiologic circles because of the following properties:

1. It is invariant under the interchange of rows and columns.
2. It is invariant under row and column multiplications.
3. The same values of the odds ratio are obtained using cell probabilities or counts.

Thus, the exposure odds ratio equals the disease odds ratio, a useful symmetry, especially in case reference studies. That is, $(a/c)/(b/d)$ is equal to $(a/b)/(c/d)$.

The rate difference (RD), sometimes called attributable risk or excess risk, is the difference between the proportion of disease among the exposed and the proportion of disease among the nonexposed. The rate difference does not enjoy the invariant qualities of the odds ratio. One specific disadvantage is that the prevalence of exposure in the population is not directly available in a case reference study, and, consequently, the rate difference cannot be calculated directly. One fine utility of the rate difference is that it takes into consideration the actual numbers of persons having the disease.

A comparison in Table 38-4 of the odds ratio (OR) and rate difference (RD) for smoking and its association with both lung cancer and cardiovascular disease illustrates the strengths of each measure. If one only looks at the odds ratio between smoking and the two diseases, it seems appropriate to conclude that smoking is more highly associated with lung cancer than it is with cardiovascular disease. The odds ratio is a relative measure and has accomplished its task. A relative measure, however, gives us no appreciation for the absolute risk involved, no consideration for the prevalence (or incidence) of the disease or the exposure. A comparison of the rate differences reveals a larger number of cases of excess cardiovascular disease due to smoking than cases of lung cancer. This occurs because the incidence (and the prevalence) of cardiovascular disease is much higher in the United States than that of lung cancer. Thus, according to one's goals in research, both measures of association are illuminating of the exposure–disease association.

This brief comparison of selected measures of association for the 2×2 contingency table illustrates their potential vulnerability to (1) marginal distributions, (2) row and column interchanges, (3) type of study design, (4) reaching the upper limit under varying definitions of perfect association, and (5) assumptions about rarity of disease. An appreciation for the numerous factors inherent in our choice of a measure of association in the *seemingly simple* 2×2 contingency table should help us be aware of how careful our selection of more complex multivariate models of association and testing must be.

Matching Measures of Association with Theory. In choosing quantitative techniques, we should creatively strive to match the analysis to the theoretic foundations of the concepts. For example, if we use a measure that is curvilinear in nature, such as the cohesion dimension of FACES (the Family Adaptability and Cohesion Evaluation Scales) (Olson, Sprenkle, & Russell, 1979), we need an analytic approach that utilizes this curvilinear component. Dividing cohesion scores at the mean or median and making comparisons using an array of tests from *t*-tests to discriminant analysis would obviously underutilize the theoretic strength of the concepts and bias the results of any estimates of association.

Theory and analysis sometimes seem an asymmetric pair. Theory, especially systemic and cybernetic approaches, can appear so dynamic and fluid. Quantifying a relationship especially seems to freeze reality. (It is true that language can freeze a process. I think that is one reason that novels are sometimes needed instead of paragraphs.) Despite our talk of process measures and longitudinal frameworks, most of our data analysis seems far too linear, reductionist, and static for our theoretic strivings.

Table 38-4. Comparison of the Odds Ratio (OR) and the Rate Difference (RD) as Measures of Association

	Smokers[a]	Nonsmokers[a]	OR	RD[a]
Cancer of the lung	48.33	4.49	10.8	43.84
Coronary artery disease	294.67	169.54	1.7	125.13

Source: From *Smoking and Health,* Report of the Advisory Committee to the Surgeons General of the Public Health Service, 1964, Princeton, N.J.: Van Nostrand, pp. 109–110.

[a]Mortality rates per 100,000 person-years.

Multivarate Measures of Association. Appearing from time to time are multivariate techniques that allow simultaneous assessment of a large number of variables. LISREL (Joreskog & Sorbom, 1978) is one such technique and may prove to be complementary to our theory in family-oriented health research. I have chosen not to pursue these approaches in detail. This is not because I do not appreciate the unique contribution of multivariate techniques and the accompanying model building. It is my hunch that we will interact better with our theories if we can first think through the possible meanings of the simpler associations in our data. We can utilize multivariate tools, and the distributional assumptions underlying them, after we have systematically exhausted the techniques and measures of association that make fewer underlying distributional assumptions about our populations and our data.

I do believe causal modeling, such as path analysis, can be an illuminating and humbling experience. Systems thinking occasionally deteriorates into an "everything is related to everything else" orientation. It is true that prenatal events are associated with characteristics of the infant at birth, and that, subsequently, infant outcome interacts with the original family factors leading to the outcome. It can, however, be a useful punctuation to focus only on the lineal determinants of infant outcome. At one level, a thing is associated with all other things; the universe is one. But, as Don Bloch (1984) aptly said, "The sun also rises." There is a time to be lineal, directional, causal, reductionist. I say to medical students in epidemiology class, "Be as holistic as possible, as reductionist as necessary." I feel almost as comfortable in saying, "Be as reductionist as possible, as holistic as necessary." I do not believe our cybernetic theory of family and health (if we have one) is so comprehensive as to preclude causal, reductionist thought. I believe causal modeling can expose agnosticism and ignorance in our knowledge and sloppiness in our thinking. Holism and reductionism are complementary visions, and the tension between them is at the epistemologic base of human perception.

MISCLASSIFICATION AND MEASURES OF ASSOCIATION

Kupper (1984) recently focused on the effects of unreliable surrogate measures on measures of association. It has been rather standard dogma in research circles that the true correlation between the exposure and the disease will be underestimated when using less than perfectly reliable surrogate measures. This is the case if the exposure and/or disease variables are unreliable surrogates and the surrogate confounder variable is reliable. If both exposure and disease variables are reliable, however, but the surrogate confounder variable is unreliable, the estimated correlation between the exposure and the disease could be positive, zero, or negative, depending on the size of the unreliability. Kupper advocates that sensitivity comparisons be carried out, with analyses based on several different specifications of reliability coefficients for the confounder variable. Kupper contends that such sensitivity analyses "be included as part of the published report of any study involving the use of potentially unreliable surrogate variables" (1984, p. 648).

Conclusion

Description emphasizes the initial focus of the hypotheses themselves. Is factor *E* related to factor *D?* What is the magnitude of the association? Does the magnitude increase or decrease with "adjustment" for potential confounding factors? Next, we shall shift our focus to inferential judgments, including those based on tests of statistical significance. For now, we can be reminded that all tests of statistical significance rely on two factors: (1)

effect size—manifested, for example, in differences in central tendency or dispersion or both, and (2) sample size. We can describe well our sample, the individual variables, and the estimate of effect. These descriptions are not just a prelude to statistical testing. Statistical testing is one needed postscript to our described results.

INFERENCE

Science is more than measurement, more than description. John Dalton (1766–1844) carefully and consistently collected information of the weather in his English township for years: temperature, barometric pressure, rainfall, wind direction, and speed. This work came to nothing. No scientific advances resulted. Data do not speak for themselves. Meaning is not inherent in the thing, event, or measurement.

Although observation is a foundation insofar as scientific theories are tested by observation, "the data" are not raw, natural units standing alone. The information we collect is in response to our collecting net. A butterfly net used in seining the ocean for microscopic organisms will result in no catches. Science lives in the world of a reality or tradition created by an observer community (Varela, 1979, p. 85).

Science, however, goes beyond the realm of the observable: the farthermost reaches of the cosmos, the beginnings of our universe, the future, the yet-to-be measured individual. An essential ingredient of science is inference—the attribution of "truth" to the *unobserved* based on the "truth" of the observed. For epidemiologic and medical reasoning, inferential judgments are central.

- All *Homo sapiens* have not had their blood pressure, temperature, or height measured; yet we speak of average values of each.
- All human pregnancies have not been monitored, but we set 40 weeks gestation as the norm.
- Having no noninvasive way to measure vascular disease directly, we measure blood pressure and use this surrogate information as a diagnostic and predictive tool. We do the same with CAT scans, radioimmune assays, and thermometers.
- There is no science of the individual—atom, cell, or human. Daily, however, science successfully takes information about groups and infers applicability to an individual case.

It is not realistic to assume that all description is complete before inference takes place. We infer meaning at every stage of the research process, from the very beginning of the planning. We formally apply systematic tests to our descriptions once the descriptions are complete.

We are concerned with four major threats to the validity of our data: systematic and random threats to both internal and external validity. Only one of the four—random threats to internal validity—relies primarily on tests of statistical significance. It is to this threat I first turn.

Random Threats to Internal Validity

Variation exists—in measurements, perceptions, observations, treatments, classifications, judgments, persons, settings, and times. Some people die younger than others; mortality varies. Some people manifest more disease than others; morbidity varies. All known physiologic processes vary from infancy to old age. These variations may be highly patterned, and we may be able to infer the determinants; or they may be random and, from our current knowledge and perspective, we may be able to discern no determinants.

Random variation is always with us. The smaller the sample, the more likely the seemingly strange occurrences. Even random assignment of exposure in a double-blind clinical trial does not preclude random error effecting an association. In the winter of 1983–1984, we conducted a clinical trial investigating the efficacy of rimantidine prophylaxis on the incidence of Type A influenza (Clover *et al.*, 1986). We were also interested in the association between family functioning and the incidence of influenza. Examination of the double-blind assignment of rimantidine found the treatment to be highly associated with type of family functioning. Even though "on the average" random assignment of exposure will tend to minimize any association of the treatment with another main determinant of outcome, it does not always happen.

We first extract information from numeric data; our description is of one sample or study. In making inferences about the descriptions of this sample, we are aware of the threat of random variation to the validity of any inferential judgment. Just as there is no science of the individual, there is no probability of the one study. Statisticians, fortunately, have provided us with a conceptual tool to help us see our study against the backdrop of numerous similar studies, real or hypothetic.

While evaluating potential random threats to internal validity, we entertain the notion that *random fluctuation alone* is responsible for our obtained results. We assume that (1) systematic error (bias) and (2) the biopsychosocial process inherent in the hypothesis are not responsible for our results.

In our attempt to test the role of random error upon our results, we need a model or mechanism of chance that is appropriate to the biopsychosocial mechanisms inherent in our hypothesis. The normal distribution, *t* distribution, or chi-square distribution approximate many of the measures of association we desire to test. Although an explanation of the process for selecting an appropriate probability distribution and accompanying statistical test is beyond our current scope, the choice is based on a series of factors: (1) type of measure of disease, (2) level of measurement, (3) research design, (4) characteristic to be emphasized in the measure of association (central tendency, variance, distributional shape), (5) number of samples, (6) relationship of samples (related, independent), (7) sample size, (8) probability distribution inherent or assumed by the biopsychosocial processes underlying the hypothesis, (9) knowledge of population parameters, and (10) directionality of the hypothesis.

No matter which we choose, probability distributions make explicit two pieces of information: (1) What are all the possible outcomes? and (2) what is the probability associated with each possible outcome? Even though statistical testing is usually a complex procedure, it always leads us back to one point: a probability statement or *p* value that gives the probability of such a value *if* all other processes are assumed to be inoperative (i.e., the null state).

ONE STUDY VERSUS MANY

One factor is a major determinant of our style of inferential decision making concerning random error. This key ingredient is whether we see the current study as one in a series of continual inquires in our professional careers or as perhaps our only or last attempt in this particular line of investigation.

Research in the United States during this century, whether it be in agriculture, eco-

Table 38-5. Type I and Type II Errors: Decisions and the Null State

		"True" situation	
		Null true	Null false
Decision of researcher	Fail to reject null	Correct acceptance probability $= 1 - \alpha$	Type II error probability $= \beta$
	Reject null	Type I error probability $= \alpha$	Correct rejection probability $= 1 - \beta$ "power"

nomics, education, psychology, anthropology, epidemiology, or medicine, has become painfully aware of the Type I error (see Table 38-5). We have learned that when we reject the null hypothesis, when we state something new, random variation is often a chief nemesis. It may be due to having too small a sample; too much variation or dispersion in the variables themselves; or, of course, too small an effect size. We have become so aware of the probability of committing this brash error that every study lists a *p* value and assumes we all understand this to be the probability of a Type I error.

This emphasis on alpha and the probability of committing a Type I error, has usually been well placed. We are all aware of the new drug, the new surgical technique, the new diet—new hypotheses inadequately tested; we desire a theoretic backdrop based on random fluctuation. We want to know the consistency of the data with the null state or "how often would we get an estimate of effect this large, given the variance of the variables and the sample size, due only to random variation"? Once we get such a probability estimate, in this case, the probability of a Type I error, then we must decide where this study stands. Remember, there is no science of the one study. Even if the probability of alpha is .01, we can never know if this study is that one study in a hundred that would find such an effect size, given random variation and the null state being true. At this stage we must use our best logical and intuitive skills. Is this effect size consistent with our theoretic foundation? With other studies? Are the data internally consistent? We are cognizant that sample size can be as crucial as the magnitude of association in determining statistical significance. We are left with a probability estimate against a backdrop of hypothetic studies of similar size and design, and just as important, a backdrop of probability density functions or population distributions.

The scientific tradition has been to err on the conservative side in making use of the alpha probability. The .05 level became a benchmark for interpreting alpha. (There is no doubt that many of us often have misused even the .05 level by fishing for associations at that level of significance, for example, by searching through a series of 40 or 50 *t*-tests looking for differences of means significant at the .05 level. Not surprisingly, we always found two or three.) By insisting on the .05 or the .01 level of significance, we are saying to our colleagues and the world that we will remain very skeptical about anything new unless random threats to validity have been probabilistically reduced to a minimum.

There are many good reasons and times for such conservatism. Part of the growth of Western science has been due to this dogged conservatism. We tend to trust only that which can be repeated, even if only hypothetically repeated in a probability distribution. There are times that we get into a line of research for reasons of convenience. As residents, we are invited to participate in an ongoing project. As faculty, we are asked by a colleague to work together on a project that is of theoretic concern primarily to the colleague. We sometimes tackle a problem that is paramount to the working of our clinic or community, but is not a central part of our long-term professional goals. In these cases, the project at hand may be a one-shot study. We may not intend to pursue the research further.

At such times, it is appropriate to be conservative in our desire to avoid a Type I error. We do not wish to make statements about associations that may well be untrue or misleading. Thus, we may decide to accept the null unless the probability of alpha is extremely low.

But so much emphasis has been placed on alpha, on the probability of committing a Type I error, that we, as a scientific statistical community, have often underemphasized beta, the probability of making a Type II error. As family medicine researchers, we face a dilemma. We do not have strong advocates in the federal funding agencies for our family-oriented health research. Consequently, we often operate our research on a meager budget. The result is small sample size. With small samples, we can set our level of acceptance or rejection for alpha at the .01 or even the .001 level and protect ourselves from a Type I error. But what if the alternative hypothesis is true?

What if family cohesion is a determinant of infant birth weight? What if family coping patterns are crucial in rehabilitation from a spinal cord injury? Our measures of psychosocial phenomena are crude at best. There are measurement errors, natural fluctuations, and problems of construct validity. With a small sample and less than optimal measurement, where are we left? We face the possibility of spending our professional careers committing a series of Type II errors. We cannot expect our family variables to explain large proportions of the explained variance in outcome. We know family factors interact with known biomedical determinants. We begin a project with such low *power,* with such meager probability of detecting an association or a treatment effect even if it does exist in our target population. In many ways, we set ourselves up for probable failure.

It seems paramount that we calculate the needed sample size for the a priori level of beta. Or, conversely, if we know that we have access only to a certain sample of pregnant women or spinal cord patients, we need to calculate our probability of detecting a clinically relevant effect size before we begin our study. We may well decide not to undertake the project. Or we may vote to forge ahead, but at least we are aware of the probability of success. We might desire to calculate the magnitude of effect that could be detected, given the sample size, the variances expected in the study, and our chosen levels of alpha and beta.

BAYESIAN VERSUS FREQUENTIST INFERENCE

In some ways, the frequentist approach to statistical inference, acceptance or rejection of a hypothesis at an a priori probability level, ignores previous experience or theory. Acceptance or rejection at a predetermined level puts the entire focus upon random fluctuation against the backdrop of a selected probability distribution with an assumption of the null state as the prior. Such was the original goal of statistical testing.

A Bayesian approach to statistical inference takes into consideration prior probabilities other than just the null. Study associations are used to revise the prior probability; the researcher must then decide if the post probability lowers or raises her confidence in the hypothesized association (see Weinstein & Fineberg, 1980, for an introduction into Bayesian thinking).

G. E. P. Box (1983) points to the differing left brain/right brain processes as the foundation for his distinction concerning inference. Box considers the left brain's concern with language and logical relationships and the right brain's activity with images and patterns as the bases for deductive and inductive inference, respectively. Box proposes "while there is an essential need for two kinds of inference, there seems an inherent propensity among statisticians to seek for only one" (p. 56). Aware that there are proponents in philosophy, mathematics, and scientific epistemology who contend there is no such thing as induction, Box stands counter and speaks of the right brain's ability to "appreciate patterns in data" and to find patterns in discrepancies between the data and tentative models as inductive inference (p. 57). Box maintains that induction is crucial to scientific discovery. The problem arises, says Box, in that some pattern can be seen in any set of data—there needs to be a check of the brain's pattern-seeking ability. "This is the object of diagnostic checks and tests of fit which, I will argue, require frequentist theory significance tests for their formal justification" (p. 57). Box suggests that frequentist (or sampling) and Bayesian principles are both needed:

> As might be expected the mistaken search for a single principle of inference has resulted in two kinds of incongruity: attempts to base estimation on sampling theory, using point estimates and confidence intervals; and attempts to base criticism and hypothesis testing entirely on Bayesian theory. (p. 76)

We are left, by Box, with an iterative play between criticism and estimation, between pattern seeking and logical checks. From the perspective of the Bayesian, the frequentist straw person exercises all his judgment and intelligence before the data arrive; afterwards, all that is left is to compute the results. The Bayesian views "reasoning in the presence of data to be the crux of data analysis" (Dempster, 1983, p. 126).

Bayesian approaches seem most applicable in clinical inferences associated with diagnostic testing. Clinical decisions, by necessity, are often immediate and practical. Clinicians cannot afford the luxury of careers full of Type II errors. If the predictive value of a positive diagnostic test is significant at *only* the .12 level, the clinician may well decide to go with the probability of .88 rather than accept the null at .12. Researchers who plan to conduct continuous projects in the same field, but who are often constrained by relatively small samples, may find a Bayesian approach to statistical inference well suited to their needs. Though not without its critics (Fleiss, 1981), Bayesian statistics does offer the family medicine researcher an alternative that encourages continuation of a line of research if the study association strengthens prior probabilities, whether those probabilities were established from theory or experience.

There are at least two ways to test a model. One is to test statistical significance. Another is to examine the robustness of that model, checking to see if small changes in the model lead to changes in the implications (Good, 1983). Earlier I mentioned the sensitivity of unreliable surrogate confounder variables on the measure of correlation. It is appropriate to go beyond the robustness of any one measure and speak of the robustness of our inferences.

> Statistical answers rely on prior assumptions as well as data, and better real world answers generally require models that incorporate more realistic prior assumptions as well as provide better fits to data. . . . In general, inferences are sensitive to features of the underlying distribution of values in the population that cannot be addressed by the observed data. (Rubin, 1983, p. 217)

> The critical issue . . . is that robustness is not a property of data alone or questions alone, but particular combinations of data, questions and families of models. (Rubin, 1983, pp. 239, 241)

Systematic Threats to Internal Validity

Although statisticians have provided invaluable contributions in ruling out random threats to internal validity, the family medicine researcher must develop her own expertise in evaluating potential systematic threats to internal validity. Three of the major sources of systematic bias in inferential judgments—selection bias, observation or information bias, and confounding—are issues that can be handled well by the family physician or family therapist. It is the clinician's medical or therapeutic knowledge that suggests the potential confounders to be measured for statistical adjustment. It is the systematic decision-making skill already honed in clinical practice that can uncover selection and observation bias in previous comparative thinking and better avoid them in the future.

We have all been warned since undergraduate days that "correlation does not mean causation." We are aware that *we* infer causality. Only in the laboratory does causality seem rather self-evident. Monitoring the course of disease in natural settings and assigning exposure in quasi-experimental clinical trials requires the scientist to become adept at dealing with systematic threats to internal validity. Hill (1965, p. 272) provides us with a beginning set of criteria as we attempt to infer causation from associations: (1) strength of association, (2) consistency, (3) specificity, (4) temporality, (5) biologic gradient, (6) plausibility, (7) coherence, (8) experimentation, and (9) analogy.

It is not surprising that a clinician, David Sackett (1979), would produce an almost exhaustive list of types of systematic bias. It is the clinician's continued involvement in decision making in cases of individual patients that provides the contextual insight necessary for avoiding systematic bias in research.

Confounding, as a systematic threat to validity, can be addressed in the analysis only if the potentially confounding variables have been measured. For a variable to be a confounder in a study, it must be associated with the outcome, independently of the exposure, and associated with the exposure of interest. Clinical insight, detailed descriptive statistics, and multivariate techniques offer the opportunity to address potential confounding. Randomization, of course, helps to remove bias due to unknown "lurking" variables.

> The problems of how to hunt out lurking variables, or how to analyse data in the presence of lurking variables is one of the most important real issues which statisticians are faced with, particularly when analysing, say, medical or economic data, rather than data from designed experiments. (Leonard, 1983, p. 17)

Although quantitative assessment can provide estimates extremely helpful in attempting to rule out systematic threats to validity—(1) standardized rate ratio or the Mantel-Haenszel (1959) odds ratio in analyzing potential confounders, for example, or (2) quantitative comparisons of the characteristics of cases and controls in evaluating selection bias, or (3) comparisons of length of interviews between cases and controls in assessing observation bias)—causality must still be inferred. The researcher uses the breadth and depth of intellectual resources—in a series of mental experiments—to attempt to rule out threats to causal validity. The key question is continually asked: Is there any way to explain the observed relationship other than cause and effect?

Internal validity potentially can suffer from both systematic and random threats. One camp in epidemiologic thought stresses the elimination of systematic threats. The emphasis is on logical deduction. The overriding reminder is that *one newly analyzed confounder and all estimates of the magnitude of effect disappear*. Concern over sampling is minimized. Thought experiments and logical attempts at ruling out systematic threats are paramount (see Maclure, 1985, for a concise presentation of this view). Another camp points to the ever-present threat of random variation. No matter how logical the design, no matter how sophisticated the adjustment for potential confounders, the *predictive estimates shrink when the model is applied to a new sample.* Both threats remain.

Systematic and Random Threats to External Validity

Up to this point we have concentrated only the covariation in our sample. We have evaluated only the data we gathered. As mentioned earlier, however, science has progressed by inferring beyond the sample.

CONSTRUCT VALIDITY

Construct validity focuses generalizations about higher order theoretic construction from the operational measurements in the research. We use blood pressure as a surrogate measure for vascular disease, functional ability as a surrogate for Alzheimer's disease, and radionuclide angiography as a surrogate for coronary artery disease. In each case we would prefer a measure that theoretically and practically (predictively) is closer to reality. For example, coronary artery disease measured by catheterization or autopsy is considered a more valid diagnosis, but the these measures are often too invasive or inappropriate. Again, we live in an observer-created reality. We test people against our measurement tools. We do not speak of coronary artery disease, but of angiographically confirmed coronary artery disease. Using prediction and theory, we must infer construct validity as we generalize from our measurements to larger theoretical problems.

As participants in the "new epistemology," we are keenly aware of reality as created, in Varela's (1979) terms, by the "observer-community." We do not need to despair, however, thinking that our lack of construct validity or objectivity is unique to the human sciences. Jacob Bronowski (1973) elegantly portrays the limits of man's research pertubations as he examines an object, examined by instrumentation across the entire spectrum of electromagnetic information from sound waves to the electron microscope. At each probe, we are limited by the wavelength itself. "The fact is that at any wavelength we can intercept a ray only by objects about as large as a wavelength itself; a smaller object simply will not cast a shadow" (Bronowski, 1973, p. 355). The perfect image, and absolute knowledge, are still elusive.

One tension in human research centers around the trade-offs between in-depth, time intensive, observational, open-ended inquiry and survey, pen-and-paper techniques. The stereotypes at either end of the continuum are valid information on a few persons and superficial information on large populations. Given our awareness of the potential threat to internal validity from random variation, and the extreme vulnerability of small samples to this threat, we feel the need to "get our numbers up." This often results in measures that we know have weak construct validity.

Ethnographers and clinicians acclaim the merits of in-depth probing. Most of us would not deny the need for such approaches and welcome the insight gained. But there is one potential methodologic problem in open-ended research. Let me begin by analogy. We are familiar with the statistical issues involved in the binomial probability of counting the number of successes in a set number of trials (e.g., the number of times "heads" appears in 10 coin tosses). Decades of research have shown the faulty statistical reasoning involved in changing the problem to "the number of trials until a success is achieved" (e.g., the number of tosses necessary to get the first "heads" in a coin toss). In the name of achieving greater construct validity, do we not run the danger of observing or asking until we get what we want? We probe until we get our predetermined success. Thus, it is possible that we both introduce observation bias and commit a statistical error in our desire to improve our construct validity.

GENERALIZATIONS ACROSS PERSONS, PLACES, AND TIMES

Generalizations across persons, settings, and times is the second issue of external validity. There can be systematic reasons that our data are not applicable to populations pertinent to our continued work (e.g., our patient population) or the general population. There can also be random causes of nonrepresentativeness. Although statistical testing assumes a representative sample in application of its probability estimates, it is not itself a *test* of representativeness. Inference as to generalizability relies on descriptions of the general population, the target population, and the sample, and on intellectual reasoning concerning applicability.

In the final analysis, external validity is an issue of replication. The testing of one predictive model on another population can add credibility to inferences concerning external validity. As family health researchers, we do have one fine method available to us in evaluating the generalizability of our results across other settings, persons, and times. We can test our predictive weights on a different set of data. We realize there will be shrinkage (Lachenbruch, 1968), the tendency of predictive models to overestimate what might be obtained in application to other than the initial sample. It is clear why this will tend to happen. In the analysis of our own data, we have made optimal use of any random variation that might improve our hypothesized association or distinction. Whether we used contingency table analysis, zero-order correlation, analysis of variance, or multiple regression, we maximized the associations in our data.

If, for example, we attempt to find those factors most highly associated with infant birth weight, multiple regression will provide us weights via regression coefficients that maximize our prediction of birth weight. Percentage of explained variance certainly is one way to gauge how well our hypothesized variables correlate with the outcome. We could use this regression equation to produce expected infant birth weights and compare these predictions on the actual weights. A 2×2 contingency table gives us a summary view of the predictive value of our weighting scheme. The generalizability of our results could be tested by applying these regression coefficients or weight to a new set of data, calculating predicted infant birth weights using the new data's characteristics, and displaying the predictive value in a 2×2 contingency table. A predictive value high enough for clinical, programmatic, or continued research purposes would lend credence to the generalizability of the original study data to new settings, persons, and times, and would give support to the usefulness of our constructed measures, no matter how subjective their origin.

On this one issue, medical research is an advantageous arena. Health, disease, and mortality are of great concern to politicians, the media, and much of the population. There *will* be more studies. Unlike stratification studies in sociology, anthropology, and economics that cost millions and rarely are replicated, studies focusing on the majority of medical issues will be replicated in one fashion or another.

There is a case to be made that a Framingham Study (Kannel & Gordon, 1971) or a National Collaborative Perinatal Project (Naeye & Trafari, 1983) does not answer some questions that a series of more moderately sized projects could. Refinement, replication, and serial testing of prior predictive models are paramount steps in addressing the issue of generalizability.

Our style may be to set very conservative levels for alpha, whether we will be conducting other similar studies or not. We may feel more comfortable or intellectually honest by rejecting the null only when the data are extremely improbable. Such a style has practical ramifications. We hunger for minute manifestations of some associations and turn our professional backs on others. It is our humanness. As long as we are aware, we can put this selective passion to good use.

Some statisticians have lamented the availability of powerful and flexible statistical software, such as SAS, SPSS, and BMDP, pointing to the often inappropriate match between the data and the selected analytic technique. I welcome these software additions on a fundamental epistemologic level. Jacob Bronowski (1973) interprets as a strength of the Western scientific tradition that the hand helps guide the brain. There is no doubt that the finest scientific tool we have is our brain. It can conduct hypothetical experiments and locate systematic flaws in prior thinking. But the brain must get its hands on stuff: probe, measure, touch, manipulate, play. It is this creative play that has been the hallmark of the learning process among *Homo sapiens* sapiens.

One fine advantage of the new powerful statistical softwares is the involvement of the scientist, the content expert, in the analysis process. Bayesian statisticians especially welcome the content researcher, realizing that the introduction of the prior often comes best from external sources—the nonstatistical experts. Bayesians and frequentists alike are aware that much of the action is in the tails of a distribution, exactly where there is a paucity of data. Content-based (i.e., "real-world") limits and guidelines must be set for the modeling process. Statisticians alone cannot decide on outliers and maximal values. It is here that the statistical and scientific models must interface. For most of us, it is not the statistical model, but the scientific conclusions given the model, that need checking. Scientific inference, in the final analysis, concerns an evaluation of (1) the clinical importance of the effect size; (2) the random and systematic threats to internal validity; (3) the generalizability of the effect size across other constructs, persons, places, and times; and (4) the contextual interplay of all these factors.

PRESCRIPTION

Once we describe our sample, variables, and associations and make inferential judgments about the internal validity and generalizability of our descriptions, we are left at a new point for decisions. What now? I chose the word "prescription" because it connotes both prediction and and action. Our description leaves us with a prediction, with information that, we hope, is more useful than our original impressions. Now we must act.

With a patient, the action may be to wait and observe. A few additional hours of observation provide a wealth of information. The action may be more invasive treatment. As a clinician or administrator, the action may be the initiation of screening or intervention programs, the raising or lowering of costs, or the discontinuation of a diagnostic procedure on a routine basis. As a researcher, the action may include embarking on an additional study or steps to avoid systematic biases that plagued the previous work.

Our inferential judgments and pursuant action are contextual. Not only our personal values, but also the historical precedences of our disciplines, greatly influence the action alternatives we consider. Consider the different inferences and subsequent action surrounding the Lipid Research Clinics' (1984) Coronary Primary Prevention Trial and the Rand Health Insurance Experiment (Brook *et al.*, 1983). Results from the Lipid Research Trial were presented in the *Journal of the American Medical Association* (Lipid Research Clinics, 1984) and the *New York Times* covered the findings in a front-page story (Boffey,

1984). The study authors conclude that the trial "leaves little doubt of the benefit of cholestyramine therapy. . . . The benefits that could be expected from cholestyramine treatment are considerable" (Lipid Research Clinics, 1984, p. 364).

The Rand Health Insurance Experiment compared the benefits and costs of several health insurance plans, including one at no cost. The result of the no-cost plan was an increase in the use of services and a slight decrease in the risk of early death for persons at high risk. The initial report concludes, "These mortality reductions in and of themselves are not sufficient to justify free care for all adults" (Brook *et al.*, 1983, p. 1433). Even the newsletter of the American Public Health Association carried the headline, "Health Does Not Seem Improved When Medical Care Is Free" (Nation's Health, 1984).

In response to the quite different reactions these two randomized trials invoked, Himmelstein and Woolhandler (1984) compared the two studies as to cost-effectiveness. The cost per death prevented with cholestyramine treatment of high-risk men, approximately aged 50, is estimated to be $9,307,500; with free medical care for high-risk 50-year-old men, the cost per death prevented is between $90,000 and $155,700. The authors conclude that free care is between 3 and 100 times as cost-effective as cholestyramine therapy in preventing death.

> Our intent is not to denigrate the achievement of the Lipid Research Trial, which has at last shown that lowering cholesterol decreases the risk of coronary heart disease and which may pave the way for more broadly applicable interventions such as changes in diet. Nor are we indifferent to the problems of skyrocketing costs. Rather, our purpose is to demonstrate that the selection of options for evaluation and cost effectiveness comparison involves many implicit value judgments. (Himmelstein & Woolhandler, 1984, p. 1514)

Many discussions of the research process focus only on analysis and inference. I have included prescription (or action) as a third component because I believe our action feeds back into our analytic and inferential styles. One process is the inferential decision making about the meaning of our observed results. A larger contextual issue—perhaps a meta issue—is the process of my acting on the scientific inferential judgments made about the data. Thus, one issue is, "Does the exposure E lead to the disease D?" A second issue is, "Given that E leads (or does not lead) to D, what will I do about it?" Each is a distinct inferential or decision-making process (see Fodor, 1985).

The danger of not evaluating our action as an additional step in the research process is exemplified by the cholestyramine–free medical care comparison (Himmelstein & Woolhandler, 1984). Sigmund Freud wrote persuasively about our investment of energy. Once we take a path of action, our investment can positively reinforce even a poor choice. If all my life I work in a laboratory, I will see controlled experimental trials as the best, if not the only, "scientific" path. Our decisions of action "after the research is over" dramatically effect our future research.

CONCLUSION

Cybernetically inclined researchers, especially in family therapy, question the appropriateness of traditional research designs and methods (Colapinto, 1979; Sheehan, Storm, & Sprenkle, 1982). Alan Gurman (1983) responds; "While the complex processes of family therapy, viewed as a whole, are admittedly and necessarily circular, subprocesses in the therapeutic encounter can be shown to be decidedly linear" (p. 229). To be closer to correct, we might use Varela's (1979, p. 65) lead and say there are subprocesses in the research encounter that we, the researchers, choose to punctuate as lineal and linear.

The issue is not, "Am I to be reductionist?" The wholeness of the universe cannot be experienced, thought, or spoken all at once. The key issue becomes, "Can I be aware of how I punctuate and can I make fruitful punctuating decisions in research?" Look at some of the processes we have chosen to punctuate as lineal. Focusing on a life span is a highly egocentric gaze. Many of you have taken professional oaths to support life as defined lineally. (Of course, cost/benefit and cost-effective approaches are the beginnings of our culture's considering other punctuations.) In pregnancy research, I unapologetically close off many cybernetic alternatives. There is a serious existential component to our research styles and perceptual rhythms.

Although I would be one of the first to criticize approaches antithetical to the "new epistemology," I think some of the discord has to do with individuals and not necessarily with disciplines. For example, I am afraid our mathematical straw person is several hundred years old. Most physicians, researchers, therapists, and the like have not been exposed to any mathematical concepts developed in the last 200 years (although this is not quite so in some of our statistical knowledge). Imagine if this were true in all of medicine, nursing, social work, family studies, cybernetics, or therapy. I cannot, for example, adequately follow the mathematics in Varela's (1979) modeling of biologic systems. Many in the new epistemology only know old math.

I agree with Gurman (1983) that the use of inferential statistics itself is founded upon *context*. Just as Gordon Paul, in 1967, posed the question, "What therapy is most effective for what problems, treated by what therapists, according to what criteria, in what setting?" (p. 111), frequentist and Bayesian statisticians have been asking for decades:

1. What measure of association?
2. Against a backdrop of what assumptions about underlying population distributions?
3. With what variance in individual variables?
4. Given what probabilistic levels of alpha and beta?
5. What sample of persons, stratified in what ways, under what tolerances to measurement errors?
6. How sensitive to inferential assumptions?

When statisticians profess that inferential robustness is a contextual issue of the data, the questions, and the models, I believe we have found epistemologic cohorts.

There has never emerged an etiologic formula for invention, innovation, and insight. It is impossible to ensure creativity. There is no series of steps that guarantees movement beyond the current level of understanding. The "aha" experience comes at strange times. But most likely the individual has been highly immersed with the problem and actively engaged with the data. That is, the brain and the hand stimulate each other. Just as clinical insight and wisdom are heightened with intensive interaction with patient after patient, scientific leaps are often made during the analysis stage as anomalies catalystically bring forth insight that was on the tip of your brain. We have a wealth of problems to overcome in family-oriented health research. May I encourage you to remember: They're your data. Play with them! Plot them. Chart them. Contrast them. Classify them. Shake them up and stratify them in a new way. Data never speak for themselves. But your analytic brain can make much of this playful sculpting.

References

Bloch DA. The sun also rises: an editorial. Family Systems Medicine 1984; 1:3–4.

Boffey PM. Study backs cutting cholesterol to curb heart disease risk. New York Times 1984; January 13:1, 10.

Box GEP. An apology for ecumenism in statistics. In: Box GEP, Leonard T, Wu CF, eds. Scientific inference, data analysis, and robustness. New York: Academic Press, 1983: 51–84.

Bronowski, J. The ascent of man. Boston: Little, Brown, 1973.

Brook RH, Ware JE Jr, Rogers WH, Keeler EB, Davies AR, Donald CA, Goldberg GA, Lohr KN, Masthay PC, Newhouse JP. Does free care improve adults' health?: Results from a randomized controlled trial. New England Journal of Medicine 1983; 309:1426–1434.

Clover RD, Crawford S, Abell TD, Ramsey CN Jr, Glezen WP, Couch RB. Effectiveness of rimantadine prophylaxis of children within families. American Journal of Diseases of Children 1986; 140:706–709.

Colapinto J. The relative value of empirical evidence. Family Process 1979; 18:427–441.

Combs-Orme T, David R. A decline in the quality of vital statistics data: evidence and implications for reproductive research [Abstract]. American Journal of Epidemiology 1984; 120:496.

D'Andrade RG. Memory and the assessment of behavior. In: Blalock T, ed. Measurement in the social sciences. Chicago: Aldine-Atherton, 1974.

Dempster AP. Purposes and limitations of data analysis. In: Box GEP, Leonard T, Wu CF, eds. Scientific inference, data analysis, and robustness. New York: Academic Press, 1983:117–133.

Fisher RA. Statistical methods for research workers. Edinburgh: Oliver and Boyd, 1925.

Fleiss JL. Statistical methods for rates and proportions, 2nd ed. New York: Wiley, 1981.

Fodor J. A compilation theory of mind: an interview with Jerry Fodor. Interview: A publication of the Oklahoma Foundation for the Humanities, 1985; 3:1–14.

Good IJ. The robustness of a hierachial model for multinomials and contingency tables. In: Box GEP, Leonard T, Wu CF, eds. Scientific Inference, data analysis, and robustness. New York: Academic Press, 1983:191–211.

Gurman AS. Family therapy research and the "new epistemology." Journal of Marital and Family Therapy 1983; 9:227–234.

Hill AB. The environment and disease: association or causation. Proceedings of the Royal Society of Medicine 1965; 58:295–300.

Himmelstein DV, Woolhandler S. Free care, cholestyramine and health policy. New England Journal of Medicine 1984; 311:1511–1514.

Joreskog KG, Sorbom D. LISREL IV: Analysis of linear structural relationships by the method of maximum likelihood. Chicago: National Educational Resources, 1978.

Kannel WB, Gordon T, eds. The Framingham Study: an epidemiological investigation of cardiovascular disease. Washington D.C.: U.S. Government Printing Office, 1971.

Kleinbaum DG, Kupper LL, Morgenstern H. Epidemiologic research: principles and quantitative methods. Belmont, Calif.: Lifetime Learning Publications, 1982.

Kupper LL. Effects of the use of unreliable surrogate variables on the validity of epidemiologic research studies. American Journal of Epidemiology 1984; 120:643–648.

Lachenbruch PA. On expected probabilities of misclassification in discriminant analysis, necessary sample size, and a relation with the multiple correlation coefficient. Biometrics 1968; 24:823–834.

Lee JL, Kolonel LN. Are body mass indices interchangeable in measuring obesity–disease associations? American Journal of Public Health 1984; 74:376–377.

Leonard T. Some philosophies of inference and modeling. In: Box GEP, Leonard T, Wu CF, eds. Scientific inference, data analysis, and robustness. New York: Academic Press, 1983: 9–23.

Lipid Research Clinics Program: The Lipid Research Clinics Coronary Primary Preventions Trial results I: reduction in the incidence of coronary heart disease. Journal of the American Medical Association 1984; 251:351–364.

Maclure M. Popperian refutation in epidemiology. American Journal of Epidemiology 1985; 121:343–350.

Mallows CL. Data description. In: Box GEP, Leonard T, Wu CF, eds. Scientific inference, data analysis, and robustness. New York: Academic Press, 1983:135–151.

Mantel N, Haenszel W. Statistical aspects of the analysis of data from retrospective studies of disease. Journal of the National Cancer Institute 1959; 22:719–748.

Moses LE, Emerson JD, Hosseini H. Statistics in practice: analyzing data from ordered categories. New England Journal of Medicine 1984; 311:442–448.

Mosteller F, Tukey JW. Data analysis and regression. Reading, Mass.: Addison-Wesley, 1977.

Mueller WH. The genetics of human fatness. Yearbook of Physical Anthropology 1983; 26:215–230.

Murray LW, Dosser DA Jr. Problems with the measurement of magnitude of effect: implications for family research. Presented at the Annual Meeting of the National Council on Family Relations, St. Paul, Minnesota, October 1984.

Naeye RL, Tafari N. Risk factors in pregnancy and diseases of the fetus and newborn. Baltimore: Williams & Wilkins, 1983.

Nation's Health. Health does not seem improved when medical care is free. Nation's Health 1984; January:1, 6.

Olson DH, Sprenkle DH, Russell CS. Circumplex model of marital and family systems: 1. Cohesion and adaptability dimensions, family types, and clinical applications. Family Process 1979; 18:3–28.

Paul GL Strategy of outcome research in psychotherapy. Journal of Consulting Psychology 1967; 31:109–118.

Reynolds HT. Analysis of nominal data. Beverly Hills, Calif. Sage Publications, 1977.

Rubin DB. A case study of the robustness of Bayesian methods of inference: estimating the total in a finite population using transformations to nomality. In: Box GEP, Leonard T, Wu CF, eds. Scientific inference, data analysis, and robustness. New York: Academic Press, 1983: 213–244.

Sackett DL. Bias in analytic research. Journal of Chronic Disease 1979; 32:51–63.

Sheehan R, Storm CL, Sprenkle DH. Therapy based on a cybernetic epistemology: problems and solutions for the researcher. Panel presented at the Annual Meeting of the American Association for Marriage and Family Therapy, Dallas, Texas, October 1982.

Smoking and health. Report of the Advisory Committee to the Surgeons General of the Public Health Service. Princeton, N.J.: Van Nostrand, 1964.

Varela FJ. Principles of biological autonomy. New York: North Holland, 1979.

Weinstein MC, Fineberg HV. Clinical decision analysis. Philadelphia: Saunders, 1980.

39

Biologic Mediators in Family Systems

JOHN L. RANDALL
Maine Medical Center, Portland

> Life does not work by following a single thread, nor yet by fits and starts. It pushes forward its whole network at one and the same time. So is the embryo fashioned in the womb that bears it. This we have reason to know, but it is satisfying to us precisely to recognize that man was born under the same maternal law. And we are happy to admit that the birth of intelligence corresponds to a turning in upon itself, not only of the nervous system, but of the whole being. (DeChardin, 1975, p. 171)

This chapter is devoted to exploring several biologic models concerned with behavior. This discussion is included to give the reader a glimpse of behavioral systems in which the molecular basis for behavior has been explored and defined.

One system deals with the vertical transmission of information in *Drosophila* (the fruit fly), which demonstrates how genetics plays a role in behavior. The other system is the horizontal transmission of behavior in the *Aplysia* sea slug, in which the mediators responsible for induction and storage of information are defined. Both of these systems deal with very simple animals but, at the same time, reveal the incredible complexity that exists even in the simplest forms of life.

Why should a book on family medicine be concerned with these systems? If, indeed, these molecular systems represent the foundation on which behavior is formed, then the instruments and designs for our studies in search of markers and explorations for ways to modify behavior should take into consideration the knowledge gained from these models.

In general, several conclusions emerge:

1. A portfolio of genes exists that provides a framework or structure for governing or producing behavioral activity.
2. Determining the molecular basis for habituation, sensitization, and associative learning, even for relatively simple behaviors, may help to define the molecular basis for higher levels of functioning.
3. The maternal–fetal axis in mammalian systems provides a method for non-Mendelian selection of the structure of behavioral activity.
4. Culture serves as a repository for storage of symbolic representations of previously learned behavior and can function as an inducer within the framework of human behavioral activity; it is also one of our flexible mediators.

ASSUMPTIONS

Any attempt to correlate human systems with those in other species must be based on several assumptions. The first of these is that the building blocks of all biologic systems repeat themselves within both "higher" and "lower" forms of life. That the tune of life is played on the same keys is apparent from the discovery of the genetic code and its universal presence in all biologic systems. Not only is there universality in the code and in the way that cells are directed, but the enzymes, the chemical bonds, and the atomic structure of living organisms remain the same.

Science tends to select simpler systems for study, not because they provide easy answers but because they tend to provide a setting where controls and careful design are less difficult. Frequently, work done on simpler organisms provides vital clues for research on higher organisms. For example, the early work done on bacterial genetics with lambda phage has paved the way for understanding the genetics of animal viruses and genetics in general. The simple and more easily accessible system of viral genetics interacting with a simple bacterial gene provided the groundwork for studying the interface of viruses and hosts, such as herpes simplex interactions with much more complicated animal systems.

If one assumes that human systems are indeed part of a universal biologic system and that underneath the careful observations of behavior there lies a physical underpinning that is similar to that of other life forms, then observations of animal systems take on greater relevance in attempts to unravel the complicated and "unique" behavior of the human species and its interactions in the complex structure of family and society.

If universality of the genetic code exists, is there universality in the structure of behavior? If we study *Aplysia* (the sea slug) or *Drosophila* (the fruit fly), can we determine information that may lead to some understanding of human behavior? Although it would be preposterous to imply that the actions of a fruit fly and those of a human being have a great deal in common, nevertheless it would be equally absurd to propose that neuronal structure—the transmitters, the cation channels, the neuronal bonds—and the methods by which genetics influences behavior in fruit flies do not have some correlation with higher organisms.

The second assumption is that the information of the descriptive phase of our discipline, family medicine, has at its roots a chemical–electrical–physical base that ultimately would be subject to the same dissection that simpler behavior patterns have already undergone in other species.

Although the idea of looking at a molecular basis for behavior may seem reductionist, it seems highly unlikely that a simple cause–effect relationship will exist. It is much more likely that the complex relationships between individual and family will be better understood in a reticular or networking framework—one in which many factors are interrelated.

The observer of reticular systems needs continuity with the system, or very sophisticated data retrieval systems. To date, complete mathematical analysis of reticular systems has not been possible. Predictions such as weather or economic forecasting require analysis of oscillating reticular systems, and the accuracy of these forecasts is well known. Therefore, an additional determinant in the development of a science of family medicine will be the development of higher mathematical systems for reticular systems analysis. Primate behavior viewed in the context of the single organism is difficult to comprehend; viewed from a family or a group perspective, it becomes even more complex.

CLINICAL OBSERVATION—RETICULAR SYSTEMS

In his book, *Epidemiology in Country Practice,* William Pickle (1939) argues as follows for the unique position of a country doctor to act as an epidemiologist (an observer of reticular systems): "He has greater knowledge than any inhabitant, he knows the relationships, friendships, and love affairs of all his patients because he is interested in people and they are a major part of his life. He knows the markets they frequent, the schools which their children attend and the memorable trips to the seaside or the pantomine" (p. 4). Many family physicians know the things Pickle wrote down and documented carefully and passed on to us as a unique body of information collected by a good "people watcher." Pickle was able, 50 years ago, to document from his tours of the countryside and office practice descriptions of epidemic pleurodynia. He estimated the incubation period of infectious hepatitis.

Similar work has been done to delineate family dynamics and behavior patterns in Holland by Huygens (1982). Over four generations of general practice, he made careful documentation not only of the vertical transmission of "biologic effects of disease," but also of patterns of behavior within families toward health and illness. New methods of documentation and record keeping are needed to adapt to computer technology in order to allow the extension of our observation beyond three or four generations. When this is possible, a clearer picture of both vertical and horizontal transmission patterns of behavior will become clearer, and reticular patterns may well unfold, a phenomenon that was only sensed previously by our "observing physicians."

BIOLOGIC MEDIATORS

Information Transfer

The word "mediator" is important to define for purposes of discussion. "Mediator" implies interaction between two points. For our purposes, however, in reticular systems, mediation may mean more than two points at one time. Thus, "mediator" represents a structure or a substance conveying information and energy. In a sense, mediators can be defined as transmitters; they are involved with information transfer. A good example is the common phenomenon seen in sports events in big stadiums—the human wave. In this setting, the individual in a crowd, sensing the movement of a person next to him, rises and sits. The combined movement of all the individuals in the stadium creates an undulating wave around a circular stadium. The purpose or goal of this wave is to encourage the team to perform well and to raise the energy level of the team. the intrinsic idea and assumption of the group is that when one person rises next to you, you also rise. The mediators are the human bodies that perform this function. In a molecular sense, the mediators are the muscles, nerves, neurons, and neuronal connectors that allow the body to rise and fall.

Perhaps information in families follows similar patterns. An idea originates from the family history, the "family myth," and is transmitted horizontally and vertically in response to an external stimulus such as a life event—marriage, birth, death, and so on. The horizontal mechanisms for transmission of behavior activate, and each individual reacts in his or her own individual way as determined by his or her specific biologic nature and by the influence of the idea or myth on the family structure. The idea and reaction to the stimulus thus move in a wavelike fashion via the mediators in each individual, and family behavior then occurs. What are the mediators in family systems and in the family tree? How is information passed down from generation to generation? How is it stored? How is it learned?

It is tempting to subdivide mediators, differentiating between those that seem to provide vertical (genetic and maternal fetal) versus those that provide horizontal (neuronal conduction) transmission. When viewing a system from a reticular standpoint, however, it may make more sense to distinguish between those mediators that are fixed and those that are flexible. It is also tempting to suspect that, in molecular terms, those elements that are fixed are "pretranscriptional," and those that are more flexible are "posttranscriptional" material. ("Transcriptional" refers to the transcribing of DNA into RNA and of RNA into protein.) Pretranscriptional material exists in the template of DNA transcribing into DNA (meiosis and mitosis). These systems are required by their biology to remain conservative and fixed. Response to the environment may be possible in posttranscriptional material through production of either RNA or protein; thus, in the search for various mediators, in terms of overall function, it is valuable to think of mediators in terms of "fixed" or "flexible" and of the neurobiologic legacy as functioning at a pre- and a posttranscriptional level.

The Drosophila Model

In an article written for *Scientific American* in 1973, Seymour Benzer describes the "genetic dissection of behavior." Benzer was able to subdivide a group of mutant fruit flies *(Drosophila melanogaster)* from wild type by the variable behavior characteristics that were passed on from generation to generation. Under prescribed environmental conditions, various traits could be induced, stabilized, and selected to become fixed behavioral characteristics. Geneticists prior to Benzer attempted to observe the same phenomenon. In those systems, the multiplicity of genes associated with a behavior frequently caused reversion back to the wild-type behavior when environmental change occurred. Benzer selected a highly inbred, uniform species and transformed genes one at a time in an attempt to find single gene mutants that would modify behavior. Flies were mutated with chemicals and radiation. These mutations led not only to structural changes, for example in eye color and bristle conformation, but to behavioral changes as well. Fruit fly behavioralists then began to develop a long list of mutants capable of affecting behavior. Some of these mutants exhibited behavior developed as a reaction to structural modifications, such as wing function and leg function. On the other hand, the behavioralists described mutants that appeared directly related to the central nervous system function. In some cases mutations seemed directly related to learning itself. For example, some flies had discrimination in sexual patterns, others in locomotion. Dr. Benzer describes one mutant, dubbed Easily Shocked, that, when stimulated by mechanical shock, fell on its back and appeared to have a seizure, then recovered, and walked around after several minutes.

Geneticists were able to pinpoint the anatomic site of the expression of the gene mutation using a "fate" map developed by A. H. Sturtevant in 1929 (Benzer, 1973). The fate map, a two-dimensional representation of the blastoderm, takes advantage of the fact that very early embryologic anatomy persists and maintains specificity in the fully developed embryo. For example, in the case of the mutant Hyperactive, the neurons in the thoracic ganglia have been shown to behave abnormally.

Mutants developed in *Drosophila* related to learning are of particular interest to geneticists and neurobiologists. A large list of *Drosophila* mutants related to neurobiology has been assembled (Hall & Greenspan, 1979).

Ten years after Benzer's work began, Aceves-Pina and colleagues (1983) succeeded in training a group of flies to avoid odor when it was paired with shock. It should not be surprising that fruit files have some way of learning about odors, since their survival is dependent on it. After developing a method of training the flies, they then identified a group who had difficulty in learning. These mutant flies (Dunce, Cabbage, Turnip, and Rutabaga), all affecting different genes, were isolated and put under further molecular examination. Another fly mutant, Amnesiac, learned but forgot what it had learned within an hour. Analysis of these flies after long and tedious work showed a linkage between behavioral changes and the function of cyclic adenosine monophosphate (cAMP) and monoamines. Specifically, Dunce and Rutabaga mutations both affect cAMP metabolism but in opposite ways. Dunce mutations decrease phosphodiesterase activity; Rutabaga, which decreases activity of adenylate cyclase, decreases cAMP levels (Livingstone, 1984). Why these mutations affect learning is not clear.

An additional group of experiments involved the use of temperature-sensitive, dopa-decarboxylase mutants. Behavioral modification was studied switching the activity off and on with temperature change (Tempel, Livingstone, & Quinn, 1984). As exploration of the basis of these behavioral mutants continues, future work will undoubtedly unravel the mechanism more clearly. *Drosophila* is an excellent organism for study because its genetics have been so clearly defined by classical geneticists, its replication time is quite rapid, and it is inexpensive to grow. This cannot be said for experiments involved in the search for mediators in higher organisms. New methods such as gene probes, the use of monoclonal antibodies (Zipursky, Venkatesh, & Benzer, 1984), and the search for variation in bioamine receptor sites may help to circumvent some of the time and expense.

The Aplysia Model

As discussed in the previous section, genetic experiments in fruit flies have allowed scientists to select specific mutants that would contribute to a greater understanding of the molecular basis for vertical transmission of behavior and learning. A different animal system, the *Aplysia* (sea slug) snail, has been studied in detail by Kandel (1983), who describes the molecular dissection of the siphon reflex in the *Aplysia*. The sea slug has been the focus of anatomic dissection by the neuroanatomists for many years, paralleling the way the *Drosophila* has been dissected genetically. The sea slug provides an excellent model for analysis of the molecular interaction of neuronal networks.

The sea slug, *Aplysia californica*, readily performs the vegetative functions of eating, mating, and crawling, and can make use of several avoidance mechanisms; that is, the animal appears to be able to alter its behavior on the basis of *experience*. the sea slug is able to do all this with 20,000 neurons grouped in 9 ganglia. Whereas *Drosophila* has giant chromosomes, *Aplysia* has giant neurons, the largest being about 1 mm in diameter.

Kandel (1983) describes a conditioned response system in which a sea slug with dissected neuronal circuits is placed into a learning mode of conditioned reflex response. The relative simplicity of the nervous system of these animals permits close observation of the networks and allows the effects of different types of stimulation to be recorded. Exploration of the neuronal circuits involved with the gill withdrawal reflex in *Aplysia* has led to considerable understanding of how behavioral circuitry occurs. Kandel and colleagues (1983) had previously studied habituation (the ability of an animal to cause extinction of a sensory stimulus after repeated low-level stimulation) and sensitization (the ability of the animal to become activated by high-level stimulation). They found 24 sensory neurons leading from the siphon skin to the exciting interneuron. If intermittent stimulation is given to the facilitary neuron attached to the head, an excited circuitry neuron will contribute to a defense arousal of its system. These neuronal connections serve as a junction between the skin and sensory organs, which will field the head shock. The stimulus of the head shock will then cause the gill to withdraw.

The analysis of habituation and sensitization led these investigators to understand the circuits and their normal behavior in both habituation and sensitization. Now the question is, "What changes occur when a classical Pavlovian model is applied to the sea slug?" The sea slug can also sense the smell or taste of a shrimp, although it does not eat shrimp. Therefore, it is possible to use the smell of shrimp as the conditioned stimulus (weak stimulus) and a head shock as the unconditioned stimulus (strong stimulus). If the conditioned stimulus precedes the unconditioned stimulus in a defined time, it will lead to a gill withdrawal. If the stimulus is repeated several times, the *Aplysia* learns that the smell of shrimp may cause it trouble. Analysis of the neuronal circuits is then possible at the molecular level to explore molecular change related to associative learning. Kandel (1984) describes changes that occur within the circuits at the synapse and describes in detail a model for nerve impulse conduction. Although the details of this model are not necessary for this discussion, it is interesting to note how the tune is played. Kandel (1984) proposed that the network of cation channels are responsible for the release of a neurotransmitter. In the case of the *Aplysia* circuit studies, serotonin-like bioamines play a role. The sodium channel acts on the calcium channel, which acts in turn on the potassium channel. Entry of calcium into the cell activates the neurotransmitter (serotonin), and serotonin then acts on cAMP to extend the life of the conduction.

cAMP functions by increasing phosphorylation, which works on protein kinase, changes its conformation, and allows it to modulate the duration of the action potential. The result is a system that develops the ability to modulate the duration of a synaptic impulse, and it appears to occur as the result of *de novo* protein synthesis. Workers previously had demonstrated morphologic changes at the synaptic level in habituation and in sensitization (Kandel, 1983). These appear to occur in learning.

Kandel (1984) proposed that the conformational change occurs in the protein kinase and is related to the amount of phosphorylation. Phosphorylation and its failure were also observed in the learning-disabled fruit fly mutants Dunce and Rutabaga.

A combination of these two models, that of the fruit fly and that of the sea slug, has lead to the conclusion that scientists are now not only closer to defining the genetic basis under which the potential for behavior function is transmitted vertically, but also closer to defining the underlying structure on which these behavioral mutations are carried out. They are also describing, at a very simplistic level, the "keyboard" on which the tune is played.

We conclude that for each structure defined in the network, a gene exists. If the gene exists, it is then subject to the laws of genetics, which include polymorphism, selective regulation, genetic repair, genetic redundancy, and genetic mutation, to mention a few. How evolutionary dynamic a specific section of the nervous system will be may be defined in terms of the stability of genetic structure for that specific section (Britten, 1986). In addition, information encoded in the DNA that is delivered to the next generation in a "pretranscriptional" form may be in a less dynamic state than "posttranscriptional" structures mediated by RNA. Posttranscriptional material—material that the organism acquires from experience—is stored in memory and externally constitutes the symbols of culture and language and other artifacts of civilization. Other genetic mechanisms for non-Mendelian delivery of DNA, such as movable genetic elements (Temin, 1980) and reverse transcriptase systems, remain to be defined.

Thus, organisms are equipped with fixed and flexible mediators allowing transfer of fixed structure and modulation of information received from the external environment.

HUMAN SYSTEMS

It is a great jump to move from the from the fruit fly and the sea slug to humans. Many factors have led us to have difficulty looking at ourselves: the diversity of our population; the inability to maintain careful records; and, most import, a belief that the sanctity of the human spirit is changed by studies investigating whether behavior is genetically transmitted, and the potential political implications thereof. In the past 30 years, it has become apparent, from psychopharmacology, our illicit drug culture, studies in viral encephalopathy, and so forth, that we, like animals, have the same mediators that help us think or not think.

One of the populations on the east coast that has lent itself to genetic studies is the Amish people of Lancaster County, Pennsylvania. Here, in a farm setting, an isolated population of people not unlike those with whom Pickle (1939) worked in the Yorkshire Dales have been living and raising their families segregated from the rest of the world, and have remained genetically isolated for 300 years. They keep good family records and, on rare occasions, will allow "English" to come into their homes. Egeland and Sussex (1985) studied manic-depressive disorders in the Amish. When they evaluated suicide in the Amish, they found that 92% of the cases were situated in multigenerational families with heavy loading for bipolar, unipolar, and other affective disorders.

That manic depression shows a genetic association is not surprising. For example, if one identical twin suffers from manic-depressive disease, a second identical twin has an 80% chance of having the disease (Kolata, 1986). Workers are now looking for a biologic marker for manic-depressive psychosis. They have explored the chromosomes and suggest that it may be located on the tip of the short arm of chromosome #11 (Egeland *et al.*, 1987). With gene probes, it will then be possible to identify the population who are carriers of this gene (Kolata, 1986). Others have evaluated the genetic pedigree in the Amish and suggest that manic-depressive disease probably is related to a dominant gene with incomplete penetrance (Kolata, 1986). Once the gene is identified and its bases are synthesized, then the general population may be screened for this abnormality. How widespread that particular behavioral mutation will be is unknown. One would expect, however, that manic-depressive disease, like so many other genetic disorders, would have a polymorphic expression. Clearly, how this information is used represents another set of challenges (e.g., in understanding such diseases as Lesch-Nyhan disease, Gilles de la Tourette syndrome, or phenylketonuria). Suffice it to say that here is an example in human systems similar to what has been found in *Drosophila*. It would be very surprising if these lesions will not in some way be involved with the intricate network of neuronal conduction discussed in the *Aplysia* model. Time will tell!

MATERNAL–FETAL DEVELOPMENT

We have reviewed the genetic and experiential mediators. What are those mediators that function aside from the genetic and learned behavior that mediates development? Although the potential of the cell exists partly in the germ plasm, the fully developed organism progresses through experience. Mammalian systems have a unique developmental pressure, which depends on the intrauterine environment through the maternal–fetal axis, where a unique exchange of information occurs. It is within this relationship that the primary development of the neurologic system and, therefore, behavioral potential takes place. This most likely represents one of the opportunities for the family to play a significant role in determining behavior.

The fetus is in constant physical contact with the maternal system during the first 40 weeks of life, and then in close proximity during the first several years (depending on social circumstances). It is also at this time of early molding of the new biologic structure that the first sketches of the permanent outline of individuality occur. Again, we will need to look at animal data, but there certainly are several areas that should be of interest to those studying families and the effects of family on the outcome of future generations.

Family nutrition—calories, type of diet, trace minerals, food additives—clearly affect the fetus. Certainly, the effects of alcohol and smoking on fetal development have been well documented. The maternal legacy then becomes a vertical system. Cell growth or cell damage becomes an option within the family system. In a sense, infection acquired *in utero,* or during the birth process, or in childhood from the mother or other family member is a strong determinant; devastating effects of rubella and cytomegalovirus have been well described, but what about normal flora that are acquired? What are the effects on the immunity of the child of the normal flora?

The model of Rh disease is interesting, as it represents a system in which the immunity of the mother can select cells or destroy fetal cells. How much selection of cells occurs early in development? How much fetal antigen is repressed or recognized in the first, second, and third trimesters of pregnancy? Are neuronal cells selected? Is there maternal immunologic control as well as hormonal control in development, and does this immunologic control have any effects on the development of the central nervous system or the selection of cells that finally develop? What are the effects of the circadian rhythms of the maternal system? There is evidence from animal data that the fetus is within the circadian rhythm system of the mother at the time of birth (Reppert & Schwartz, 1983). What are the effects of behavior when the rhythms are modified? What are the effects on the fetus of a mother whose circadian rhythms are not clearly established during pregnancy? How does this affect behavior? The understanding of the maternal role in fetal development will surely lead to definition of new patterns of mediation.

THE FAMILY AND MEDIATORS

The family represents a major part of the reticular system of behavior. It is the first-level move for the individual to a system of more than one. The laws that govern family networking may well represent laws that encompass behavior in a much larger sense. How then does the individual, with its intricate neuronal structure, its pretranscriptional legacy, interface with other individuals and adapt its behavioral characteristics? How does the family influence the flexibility or the rigidity of the vertical legacy?

If learning and adaptation are a result of an interface between a chemical substrate and an oscillating environment, then it is this event between the substrate and the environment that determines the posttranscriptional activity. Family myth, culture, political ideas, and the like then become "fixed" representations of posttranscriptional activity. The human system has adapted so that memory is stored in a society and culture in symbols. The process of education becomes, in a sense, a biologic process of induction; the symbols of society and culture are the substrates or inducers. In simpler systems, the substrate induces an enzyme and then the kinetics of the enzyme induction are observed and measured. In family systems, the observation and kinetics are much more complicated in that they occur in a networking system. To understand this mediation, a new mathematical system is needed.

The reticular nature of life itself makes study very difficult and, in a sense, ultimately immune to complete dissection with our present technology. This type of thinking does not eliminate the emphasis on the environment, for if behavior requires induction from external stimulation and if the form of stimuli determines the type of reaction that is to occur, then the environment and its symbolic representations become even more significant.

The individual sits in an ever-enlarging circle equipped with an endowment of cells, connections, bioamines, and sensors. The individual is surrounded concentrically by family, town, country, world, and the biosphere. Movement and reception of outside cultural symbols will have less or greater impact depending on the strength of the symbol and the timing of its presentation. For example, the presentation of a religious icon to a 4-year-old will not have the same impact as the presentation of the same symbol to a 40-year-old who has no prior experience with the icon. The point at which the contribution of external stimuli and internal representation reach a threshold that will allow self-reflection and creativity then becomes crucial to healthy functioning. This is a state not available to all, but the potential for its exists within each and every one of us. Therefore, the understanding of the keyboard and the instrument should not in any way preclude the enjoyment of the symphony or its creation.

Family medicine, in its search for explanation of function and searches for mediators, should not lose sight of the work with *Drosophila* and *Aplysia* as we begin to understand family myth, family language, and the reticular system as it proceeds over time. We will begin to appreciate that culture represents a symbolic construct of biologic activity and, in a sense, becomes the greatest biologic mediator of all.

As the human species evolves, it is crucial to understand which sections of the neuronal genetic portfolio remain stable and which sections are subject to change. Aside from the ability to repair our genes, the genetic structure that underpins individual neurobiology may well be the most crucial determinant of evolution.

References

Aceves-Pina EO, Booker R, Duerr JS, Livingstone MS, Quinn WG, Smith RF, Sziber PP, Tempel BL, Tully TP. Learning and memory in Drosophila, studied with mutants. Cold Spring Harbor Symposia on Quantitative Biology 1983; 48:831–840.

Benzer S. Genetic dissection of behavior. Scientific American 1973; 229:24–37.

Britten RJ. Rates of DNA sequence evolution differ between taxonomic groups. Science 1986; 231:1393–1398.

DeChardin PT. Phenomenon of man/Teilhard DeChardin. New York: Harper & Row, 1975. (Original work published 1923)

Egeland JA, Gerhard DS, Pauls DL, Sussex JN, Kidd KK, Allen CR, Hostetter AM, Housman DE. Bipolar affective disorders linked to DNA markers on chromosome 11. Nature 1987; 325:73–77.

Egeland JA, Sussex JN. Suicide and family loading for affective disorders. Journal of the American Medical Association 1985; 254(7):915–918.

Hall JC, Greenspan RJ. Genetic analysis of Drosophila neurobiology. Annual Review of Genetics 1979; 13:127–195.

Huygens FJA. Family medicine. New York: Brunner/Mazel, 1982.

Kandel E. From meta-psychology to molecular biology: explorations into the nature of anxiety. American Journal of Psychiatry 1983; 140:1277–1293.

Kandel E. Steps toward a molecular grammar for learning: explorations into the nature of neurology in medicine, science, and society. In: Isselbecher KJ, ed. Symposia celebrating the Harvard Medical School bicentennial. New York: Wiley, 1984: 556–604.

Kandel ER, Abrams T, Bernier L, Carew TJ, Hawkins RD, Schwartz JH. Classical conditioning and sensitization share aspects of the same molecular cascade in Aplysia. Cold Spring Harbor Symposia on Quantitative Biology 1983; 48:821–830.

Kolata G. Manic-depression: is it inherited? Science 1986; 232:575–576.

Livingstone MS. Genetic dissection of Drosophila adenylate cyclase. Proceedings of the National Academy of Science 1984; 82:5992–5996.

Pickle W. Epidemiology in country practice. Bristol: John Wright & Sons, 1939.

Reppert SM, Schwartz WJ. Maternal coordination of the fetal biological clock in utero. Science 1983; 220:969–971.

Temin HM. Origin of retroviruses from cellular moveable genetic elements. Cell 1980; 21(3):599–600.

Tempel BL, Livingstone MS, Quinn WG. Mutations in the Dopa decarboxylase gene affect learning in Drosophila. Proceedings of the National Academy of Science 1984; 81:3577–3581.

Zipursky S, Venkatesh T, Benzer S. From monoclonal antibody to gene for a neuron-specific glycoprotein in Drosophila. Proceedings of the National Academy of Science 1984; 82:1855–1859.

40

Challenges to Integration: Research and Clinical Issues

WILLIAM J. DOHERTY
University of Minnesota

The theme of this book is the creative integration of biologic science and family psycho-social science. Previous chapters have discussed how these sciences together can try to illuminate a number of difficult problems in human health and disease. This chapter will describe the challenges and possibilities faced by theoreticians, researchers, and clinicians as they bring their own intellectual and social contexts to the task of integration and collaboration. My main points are that optimal collaboration between biologic and psychosocial scientists, and between researchers and clinicians, will require nothing less than a paradigm shift for all parties and, consequently, that progress is likely to be both difficult and exciting.

The chapter begins with a discussion of the different intellectual and cultural worlds occupied by the scientists and clinicians and by biomedical scientists and psychosocial scientists. (I will use the terms ''psychosocial'' and ''family'' science interchangeably in this discussion, since the main issues apply both to the sociobehavioral sciences in general and to family science in particular.) The second section describes a new emerging paradigm, based on developments in the physical sciences, that holds promise of bridging the gaps between these intellectual and cultural worlds. The third section describes the movement away from reductionism that both biomedical adherents and psychosocial adherents must make if integrative work is to occur. The final section lays out several challenges facing individuals who would work at the interstices of the biologic and psychosocial dimensions of science and clinical practice. A number of ideas in the chapter are drawn from my previous work (Doherty, 1986; Doherty & Baird, 1983, 1987; Doherty, Baird, & Becker, 1987) and from conversations with several colleagues.

FOUR DIFFERENT WORLDS OF COLLABORATION

Figure 40-1 expresses four different activities practiced by authors in this book and by individuals who would seek an integration of family systems theory and the biologic sciences. The axes represent research versus practice and the biologic/biomedical science versus psychosocial/family science. The main point is that these cells tend to constitute different world views. Functioning in two of these cells (e.g., biomedical researcher and medical clinician) is difficult enough, but practicing in three is extraordinarily difficult. Combining all four in one individual is practically unheard of since the time of Albertus Magnus in the Middle Ages, by reputation the last scholar who was on top of all fields of knowledge.

What are different world views in the four activities? The following discussion will counterpose the perspectives along two axes. The first contrast is between the world views of the researcher and the clinician. This split can occur between groups (full-time researchers and full-time clinicians) and within individuals (as when a researcher/clinician is not

Biomedical   Psychosocial

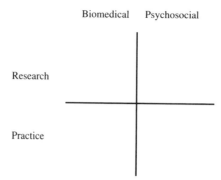

Research

Practice

Figure 40-1. Four worlds of collaboration.

able to integrate both perspectives). I frequently use the qualifier ''traditional'' to characterize the research models learned and practiced by most contemporary biomedical and family scientists; the newer paradigm to be described later is not yet widely subscribed to in either area.

Research versus Practice

1. *Traditional research emphasizes simplifying assumptions; clinicial practice emphasizes complexity.* Although researchers deal with complex phenomena, their approach stresses the core assumption ''all else being equal.'' For example, when physicists maintain that according to Newton's law of gravity objects fall at the same rate regardless of their mass, the simplifying assumption is that environmental conditions are held constant. A strong wind would obviously affect some objects more than others, but such real-world contingencies are not relevant to the basic scientific proposition. In the psychosocial sciences, scientists generally make the simplifying assumptions that respondents are putting the same amount of effort into the self-report instrument or the experimental procedure and that subjects are taking the procedure seriously. With the exception of a few instruments with ''lie'' scales, this assumption is hardly ever questioned in social science research.

Clinical practice, on the other hand, deals forthrightly with the complex contextual issues for which scientists try to control. Whereas a biomedical researcher conducting a clinical trail of a new drug for hypertension can recruit a homogeneous sample of patients without concurrent disease and with high likelihood of compliance with the drug regimen, a clinician must deal with hypertensive patients with heterogeneous medical histories and uncertain potential for compliance. A family researcher uses a large sample to try to minimize the problem of differences in subjects' desire to disclose family problems, on the assumption that in a large sample idiosyncratic family disclosure patterns will average out. A family therapist, however, is likely to emphasize the nuances of family members' ambivalence about disclosing painful aspects of their family life. Complexities that to researchers are ''confounds'' to be controlled for are, to clinicians, the very stuff of clinical practice.

2. *Traditional research has a narrow focus; clinical practice, a broad focus.* Traditional research proceeds by investigating narrowly defined problems in great detail. Generally, the same study does not simultaneously search for a gene that causes multiple sclerosis and also examine the natural history of this disease. Similarly, family scientists

generally do not simultaneously study both how family factors precipitate a disease process and how the disease affects the family. There is no reason, in principle, that both areas could not be addressed in the same study, but the traditional norms of research design and funding push researchers to confine the scope of their research questions.

Clinical practice, particularly in primary care and general family mental health care, takes as its unit of analysis not a study question but a person or a family. The scope must be as wide as the presenting problems. Each problem must be evaluated in the context of other problems and other strengths of the individual and family. Multiple sclerosis must be examined within the context of concurrent medical, psychologic, social, and economic problems. Awareness of the continuing arcs of influence among these factors is the heart of the clinical perspective.

3. *Traditional research emphasizes information; clinical practice emphasizes decisions and actions.* Although science is not without its ethical dilemmas, they pale in comparison with the clinician's continual struggle to weigh benefits and risks for individuals and families. The end point for scientific research is data that support or refute a theory. The end point for clinical investigation is a decision on actions that directly affect human lives. For example, in the mid-1980s there is mounting evidence for a link between elevated serum cholesterol and heart disease, and for the potential benefits of reducing serum cholesterol (Grundy, 1986). Researchers who have devoted their careers to gathering information about this linkage seem ready in 1986 to prescribe therapeutic and public health action to lower cholesterol (Rifkin & Lenfant, 1986). But clinicians who are faced with difficult decisions about how to treat individual patients for whom dietary changes may be difficult and long-term drug use risky are less enthusiastic about the clinical implications of current research (Grouse, 1986). It is not uncommon for clinicians, who face the responsibility for individuals' well-being, to demand a higher level of proof than scientists and public health leaders demand. The way the world looks depends on where you perch.

4. *Traditional research stresses the impersonal and objective; clinical practice, the personal and subjective.* Human subjects in research are faceless and nameless; in fact, human subjects requirements generally insist on this anonymity. Their experiences usually are summarized in numbers, not in stories. Often the principal investigators have little or no personal contact with research subjects. By traditional standards, it is scientifically inappropriate to recruit a sample from one's circle of acquaintances; sampling should be as objective and nonarbitrary as possible. Clinical practice, on the other hand, is based on personal relationships between clinicians and patients; the success of a practice, especially in primary care, often depends on the clinician's ability to attract a "following" from among his or her social network. Both scientists and clinicians gain something and lose something because of these differences. Scientists gain the perspective and freedom from bias that comes from distance, but lost the details viewed close up by clinicians. Clinicians gain insight into individual cases but miss the big picture and the generalizability that researchers achieve with their methods. Although ideally these two perspectives complement each another, the linkages are usually obscure in daily work. The *distinctions* between the objective and the subjective, between the impersonal and the personal, become *dichotomies*—chasms that are hard to bridge.

Biomedical Research versus Family Systems Research

This contrast is within the research community itself. The gulf between biomedical researchers and psychosocial/family researchers may be wider than that between biomedical researchers and biomedical clinicians, who at least know they need one another to make medical progress. Biomedical and social scientists generally view themselves as having different goals and speaking different tongues. In addition to these general differences, the following are contrasting aspects of the activities and world views of each group.

1. *Biomedical scientists often deal with directly observable objects or processes; family researchers more often deal with indirectly observed, inferential processes.* In studying important aspects of family dynamics, family scientists have no counterpart to the direct observation of the microscope. As Kenneth Gergen (1982) has pointed out, although social scientists can observe human behavior directly, actual behavior is usually of minor interest compared to the processes or characteristics inferred to underlie the behavior. Checks on a questionnaire are of trivial importance; the subject's thoughts and feelings, indirectly measured through the questionnaire, are the variable of interest. Similarly, behaviors (such as interruptions) observed during a laboratory procedure are meaningful only insofar as social scientists takes them for a proxy for other inferred variables (such as enmeshment or power struggle). Because human behavior can be taken to mean different things to different researchers, social science *lacks* as many common reference points as biology *has*. For example, when two biologists observe cells dividing under a microscope, they will probably agree that they are observing the process labeled by scientists as "mitosis." But when two family scientists—say, a psychoanalytically oriented one and a behaviorally oriented one—observe a married couple disagree repeatedly with each other during an interaction, they are likely to draw different, equally plausible inferences about the underlying marital process they are observing. If social scientists have difficulty talking with one another, it is not surprising that biomedical and social scientists have a large communication gap related to describing the objects and processes they are studying.

2. *Biomedical scientists have developed relatively strong methods for laboratory controls; by comparison, family scientists have few controls.* In studies of the effects of stress on immune functioning, for example, biologists are able to use a group of genetically similar mice in a controlled environment with a carefully defined stressor. Social scientists studying the influence of family stress on immune functioning have virtually no control over genetic and concurrent environmental factors; even if the stressor is well defined objectively (e.g., death of a spouse), the subjective aspects of the stressor are likely to be quite variable among individuals. Social scientists, of course, do their best to use controls available to them, such as specifying the cause of death of the spouse and using one age group of subjects. But the world of the social scientist is far more experimentally "sloppy" than the world of the biologist.

3. *Biomedical findings inherently are more likely to be generalizable than are family science findings.* When the gene for Huntington's disease is located in a representative sample of people, biologists are likely to agree that this gene causes Huntington's all over the world. When biomedical scientists discovered the role of insulin in metabolizing blood sugar, they had every reason to be confident that this process occurs universally in humans. But as Gergen (1982) has pointed out, the findings of social science generally must be specified as to culture and historical time period. For example, several studies using samples in England, Canada, and the United States have supported Brown and Harris's (1978) initial finding that perceived lack of marital intimacy is a risk factor for the onset of depression among married women. However, there is good reason to doubt that this finding would generalize to other non-Western cultures, where marital intimacy is not so highly valued and where the extended family is more important. Similarly, the same finding may not have held two centuries ago in the same Western countries and may not continue to be found in future generations if expectations of marriage change.

These points are not meant to undermine the importance of this body of research, which has important implications for clinicians in Western countries, but to suggest that the findings of social science research are far more circumscribed than those of biomedical science. An example of the "slipperiness" of biomedical findings analogous to much social science research is the tendency of disease-causing microorganisms to mutate in response to effective antibiotics; the medicine that works today may not work next month.

In order to avoid repetition, I will not discuss in depth the contrasting world views of all the cells in Figure 40-1. The diagonal groups—biomedical researchers and family clinicians, and family researchers and biomedical clinicians—have little in common in activities and world views. Nor will I discuss the differences between biomedical and family clinicians, since these issues have been dealt with in other writings (Doherty, 1986; Doherty & Baird, 1983).

This discussion has contrasted the world of *traditional* research with that of clinical practice. Part of the gap between the two can be explained by the adherence of most natural scientists, and many social scientists, to a scientific paradigm that is unsuited to the complexities of the biopsychosocial phenomena under study. In the next section, I argue for the new scientific paradigm that is emerging in the physical and social sciences, one that potentially can close the dichotomies between research and practice, and between the biomedical and social sciences.

THE "NEW" SCIENTIFIC PARADIGM

Modern physics, through the revolution known as quantum mechanics, has moved away from the rigid dichotomies that underlie the separate worlds of traditional research and clinical practice, and of traditional natural science and social science. In particular, quantum physics has called into question the Newtonian principles that separated subject from object, object from its context, and static entities from mobile process. My main argument here is that the scientific world view or paradigm of quantum physics creates the possibility that sound science can be conducted according to assumptions that clinicians, natural scientists, and social scientists can all embrace. The new paradigm will be articulated in the form of three contrasts with ideas from the old paradigm. The discussion here is elaborated more fully in Doherty (1986).

Relations versus Objects

The traditional scientific world view, based on Newtonian physics, has divided the world into discrete objects, which scientists can isolate and study in isolation. According to modern physics, however, the stuff of nature fundamentally involves relations or connections among entities. The basic building blocks of matter, the elementary particles, interact in such a way that they are continually transformed in and out of existence. There is no such thing as an electron existing with an identity independent of its relationships. Classical Newtonian physics, according to Alfred North Whitehead (1929), suffered from the "fallacy of misplaced concreteness"—the illusion that the world consists of self-contained isolated entities. According to Whitehead (1929) and the quantum physicists, there are no objects existing completely independent in space and time; there are no self-contained entities that can be fully explained outside their context. Werner Heisenberg (1958), one of the founders of quantum physics, wrote late in his life that, although the same matter and the same forces operate in every object of nature,

> what can be distinguished is the kind of connection which is primarily important in a certain phenomenon. . . . The world thus appears as a complicated tissue of events, in which connections of different kinds alternate or overlap or combine and thereby determine the texture of the whole. (p. 107)

This philosophic principle of relations versus isolated objects has implications not only for the importance of studying objects in their context (the clinician's perspective), but also for the relationship between researchers and the objects of their study. A cardinal notion in quantum physics is that the observer cannot be separated from the object of observation. In fact, the proper unit of measurement in a scientific study is always the *interaction* between the object and the measurement device set up according to the intentions of the investigator. Hence, the traditional notion of complete scientific objectivity as based on an absolute separation of the scientist from the object of study has broken down in modern physics. Along with absolute objectivity has gone the absolute dichotomy between the objective and the subjective. The two become inseparable elements of both scientific and clinical interactions.

Process versus Static Reality

The classical scientific paradigm separates objects of nature from the process of transformation; objects were thought to endure with stable characteristics over time. Quantum physics found that the basic ingredients of matter—the atomic particles—are not static entities existing unchanged over time. They go in and out of existence. Indeed, according to Heisenberg's (1958) uncertainty principle, particles with definite location and momentum cannot be found in nature. This discovery paved the way for what philosopher of science Capek (1961) termed "the reinstatement of becoming in the physical world." This notion of "becoming" as transformations over time has been most forcefully articulated by Nobel Prize-winning chemist Ilya Prigogine (1980). Prigogine has demonstrated that complex open systems, including all organic systems, are susceptible to qualitative transformations as they interact with their environment.

In biomedical research, time tends to be viewed in terms of the minutes or days required to grow cultures or perform experiments or test, not in terms of the lifetimes over which disease may develop in people. This constraint helped give rise to the notion that a disease is a "thing" existing at a point in time. It is something a person "has." Less consideration is given to the permutations of a disease process over an individual's life, as when hypertension or Type II diabetes wax and wane with the individual's weight and diet, or when the herpes simplex virus, always present, manifests itself at some times and is dormant at others (Schmidt, Zyzanski, Ellner, Kumar, & Arno, 1985). The world of the clinician inevitably is caught up in the flow of change as patients age and disease processes permutate over time. The "snapshots" of the statically focused researcher do not capture the "movie reel" of the clinician.

The reinstatement of process and change into scientific parlance in physics parallels a similar development in evolutionary biology (Mayr, 1982). These notions have been less fully embraced in laboratory biology, biomedical science, and many areas of traditional social science. But if the worlds of researcher and clinician and the domains of biomedical systems and family systems are to be linked, a shared dynamic view of reality will be essential.

Dynamic Causation versus Mechanical Determinism

Quantum physics rejected the classical notion of determinism, the idea that physical events of the present can predict fully all events of the future. In its place, quantum physicists such as Heisenberg and Bohr substituted the idea of objective probability: The past influences the present and the present influences the future, but in ways that allow for spontaneous behavior even in physical systems. Indeterminism, then, does not rest just on our imperfect methods of measuring important predictors of the future, but on the inevitable "fuzziness" of nature and the presence of real novelty in nature.

The notion of dynamic causation introduces into science what clinicians have sensed all along. Whether Mrs. Jones responds well to her insulin regimen depends not just on the biochemical interactions, but also on her level of personal stress, her husband's support of her diet, her work supervisor's attitude toward her, and any number of "surprise" elements no one could predict—including an invisible decision Mrs. Jones makes about whether or not to buckle down to control her diabetes. Each of these factors can be studied in isolation, as could the biochemical pathways, but a full scientific explanation of diabetes control would be closer to the dynamic model of the clinician than to the mechanical model of the laboratory researcher, whose simplifying assumptions inevitably break down in the complex world of human interactions. Although these ideas pose a threat to the security of traditional science, they open up new vistas for the new paradigm. I will end this section with a quote from Prigogine and his collaborator Isabelle Stengers (1984) about the profound changes occurring in Western science, changes that I am arguing can serve to break down the gaps among researchers and between researchers and clinicians:

> The artificial may be deterministic and reversible. The natural contains essential elements of randomness and irreversibility. This leads to a new view of matter in which matter is no longer the passive substance described in the mechanistic world view but is associated with spontaneous activity. This change is so profound that . . . we can really speak about a new dialogue of man with nature. (p. 9)

This section has summarized the new scientific paradigm emerging from quantum physics, from chemists such as Prigogine, and from philosophers of science. The implications of paradigm choice for the emerging family medicine science are twofold. First, I believe that the reductionist, mechanical scientific paradigm will not be adequate to the task of a biopsychosocial, systems-oriented science. It would be new wine in old wineskins. We will search for isolated family variables that "determine" certain biologic processes—and we will come up short of capturing enough complexity to satisfy. The new paradigm will require development of new concepts and new methods, and the redefinition of the findings from traditional methods, but in the end I believe that progress will be more satisfying (Doherty, 1986). Second, the use of the new scientific paradigm will allow for unprecedented collaboration between researchers and clinicians, because each has skills needed to wed traditional, "simplifying" methods with newer, "complexifying" methods.

The scientist has specialized in controls and the clinician in context. The two together make for an exciting new science.

INTEGRATING BIOMEDICAL AND PSYCHOSOCIAL SCIENCES

The previous section described how the new scientific paradigm can allow for common ground between scientists and clinicians. This section tackles the other polarity—between biomedical specialists and psychosocial specialists. Here, the task is even more difficult because differences are created not only by different daily activities but also by widely divergent areas of interest. To collaborate across domains of interest—the biomedical and the psychosocial—requires extraordinary efforts on both sides.

The biomedical model (which I term the "radical" biomedical model in the following discussion) has been characterized by George Engel (1977) as one that views disease and its treatment as reducible to definable biologic processes. The scientist uses the tools of biology, and the clinician serves as an applied biologist. In contrast, Engel (1977) describes a proposed biopsychosocial model as one that views disease and its treatment as a seamless web of biologic, psychologic, and social phenomena. The biopsychosocially oriented scientist uses the tools of the behavioral and social sciences along with those of the biologic sciences, and the biopsychosocially oriented clinician attends to all three dimensions of the patient's problem.

In attempting to locate contemporary family medicine within Engel's two models, I have proposed elsewhere a third, intermediate and possibly transitional model—the split biopsychosocial model (Doherty, Baird, & Becker, 1987). In this framework, psychosocial issues are viewed as important but as not yet integrated with biological issues. Mind and body are valued but dichotomized. Problems are either primarily organic or primarily psychosocial; treatment follows the same split. The split biopsychosocial model is inherently unstable in our intellectual culture; it lacks the purity of the biomedical model and the integrative complexity of the biopsychosocial model. Hence, when scientific or clinical doubt arises, its medical adherents are apt to fall back on the dominant biomedical model. This resolution of ambiguity typically rules out all possible biologic causes and treatments for a set of symptoms before calling on psychosocial causes and treatments.

In addition to this description of the three models of medicine—the biomedical, the split, and the biopsychosocial—I propose that many psychosocial scientists and clinicians adhere to a fourth model—the radical psychosocial model. The radical psychosocial model ignores biology and, in fact, is often antagonistic to biologic explanations and treatments for human problems. Mental illness in particular is viewed as strictly a psychosocial phenomenon; biology is viewed as a competing, unacceptable alternative to a purely psychosocial perspective. Given the cultural acceptance of the mind–body split, it should not be surprising that many psychosocial scientists and clinicians would be weaned on this radical psychosocial model for understanding problems within their fields.

In response to the widely acclaimed advances in the biologic understanding of and treatment for psychologic problems, many psychosocial scientists and clinicians have moved into the split biopsychosocial model. Thus, depression is dichotomized into endogenous (biologic) and reactive (psychosocial). The psychoses are handed over to a biologically oriented psychiatrist, with the neuroses held tight by the psychotherapists. From this split model, it is quite difficult to understand the interplay between biologic and psychosocial factors in family dysfunction—how, for example, neuroendocrine and family interaction activities can be both causes and effects within an ongoing experience of diabetes in a family member. Just as the biomedical side of the split model accepts the need for psychosocial variables but emphasizes the primacy of the biologic in "real" disease, the psychosocial side of the split model accepts the need for the biologic but guards the primacy of the psychosocial for "mental" and "social" problems.

Naturally, there is more at stake here than intellectual paradigms. The reductionist biomedical and psychosocial traditions are supported by powerful political and economic interests. Each side struggles to maintain its turf in an increasingly competitive scientific and clinical world. The ascendancy now seems to be going to the biomedical side, which makes the psychosocial advocates even less likely to give ground voluntarily. From this point of view, the split biopsychosocial model represents progress toward a synthesis and allows for the necessity of collaboration between biomedical specialists and psychosocial specialists for at least some problems. Both the radical models and the split model, however, tend to emphasize the primacy of the expert who is in charge of clinical relationships (Doherty *et al.*, 1987). The politics of these contemporary models, then, are essentially similar: Scientists and clinicians know what's best, and patients and the public should follow suit. What is at stake in maintaining one's turf as a biomedical or psychosocial specialist, then, is the claim to unique expertise over important human problems, expertise that brings grant monies and patients.

Figure 40-2 expresses my view of how these models come together in the biopsychosocial model, a "turf" that cannot be claimed by any one intellectual, scienfitic, or clinical tradition. This model, still in its infancy both theoretically and clinically, integrates the radical biomedical and radical psychosocial models. In Figure 40-2, the split model represents a possibly necessary transition between the more radical frameworks. The biopsychosocial model is represented as transcending the others, combining their knowledge into a broader integration. The top horizontal line is intended to indicate that the biopsychosocial framework on problems is not an end point, a "mountain peak," but, rather, a starting-off place, a foundation, for the important work to follow. Having achieved a biopsychosocial perspective, scientists and clinicians, biomedicalists and psychosocialists, are positioned to ask the important questions in ways that might lead to satisfying answers.

In keeping with the spirit of Engel's (1977) work, I propose that in the integrated biopsychosocial model, expertise belongs to a *community* of scholars, clinicians, and lay people (Doherty *et al.*, 1987). Because it acknowledges, along with the new scientific paradigm, the interrelatedness of ideas and of people, the politics of the biopyschosocial model are inherently collaborative. For example, in the contemporary debate about cholesterol and heart disease, the combined perspectives of biomedical scientists, medical and other health professionals, mental health professionals, behavioral and social scientists, the government, and the community of citizens will be necessary to resolve the best direction to take. The importance of the community and government becomes evident in their role in setting priorities for funding and their effective veto over efforts to influence the public

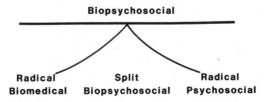

Figure 40-2. Four models of science and practice.

health. Scientists and clinicians function as experts, but only in roles delegated by the community of patients and citizens.

THE CHALLENGE OF COLLABORATION

I propose three areas of change among scientists and clinicians if we are to achieve the goals of biopsychosocial, family systems science and clinical practice. These "prescriptions" follow from the preceding "diagnosis" of the current problem, the splits and dichotomies that derive from our scientific, clinical, and cultural heritage.

First, we must be committed to changing our paradigms-of-origin. If indeed we have all been weaned either in a radical model or a split model of science and practice, then these paradigms will have to be revised. The intellectual heritage of Newtonian science simply cannot allow for the complexity and fluidity required to understand systems phenomena that cut across the physical, the biologic, the psychologic, and the social/cultural. Similarly, the clinical heritage of the applied medical biologist or the biologically innocent psychotherapist are not adequate to the complexities of biopsychosocial problems and treatments. The split model represents genuine progress in one's paradigm development because it introduces greater complexity into one's thinking. A second shift, toward biopsychosocial integration, requires a more profound reorientation of one's world view toward an integrated approach. Such changes do not come without uncertainty, and frequent "relapses" occur, back into one's paradigm-of-origin, which has more cultural support and more economic incentives, or into the split model, which does not take as heavy an intellectual or clinical toll on its adherents.

Second, we must be willing to share knowledge and power. Part of the paradigm shift involves the realization that the problems we are studying and treating are ultimately addressed by communities of scholars and clinicians and citizens. Sharing knowledge with intellectual or clinical "competitors" is the only path toward achieving this community. The trend toward specialization in our culture runs opposite this goal of sharing knowledge; others are considered not equipped to partake of the secrets of one's profession. Guarding knowledge, of course, is a way to guard power. Nothing meaningful will change in the direction of biopsychosocial treatment until physicians learn to share economic and decision-making power with nonphysicians, and until nonphysicians learn to share their expertise on human problems and social systems with physicians. The integrated model involves knowledge and skill no one profession possesses. It is inherently collaborative, which means a new, almost unprecedented approach to sharing knowledge and power. (I refer the reader to a book by Michael Glenn, 1987, a family physician who is a champion of collaborative health care.)

Third, we must be willing to be different from our own professional families. In a world where specialization and its attendant turf issues dominate, professionals who work at the interface of disciplines risk serious consequences from their professional peers. Changing one's paradigm-of-origin may be perceived as a betrayal of one's professional family-of-origin. Sharing knowledge and power with "outsiders" is not likely to endear one to professional peers who have spent a career trying to solidify the unique claims of the profession. Investigating topics outside the tradition of one's academic discipline leaves the scientist without clear direction for where to send a manuscript for review and which federal agency to ask for funding support. The journal system and the federal research funding system, after all, are organized around the mind–body split and around traditional specialties. Exploring the terrain of collaboration, therefore, is not for the fainthearted traveler. The opportunities to see new vistas with new colleagues are exciting, but the prospects of the welcome home are sometimes distressing.

CONCLUSION

An old song says, "We live in two different worlds." This chapter has argued that the professionals represented in this book come from at least four different worlds: those of science versus practice, and those of biomedical orientation versus psychosocial orientation. These professionals working toward an integrated biopsychosocial, family systems approach to health and illness come from traditions that are as different as the major religious faiths of the world. We tend to feel at home with the assumptions, methods, and practice style of our own disciplinary tradition. We feel inspired, adrift, dazzled, suspicious, enriched, and befuddled—when dealing with a different tradition. The challenge for collaboration represented in this book is akin to the ecumenical movement in contemporary religion: to respect diversity and to learn from it while searching for common ground from which to better understand our world and improve the lot of humankind.

Acknowledgment

Conversations with Howard Stein, Macaran Baird, Alvah Cass, and Lorne Becker contributed to my understanding of the issues discussed in this chapter.

References

Brown GW, Harris T. Social origins of depression: a study of psychiatric disorder in women. London: Tavistock, 1978.

Capek, M. The philosophical impact of contemporary physics. Princeton: Van Nostrand, 1961.

Doherty, WJ. Quanta, quarks, and families: implications of quantum physics for family research. Family Process 1986; 25:249–264.

Doherty WJ, Baird MA. Family therapy and family medicine: toward the primary care of families. New York: Guilford Press, 1983.

Doherty WJ, Baird MA, eds. Family-centered medical care: a clinical casebook. New York: Guilford Press, 1987.

Doherty WJ, Baird MA, Becker LA. Family medicine and the biopsychosocial model: the road toward integration. In: Doherty WJ, Christianson CE, Sussman MB, eds. Family medicine: the maturing of a discipline. New York: Haworth Press, 1987.

Engel, GL. The need for a new medical model: a challenge for biomedicine. Science 1977; 196:129–136.

Gergen KJ. Toward the transformation in social knowledge. New York: Springer-Verlag, 1982.

Glenn MJ. Collaborative health care: a family-oriented model. New York: Praeger, 1987.

Grouse L. Taking on the fat of the land: cholesterol and health. Journal of the American Medical Association 1986; 256:2873–2874.

Grundy SM. Cholesterol and coronary heart disease. Journal of the American Medical Association 1986; 256:2849–2858.

Heisenberg W. Physics and philosophy: the revolution in modern science. New York: Harper & Row, 1958.

Mayr E. The growth of biological thought. Cambridge, Mass.: Harvard University Press, 1982.

Prigogine I. From being to becoming: time and complexity in the physical sciences. San Francisco: Freeman, 1980.

Prigogine I, Stengers I. Order out of choas. New York: Bantam Books, 1984.

Rifkin BM, Lenfant C. Cholesterol lowering and the reduction of coronary heart disease risk. Journal of the American Medical Association 1986; 256:2872–2873.

Schmidt DD, Zyzanski S, Ellner J, Kumar ML, Arno J. Stress as a precipitating factor in subjects with recurrent herpes labialis. Journal of Family Practice 1985; 200:359–366.

Whitehead AN. Process and reality. New York: Macmillan, 1929.

41

Toward a Theory of Family Medicine

CHRISTIAN N. RAMSEY, JR.
University of Oklahoma

A major goal of the science of family medicine is to develop a theory of family medicine that describes the precise ways in which the family system is related to and regulates human biosystems.

This chapter has three objectives: (1) to define the initial or basic conditions that must be met in developing a theory of family medicine; (2) to review the experimental evidence and approaches (or lack thereof) that support the essential conditions for a theory of family medicine; and (3) to identify issues and questions for future study in the development of the theory of family medicine.

BASIC CONDITIONS OF A THEORY OF FAMILY MEDICINE

At least five fundamental requirements or conditions should be met to validate a theory of family medicine. In this section, these conditions are stated and discussed, and the supporting experimental evidence is presented. The five basic conditions are:

1. There must be a family theory to account for and/or explain the following processes: (a) family system growth and development; (b) family system response to stimulus/stress; (c) family system influences on individual behavior; (d) family system information processing; and (e) famiily system relationship to symptom production. Techniques must exist for the reliable and repeatable assessment of family structure and functioning, including documentation of the mechanisms through which symptoms or biologic dysfunction occur in individual family members.

2. The nervous systems of individual family members should express specific receptors/circuits for processing family system information and transmitting such information to end organs through the nervous, endocrine, or immune systems.

3. Dynamic family systems–psychoneuroendocrine/immune (PNEI) interactions should be demonstrated, resulting in (a) demonstration of the family system's role in the maintenance of the normal tone of the PNEI systems (resting) potential, and (b) reflex pathways through which the PNEI and the family system influence each other. One implication is that messengers from the PNEI to the family system would provide information about PNEI status, and messengers from the family system to the PNEI would transmit changes in the activity of family systems.

4. Severe emotional or mental dysfunction should be accompanied by both PNEI system and family system abnormalities.

5. Family system dysfunction should interfere with processes related to hormone production (endocrine function) and/or immune response. Experimental manipulation of the family system should affect the PNEI response.

EVIDENCE TO SUPPORT THE REQUIREMENTS
FOR A THEORY OF FAMILY MEDICINE

Family Theory Development

This requirement defines the theoretic framework for understanding the family system. At a minimum, there must be a family theory that describes the following processes: (1) family system growth and development, (2) family system response to stimulus/stress, (3) family system influence on individual behavior, (4) family system information processing, and (5) family system relationship to symptom production. Techniques must exist for the reliable and repeatable assessment of family structure and functioning, including documentation of the mechanisms through which symptoms or biologic dysfunction occur in individual family members.

Developing a theory of family medicine requires definition and understanding of the functioning of the family system specifically as it relates to biologic phenomena and response. An implicit assumption is that the fundamental purpose of the family is to organize information from the external environment to aid in the survival, adaptation, and preservation of biologic and behavioral material and processes. Thus, there is a need for a solid theoretic basis for the family's growth processes, response to various stimuli, and information interchange with both the social environment and individual family members through its boundaries.

With reference to family boundary, Chorover and Chorover's (1982) definition of the family boundary is relevant: a semipermeable membrane or spatiotemporal boundary consisting of an "orderly set of processes through which the family develops and maintains itself as a composite entity" (p. 145). Understanding the family system as a major regulator of PNEI systems requires knowledge and understanding of the ways in which the family boundary serves to define and facilitate communication both inside and outside the family system.

CONCEPTS TO BE ADDRESSED IN FAMILY THEORY

Family theory has progressed substantially during the past two decades but still lacks definition of the specific mechanisms that could account for biologic impacts. Three aspects of family theory are particularly relevant to a theory of family medicine and need further development: (1) family information processing, (2) family response to stress/stimulus, and (3) symptom processes and formation.

Family Information Processing. A key to understanding the functioning of the family system with reference to its relationship to PNEI is to understand the ways in which information that ultimately has biologic response is processed by the family system. Family information processing is defined as the way in which the family system gathers, transduces, codes, stores, integrates, and acts on internal and external environmental input. To "process" means to change something from one state to another in an orderly fashion. In a broad sense, information can be defined as nonrandom interaction with the environment. In this context, information not only includes verbal information but may also involve changing language or feelings to electrical impulse, changing electrical impulse to chemical molecules, and so forth. The importance of information processing in the family system is analogous to that of information processing in the nervous system.

It is now possible to relate the anatomy, function, and chemical mechanisms for information processing in a single neuron. One action potential is like another in a different part of the nervous system. Understanding how the action potential is generated, however, is not the same as knowing how information is coded by that action potential within a given neural circuit. According to Christensen, Krausz, Perez-Polo, and Willis (1980), the difference between neural circuits is not that they are composed of different modular blocks but that they possess different information. In a similar way, genetic information is stored in complex macromolecules composed of similar building blocks (purines and pyrimidines) but in different combinations. In order to analyze the relevance of the information being processed, it is necessary to know how the circuits interface with reference to input and output.

Existing family theories do not adequately address family information processing. The specific factors of family information processing that must be described and accounted for in a theory of family medicine include how the family and its members (1) survey the environment to collect information, (2) decide whether to process information to memory/behavior or ignore it, (3) construct family standards (paradigms) with which to compare new information, (4) maintain (store) family memory, (5) store and transmit transgenerational behavioral patterns, and (6) transmit information from family memory to individual family members.

Two lines of work may provide the knowledge of family information processing needed in theory development: experimental confirmation of Reiss's Cycle Hypothesis (1981) and the use of mathematical modeling techniques to simulate family information processing. The Cycle Hypothesis comprises six sequential, partly duplicated steps developed to explain how the family paradigm is formed and stabilized over time. The steps involve specification of patterns of interaction with the environment, development of a specific link with the environment, and selection of specific environments. Reiss has developed a number of variables for each step of the process. The number of potential combinations of variables and the potential complexity of the paradigm building provide an impressive array of information-processing capacities.

Moore (1980) described the use of mathematical techniques to model information processing in the nervous system. Of particular interest to family social scientists may be the newer, random stimulus techniques that permit concurrent manipulation of multiple input variables so that the effect of each variable on the system output can be determined and interactions between input variables that alter the time course of their absolute effectiveness can be detected. Since the power of the family is related to its complex ability to respond differentially to the impact of many variables, one can scarcely hope to document or even detect subtle modes of information processing unless stimuli or other variables of relevance have the potential interactive complexity to match that of the family system. These newer mathematical techniques, which allow concurrent manipulation of several independent variables, have the potential for freeing investigators from the single input–single output experimental designs that have prevailed up until now.

Family Response to Stress/Stimulus. The concept of the family system as a stimulus–response system is crucial to the evaluation of a theory of family medicine. Living, biologic systems usually must be provoked to be fully understood. Three recent contributions from the fields of physiology, biochemistry, and psychology may be helpful in refining knowledge of the family system as a stimulus–response system. The concepts may be relevant to family theory as a way of explaining the variable reactions and multiple accommodations to stress.

1. *Stimulus definition:* Terman, Shavit, Lewis, Cannon, and Leibeskind (1984) have worked to understand the neural and neurochemical basis of pain perception and have

recently extended their investigations to the areas of tumor growth and immunocompetence. In elegant experiments, they have demonstrated that painful stress can activate either of two different analgesia mechanisms in the brain stem—one opioid-based and the other non-opioid-based. The stimulus paradigm *alone* determines which of these two systems will be activated. Relatively small differences in stimuli are all that are needed to switch back and forth between the two systems. These workers have studied the effects of dissection of the stimulus on both tumor growth and immune function as measured by mitogen reactivity and have found that only stress that activates the opioid-based system causes tumor enhancement and change in lymphocyte stimulation. Both stress effects are blocked by naltrexene, a narcotic antagonist.

These studies show that minor differences in stress parameters (intermittent versus continuous) determine whether or not a stimulus will cause analgesia, be immunosuppressive, or be tumor-enhancing. Thus, different parameters of a single stressor have different psychologic, neurochemical, endocrine, and immune consequences.

This work is of major interest to the development of family theory, as it implies that variation in biologic response could be attributed to subtle differences in the family stimulus paradigm. As Patterson (Chapter 7, this volume) stated, we must look at multiple stimuli or variations to explain the full results.

2. *Accommodation to stress:* Mason (1968), working with primates and humans, found that physiologic stressors do not elicit a stress response when they are presented in a way that eliminates their psychologic sequelae of uncertainty and fear. Further, Sakellaris and Vernikos-Danellis (1975) demonstrated a conditioning of the stress response. Burchfield (1979) suggested that all organisms are genetically predisposed to adapt to stress and that the adaptation consists of a conditioned endocrine response, before the stressor is presented, accompanied by a decrease in arousal during stress. She suggests that the pattern is adaptive because it conserves resources and promotes homeostasis.

Clearly, if families accommodate to stress and react in adaptive rather than outright responses, results will be confounded. Perhaps the answer will come through laboratory study and manipulation of family systems with standardized, quantitative, multivariate stressors—coupled with protocols designed to detect accommodation—using biologic markers. Family stress theory could then be modified to deal with the phenomenon of accommodation.

3. *Reactivity to stress:* Reactivity is almost an opposite response to stress from that of accommodation. Reactivity, or physiologic responsiveness, to emotional stress has been suggested as a marker for the pathogenic processes involved in the etiology of coronary-heart disease or essential hypertension (Eliot, Chapter 19, this volume; Eliot, Buell, & Dembroski, 1982). Large-scale cardiovascular and neuroendocrine responsiveness has been observed to both laboratory or naturalistic stressors. Krantz and Manuck (1984) recently reviewed the evidence linking behaviorally induced cardiovascular and endocrine changes to coronary heart disease and essential hypertension, and have concluded that reactivity to stress is a construct with many dimensions: Different testing and situations appear to elicit different patterns of physiologic responses. They recommend more effort toward methodologic studies of stimulus diversion and response.

From the standpoint of family theory development, it would be enormously helpful to know whether or not there are "family reactor groups" or whether the index patient in a family system is a "reactor." Work is currently underway at the Department of Family Medicine, University of Oklahoma College of Medicine (S. J. Spann, personal communication, December 1986) to measure simultaneously cardiovascular and neuroendocrine reactivity in family groups, which may shed some light in this area.

Symptom Processes. Utilizing scientific methods, one should be able to explain or predict the way in which a specific family member will display dysfunction or possess symptoms. Even in cybernetic systems, there is a hierarchic transmission of information as it proceeds down the chain to cause a biologic consequence.

Symptoms are important because they are an indicator of the family's functional level—either the need for change or the prohibition against change in the family system. Symptoms can mean one of three things:

1. They may serve a homeostatic or, according to Ashby (1960, cited in Hoffman, 1980), a "bimodal feedback" function.
2. A symptom may be the herald of major change, what Platt (1970, cited in Hoffman, 1980) called the "time emergence" form of systems change, likening change, or transformation, to a kaleidoscope, in which "one can never go back" (pp. 55–56).
3. A symptom may represent a holdover from the past—a "failed transformation."

The importance of understanding symptom processes from the standpoint of the science of family medicine is that different types of family symptoms may have different biologic consequences—or different symptoms may have the same biologic consequences. It seems likely that the family system can have both direct and indirect effects on symptom production processes.

Indirect family effects on symptom processes would involve those situations in which the family system facilitates or inhibits the response to an outside factor. These indirect effects include (1) genetic effects through the expression or repression of a gene or through influencing the time of expression of a gene, and (2) regulation of the PNEI to modulate a response to a specific stimulus, such as exposure to a pathogen.

Direct effects of the family system on symptom processes can occur through two mechanisms: (1) change in family structure or (2) direct influence on family processes. Change in family structure primarily involves change at the time of addition or loss of a family member. The biologic consequences associated with reproductive process (i.e., low birth weight; Ramsey. Chapter 23, this volume) or at the time of death of family members (immunoincompetence) are well documented. The direct influence of family processes on symptom production has been addressed by many family theories. Sluzki and Ransom (1976) suggested that symptoms can be viewed from the standpoint of production or maintenance and family theory has addressed each aspect.

The Bowen Theory (Bowen, 1959, 1960; Bowen, 1978, cited in Hall, 1981; Hall, 1981) suggests that the process of triangulation is a major symptom-producing mechanism in an undifferentiated child. Haley (1973) and Terkelsen (1980) suggest that pathologic response (symptom) surfaces when the process of disengagement from one generation to another is detained or prevented. The typologic theories suggest that the position or type of family with reference to cohesion and adaptability will be predictive of symptom production.

Reiss and Oliveri (Oliveri & Reiss, 1982; Reiss & Oliveri, 1983) suggest that certain family paradigms will maintain symptomatology (i.e., interpersonal distance-sensitive or consensus-sensitive). Stanton and Todd (1982, pp. 16–17) have suggested that drug addiction has many functional or adaptive qualities for the addict and family and provides a paradoxical resolution to the dilemma of maintaining or dissolving the family through the pharmacologic effects of the drug (i.e., the drug allows the addict to be physically "close" to the family, while the narcotic effects of the drug keep the addict separated). This concept is corroborated by Steinglass's model of the alcoholic family system (Steinglass, 1980, Chapter 7, this volume). The idea demonstrates how symptom incorporation can begin a vicious cycle leading to social and biologic deterioration.

To summarize, the study and elucidation of symptom processes is of major importance in developing a theory of family medicine because (1) different symptom mechanisms may cause different or similar biologic consequences; (2) the understanding of the interplay between family systems and biologic aspects of symptoms will allow for more effective interventions; that is, interventions to repair the biologic symptom will not be undertaken without preparing for family system effects; and (3) in highly recursive systems, the symptom—particularly biologic dysfunction—provides us a good place to start examining inter-relationships.

Neural Circuits for Information Processing

The nervous system of individual family members should express receptors/circuits for processing family system information and transmitting such information to end organs through the nervous, endocrine, or immune systems.

This requirement deals with the ways in which the nervous system of the individual biologic organism receives, codes, stores, integrates, and acts on family systems information output. Clearly, if the family system is a major regulator of the PNEI, there must be a neural basis for the receipt and processing of family systems information. In this requirement, we are interested in several characteristics of nervous system circuits:

1. What are the neural circuits for processing family/social information?
2. How is social behavior integrated, learned, and stored within the nervous system?
3. How is such family information transmitted or translated into a biologic response?

In this section, we will review the aspects of neuroanatomy and physiology that are pertinent to family systems information processing, and then consider several neural responses to family behavior.

As will be seen, much of the work has been focused on *social* behavior in general rather than on family behavior in particular.

NEURAL CIRCUITS IN FAMILY INFORMATION PROCESSING

Four central nervous system processes related to social behavior have been investigated. First, work has been done to elucidate the mechanism of learning social behavior. Second, work has been done to show the role of the hippocampus in responding to uncertainty and in social withdrawal. Third, the amygdala has been shown to play a central role in challenging social attachments and in arousal responses. Fourth, work has been done that links behavior to specific endocrine and immune responses (see Borysenko, Chapter 15, this volume). Each of these lines of work addresses an aspect of neural function with potential for understanding family information processing.

Neural Processes in the Integration and Learning of Social Behavior. Watson and Henry (1977) have studied the learning of social behavior in mice. Their work was based both on the knowledge of (1) the importance of REM sleep in learning and (2) the need for animals to learn social behavior in *early* life. Many workers have demonstrated the necessity of REM sleep for learning activity, and several groups have observed that the duration of REM sleep increases after learning activity (Fishbein, Kastaniotis, & Chattman,

1974; Hennevin, Leconte, & Bloch, 1974, cited in Henry & Stephens, 1977; Smith, Kitahama, Valatx, & Jouvet, 1974). Furthermore, Kitahama, Valatx, and Jouvet (1975, cited in Henry & Stephens, 1977) demonstrated that if REM sleep is prevented for several hours after an experience, a deficit in learning occurs. Concurrently, work has shown the necessity of peer interaction early in life in the development of social behavior in animals. Watson, Henry, and Haltmeyer (1974) showed that when socially isolated mice were exposed to each other for 30 minutes of social interaction, they had a much higher plasma cortisone response than group-reared mice, were less active in the open field, and demonstrated high levels of aggression when put into complex population cages.

In questioning how social interactions were learned, Watson and Henry (1977) reasoned that dreaming, or REM sleep, may be important to the developing central nervous system as it integrates and reprograms new experiences into social-behavioral patterns. They developed a protocol that exposed a group of young mice to a treadmill experience after a period of social peer interaction, while allowing the controls to sleep. In the experimental group, repeated attempts at socialization were futile because the mice were forced to wait on the treadmill following each social encounter before they could sleep and, presumably, integrate and consolidate their social experiences. These mice were as aggressive as isolated mice and were also hypertensive.

Thus, an explanatory basis exists for the neural integraton of social experience in the developing organism.

Information Processing in Social Hierarchy Behavior. Social organizations, such as family systems, require their members to have an acute sense of position and to "know their place" in both the physical and hierarchic senses. Loss of position, whether physical territory or social status, is often accompanied by depression. Recent work has confirmed that the hippocampus is the basic neural circuit concerned (1) with territoriality and (2) with hypothalamic interactions that control and regulate the secretion of adrenocorticotropic hormone (ACTH) and activate the pituitary–adrenocortical system (depression hormones). O'Keefe, Nadel, Keightley, Kill, and Fornix (1975) have proposed that the hippocampus functions as a cognitive mapping system, and this mapping function applies not only to space in the physical sense but to the concepts of territory and home range.

Ely, Greene, and Henry (1976) studied the behavior of mice in the social hierarchy and demonstrated that, following hippocampal lesions, there was a loss of behavior patterns between the dominant and subordinate. These workers further suggest that there is a modification of emotional control in the colony following lesioning of the hippocampus. Isaacson (1974) proposed that the hippocampus is a mechanism by which the most well established patterns are turned off when the unexpected happens and control of territory is lost. He perceives that the hippocampus functions by regulating other regions during mismatches between stored representation and present perception of environment, or when old and established response patterns fail to induce with expected rewards.

In addition to its direct neural control of territoriality, the hippocampus also exerts significant control over the pituitary adrenocortical mechanism, as exemplified by the numerous demonstrations of the correlation of social rank with level of ACTH secretion. Bronson and Eleftheriou (1965) showed that the mice previously exposed to a fighter will develop increased corticosterone levels when they see their opponent again. Davis and Christian (1957) showed that the higher the social rank of the rodent, the less its adrenal corticogenesis was affected when it was placed with other rodents. Christian (1971) showed that dominant mice that initiate and win their fights show no increase in plasma corticosteroids, but that subordinate mice that do so show a significant increase. He concluded that defeat was an important stimulus acting on mice to produce an adrenal response after fighting. The central effect of cortisone is depressed feelings, and therefore it is thought that cortisone is a biologic mechanism that reinforces subordination or accommodation to a subordinate role.

Thus, it appears that the hippocampus provides regulation of both territory mapping and the ACTH response to loss of territory. Further, when old behavior patterns fail or when control of space/hierarchy is lost, a depressive response is reinforced by the release of ACTH and activation of the pituitary adrenal system, which aids in adaptation to a subordinate social position.

Neural Processes in Attachment and Defense Responses. The amygdalar nuclei are located in the anterior portion of the temporal lobes and appear to have many functions. First, the amygdalar nuclei appear to maintain blood pressure throughout the sympathetic nervous system. Lang (1975) and Lang, Innes, and Tansy (1975) demonstrated the controlling influence of the amygdala on the sympathetic nervous system. They showed that the rise in blood pressure that follows stimulation of the vagus could be inhibited by simultaneously stimulating the amygdala. Second, amygdalar lesions upset the ease with which new behavior can be elicited; attachment is disturbed, and lack of induced competitiveness results in a loss of social status. Third, the amygdala can activate the hypothalamic neuronal substrate for the expression of emotions (Isaacson, 1974). Both inhibitory and facilitory influences on the fight or flight reaction have been demonstrated with amygdalar stimulation.

The biologic impact of activation of the amygdala is thus the activation of the sympatho-adrenal-medullary pathway. If circumstances are appropriate (e.g., meeting a rival who has been defeated previously), the amygdala is activated and impulses are sent to the posterior hypothalamus, which causes a rise in blood pressure and a defense response. Adrenal catecholamine synthesis will be stepped up, cardiac output and peripheral resistance will increase, and blood pressure will be elevated as the organism assumes the posture appropriate for fight or flight and the accompanying rapid expenditure of energy. Thus, a chain of events and behavior following a certain type of social perception leads to a significant biologic response.

To summarize, the amygdala—with inputs from the frontal cortex—is associated with the reinforcement of behavior/response. Amygdalar control leads to a chain of responses in which sympathetic efferents are activated, which in turn leads to elevated epinephrine during general arousal and plasma norepinephrine during a fight. By contrast, the hippocampus—with inputs from other areas of the frontal cortex—regulates the activities of corticotropin in producing hypothalamic cells when control of territory has been lost during conditions of uncertainty. When control of surrounding space is lost, the depressive response is precipitated, along with the release of ACTH and activation of the pituitary–adrenocortical system.

In summary, it is possible to identify specific neural circuits for processing social information that are compatible with family information processing. Further neural mechanisms that link social behavior with endocrine and immune responses have been identified. A major question concerns the application of family information processing to the knowledge of neural circuits and neuroendocrine and immune information processing.

Family Systems–Psychoneuroendocrine/Immune Interactions

Dynamic family systems–psychoneuroendocrine/immune (PNEI) interactions should exist, resulting in (1) demonstration of the family system's maintenance of the normal tone of the PNEI systems (resting potential) and (2) reflex pathways through which the PNEI and family systems influence each other. An implication is that messengers from the PNEI to the family system would provide information about PNEI status, and messengers from the family system to the PNEI would transmit changes in the activity of the family system to the PNEI.

This requirement deals with two fundamental properties of living systems: one that is inherent and independent within a single cell, and one that is dependent on the living organism's relationships. The first is exemplified by the resting potential. The resting potential in a muscle cell is the amount of energy expended to maintain a differential concentration of ions across the cell membrane, so that the inside of the cell is strongly negatively charged with respect to the outside of the cell. Maintaining the resting potential is an absolute requirement for maintaining the integrity of the cell. To be functional, the muscle cell has a second property called "tonus," or tone, in addition to the resting potential. Tone is not inherent in the cell but depends on the existence of a neuronal connection. If the neural circuit is interrupted, the muscle cell's tone is lost and it literally withers. In relating this connection between the neuron and muscular tone to the family system, it is postulated that the family system is essential to provide tone for the individual family members. Thus, this requirement deals with the proposition that the family system is essential to provide tone for the individual family member—that the family system, as a major regulator of an individual human system, is involved in maintaining the tone of the psychologic and biologic subsystems within the individual family member.

A good example of tone maintenance in a biologic system involves the stretch reflex of the motor unit—a single neuron and a muscle cell. In this section, the concept of maintenance of tone will be illustrated with the example of the stretch reflex, and then three lines of evidence suggesting a family system role in tone maintenance of individual family members will be presented. The description of the stretch reflex is adapted from Jensen's *Principles of Physiology* (1976).

The stretch, or myotactic, reflex is the fundamental neural mechanism for maintaining tone in skeletal muscle. It serves two basic functions: (1) keeping muscles in a state of slight partial contraction at all times and (2) increasing the contractile state of certain muscle groups under physiologic conditions, thereby providing a background of postural muscle position on which voluntary movements can be superimposed. Thus, skeletal muscles are never fully relaxed; they are in a partially contracted state at all times. If the nerve (either sensory or motor) to a muscle is cut or sectioned, muscle tone is immediately abolished, indicating that the contractile state is caused by a reflex activity and is not a property of skeletal muscle per se.

Thus, in biologic systems, (1) tonus is a requirement of maintenance of reflexivity (functionality), and transection of the nerve causes instant loss of tonus and paralysis; (2) tonus is not inherent but is provided for the muscle cell through connection with a neuron, which is regulated in turn by higher centers; and (3) maintenance of tonus requires little energy expenditure.

Evidence of a link between an individual's ability to maintain tone and that individual's personal relationship within the family system comes from four sources: (1) studies of parental deprivation, (2) immune and hormonal responses to bereavement in the loss of a spouse, (3) endocrine and metabolic response to social isolation, and (4) immune and endocrine response to loneliness.

Studies of maternal deprivation have demonstrated that severe cases of deprivation are associated with sociopathic personality and delinquency, while less severe cases are subject to neurosis. Earle and Earle (1961) studied 1,423 patients and found 100 who had had maternal deprivation of at least 6 months duration in the first 6 years of life. These 100 were age- and sex-matched with controls who did not have maternal deprivation. The incidence of childhood personality disorder and sociopathic personality disorder was significantly greater in the deprivation cases than in the controls.

A second line of evidence comes form work related to fracture of the family system by death of a spouse. Studies by Bartrop, Luckhurst, Lazarus, Kiloh, and Penny (1977) and others (e.g., Schleifer, Chapter 16, this volume; Schleifer, Keller, Camerino, Thornton, & Stein, 1983) have demonstrated that, following death of a spouse, there is immunoincompetence in the survivor as evidenced by decreased reactivity of lymphocytes to mitogen stimulation. Another effect of loss of a spouse involves the endocrine system. Carroll (1976) showed that bereavement activates the ACTH pituitary and adrenal cortical hormonal systems and that production of steroids increases, all of which phenomena are associated with depression. Carroll further showed that there was an impaired response to dexamethasone, which normally suppresses cortisone release by blocking ACTH release by competing with cortisone for pituitary and hypothalamic receptor sites, and thus eliminates feedback to the ACTH mechanism.

A third line of evidence for a family role in tone production and maintenance relates to the endocrine and metabolic effects of experimental social isolation of elderly patients (Arntez, Theorell, Levi, Kallner, & Eneroth, 1983). An experimental activity program was instituted for half of the residents (30 individuals) of a senior citizen apartment building; the other 30 constituted the control group. Psychosocial and blood testing were done initially, and again 3 and 6 months after starting the activities program. Social activation increased threefold in the experimental group. Plasma testosterone, dihydroepiandrosterone, and estradiol increased significantly in the experimental group, while hemoglobin A1-C decreased. Cortisol and growth hormone were not changed.

A final line of evidence comes from work on the biologic consequences of loneliness. Kiecolt-Glaser *et al.* (1984a) studied the immune effects of loneliness on medical students and found that those who scored high on loneliness had higher Epstein-Barr virus (EBV) titers than did low scorers. In EBV infections, higher titers reflect poor cellular immune response, since after an active infection the virus genome is repressed in a latent state within the host B-lymphocytes. Several months after the first sampling, students were tested to study cellular transformation by EBV. The investigators found that high-loneliness subjects had lower transformation levels than did low scorers. These same workers examined the association between loneliness, stressful life events, urinary cortisol, and cellular immunocompetency in psychiatric patients (Kiecolt-Glaser *et al.*, 1984b). The high scorers on the loneliness scale had higher urinary cortisol levels, lower levels of natural killer cell activity, and poorer T-lymphocyte response to phytohemagglutinin (PHA).

Though not as direct as transsection of a nerve, these studies give considerable support to the notion that the family system may be responsible for maintaining the tone of the individual human system.

The nature of the processes or mechanisms by which family systems might produce tone have not been investigated. Although it is probable that, as in many other biologic systems, there is a stimulus–response and feedback system, it is also likely that tone is maintained by a higher center or level in the biosociosphere. In this vein, it would be reasonable to suspect that family ties with the social and physical environment are partly responsible for maintenance of tone between the family system and the biologic system.

It is widely held that normal family functioning is associated with healthy biologic and psychologic systems and maintenance of individual member tonus. With reference to overall family competence and global health measures, Pratt (1976) found that energized families and their members (1) had a high level of health, (2) had better health practices than other groups, and (3) made better use of health services than did nonenergized families. Characteristics of the energized family included (1) regular interaction between family members; (2) varied and active contacts with many groups in the community; (3) attempts by family members to master their lives and environment; (4) fluid internal organization, shared power, and mutual support; and (5) a high degree of personal autonomy. In many ways, Pratt's energized family is very much like the "competent" family of Lewis, Beavers, Gossett, and Phillips (1976) or the environment-sensitive family described by Reiss (1981); all three are examples of healthy families. These examples of healthy functioning families suggest that physiologic tonus is a dynamic, active, energy-consuming process between the individual family member, the family system, and the larger community (environment).

Family System–Psychoneuroendocrine System Interaction in Mental Illness

The fourth requirement for a theory of family medicine states that severe emotional or mental dysfunction should be accompanied by both PNEI system and family system abnormalities. Evidence for linkages between (1) the family system, (2) the central nervous system, and (3) endocrine/immune function can only be inferred from studies of a variety of endocrinologic and immunologic abnormalities in conjunction with major central nervous system dysfunction, particularly depressive illness and schizophrenia. Although there have been a number of studies of family functioning with reference to depression and schizophrenia, there are none in which the family system, mental illness, and endocrine or immune dysfunction have been studied simultaneously in the same patients and families.

A number of effects of depression on family systems have been observed. These include (1) change in health behavior of family members, (2) change in the type of family complaints as the reason for a medical visit, and (3) the impact of a depressed patient on the mood of others. A great deal of work has been done by Widmer (see Chapter 36, this volume) on the impact of depressive illness on the family. He found significant changes in the health behavior of family members of depressed patients, including more visits by spouses, more visits by children, and increased incidence of pain and of functional or anxiety complaints in family members. Cadoret, Widmer, and Troughton (1980) found increased doctor visits by family members of depressed patients for complaints related to family problems (e.g., parent–child problems or marital conflict). Coyne and colleagues (Coyne, 1976a, 1976b; Coyne, Aldwin, & Lazarus, 1981) found that telephone conversations with depressed patients made interviewers depressed, hostile, anxious, and rejecting.

From a biologic standpoint, depressive illness has been shown to have a significant effect on the neuroendocrine system. In 1966, Rubin and Mandell predicted future developments in the field by stating that "functional" depressive states are concomitants of suprahypophyseal brain dysfunction, which is also responsible for hyperstimulation of the anterior pituitary. Sachar (1976) showed that the mean hourly cortisol concentration in depressed patients is significantly higher in the afternoon, evening, and early morning hours. He concluded that there is either excess stimulation or removal of inhibition of the hypothalamic cells secreting corticoid-releasing factors as an intrinsic part of severe depressive illness.

A specific link between the hypothalamic–pituitary–adrenal (HPA) axis and depressive illness has been identified by three independent groups (Butler & Besser, 1968; Carrol, Martin, & Davies, 1968; Stokes, 1972). These groups studied the central mechanism that regulates ACTH release, and all reported that depressed patients failed to exhibit a normal suppression to dexamethasone. Other psychiatric and normal patients—no matter how anxious, distressed, or psychotic they were—had normal HPA function. After clinical recovery, response of depressed patients to dexamethasone was normal. There is evidence to support the hypothesis that depressive illness is associated with functional depletion of limbic system norepinephrine, including the fact that antidepressant drugs decrease norepinephrine catabolism. Reserpine, which can produce depression, depletes brain norepinephrine. Finally, there is evidence that growth hormone and luteinizing hormone (also regulated by HPA) are both lowered in depressive illness (Sachar, Finkelstein, & Hellman, 1971; Sachar, Frantz, Altman, & Sassin, 1973).

Family dysfunction in schizophrenia has been studied extensively and is the subject of different approaches by different workers. Fromm-Reichmann (1948) attributed schizophrenia to a schizophrenogenic mother; Bateson, Jackson, Haley, and Weakland (1960) suggested that schizophrenia is caused by the family's double-binding communication. Theodore Lidz (1973) suggested that schizophrenia is due to the narcissistic egocentricity of parents and to the schism and skew in their marriages, while Wynne and Singer (1963) attribute it to parents' fragmented or amorphous style of communications. From a systemic view, Reiss (1971a, 1971b, 1971c) has characterized schizophrenic families as "consensus-sensitive." He found that in this type of family, there is a joint perception that problem analysis and solution are simply a means by which close and uninterrupted agreement can be maintained at all times. In addition, work by several investigators (Brown, Monck, Carstairs, & Wing, 1962; Falloon, Liberman, Lillie, & Vaughn, 1981; Vaughn & Leff, 1976; Vaughn *et al.*, 1982) demonstrated decreased use of drugs and fewer hospital days for schizophrenics in a family-treated group.

With reference to PNEI changes in schizophrenia, abnormalities have been found in immunoglobulins, autoantibody levels, immune responsivity, and lymphocyte reactivity. With reference to immunoglobulins, Fessell and Grunbaum (1961, cited in Solomon & Amkraut, 1981) found both quantitative and qualitative changes in serum globulins. Solomon and Amkraut (1979) found a correlation between severity of psychotic symptoms and IgM, elevation of IgA, and poorer prognosis in patients with a diffuse increase in immunoglobulins. An increased incidence in a variety of autoantibodies has also been found, including rheumatoid factor (Burian, Kubikova, & Krejeova, 1964, cited in Solomon & Amkraut, 1981), antinuclear factor (Fessel, 1961, cited in Solomon & Amkraut, 1981), and antithymic antibodies (Domashneva & Maznina, 1976, cited in Solomon & Amkraut, 1981). Diminished or decreased immunologic response to antigen has been demonstrated with pertussis (Vaughan, Sullivan, & Elmadjian, 1949, cited in Solomon & Amkraut, 1981), guinea pig serum (Molholm, 1942, cited in Solomon & Amkraut, 1981), and a variety of other antigens. Finally, Fessel and Hirata-Hibi (1963, cited in Solomon & Amkraut, 1981) found abnormal lymphocytes in the peripheral blood of most schizophrenic patients. In a blind study of 50 patients and 50 controls, 49 were correctly diagnosed. Families of process schizophrenics (insidious onset, poor premorbid history, little precipitating stress), but not of reactive schizophrenics, had 30 times as many schizophrenic lymphocytes as did controls (Fessel, Hirata-Hibi, & Shapiro, 1965, cited in Solomon & Amkraut, 1981). This work has been confirmed in chronic schizophrenics and their family members (Sethi, Sethi, & Kumar, 1973, cited in Solomon & Amkraut, 1981) and in schizophrenic children (Fowle, 1968, cited in Solomon & Amkraut, 1981). At a functional level, deficient response to T-cell mitogens by lymphocytes in schizophrenic patients has been reported (Liedermann & Prilipuko, 1978, cited in Solomon & Amkraut, 1981) as has the ability of the serum of schizophrenic patients to inhibit PHA stimulation in normal individuals (Vartanian, Koly-askina, Lozovsky, Burbaeva, & Ignatov, 1978, cited in Solomon & Amkraut, 1981).

Thus, there is a good deal of evidence to link severe emotional or mental dysfunction/ illness, family system dysfunction, and changes in either the neuroendocrine or the immune system. The relationship between the functioning of the family system, central nervous system dysfunction, and immune or endocrine changes is unclear as to the etiology and pathogenesis of mental illness.

Family System/Endocrine System/Immune System Physiology

Family system dysfunction should interfere with processes related to hormone production (endocrine function) and/or immune response. Experimental manipulation of the family system should affect the PNEI response.

FAMILY SYSTEM DYSFUNCTION, HORMONE PRODUCTION, AND IMMUNE RESPONSES

A great deal of work supports a role for the dysfunctional family system interfering with the production of hormones or with immune competence. A significant amount of work with animals has provided answers to some basic questions with regard to the manipulation of social variables. Data from animal studies will be presented, as will human studies beginning with the endocrine system.

Endocrine System. In animals, studies of social forces on the neuroendocrine system have centered on either the pituitary–adrenal–cortical axis or on the sympathoadrenal med-ullary system. Design of studies in animals usually involves measurement of plasma levels of a hormone in response to social manipulation.

Studies have shown that social isolation produces adrenal hyperactivity, social support modulates endocrine response to stress, social deprivation causes adrenal hyperresponsive-ness, and change in social attachments causes higher rates of cardiovascular morbidity. Conner, Vernikos-Danellis, and Levine (1971) found that single rats, isolated and exposed to repeated foot shocks, had higher plasma ACTH levels than did paired rats receiving shocks of the same intensity. The investigators had expected to find higher levels in the paired rats since there was, in a sense, a double stimulus, and since two rats fight each other when shocked. They concluded, however, that pairing changes the animals' percep-tions, reasoning that the single animal probably experiences helplessness and depression due to uncontrollable shock; the fighting pair experience an arousal of the classic sympa-thetic adrenal medullary response.

As mentioned previously, Watson and colleagues (1974) showed that when socially deprived mice were exposed to each other for 30 minutes of social interaction, they had much higher plasma cortisone levels than did group-reared mice. Kaplan and co-workers (1983) manipulated tribal membership in groups of rhesus monkeys on a regular basis. All experimental and controlled monkeys were housed, fed, and treated similarly, with the exception of rotating one member of each experimental group to another group every 2 months. After 2 years, at the conclusion of the experiment, all animals were sacrificed, and the cross-sectional areas of atheromatous plaque in the coronary arteries were com-pared. All monkeys in the experimental group had significant and pathogenic plaque, whereas those in the control group did not.

To summarize, workers have shown that manipulation of social forces in animals has significant endocrine effects. The biologic effects of a large number of social forces—from isolation to novel situations to disruptions from tribal ties—have been studied.

The evidence for human family dysfunction having a direct impact on the neuroendocrine system is much less direct than that for animals. Neser, Tyroler, and Cassel (1971) investigated the relationship of stroke mortality to family disorganization and found that stroke mortality increased as family organization became greater. Stroke mortality is related to hypertension, which is generally related to dysfunctioning of the sympathoadrenal medullary system. Therefore, there is some evidence for a relationship between the family system organization and dysfunction of the sympathoadrenal medullary system. An additional indirect piece of evidence to support a relationship between the family system and coronary artery disease is the work of Medalie, Snyder, Groen, Neufeld, and Goldbourt (1973), who examined the incidence of family problems in 10,000 Israeli men and related the severity of family problems (as measured by self-report) to the incidence of angina over a 5-year period. They found a threefold increase in the incidence of angina, after all other risk factors were controlled for, in those men with the most severe family problems.

Perhaps the most direct experiments involving a family system–endocrine relationship comes from the work of Minuchin, Rosman, and Baker (1978), who measured free fatty acid (FFA) production in families with diabetic children during provocative family testing. In one group of families, the parental FFA fell when the child was brought into the room— a striking depiction of "biologic" triangulation. During the experiments, FFA generally rose as family stress was increased.

Immune System. Animal model systems for the study of immune response to social manipulation have provided a great deal of evidence that confirms a relationship between social forces and immune status. Borysenko, Turesky, Borysenko, Quimby, and Benson (1980) showed that crowding and inescapable shock increased both the incidence and the severity of dental caries in rats who were infected intraorally with *Streptococcus mutans* and maintained on a high-sugar diet. Similarly, the stress of crowding markedly increased susceptability to *Salmonella typhimurium* (Edwards & Dean, 1977). With regard to tumorogenesis, stressful social conditions—isolation or physical stress—have been shown by a number of investigators to influence tumor growth and development. Several investigators have reported that individual housing of mice increased the frequency of spontaneous tumors or enhanced the growth of transplanted tumors (Adervont, 1944; Dechambre & Gosse, 1973; Sklar & Anisman, 1980). An interesting finding is that, unlike physical stressors, immunosuppression induced by social stress is not altered under chronic conditions. Thus, social isolation, overcrowding, and predator stress suppress immunologic functioning and will do so even if chronically applied (Brayton & Brain, 1974; Friedman, Glasgow, & Ader, 1969; Nieburgs *et al.*, 1979, cited in Sklar & Anisman, 1980; Solomon & Amkraut, 1979). These social stressors inhibited the responsiveness of both T- and B-cell systems.

Acute and chronic social stress apparently affect immunologic alterations just as they affect neurochemical and hormonal activity. In animal studies designed to evaluate specific immune function after social stress, deficiencies in both cell-mediated and humoral responses have been demonstrated, including decreased responsivity to mitogen stimulation (Gisler, 1974; Monjan & Collector, 1977), antigen stimulation (Joasod & McKenzie, 1976), and reduced lymphocyte toxicity (Monjan & Collector, 1977). Prolongation in time of rejection of skin allografts (Wistar & Hildemann, 1960), reduced graft-versus-host responsiveness, and diminished delayed hypersensitivity reactions (Pitkin, 1965) indicate suppression of cell-mediated immunity following stress. Thus, there is significant evidence to suggest a connection between social force (stress) and immune interactions in animals.

The study of the impact of family dysfunction on the human immune system has been conducted mainly within an epidemiologic framework. Meyer and Haggerty (1962) found an increased incidence of Group A streptococcal pharyngitis infections in families with high levels of family problems coupled with chronic stress. Similarly, we have found increased incidence of both Type A and Type B influenza infection in dysfunctional families. In the case of Type A infections, the families were enmeshed, while in the case of Type B the families were both enmeshed and chaotic. Kraus and Lillienfield (1959) reviewed morbidity and mortality data of young widowers (ages 26 to 35 years) from an epidemiologic standpoint, and found substantially increased mortality from infectious diseases and neoplasms, ranging from 4 to 8 times that for the nonwidowed cohort population. LeShan (1966) studied the life history pattern of 450 adult cancer patients and found that 72% of those studied had experienced the loss of a central relationship. To summarize, there is evidence at the epidemiologic level to suggest family system influences on immune status.

CONCLUSION

Clearly, the evidence supporting the fundamental tests of a theory of family medicine is incomplete. Yet, one senses "reality" and plausibility in the theory as the work of many investigators is synthesized and integrated into a new paradigm. Much work needs to be done to complete the picture, but the science of family medicine is in its infancy and will be an active science for many years to come.

In looking to the future, a priority for researchers will be to correlate the development of family systems theory with the results of experiments in which family and biologic systems are measured simultaneously. Work is needed that utilizes stressors and markers that cause predictable, replicable responses. A great deal of work is needed to develop methods to quantify information processing in family systems. Finally, longitudinal experiments must be designed that treat family and biologic systems as dynamic, living, and communicating systems. This is not to say that cross-sectional studies are not important, but only to emphasize that such work needs to be expanded to include studies of the impacts of the flow of information-intense systems over time.

In conclusion, the family system appears to provide the domain in which individual family members continuously participate in the production, maintenance, and transgenerational reproduction of beliefs, values, and behavior that serve to maintain the tone of and regulate/modulate psychologic, endocrine, and immune processes. Surrounded by a semipermeable boundary, family members interact with and relate to each other on social, psychologic, and biologic levels. The family system and its members develop and create similar and dissimilar feelings, thoughts, and actions, all the while producing and reproducing in themselves and each other patterns of differentiation and integration that regulate and control human psychologic and biologic systems. The science of family medicine offers a method for understanding and harnessing these phenomena in the service of patients and their families. Working with families to develop ways of understanding their complex processes is a rare privilege for scientists. Developing the science of family medicine is a unique and difficult challenge, one that will require discipline and commitment to critical inquiry and to the highest levels of excellence.

References

Adervont EB. Influence of environment on mammary cancer in mice. Journal of the National Cancer Institute 1944; 4:579–581.

Arnetz, BB, Theorell T, Levi L, Kallner A, Eneroth P. An experimental study of social isolation of elderly people: psychoendocrine and metabolic effects. Psychosomatic Medicine 1983; 45:395–406.

Bartrop RW, Luckhurst E, Lazarus L, Kiloh LG, Penny R. Depressed lymphocyte function after bereavement. Lancet 1977; April 16:834–836.

Bateson G, Jackson D, Haley J, Weakland J. Toward a theory of schizophrenia. In: Jackson D, ed. The etiology of schizophrenia. New York: Basic Books, 1960:346–371.

Borysenko M, Turesky S, Borysenko JZ, Quimby F, Benson H. Stress and dental caries in the rat. Journal of Behavioral Medicine 1980; 3:233–243.

Bowen M. Family relationships in schizophrenia. In: Auerback A, ed. Schizophrenia—an integrated approach. New York: Ronald Press, 1959:147–178.

Bowen M. A family concept of schizophrenia. In: Jackson D, ed. The etiology of schizophrenia. New York: Basic Books, 1960:346–372.

Brayton AR, Brain PF. Studies on the effects of differential housing on some measures of disease resistance in male and female laboratory mice. Journal of Endocrinology 1974; 61:48–49.

Bronson FH, Eleftheriou BE. Adrenal response to fighting in mice: separation of physical and psychological causes. Science 1965; 147:627–628.

Brown GW, Monck EM, Carstairs GM, Wing JK. Influence of family life on the course of schizophrenic illness. British Journal of Preventive Social Medicine 1962; 16:55–68.

Burchfield SR. The stress response: a new perspective. Psychosomatic Medicine 1979; 41(8):661–672.

Butler PWP, Besser GM. Pituitary–adrenal functioning severe depressive illness. Lancet 1968; 2:1234–1236.

Cadoret RJ, Widmer RB, Troughton EP. Somatic complaints: harbinger of depression in primary care. Journal of Affective Disorders 1980; 2:61–70.

Carroll BJ. Limbic system–adrenal cortex regulation in depression and schizophrenia. Psychosomatic Medicine 1976; 38:106–121.

Carroll BJ, Martin FIR, Davies BM. Resistance to suppression by dexamethasone of plasma 11-OCHS levels in severe depressive illnesses. British Medical Journal 1968; 3:285–287.

Chorover SL, Chorover B. Towards a theory of human systems. In: Rose S, ed. Towards a liberatory biology. New York: Allison & Busby, 1982:134–149.

Christensen B, Krausz H, Perez-Polo R, Willis WD Jr. Communication among neurons and neuroscientists. In: Pinsker HM, Willis WD Jr, eds. Information processing in the nervous system. New York: Raven Press, 1980:339–359.

Christian JJ. Population density and reproductive efficiency. Biological Reproduction 1971; 4:248–294.

Conner RL, Vernikos-Danellis J, Levine S. Stress, fighting and neuroendocrine function. Nature (London) 1971; 234:564–566.

Coyne JC. Depression and the response of others. Journal of Abnormal Psychology 1976a; 85:186–193.

Coyne JC. Toward an interactional description of depression. Psychiatry 1976b; 39:28–40.

Coyne JC, Aldwin C, Lazarus RS. Depression and coping in stressful episodes. Journal of Affective Psychology 1981; 90:439–447.

Davis DE, Christian JJ. Relation of adrenal weight to social rank of mice. Symposia of the Society of Experimental Medical Biology. 1957; 94:728–731.

Dechambre RP, Gosse C. Individual versus group caging of mice with grafted tumors. Cancer Research 1973; 33:104–144.

Earle AM, Earle BV. Early maternal deprivation and later psychiatric illness. American Journal of Orthopsychiatry 1961; 31:181–186.

Edwards EA, Dean LM. Effects of crowding of mice on humoral antibody formation and protection to lethal antigenic challenge. Psychosomatic Medicine 1977; 39:19–24.

Eliot RS, Buell JC, Dembroski TM. Biobehavioral perspectives on coronary heart disease, hypertension, and sudden cardiac death. Acta Medica Scandinavica 1982; 13 (Suppl 606):203–219.

Ely DL, Greene EG, Henry JP. Minicomputer monitored social behavior of mice with hippocampus lesions. Behavioral Biology 1976; 16:1–29.

Falloon IRH, Liberman RP, Lillie FJ, Vaughn CE. Family therapy of schizophrenics with high risk of relapse. Family Process 1981; 20:211–221.

Fishbein W, Kastaniotis C, Chattman D. Paradoxical sleep: prolonged augmentation following learning. Brain Research 1974; 79:61–75.

Friedman SB, Glasgow LA, Ader R. Psychological factors modifying host resistance ot experimental infections. Annals of the New York Academy of Science 1969; 164:381–392.

Fromm-Reichmann F. Notes on the development of treatment of schizophrenia by psychoanalytic psychotherapy. Psychiatry 1948; 11:263–273.

Gisler RH. Stress and hormonal regulation of the immune response in mice. Psychotherapy and Psychosomatics 1974; 23:197–208.

Haley J. Uncommon therapy: the psychiatric techniques of Milton Erickson, MD. New York: Norton, 1973.

Hall MC, ed. The Bowen family theory and its uses. New York: Jason Aronson, 1981.

Henry JP, Stephens, PM. Stress, health, and the social environment. New York: Springer-Verlag, 1977.

Hoffman L. The family life cycle and discontinuous change. In: Carter EA, McGoldrick M, eds. The family life cycle: a framework for family therapy. New York: Gardner Press, 1980:53–68.

Isaacson RL. The limbic system. New York: Plenum, 1974.

Jenson D. The principles of physiology. New York: Appleton-Century-Crofts, 1976.

Joasod A, McKenzie JM. Stress and immune response in rats. International Archives of Allergy 1976; 50:659–663.

Kaplan JR, Manuck SB, Clarkson TB, Lusso FM, Taub DM, Miller EW. Social stress and atherosclerosis in normocholesterolemic monkeys. Science 1983; 220:733–735.

Kiecolt-Glaser JK, Garner W, Speicher C, Penn GM, Holliday J, Glaser R. Psychosocial modifiers of immuno-competence in medical students. Psychosomatic Medicine 1984a; 46:7–14.

Kiecolt-Glaser JK, Ricker D, George J, Messick G, Speicher CE, Garner W, Glaser R. Urinary cortisol levels, cellular immunocompetency, and loneliness in psychiatric inpatients. Psychosomatic Medicine 1984b; 46:15–23.

Krantz DS, Manuck SB. Acute psychophysiologic reactivity and risk of cardiovascular disease: a review and methodologic critique. Psychological Bulletin 1984; 96(3):435–464.

Kraus AS, Lillienfeld AM. Some epidemiological aspects of the high mortality rate in the young widowed group. Journal of Chronic Diseases 1959; 10:207–217.

Lang IM. Limbic system involvement in the vagosympathetic arterial pressor response of the rat. Unpublished master's thesis, Temple University, Philadelphia, 1975.

Lang IM, Innes DL, Tansy MF. Areas in the limbic system necessary to the operation of the arterial pressure reflex in the rat. Federal Proceedings, Federation of the American Society of Experimental Biology 1975; 34:420 (Abstract).

LeShan L. An emotional life history associated with neoplastic disease. Annals of the New York Academy of Science 1966; 125:780–793.

Lewis JM, Beavers WR, Gossett JT, Phillips VA. No single thread: psychological health in family systems. New York: Brunner/Mazel, 1976.

Lidz T. The origin and treament of schizophrenic disorders. New York: Basic Books, 1973.

Lucero MA. Lenthening of REM sleep duration consecutive to learning in the rat. Brain Research 1970; 20:319–322.

Mason JW. Organization of the multiple endocrine responses to avoidance in the monkey. Psychosomatic Medicine 1968; 30:774–790.

Medalie JH, Snyder M, Groen JJ, Neufeld HN, Goldbourt U. Angina pectoris among 10,000 men. American Journal of Medicine 1973; 55:583.

Meyer RJ, Haggerty RJ. Streptococcal infections in families: factors altering individual susceptibility. Pediatrics 1962; 29:539–549.

Minuchin S, Rosman BL, Baker L. Psychosomatic families: anorexia nervosa in context. Cambridge, Mass.: Harvard University Press, 1978.

Monjan AA, Collector MI. Stress-induced modulation of the immune response. Science 1977; 196:307–308.

Moore GP. Mathematical techniques for studying information processing by the nervous system. In: Pinsker HM, Willis WD Jr, eds. Information processing in the nervous system. New York: Raven Press, 1980:17–30.

Neser WB, Tyroler HA, Cassel JC. Social disorganization and stroke mortality in the black population of North Carolina. American Journal of Epidemiology 1971; 93:166–175.

O'Keefe J, Nadel L, Keightley S, Kill D. Fornix lesions selectively abolish place learning in the rat. Experimental Neurology 1975; 48:152–166.

Oliveri ME, Reiss D. Families' schemata of social relationships. Family Process 1982; 21(3):295–311.

Pitkin DH. Effect of physiological stress on the delayed hypersensitivity reaction. Proceedings of the Society of Experimental Biology and Medicine 1965; 120:350–351.

Pratt L. Family structure and effective health behavior: the energized family. Boston: Houghton Mifflin, 1976.

Reiss D. Varieties of consensual experience: I. A theory for relating family interaction to individual thinking. Family Process 1971a; 10:1–28.

Reiss D. Varieties of consensual experience: II. Dimensions of a family's experience of its environment. Family Process 1971b; 10:28–35.

Reiss D. Varieties of consensual experience: III. Contrast between families of normals, delinquents and schizophrenics. Journal of Nervous and Mental Disease 1971c; 152:73–95.

Reiss D. The family's construction of reality. Cambridge, Mass.: Harvard University Press, 1981.

Reiss D, Oliveri ME. Sensory experience and family process: perceptual styles tend to run in but not necessarily run families. Family Process 1983; 22(3):289–308.

Rubin R, Mandell A. Adrenal cortical activity in pathological emotional states: a review. American Journal of Psychiatry 1966; 123:387–400.

Sachar EJ. Neuroendocrine abnormalities in depressive illness. In: Sachar EJ, ed. Topics in psychoendocrinology. New York: Grune & Stratton, 1976:135–156.

Sachar EJ, Finkelstein J, Hellman J. Growth hormone responses in depressive illness. Archives of General Psychiatry 1971; 25:263–269.

Sachar EJ, Frantz AG, Altman N, Sassin J. Growth hormone and prolactin in unipolar and bipolar depressed patients: responses to hypoglycemia and L-DOPA. American Journal of Psychiatry 1973; 130:1362–1367.

Sakellaris PC, Vernikos-Danellis J. Increased rate of response of the pituitary–adrenal system in rats adapted to chronic stress. Endocrinology 1975; 97:597–602.

Schleifer SJ, Keller SE, Camerino M, Thornton JC, Stein M. Suppression of lymphocyte stimulation following bereavement. Journal of the American Medical Association 1983; 250:374–377.

Sklar LS, Anisman H. Social stress influences tumor growth. Psychosomatic Medicine 1980; 42:347–465.

Sluzki CE, Ransom DC, eds. Double bind: the foundation of the communicational approach to the family. New York: Grune & Stratton, 1976.

Smith CI, Kitahama K, Valatx JL, Jouvet M. Increased paradoxical sleep in mice during acquisition of a shock avoidance task. Brain Research 1974; 77:221–230.

Solomon GF, Amkraut AA. Neuroendocrine aspects of the immune response and their implications for stress effects on tumor immunity. Cancer Detection and Prevention 1979; 2:197–223.

Solomon GF, Amkraut AA. Psychoneuroendocrinological effects on the immune response. Annual Review of Microbiology 1981; 35:155–184.

Stanton MD, Todd TC, & Associates. The family therapy of drug abuse and addiction. New York: Guilford Press, 1982.

Steinglass P. A life history model of the alcoholic family. Family Process 1980; 19(3):211–226.

Stokes P. Studies on the control of adrenocortical function in depression. In: Williams TA, Katz MM, Shield JA Jr, eds. Recent advances in the psychobiology of the depressive illnesses. Washington, D.C.: U.S. Government Printing Office, 1972:199–220.

Terkelsen KG. Toward a theory of family life cycle. In: Carter EA, McGoldrick M, eds. The family life cycle: a framework for family therapy. New York: Gardner Press, 1980:21–52.

Terman GW, Shavit Y, Lewis JW, Cannon JT, Leibeskind JC. Intrinsic mechanisms of pain inhibition: activation by stress. Science 1984; 226:1270–1277.

Vaughn CE, Leff JP. The influence of family and social factors on the course of psychiatric illness. International Journal of Psychiatry 1976; 129:125–137.

Vaughn CE, Snyder KS, Freeman W, Jones S, Falloon IRH, Liberman RP. Family factors in schizophrenic relapse: a replication. Schizophrenia Bulletin 1982; 2:425–426.

Watson FMC, Henry JP, Haltmeyer GC. Effects of early experience on emotional and social reactivity in CBA mice. Physiological Behavior 1974; 13:9–14.

Watson FMC, Henry JP. Loss of socialized patterns of behavior in mouse colonies following daily sleep disturbances and maturation. Physiological Behavior 1977; 18:119–123.

Wistar R, Hildemann WH. Effect of stress on skin transplantation immunity in mice. Science 1960; 131:159–160.

Wynne L, Singer M. Thought disorder and family relations of schizophrenics, I and II. Archives of General Psychiatry 1963; 9:191–206.

Index

601

Health vs. illness, definitions (*continued*)
  pathology, question of, 152
  punctuation of process, 153
  unequivalences, 154
Heart problems and personality
  adaptation vs. survival, 288
  biological signs, 288
  type A, 287, 288
  type B, 288
Helplessness, learned, 284, 364
Herpes simplex type I, as psychoneuroimmunology
    model
  catecholamines, 268, 269
  vs. family behavior, 7
  interleukin 2, 270, 271
  lymphocyte formation, 269, 270
  population, 269
  psychological states, 269, 270
  T4/T8 ratio, 269, 270
  T8 values, 269, 270
HMOs, 413, 414
Homeostasis
  diabetes, 295
  family health, 30, 31, 135, 136
  oscillation, 60
Homes, sketches of, 380, 381
Hypertension
  animal studies, 285
  birth weight, 334, 335
  catecholamines, 285
  endocrine system, 596
  personality for, 285
Hypothalamic–pituitary unit
  ACTH, 40
  adenohypophysis, 38, 39
  amphetamines, 40
  anterior pituitary, 40
  CRH, 40
  dopamine synthesis, 40
  FSH, 40
  glands, parts of, 38, 39
  GnRH, 39
  growth hormone, 40
  luteinizing hormone, 39
  nerve tracts, 39
  neurohypophysis, 39
  neurotransmitters, 40
  neurovascular complex, 39
  noradrenergic pathways, 40
  oxytocin, 39
  prolactin, 40
  TRH, 39
  TSH, 39
  tuberoinfundibular neurons, 39
  vasopressin, 39
Hypothalamic–pituitary–adrenal axis and bereave-
    ment, 260
Hypothalamus
  lesions, 260, 261

norepinephrine, 261
secretions, 39
stress, 260, 261

Illness, behavior in vs. patient's reality perceptions,
    374, 375
Illness episodes, reconstruction, 378, 379
Illness and FAAR, 113, 114
  hurdles in, 114
Illness, and family system changes
  balanced families, 88
  heart attack, 88, 89
Illness system, and family system
  abdominal pain syndrome, 324–326
  altered cell function, 325
  cervical cancer, 328, 329
  class, social, of patients, 327, 329, 330
  conflicts between parents, 324, 325
  drug addiction, 327, 328
  families of drug addicts, 327, 328
  geometry of family, 324, 325
  illness pattern, self-maintenance of, 325
  limit setting, 327, 328
  organ transplant, 328
  paralysis in children, 329, 330
  pattern isomorphism, 327
  postpartum depression, 326, 327
  time boundaries, 326
  treatment centers for drugs, 327
  tumor stroma, 325, 326
  virology, comparison with, 325
  wound healing, 325, 326
Illness theory
  completeness of description, 322
  ecological event shape, 323, 324
  and families, 322
  intervention, problems with, 322, 323
  problem-generated system, 323
  recent theory, 323
  storytellers in, 322, 323
Immune system
  antibodies in, 46
  complement system in, 49, 51
  early work, 45
  laboratory evaluation, 51
  phagocytosis, 45
Immunity
  and family systems
    infections vs. family behavior, 7
    information processing, 5
    interactions, diagram, 6
    secretions, 5, 6
    spouse death, effects, 6, 7
    stress model, 6, 7
    tumors, growth of, 7
  modulation of
    antigens, 247
    B-cells, 246, 247